"The republication of this volume is most welcome. Fully consistent with the apostolic demand to bring every thought captive in obedience to Christ as that is to be done under the final authority of the self-attesting Christ of Scripture, the robust and penetrating theological epistemology this book provides is needed as much today as when it first appeared. Oliphint's copious annotations throughout enhance its usefulness."
—Richard B. Gaffin, Jr., Distinguished Professor Emeritus of Biblical and Systematic Theology, Westminster Theological Seminary

"Every time I revisit his writings—which is often—I find my conviction reinforced that Cornelius Van Til is the most important and incisive Reformed thinker of the last hundred years. I'm therefore delighted that Westminster Seminary Press is reissuing *A Christian Theory of Knowledge*. The book makes for a challenging read, but it is replete with profound and illuminating insights, and Dr. Oliphint's superb foreword and explanatory notes make it much more accessible to readers unfamiliar with Van Til's thought and the theological principles that undergird his philosophical analyses."
—James N. Anderson, Carl W. McMurray Professor of Theology and Philosophy, Reformed Theological Seminary

"Cornelius Van Til's writings continue to prove themselves helpful and incisive as the decades move forward. If anything, they grow in importance as the antithesis between Christ and the world becomes more evident in the twenty-first century. I commend this new edition of his work."
—Vern S. Poythress, Distinguished Professor of New Testament, Biblical Interpretation, and Systematic Theology, Westminster Theological Seminary

"I don't agree with everything Van Til argued, but I never fail to be edified by his overall concern. The overwhelming *emphasis* has to be the attitude of Christian apologetics: We are not God. God has revealed himself, but we systematically 'suppress the truth in unrighteousness.' The way things are (ontology) precedes how we know them (epistemology). The humility of covenant servants before the covenant Lord must be preeminent in our thinking about how dependent creatures encounter an independent Creator. This emphasis, at the heart of Van Til's *Christian Theory of Knowledge*, is a bracing challenge at a time when we think we are in the driver's seat."
—Michael S. Horton, J. Gresham Machen Professor of Systematic Theology and Apologetics, Westminster Seminary California

"Cornelius Van Til has been called the most original apologist of the 20th century (Pierre Courthial). . .[yet] the premise of this book, as with everything he wrote, is simple but profound: God is self-defining and sovereign over all things, including 'epistemology' or knowledge. Yet this does not make him the author of sin. We have here a felicitous mystery. The fruit of this conviction enlivens all the pages of this book. Within this central principle, they are surprisingly diverse. By reading them, if not already the case, the reader will become convinced of the centrality of such knowledge for all of life. The pioneering foreword by K. Scott Oliphint is worth the price of the volume. We are grateful to Westminster Seminary Press for providing this updated edition."

—WILLIAM EDGAR, Professor Emeritus of Apologetics, Westminster Theological Seminary

"This edition of *A Christian Theory of Knowledge* continues Scott Oliphint's highly useful work of annotating Cornelius Van Til's most influential volumes on Christian apologetics and theology. In the form of 350 footnotes added to this work, Oliphint's glosses make Van Til's inferences more readily accessible to contemporary readers, repeatedly relate the point under discussion to other points Van Til makes in his larger body of work, translate every one of Van Til's Latin and German quotations into English, and add substantive biographical synopses of the scores of thinkers discussed by Van Til (especially patristic sources and modern theologians). Along the way, Oliphint fully documents Van Til's consilience with the Reformed systematic theologian Herman Bavinck, and his foreword explains how Van Til's dialectic makes use of principles of plenitude, continuity, and discontinuity. This is an impressive re-presentation of Van Til for the next generation."

—GREG WELTY, Professor of Philosophy, Southeastern Baptist Theological Seminary

"This splendid annotated edition will make key elements of Van Tilian thought accessible to a new generation of scholars. Readers already familiar with Van Til's approach, and those new to the work of this most remarkable of theologians, will alike find much in these pages to help revivify, reinforce, and indeed rethink the apologetic enterprise in the twenty-first century."

—CHRISTOPHER WATKIN, Associate Professor in French Studies, Monash University

"Cornelius Van Til's work represents an influential stream of reception of the Dutch neo-Calvinist tradition in North America, and is often misunderstood by both critics and enthusiasts alike. His *Christian Theory of Knowledge* clearly presents his vision for a Reformed apologetic, along with his contested critiques of other major thinkers that have come before him. Westminster Seminary Press is to be thanked for making this representative work newly available again for a fresh reading."

—NATHANIEL GRAY SUTANTO, Assistant Professor of Systematic Theology, Reformed Theological Seminary

A CHRISTIAN THEORY *of* KNOWLEDGE

A CHRISTIAN THEORY *of* KNOWLEDGE
CORNELIUS VAN TIL

EDITED *by* K. SCOTT OLIPHINT

A Christian Theory of Knowledge
Copyright © 2023 Westminster Seminary Press

First published 1969 by Presbyterian and Reformed Publishing Company

All Rights Reserved. No part of the copyrighted material may be
reproduced without the written consent of the publisher, except
for brief quotations for the purpose of review or comment.
For inquiries and information, contact Westminster Seminary Press:
2960 Church Road, Glenside, Pennsylvania 19038, or at wsp@wts.edu.

Unless otherwise indicated, all English Scripture
quotations are from the original work.

Printed and Bound in the United States of America

Creative Direction and Design by Foreknown
Typeset in Adobe Garamond Pro by Angela Messinger

Hardcover ISBN: 978-1-955859-08-0

CONTENTS

Foreword by K. Scott Oliphint xi
A Note on the Text and Acknowledgments xxxi
Preface xxxiii
Introduction xxxv

I. Preliminary Survey 1

II. The Holy Scriptures 17
    A. The Self-Sufficiency of Scripture 18
    B. Facts 26
        1. The Phenomena of Scripture 26
        2. Facts Outside of Scripture 28
    C. Logic 28

III. The Autonomous Man 33
    A. The Necessity of Scripture 44
    B. The Question of Authority 48
        1. Schleiermacher 52
        2. Recent British Theologians 52
        3. Dialectical Theology 54
    C. The Sufficiency of Scripture 57
    D. The Perspicuity of Scripture 61

IV. The Church Fathers 67
    A. Philo Judaeus 67
    B. The Church Fathers in General 69
    C. The Apostolic Fathers 71
        1. Clement of Rome—Ethics 72
        2. Ignatius—Heresy 72
        3. Polycarp—Authority 73

CONTENTS

- D. The Apologists 71
  - 1. Justin Martyr 71
  - 2. Athenagoras 76
  - 3. Irenaeus 77
  - 4. Tertullian 80
    - a. B. B. Warfield on Tertullian 81
    - b. *Apology* 84
    - c. *An Answer to the Jews* 86
    - d. *The Soul's Testimony* 86
    - e. *A Treatise on the Soul* 88
    - f. Authority 101
  - 5. Alexandrianism (Clement and Origen) 106
    - a. Clement on Authority 111
    - b. Origen on Epistemology 114
- E. Saint Augustine 115
  - 1. Early Writings 116
    - a. Augustine's Rationalism 116
    - b. Augustine's Irrationalism 122
  - 2. Later Writings 133
    - a. The Two Cities 134
    - b. True Freedom 136

V. From Sovereign Grace to Synergism 141
- A. Plotinus 141
- B. The Aereopagite 145
- C. Johannes Scotus Erigena 148
- D. Natural Theology 149
- E. Mystical Theology 151

VI. Autonomy Plus Authority: Roman Catholicism 155
- A. Earlier Official Writings 155
  - 1. Trent 155
  - 2. Vatican I 157
- B. The Attributes of Scripture 161
  - 1. Necessity 162
  - 2. Authority 164
  - 3. Perspicuity 165
  - 4. Sufficiency 167
- C. The Thomistic Paideia 169

CONTENTS

    D. Vatican II... 175
        1. Herman Bavinck on Trent 176
        2. G. C. Berkouwer on Vatican II 178
        3. The Documents of Vatican II..................... 188

VII. Evangelicalism and Scripture............................. 197
    A. Lutheranism... 200
        1. Francis Pieper..................................... 200
        2. Karl Francke 206
    B. Arminianism 212
        1. Richard Watson................................... 216
        2. Joseph Butler..................................... 219
        3. John Miley....................................... 221

VIII. Natural Theology and Scripture.......................... 225
    [A.] Kuyper and Warfield on Apologetics 233

IX. Hamilton's *Basis of Christian Faith*........................ 259
    A. The Existence of the Soul 263
    B. The Nature of the Reasoning Process 264
    C. The Insuperable Problem 266

X. Buswell's *Systematic Theology*.............................. 279
    A. Natural Theology 283
    B. What Is God?....................................... 284
        1. The Cosmological Argument 286
        2. The Teleological Argument 288
        3. The Anthropological Argument 289
        4. The Moral Argument............................. 290
        5. The Ontological Argument 290
    C. Evaluation 292
        1. Buswell Modifies Thomas......................... 292
        2. Buswell Rejects Presuppositionalism 294
            [a.] A Basic Misunderstanding.................. 296
        3. Buswell's Natural Theology 314
        4. The Unbeliever Replies to Buswell................. 315

XI. The Dilemma of Western Thought 319
    A. Demythologization.................................. 321

B. Existential Interpretation 321
   C. Dimensionalism Is No Help. 331
   D. Demythologization Again 340
   E. Peace On Earth 346
   F. Traditional Apologetics 348

XII. The Dilemma of Modern Theology 353
   A. A New Quest of the Historical Jesus. 353
   B. Christ without Myth 360
   C. Primal Thinking. 366
   D. Preaching the New Objectivism. 367

Index of Subjects and Names. 373
Index of Scripture References 383

FOREWORD

In the first chapter of this book, Cornelius Van Til notes that:

> It is of critical importance in the current scene that a consistently Reformed apologetic be set forth. The non-Christian point of view is much more self-consciously hostile to Christianity than it has ever been. The fact that the assumption of human autonomy is the root and fountain of all forms of non-Christian thought is more apparent than it has ever been in the past. Any argument for the truth of Christianity that is inconsistent with itself should not expect to have a hearing. Only a position which boldly and humbly challenges the wisdom of the world and, with the Apostle Paul, brings out that it has been made foolishness with God will serve the purpose. Only such a method which asks man to serve and worship the Creator rather than the creature honors God and assigns to him the place that he truly occupies. Only such a method is consistent with the idea that the Holy Spirit must convict and convince the sinner. The Holy Spirit cannot be asked to honor a method that does not honor God as God.[1]

Van Til's concern, throughout his career, was for a "consistently Reformed apologetic." That apologetic, as has too rarely been emphasized, especially in literature critical of Van Til, has its *animus* in the biblical theology that came forth from the Reformation. As Van Til notes, the Reformers and theologians of the post-Reformation era were not *centrally* concerned with a biblically consistent defense of Christianity. But they did lay the groundwork for such a defense. It was in this context that Van Til set himself to the application of Reformed theology to Christian apologetics, the challenge that motivated his entire career.

But Van Til's work was no mere historical enterprise. His words, written

---

1. See page 12–13 in this volume.

more than fifty years ago, are more relevant today than they were when they were first penned. Authority of all kinds was challenged in the decade of the sixties and "freedom" was set forth as *summum bonum*. But he could not have seen how twenty-first century notions of "freedom" and of autonomy, as well as a militancy against authority, would make the sixties pale by comparison.

For the malcontents of the sixties, it was primarily familial, institutional, and governmental authority that was being challenged by the younger generation. In our current day, the entire history of humanity, as well as the most basic and intuitive laws of nature, are regarded as nothing but outdated, superficial and rigid prejudices—fetid as rotten fish—that must be discarded in the waste bin so that we all, together, can celebrate our now-enlightened enfranchisement. Autonomy, on vivid display in the sixties, is now the putrid air to which everyone is constantly exposed, threatening to suffocate any trace of opposition to it. The chaos that the sixties initiated has descended the ladder of irrationalism as hostility to Christianity continues to grow at an almost blinding pace.

The good news in the midst of this chaos is that the "wisdom of the world" looks more and more like utter foolishness. Cultural authorities, who claim to "follow the science," are adept at ignoring and suppressing any science that will not fit their own cultural model. Thus, "science" itself loses all objectivity, and a purportedly objective notion like "follow the science" becomes the opposite of itself; its translation, in practice, is "follow *me*." Autonomy reigns and chaos results. Objectivity becomes subjectivity; the rational becomes irrational.

In the midst of our present cultural crises, Van Til's analysis in *A Christian Theory of Knowledge* is even more relevant than when he wrote it. Some of the names, ideas, and philosophical systems are no longer the cultural touchpoints they were in Van Til's day. Many of them have already been consigned to their proper dustbins (which is a fitting reminder about our present context). However, the *critiques* that he offers to those names, ideas, and philosophical systems endure and remain useful for mounting a Christian defense in today's world. These critiques remain so because they rest on the unchanging Word of God, and on the Reformed theology that flows from that Word.

PLENITUDE, CONTINUITY, AND DISCONTINUITY

As I read through this book one more time, with "fresh eyes" in order to annotate it, it struck me that it might be useful to explain in a bit more detail the dialectic that Van Til utilizes—in this book more than any of his other works—as he both critiques unbelieving ideas, and as he presents, defends, and explains Christian truth in light of those ideas.

There is a triplex of inextricably related principles that Van Til deploys in various ways throughout this book that can benefit from a little explanatory background. They are (1) the principle of *plenitude*, (2) the principle of *continuity*, and (3) the principle of *discontinuity*. Though all three principles are rarely found in contemporary literature, the latter two especially should be recovered as useful, at least structurally if not specifically, in a Christian apologetic.

It is my opinion that Van Til, in his use of these three principles, was influenced, at least in his language, by Arthur O. Lovejoy's highly influential book (during Van Til's career), *The Great Chain of Being*.[2] Much of Lovejoy's influence on Van Til is not seen explicitly in Van Til's published work. It is, however, a significant part of Van Til's unpublished syllabus, "Christianity in Conflict,"[3] a course he taught at Westminster Theological Seminary for decades. His use of the three principles listed above in that syllabus will be helpful in understanding his use of them in this book.

The Principle of Plentitude

First, what does Van Til mean by the "principle of plenitude" and why is it useful for his apologetic purposes? Quoting Lovejoy, Van Til says, "This principle shows that, after all, 'a God unsupplemented by nature in all its diversity would not be "good,"' and, therefore 'would not be divine.'"[4]

Anyone who has followed Van Til's career will know why this "principle of plenitude" was of such interest to him. As he set out, from the point of his doctoral dissertation onward, to critique philosophical idealism in its various forms, one of his primary critiques was that the "Absolute" of idealism was, in the end, *not* absolute at all. Even as some were wanting to adopt idealism as a Christian philosophy, Van Til argued instead that the "Absolute" of idealism could only be what it was if it had, over against itself, a "relative" by which it is defined and according to which it *must be* related. This, structurally, is what the "principle of plenitude" holds as well.

The "principle of plenitude," according to Lovejoy, *requires* that "the Good," as the ultimate reality, *must* express itself. If it did not express itself, how could it be good at all? Here is Lovejoy (quoted by Van Til),

---

2. For a useful assessment of Lovejoy's significance, see Daniel J. Wilson, "Lovejoy's the Great Chain of Being After Fifty Years" in the *Journal of the History of Ideas* 48, No. 2, (1987): 187–206. Wilson notes Jaakko Hintikka's assessment that Lovejoy's book has been "the most influential single work on the history of ideas in the United States during the last half century" (p. 202).
3. Cornelius Van Til, "Christianity in Conflict" in *The Pamphlets, Tracts, and Offprints of Cornelius Van Til*, ed. Eric H. Sigward. Labels Army Company: New York, 1997. LOGOS Bible Software.
4. Ibid.

> . . .the concept of Self-Sufficing Perfection, by a bold logical inversion, was—without losing any of its original implications—converted into the concept of a Self-Transcending Fecundity. A timeless and incorporeal One became the logical ground as well as the dynamic source of the existence of a temporal and material and extremely multiple and variegated universe. The proposition that—as it was phrased in the Middle Ages—*omne bonum est diffusivum sui*[5] here makes its appearance as an axiom of metaphysics.[6]

The "principle of plenitude," in other words, defines ultimate goodness as including a *necessity* of diffusion and expression. Goodness would not be ultimately good unless it actualized everything of itself that could possibly be actualized. How could "the Good" be ultimately good if there were possible existents that the Good *would not* actualize? This principle moves, according to Lovejoy, from Plato, through to Aristotle, into much of the Christian tradition.

> With this. . . there was introduced into European philosophy and theology the combination of ideas that for centuries was to give rise to *many of the most characteristic internal conflicts*. . . the conception. . . of a divine completion which was yet not complete in itself, since it could not be itself without the existence of beings other than itself and inherently incomplete; *of an Immutability which required, and expressed itself in, Change; of an Absolute which was nevertheless not truly absolute because it was related*, at least by way of implication and causation, to entities whose nature was not its nature and whose existence and perpetual passage were antithetic to its immutable subsistence.[7]

In this quotation we see again why Lovejoy's analysis of the "great chain of being" so resonated with Van Til. Van Til himself was tireless in his efforts to show "many of the most characteristic internal conflicts" of unbelieving thought. He would display those internal conflicts brilliantly throughout this book.

He also continually brought out the inconsistency of Arminian and Roman Catholic thought, for example, as thought that imagines a God who is *not* in the end "most absolute," but who is, instead, necessarily dependent on his creation to be who he is and to do what he does. For Van Til, Lovejoy's analysis of the "principle of plenitude" was further confirmation of a compromise—both

---

5. That is, "all good is self-diffusive."
6. Ibid.
7. Ibid., my emphases.

of philosophy and of some systems of theology—that displayed the "internal conflicts" present in their respective systems of thought.

It is this "internal conflict" that Van Til (as well as Lovejoy, though in a vastly different way) applied to various systems of thought, and which is delineated by the other two key, dialectical, and related principles—the "principle of continuity" and the "principle of discontinuity."

The Principle of Continuity

The "principle of continuity" follows from the "principle of plenitude." Lovejoy argues that the "principle of plenitude" *inevitably* results in the "great chain of being," which displays the "principle of continuity." The "great chain of being," says Van Til (quoting Lovejoy) is,

> composed of an immense, or—by the strict but seldom rigorously applied logic of the *principle of continuity*—of an infinite number of links ranking in hierarchical order from the meagerest kind of existents, which barely escape non-existence, through 'every possible' grade up to the *ens perfectissimum*—or, in a somewhat more orthodox version, to the highest possible kind of creature, between which the Absolute Being the disparity was assumed to be infinite—every one of them differing from that immediately above and that immediately below it by the 'least possible' degree of difference.[8]

Here, then, is the "principle of continuity." It is a principle, entailed and motivated by the "principle of plenitude," which recognizes "Being" to be of a transcendental nature—that is, it necessarily actualizes and applies to all that exists. It also distinguishes between existent things according to their respective *modes* and *degrees* of existence. There is a "chain of *being*" because "Absolute *being*" must express itself by a diffusion of *existence*; and there is a "*chain* of being" because the expression or diffusion of "Absolute being" can only emanate downward, as it were, to actualize other existent things. The "lowest" expression of being is perilously close to non-being; the highest is closest to the Absolute. Whether low or high, however, there is, throughout *all* that exists, a *chain*, and that chain is exhaustively linked by "Being" or existence itself.

The "principle of continuity," as Lovejoy described it, and as Van Til affirmed, is, in and of itself, a principle of *necessity* or of *determinism*. Lovejoy

---

8. Ibid. This "scale of being" idea has been replete in theology as well. For a discussion of the great scale of being applied to "Perfect Being Theism," see Yujin Nagasawa, *Maximal God: A New Defence of Perfect Being Theism*, (Oxford University Press, 2017).

argued that, while Plato introduced the "principle of plenitude," it was Aristotle who showed that the "principle of continuity" is directly deducible from it.

> From the Platonic principle of plenitude the principle of continuity could be directly deduced. . . . If there is between two given natural species a theoretically possible intermediate type, that type must be realized—and so on *ad indefinitum*; otherwise, there would be gaps in the universe, the creation would not be as 'full' as it might be, and this would imply the inadmissible consequence that its Source or Author was not 'good,' in the sense which that adjective has in the *Timaeus*.⁹

In Van Tilian terms, the principle of continuity, since it flows from the necessity entailed by the "principle of plenitude," is a principle of *determinism*. The "great chain of being" is a chain that *must* be what it is, without gaps and without remainder.¹⁰ It is, necessarily and from first to last, a *plenitude*—all that *could* exist, *must* exist. Thus, when Van Til employs the notion of a non-Christian "principle of continuity," he means by that some non-Christian notion of *necessity*, or of *determinism*, or, more generally, of *rationality* or *unity*. It is this principle, as employed by the non-Christian, that is supposed to make sense of, or properly and meaningfully interpret, the facts around us.

The Principle of Discontinuity

Van Til recognized that, as Lovejoy argued, it isn't possible to live with such a stark view of necessity or determinism. The "internal conflict" which Lovejoy mentioned, and which Van Til himself had seen in unbelieving thought from the beginning of his career, is manifested when the notion of "pure contingency" is introduced or affirmed to counteract or complement such determinism. With the introduction of "pure contingency," we have the third key principle, the "principle of discontinuity." So, according to Van Til,

> . . .if men draw back in horror from the logical consequences of their allegiance to the determinist principle [of continuity] of Parmenides then they have no way of escape except by somehow adding the principle of abstract contingency [discontinuity] to their principle of abstract determinism [continuity].¹¹

---

9. Arthur O. Lovejoy, *The Great Chain of Being: a Study of the History of an Idea* (Cambridge, Mass.: Harvard University Press, 1936), 71.
10. Ibid., 246, Lovejoy notes that *"natura non facit saltus,"* nature does not produce gaps.
11. Van Til, "Christianity in Conflict."

It is this dialectic, according to Van Til, of the "principle of continuity" together with the "principle of discontinuity" that characterizes all non-Christian thought, as well as less-than-Reformed systems of theology. Lovejoy sees it preeminently in medieval theology. Van Til puts it this way:

> There was in the thinking of these medieval philosophers, Lovejoy boldly argued, first the *principle of continuity* which, he said, must be traced back to Parmenides. By using this principle the medieval thinkers indeed got unity into everything, even into all the changing things of this world. But the unity they found in this change is the unity of *rational determinism*. And the employment of this principle of unity would naturally lead to the reduction of all individuality and change to abstract identity. But then, added Lovejoy, in order to escape this determinism they employed a *principle of discontinuity* which is purely *irrational*. Using this principle would naturally lead to a God who is unknown and unknowable, even to himself as well as to a man wholly unknown and unknowable to himself. Using this principle of discontinuity consistently would mean the destruction of all unity.[12]

That is, in sum, and as Van Til illustrates in the pages of this book, unbelieving thought sought for a principle of unity, and some thought they had found it in the principle of continuity. But, as the changing facts of the world were referred to this principle, only "abstract identity" could be affirmed. When affirmed, the facts of this world lost all individuality. Thus, discontinuity had to be affirmed as well. But a principle of discontinuity destroyed, by definition, all unity. This is the inescapable and irresolvable dilemma of dialectical thought.

This elucidation of the principles of continuity and discontinuity, in my view, is one of the definitive marks of Van Til's genius in his Reformed apologetic approach. While there will be certain *emphases* on the rational or the irrational in unbelieving thought, Van Til consistently argued that all unbelieving thought rests on a rational/irrational dialectic, is self-contradictory, and thus, *on its own terms*, is self-destructive. It is self-destructive because such a dialectic cannot, in fact, provide the metaphysical or explanatory foundation that is needed for the system of thought to be coherent. Instead, any and all non-Christian systems of thought—and any Christian theology that smuggles in non-Christian assumptions—will inevitably vacillate between two incommensurate principles. To put it in concrete terms, non-Christian systems will, at one and the same time, argue that the traffic light is dialectically both green and red at the same time. No such

---

12. Ibid., my emphases.

light could exist, much less do the work it is meant to do. Such is the case with theologically inconsistent systems as well.

So, in reading this book, it will be helpful if, when Van Til employs the notion of a non-Christian "principle of continuity," one can see in that principle the non-Christian "principle of plenitude," which itself reduces reality to a necessary, rationalistic determinism. When Van Til employs the notion of a non-Christian "principle of discontinuity," one can see in that principle the affirmation of "pure contingency," which refers to a process of pure chance, which, by definition, can have no rational foundation. The former principle is equivalent to a non-Christian notion of rationality; the latter is equivalent to a non-Christian notion of irrationality. With this dialectic in play, meaning, at root, is sacrificed at the altar of autonomy. That, in itself, is a useful commentary on our present age.

THE CHRISTIAN ALTERNATIVE

As Van Til offers his critique, showing the incoherent dialectic of non-Christian thought, as well as "sub-Christian" or non-Reformed theologies, he also offers a Christian alternative. With respect to the "principle of plenitude," Van Til recognizes that Christianity must reject it wholesale.

> The first thing to be said by the Christian believer today is: (1) That taking full account of the significance of the principle of plenitude, he rejects it *in toto*. This principle of plenitude is the product and expression of apostate faith. It is the natural man, blind to the truth about God, about himself, and about the world, who employs this principle as his weapon against the truth as it is in Jesus. Thus faith stands against faith. True faith stands over against false faith. Faith which thinks and speaks of everything on the presupposition of the truth of the Christian framework of things revealed by Christ in his Word stands over against the faith which thinks and speaks of everything on the presupposition of the falsity of that framework. But for man to presuppose the falsity of the Christian framework of things requires that he assumes the truthfulness of its opposite. And the truthfulness of the framework opposite to that of Christianity rests upon the assumption of human autonomy.[13]

Because the "principle of plenitude" *necessarily requires* the relative and contingent with respect to the highest "Being," or with respect to God, Christians

---

13. Ibid.

must reject it. In no sense can the Infinite *necessarily require* the finite, the Immutable *necessarily require* the mutable, the One God *necessarily require* the diversity of creation. The Christian God's relation to creation originates in the free determination of his will; creation could in no wise be necessary. Not only so, but God's relation to creation could in no way change his character. He is, as he *must* be and remain, eternally, infinitely, and immutably the "I Am Who I Am." The "principle of plenitude" must be rejected by Christians, as Van Til says, *in toto*.

Christian Continuity and Christian Discontinuity

However, with respect to the other two principles—of continuity and discontinuity—Van Til, in this volume more than any other of his published works, co-opts the same language and argues for a *Christian* understanding of each of these two principles. He offers to his readers a *Christian* "principle of continuity" and a *Christian* "principle of discontinuity."[14] Van Til's analysis of the history of Christian thought depends on his assessment of both the non-Christian and the Christian principles of continuity and discontinuity, so we need to provide a "working knowledge" of the *Christian* principles in order properly to assess his arguments herein. With respect to a Christian "principle of continuity," Van Til says, "This involves the idea that God himself is wholly known to himself and that the created universe is also wholly known to him because wholly controlled by him. This is the Christian principle of continuity."[15]

To put it in Christian vernacular, the Christian "principle of continuity" refers to the aseity and the consequent all-controlling sovereignty and providence of God. What makes it a principle of *continuity* is the fact that there are no "gaps" in God's character, because of his exhaustive and *a se* knowledge of himself and of everything that is.[16] Thus, "continuity" is defined, not in terms of a "principle

---

14. Whether or not this co-opting of philosophical language is the best way to combat unbelieving thought can be debated. What is certain is that Van Til uses this language as a point of *persuasion*. That is, instead of defaulting immediately to the language of Reformed theology, he is wanting to communicate to those who are not familiar with Christian language. He is saying to his non-Christian opponents that if it is a "principle of continuity" they want, or a "principle of discontinuity," such principles can only be found and have meaning *within* the Reformed faith; he defines these very principles with Reformed content. Outside of that faith, they inevitably reduce to incoherence. For a stimulating discussion of Van Til's use of philosophical language, see Hendrik G. Stoker, "Reconnoitering the Theory of Knowledge of Professor Dr. Cornelius Van Til," in *Jerusalem and Athens: Critical Discussions on the Philosophy and Apologetics of Cornelius Van Til*, ed. E. R. Geehan, (New Jersey: Presbyterian and Reformed Publishing Co., 1977), 52–53.

15. See page 48 in this volume.

16. This is in contrast to Molinism and Arminianism wherein aspects of God's knowledge are *conditioned* according to what human beings would choose in any given situation. This makes God dependent on man, and it denies the self-sufficiency of God's character and knowledge.

of plenitude" which *requires* that all that is possible be actual and that disallows for gaps of "Being" in all that exists. Instead, "continuity" is defined in terms of God's own *a se* character, and the implications of that character with respect to all that he determines to create.[17]

Importantly, and perceptively, Van Til defines the Christian "principle of discontinuity" in the context, initially, of a Reformed doctrine of Scripture:

> Moreover, to say that every fact in the world is what it is because of its place in the system of truth set forth in Scripture, is to establish the legitimacy of the *Christian principle of discontinuity*. The system of truth set forth in Scripture cannot be fully understood by the creature. The point here is not merely that creatures who are sinners are unwilling to believe the truth. The point is further that man as finite cannot understand God his Maker in an exhaustive manner. As he cannot understand God exhaustively, so he cannot understand anything related to God in an exhaustive way, for to understand it we would have to penetrate its relation to God and to penetrate that relation we would have to understand God exhaustively.[18]

This is a fascinating and ingenious application of a philosophical principle, now applied to one of the most contentious aspects of Reformed theology, the doctrine of the self-attestation and absolute authority of Scripture. Quoting Herman Bavinck, Van Til argues,

> It must be said, therefore, that there is a sense in which the orthodox believer holds to his doctrine of Scripture "in spite of appearances." He believes in the Bible as the Word of God because God has said that it is his Word. "With respect to the inspiration of Scripture as is the case with every other doctrine the question *is not in the first place how much can and may I believe without coming into conflict with science, but what is the witness of Scripture and what is accordingly the expression of Christian faith.*"[19]

---

17. To the extent that Arminian and Roman Catholic theology depend on a Molinistic view of human freedom, they would not be able to affirm this Christian "principle of continuity." Nor could they affirm that God is "most absolute." The fact that God depends on pre-volitional counterfactuals of human freedom as a prerequisite to his determination to create requires that his knowledge is not altogether from or of himself. *What* he knows with respect to human beings, he only knows *because* of their free choices, and not because of his unconditional, comprehensive knowledge of all that is.

18. See page 27 in this volume.

19. See page 27 in this volume, my emphasis.

It is just *because* we cannot penetrate exhaustively into the "gapless" counsel, sovereignty, and providence of God that we must affirm a Christian "principle of discontinuity." That principle requires us to take God at his Word, and to frame the facts of the world, as best we are able, in light of what God has said in his Word. As noted above, any other view that claims, for example, to "follow the science" winds up with pure subjectivism, and thus with a dialectic of determinism ("science") and abstract contingency at its root.

But there is more to Van Til's Christian interpretation of the "principle of discontinuity" as it exhibits the deep roots of Reformed theology in Van Til's thinking. Note:

> . . .the Christian idea of God's control of all things—the Christian principle of continuity—*requires a Christian principle of indeterminism.* These two are correlative of one another, and the relationship between them cannot be penetrated by the mind of man. *This relationship is not contradictory since in God there is full internal coherence.* But for the human mind they must in the nature of the case have *the appearance of being contradictory.* The idea of their unity must therefore be given on authority. Hence the need of supernatural revelation, and, after the fall, of the inscripturation of this supernatural revelation. The biblical idea of unity presupposes the self-identification of God and of his finished revelation to men in history. It involves the idea of God's giving in this self-identified revelation a system of truth, which is *anthropomorphic in its expression* and yet *all-determinative in its content.* These two ideas, that of self-identification and of an authoritative system, are involved in one another.[20]

This is a brilliant insight from Van Til. Some elaboration should help show its grounding in Reformed theology. First, what does Van Til mean when he says that God's control of all things—which is included in Van Til's Christian use of the "principle of continuity"—*requires* a Christian principle of indeterminism? How, in other words, could there *be any* "indeterminism" if, in fact, God ordains "whatsoever comes to pass," and is in control of *all things*?

Christian Indeterminism and the Westminster Confession of Faith

We should recognize, in order to address this question, that Van Til uses the term "indeterminism" in its Christian sense, as including or entailing the Reformed notion of contingency and of free will. All of these represent, for Van Til, the

---

20. See page 71 in this volume, my emphases. Van Til applies the principle of continuity/discontinuity both epistemologically and metaphysically. The principle relates to our knowledge and to the way the world is, including the relationship of God's exhaustive control over the world and the reality of our free choices. My thanks to Greg Welty for pointing this out.

Christian "principle of discontinuity." With that in mind, and to better grasp those Reformed notions, we can be helped by two places in the Westminster Confession of Faith.

First,

> God, from all eternity, did, by the most wise and holy counsel of his own will, freely, and unchangeably ordain whatsoever comes to pass: yet so, as thereby neither is God the author of sin, nor is violence offered to the will of the creatures; nor is the liberty or contingency of second causes taken away, but rather established.[21]

Included in this one section is both the Christian "principle of continuity" as well as the Christian "principle of discontinuity." With respect to the "principle of continuity," the Confession affirms that God unchangeably ordains *whatsoever comes to pass*. There is, in history, from the beginning of creation and into eternity future, *nothing* that is outside of God's ordaining providence and control. *Whatever* happens, in all of creation, happens by virtue of God's *a se* ordination of all things.

Just as the "principle of plenitude" attempts to ensure that there are no "gaps" in all that exists, so also, in rejecting such a principle, the Reformed view of all that exists is that the self-sufficient and *a se* God ordains it all. There are no "gaps" in anything in God's creation since he is utterly and exhaustively *of himself*, entirely self-sufficient, and thus he "works all things according to the counsel of his will," (Eph. 1:11, ESV).[22]

In keeping with this Christian notion of the "principle of continuity," the Confession goes on to affirm the following:

> Although God knows whatsoever may or can come to pass upon all supposed conditions, yet hath he not decreed anything because he foresaw it as future, or as that which would come to pass upon such conditions.[23]

Van Til's Christianized "principle of continuity" includes God's exhaustive self-sufficiency, aseity, and knowledge. This section of the Confession staves off any notion, as in Molinism, that there are states of affairs over which God has

---

21. Westminster Confession of Faith (WCF) 3.1
22. The Molinist might agree that God "works all things according to the counsel of his will," but they understand "the counsel of his will" to be logically consequent to his middle knowledge. Thus, the "counsel of his will" is a *conditional* counsel in that it depends on what free creatures would do. This is not, we should recognize, what Paul meant in that verse.
23. WCF 3.2

no control, and on the basis of which God determines His decree. That is, this section of the Confession affirms that God's decree and providence, which are inclusive of *everything in creation*, were in no way conditioned on some notion of God prevolitionally "foreknowing" or "foreseeing" what *would* take place, in order then to decree what *will* take place. In sum, the Confession is in direct opposition to any kind of Molinistic understanding of God's counsel and will. Thus, a Christian view of the "principle of continuity" includes God's aseity and exhaustive self-sufficiency, as well as his meticulous sovereignty and control over everything, at all times and into eternity, in and over all of creation.

However, given the succinct brilliance of the Confession, the writers anticipated objections that would arise, since they affirmed God's exhaustive control over all things. Without arguing their points (which is not the purview of a confession), they went on to state that God ordaining everything does *not*, in fact, make God the "author of sin." Neither does his exhaustive ordination of all things coerce the human will or remove the liberty and contingency of second causes. As a matter of fact, they affirmed—and here the Confession combines for us, in a way that we cannot exhaust, the principles of "continuity" and of "discontinuity"—that the freedom of the human will (more on this below), as well as the liberty and contingency of second causes, are *established* by God's ordaining of all things. This point is too often ignored or overlooked.

Free Will

It might be a surprise that the Westminster Confession of Faith dedicates a chapter (9) to addressing the topic of free will. That phrase is often found in Molinist and Arminian theologies. It is significant that the Reformed authors of the Confession wanted to include it, to define it, and to affirm it. There is much that could profitably be discussed in that chapter, but we will need to be content with a quick review of section 1:[24] "God hath endued the will of man with that natural liberty, that it is neither forced, nor, by any absolute necessity of nature, determined to good, or evil."[25]

There is a mountain of theology packed into this one sentence. We first recognize that the Confession affirms that the human will retains, by virtue of what it is, a "natural liberty." This natural liberty, the Confession wants us to recognize, has not been lost because of the fall. Sections 3 and 4 of chapter 9 will go on to describe the will before the fall and after the fall. But, in each case,

---

24. It is worth noting that Van Til wrote a paper in 1924, while a student at Princeton Theological Seminary, titled, "The Will in its Theological Relations." He was awarded a fellowship in systematic theology for that paper.
25. WCF 9.1

both before and after the fall, the will of each and every human being, because of the way in which God has made it, has as an aspect of its *essential* character a "natural liberty."

Section one goes on to describe what is meant by "natural liberty." It means the human will is never *forced* or *coerced* to decide what it decides, nor is it naturally *determined* to good or evil. These truths require some theological distinctions which can only be briefly broached here.

First, the Reformed have maintained that the will functions, at all times, without any *natural* necessity. This means, in part, that for every human being there is no point in our choosing in which our wills are naturally or necessarily *coerced* to make the choices we make. We should recognize, however, (and section three makes this clear) that, since the fall, there is, indeed, a *moral* necessity attached to our choices. That moral necessity does not eclipse, but rather presupposes, the lack of natural necessity of the human will.

Second, it is because we retain the ability *actually* to choose, without coercion, that our wills are not *naturally* determined to good or evil. So, whatever notion of theological determinism one might want to support, that determinism *cannot*, from a Reformed perspective, include a *natural necessity* of the human will. Along with this, two more points need to be mentioned.

In order to try to articulate what this denial of a natural necessity of the human will might look like, another important distinction was, and is, utilized by the Reformed—the distinction between the "necessity of the consequent," and the "necessity of the consequence." The former the Reformed deny, the latter they affirm. In the "necessity of the consequence" the Reformed affirm God's all-controlling decree. The "necessity of the consequence" recognizes that, whatever the outcome of any given event, including any given choices required in that event, God has ordained its outcome, and thus, in that sense, the outcome is determined by his decree and providence. The necessity of the consequence is what it is because God ordains "whatsoever comes to pass."

With the "necessity of the consequent," which the Reformed deny, the actual choice required in a given circumstance is not, in and of itself *as a choice*, *necessary*, but is, instead, *contingent*. For example, if we take the if-then proposition, "If Abraham is commanded to sacrifice Isaac on Mt. Moriah, he will obey," the "If" clause is the antecedent, and the "he will obey" clause is the consequent. The question with respect to Abraham's choice is, when he is commanded to sacrifice Isaac, is there, in reality and at that moment, a *real choice* for Abraham? To put it another way, given God's all-controlling decree and providence, does Abraham *really* have a choice on Mt. Moriah? Would the Reformed change the consequent to "he *must and necessarily will* obey"? The answer is "no" with respect to the consequent itself.

FOREWORD

Since the Reformed deny the necessity of the consequent—the "he will" clause in our example—Abraham's choice on Mt. Moriah is, itself, historically *contingent* and not necessary. Abraham retains the *natural* ability to choose either to obey or to disobey the Lord on that mountain. There is real *contingency* involved in Abraham's decision at that point. That contingency does not, because it could not, eclipse, undermine, or supersede God's ordination of every facet of that event; instead, God ordaining that event, including Abraham's choice, *establishes* the contingency involved in the choice, even as it denies any autonomy of choice. The same is true of any and every human choice; there is *real* contingency in the choosing, such that *we* are responsible for what we decide.

Included in this discussion of the contingency of our choices is a Reformed notion of *concursus*. Here, Bavinck's explanation is among the best:

> With his almighty power God makes possible every secondary cause and is present in it with his being at its beginning, progression, and end. It is he who posits it and makes it move into action (*praecursus*) and who further accompanies it in its working and leads it to its effect (*concursus*). He is "at work" [in us] "both to will and to do for his good pleasure" (Phil. 2:13). But this energizing activity of the primary cause in the secondary causes is so divinely great that precisely by that activity he stirs *those secondary causes into an activity of their own*. "The providence of God does not cancel out but posits secondary causation." Concurrence is precisely the reason for the *self-activity of the secondary causes*, and these causes, sustained from beginning to end by God's power, work with a strength that is appropriate and natural to them. So little does the activity of God nullify the activity of the creature that the latter is all the more vigorous to the degree that the former reveals itself the more richly and fully. Hence, the primary cause and the secondary cause *remain distinct*. The former does not destroy the latter but on the contrary confers reality on it, and the second exists solely as a result of the first. Neither are the secondary causes merely instruments, organs, inanimate automata, but *they are genuine causes with a nature, vitality, spontaneity, manner of working, and law of their own*.[26]

LIMITING CONCEPTS

In tandem with the Christian "principle of continuity" is the Christian "principle of discontinuity," the latter of which includes, says Van Til, a Christian notion

---

26. Herman Bavinck, John Bolt, and John Vriend, *Reformed Dogmatics: God and Creation* (Grand Rapids, MI: Baker Academic, 2004), 614, my emphases.

of *indeterminism*. The reality and "establishing" (as the Confession puts it) of *contingency* is what Van Til means by a Christian notion of *indeterminism*, and is, in part, included in his notion of a Christian "principle of discontinuity."

This is all-important because of (1) the determinism that is entailed by the "principle of plenitude," and because (2) many see the affirmation of God controlling "whatsoever comes to pass" as entailing a determinism that disallows for the reality of the contingent. From the beginning, the Reformed have never argued for such a determinism. As a matter of fact, notwithstanding claims to the contrary by Arminian and Molinist theologians, the Reformed have always affirmed *both* that God ordains whatsoever comes to pass *and* that he is in no wise the author of sin. The contingency, or indeterminism, established by God's ordaining of all things is embedded in a Reformed view of secondary causes, and of the human will.

There is one more salient point that should be briefly elaborated. In his affirmation of a Christian conception of both continuity and discontinuity, Van Til says, "These two are correlative of one another, and the relationship between them cannot be penetrated by the mind of man. *This relationship is not contradictory since in God there is full internal coherence.* But for the human mind they must in the nature of the case have *the appearance of being contradictory*."[27] Here I think Van Til's introduction of a Christian view of "limiting concepts" can be useful.[28]

We need initially to recognize what a *Christian* version of "limiting concepts" is, according to Van Til:

> If we hold to a theology of the apparently paradoxical we must also hold, by consequence, to the Christian notion of a limiting concept. The non-Christian notion of the limiting concept has been developed on the basis of the non-Christian conception of mystery. By contrast we may think of the Christian notion of the limiting concept as based upon the Christian conception of mystery. The non-Christian notion of the limiting concept is the product of would-be autonomous man who seeks to legislate for all reality, but bows before the irrational as that which he has not yet rationalized. The Christian notion of the limiting concept is the product of the creature who seeks to set forth in systematic form something of the revelation of the Creator.[29]

---

27. See page 71 in this volume, emphases mine.
28. For a fuller discussion of "limiting concepts," see my foreword in Cornelius Van Til, *Common Grace and the Gospel* (Phillipsburg, N.J.: Presbyterian and Reformed Publishing Company, 2016), xxxvi–xliii.
29. Van Til, Cornelius, *Defense of the Faith*, 4th ed., ed. K. Scott Oliphint, (Phillipsburg, N.J.: Presbyterian and Reformed Publishing Company, 2008), 16.

FOREWORD

The phrase "limiting concept," as used by Van Til, is a term that helps to explain a biblical concept of mystery based on the God of Scripture. Not only so, but to employ the non-Christian notion of a "limiting concept" and, thus, of mystery, destroys any basis at all for understanding human experience.

Hyperdox

Mystery, as Bavinck reminds us, is at the root of all Christian theology.[30] When we affirm the ontological Trinity, the incarnation, the covenant of God with man, etc., we are articulating the *truth* of the matter, according to Scripture, but we also affirm that our minds are not able to put the truth of the matter together in a way that is completely amenable to our usual ways of thinking. Perhaps the best word to denote a teaching that requires that we *affirm* that which cannot be *delimited* by our laws of thought is "hyperdox," i.e., a teaching of Scripture that must be affirmed, though it does not conform to, but rather transcends, standard rules of thought.[31] That is, these are teachings (*dox*) that are *above* (*hyper*) our typical (and proper) ways of thinking.

Van Til refers to these teachings as "apparent contradictions."[32] By that, he does not mean that they are explicit and obvious violations of the law of non-contradiction or some other canon of formal logic. That is, we do not affirm, for example, that God's attitude toward all men is gracious *in the same way* that God's attitude toward all men is not gracious. Similarly, to use another example, with respect to God's triunity, we do not affirm that God is three *in the same way* that he is one. Nor do we affirm that Christ is God *in the same way* that he is man. There are deep and abiding issues in these truths of *compatibility*, but incompatibilities are not, *per se*, contradictions.

Van Til's notion of "apparent contradiction" is shorthand for recognizing that what we do affirm with respect to (much of) biblical teaching is that we are not able completely to subsume such teaching under our standard laws of thought. Our laws of thinking are not able exhaustively to demarcate the meaning of what we affirm to be true in Scripture. The problem is *not*, we should note, with our standard ways of thinking. God has created us so that, typically, when we affirm something to be true we are not meant, at the same time and in the

---

30. Herman Bavinck, John Bolt, and John Vriend, *Reformed Dogmatics: God and Creation* (Grand Rapids, MI: Baker Academic, 2004), 29.

31. Standard rules of thought would typically include the law of identity, the law of non-contradiction, and the law of excluded middle. The term "hyperdox" is from H.G. Stoker and may be preferable to the term "paradox." A paradox refers to two mutually implied teachings that are set side-by-side; a hyperdox includes those two (or more) teachings, but affirms that they are above and beyond our human ability to understand. See Stoker, "Reconnoitering the Theory of Knowledge of Professor Dr. Cornelius Van Til," 30.

32. Cornelius Van Til, "Christianity in Conflict."

same way, to deny its truth. He has created us so that we distinguish one thing from another (i.e., diversity). He has created us to see and affirm the myriad relationships of differing things (i.e., unity) that is replete through the entirety of creation and of our experiences. This is all a part of "thinking God's thoughts after him."

The issue with respect to "hyperdoxes," then, is that an understanding of the character of God and his activity in the world will always transcend the typical ways we are meant to understand and know the world. More importantly, it is the mystery of biblical teaching, the hyperdoxes given to us in Scripture, that should form the *foundation and basis* for our typical ways of thinking. That is, it is not as though we're meant to apply our laws of thinking as far as we possibly can and then, in the end, to refer the remainder to mystery. Rather, we *begin* with mystery because we *begin* with the triune God himself. In that way, at minimum, we recognize our typical ways of thinking themselves to be limited, to be in need of their own foundation, and to have their own God-given boundaries.

Another important aspect to this notion of "limiting concepts" is that, unlike dialectical thinking, which posits contradictory or incommensurable notions without the possibility of any resolution, the limiting concepts posited, because they are biblical and thus are integral to a Reformed theological system, *depend on* and *interpret* each other. Given that they have their ultimate resolution in the mind of God, it is incumbent on the Christian to see each "side" of the two as properly modifying, explaining, and elaborating the other "side." In this way, we affirm their ultimate unity, even if that unity is beyond our ability comprehensively to articulate.

CONCLUSION

In sum, one of Van Til's most helpful insights throughout his career was his insistence that unbelieving thought is necessarily dialectical. When we see this properly, we are better equipped to "destroy the strongholds raised up against the knowledge of God."(1 Cor. 10:5, ESV) If the principles of continuity and discontinuity are not as clear or useful, another way that Van Til expresses the dialectic is "rational/irrational." In all unbelieving thought, there will be attempts at unity, at an overall interpretation or meaning. But there will, at the same time, be pronouncements of freedom, of individuality, of the indeterminate. These two—the universal (unity) and the particular (individuality)—lay at the root of unbelief, and it is useful, apologetically, to recognize them and perhaps point to them as providing the destruction of thought and meaning. All unbelieving thought is caught in an irresolvable dialectic, and thus is built on quicksand.

The reason for this dialectic, as I have tried to show elsewhere,[33] is that all people, because they are made in the image of God, have, by God's activity and providence, the true knowledge of God. This is what Calvin called man's *sensus divinitatis*, or sense of divinity. It is this *sensus* that motivates people to subsume what they believe into some kind of meaningful unity. No matter how disparate people may claim their own views to be, there will always be this push to bring together their thinking and their lives under something beyond their own existence. This was the force of the statement, quoted by the apostle Paul, "In him we live and move and have our being," (Acts 17:29, ESV). That statement, borrowed from Epimenides, was an attempt to bring human existence into some kind of unity.

But, always and everywhere, along with this *sensus*, there is suppression of the truth that we know. So, even as Epimenides wrote that statement, the "him" that was meant to unify humanity was Zeus, and not the true God. Thus, the rational *sensus* was distorted and perverted by the irrational *suppression* so that the statement made by Epimenides was caught in the dialectic that is everywhere typical of unbelief.[34] Paul, of course, redeemed the statement by referring it, not to Zeus, but to the true God whom he had just proclaimed to them in Athens. Thus, the rational/irrational dialectic of pagan Greek thought was transformed into the biblical "limiting concepts:" "in him" ("principle of continuity") and "we live and move and have our being." ("principle of discontinuity").

With this, we can close our introduction to this important work by Dr. Van Til, which he saw as a supplement to his *Defense of the Faith*. This is a book that shows Van Til's application of Reformed apologetics to numerous ideas, various people in the history of the church, and contemporary Protestant and Catholic theologians. Van Til was able to see the "big ideas" in these many thinkers and theologians, expose the unbelief resident in those ideas, and point a Christian way forward in each case. *A Christian Theory of Knowledge* is, in one sense, a bird's-eye view, albeit a critical one, of church history, from the 2nd century A.D. to Van Til's day, wherein the value of Reformed theology is seen and applied apologetically by Van Til's constant defense of it.

If I were to recommend a course of reading and study in Van Til's works, I would recommend that one begin with *The Defense of the Faith*, followed by *Common Grace and the Gospel*, and then work through this excellent study. With those

---

33. See, for example, K. Scott Oliphint, "The Irrationality of Unbelief" in *Revelation and Reason: New Essays in Reformed Apologetics*, K. Scott Oliphint, and Lane G. Tipton, eds. (Phillipsburg, NJ: Presbyterian and Reformed Publishing Co., 2007), 59–73.

34. I attempt to frame Van Til's rational/irrational dialectic in the biblical categories of sensus/suppression. See K. Scott Oliphint, *Covenantal Apologetics: Principles and Practice in Defense of Our Faith*, (Wheaton, IL: Crossway Books, 2013), esp. 148–150.

three books, the substance of Cornelius Van Til's long and productive career, as he sought to reform the discipline of Christian apologetics, will be well in hand. With those three, a Reformed covenantal apologetic should be well understood.

K. Scott Oliphint
Westminster Theological Seminary
August, 2022

A NOTE ON THE TEXT AND ACKNOWLEDGMENTS

The complete text of *A Christian Theory of Knowledge* is reproduced here from the first edition published by Presbyterian and Reformed Publishing Company (P&R) in 1969 with minor adjustments. In two instances headings have been lettered to better signal their location in the structure of the book. These are indicated by brackets. Van Til's extended quotations have also been set in block quotes. Otherwise, corrections have been made only in cases of clear errors or typos.

In previous reissues of Van Til's works annotations were indicated by variations in font. For this edition, annotations are attributed to the volume editor ("KSO") at the beginning of the footnote. Unattributed notes are original to the 1969 edition.

P&R published many of Cornelius Van Til's major works during his lifetime and, in the years since his passing, has released trailblazing annotated editions of his *Christian Apologetics, Introduction to Systematic Theology, The Defense of the Faith, Christian Theistic Evidences,* and *Common Grace and the Gospel.* Westminster and students of apologetics worldwide owe P&R and the Craig family a debt of gratitude for this fine service. It is an honor for WSP to contribute this volume to that body of work.

Finally, we extend a very special debt of thanks to Gabe Fluhrer and Ransey Bowers. Without Mr. Bowers's generous gift toward Reformed apologetics this new edition of Van Til's seminal work may not have come to be.

Westminster Seminary Press

·———·

My thanks go to P&R for their gracious permission to reprint this volume. I also wish to thank Andrew Becham, Caleb Burkhart, Ruben Cabrera, Handa Chun, Josh Currie, Gabe Fluhrer, David B. Garner, Pierce T. Hibbs, Chun Lai, Peter

A. Lillback, Angela Messinger, Randall Pederson, Josiah Pettit, Uriah Renzetti, Jim Sweet, Jerry Timmis, Bridger Ueeck, and Kyle Whitgrove, for their hard work and support in seeing this book to completion. Finally, I'm grateful to Greg Welty, Todd Rester, and Dick Gaffin for reading and suggesting clarifications and corrections prior to publication.

K. Scott Oliphint
December, 2022

PREFACE

This work is to a large extent an expansion of and supplement to my *The Defense of the Faith* (1955, 3rd. ed., 1967). In particular it picks up some of the major themes touched on in "The Christian Philosophy of Knowledge," a chapter of that work. In the present volume I attempt to work out in greater detail the nature and implications of our commitment to Scriptural authority in relation to our activity as Christian theologians and philosophers today.

In addition several men discussed in *Defense of the Faith* are given a deeper analysis. Among these are Warfield, Kuyper, Buswell and Hamilton.

I have added footnotes to indicate the location of further discussions of some areas not fully taken up in the present work. There are two works which may be mentioned in particular. They are *The Doctrine of Scripture* (1967), a classroom syllabus which works out the doctrine of Scripture more or less assumed in the present work, and *The Reformed Pastor and the Modern World*, a work to be published shortly, which attempts to root more firmly the argument of this book in the thought of Calvin as well as providing much more extensive discussions of Aquinas, modern Catholic philosophy and Immanuel Kant.

Needless to say to those acquainted with *Defense of the Faith*, the whole of my work presupposes a certain understanding of *Common Grace*, a discussion of which may be found in my book by that title.

All three of these works may be obtained from the Presbyterian and Reformed Publishing Company.

I wish to thank Mrs. Travis J. Reimer for the excellent typing of the manuscript and Mr. Robert Geehan for invaluable help of various kinds.

Cornelius Van Til
January, 1969

INTRODUCTION

This work seeks to present a Christian and, more especially, a Reformed theory of knowledge.

The present writer holds with the late B. B. Warfield that the Reformed Faith is the most consistent expression of Christianity. *Christian* apologetics is therefore considered identical with *Reformed* apologetics. No depreciation of non-Reformed views of Protestantism is implied. On the contrary, it is the writer's conviction that the cause of evangelical, that is, non-Reformed Protestantism, is bound to profit from a defense of the Reformed Faith, for a defense of the Reformed Faith is not primarily a defense of the "five points of Calvinism." A defense of the Reformed Faith is a Reformed method of the defense of Christianity and this should be to the profit even of Roman Catholic Christianity.[1]

Reformed apologetics wants first of all and above all to be biblical apologetics. Its aim is to interpret all of life in terms of basic truths derived from the Scriptures of the Old and New Testaments as the infallible rule of faith and practice. The writer is therefore greatly indebted to the great Reformed exegetes of Scripture. In modern times many excellent commentaries written by Reformed scholars have appeared. He is also greatly indebted to the great Reformed dogmaticians of modern times, such as Charles Hodge, Thornwell, Dabney, Shedd, Kuyper and especially Herman Bavinck. Back of all of them stands that master theologian and exegete of Scripture, John Calvin, whose writings have been constantly consulted.

The present work seeks specifically to show the relevance of Christianity to modern thought. Its main contention is that Christianity has the answer that

---

1. KSO: The reason Van Til avers that non-Reformed and Roman Catholic people could "profit" from a Reformed apologetic is because (1) as he says, Reformed theology is the most consistent expression of Christianity and therefore (2) non-Reformed and Roman Catholics would see how such a theology is applied to the discipline of defending Reformed Christianity. To see Reformed theology applied to apologetics would highlight the consistency of the former for the sake and use of the latter. Van Til's sole concern throughout his career was the application of a consistently Reformed theology to apologetics.

modern thought seeks in vain. Modern thought in general is largely controlled by the basic principles of modern philosophy. To evaluate these basic principles from the point of view of Christianity is therefore of paramount importance. Much help has been received on this matter from the writings of D. H. Th. Vollenhoven and Herman Dooyeweerd of the Free University of Amsterdam, and from G. H. Stoker of Potchefstroom, South Africa.[2] It is the writer's hope that something in the way of a beginning may herewith be made in the utilization of all the wealth of Reformed scriptural exegesis, theological research, and philosophy that has appeared in recent times for purposes of a Reformed or consistently Christian theory of knowledge and a consistently Christian apologetics.

---

2. KSO: Herman Dooyeweerd (1894–1977), D. H. Th. Vollenhoven (1892–1978), Dooyeweerd's brother-in-law, and Hendrik G. Stoker (1899–1993) were all philosophers who sought to apply Reformed principles to the discipline of philosophy in order to set forth a specifically Christian philosophy. With Van Til, they began a periodical, *Philosophia Reformata*, in 1935. Dooyeweerd and, to a lesser extent, Vollenhoven developed what they called "The Philosophy of the Law-Idea" (*Wijsbegeerte der Wetside*), which asserted "Law" as the boundary between God and creation. Stoker argued in a similar way but saw creation, rather than law, as the distinguishing "boundary." His philosophy was called "The Philosophy of the Creation Idea" (*Wysbegeërte der Skeppingsidee*). In the end, Van Til was not able to follow Dooyeweerd and considered his own work more consistently applied in Stoker's attempt at a Christian philosophy. Readers interested in more details can consult E. R. Geehan, *Jerusalem and Athens: Critical Discussions on the Philosophy and Apologetics of Cornelius Van Til* (Nutley, New Jersey: Presbyterian and Reformed Publishing Co., 1977): 23–128.

A CHRISTIAN THEORY *of* KNOWLEDGE

1

PRELIMINARY SURVEY

The present chapter offers to the reader a preliminary survey of the contents of this work. It strives especially to indicate in a broad way the method of reasoning that is to be pursued.

In this work the Christian position will be set forth first. Then the non-Christian view will be presented. After that the argument for the truth of the Christian position will be put forward.

As already indicated in the preface, it is impossible to set forth the Christian position without considering the different interpretations that have been given of it. In particular, the difference between Protestantism and Roman Catholicism must be noted. This implies that the difference in method of reasoning between a Protestant and a Romanist defense of Christianity must be explained.

Another difference also comes into view at this point. All Protestants will agree with one another that the doctrines of Protestantism must be defended as over against Romanism. But not all agree that there is a distinctly Protestant method of defending Christianity as a whole. Some hold that Protestants should first join the Romanists in order with them to defend the doctrines that they have in common. All Christians, we are told, believe in God. All believe that God has created the world. All Christians hold that God controls the world by his providence. All believe in the deity of Christ. These and other doctrines may therefore be defended in the same way by all Christians. There is no specifically Protestant way of defending the Christian doctrine of God. How could there be since this is the common property of all Christians?

Other Protestants contend that there must be a specifically Protestant defense of all Christian doctrines. Their argument is that all Christian doctrines are interdependent. Each major doctrine implies all of the others and colors all of the others. A Protestant's doctrine of the atonement will, to some extent, color his doctrine of God and vice versa. In fact, the difference with respect to all other doctrines rests ultimately on a difference with respect to the notion one has of God.

But what, it will then be asked, is the difference between a Protestant and a Romanist doctrine of God? The answer given is that the Protestant doctrine of God stresses his self-sufficiency and therefore his ultimate control over all that comes to pass in the course of the history of the world. The Romanist doctrine of God, while also speaking of God's self-sufficiency, none-the-less compromises it to some extent. It does this by virtually ascribing to man a measure of self-sufficiency. And by ascribing a measure of self-sufficiency or ultimacy to man, God is in a measure made dependent upon man.[1]

It is natural, then, to ask how this difference between the Romanist and the Protestant concept of God should necessitate a specifically Protestant defense of Christianity as a whole. The reply would be as follows: The Protestant doctrine of God requires that it be made foundational to everything else as a principle of explanation.[2] If God is self-sufficient, he alone is self-explanatory. And if he alone is self-explanatory, then he must be the final reference point in all human predication. He is then like the sun from which all lights on earth derive their power of illumination. You do not use a candle in order to search for the sun. The idea of a candle is derived from the sun. So the very idea of any fact in the universe is that it is derivative. God has created it. It cannot have come into existence by itself, or by chance. God himself is the source of all possibility, and, therefore, of all space-time factuality.[3]

On the other hand, if God is not self-sufficient and self-explanatory then he is no longer the final reference point in human predication. Then God and man become partners in an effort to explain a common environment. Facts then are not what they are, in the last analysis, by virtue of the plan of God; they are partly that, but they partly exist in their own power. The human mind, then, need not subject itself to the revelation of God as absolutely authoritative for him.

---

1. KSO: Van Til has in mind here the teaching of the Roman Catholic Church on free will. Note: "If anyone says that man's free will moved and aroused by God, by assenting to God's call and action, in no way cooperates toward disposing and preparing itself to obtain the grace of justification, that it cannot refuse its assent if it wishes, but that, as something inanimate, it does nothing whatever and is merely passive, let him be anathema," Henry Joseph Schroeder, ed., *Canons and Decrees of the Council of Trent* (Charlotte, N.C.: TAN Books, 2011): Canon 4, p. 76. Such a view of free will amounts to human autonomy, which the Reformed summarily rejected. This view of autonomy informs virtually everything Van Til will say about the Roman Catholic position, and so should be kept in mind all along.

2. KSO: Van Til is highlighting the Reformed affirmation that God is the *prinicipium essendi*, the principle or foundation of existence. He alone exists in and of himself; everything else that is exists by his free determination. See Richard Muller, *Post-Reformation Reformed Dogmatics: The Rise and Development of Reformed Orthodoxy, ca. 1520 to ca. 1725: Prolegomena to Theology*, Volume 1, 126.

3. KSO: As Van Til will go on to elaborate, this is crucial to recognize when we speak of "facts" in apologetics. True knowledge of any fact must include the reality that God is its creator and sustainer, and is revealed in and through the facts of creation. Without that recognition, knowledge of a fact is fundamentally, *principially*, flawed.

Man may then defer to God as to an expert who has had greater experience than himself, but he need not make all thoughts captive to the obedience of Christ.[4]

The Christian cannot, on this view, indicate to the non-Christian that the non-Christian position is destructive of experience. Nor can he make plain to the non-Christian that Christianity will give him, and will *certainly* give him, what he needs. The essence of the non-Christian position is that man is assumed to be ultimate or autonomous. Man is thought of as the final reference point in predication. The facts of his environment are "just there"; they are assumed to have come into being by chance. Possibility is placed above both God and man alike. The laws of logic are assumed as somehow operative in the universe, or at least as legislative for what man can or cannot accept as possible or probable. If a god exists, he must at least be subject to conditions that are similar to, if not the same as, those to which humanity itself is subject.

How then we ask is the Christian to challenge this non-Christian approach to the interpretation of human experience? He can do so only if he shows that man *must* presuppose God as the final reference point in predication. Otherwise, he would destroy experience itself. He can do so only if he shows the non-Christian that even in his virtual negation of God, he is still really presupposing God. He can do so only if he shows the non-Christian that he cannot deny God unless he first affirm him, and that his own approach throughout its history has been shown to be destructive of human experience itself.[5]

The Romanist method of defending God does no such thing. It does not, to be sure, agree with the non-Christian position in assuming that *man* must deliberately be made the final reference point of human predication. On the other hand, it does not clearly insist that *God* be made the final reference point. In other words, the Romanist position is a compromise between the Christian and the non-Christian view on the matter of the final reference point of human experience. Hence it cannot distinguish clearly between the two positions. On

---

4. KSO: See 2 Cor. 10:1–5.

5. KSO: This paragraph highlights the various ways the notion of "presupposition" or "presupposing" is used by Van Til. He first asserts that man "must presuppose God as the final reference point in predication." The force of this "must" is not only *ethical*, in that God requires that we see him and his character in all that exists, but it is also the case that there is no meaning to human experience unless God is recognized as its foundation. That is a crucial part of our apologetic argument. But Van Til then notes that the non-Christian "even in his virtual negation of God. . . is still really presupposing God." This may seem initially to be at odds with his first notion of presupposition. How is it that the non-Christian "must" presuppose God when, even in his negation of God, the non-Christian "really" presupposes God? This second use of "presupposition" is a recognition of the state of affairs as they *actually* ("really") obtain. The non-Christian could not utter a word, think a thought, or even argue *against* Christianity, unless God had created him, sustained him, and gave him "life and breath and all things," (Acts 17:25). It is important and crucial, apologetically, to recognize these distinctions in the notion of "presupposing" or "presupposition."

the one hand, it cannot consistently show that the non-Christian view is ruinous to man. On the other hand, it cannot consistently show that the Christian position means salvation for human experience.

·———·

Up to this point in our discussion it has been assumed that all Protestants agree in thinking of God as all-sufficient and as self-explanatory. This assumption must now be examined. Why does one group advocate the idea that there is a distinctly Protestant method of defending Christianity in all of its doctrines? Why does the other group maintain that Protestants should first join Roman Catholics in defending doctrines they have in common with them in order then to go on to the defense of the specific Protestant teachings? The only reason that can be found is that the second group is basically sympathetic to the Romanist view of man as being, in part, autonomous.

We refer now to those Protestants who are usually spoken of as *evangelicals* as distinct from those who embrace the Reformed Faith. Under the term *evangelicals* we include all those who hold to the Remonstrant or Arminian view of man in his relation to God. We include also the Lutherans. To be sure, Lutherans are not by any means to be identified as Arminian in every respect. But on the point at issue their view is basically the same as that of the Arminians. The point is that both Arminians and Lutherans maintain that man has a measure of ultimacy or autonomy. In this respect they resemble the Roman Catholics. The measure of autonomy ascribed to man is much smaller in the case of many Arminians and Lutherans than it is in the case of the Roman Catholics. Even so, *any* measure of autonomy ascribed to man implies a detraction from the self-sufficiency of God. It implies that God can no longer be taken as the final reference point in human predication. It is expected, then, that evangelicals, holding as they do in their theology to the idea of man as having some measure of ultimacy, will also maintain that Protestants may and even must join with Roman Catholics in defending certain doctrines that they have in common. They will hold that only after certain doctrines that Roman Catholics and Protestants hold in common have been defended against the non-Christian by both groups standing side by side, will there be occasion for Protestants to go on to the defense of their own teachings.[6] Then

---

6. KSO: Consistent with and entailed by the notion of "free will" mentioned above in footnote 1, is the supposition of human reason as virtually unaffected by the fall of man into sin. This is a serious problem that the Reformed had to address during the time of the Reformation. Note: "The critique leveled by the Reformation at medieval theological presuppositions added a soteriological dimension to the epistemological problem. *Whereas the medieval doctors had assumed that the fall affected primarily the will and its affections and not the reason, the Reformers assumed also the fallenness of the rational faculty:* a generalized or "pagan" natural theology, according to the Reformers, was

this defense of their own teachings will have to be against Roman Catholics as well as against unbelievers.

Over against these convictions of the evangelicals with respect to the method of defense of the Christian Faith stands the position of Reformed theology. Reformed theology holds to the self-sufficiency of God without compromise. It therefore rejects every form of human autonomy. Only on the assumptions of divine self-sufficiency and man's complete dependence upon God can the difference between the Christian and the non-Christian points of view be clearly made out. Only thus can the issue be clearly drawn. The non-Christian assumes that man is ultimate, that is, that he is not created. Christianity assumes that man is created. The non-Christian assumes that the facts of man's environment are not created; the Christian assumes that these facts are created. The Christian has derived his convictions on these matters from Scripture as the infallible Word of God. *As self-explanatory, God naturally speaks with absolute authority. It is Christ as God who speaks in the Bible. Therefore the Bible does not appeal to human reason as ultimate in order to justify what it says. It comes to the human being with absolute authority.*[7] Its claim is that human reason must itself be taken in the sense in which Scripture takes it, namely, as created by God and as therefore properly subject to the authority of God.[8]

---

not merely limited to nonsaving knowledge of God—it was also bound in idolatry. This view of the problem of knowledge is the single most important contribution of the early Reformed writers to the theological prolegomena of orthodox Protestantism. Indeed, it is the doctrinal issue that most forcibly presses the Protestant scholastics toward the modification of the medieval models for theological prolegomena," Richard A. Muller, *Post-Reformation Reformed Dogmatics: The Rise and Development of Reformed Orthodoxy, Ca. 1520 to Ca. 1725: Prolegomena to Theology* (Grand Rapids, Mich.: Baker Books, 2003): 108, my emphasis.

As Van Til notes, many Protestants join with the medievals in this notion of human reason. See, for example, Norman L. Geisler, *Christian Apologetics* (Grand Rapids: Baker Book House, 1976). Note also a less-than-Reformed assessment of total depravity, "We suggest that classic Reformed orthodoxy saw the noetic influence of sin *not as direct through a totally depraved mind,* but as indirect through the totally depraved heart." R.C. Sproul, John Gerstner and Art Lindsley, *Classical Apologetics: A Rational Defense Of The Christian Faith And A Critique Of Presuppositional Apologetics,* (Zondervan Publishing House, Grand Rapids, MI, 1984), 537, my emphasis. This is one of the primary reasons why a so-called "classical" apologetic approach goes against the theology of the Reformation.

7. KSO: Alongside the *principium essendi*, noted above, the second of two *principia* argued by Reformed theology, is the *principium cognoscendi*, the foundation of knowledge. Our foundation of knowledge can be none other than God's self-attesting revelation. These two *principia* entail each other, given creation. If one really holds to the self-sufficiency of God, one must hold as well to the self-sufficiency and self-attestation of his revelation.

8. KSO: This is a standard Reformed understanding of reason. Note, for example, Francis Turretin: "The question is not whether reason is the instrument by which or the medium through which we can be drawn to faith. For we acknowledge that reason can be both: the former indeed always and everywhere; the latter with regard to presupposed articles. *Rather the question is whether it is the first principle from which the doctrines of faith are proved; or the foundation upon which they are built,* so that we must hold to be false in things of faith what the natural light or human reason

It is, therefore, required of man that he regard himself and his world as wholly revelatory of the presence and requirements of God. It is man's task to search out the truths about God, about the world and himself in relation to one another. He must seek a "systematic" arrangement of the facts of the universe. But the "system" that he thus tries to form is not the sort of system that the non-Christian is seeking to make for himself.

The two systems, that of the non-Christian and that of the Christian, differ because of the fact that their basic assumptions or presuppositions differ. On the non-Christian basis man is assumed to be the final reference point in predication. Man will therefore have to seek to make a system for himself that will relate all the facts of his environment to one another in such a way as will enable him to see exhaustively all the relations that obtain between them. In other words, the system that the non-Christian has to seek on his assumption is one in which he himself virtually occupies the place that God occupies in Christian theology. Man must, in short, be virtually omniscient. He must virtually reduce the facts that confront him to logical relations; the "thingness" of each thing must give up its individuality in order that it may be known; to be known, a thing or fact must be *wholly* known by man.[9]

It is true that in modern thought there seems to be no such striving after exhaustive knowledge. But the reason for this seeming "irrationalism" of modern thought lies in the fact that it puts great stress upon another non-Christian assumption: that all reality is temporal throughout.[10] Hence all facts are assumed

---

cannot comprehend. This we deny," Francis Turretin, *Institutes of Elenctic Theology*, ed. James T. Dennison Jr., trans. George Musgrave Giger, vol. 1 (Phillipsburg, NJ: P&R Publishing, 1992–1997), 24, my emphasis.

9. KSO: There are a number of epistemological assumptions in this paragraph. It is important to note that Van Til is discussing *systems* of knowledge. People, of necessity, think in terms of systems. A particular thing—a tree, for example—is known according to its own properties, including its species. That species is known according to its genus, and a genus is related to a family, an order, a class, a phylum, and a kingdom. Even if such categories are not known, we always relate particular "things" to properties of its species. When we say, "There is a tree," we have some, perhaps rudimentary, knowledge of what "treeness" is and how that tree and its class are related to and different from other trees, shrubs, etc. We also know how such trees are not rocks, dogs, or stars. This "*systematic*" understanding of knowledge requires, in principle, knowledge of all things, both as *related* ("treeness") and as *distinct* (not a rock or a dog) in order to know that fact for what it is. Thus, there must be exhaustive knowledge *somewhere* if there is to be true knowledge *anywhere*. For the non-Christian, the only point of reference is man himself. Man must have, in principle, exhaustive knowledge in order truly to know a thing and its "thingness." For the Christian, God has exhaustive knowledge. The Christian need not refer all things to human knowledge, but instead recognizes each thing according to that which God creates and sustains, and through which he "speaks" (cf. Ps. 19:1–2). This is, in part, what it means for the Christian to "think God's thoughts after him."

10. KSO: Since modern thought denies the existence of God, and since it relies only on its own resources for knowledge, reality must itself be *only* temporal.

to be what they are simply as products of chance. This assumption was implied in ancient non-Christian thought as well as in modern non-Christian thought. But it was not until modern times, especially since the time of Kant, that this assumption has come clearly to the foreground. In consequence, modern thought speaks of its systems as being limiting concepts or ideals. The ideal is still that of complete comprehension for man.

The system that Christians seek to obtain may, by contrast, be said to be *analogical. By this is meant that God is the original and that man is the derivative. God has absolute self-contained system within himself.* What comes to pass in history happens in accord with that system or plan by which he orders the universe. *But man, as God's creature, cannot have a replica of that system of God. He cannot have a reproduction of that system.* He must, to be sure, think God's thoughts after him; but this means that he must, in seeking to form his own system, constantly be subject to the authority of God's system *to the extent* that this is revealed to him.[11]

For this reason all of man's interpretations in any field are subject to the Scriptures given him. Scripture itself informs us that, at the beginning of history, before man had sinned, he was subject to the direct revelation of God in all the interpretations that he would make of his environment.

It is of basic importance to understand what is meant by saying that the human system should be *self-consciously analogical.* For there are many non-Christians who also speak of their systems as analogical. But when they do, they simply mean that man cannot exhaustively explain reality to himself, and that, therefore, he projects the idea of a god who does. Then he adds that man is dependent upon this god, but in reality this is not true. For the god whom the non-Christian speaks of is in fact a projection, or limit. He is not self-contained. It is man who is assumed to be original and God is assumed to be derivative. So non-Christian systems should not be called analogical.[12]

---

11. KSO: The notion of "analogical knowledge" has a long and complex history. The term itself is not as perspicuous as it might be. It is best to see it as identical with the Reformed affirmation of human knowledge as *ectypal*. Herman Bavinck puts it this way, "The relation of God's own self-knowledge to our knowledge of God used to be expressed by saying that the former was archetypal of the latter and the latter ectypal of the former. Our knowledge of God is the imprint of the knowledge God has of himself but *always on a creaturely level and in a creaturely way.* The knowledge of God present in his creatures is only a weak likeness, a finite, limited sketch, of the absolute self-consciousness of God accommodated to the capacities of the human or creaturely consciousness," Herman Bavinck, John Bolt, and John Vriend, *Reformed Dogmatics: Prolegomena*, vol. 1 (Grand Rapids, MI: Baker Academic, 2003), 212. See also Ibid., vol. 2, pp. 134, 137. Or, to put it another way, since we are image of God, we should see all of our knowledge as an "image" of God's knowledge, never identical with the archetypal knowledge of God in any way.

12. KSO: It is likely, given Van Til's philosophical education, that he has Immanuel Kant in mind here. According to Kant, "If I say that we are compelled to look upon the world as if it were the work of a supreme understanding and will, I actually say nothing more than: in the way that

Then there is the Romanist use of the idea of analogy. Romanism thinks that it has the true idea of analogy. It holds that Protestantism, and especially the Reformed Faith, does not have a true notion of analogy since it does not do justice to man as in some measure autonomous. Roman Catholic theology will not make man fully and exclusively dependent upon God, and therefore, from a Reformed point of view, cannot do justice to the idea of analogy. It will not make a clear-cut choice between the Christian and the non-Christian position on the question of the final point of reference in predication. If man is made or assumed to be ultimate, then he is not analogous of God. Only if God is taken to be ultimate is man really analogous of God. It is only in the Reformed Faith that God is really taken to be ultimate. Hence the Reformed idea of *system* is different, not only from the non-Christian and from the Romanist, but even from the evangelical idea. We mean that so far as the evangelical holds with the Romanist that man has some measure of autonomy, he cannot do justice to the idea that the human system should aim to be analogical *and no more*.[13]

The difference between a Christian system that seeks to be consistently analogical and one, like that of Romanism and evangelicalism, that does not, is that only in the former is the *false ideal of knowledge* of the unbeliever rejected. *If one does not make human knowledge wholly dependent upon the original self-knowledge and consequent revelation of God to man, then man will have to seek knowledge within himself as the final reference point.* Then he will have to seek an exhaustive understanding of reality. Then he will have to hold that if he cannot attain to such an exhaustive understanding of reality, he has no *true* knowledge of anything at all. Either man must then know everything or he knows nothing. This is the dilemma that confronts every form of non-Christian epistemology. The

---

a watch, a ship, and a regiment are related to an artisan, a builder, and a commander, the sensible world (or everything that makes up the basis of this sum total of appearances) is related to the unknown—which I do not thereby cognize according to what it is in itself, but only according to what it is for me, that is, with respect to the world of which I am a part. *This type of cognition is cognition according to analogy,* which surely does not signify, as the word is usually taken, an imperfect similarity between two things, but rather a perfect similarity between two relations in wholly dissimilar things. By means of this analogy there still remains a concept of the supreme being sufficiently determinate for us, though we have omitted everything that could have determined this concept unconditionally and in itself; for we determine the concept only with respect to the world and hence with respect to us, and we have no need of more," Immanuel Kant, *Prolegomena to Any Future Metaphysics* (Cambridge University Press, 2004): 108–109.

13. KSO: Roman Catholicism and evangelicalism would both affirm that man is *metaphysically* dependent on God; they would affirm that God is the Creator of all that is. However, as we noted above, because they ascribe a measure of autonomy to man's reason and will, they would hold that our reasoning faculty is *epistemologically* not dependent on God, but instead is its own initial authority. In that sense, man's reason and will cannot be *ectypal*, but are thought to be *archetypal*, even though created.

Romanist or evangelical type of argument for Christianity is not able to indicate this fact with clarity. The only way by which this dilemma can be indicated clearly is by making plain that the final reference point in predication is God as the self-sufficient One.

. ——— .

So far in this chapter the general difference between a consistently Protestant or Reformed and a more generally evangelical method of reasoning has been pointed out. The Romanist-evangelical method would start reasoning with the non-Christian on a neutral basis. It would not challenge the presuppositions of the non-Christian at the outset of the argument. The reason for this is obvious. The Romanist and the evangelical are in some measure in agreement with the non-Christian on his presuppositions. They, too, attribute a measure of autonomy to man. They therefore hold that the non-Christian quite legitimately demands that Christianity shall be shown to meet the demands of the autonomous man.

These demands are, first of all, that Christianity shall be shown to be in "accord with reason." By "reason" is meant the reason of man as the determiner of the possible and the impossible by means of "logic." Only that is said to be possible which is in accord with, or at least is not against, the law of contradiction. Secondly, Christianity must be shown to be "in accord with the facts." These facts are the facts as reason, the determiner of the possible and impossible, has "discovered" or observed them.[14]

The Romanist-evangelical method of defending Christianity therefore has to compromise Christianity while defending it. If the demands of "reason" as the non-Christian thinks of it are assumed to be legitimate, then Christianity will be able to prove itself true only by destroying itself. As it cannot clearly show the difference between the Christian and the non-Christian view of things, so it cannot present any clear-cut reason why the non-Christian should forsake his position.

The Reformed method of apologetics seeks to escape this nemesis. It begins frankly "from above." It would "presuppose" God. But in presupposing God it cannot place itself at any point on a neutral basis with the non-Christian. Before

---

14. KSO: For example, Thomas Aquinas, and his followers, would affirm: "Now in those things which we hold about God there is truth in two ways (*duplex veritatis modus*). For certain things that are true about God wholly surpass the capability of human reason, for instance that God is three and one: while there are certain things to which even natural reason can attain, for instance that God is, that God is one, and others like these, which even the philosophers proved demonstratively of God, being guided by the light of natural reason," Thomas Aquinas, *The Summa Contra Gentiles of Saint Thomas Aquinas*, trans. the English Dominican Fathers, 5 vols. (London: Burns Oates & Washbourne, 1923–29), 1:4–5. According to Thomas, "even the philosophers proved demonstratively" that God is, and is one. This inevitably gives undue weight to unbelieving reason, assuming that all can truly know certain characteristics of God.

seeking to prove that Christianity is in accord with reason and in accord with fact, it would ask what is meant by "reason" and what is meant by "fact." It would argue that unless reason and fact are themselves interpreted in terms of God they are unintelligible.[15] If God is not presupposed, reason is a pure abstraction that has no contact with fact, and fact is a pure abstraction that has no contact with reason. Reason and fact cannot be brought into fruitful union with one another except upon the presupposition of the existence of God and his control over the universe.

Since on the Reformed basis there is no area of neutrality between the believer and the unbeliever, the argument between them must be *indirect*. Christians cannot allow the legitimacy of the assumptions that underlie the non-Christian *methodology*. But they can place themselves upon the position of those whom they are seeking to win to a belief in Christianity for the sake of the argument. And the non-Christian, though not granting the presuppositions from which the Christian works, can nevertheless place himself upon the position of the Christian for the sake of the argument.

The Christian knows the truth about the non-Christian. He knows this because he is himself what he is by grace alone. He has been saved from the blindness of mind and the hardness of heart that marks the "natural man." The Christian has the "doctor's book." The Scriptures tell him of the origin and of the nature of sin. Man is dead in trespasses and sins (Eph 2:1). He hates God. His inability to see the facts as they are and to reason about them as he ought to reason about them is, at bottom, a matter of sin. He has the God-created ability of reasoning within him. He is made in the image of God. God's revelation is before him and within him. He is in his own constitution a manifestation of the revelation and therefore of the requirement of God. God made a covenant with him through Adam (Rom 5:12). He is therefore now, in Adam, a covenant-breaker. He is also against God and therefore against the revelation of God (Rom 8:6–8). This revelation of God constantly and inescapably reminds him of his creatural responsibility. As a sinner he has, in Adam, declared himself autonomous.

Thus, intellectual argument will not, as such, convince and convert the non-Christian. It takes the regenerating power of the Holy Spirit to do that. But as in the case of preaching, so in the case of apologetical reasoning, the Holy

---

15. KSO: This is the case, as we noted above (fn. 9), because the responsibility of reason is to think God's thoughts after him, and to systematize the facts of creation in terms, first of all, of what God has said about them. Non-Christians still *use* their reason, and *seek* to know the facts. But if their use of reason and method of knowing eliminates who God is and what he has done, then the only referent available to them is their own mind. Knowledge, then, is only and always *self*-referential, thus relative, and ultimately unintelligible.

Spirit may use a *mediate* approach to the minds and hearts of men.[16] The natural man is quite able intellectually to follow the argument that the Christian offers for the truth of his position. He can therefore see that the wisdom of this world has been made foolishness by God.[17] Christianity can be shown to be, not "just as good as" or even "better than" the non-Christian position, but the *only* position that does not make nonsense of human experience.

To this point no notice has been taken of the fact that not all Reformed theologians follow the method briefly suggested so far. What has been called the Reformed method in the preceding discussion is implied in the basic contention of Reformed theology, namely, the self-sufficiency and self-explanatory character of the triune God. But that such is the case has not always been recognized. The Reformed theologians of the Reformation period did not work out a Reformed apologetical methodology. This is not to be marveled at. They laid the groundwork for it. Some later Reformed theologians continued to use the Romanist-evangelical method of defending Christianity. At least they did so up to the point where the specifically Reformed teachings on the sovereignty of God in soteriology came up for discussion. Thus the apologetics of the Reformed theologians at Princeton Theological Seminary (prior to its reorganization in 1929 when the Reformed Faith was rejected in principle) used a method of argument similar to that employed in Bishop Butler's *Analogy*.[18] Now Butler's work is perhaps the most outstanding historical example of evangelical non-Reformed methodology. It starts with assuming that man, though he has not taken God into account, has by his own principles been able to interpret the course and constitution of nature aright.[19] Butler's argument is to the effect that, if men would only follow the same method they have employed for the interpretation of nature when they

---

16. KSO: This point should not be underestimated or overlooked. An apologetic that is consistent with Reformed theology is an apologetic that communicates the truth of God and his Word to those who are outside of Christ. As with preaching, therefore, the communication of that truth may be used by the Holy Spirit to soften hard human hearts.

17. KSO: Notice that Van Til affirms that unbelievers can "follow the argument" that we give and can "see that the wisdom of this world has been made foolishness by God." They can do this, because they remain in God's image and they know the God of whom we speak (Rom. 1:18). In other words, they *do not* do this because of a neutral notion of reason, but because of what God says about us, and about himself in and through all that is made.

18. *The Works of Joseph Butler*, D. C. L. ed. by The Rt. Hon. W. E. Gladstone, Vol. I (New York: Macmillan and Co., 1896).

19. KSO: Van Til might have been more specific in his critique of Old Princeton and its apologetic. Since Van Til studied apologetics at Princeton under William Brenton Greene, Jr., he would have recognized Greene's allegiance to Scottish Common Sense Realism. However, both Butler and Greene argue that there are a host of commonalities between the natural man and the Christian with respect to knowledge. For more on Greene's commitment to common sense realism, see my foreword in Cornelius Van Til, *Christian-Theistic Evidences* (Phillipsburg, New Jersey: Presbyterian and Reformed Publishing Co., 2016).

are confronted with the claims of Christianity, they will be driven to accept the latter as true. Men have seen evidence of substitution in nature and they have recognized it as such. So then, why should they not also accept the idea of the substitutionary atonement by Christ, the Son of God, as presented in Scripture? Men have admitted that the exceptional, the inexplicable, takes place in nature. There is a principle of discontinuity as well as a principle of continuity that men recognize in the world. Why then should they object to the possibility of the supernatural and of miracle? They can allow for these without in the least giving up their own basic principle of interpretation.[20]

It was against a position similar to this that Dr. Abraham Kuyper protested in his famous work *Principles of Sacred Theology*.[21] His argument is to the effect that apologetics of this nature gives over one bulwark after another to the enemy. Kuyper's contention is that the Christian must take his place directly upon the presupposition of the truth of the Christian religion as it is presented in Scripture.

In similar fashion Dr. Herman Bavinck argued that there is only one principle of interpretation for the Christian, namely, as it is objectively expressed in Scripture and as this is testified to by the Holy Spirit in the mind and heart of the believer.

Even so, both Kuyper and Bavinck did not work out their own principles fully; their primary interest was theological rather than apologetical. When they did engage in apologetical argument they sometimes employed the method which they themselves had criticized in others.

What has been called the Reformed method in the preceding discussion was, however, employed by both the men of Princeton and of Amsterdam to which reference has been made. At one point or another all the Reformed theologians of modern times argue that unless the "reason of man" and the facts of the universe be taken as they are taken in terms of the infallible revelation of God given to man in the Bible, human experience runs into the ground.[22]

It is to this basic approach of Kuyper and Bavinck, of Charles Hodge and B. B. Warfield and Geerhardus Vos (ignoring or setting aside the remnants of the traditional method that is found in their works) that appeal is made in this work.

It is of critical importance in the current scene that a consistently Reformed apologetic be set forth. The non-Christian point of view is much more

---

20. Cf. B. B. Warfield, "Apologetics," *The New Schaff-Herzog Encyclopaedia of Religious Knowledge*, ed. by Samuel M. Jackson (Grand Rapids: Baker Book House, 1951).

21. Abraham Kuyper, *Principles of Sacred Theology*, tr. by J. H. DeVries (Grand Rapids: Wm. B. Eerdmans, 1954). This is an abridgment of Kuyper's three volume work *Encyclopaedie der Heilige Godgeleerdheid* (Kampen: J. H. Kok, 1908–09).

22. KSO: Importantly, Van Til recognizes that these Reformed theologians *were*, at times, consistent with their theology in their defense of Christianity.

self-consciously hostile to Christianity than it has ever been. The fact that the assumption of human autonomy is the root and fountain of all forms of non-Christian thought is more apparent than it has ever been in the past. Any argument for the truth of Christianity that is *inconsistent with itself* should not expect to have a hearing. Only a position which boldly and humbly challenges the wisdom of the world and, with the Apostle Paul, brings out that it has been made foolishness with God will serve the purpose. Only such a method which asks man to serve and worship the Creator rather than the creature honors God and assigns to him the place that he truly occupies. Only such a method is consistent with the idea that the Holy Spirit must convict and convince the sinner. The Holy Spirit cannot be asked to honor a method that does not honor God as God.

To be sure, however, objection has been raised to what has been called the Reformed method of apologetics. In his book *General Revelation and Common Grace*,[23] Dr. William Masselink, formerly of the Reformed Bible Institute at Grand Rapids, Michigan, takes exception to the position of the present writer. It will be necessary therefore to deal with this matter later. The question hinges largely on the problem of the value of the knowledge of the non-Christian. Masselink's contention is that, on the basis of the position taken by this writer, no value can be assigned to the knowledge of the unbeliever at all. This, he argues, is against the Reformed confessions. For these confessions speak of the natural light of reason by which men, though they are sinners against God, yet have natural knowledge of God and morality. In particular, God has, by his "common grace," not only restrained the sin of man but maintained the image of God in him. He thus enables him to make contributions to science and to practice "moral virtue."

In dealing with this contention an attempt will be made to show that the doctrine of general revelation and of common grace must not be taken as justifying a neutral area between the non-Christian and the Christian. There is no escape from taking it as such unless, with Calvin, appeal is made to the knowledge of God which the natural man inescapably has (Rom 1:19–20; Rom 2:14), but which he seeks to, but cannot wholly, suppress (Rom 1:18).[24]

As far as the principle of interpretation is concerned, the natural man makes himself the final point of reference.[25] So far, then, as he carries through his principle, he interprets all things without God. In *principle* he is hostile to God. But he cannot carry through his principle completely. He is restrained by God from

---

23. William Masselink, *General Revelation and Common Grace* (Grand Rapids: Wm. B. Eerdmans, 1953).

24. KSO: This one sentence is as concise a summary of Van Til's apologetic approach as one is likely to find.

25. KSO: Van Til refers here to the "principle" of interpretation. This is the all-important apologetic point. On what *principle*, or *foundation*, does the natural man purport to know anything?

doing so. Being restrained by God from doing so, he is enabled to make contributions to the edifice of human knowledge. The forces of creative power implanted in him are to some extent released by God's common grace. *He therefore makes positive contributions to science in spite of his principles and because both he and the universe are the exact opposite of what he, by his principles, thinks they are.*

As against this method of approaching the question of the knowledge of the non-Christian, Masselink argues, with the late Dr. Valentine Hepp of Amsterdam, that there are *central* truths about God, man, and the world on which Christians and non-Christians do not greatly differ. That is to say, Masselink, following Hepp, does not signalize, first, the difference between the two principles of interpretation, the one based on the assumption that man is ultimate and the other based on the assumption that man is the creature of God. Common grace is, in effect, used to blur the differences between these two mutually exclusive principles. There is supposed, then, to be some area where the difference between these two mutually exclusive principles does not very greatly count. There is a "twilight zone" where those who are enemies fraternize and build together on the common enterprise of science; there is an area of commonness without difference, or at least without basic difference. It is the contention of this writer that in this manner the doctrine of common grace becomes a means by which a specifically Reformed conception of apologetics, and therefore a consistently Christian method of apologetics, is suppressed. In other words, it will be shown that what was done at Princeton when Butler was used as a sample of true methodology is now being done more self-consciously by means of "common grace." Naturally, a method such as is set forth in this book will need to relate the doctrine of common grace to the sovereignty of God in such a way as to express instead of blur it.

It will be plain from the foregoing that the question of a truly Christian method of defending Christianity is very much a matter of dispute. Naturally, a method such as is set forth in this book will appear to many to be very "dogmatic and absolutistic." The non-Christian is to be told that his basic assumption is mistaken, that on his assumption experience is reduced to that which has no meaning. The Roman Catholic is to be told that his theology involves a compromise with the "natural man" and that therefore his method of apologetics is internally inconsistent and cannot challenge the natural man. The evangelical is to be told that he, too, has to some extent made compromise with "the enemy," allowing him such rights as no creature should claim for himself. The time-honored method of apologetics followed by great Reformed theologians of "old Princeton" is to be assailed as inconsistent with the theology that these very men taught us to embrace. And, finally, the theory of common grace, we are boldly told, is not given its proper place by such great Reformed theologians as Kuyper, Bavinck and Hepp.

Here the following remarks are in order. In the first place, every Christian must tell the non-Christian that he must be *saved* from his false views of God and himself. The greatest love can be shown for the lost only by those who have themselves sensed most deeply the lost condition from which they have been saved. The best physician is he who tells the patient who needs surgery that he must be rushed to the hospital, not he who tells him to take a strong sedative. It is this that the present writer has learned from those from whom he has been bold enough to differ at points. It is only in a subordinate way that he differs from the great theologians of the preceding generation. The greater part of what is presented here is due to the fact that the writer stands on the shoulders of the great Reformed thinkers mentioned above. He is merely gathering together the thoughts found over a widely diversified body of their writings in order to present briefly that which basically they have taught. The present book is no more than an effort to stimulate thinking along the lines of a consistent Christian approach to modern thought. The message of Christianity must ring out clearly in the modern tumult. If Christianity is to be heard above the din and noise of modern irrationalism and existentialism, it must think in terms of its own basic categories. If it has to import some of its materials from the enemy, it cannot expect effectively to conquer the enemy. It is the Christian Faith that alone has the truth; this should be its claim. It should be made with all modesty; those who have accepted it once were blind. They have been saved by grace. Little would it behoove them to regard themselves as the source of wisdom. But disclaiming themselves as the source of wisdom, they cannot make apology for God and for Christ the Son of God. If men would be saved, if they would save their culture as well as themselves, they must meet the requirements of God. There is no other way to truth. "Hath not God made foolish the wisdom of this world? For after that the world by its wisdom knew not God, it pleased God through the foolishness of preaching to save those that believe" (1 Cor 1:20–21).

II

THE HOLY SCRIPTURES[1]

In presenting an argument for the truth of Christianity it is essential to know what is meant by Christianity. So the question at once comes up as to how this is to be discovered. This leads directly to the Scriptures. For the Scriptures of the Old and New Testaments are the source book of knowledge for Christians. True, not all Christians have the same view of Scripture. Not all regard it as the exclusive source book of knowledge with respect to the nature of Christianity. Roman Catholic theology places tradition alongside of Scripture as a source of information. Its position will therefore need separate discussion. We first set forth the Protestant doctrine of Scripture.

But is there, it will at once be asked, such a thing as a doctrine of Scripture on which all Protestants agree? Bavinck's words to the effect that there is no dogma on which there is more unity than the dogma with respect to Scripture comes to mind at once when we seek a reply to this question.[2] But in saying this Bavinck does not mean to deny the basic difference between Protestants and Roman Catholics on the doctrine of Scripture. He himself works out a doctrine of Scripture with which only Reformed Christians can fully agree. This is to be expected. For only those who hold to the doctrine of God as self-sufficient will naturally also hold to the doctrine of Scripture as wholly self-interpretative. The difference between a specifically Reformed and an evangelical doctrine of Scripture will appear more clearly at a later point. For the moment we proceed to set forth the idea of Scripture as the Reformed confessions and the Reformed theologians have taught it.

---

1. KSO: This is a centrally and foundationally crucial aspect of Reformed theology, and thus of Van Til's apologetic. Only in Reformed theology is the *principium cognoscendi* affirmed to be utterly self-attesting, and thus not dependent on anything for its authority except itself. Moreover, it seems the doctrine of Scripture, and what it teaches, has been the perennial target of detractors, both within and without Christianity.

2. Herman Bavinck, *Gereformeerde Dogmatiek*, Vol. I (Kampen: J. H. Kok, 1928), p. 442. KSO: Herman Bavinck, *Reformed Dogmatics: Prolegomena* ed. John Bolt, trans. John Vriend, Vol. 1 (Grand Rapids, Michigan: Baker Academic, 2003), 598.

A. THE SELF-SUFFICIENCY OF SCRIPTURE

The first point about a truly Protestant or Reformed doctrine of Scripture is that it must be taken exclusively from Scripture. It is, says Bavinck, exclusively from the Scriptures that we learn about Christ and his work of redemption for man. From the Scriptures alone do we learn about God's work of redemption for man. On its authority as the Word of God do we know the whole "system" of Christian truth. Therefore also, on its authority alone do we believe what the Scripture says about itself. The Scripture testifies to itself because in it Christ testifies of himself. "Now, in order that true religion may shine upon us, we ought to hold that it must take its beginning from heavenly doctrine and that no one can get even the slightest taste of right and sound doctrine unless he be a pupil of Scripture. Hence, there also emerges the beginning of true understanding when we reverently embrace what it pleases God there to witness of himself."[3]

Reformed theologians have pointed out that the idea of Scripture as self-attesting is involved in the fact that in it we have the message of redemption for man. This message of redemption is not a piecemeal affair. It centers around the person and work of Jesus Christ. His incarnation, his death and resurrection, Bavinck points out, cannot be repeated. They are historically unique.[4] The Son of God became like unto men in all things, sin excepted. So the question of identification becomes at once important. Who is the Christ? Is it this man Jesus of Nazareth? But he does not seem to differ greatly from other men. How can he be identified as being the Son of God as well as the son of Mary?

Can there be identification unless there be complete or exhaustive description? How is he, if he is wholly unique, to be indicated for what he is to those who are wholly different from him? Or, if he is not wholly different, if he is like them and yet also unlike them, where is the boundary line between likeness and difference? When we can only recognize him at the point where he is like us or identical in nature with us, we can not recognize him where he is different from us.

The upshot of such considerations is that the identification of Jesus Christ must be by his own authority. Without authoritative identification, the Christ is lost in the ocean of relativity.

A distinction must be made at this point. Authority is needed for purposes of identification in history. But the authority of Scripture, as has already been mentioned, has to do with the question of redemption through Jesus Christ as the Son of God. Christ came to redeem sinners. Sinners are covenant-breakers. They

---

3. Calvin: *Institutes of the Christian Religion*, ed. by John T. McNeill, tr. by Ford Lewis Battles ("The Library of Christian Classics," Vol. XX, XXI, ed. by J. Baillie, J. T. McNeill and H. P. Van Dusen; Philadelphia: Westminster Press, 1960), I:6.2.
4. Bavinck, *op. cit.*, p. 399. KSO: Bavinck, *Prolegomena*, 379.

are descendants of Adam in whom, as their representative, they turned against God. The natural man, the sinner, the covenant-breaker in Adam, is spiritually blind. He is willfully blind. He cannot see the truth because he will not see it. He seeks to suppress the truth in unrighteousness (Rom 1:18). Sinners hate the idea of a clearly identifiable authority over them. They do not want to meet God. They would gladly make themselves believe that there is no clearly discernible, identifiable revelation of their Creator and Judge anywhere to be found in the universe. God's work of redemption through Christ, therefore, comes into enemy territory. It comes to save from themselves those who do not want to be saved, because they think that they do not need to be saved.

It is this situation, as has been indicated by Reformed theologians, that accounts for the need of inscripturation of the authoritative and redemptive Word of God.

But this view of sin itself comes from Scripture as authoritative. Experience apart from Scripture does not teach such a doctrine. Only he who accepts the Scripture as the authoritative revelation of God and of the self-identifying Son of God, will accept what it says about himself as a sinner. So we are of necessity moving about in circles. Those who accept the fully biblical conception of sin will accept the Bible as authoritative. And those who accept the fully biblical view of sin do so because they accept the Bible as the authoritative Word of God.

The inscripturation of the Word of God with respect to God's plan of redemption through Christ, therefore, is the Bible. Because of sin in the heart of man, the Word of God thus acquires the greatest possible permanence of form. It is, as the inscripturated Word of God, less liable to perversion than mere tradition would be.

That the Bible is the Word of God pertains only to the original autographs. The versions and translations may fairly be said to be faithful reproductions of the autographs. But they cannot be said to be exact replicas of them.

It has been said at this point that if this be the case, we have no identifiable revelation of God after all. The *autographa* are not available and none of the manuscripts from which our Bible is taken are perfect. Why then speak of an absolutely identifiable Word of God? Why then claim that we have the direct revelation of God in the Bible? Do we not in any case have to rely on that which we think is *generally* reliable without its being *absolutely* infallible?

In reply to this objection the following remarks are in order. There would be no *reasonably reliable* method of identifying the Word of God in human history unless human history itself is controlled by God. The doctrine of Scripture as self-attesting presupposes that whatsoever comes to pass in history materializes by virtue of the plan and counsel of the living God. If everything happens by virtue of the plan of God, then all created reality, every aspect of it, is inherently revelational of God and of his plan. All facts of history are what they are ultimately because of what God intends and makes them to be. Even that which is accomplished in human history through the instrumentality of men still happens by virtue of the plan of God. God tells the stars by their names. He identifies by complete description. He knows exhaustively. He knows exhaustively because he controls completely.

It is of such a God the Bible speaks. So it is once again a matter of moving about in circles. It is impossible to attain to the idea of such a God by speculation independently of Scripture. It has never been done and is inherently impossible. Such a God *must* identify himself. Such a God, and only such a God, identifies all the facts of the universe. In identifying all the facts of the universe he sets these facts in relation to one another.

Such a view of God and of human history is both presupposed by, and in turn presupposes, the idea of the infallible Bible; and if such a God is presupposed then it is not a matter of great worry if the transmissions are not altogether accurate reproductions of the originals. Then the very idea of "substantial accuracy" or "essential reliability" has its foundation in the complete control of history by God. Then it is proper and meaningful to say that God in his providence has provided for the essentially accurate transmission of the words of the original.

Without such a view of history as wholly controlled by the plan of God the idea of essential dependability would be without foundation. If history is not wholly controlled by God, the idea of an infallible Word of God is without meaning. The idea of an essentially reliable Bible would have no foundation. In a world of contingency all predication is reduced to flux.

It thus appears afresh that a specifically biblical or Reformed philosophy of history both presupposes and is presupposed by the idea of the Bible as testifying to itself and as being the source of its own identification.

To what has been said one further point needs to be added. It has been stressed that the Reformed concept of Scripture and the Reformed view of history imply one another. It has been stressed that the inscripturation of the Word of God is necessary because of the sin of man. Thus we have the idea of an authoritative revelation of God as self-attesting in a world of sin. But the world was not always a world of sin. Before the fall of Adam, man walked and talked with God in intimate fellowship. Then no Bible was required. Man was not alienated from God. No Christ was needed for man's redemption. But shall we add that therefore no supernatural authoritative revelation was necessary for him? Shall we say that man could originally identify himself and the facts of the universe without supernatural thought communication on the part of his Creator? The answer must be in the negative.

The necessity of an authoritative self-revelation of God in supernatural fashion is inherent in the human situation. It is "natural" that there should be supernatural revelation. Apart from and prior to the entrance of sin, God actually spoke to man. God *identifies* one tree among many in order to indicate to man his task on earth. Man's task is to cultivate the earth and subdue it. He can do so only if he thinks and acts in obedience to his Maker. So his obedience must be tested. He must become even more self-consciously desirous of keeping the covenant with his God than he was. Hence supernatural thought communication is from the outset of history added to revelation through the facts of the universe in order thus to intimate to man his cultural task. Self-conscious covenantal reaction on the part of man presupposes identification of the facts of history and nature as clearly and directly carrying the will of God.

Man was to deal covenantally with every fact of history. He must therefore have available to him in history the direct confrontation of God and his requirements. Man must be able to identify all facts about him as the bearers of God's requirements; hence he needs a special supernatural test at the outset. He needs to learn by way of one example what he is to do with all the facts of history.

Thus the idea of supernatural thought communication on the part of God to man is inherent in the human situation. It is important to emphasize this point. Without clearly seeing that such is the case, there is no good argument for the necessity of Scripture. The idea of the Bible as the infallible Word requires, as has been noted, the idea of God's complete control over history. In similar fashion the idea of the Bible as supernatural revelation and as self-attesting, presupposes the idea that God's supernatural identification of his will in history took place before the fall of man. *It was against such a specific self-identification that man sinned.* The idea of sin is precisely that of the willful setting aside of that which has been clearly identified to him as the will of God by God himself. So *pre-redemptive* supernatural revelation is the presupposition of *redemptive* supernatural revelation.

A further point remains to be made. It has been pointed out that the Bible tells the story of God's redemptive work for man. This work is accomplished through Christ, the Son of God, who is also completely human. The Word tells us of the person and work of Christ. But Christ himself tells about the Word as being authoritative because it is the Word of God. Christ testified to the Old Testament as being the Word of God that cannot be broken. He performed his work on earth in accordance with the program outlined for him in the Word. Thus the Christ as testifying to the Word and the Word as testifying to the Christ are involved in one another.

But the work of Christ was not finished while he was on earth. He accomplished much of his work through his apostles after him. So he promised them his Spirit that they might write the New Testament as a supplement to the Old Testament. But who should identify the New Testament as being the Word of

God after it was written? Should the church do this? Protestant theologians have replied that the church cannot and did not authenticate the New Testament Scriptures as being the Word of God.[5] The New Testament as well as the Old is self-attesting. The church merely recognized the Word in its self-attestation. It is Christ whose voice the church hears in Scripture.

It is only if, in this manner, both the Old and New Testaments are regarded as a unit, and as a self-attesting unit, that justice is done to the idea of the Scriptures as the Word of God.

It is only thus, too, that the unity of the work of Christ can be maintained. The work of Christ is the work of establishing and perfecting the covenant of grace in a world of sin. He came to redeem a people for the Father. That people is a unit by virtue of their common redemption through Christ. But they are taken out of a broader unit, namely the human race. This work has the greatest possible significance for the human race as a whole. Christ's work is of cosmic significance. He came to save the *world*. So there is through him and through his Word an authoritative interpretation given to mankind of the whole of the cosmic scene. Every fact in the universe must be Christologically interpreted. Through Christ the new heavens and the new earth are to come into being, as sprung from the old, through the redemptive power of the risen Christ. In greater or lesser degree, all the facts of the universe are what they are because of the work of Christ. For it is through the work of Christ that God accomplishes his plan for the world.[6]

Accordingly, the Bible must be identified in its entirety in all that it says on any subject as the Word of God. It is, again, only if history is considered to be what it is because of the ultimate controlling plan of God, that such a relationship between God's Word and all the facts of the universe can be obtained.

In several of the preceding sections we have seemingly gone beyond the matter of Scripture's self-attestation. It has been impossible to avoid dealing with the question of what Scripture teaches even in a discussion of where the Scriptures may be found. In other words, the question of the identity of Scripture could not be discussed without asking about the truth of the content of which it speaks. The *that* and the *what* overlap. Unless we conjoin the message of the Scripture and the idea of Scripture, the latter becomes an abstraction.

This is but to be expected. It is of the utmost apologetical importance. It is precisely because God is the kind of God he is, that his revelation is, in the nature of the case, self-attesting. In particular, it should be noted that such a God as

---

5. KSO: See WCF 1.4.
6. KSO: In this sense, any other "kingdom"—whether the kingdom of darkness, or the kingdom of this world—is subservient to, and meant to be in subjection to, the all-encompassing kingdom of Christ.

the Scripture speaks of is everywhere self-attesting. It is not now our purpose to deal fully with the problem of general or natural revelation. But so much must be said of it as to bring out the full significance of the Scriptures as self-attesting. To see the import of this doctrine it must be noted that man cannot look anywhere but that he confronts God, and God as self-attesting. Natural or general revelation speaks with as much authority and as directly as does the Bible, albeit in a different manner and not on redemption.

It is this complementary and supplementary character of supernatural and natural revelation that must be borne in mind when approach is made to the question of the indications of the divinity of Scripture. The Westminster Confession of Faith speaks eloquently of the heavenly character, the consent of all the parts, etc., of Scripture.[7]

Says Calvin on this subject: "What wonderful confirmation ensues when, with keener study, we ponder the economy of the divine wisdom, so well ordered and disposed; the completely heavenly character of its doctrine, savoring of nothing earthly; the beautiful agreement of all the parts with one another—as well as such other qualities as can gain majesty for the writings."[8]

Then after considerable discussion on the various matters he adds:

> There are other reasons, neither few nor weak, for which the dignity and majesty of Scripture are not only affirmed in godly hearts, but brilliantly vindicated against the wiles of its disparagers; yet of themselves these are not strong enough to provide a firm faith, until our Heavenly Father, revealing his majesty there, lifts reverence for Scripture beyond the realm of controversy. Therefore Scripture will suffice for a saving knowledge of God only when its certainty is founded upon the inward persuasion of the Holy Spirit."[9]

In this passage Calvin brings into contact the fact that objectively the Scriptures have on their face the appearance of divinity while yet none will accept its self-attestation unless the Holy Spirit, himself divine, witness to the Word which he has inspired the prophets and apostles to write.

First then, argues Calvin, we are not to separate the fact of Scripture from the nature of Scripture. The identification of the fact of Scripture is an identification accomplished by the setting before us of the content of Scripture, the system of truth centering in the ideas of God as self-contained and of his plan for the

---

7. KSO: See WCF 1.5.
8. *Institutes*, I:8.1.
9. Ibid., I:8.13.

universe which controls whatsoever comes to pass. The identity is not that of an unknown quantity. Faith is not blind faith.

> The nature of faith is acceptance on the basis of testimony, and the ground of faith is therefore testimony or evidence. In this matter it is the evidence God has provided, and God provides the evidence in his Word, the Bible. This means simply that the basis of faith in the Bible is the witness the Bible itself bears to the fact that it is God's Word, and our faith that it is infallible must rest upon no other basis than the witness the Bible bears to this fact. If the Bible does not witness to its own infallibility, then we have no right to believe that it is infallible. If it does bear witness to its infallibility then our faith in it must rest upon that witness, however much difficulty may be entertained with this belief. If this position with respect to the ground of faith in Scripture is abandoned, then appeal to the Bible for the ground of faith in any other doctrine must also be abandoned.[10]

It is this interdependence of the idea of *the fact* and *the content* of Scripture that is all important. The *that* and the *what* are correlative or supplementative the one to the other. It is this interdependence that enables Calvin to exult in the absolute assurance that he has before him in the Bible, not the word of man, not the word of man as it speaks in a church that claims to authenticate the Word, but the very Word of God himself. "As to their question—How can we be assured that this has sprung from God unless we have recourse to the decree of the church?—it is as if someone asked: Whence will we learn to distinguish light from darkness, white from black, sweet from bitter? Indeed, Scripture exhibits fully as clear evidence of its own truth as white and black things do of their color, or sweet and bitter things do of their taste."[11]

It is through the heavenly content of the Word that God speaks of himself. Faith is not blind faith; it is faith in the truth, the system of truth displayed in the Scriptures.

At the same time the interdependence of the *that* and the *what* of Scripture fits in with the idea of the witness of the Holy Spirit to the divinity of Scripture as alone able to convince men of its divinity.

It is this whole system of truth that is set forth in the Bible. The writers of Scripture were inspired by the Holy Spirit to set forth this system of truth. Thus

---

10. John Murray, "The Attestation of Scripture," *The Infallible Word, a Symposium by the Members of the Faculty of Westminster Theological Seminary*, ed. by N. B. Stonehouse and Paul Woolley (Philadelphia: The Presbyterian Guardian, 1946), pp. 7–8. Revised, Presbyterian and Reformed Publishing Co., 1968.

11. Calvin, *Institutes*, I:7.2.

THE HOLY SCRIPTURES

the system is self-attesting. The testimony or influence of the Spirit in the heart of man cannot be in the nature of new information. The whole system of truth is already contained in Scripture and is being identified as such. It would not be identified by the Spirit as such if the Spirit gave other additional revelation. The Scripture would no longer be self-attesting if the Spirit gave additional information. On the other hand it is by the sovereign act of the Holy Spirit that the Scripture can be seen to be the self-attesting Word of God. For sin is that by which men seek to interpret facts apart from the revelation of God. The sinner seeks a criterion of truth and knowledge independent of the revelation of God. The sinner wants to test that which presents itself as the revelation of God by a standard not itself taken from this revelation. He complains of the circular reasoning that would be involved in accepting the word of Scripture about the nature of Scripture. So then, to overcome this hostile attitude of the sinner it is necessary that the Holy Spirit convict him of his sin in not accepting the Bible as the Word of God. The miracles, the prophecies fulfilled, the symmetry of its parts, etc., will all be misinterpreted because interpreted by the wrong standard, unless the Spirit convicts and convinces the sinner that he is dealing with the Word of God.

"For as God alone is a fit witness of himself in his Word, so also the Word will not find acceptance in men's hearts before it is sealed by the inward testimony of the Spirit. The same Spirit, therefore, who has spoken through the mouths of the prophets must penetrate into our hearts to persuade us that they faithfully proclaimed what had been divinely commanded."[12]

It should be noted that this view of Scripture thinks of God as here and now speaking to men through his Word. "Scripture is not a dry tale or an old chronicle, but it is the ever living, ever youthful Word which God at the present time and always sends out to his people. It is the ever continuing speech of God to us—It is the *viva vox Dei epistola omnipotentis ad suam creaturam.*"[13] [14]

· ——— ·

The foregoing brief statement of the doctrine of Scripture is quite out of accord with the modern view of Scripture. We shall deal with the modern view of Scripture in the next chapter. For the moment, reference is made to it only insofar as to make plain the historic Christian view. We shall, however, view and discuss two classes of objections that are raised against the orthodox view. The

---

12 Ibid., I:7.4.
13. Bavinck, *op. cit.*, p. 405.
14. KSO: "It is the living voice of God, the letter of the omnipotent God to his creature." Bavinck, *Prolegomena*, 385.

first is that it is based on pure *a priori* assumptions, without regard to the facts as they are ascertainable by scientific research. The second is that the system of truth supposedly contained in Scripture is no system at all; Scripture is said to contain doctrines logically incompatible with one another. In other words, the orthodox Christian is said to disregard both facts and logic when he accepts on mere authority a doctrine of Scripture such as has been outlined.

B. FACTS

The question of facts in relation to Scripture may be divided into two parts. One part deals with the facts or phenomena of Scripture itself and the other part deals with the facts of nature and history with which science and philosophy deal apart from Scripture. There are many works dealing with these questions; a word about each point must suffice here.

1. The Phenomena of Scripture

It has already been pointed out that the claim to infallibility for the Scripture does not pertain to anything but the originals and that the originals are not available for inspection. It is therefore to be expected that there will be "discrepancies" in the Bible. Orthodox scholars have labored to show that these are of no great moment for the "system of doctrine" contained in the Bible. But the point is, we are told, that in an infallible Bible there should not be any discrepancies. There should be no statement of historical fact in Scripture that is contradictory to a statement of historical fact given elsewhere. Yet higher criticism has in modern times found what it thinks are facts that cannot possibly be harmonized with the idea of an infallible Bible.

What shall be the attitude of the orthodox believer with respect to this? Shall he be an obscurantist and hold to the doctrine of authority of the Scripture though he knows that it can empirically be shown to be contrary to the facts of Scripture themselves?

It goes without saying that such should not be his attitude. He should, on the contrary, freely admit that orthodox scholarship has not solved all of the difficulties deriving from the phenomena of Scripture. It is not even likely that these difficulties will ever be fully resolved. "But some difficulties, perhaps many, remain unsolved. The earnest student has no adequate answer and he may frankly confess that he is not able to explain an apparent discrepancy in the teaching of Scripture."[15]

It must be said, therefore, that there is a sense in which the orthodox believer

---

15. John Murray, *op. cit.*, p. 6.

holds to his doctrine of Scripture "in spite of appearances."[16] He believes in the Bible as the Word of God because God has said that it is his Word. "With respect to the inspiration of Scripture as is the case with every other doctrine the question is not in the first place how much can and may I believe without coming into conflict with science, but what is the witness of Scripture and what is accordingly the expression of Christian faith."[17]

In these words of Bavinck we would take our starting point. To do so is consistent with what has been said above about the Scripture as self-testifying. To say that Scripture testifies to itself and therefore identifies itself is to imply that it also identifies every fact in the world. That is to say the God of which the Scriptures speak is the God who makes the facts to be what they are. There can therefore be no fact which is ultimately out of accord with the system of truth set forth in Scripture. Every fact in the universe is what it is just because of the place that it has in this system.

Moreover, to say that every fact in the world is what it is because of its place in the system of truth set forth in Scripture, is to establish the legitimacy of the *Christian principle of discontinuity*. The system of truth set forth in Scripture cannot be fully understood by the creature. The point here is not merely that creatures who are sinners are unwilling to believe the truth. The point is further that man as finite cannot understand God his Maker in an exhaustive manner. As he cannot understand God exhaustively, so he cannot understand anything related to God in an exhaustive way, for to understand it we would have to penetrate its relation to God and to penetrate that relation we would have to understand God exhaustively.

The objections against the phenomena of Scripture would therefore be legitimate if those who make them could show us the positive foundation on which they are standing. This foundation should enable them to explain the facts in terms of a system of truth other than that which is offered in the Bible. This point will later concern us more fully. For the moment, the difference between the final point of reference of the Christian and the final point of reference of the non-Christian is indicated so as to make plain that no discussion of "fact" can be said to settle final issues unless it takes this difference into consideration. The Christian's belief in the Bible as the Word of God is involved in, and is an expression of, his belief in the triune God as the only final point of reference in all human predication. The Christian holds to the authority and finality of the Bible not because he can clearly, that is exhaustively, show the coherence of every fact with every other fact of Scripture. He rather holds to

---

16. Bavinck, *op. cit.*, p. 461. KSO: Bavinck, *Prolegomena*, 436.
17. Ibid., p. 462. KSO: Ibid.

this doctrine of Scripture because, unless he does, there is no resting point for the search of facts anywhere.[18]

2. Facts Outside of Scripture

Having dealt with the question of the facts of Scripture as they are related to the divinity of Scripture, little needs to be added on the second point mentioned above. The facts of the universe in general may either be regarded in the light of the system of truth presented in Scripture or they may be seen in the light of some other system of truth that men think they possess. The Christian is convinced that there is no other system of truth in the light of which the world may properly be regarded; this point will reappear later. The question is not whether the teachings of Scripture are in accord with the facts of science as science is often understood. As often understood, science may properly interpret the facts of the universe without reference to the system of truth set forth in the Bible. It is then assumed that science has performed its task and has been successful in doing so. It has therefore a field of its own, a territory in which it is autonomous. So the Christian must see to it that what he regards as truth revealed in Scripture is in accord with these "assured results of science."

Now it is, of course, true that many of the sciences do not, like theology proper, concern themselves directly with the question of religion. Granting this, it remains a matter of great significance that ultimately all the facts of the universe are either what they are because of their relation to the system of truth set forth in Scripture or they are not. In every discussion about every fact, therefore, it is the two principles, that of the believer in Scripture and that of the non-Christian, that stand over against one another. Both principles are totalitarian. Both claim all the facts. It is in the light of this point that the relation of the Bible as the infallible Word of God to the "facts" of science and history must finally be understood.

C. LOGIC

The second objection mentioned, namely that the system of truth is out of accord with logic, must be answered in a similar manner. In fact, in dealing with the question of facts, it has been impossible to disregard the question of logic. We

---

18. KSO: This sentence illustrates what Van Til sometimes calls a "transcendental" approach, sometimes also called by him the "impossibility of the contrary." We believe Christianity because it is not possible consistently to believe (or to live according to) anything contrary to it. Notice how this approach is entailed, in this section, by a Reformed view of Scripture and its self-attestation. Anyone who believes Scripture to be self-attesting should also recognize the "transcendental" approach that such a belief entails.

have repeatedly asserted that the facts of the universe are what they are because they express together the *system of truth* revealed in the Bible. *What is meant by the idea of truth as found in Scripture does not*, as noted, *mean a logically penetrable system. God alone knows himself and all the things of the created universe exhaustively.* He has revealed himself to man. But he did not reveal himself exhaustively to man. Neither the created universe nor the Bible exhaustively reveals God to man. Nor has man the capacity to receive such an exhaustive revelation. God reveals himself to man according to man's ability to receive his revelation. *All revelation is anthropomorphic.*[19] Moreover, when we say that man understands the revelation of God what is meant is not that he sees through this revelation exhaustively. Neither by logical reasoning nor by intuition can man do more than take to himself the revelation of God on the authority of God. *Bavinck has well said that dogma begins and ends in mystery.*[20] The entire revelation of God points to the self-contained God. This God as self-contained makes every fact to be what it is. Therefore man's study and understanding of any fact is an understanding of something of the ways of God in the world. Man's system of truth, even when formulated in direct and self-conscious subordination to the revelation of the system of truth contained in Scripture, is therefore not a deductive system. God has in himself absolute truth. God is truth. We need not call it a system of truth because there is, in his case, no gathering of facts into coherent relationships with one another. Secondly, God reveals to man in Scripture a system of truth. But this system is not an exhaustive replica of the truth as it is in God himself. It is a system that is adapted to human understanding. Third, the church's restatement of this revealed system of truth is a reworking of the system of truth in Scripture. It cannot therefore claim to be of the same authority as the system of the Bible. But the church must, of necessity, set forth a system of truth in the form of Confessions. It must do so in order the better to understand the truth of Scripture and in order to oppose error.

The main point to be emphasized here is that the system of truth as the Christian thinks of it, as found in Scripture is, as already suggested above, an analogical system. To be faithful to the system of truth as found in Scripture one must not take one doctrine and deduce from it by means of syllogistic procedure

---

19. KSO: Van Til is repeating Bavinck here: "All revelation is anthropomorphic, a kind of humanization of God. It always occurs in certain forms, in specific modes. In natural revelation his divine and eternal thoughts have been deposited in creatures in a creaturely way so that they could be understood by human thought processes. And in supernatural revelation he binds himself to space and time, adopts human language and speech, and makes use of creaturely means." Bavinck, *Prolegomena*, 310.

20. KSO: "Mystery is the lifeblood of dogmatics." Ibid., *God and Creation*, vol. 2 (Grand Rapids, MI: Baker Academic, 2004), 29.

what he thinks follows from it. One must rather gather together all the facts and all the teachings of Scripture and organize them as best as he can, always mindful of the fact that such ordering is the ordering of the revelation of God, who is never fully comprehensible to man.

In the Westminster Confession of Faith the statement is made that that is true which by good and necessary consequence may be deduced from Scripture.[21] *This statement should not be used as a justification for deductive exegesis.* One must not start with the idea of the sovereign control of God over all things and deduce from it the idea that there is no human responsibility. Nor must one begin with the doctrine of human responsibility and deduce from it the idea that there is no absolute control by God over the wills of men.[22] *But to say that one must not engage in this sort of deduction is not to say that the Bible can teach that which is contradictory.* It is not to say that the Bible can teach both that God elects men to salvation and at the same time that they have the power to reject the grace of God. To say such things is to say that the Bible does not identify itself as the Word of the God of truth. It would be to violate the whole doctrine of Scripture as set forth above. For that doctrine implies that God identifies his Word as the Word of truth, as the Word of himself as the God of truth. Thus the fact and the meaning of the fact, the *that* and the *what* of God's revelation, are seen to be involved in one another. There is therefore an ascertainable system of truth in the Bible. That which, in its very statement, involves a denial of the idea of the Word of God as containing absolute, consistent truth-content involves, in effect, a denial of the Bible itself as the Word of God. It is to deny the fact that God through Christ in the Bible identifies himself as God.

In conclusion it should be pointed out that the doctrine of Scripture set forth above sets before men the face of God. God requires of men that they love and obey him. He made them perfect in his image. They rebelled against him. Now he is, in grace, calling them to repentance through his Son. He tells them about this call to repentance and love in the Bible. So Christ, the Redeemer, the Son of God, speaks directly to us in the words of Scripture.

It follows that those who take the Bible to be what it says it is, must present this Bible as conveying a challenge of Christ to men. They must use it always as a means with which to send forth a clarion call of surrender to those who are rebels against God. To be sure, it is the grace of God that is offered to men. Just

---

21. KSO: See WCF 1.6.

22. KSO: Reformed theology has been clear that God's control over all things does not eliminate human responsibility. To think that God's sovereignty means that people are puppets was an argument recognized and addressed by Reformed theologians. See, for example, Willem J. van Asselt, J. M. Bac, and R. T. te Velde, *Reformed Thought on Freedom: The Concept of Free Choice in the History of Early-Modern Reformed Theology* (Grand Rapids, MI: Baker Academic, 2010).

as Jesus wept over Jerusalem and her children, desiring that they might repent, so those who are believers must be filled with deep concern and love for the lost. But in their love for the lost they must, none the less, not lower the claims of God revealed in Christ who calls upon "all men everywhere" to repent (Acts 17:30). This call to repentance has application for the whole of human life and for all the activities of men.

"The authority of Scripture extends itself over the whole man and over the whole of humanity. It stands above mind and will, above heart and conscience; it cannot be compared to any other authority."[23]

Men must therefore be asked to repent for the way they have carried on their scientific enterprises, no less than for the way they have worshiped idols. Scripture is the Word, the living Word of God who is the Creator and Redeemer of men and of mankind. It presupposes that he to whom it comes is ". . . corrupted in his religious attitude and therefore in need of redemption. It would therefore be to deny itself if it recognized the natural man as its competent judge. If Christianity is in the full sense of the term a religion of redemption and therefore wants to redeem man from the error of his intellect as well as from the impurity of his heart, if it wants to save man from the death of his soul as well as from that of his body, then it can in the nature of the case not subject itself to the criticism of man, but must subject man to the criticism of itself."[24] "The revelation of God in Christ does not seek support or justification from men. It posits and maintains itself in high majesty. Its authority is not only normative but also causative. It fights for its own triumph. It conquers for itself the hearts of men. It makes itself irresistible."[25]

---

23. Ibid., p. 492.
24. Ibid., p. 533.
25. Ibid.

III

THE AUTONOMOUS MAN

In the previous chapter the biblical notion of Scripture has been set forth. This has been done only insofar as it has direct apologetical significance. Stress has been laid on the fact that the Bible speaks of the Word of God as self-contained. That is, the Bible is the Word of him who, as Creator-Redeemer alone can identify himself. God in Christ identifies himself in terms of himself because he exists exclusively in terms of himself. There is no non-being over against him that influences him.[1] There are no laws of logic above him according to which he must measure his own internal consistency.[2] This God of the Bible is, therefore, the final reference point for predication of his rational creatures. They, and with them all things in the universe, must be explained in terms of him, and he is never wholly comprehensible to them. Therefore no fact in the universe is ever wholly comprehensible to them. They therefore need to live by authority. They have to be told who they are and what the things of the universe mean in relation to themselves and finally in relation to God. God's supernatural revelation is presupposed in all successful rational inquiry on the part of man. And all revelation of God to man is anthropomorphic. It is an adaptation by God to the limitations of the human creature. Man's systematic interpretation of the revelation of God is never more than an approximation of the system of truth revealed in Scripture, and this system of truth as revealed in Scripture is itself anthropomorphic. But being anthropomorphic does not make it untrue. The Confessions of the Church pretend to be nothing more than frankly approximated statements of

---

1. KSO: That is, before creation existed, there was *only* God. There was not God plus "not-God" outside of him. He alone existed, and there was no such thing as "outside of him," or "contrary to him."

2. KSO: In other words, contra Aristotle, the law of non-contradiction cannot be the first principle. God himself is the first principle and the law of non-contradiction must presuppose him and his existence. For an elaboration of this point in a Reformed context, see, for example, Aza Goudriaan, "Samuel Rutherford on the Divine Origin of Possibility," in *Reformed Orthodoxy in Scotland: Essays on Scottish Theology 1560–1775*, ed. Aaron Clay Denlinger, (Bloomsbury Publishing, 2014).

the inherently anthropomorphic revelation of God. For it is such a system that is directly involved in the idea of the self-contained God.

As over against this Christian view of God, speaking in Christ through the Scriptures, as the final reference point in predication, there stands that of fallen man. For fallen man the final point of reference is himself. It is of the utmost significance for Christian apologetics that this point be carefully noted.

The picture of fallen man as given in Scripture is that he knows God but does not want to recognize him as God (Rom 1). That he knows God is due to the fact that all things in the universe about him and within him speak clearly of God. It is as "knowing God" that man rebels against God. Moreover, at the beginning of history Adam, representing mankind, received from God direct supernatural communication about himself and his task in the world. All men are responsible for this revelation. Speaking of the Gentiles, Paul says that "when they knew God, they glorified him not as God, neither were thankful; but became vain in their imaginations, and their foolish heart was darkened" (Rom 1:21). And further, that they "changed the truth of God into a lie, and worshiped and served the creature more than the Creator, who is blessed forever" (Rom 1:25). In consequence of their rejection of God as their Creator and Lord they are now subject to the wrath of God. "Wherefore as by one man sin entered the world, and death by sin; and so death passed upon all men, for that all have sinned" (Rom 5:12), and having sinned in Adam they are now by nature born dead in trespasses and sins (Eph 2:1). They are "children of disobedience" (Eph: 2:2); and ". . . by nature the children of wrath" (Eph 2:3). They walk "in the vanity of their mind," "having the understanding darkened, being alienated from the life of God through the ignorance that is in them, because of the blindness of their heart" (Eph 4:18). Paul speaks of fallen man as having a "carnal mind," and says that ". . . to be carnally minded is death; but to be spiritually minded is life and peace. Because the carnal mind is enmity against God, for it is not subject to the law of God, neither indeed can be" (Rom 8:6).

Here then is the heart of the matter: through the fall of Adam man has set aside the law of his Creator and therewith has become a law to himself. He will be subject to none but himself. He seeks to be autonomous. He knows that he is a creature and ought to be subject to the law of his Creator. He knows that his Creator has made him to be his image; he knows that he *ought* therefore to love his Maker and bountiful Benefactor. He knows that the light of knowledge depends for him upon his walking self-consciously in the revelation of God. Yet he now tries to be the source of his own light. He makes himself the final reference point in all predication. What is said above has been, of course, taken from Scripture. It is not what fallen man says about himself. This at once raises an important question of procedure. Is it fair for us to take the picture of man from Scripture alone and to ignore what the fallen man says about himself? Is it not of the first importance to look into the problematics of men sympathetically and to see them from their own point of view? Are we not condemning without hearing what the accused has to say for himself?

In reply it must be said that those who are by nature "as others children of wrath" but who have been saved from the "wrath to come" ought to be utterly sympathetic with those who have not yet become the objects of God's saving grace. Believers themselves have not chosen the Christian position because they were wiser than others. What they have they have by grace alone. But this fact does not mean that they must accept the problematics of fallen man as right or even as probably or possibly right. For the essence of the idea of Scripture is that it *alone* is the criterion of truth. The standards by which the fallen man judges himself are false standards. That is the most important point in his case. Fallen man cannot by his own adopted criteria make a true analysis of his own condition. The remedies that he employs for his own salvation are the wrong remedies just because the diagnosis that he has made of his own disease is made by the wrong criterion. A medical doctor is able to prescribe the right medicine for a patient just because he, rather than the patient himself, has given the correct diagnosis of the patient's disease. In an infinitely deeper sense only Christ, the great physician, can diagnose the disease of men.

Thus the Christian apologist should, to be sure, look sympathetically into the efforts of men in general when they seek to analyze themselves and their problems. There will be no doubt "elements of truth" in such an analysis; even so, ultimately, the idea of a standard of truth is involved in any "system of truth." The Bible is the only ultimate standard of truth. And therefore the analysis of man's sin and evil must be made by means of Scripture, as the "medicine book" by which men are to be judged.

Just now we spoke of "elements of truth" that may be found in the non-Christian diagnosis of sin and evil. This points to the necessity of qualifying the analysis of fallen man given above. What we have said of him is true only *in principle*. Fallen man does *in principle* seek to be a law unto himself. But he cannot carry out his own principle to its full degree. He is restrained from doing so. God himself restrains him; God is long-suffering toward him. He calls man to repentance. He keeps fallen man from working out the full consequence of his sin. Reformed theologians speak of this restraint of God upon mankind in general as due to *common grace*. The restraint of God upon fallen mankind enables it to help build the culture of the race. At the beginning of history man was given the task of subduing the earth. He was to subdue it "under God" and thus to the glory of God. But as a sinner man seeks to make himself, instead of God, the ultimate aim as well as the ultimate standard in life. Yet he cannot ultimately change the practical situation. He is still a creature. The universe is still what God has made it to be, and it will be what God intends it to be. So fallen man cannot destroy the program of God. He cannot even destroy himself as inherently a builder of culture for God. In spite of what he does against God, he yet can and *must* work for God; thus he is able to make a "positive contribution" to human culture.

Thus it comes to pass that they of whom Scripture says that their minds are darkened can yet discover much truth. But this discovery of truth on their part is effected *in spite of* the fact that *in principle* they are wholly evil. Their discovery of truth is adventitious so far as their own principle is concerned. They are not *partly* evil, they are not just sick; they are *wholly* evil, they are spiritually *dead*. But in spite of being dead in sins, they can, because of God's common grace, discover truth. The universe is what the Scripture says it is, and man is what the Scripture says he is. On both of these points it says the opposite of what fallen man says. Fallen man knows truth and does "morally good" things in spite of the fact that *in principle* he is set against God.[3]

In view of the facts mentioned above we shall have to concern ourselves first and primarily with the two opposing *principles* of interpretation. The Christian principle of interpretation is based upon the assumption of God as the final and self-contained reference point. The non-Christian principle of interpretation is that man as self-contained is the final reference point. It is this basic difference that has to be kept in mind all the time. It will be difficult at times to see that such is actually the case. The very fact that by God's common grace fallen man is "not as bad as he could be" and is able to do that which is "morally good" will make the distinction between two mutually exclusive principles seem an extreme oversimplification to many.

In fact, it is *in spite of appearances* that the distinction between the two principles must be maintained. The point is that the "facts of experience" must actually be interpreted in terms of Scripture if they are to be intelligible at all. In the last analysis the "facts of experience" must be interpreted either in terms of man taken as autonomous, or they must be interpreted in terms of God. There is no third "possibility." The interpretation which takes the autonomous man as self-interpretive is an "impossible possibility."

It is our task now to indicate how fallen man, the man who *in principle* assumes himself to be a law unto himself, will estimate the idea of Scripture as outlined in the preceding chapter. The Scriptures speak of the self-identifying

---

3. KSO: This paragraph may surprise some who have relied on caricatures of Van Til's thought rather than on what he actually said. Because all people remain in the image of God, and because God's common grace restrains sin and evil in multiple ways, unbelievers can act in ways that accord with God's law (but only superficially).

Christ as the self-identifying God and therefore of his self-attesting revelation to man. Scripture requires that man renounce himself as autonomous and submit himself to the will of God as expressed in Christ. The Scripture requires repentance. It says to the natural man that he is blinded in mind and rebellious in heart. It tells him that he cannot of himself see the truth which he yet ought to see, and that he cannot do that which he yet ought to do. True, as noted above, Paul says that man knows God and that he recognizes, in a sense, the difference between right and wrong. But when Paul speaks of the natural or fallen man as knowing God and as knowing and even in a sense doing good, he is not speaking of that knowledge which is according to truth, that knowledge which man needs in order to be what God at the first made him to be. There are two senses to the word "knowledge" used in Scripture. There is the sense in which Paul uses it when he says that men by virtue of their creation by God in his image have knowledge of God. They cannot at any point of their interest succeed in escaping from the face of God. Their sin is always sin against better knowledge.

This point is of the utmost importance for Christian apologetics. It alone offers a point of contact with the mind and heart of the natural man. For the moment it may suffice to stress the fact that the Bible itself would come to man in a vacuum and its whole claim would be without meaning except for the assumption that all the facts of the universe, including man himself, are revelational of God. The revelation of grace comes to those who have sinned against the revelation that came to man previous to his need for grace. Men could not have sinned in a vacuum. The very idea of sin is sin against the revelation of God.

Though it is of the greatest possible importance to keep in mind that man knows God in this original sense it is of equally great importance to remember that he is now, since the fall, a sinner without *true* knowledge of God.[4] He is spiritually blind. He will not see things as he, in another sense, knows that they are. He hates to see them that way because if he admits that they are what they really are, then he therewith condemns himself as a covenant-breaker. He therefore cannot see the truth till he at the same time repents.

This is but to emphasize the fact that it is with the human person as a unit that we deal. We are not merely concerned with the intellect of man and its supposedly legitimate demands. We are not dealing with some abstract "rational

---

4. KSO: Van Til's point here requires the proper context, since he has just affirmed above that all people know God truly. Like Paul, who says that unbelievers "know God" (Rom. 1:19–20), and that they "do not know God" (1 Thess. 4:5; 2 Thess. 1:8), context is all-important. It might be best to think of the unbeliever as having "true-but-suppressed" knowledge of God, and the Christian as having "true-and-embraced" knowledge of God. Because of the darkness of sin, those who are apart from Christ remain in a "knowing but not knowing" condition until and unless they repent and trust Christ.

man" who is seriously and open-mindedly seeking the truth. There is a sense in which fallen man, in natural things, may be said to be looking for the truth. But we are now concerned with ultimate principles of interpretation. We are looking for a final point of reference, and that final point of reference must be said to lie in God as revealed through Christ in Scripture instead of in man.[5] Fallen man will use his intellect. It will be like the saw of a carpenter with which he fits the boards that he wants to use for the construction of his building. The set of the saw is all-important. The saw may be very shiny and ever so sharp; if the set is wrong it cannot but do damage. So the intellect of fallen man may be ever so brilliant, since the set of his person, as a covenant-breaker, is wrong it will, in the ultimate sense, do all the more damage. It may also at the same time, because of God's common grace, do all the more good for the progress of culture.[6]

Again it must be borne in mind that when we say that fallen man knows God and suppresses that knowledge so that he, as it were, sins self-consciously, this too needs qualification. Taken as a generality and in view of the fact that all men were represented in Adam at the beginning of history, we must say that men sin against better knowledge and also self-consciously. But this is not to deny that when men are said to be without God in the world they are ignorant. Paul speaks of the ignorance of men to whom the gospel has not been preached. There is therefore a gradation between those who sin more and those who sin less self-consciously, as some are closer and others are further removed in history from the original direct supernatural revelation of God to man. Even so when we speak of the human race as a whole, as fallen in Adam, we must think of it as *in principle* being opposed to the truth of God. In Adam mankind has set aside the truth of God.

Now since it was in Adam as their representative that men have sinned, it is well that the implications of this fall for the Christian theory of knowledge be ascertained as far as possible.

The story of Adam in paradise is familiar. It is part of the orthodox view of things to regard this story as historical. It is so presented in Scripture, and it is in accord with the idea of Scripture as identifying to man in this story a clear-cut expression of the will of God. Those who would make a myth or a *saga* out of

---

5. KSO: It is important to keep in mind that in apologetics the crucial and ultimate point is the *final* point of reference. In that way, we seek to show how everyday aspects of thinking and living lack meaning, coherence, and purpose unless they can point to something beyond themselves, specifically to the true God.

6. KSO: Again, Van Til is attempting to strike the biblical balance in affirming that apart from Christ people can still accomplish some good things. Even those good things, however, are ultimately judged negatively by Christ in that they do not and cannot be accomplished to and for his glory. To put it in ethical categories, even if the "standard" is, in some limited and superficial sense, met by an unbeliever, the *"goal"* and *"motive"* will inevitably be directed toward the self rather than toward God.

this narrative do so in the interest of a philosophy that holds that no dear and direct revelation of God to man can be given in and through the facts of history.[7]

The tree of the knowledge of good and evil was indicated to Adam as a test by which God would bring man to a fully self-conscious reaction to his will. Man was created good. He was not created with a will that could as well turn in the direction of evil as in the direction of the good; even so God would have man become fully and wholly spontaneous and self-conscious in every sense of the word in his attitude toward God. God wanted man to accept God's judgment or criterion as that to which man would gladly and lovingly submit.

At the instigation of Satan man decided to set himself up as the ultimate standard of right and wrong, of the true and false. He made himself, instead of God, the final reference point in predication.

For the question of knowledge this implied the rejection of God as able to identify himself in terms of himself to man and with it the rejection of God as the source of truth for man. Instead of seeking an analogical system of knowledge, man after this sought an original system of knowledge. This means that God was reduced with him to the necessity of seeking truth in an ultimately mysterious environment. In other words, it implied that in setting up himself as independent; man was declaring that there was no one above him on whom he was dependent. But man even then knew that he was not ultimate. He knew that he had no control of reality and its possibilities. So what his declaration of independence amounted to was an attempt to bring God down with himself into an ocean of pure contingency or abstract possibility.[8]

Moreover, pure contingency in metaphysics and pure irrationalism in epistemology go hand in hand. Abstract possibility in metaphysics and ultimate mystery in epistemology are involved in one another. To this must be added that in ethics this involved the denial of God's right to issue any commandment for man. For the natural man reality, truth and goodness must be what he thinks they must be. They cannot be what Christ says they are.

At the fall then, man virtually told God that he did not and could not know what would happen if he (man) should eat of the "forbidden tree." Why

---

7. Neo-orthodox theologians do not take the Genesis creation and fall accounts seriously as historical narratives in the common sense notion of 'historical' (events in the phenomenal world). In recent years some Reformed theologians under the influence of neo-orthodoxy are trying to make adjustments on this point.

8. KSO: By "ocean of pure contingency or abstract possibility" Van Til means that Adam sinfully decided that what God has said was *not* true, and therefore that it was "up to Adam" to determine his own status in the garden. In that way, he attempted to "bring God down," as it were, into the contingency of Adam's choice. God said to Adam that he would surely die; Satan said Adam would not die. Adam sinfully thought his own choice to follow Satan would be the determining factor of history, rather than what God had surely said.

was this called a "forbidden" tree? Was it not perhaps because God arbitrarily called it thus? God was first upon the scene of history. No one had as yet had any experience with eating of this tree; there were no inductively gathered records to indicate even as much as a tendency to evil being involved in the use of the fruit of this tree. It was the "inductive method" with its assumption of ultimate mystery involved in pure possibility that Adam introduced. This was utter irrationalism. It was therefore by implication a fiat denial of God's being able to identify himself. It was in effect a claim that no one, neither God nor man, can really know what he is or who he is. How could there be any ultimate or final distinction or preference made in an ocean of Chance? Anyhow why should one "rational being" who had become rational by Chance, seek to lord it over another "rational being" ~~who also~~ had become rational by Chance? In a world of Chance there can be no manner of self-identification. There can be no system of truth and therefore no intelligible use of the "law of contradiction." There can therefore certainly be no authoritative identification of truth and law by one "rational being" for another "rational being." There can be no such thing as authority in the biblical sense of the term.[9]

But there is another side to the story of the fall of man. How could man be sure that he could safely ignore the command of God? How did he presume to know that God did not know what would come to pass should he eat of the forbidden tree? If there was to be any seeming sense to such an action, it would have to be on the assumption that man himself knew that the evil threatened would not take place. Satan told man that the issue would be quite otherwise than God said it would be. He said that God knew that it would be otherwise. Satan suggested that God too knew that man would be as God, knowing good and evil if man should eat of the tree. Reality, said Satan in effect, is wholly lit up, lit up for the "creature" as well as for the "Creator." Man therefore does not need to live by the authoritative assertions of the Creator. He can discover by his own independent inspection, by *Wesensschau*,[10] what will take place in the course of time. Man as well as God can ascertain the laws of being by means of the laws of rationality in his mind. Is not the law of rationality in the minds of men and of gods ultimately one with the law of being in reality as a whole? Surely reality cannot be "deeper than logic."

---

9. KSO: This paragraph is a brilliant explanation of the philosophical implications of Adam's sinful choice. Not only did it entail radical disobedience, but it entailed an entire picture of God and the universe that Adam thought needed to be defined by his act of eating from the forbidden tree.

10. KSO: Van Til uses a phenomenological term here, likely from Edmund Husserl (1859–1938), in which it is supposed that one can grasp the essence of something by an "objective" vision of it, and thus discern its true character.

It was thus that man, in rejecting the covenantal requirement of God became at one and the same time both irrationalist and rationalist. These two are not, except formally, contradictory of one another. They rather imply one another.[11] Man had to be both to be either. To be able to identify himself apart from God, man had to distinguish himself as an individual from all the relationships of the system of which he actually is a part. If he were not part of the God-ordained system of relationships, he would be an entity in a vacuum; he would not be distinguishable to himself from any one or anything else. In fact he would not be self-conscious at all. He or it would be part of "the great buzzing blooming confusion"[12] that would constitute Chaos. On the other hand, being part of a system of relations "created" by himself man would have to know this system exhaustively in order to know it at all. Reality then must be "wholly lit up" to himself without any appeal to authority. Only then can he rightly say that he does not need to be identified and set in a system of relationships by God his Creator.

It is with this background in mind, frankly taken from Scripture as authoritative, that we can interpret with some measure of intelligence the history of human thought. There are many schools of philosophy with which the college student has to make his acquaintance. The textbooks speak of some of them as objective and of others as subjective. Some are spoken of as monistic and others as pluralistic. Some are said to be pantheistic and others deistic, some rationalist and others irrationalist. Recently we have existential, analytical and positivist systems of philosophy. But all these schools must be seen in the light of the analysis made of them in Scripture. The main question that can be asked about any system of thought is whether it is man-centered or God-centered. Does it make the Creator-Redeemer or the creature the final reference point in prediction? If an answer to this question is found, then the problematics presented by the various schools of philosophy become intelligent to us.

When man seeks to identify himself as the final reference point in predication, he will deny that it is possible to know *anything* about such a God as Christianity presents. He will say that mystery is ultimate, that *any* God of which man speaks must be merely a limit and an ideal, an ideal of which when anything

---

11. KSO: When Van Til says that the rational and irrational "imply one another" he is referring to the thinking of those who are outside of Christ (see the foreword in this volume for more on this dialectic). If God is not the standard of rationality, then man is his own standard. When man is his own standard of rationality there will inevitably be things we think we know (rational), as well as others that cannot "fit" with our own presumed standard (irrational), since we are inherently unable consistently to think and live as God's creatures, in his image, in the world he has made.

12. KSO: Van Til is likely referring here to a quote, from the pragmatist William James (1842–1910), in which James describes infants bombarded with an abundance of sensory data that they are unable to synthesize, resulting in chaos and confusion. In his doctoral dissertation, Van Til dealt both with Idealism and Pragmatism.

positive is said at all, it is admittedly said by way of symbol or allegory. God is "beyond" anything that any man can say of him. He is not the self-conscious self-identifying being who identifies and gives orders to man.[13]

Again, when man seeks to identify himself in terms of himself he will also demand that any God he is asked to believe in must be "rationally connected with his own experience," that is, he must be wholly known to man. God must with man be wholly mysterious and unknown and at the same time wholly rational to both God and man and therefore systematically or speculatively controllable by man.

Of these two demands, first one and then the other, may come to the fore. But each is involved in the other. In ancient philosophy the rationalistic motif seemed to dominate the scene; in modern times the irrationalistic motif seems to be largely in control. But the one never lives altogether independently of the other.

Professors D. H. Th. Vollenhoven and Herman Dooyeweerd of the Free University of Amsterdam have worked out a Christian system of philosophy.[14] They stress the fact that man should by virtue of his creation by God stand self-consciously under the law of God. Then they point out that since the fall man seeks his reference point in the created universe rather than in the Creator of the universe. They speak of non-Christian systems of philosophy as being immanentistic in character, which refuse to recognize the dependence of human thought upon divine thought. They indicate that on the basis of immanentistic philosophies there has been a false problematics. Immanentistic systems have absolutized one or another aspect of the created universe and have therewith been forced to do injustice to other equally important or more important aspects of the created universe. So for instance the Pythagoreans contended that all things are numbers. By thus taking the idea of the numerability of created things, which is the lowest and therefore the least informative aspect of reality as the whole of it, as the final principle of interpretation, they have done grave injustice to other and higher aspects of reality. But in thus arguing for the significance of higher

---

13. KSO: In this paragraph, Van Til explains what a belief in God would be like if there were no revelation from God. Since man is the final reference point, any notion of God would have to be defined by man himself. Thus, God could not be known in any positive sense at all.

14. KSO: Van Til's personal history with his Dutch contemporaries Vollenhoven (1892–1978), and primarily Dooyeweerd (1894–1977), is long and complicated. As noted above, they both adhered to what was called "The Philosophy of the Cosmonomic Idea" (*Wijsbegeerte der Wetsidee*). For much of his career, Van Til sought to be supportive of their overall project, in that they were attempting to develop a fully Christian philosophy. That philosophy can be seen in Dooyeweerd's *A New Critique of Theoretical Thought*. Those aspects that are most helpful in their philosophy are highlighted by Van Til in this paragraph. However, by the end of his career, Van Til found himself in disagreement with their overall approach.

dimensions of created reality they do so by insisting that no dimension of created reality has justice done to it unless it is seen in the perspective of its being subject with all other dimensions to the law of God for all created reality. In other words, there is a non-Christian as well as a Christian dimensionalism.[15] Some schools of immanentistic philosophy want to maintain the reality and significance of higher dimensions than numerability and spatiality, etc. But only a Christian dimensionalism is able to keep from reducing all dimensions to one stark identity, for only a Christian dimensionalism keeps the intellect of man within its place. It requires the intellect of man to *find* the dimensions of created reality, without *legislating* for reality. On the other hand even the highest form of non-Christian dimensionalism is still rationalistic in that it would reduce all reality, in all of its dimensions, to a penetrable system. Merely to say that science is not by itself able to interpret the whole of life is not to present the claim of Christ. There are many vague, non-Christian "spiritualist" interpretations of life which are in the end no better than gross materialism.

·———·

It is to be regretted that no full use of this well-worked out system of Christian philosophy can be made in this work. It would carry us too far afield. But it will be greatly helpful to us, especially in the analysis of the history of non-Christian philosophy.[16]

What then, it must be asked, is the attitude of the non-Christian to the notion of the Bible? We ask this question of individual men who have been confronted with the Bible. But by no means have all men been confronted with the Bible and its claims about itself. We shall, therefore, in any case, have to judge the race as a whole by the example of the few. We shall have to ask what would have been their attitude had they been placed before the Bible? From this point of view our reply cannot be the result of exhaustive empirical examination. It need not be. Accepting the view of Scripture as the word of the self-attesting Christ, we also accept the twofold division the Scripture presents. There are creature-worshippers and Creator-worshippers.

We shall need, however, to go further than this. We cannot even approach the examples of those who are confronted with the Bible and who have given

---

15. KSO: "Dimensionalism" is one of Van Til's ways of describing the history of philosophy in general, philosophical structures. For Plato, for example, there was the "Real" and the "Ideal" dimensions; for Kant, there was the "Phenomenal" and the "Noumenal." For Christians, there is the Creator and the creation.

16. KSO: It should be noted here that, even with Van Til's eventual disagreement with the Cosmonomic philosophy, he nevertheless appreciated and utilized its critique of non-Christian philosophy.

their answers in a "neutral" attitude. We must approach them in the light of what the Bible says about them. This is the only thing that can be done which is consistent with the idea of the Bible as the Word of God. This is not to impugn the honesty of men. If they profess to believe the Bible as the Word of God, we accept their profession at face value. We then take for granted that by the regenerating power of the Holy Spirit they have been enabled to see the Scriptures for what they really are. But we are now speaking of fallen man and the question of his ability or inability to see the need for the authority, the sufficiency, and perspicuity of Scripture in the way that Scripture itself regards them. And then the answer must be that fallen man cannot, because he will not, accept the Bible as the word of the self-identifying Christ. For in accepting the Bible he must at the same time accept what it teaches about God in relation to man. And that, fallen man will not do.

A. THE NECESSITY OF SCRIPTURE

For the purpose of doing this we may look at what are often spoken of as the attributes of Scripture to see how the fallen man reacts to them. These attributes are the necessity, the authority, the sufficiency, and the perspicuity of Scripture.[17]

The necessity of Scripture, as seen in the previous chapter, lies in the fact of the sin of man. Man does not need the Scriptures because he is finite; he needs them because he is a sinner.[18] They tell him of God's work of redemption in Christ; they *alone* tell him of this work. So every sinner needs the Scriptures as he needs the Christ. And these Scriptures telling of the Christ must identify themselves as they must identify the Christ to sinners. The Scripture is the Word of the self-identifying Christ. Moreover, this identification of Scripture is not made effective except through the testimony of the Holy Spirit which convicts and convinces sinners of their sin and of their need of salvation.

But the sinner will not of himself, from his "experience," admit the fact that he is a sinner. He may agree that he is far from being what he ought to be.

---

17. In his recent work on Scripture (*De Heilige Schrift*, Vol. I, 1966; Vol. II, 1967), G. C. Berkouwer warns against speaking of the "attributes" of Scripture in a formal manner. His point is that unless the *message* of Scripture be taken together with the *idea* of Scripture, we have an empty form. The *what* of Scripture cannot be separated from its *message*, just as the words of Christ cannot be separated from the person of Christ. It is this very point which the present writer has continually stressed. Cf. *Metaphysics of Apologetics*, 1932 (now re-issued as A Survey of Christian Epistemology, with little revision, 1969, not to be quoted). For a more thorough view see the present writer's syllabus *The Protestant Doctrine of Scripture* (Westminster Theological Seminary, 1968).

18. KSO: It is certainly the case that man needed special revelation *before* the fall. God identified man, and woman, and set their tasks in the garden by way of *speaking* to them. Van Til is here referring to the condition of man *after* the fall. See WCF 1.1.

He may admit that he is very wicked. But he will not admit that he has sinned against the revelation of God, that he has set God aside and made himself a law unto himself. He does not believe in any revelation of God. The very essence of his sin, as noted, is that it has lifted man, the creature, up to the level of God his Creator, or brought down God the Creator to the level of man, his creature. The sinner is therefore "monistic" in his thinking.[19] When Isaiah says that God's thoughts are higher than man's thoughts, fallen man will shake his head and deny it. He may allow that there may possibly be a god whose thoughts are higher than man's thoughts, but then he simply means by this that the thoughts of this god are more extensive than are the thoughts of man. The thought of God is for fallen man always essentially of the same quality as the thought of man.

Accordingly fallen man cannot admit that he has sinned against the revelation of the thought or will of the God of Scripture. There could, he argues in effect, be no expression of such a thought by such a God.

To this contention the following objection has frequently been raised. If only you look at the facts of the history of the human race, you can see that men *have* believed in God, in the revelation of God and in the idea that they have sinned against this revelation of God.

But precisely here it is of importance to apply the principle that it is *Scripture* that must interpret the facts of history for us. To be sure, there are the "redemption religions"; there is the fact of numberless altars made by all manner of religious men all over the world. But these facts only corroborate the point noted above, namely, that all men are actually created by God and, in a sense, know this to be the case. Paul says that all men know God and that they have broken his law. They have inherited an evil nature and with it an evil conscience. So they seek to appease the "gods." But the gods against whom men think they have sinned are always intra-cosmical entities; at least they are, like men, themselves surrounded by an environment more ultimate than themselves. All the "mystery religions" worship and serve the creature more than the Creator. And it is from this worship of the creature as being the essence of sin, that the Bible calls men away. Modern depth psychology and existentialist philosophy have not seen so much as a glimpse of the depth of the iniquity of the human heart. They only "cover up" this iniquity by their ersatz views of sin. It is only by grace that men can see the need of turning away from idols to the living and true God. Men do not see the need of grace till by grace they see it. They do not see the need of Christ unless through the Bible they are told of the Christ in the Scripture.

---

19. KSO: Sinners are "monistic" in their thinking because they seek to eliminate the Creator/creature distinction. Reality exists, they think, on "one" monistic level—the same for God (if he exists) and for man.

And men do not accept the Scripture as the Word of God telling about salvation through Christ unless by the Holy Spirit witnessing to its truth they believe in it and in what it says about the Christ who came to save, and God the Creator against whom they have sinned. Knowledge of sin, as well as knowledge of salvation comes, not from experience as interpreted by experience; the one is involved in the other and the two together come as a unit, but by the grace of God. The Heidelberg Catechism makes this matter plain when it asks, Whence knowest thou thy sin? The answer is, "From the law of God."[20] Not from experience, but from the revelation of the will of God comes the knowledge of sin and therewith the recognition of the need of Scripture. It is only from the Scripture that one learns of his need of Scripture. It is only by the gift of grace that one learns of his need of grace. So it is only from the law of God by grace that one learns both that it is the law of God and that he has broken the law of God.

The question of the point of contact may be briefly touched upon in this connection. This matter will be more fully considered later. At the moment it is brought into the picture because it is frequently used as an objection to the point of view just expressed. Does not Scripture itself appeal to those who are "weary and heavy laden," to those who have a realization of their own distress and need of salvation? Granted that men do not clearly know just what it is that ails them and what the remedy may be for their need, is not their vague sense of need an adequate point of contact for the gospel of redemption? Are not men ready to listen to the gospel of redemption because they know themselves to be in distress?

Full justice should be done to this question. No doubt their own sense of need makes men, in the providence of God, "ready to listen to the gospel." And the greater the sense of need the greater the readiness to listen to the gospel. Those who lie in hospital beds awaiting serious operations will be more "amenable to the gospel" than they are when "riding high" in full prosperity and health. Men know that they are creatures of God; they know that they have broken the law of God.[21] They know that they need "salvation." Even so in the worst of their condition men still rebel against the analysis of their case as given in Scripture. They may speak with Kant of the "radical evil" in man; they may speak with Freud of the utter corruption of the race. They may speak with Heidegger of being as "being unto death." Even so, they still hold that this is something that is inherent in reality as such. What else can one expect to come forth from the womb of chance? Man, they hold, cannot really be held responsible for his "sin"; he certainly is not exclusively responsible. He has not sinned in Adam against

20. KSO: Heidelberg Catechism, Q. 3.
21. KSO: See Rom. 1:18–32.

a known will of God. His sin is not to him a matter for which he himself fully deserves eternal separation from God.

Thus the patient and the doctor still have radically different analyses of the nature of the disease and radically different conceptions of the kind of remedy that will rescue the patient from death. God in his mysterious providence may use the sense of distress as a means by which the Holy Spirit convicts the sinner of what is really wrong with him. Thus God no doubt uses the fact that men are actually creatures of God, and deep down in their hearts know themselves to be such, as a fact on which he builds his work of salvation. But it is by grace that men must learn to know what it means that they are creatures of God in another sense than they already know that this is true.

It is only if we set the two principles of interpretation spoken of above clearly over against one another that the matter comes to stand in the right perspective. So far as the natural man thinks self-consciously according to his principle as a sinner he cannot accept the analysis that God gives in his Word. But since man is unable to carry through his principle of interpretation to the end, since the folly of carrying it through to the end stands clearly before him at all times, and since in many instances the love of God to sinners is preached to him and lived before him in the lives of the people of God, God can use this situation in order by means of it to enforce upon men a consideration of the fact that they are what he tells them they are.

The point of contact with the sense of need found in the sinner is therefore not simply a matter of telling him that you have what he knows he needs. Here is a man who says that he needs some groceries. He goes to the store and the storekeeper does not have quite the brands that he wants. But he assures his customer that what he has, though the customer has never used it before, is "just what he wants," in fact "just what he needs."

In contrast with this the sinner says that he has not lived up to his own ideals of a good life. He fears that this may bring him evil consequence. Somehow reality visits "sin" with punishment, and, if sin is inherent in the race, if it is endemic in man, if sin is "original" sin, then he will welcome any alleviation any one may offer. How may he get rid of his "guilt complex?" By the doctrine of "original sin," that is, by distributing his guilt over the whole human race? By making it therefore a natural something?

To men thinking in this fashion the message of the gospel comes with a quite different analysis of sin. It presents the sinner with a different meaning for every word he uses. It does so by setting man in a wholly different complex of relations. It offers him no way of escape except that of repentance before his Maker and Redeemer. "More of this sort of food" the Christian grocer says, is only poison to you. It is the bloodstream that itself must be cured. And that is beyond the power of any human doctor. Your sin is of such a nature as to need the Son of God and his death upon the cross for its removal. Its nature may be seen only in the light of what it takes for its removal. Do you own that you are rightly a child of eternal damnation? It is that from which Christ came to redeem you. That is what the Bible therefore says of sin. It is that which you must confess your sin to be. Till now you have done nothing of the sort.

With this basic contrast in mind it is then possible to speak in biblical fashion of the point of contact for the gospel in the sense of need found in the natural man. It is the original and ineradicable revelation of God and of his will within men's minds that is the background and foundation for the work of the Holy Spirit. Without this background the gospel would speak into a vacuum.[22]

B. THE AUTHORITY OF SCRIPTURE

The question of what the natural man will do when confronted with the Scripture's claim to its authority needs to be answered next. The question is whether the natural man, so far as he works self-consciously from his principle, can be in any sense favorably disposed to the biblical notion of its authority. The answer must be in the negative, for essentially the same reason that the natural man cannot recognize the necessity of Scripture. For it is the necessity of the Bible as speaking with authority that we dealt with in the previous section. It has been intimated that fallen man is both irrationalist and rationalist, and at the same time. His irrationalism rests upon his metaphysical assumption that reality is controlled by or is an expression of pure Chance. His rationalism is based upon the assumption that reality is wholly determined by laws with which his thought is ultimately identical.[23] It is to be expected that on such assumptions fallen man cannot allow for biblical authority. For this idea, as noted above, rests upon the idea of the self-contained God. This involves the idea that God himself is wholly known to himself and that the created universe is also wholly known to him because wholly controlled by him. This is the Christian principle of continuity.

---

22. KSO: This is a centrally important point. The gospel always comes to people to whom God is constantly revealing himself; it never comes to man in ""a vacuum." Since it comes to people who know God, but suppress that truth, it comes to those who cannot eradicate the knowledge that God constantly gives. So, even if the natural man rejects the gospel, that gospel nevertheless always appeals to this universal knowledge of God in all people as its proper context.

23. KSO: For Van Til, the natural man always operates with this "rational/irrational dialectic" as his basic presupposition. He does so because he cannot have any knowledge of that which comes by "pure Chance," given its irregularity and unpredictability, but he must have some way of ordering his knowledge and his life, so he depends on the "rational" regularities of reality. On both sides of the dialectic, the natural man refuses to acknowledge the God he knows, and thus is unable, ultimately, to make any sense of himself and the world.

The natural man would call this rationalism and determinism. He would say that the idea of freedom and significance for human knowledge has, on this view, disappeared. At the same time the Christian idea of authority maintains that God's thoughts are not open to the inspection of man. God must reveal himself. This is the Christian principle of discontinuity. The natural man would call this irrationalism and indeterminism. He would say that it cuts off all reasonable continuity between God and man. It requires man to be subject to the purely arbitrary pronouncements that God may make upon him.

Thus it is that a combination of the non-Christian principle of continuity correlative to the non-Christian principle of discontinuity stands over against the Christian principle of continuity correlative to the Christian principle of discontinuity. Frequently Christians are deceived in this matter. They tend to forget that the meaning of discontinuity is determined by its correlative. Thus one who defends a non-Christian principle of discontinuity will, on the surface, appear to be defending Christianity and its supernatural elements Yet one who argues against determinism and naturalism, one defending "higher dimensions" of reality, may be doing no more than defending his own supposed freedom or autonomy from the encroachments of its own principle of continuity.[24]

Vollenhoven and Dooyeweerd have pointed out how, particularly in modern times, apostate man has come to sense something of the destructive character of his own problematics. In the beginning of the modern era he seemed to have won for himself absolute freedom. At the same time he was using modern mathematics in order by means of it to control the whole of reality, including man himself. The ideal of his science was to know and control all things, including the internal movements of the human mind. But if this ideal should succeed, man would have lost his freedom which he wishes to maintain at all costs. So in the philosophy of Kant there is a sort of compromise between the ideal of science and the ideal of free personality. To the former is assigned the realm of the *phenomena*, to the latter is reserved the realm of the *noumena*. But this is merely a *modus vivendi*;[25] it is no solution to the problem. No solution is possible on a non-Christian foundation.

---

24. KSO: There is a lot of theology packed into these statements. What Van Til has in mind here is a faulty notion that "Christianity and its supernatural elements" provide the proper answer to a natural world that is irregular, uninterpretable, and disjointed. Thus, it is mistakenly thought, what is needed is an "injection" of the supernatural into the natural. This would be, as he says, "[an "argument] against determinism and naturalism" because Christianity is superimposed on the natural as a "*supplemental*" principle. Not only so, but this notion of Christianity as supplemental wants to protect some notion of "pure Chance," or human freedom (i.e., autonomy), as in Roman Catholicism or Arminianism, even as it wants to commend a certain need for Christianity for the "natural world."

25. KSO: That is, an agreement to disagree, or an agreement to allow antithetical ideas to coexist.

From the non-Christian point of view then, the idea of biblical authority is impossible. This idea is impossible if human experience is to be interpreted by the adopted principle of apostate man. On the basis of apostasy it is impossible that there should be the sort of God who speaks with authority. Kant made room for "faith" but not for biblical faith.[26] To be sure, the non-Christian principle of discontinuity demands that one hold to abstract possibility. "Anything" is possible on this principle. Thus it would seem that the existence of such a God as the Bible speaks of may also be possible. But when the natural man says that for him anything is possible and that therefore he has an open mind for the evidence of anything that may be presented to him, this assertion has a basic limitation. When he says that anything is possible, this is for him an abstraction or a limiting concept. He knows that cows cannot jump over the moon except in fairy tales. So the idea of a God whose experience is not subject to the same conditions as those that control man is not *practically* possible. Such an idea, he says, is meaningless. It is without intelligible content. It is the mere assertion of a *that* without an intelligible *what*. It is therefore pure irrationalism to say that such a God exists.

On the other hand, the Christian notion of biblical authority is said to be pure rationalism. It would require a view of rationality as controlling whatsoever comes to pass. It would give man no measure of independence, his own reason would be of a piece with that which is predetermined from all eternity by God. Thus there would be no authority at all because authority implies the freedom of one person over against another.

The non-Christian is quite consistent with his own principles when he thus rejects the Christian claim to authority as well as the Christian claim to the necessity of Scripture. How could there be any necessity for that which is inherently meaningless and outside the realm of practical possibility? How can we say that man has sinned against a God who exists in isolation from man and yet places irrational demands upon him, out of accord with the nature of human personality?

It may be objected, as it was objected to the question of the necessity of Scripture, that we have ignored the facts of history. As men recognize their evil and sin do they not also, many of them, recognize the need for authority? As they appeal for help to the gods, do they not also therewith appeal to the authority of these gods? Did not the Hellenistic schools of philosophy themselves appeal to authority? And did they not do this because of their sense of the bankruptcy of Greek philosophy?

---

26. KSO: In his "Preface" to the second edition of *Critique of Pure Reason*, Kant said that his project in the book was to deny knowledge in order to make room for faith.

THE AUTONOMOUS MAN

We answer as we did in the preceding section. The kind of sin that men admit and the kind of redemption that they want is one thing. But the kind of revolt sin is according to Scripture and the kind of redemption that men actually need according to Scripture is quite another thing. Similarly the kind of authority men will appeal to is one thing, but the kind of authority they ought to appeal to is quite another thing. A brief indication may be given of the kind of authority that man who does not begin with Scripture will accept. The kind of authority that he will accept must, in short, be consonant with his own ultimacy and with his own right to be the final arbiter of his fate. In other words the kind of authority he will allow for is such as is consistent with his principle of his ultimate self-reference.

1. Man will allow that the matter of finding the meaning of his experience is a joint enterprise. No one man can know all things. Thus there are authorities in this field and in that field. The doctor is expert in the field of medicine. The physicist is expert in his own field, and so on. Such expert authority men will of course readily own. It is quite consistent with their principle to admit that they are finite.

2. When it comes to religion men will agree that there are those who are experts in this field. So the Jews seem to have been a pre-eminently religious people, and among them Jesus of Nazareth was perhaps the greatest religious expert that the race has seen. He is the kind of man that we should like to be. So we may take him as our guide or authority. He seems to have had a sort of intuition of the nature of God or ultimate reality. Since it is in any case impossible to find exhaustive knowledge because man cannot by the laws of his thought reach further than the world of experience, it is well to appeal to one who has a feeling for the numinous. Perhaps there is more to life than appears to the eye. Perhaps reality is deeper than logic. Perhaps the great mystics were not altogether wrong. No one knows. Perhaps some have valid hunches.

In such views of authority, it is clear, the final point of reference is still the would-be autonomous man. The experts may differ; it is up to every man finally to decide for himself. This is proper; the sanctity of the human person must not be violated. Ask any man to accept anything on pure authority, the sort of authority that the Bible claims for itself, and you are virtually asking him to deny his manhood. You are then asking him to be irrational and therewith to deny him the use of the powers that constitute his personality. With Plato I may look for some great expert, and listen to mythology, as a second best but rational inquiry for better or for worse, must be my final guide. For better or for worse I must hold that I have the final criterion of truth or falsehood within myself.

The point of authority is so all-important that a note on some of the modern theologians and their views may here be appended.

1. Schleiermacher[27]

Friedrich Schleiermacher is usually called the father of modern theology. Following Kant, he held that it is impossible for man to know a transcendent God, such as historic Christianity had always taught about. He rejected the orthodox view that all things in the world are clearly revelational of God. Yet he asserted the idea of man's absolute dependence on "God." But then this god is not the God of historic Christianity. The God of Schleiermacher is *reality*.

Now man is religious when he feels his absolute dependence on this, his god. But to feel our absolute dependence we must know ourselves to be absolutely free. Absolute dependence and absolute autonomy are, according to Schleiermacher's argument, correlative one to another. Human personality, he assumes with Kant, has the final criterion of truth or falsity within itself. When the religious man says that he is wholly dependent upon God and upon Christ he virtually says that he admires them greatly for their noble attitude toward reality.

Thus there is no place in Schleiermacher's system of theology for authority in the biblical sense. It is only the authority of the expert, the sort of authority that the non-Christian scientist will also allow for in his field, that Schleiermacher will admit as having any right in the Christian scheme of things.

2. Recent British Theologians

We omit discussing Ritschl and the mediating theologians since their views are very similar to those of Schleiermacher. We turn to some of the representatives of recent British or Anglican theology.

Taking first A. E. Taylor,[28] we find in him the combination of an outstanding philosopher and an ardent churchman. Apparently Taylor has been able to harmonize reason and authority in his life and in his thought. In his great work *The Faith of a Moralist* he deals specifically and fully with the subject. But the viewpoint is again familiar. Taylor pleads for the recognition of authority in philosophy, but argues that the kind of authority to be invoked must not, in

---

27. KSO: As Van Til notes, Friedrich Schleiermacher (1768–1834) is sometimes called the father of liberalism due to his significant influence on liberal theologians that came after him, e.g. Albrecht Ritschl (1822–1899). Schleiermacher's most influential books were *On Religion* (1799) and *The Christian Faith* (1822). In sum, he defined religion as a feeling of absolute dependence. As such, the notion of the objective truth of God's revelation is all but buried.

28. KSO: "A.E. Taylor (1869–1945), was a philosophical theist, and is perhaps best known for his translation of a number of Greek philosophical texts. He was educated at Oxford and later became a fellow of Merton College from 1891 to 1898. After teaching at Manchester and in Canada, he spent most of his career at the University of St. Andrews as Professor of Moral Philosophy (1908–1924), and then at the University of Edinburgh as the Chair of Moral Philosophy from 1924 until his retirement in 1941." Cornelius Van Til, *The Defense of the Faith*, ed. K. Scott Oliphint (Presbyterian & Reformed: Philipsburg, NJ, 2008) 119.

the nature of the case, be external or infallible. Agreeing with Ferrier[29] that it is more important for a philosophy to be reasoned than true, he says: "But if we once allow an assent which is more than consciously tentative and provisional to be given to that which has not been thought out by personal effort, but taken on trust without question or criticism—and this is the kind of assent a positive religion necessarily demands when its God has spoken—the central conviction which lies at the heart of all rational philosophy—the conviction that reality has a structure which is intelligible—has been surrendered."[30] With this agree the words of another member of the Anglican Communion, Alfred Edward John Rawlinson[31] when he says: "The final appeal is to the spiritual, intellectual and historical content of divine revelation, *as verifiable at the threefold bar of history, reason and spiritual experience.*"[32] Even Archbishop William Temple[33] makes no higher claim for the authority of Scripture than that of expert advice. For the individual, he says, authority must precede experience, but for the race experience must precede authority.[34] The spiritual authority of revelation, he contends, "depends wholly upon the spiritual quality of what is revealed."[35] Whether

---

29. KSO: J.F. Ferrier (1808–1864) was a Scottish philosopher. For an analysis of his work and influence, see Arthur Thomson, "The Philosophy of J. F. Ferrier," *Philosophy*, vol. 39, no. 147, (Royal Institute of Philosophy, Cambridge University Press, 1964) 46–62. The quote Van Til cites is from his *Institutes of Metaphysics*.

30. A. E. Taylor, *The Faith of a Moralist*, Vol. II (London: Macmillian and Co., 1931), p. 200.

31. KSO: "Born at Newton le Willows, Lancashire, England, Rawlinson was educated at Corpus Christi College, Oxford University, graduating in 1907 with high honors. Ordained in the Church of England as deacon in 1909 and priest in 1910, he was a tutor at Keble College (1909–1913) and student and tutor at Christ Church College (1914–1929). In the latter year he was made canon residentiary of Durham and archdeacon of Auckland; and in 1936 he was appointed bishop of Derby, where he remained until his retirement in 1959. Between 1930 and 1936 he was chaplain to the king. Rawlinson published a commentary on Mark's Gospel in the Westminster Commentaries series. He delivered the Bampton Lectures in 1926 on the subject "The New Testament Doctrine of the Christ." He authored books on theology such as *Dogma, Fact, and Experience* (1915) and *Authority and Freedom* (1924). He also contributed to publication of several theological symposia—for example, *Foundations* (1912), *Essays Catholic and Critical* (1926), and *Essays on the Trinity and Incarnation* (1928)." N.V. Hope, "Rawlinson, Alfred Edward John," ed. J.D. Douglas and Philip W. Comfort, *Who's Who in Christian History* (Wheaton, IL: Tyndale House, 1992), 583–584.

32. A. E. J. Rawlinson, "Authority as a Ground of Belief," *Essays Catholic and Critical*, ed. Edward Gordon Selwyn (New York: Macmillan and Co., 1926), p. 95. Italics are his.

33. KSO: William Temple (1881–1944) was Archbishop both of York (1929–42) and of Canterbury (1942–44). "In these places of leadership he devoted himself to three aims. First, he attempted to present a reasoned exposition of the Christian faith, which is expounded in *Christian Faith and Life* (1931), *Reading in St. John's Gospel* (1939–1940), and *Nature, Man, and God* (Gifford Lectures, 1934). He emphasized the Incarnation and a Christ-centered metaphysical philosophy." P. Toon, "Temple, William," ed. J.D. Douglas and Philip W. Comfort, *Who's Who in Christian History* (Wheaton, IL: Tyndale House, 1992), 662.

34. William Temple, *Nature, Man and God* (London: Macmillian and Co., 1935), p. 329.

35. Ibid., p. 347.

the quality be spiritual, of that, Temple argues in effect, the autonomous man must ever remain the judge. Accordingly revelation is said to take place not by communication of propositional truth, but by means of personal impression.[36] Doctrines can never be the "vehicle or the content of that revelation; they are the exposition of it, as the textbook of Astronomy is the exposition of the starry heavens. The revelation is the fact—Jesus Christ himself."[37] And Jesus has the sort of attitude toward the universe or reality that we, as independent judges, approve.

Here then modern Protestantism, including the Church of England through its leading voices, agrees with modern philosophy in submitting all authority to the final adjudication of autonomous reason.

3. Dialectical Theology[38]

But has there not been a great and sudden reaction to all this "consciousness" theology? What of Karl Barth and Emil Brunner with their followers? Have they not bravely contended for an "absolutely other" God, for a God whose Word should admit of no appeal beyond itself? Look at the lashing Barth gives the "consciousness" theologians in his *Christliche Dogmatik* (1927)! Note with what increasing consistency through the periods of his development he has sought to set his theology over against that of Schleiermacher and "modern Protestantism"! And behold how desperately he has striven to find a theology that shall be able to outreach the vile clutches of Feuerbach's ghost and "laugh him in the face."[39] A true theology, Barth argues, has its chief canon in the first and great commandment, "Thou shalt have no other Gods before me." A true theology must break through all human systems and thus reach man in the depth of his being. It wants man to obey the voice of authority implicitly. Here then, our student may think, is at least one among the "types of modern theology" that

---

36. William Temple, contribution III, *Revelation*, ed. John Baillie and Hugh Martin (London: Faber and Faber, 1937), p. 120.

37. Ibid., pp. 120–121.

38. KSO: "Dialectical theology was a reaction against liberal theology and refers, primarily but not exclusively, to the theology of Karl Barth (1886–1968). The emphasis in dialectical theology is on contradiction and contrast—the contrast of God's "No" with respect to sin and his "Yes" in Jesus Christ. Thus, dialectical theology finds its home in Kierkegaard, and not in a Hegelian dialectic, in that there is no synthesis in view. This contrast requires that our relationship to God be by way of an encounter between the divine and the human. Virtually every central Christian doctrine is redefined and recontextualized in dialectical theology. For Van Til's analysis of the dialecticism of Barth, see Cornelius Van Til, *Christianity and Barthianism* (Philadelphia, PA: Presbyterian and Reformed Publishing Co., 1962)." Cornelius Van Til, *The Defense of the Faith*, 1–2.

39. KSO: In the 1920s, Barth was somewhat sympathetic to Feuerbach's project, but recognized some profound theological gaps. In the end, Barth surmised, the best thing to do with Feuerbach was to laugh him off. See, for example, George Hunsinger, ed., *Thy Word is Truth: Barth on Scripture* (Grand Rapids, MI: Wm. B. Eerdmans Publishing Co., 2012): 54–55.

will not agree to submit its pronouncements to human reason as a final arbiter. Here, it seems, is one theologian who dares to stand up against both modern philosophy and theology, defending the idea of absolute or unqualified rather than expert authority.

Yet Barth too, as much as the consciousness theologians he so vigorously opposes, virtually accepts Kant's idea of the autonomous man as the presupposition of all he says. The "absolutely other" God, whom Barth's man of faith obeys, is once again of the skyrocket variety: he has first been cast up by the would-be self-sufficient man before he comes to speak to him. He has been cast so far into the dark sky of non-existence by the power of pure negation on the part of autonomous man that he seems indeed to be *wholly* other. But just because he is *wholly* other and therefore has authority just so long as he does *not* speak, he remains, in company with Aristotle's *noesis noeseoos*,[40] hidden in the contemplation of his own blankness. It is again the autonomous consciousness itself that must supply the content of the revelation that is to come to man with such authority.

By the authority of the Bible Barth does not mean that what it says is, as such, an ascertainable system of truth, normative for what man should think and do. As an historical entity the Bible is written by fallible and erring men. It is through their words as a witness to revelation, says Barth, that we must seek to hear the revelation of God's will for man. We do not hear that revelation of God unless, through Christ, we are eternally contemporaneous with God. This contemporaneity, in turn, is an Event in which men participate from all eternity. Thus for Barth the idea of participation of man in God through Christ replaces the orthodox doctrines of creation, incarnation and of revelation. Naturally the Bible can no longer be taken as authoritative in the historic sense of the term. With the Creator-creature distinction removed, there can be no authoritative Bible.[41]

After this we need not spend much time on the Americanized forms of Barthianism, such as are to be found in the writings of Reinhold Niebuhr, Richard Niebuhr, Nels F. Ferré, John A. Mackay or Elmer George Homrighausen. In their theology, as in that of Barth it is in the last analysis the religious consciousness that divides itself into two sections after the style of Dr. Jekyll and Mr. Hyde. The higher aspect will then address the lower aspect and insist upon obedience

---

40. KSO: That is, "thought thinking itself."
41. KSO: This last statement sums up the discussion above on Barth. Because Barth does not begin with the self-authenticating Word of God, he necessarily begins with himself. Thus, the "wholly other" God is not the God of Scripture, but is the God of the Kantian "noumenal," who cannot be known. Dialectically, however, this God is known only in and through Jesus Christ, who, Barth argues, is eternally incarnate.

to its voice. And thus man will tell himself that he has been listening to God or to Jesus.[42]

So far then we have found a wonderful harmony between the representatives of "authority" and those of reason. The two have found each other in the notion of the expert. The clergyman sends out his questionnaire to the scientists and philosophers asking *whether* they still believe in God; the answer is reassuring. The philosopher sends out his feelers to the representatives of religion asking whether they will honor the autonomous man; he need no longer expect any opposition from them. Does not the Bible itself appeal to reason? "Come now, let us reason together . . .," said Isaiah the prophet. Was it not then mere priestcraft that spoke otherwise?

It is clear that, though many men, including many leaders of the modern church, will allow for the idea of authority, it is not biblical authority that they accept. They will accept only such an authority as is consistent with man as ultimate and as the final point of reference in all human assertion.

The question of the point of contact may therefore again be noted briefly. Is there no value then in the fact that men recognize their need of authority? Does their recognition of absolute dependence mean nothing at all? Is man's recognition of the need of gods above him as well as his recognition of wrong that he has done of no value for the question of point of contact? Is it only a head-on collision that you seek with the natural man in trying to win him over to the faith?

We answer as we did above on the question of the necessity of Scripture. In their recognition of their sin and in their expressed need of authority men do recognize, but in spite of themselves, that they are really not so self-sufficient as their principle requires them to be. They are like the prodigal son whose principle requires him to deny that he is a son of his father whom he has left, but who cannot forget his father's voice. God's authoritative Word does not speak in a vacuum. It speaks to such as are unable ever to escape the call of his voice. They have to maintain their own principle artificially by building dams anew each day against the overwhelming evidence of the presence of their Creator and Judge. Men therefore try to naturalize the idea of authority as well as the idea of sin; they say it is to be expected that finite men do not know all things and do not do fully that which is right and true. Even so they cannot fully naturalize these concepts. They will not be naturalized. In their refusal to be naturalized these concepts testify to man to the effect that he ought to accept that which his adopted principle requires him to

---

42. KSO: Van Til is referencing here what Barth called "consciousness theology" in which man begins with his own consciousness in order to move toward "God-consciousness." See, for example, Van Til's discussion of this in *The New Modernism : An Appraisal of the Theology of Barth and Brunner* (Philadelphia, PA: The Presbyterian and Reformed Publishing Company, 1947): Chapter 6 and Chapter 10.

reject. Thus the futility of his struggle with the problem of authority as well as with the problem of evil is itself a means by which God brings his pressure to bear upon men. Having a consciousness of their creaturehood and with it a consciousness of "good and evil," their need of authority is the sounding board against which the gospel comes to man. But the gospel's idea of authority is not a mere continuation of the idea of authority such as the natural man admits that he needs.[43]

C. THE SUFFICIENCY OF SCRIPTURE

By the sufficiency of Scripture is meant its finished character. In Scripture there is given a once for all and completed revelation of God's redemptive work for man. This attribute of Scripture again involves the question of the *that* and the *what*, of identification and of content or system. Here is a body of writing identifying itself in distinction from all other writings as the Word of God. Granted that human agency was used in the collection of the several books of the Bible into the canon of Scripture; it remains true that Scripture identifies itself as the Word of God. The human agents did the subordinate work of collecting that which witnessed to itself as divine in each part as well as in the whole. Then this self-identified body of writings claims to give men a finished system of interpretation of human life and history. What does the "modern mind" think of this?

Naturally it rejects this idea, as it does that of the necessity and authority of Scripture, and with vigor. Not only does it do so in the work of higher criticism, but back of this work of higher criticism lies the assumption that there cannot be such a thing as a finished revelation of God in history. And how can there be, if man is himself the final reference point in predication?

Modern man argues that on the basis of a finished Bible, a closed canon, there could be nothing new for man to discover. The idea of a finished, directly given revelation in Scripture, is opposed to the notion of the "open universe" or to the open aspect of the universe. It does not accept the modern view that human knowledge must therefore be synthetic as well as analytic. It does not realize that no fact in the phenomenal world is an entity by itself. It does not realize the fact that all human knowledge is correlative to the human mind and to that extent must be considered subjective. In fact the orthodox doctrine of a finished revelation seeks to identify as absolute something that is, as involved in the "human situation," relative.

---

43. KSO: Van Til highlights the fact that whatever is common between believer and unbeliever is only superficially so. The concept of authority, when held by an unbeliever, is not on a continuum with a Christian concept of authority; it is antithetical to it. Any concept of authority that is not Christian is, by definition, anti-Christian and thus is foundationally opposed to the Christian concept.

As the idea of a closed canon seeks to identify something as absolute in a sea of relativism, so it separates this identified object from all relations of significance with human experience. It sets off the Bible as a mechanical something over against human experience. Yet it wants this Bible, though separated out of contact with the stream of human experience, to have an all-controlling influence on this experience. It wants the Bible to be the standard of human life. It lifts this standard of life out of contact with life and then expects it to have an all-important bearing on life. It wants all of human life to be regulated rationalistically by a hard and fast pattern that is not adjustable as human experience accumulates.

Thus the idea of the sufficiency of Scripture as well as that of its necessity is charged with being both irrationalistic and rationalistic. This charge is based upon the assumption of the ultimacy of man. Thus man's ultimate irrationalism requires that he charge the Christian position with rationalism because it holds to a God who controls all things.[44] Thus man's ultimate rationalism requires that he charge the Christian position with irrationalism because it holds that God controls all things by his counsel that is itself above and prior to and therefore not involved in the "relativity" of history.

It may be well at this juncture to deal briefly with the dialectical view on the Scriptures as a finished revelation of God. For it is particularly Karl Barth who has insisted that the Bible *is* God's Word. He has insisted on this as over against the views of such modern theologians as Schleiermacher and Ritschl. At the same time Barth insists that higher criticism must have free course and that we must be done with the orthodox doctrine of the givenness of revelation. Barth is as vigorously opposed to the notion that there should be in history something directly identifiable with the written Word of God as he is vigorously opposed to the idea that we should claim to find in history a man that can as such be said to be directly identifiable with the Son of God, and therefore God himself.[45]

In his *Church Dogmatics* Barth speaks of the Word of God in its threefold form, the Word as proclaimed, the Word as written and the Word as revealed.

To understand what is meant by the Word of God, says Barth, we must start with the fact of its present proclamation. This Word as proclaimed must

---

44. KSO: Van Til is employing his complex dialectic here of the rational/irrational in unbelieving thought. Given that dialectic, man's presumed ultimacy expresses its irrationalism in its rejection of God's providence (since it irrationally supposes the universe to be controlled by chance), and it expresses its rationalism in holding that it is irrational to affirm God's counsel as absolute (since it rationally supposes that the facts of the world are what they are by way of man's interpretation of them).

45. KSO: Van Til understood Barth to hold a "mechanistic" view of the "phenomena" of history. With such a view, the Word of God and the Son of God would be "absorbed" by history's phenomena and thus, in that sense, meaningless. Barth needed to find a way for the Word and the Son to transcend the phenomena of history.

be based on definite content. Yet it is not "at hand." It takes place moment by moment (*je und je*) rather than in accord with any plan.[46] The Word of God is an Event. It is an act of God. The Word as proclaimed must be tested by the Word as written. Scripture is our canon.[47] As such it has constitutive significance for church proclamation.[48]

But the idea of the Bible as having constitutive significance for the proclamation must not be taken in the orthodox sense. The Bible is not a finished product. For the Word of proclamation is a *continuation of the same Event* as the Word of inscripturation ("*dort die Schrift als Anfang, hier die heute zu haltende Predigt als Fortsetzung eines und desselben Geschehens*").[49] [50] The written Word is therefore the antecessor to the proclaimed Word as its successor.[51]

Thus there is for Barth no identifiable body of writings that stands out from other writings or from words spoken by men as being alone the Word of God and as constituting a final norm for church proclamation. We should be doing poor honor to Scripture, says Barth, if we should identify it with revelation.[52]

The reason why the Bible must not be identified with the Word of God lies,

---

46. Karl Barth, *Die Kirchliche Dogmatik*, I/1 (Munchen. Chr. Kaiser, 1932), p. 94.
47. Ibid., p. 103.
48. Ibid., p. 105.
49. KSO: Translated as, ". . . Scripture as the commencement and present-day preaching as the continuation of one and the same event . . ." Karl Barth, ed. Geoffrey William Bromiley, and Thomas F. Torrance, *Church Dogmatics: The Doctrine of the Word of God*, Part 1, vol. 1 (London; New York: T&T Clark, 2004), 102.
50. Ibid., p. 104
51. Ibid., p. 107
52. Ibid., p. 115. Many Reformed and evangelical theologians have in recent years seen a radical change in the theology of Barth. But the disciples of Barth have seen no such change. Arthur C. Cochrane has observed in a review of *Radical Theology and the Death of God* by Altizer and Hamilton (*Journal of Ecumenical Studies*, Winter, 1967, Vol. 4, No. 1, p. 137): "Too long theology has behaved as if it were capable of communicating the truth of God to modern man, as if its God-talk were objectively true, as if kerygmatically or apologetically, in metaphysical or secular concepts, we could speak about God. In spite of repeated warnings Barth's massive *Church Dogmatics* has given the impression of what Dietrich Bonhoeffer described as 'theological positivism' and Heinrich Vogel called a *theologia gloriae*. Actually Barth has known all along that his theology, even when produced in fidelity to Scripture, is in itself nothing more than words. 'Vanity of vanity, all is vanity'! Appearances to the contrary, Barth has never abandoned the insight of his early years that 'the word of God on the lips of man is an impossibility. . . We are human and so cannot speak of God.' This is the confession of any man whom God has encountered in his revelation. It is a fearful thing to fall into the hands of the living God precisely because the living God is a consuming fire. Before him ecumenical theology can be pursued only in 'fear and trembling,' and that means in full awareness of both an immanent and transcendent crisis of Christianity. The fear of the Lord is the beginning of wisdom. The significant service which the radical theologians may render to ecumenical theology is the reminder that it too can only be 'a cry out of the depths.' Then, and only then, will it be blessed and be a blessing to the people of God and the nations of the world." See the entire review (pp. 133–137) for a very helpful discussion of the relationship of Barth to radical theology.

according to Barth, in the fact that revelation lies back of ordinary history. The Bible is therefore no more than the record of the event of revelation.[53] The event itself is a matter of supra-history. In supra-history (*Geschichte*) there is no distinction between past and future. It is the realm of exclusively personal relations. Personal relations defy all calendar distinctions; they are always in the "present." And this "present" is not the border between past and future. It is beyond the distinctions of the calendar altogether.

To be sure, this revelation took place in the "fulness of time." As such it is a "fixed event" (*abgeschlossene Geschehen*). Of it we must assert that "it is finished."[54]

But to say that it is "finished" is not to say that it took place in the past. It is unique in that it is finished as a presently continuing event. "Thus we must think of every state of revelation as a process of revelation, that is, as conditioned by the very act of revelation."[55] To identify the Bible with the idea of God's revelation would, therefore, according to Barth, be destructive of the very idea of revelation. It would be to deny, in effect, the free and sovereign character of that revelation. For revelation *is* God, and God *is* revelation. The free and sovereign God must not be identified by something that is past. Then God would be dead.

Moreover the idea of the Bible as a finished revelation would preclude man's profiting from the work of Christ. God is his revelation and this revelation is Jesus Christ. It is Jesus Christ as the Event of God in revelation. And man must profit from this Event of revelation by participating in it. Revelation *is* redemption and *is* reconciliation. Our time, our history, must therefore be taken up into this one Event which is Christ. Otherwise our time is lost, is past, is dead.

We are, as reconciled to God through Christ, contemporaneous with him. Even from all eternity we have participated in this contemporaneity with God. Our *true past* therefore lies in this contemporaneity with the eternal God in Christ as the Event of revelation.[56]

Everything therefore depends, says Barth, upon our taking the idea of revelation as that which takes place now in the one eternally present act of incarnation, reconciliation and redemption. Nothing is past, nothing is merely future. All is present. So then in our time, in history measured by the calendar, there can be no more than a witness to this contemporaneity of man with God. The witness *points to* but is not identical with revelation.

---

53. Ibid., p. 116.
54. Ibid., p. 119.
55. Ibid., p. 122.
56. Karl Barth, *Die Kirchliche Dogmatik*, I/1; (Zollikon: Verlag der Evangelischer Buchhandlung, 1938), p. 6 ff.

> *Dass sie von Gottes Offenbarung zeugt, das bedeutet ja nicht, dass Gottes Offenbarung nun in irgend einer göttlichen Offenbartheit vor uns läge. Die Bibel ist kein Orakelbuch; sie ist kein Organ direkter Mitteilung. . .Die Menschen, die wir hier als Zeugen reden hören, reden als fehlbahre, als irrende Menschen wie wir selber. Was sie sagen und was wir als ihr Wort lesen, könnte an sich selbst den Anspruch, Gottes Wort zu sein, wohl erheben, aber nimmermehr siegreich durchsetzen."*[57] [58]

He who says that he deals with the Word of God should deal with something that is wholly beyond the control of man.[59] Of the book as such we can only say that in that book we have heard the Word of God, that the Word of God has been heard in it, and so we expect to hear the Word of God again in this book.[60]

It is this activistic character of Barth's conception of God and his revelation that must, therefore, be kept in mind if we are to understand what Barth means when he asserts that the Bible's the Word of God and when he avers his belief in verbal inspiration. The Bible is never *directly* identical with the Word of God says Barth. If we took it as such we should only have something relative. How could one relative entity take precedence over other relative entities? And how could it have relevance to human experience? The Bible must therefore be taken as *indirectly* identical with the Word of God. It is that which we should mean when we say that it is the Word of God.[61] As for verbal inspiration, this fallible and erring human word is now as such taken into his service by God, and in spite of its human fallibility is to be taken and heard as God's Word.[62]

D. THE PERSPICUITY OF SCRIPTURE

Finally a word must be said about the perspicuity of Scripture in relation to those who hold to the doctrine of the autonomous man.

---

57. KSO: Translated as, "It witnesses to God's revelation, but that does not mean that God's revelation is now before us in any kind of divine revealedness. The Bible is not a book of oracles; it is not an instrument of direct impartation. . . The men whom we hear as witnesses speak as fallible, erring men like ourselves. What they say, and what we read as their word, can of itself lay claim to be the Word of God, but never sustain that claim." Karl Barth, Geoffrey William Bromiley, and Thomas F. Torrance, *Church Dogmatics: The Doctrine of the Word of God*, Part 2, vol. 1 (London; New York: T&T Clark, 2004), 507.
58. Ibid., p. 562.
59. Ibid., p. 585.
60. Ibid., p. 509.
61. Ibid., p. 597.
62. Ibid., p. 592.

The system of truth set forth in the Scriptures clearly and simply tells man who he is, what the nature of his sin is and what is the nature of the remedy that God has provided for the removal of that sin. But this idea of perspicuity or clarity is not opposed to the "incomprehensibility" of God. The system of Scripture is an analogical system. The relation between God and man is, in the nature of the case, not exhaustively expressible in human language.

Yet the sort of system the natural man requires is one in which every part is penetrable by human logic. In other words the natural man, as we saw in the analysis given of the fall of Adam, will not submit himself to a God whose thoughts are essentially higher than his own. He will gladly admit the existence of "larger" or "greater" minds than his own. But he will not admit the possible existence of a mind to which his own must be in subjection, on which the voluntary action of his own mind depends. This is what we have called the rationalism of the natural man.

In terms of this rationalism he must therefore deny that any system can be called perspicuous or clear that is not open to complete inspection by man. To be sure, the natural man does not mind if it takes many thousands or millions of years before reality should be exhaustively stated. He does not object if it is *never* exhaustively known. What he objects to is the idea of the mind of God as inherently incomprehensible to man because it is self-sufficient and therefore independent.

On the other hand the natural man, as indicated repeatedly, insists that reality is ultimately "open." It constantly produces the wholly new. It cannot then be controlled by a plan of a God who exists apart from the world. God himself must, together with the world and as an aspect of the world, be involved in a process or he cannot be honored as God. Thus the idea of a system of truth, such as orthodox Christianity pretends to have, which clearly, in readily identifiable and in directly available fashion, tells man what is true and what he ought to do, cannot exist. We must think of mystery as something ultimate, as something that envelops God as well as man. This idea of mystery as inclusive of God as well as man is taken as correlative to the notion that all reality, again inclusive of both God and man, is exhaustively lit up and wholly penetrable to man. The two notions must be taken as supplementative of one another. Only then, says modern man, do we do justice to both aspects of reality, its wholly hidden and its wholly revealed character.

A brief word may again be added on the dialectical view of the perspicuity of the Scriptures. From what has been said about Barth's view on the authority and sufficiency of Scripture it will be expected that Barth does not hold to the historic doctrine of the perspicuity of Scripture.

In the world of historical relativity there can be no such thing as a directly distinguishable entity that can as such properly be called the Word of God. As an eternal novelty, an ever-contemporaneous event, revelation therefore cannot be clear or perspicuous in the orthodox sense of the term. To be clear in the orthodox sense of the term, Barth argues, God would have to be exhaustively revealed without at the same time being completely hidden. And the very essence of a true theology is that it thinks of the revealed *Deus Revelatus*, as being at the same time the hidden God, *Deus Absconditus*. In the incarnation God is fully revealed and yet is wholly hidden.[63]

The Bible merely witnesses to this Event of revelation as wholly hidden when wholly revealed.[64]

---

63. Thus Barth is opposed to the historic Reformation doctrine at every point.

64. The viewpoint expressed here was also expressed in my *Christianity and Barthianism* (Presbyterian and Reformed, 1962) saying: "On the basis of Barth's theology, there is, says Berkouwer, no transition from wrath to grace in history. No more basic criticism of Barth's theology can be made" (p. 113).

The Reverend James Daane, a theologian of the Christian Reformed Church, reviewed that book in the *Reformed Journal* (Jan., 1963, Vol. XIII, no. 1, p. 27–29). He claimed in his review that in appealing to Dr. Berkouwer for support of my criticism of Barth, I overstated the case. Daane said that in Berkouwer's *De Triomf der Genade in de Theologie van Karl Barth* (Kok, 1954; English translation, *The Triumph of Grace in the Theology of Karl Barth*, Grand Rapids: Eerdmans, 1954) he found no stronger criticism of Barth than that in his theology "the *transition* in history from wrath to grace is obscured" (*De Triomf* etc., p. 253; E.t., p. 257). Daane claimed that I used Berkouwer "for more than he is worth."

I would like therefore to give a brief *summary* of Berkouwer's criticism of Barth's theology in general and of his criticism of Barth's view of the transition from wrath to grace in particular. (Cf. *Christianity and Barthianism*, pp. 120–135 for a full statement of this summary.)

In *Christianity and Barthianism* I pointed out that not only Berkouwer but also other European Reformed theologians have found in Barth's theology no such thing as the *biblical view* of a transition from wrath to grace in history through the death and resurrection of Jesus Christ. Barth makes no room for the idea of such a transition. The structure of his thought prohibits it. Barth holds to a *nominalist-realist* view of the relation of God to man (cf. p. 117).

In theology, nominalism, when held to consistently, would negate the possibility of God's revelation of himself in any aspect of created reality. All knowledge of God, therefore, would have to come through special revelation, i.e., it would have to come down to man from above because nature can tell man nothing about God. Nature can in no way be objectively revelational. But history is part of the natural order and therefore God cannot reveal himself in history either.

On the other hand, realism, when held to consistently, would posit that for any individual existent to be meaningful or real it must in some sense participate in the truly "real," the world of transcendent reality. Individual facts or events would be *in themselves* meaningless. Historical events, therefore, can be of no real theological importance. They can only, in some sense and at most, be *pointers* to a transcendent reality.

'Nominalism' and 'realism' have one thing in common; they posit a disjuncture between two worlds so that the 'events' of the one cannot effect the other. In nominalism, history cannot be controlled by the part of the world called God. In realism, history can accomplish nothing in the plan of God, although it is thoroughly determined due to its participation in an abstract principle of transcendence.

In his earlier works, especially his *Romans*, Barth was strongly nominalist in his views of the

Summing up now what has been said on the attitude of "modern man" to the Scripture, we have the following:

(a) Basic to all the various views present is the common assumption of man as autonomous.

(b) This basic assumption is *in principle* the exact opposite of the view that the Bible, God's Word, is autonomous.

(c) By and large, modern man therefore cannot allow for: 1. The idea of a Bible that testifies to itself by identifying itself as alone the Word of God. 2. The idea that there is in this Bible a system of truth that requires men to interpret the world and themselves in terms of it.

---

relation of God to man. In this work, Barth militated constantly against the historic Christian idea of God's revelation as once for all given to man in history. On this point, Berkouwer speaks of a "cardinal difference between Reformed orthodoxy and 'dialectic theology'" (*Geloof en Openbaring in de Nieuwere Duitsche Theologie*, 1932, p. 213). "Christ no less than the Scriptures," says Berkouwer, "stands in Barth's theology beneath the 'Vorbehalt' [condition] of the speaking of God" (Ibid.).

Barth's nominalist, or actualist, view of God and of God's revelation to man, says Berkouwer, is *speculative* rather than *biblical*. Barth's view puts him in direct relation to 'Occamistic nominalism' (Ibid., p. 215). Thus, says Berkouwer, "God's revelation is deprived of its meaning" (*Karl Barth*, 1936, p. 93). In fact, Barth's view of God is even more nominalist than that of Occam. "Occam still appealed to the direct authority of the church. Barth no longer does so" (Ibid., p. 80). For Barth, Berkouwer says, the whole of positive revelation is "uprooted and given over to an actualist, unapproachable reality of God" (Ibid., p. 92).

This is the opposite of Calvin's view. "For Calvin the sovereignty of God never becomes a threat that hangs above his given revelation... The Occamist view of God with its idea of 'absolute power' is for Calvin the fruit of useless pagan speculation" (*Christianity and Barthianism*, p. 130; cf. *Karl Barth*, pp. 87–89).

Barth's nominalist, or actualist, view of God leads him to make a distinction between special (Geschichte) and ordinary (Historie) history. This distinction, says Berkouwer, "tears apart the idea of historical revelation" (*Het Probleem der Schriftkritiek*, 1938, p. 80).

Along with Barth's view of 'special history' as distinct from ordinary history, goes the acceptance of the higher criticism of the Scriptures. But, objects Berkouwer, it is impossible to give over the Bible to historical criticism and still maintain the content of the Christian faith (Ibid., p. 83). Barth is quite inconsistent when he rejects the idea of myth once he has accepted the idea of saga and legend (Ibid.).

Nominalism, in all its implications, cuts the nerve between revelation and history. It cuts the nerve between revelation and the human nature of Christ. It cuts the nerve between revelation and Scripture. History cannot be revelational.

In Berkouwer's earlier writings he was criticizing Barth's earlier writings and therefore criticized Barth's emphasis on nominalism.

We shall turn now to the later writings of Barth and with them to the later criticism of Berkouwer. We turn, therefore, to Barth's realism. By means of his realism, Barth believes he can escape the pure contingency or pure Chance in the phenomenal world necessitated by his nominalism. By means of a virtual determinism, Barth seeks to counterbalance what is none other than pure indeterminism. Barth's theology is like a pendulum which swings back and forth between pure nominalism and pure realism. In both cases the nerve which connects revelation and history is severed.

We have seen that such a severance is, according to Berkouwer, the result of Barth's nominalist

THE AUTONOMOUS MAN

(d) The ideas of the Bible as identifying itself and of containing the divine system of truth are correlative to one another. They are together involved in the idea of God as self-contained.

(e) These ideas will therefore be charged with being both irrationalistic and rationalistic by those who make man the final reference point in predication.

1. They will be said to be irrationalistic in terms of what is actually the rationalistic notion of fallen man. Fallen man putting himself virtually in the place of God also virtually demands essential continuity between himself and God. He speaks of thought in general and of the laws of being in general. He therewith subjects the thought and being of God to the same limitations to which man is subject. In consequence the Christian's view of Scripture appears to break the continuity between God and man, as being irrationalistic.

2. On the other hand, the biblical idea of self-identification as containing the ultimate system of truth will be charged with being rationalistic by the natural man. This is the case because such an idea of Scripture involves the notion

---

principle. Berkouwer, however, is equally explicit with respect to Barth's realism. In both cases, revelation and history are divorced.

Berkouwer observes, as he sets forth Barth's view: "Our being in Adam stands 'in advance' (zum vornherein) in the light of the fact that we are in Christ" (*De Triomf* etc., p. 80; E.t., p. 86). The triumph of grace, therefore, is of an *a priori* nature. It is correlative to the ontological impossibility of sin. "This impossibility," says Berkouwer, "*is raised above all doubt in the prefiguration of the creation triumph*" (Ibid., p. 82; E.t., p. 88). Revelation and history are again divorced.

We are here "confronted with ideas that lie on a totally different plane from that of Scripture when it tells us what God is not" (Ibid., p. 215; E.t., p. 222). "If sin is ontologically impossible," says Berkouwer, "a transition from wrath to grace in the historical sphere is no longer thinkable. It is clear that *this* transition is excluded when Barth, consistent with his total view, elucidates what he means by the ontological impossibility of sin by saying that sin is substantially a grasping for that 'which has been made impossible for man and against which he has also been secured' " (Ibid., pp. 228–229; E.t., pp. 233–234, quoting Barth's K. D. III/2, p. 176). "When Barth speaks of chaos, mystery, enigma, shadow and impossibility, this last word explains all the others and forms the central category of his doctrine of sin and redemption" (Ibid., p. 229; e.t., p. 234). "We see that the triumph of grace is emphatically placed before sin and that for this reason sin is anticipated and intercepted and so made ontologically impossible. The triumph of grace is the reverse side of (in a certain sense one can say that it is identical with) the ontological impossibility of sin" (Ibid.).

The reader now has more than enough evidence of the fact that I did not misrepresent Berkouwer's analysis of Barth's notion of sin as 'ontologically impossible.' Berkouwer says that a *transition* from wrath to grace in history is *unthinkable*. Therefore my interpretation of Berkouwer given on page 113 of *Christianity and Barthianism*, although not an exact translation of his statement, still is true to Berkouwer's sense. "Barth," says Berkouwer, "speaks of the fearful reality of sin, but *at the same time* he holds to the ontological impossibility of sin, because a *transition* from wrath to grace *in history* has already been excluded and has been changed into a conception in which wrath is no more than 'the form of grace'" (Ibid., p. 248; e.t., p. 253).

"Barth's revised supralapsarianism," says Berkouwer, "blocks the way to ascribing *decisive* significance to history" (Ibid., p. 252; e.t., p. 256). "The problems Barth raises with respect to the 'ontological impossibility' of unbelief," says Berkouwer, "are wholly foreign to Reformation theology" (Ibid., p. 270; e.t., p. 274).

that God knows all things because he controls all things. Thus, it is argued, the sacredness of human personality and human freedom would be violated. In the name of the idea of science, the ideal of complete comprehension and continuity, the idea of Scripture is said to be irrationalistic. In the name of the idea of personality—the idea of freedom—the idea of Scripture is said to be rationalistic.

(f) Modern science, modern philosophy and modern theology are, broadly speaking, in agreement with one another in their assumption of the autonomy of man. We have limited our discussion largely to modern theology. Its two main schools, that of the old or traditional modernism (Schleiermacher and Ritschl) and that of the new modernism or dialecticism (Barth and Brunner) are in agreement on this. That this is true of dialecticism seems, on the surface, to be denied by the assertions of Barth and Brunner to the effect that they want to return to a "theology of the Word."

Yet when the views of dialectical theology are examined they are seen to hold to the same activistic theory of knowledge and being that controls the views of Schleiermacher and Ritschl. These views are, like those of modern philosophy, largely in accord with the philosophy of Immanuel Kant.

IV

THE CHURCH FATHERS

In the two preceding chapters the Christian and the non-Christian positions with respect to Scripture have been outlined. To make the issue clear we have taken the most consistent (some would say the most extreme) forms of the two positions. Between these two "extreme" positions lies that of Roman Catholicism. Romanism seeks to "do justice" to both "reason" and "authority." In order to do so it divides the field of human experience between them. Of course when it is asked what it means by reason Romanism says that it is the reason of man as created in the image of God. And this reason, it adds, is wounded through sin. To an extent then, Rome seeks the interpretation of human reason in terms of the Christian religion. But in practice Rome teaches that those who take reason as autonomous and who therefore make man the final point of reference in predication are essentially right in their methodology. In particular is this the case with Aristotle who is constantly called "the philosopher" by St. Thomas and frequently said to be right in his basic methodology.

The Roman Catholic system is a system that is made up of two mutually exclusive principles, the Christian and the non-Christian. Naturally it is instructive to see something of the nature of such a system, but before doing so it is well that, for background, we deal with some of the church Fathers. In them we see a struggle to do justice to the Christian view of Scripture together with frequent adjustments to systems produced by the natural man.

A. PHILO JUDAEUS

A few remarks may first be made with respect to the Jew, Philo Judaeus.[1] He was an orthodox Jew. As such he held to the authority of the Old Testament Scripture.

---

1. For an expanded discussion of Philo in the context of Jewish apologetics in general, see the present writer's Christ and the Jews (Presbyterian and Reformed Pub. Co., 1968). KSO: Philo Judaeus, "also called Philo of Alexandria (c.20 B.C.–c.40 A.D.), a contemporary of Jesus and the apostles, is the one Jewish author belonging to the Dispersion whose works have been preserved in any considerable quantity. Quite apart from the influence exercised by his writings on later Christian

But he did not think of the authority of Scripture as implying the necessity of getting basic concepts of philosophy from Scripture. In other words he seemed to think it quite possible that a system of interpretation based on human experience should be found to be consistent with the content of Scripture. In fact he did his best to show that what Greek philosophy had taught about God and man was virtually the same thing that the Old Testament taught about them.

Philo virtually makes the Old Testament teach that which Greek philosophy, based on autonomous human experience, had taught. Wherever the Old Testament obviously conflicts with the teaching based on self-interpreted experience Philo resorts to allegory. So the Mosaic account of the origin of the world and of the days of creation must not be taken as historical but as allegorical. Matter and change are eternal. Therefore creation is not the bringing of the universe into existence out of nothing but it is the molding of pre-existent material. On the one hand, there is in the universe an eternal undifferentiated matter, and, on the other hand, there is an eternal form. In other words, Philo interprets the origin and course of the world in terms of the form-matter scheme of much of Greek philosophy. Original matter has no qualities, and God has no qualities that man can know. These are virtually taken as limiting concepts of one another. They are correlatives.[2] Philo asserts belief in the idea of creation out of nothing. Yet it is his chief effort to show that the Greek philosophy form-matter scheme and Scripture accord one with another. To do this he uses allegory as a means of removing the historical character of the biblical doctrine of creation in general and of the creation of man in particular.

What is true with respect to the idea of creation is also true with respect to the fall of man. Philo says that the lower parts of the soul naturally turn to the things of sense and evil. It is the mind, the intellect, that must act as governor; it naturally does not always succeed. Thus Philo virtually denies that originally man was perfect in all aspects of his personality and because of the fall man became sinful in all the aspects of his personality. Here again it is the Greek rather than the biblical idea that dominates the scene.

For Philo it is not possible that Scripture should identify one point in history at which man is clearly confronted with the expressed will of God. History

---

thought and exegesis, his works are a primary source of information for the Judaism of the Dispersion, for the ideas current in NT times, for the ways in which Jews of the period could react to the thought and culture of a predominantly gentile environment, and for the extent to which it was possible to harmonize the OT with Greek philosophy." R. M. Wilson, "Philo Judaeus," ed. Geoffrey W. Bromiley, *The International Standard Bible Encyclopedia, Revised* (Wm. B. Eerdmans, 1979–1988), 847.

2. James Drummond, *Philo Judaeus; or, The Jewish Alexandrian Philosophy in its Development and Completion*, Vol. I (London: Williams and Norgate, 1888), pp. 257–259.

is composed in part of the wholly irrational. The temporal world is made up of "matter" that has no quality; this matter makes it impossible for any fact of history to be the medium of the revelation of God to man. Certainly then it is impossible that there should be one particular point in history which is of all-determinative significance.

Again the temporal world is determined in part by the idea of an all-inclusive Form, a universal that includes all forms of consciousness, the consciousness of God no less than the consciousness of man. It is impossible then that there should be conveyed to man as a finite consciousness a system of truth by another form of consciousness standing above it. The two forms of consciousness are continuous, the one with the other.

Thus the Greek principle of discontinuity and the Greek principle of continuity as involved in one another kept Philo from accepting the notion of Scripture as testifying to itself and as authoritatively conveying to man its system of truth.[3]

B. THE CHURCH FATHERS IN GENERAL

Coming now to the church Fathers we use a few illustrative examples. They show that these Fathers were no doubt seeking to be true to the Scriptures as the Word of God. But they also show that the church Fathers did not as yet clearly see the implication of this position. They, like Philo Judaeus, some in smaller and some in greater degree, failed to realize that the Scripture must identify itself, and that its system of truth is therefore the opposite of such systems as are built upon human experience assumed to be ultimate.

In particular the early church Fathers did not clearly observe that the Christian principle of continuity and the Christian principle of discontinuity are involved in one another. That such is the case may be learned from one constantly recurring fact. In their apologetical presentation of Christianity to unbelievers they were, of course, confronted with both the non-Christian principle of continuity and with the non-Christian principle of discontinuity. The former is found in particular in the idea of Form as the all-embracing universal idea. The latter is found in particular in the idea of indeterminate matter as an original constitutive factor of reality.[4] Now the church Fathers tended, by and

---

3. Ibid.
4. KSO: In Platonic and Neo-Platonic philosophy, the world of Ideas, or of the Forms, is the "real" and highest world. The everyday world, the world of our senses, participates in the world of Forms to the extent that "matter" is conformed to the Forms. Typically, in Greek philosophy, matter is seen as the substratum which cannot be known by the mind unless actualized by the Forms.

large, to identify the non-Christian principle of continuity with the Christian principle of continuity and therefore the non-Christian idea of system with the Christian or biblical idea of system. But the non-Christian idea of system was rationalistic and deterministic. It implied the disappearance of human personality and with it of the individual reason of men.[5] Some non-Christians charged the Christians with holding to rationalism and determinism. Then—and this is the point of importance—the Christians would reply that they believed in free will. They were not determinists or rationalists. The biblical system permitted them and required them to do full justice to the freedom or autonomy of man. Thus, because they had mistakenly identified the principle of system or continuity with the non-Christian idea of system or continuity, they also appealed to the non-Christian idea of discontinuity in order therewith to remedy the situation.[6]

On the other hand the Christian position was frequently charged with being irrationalistic and arbitrary. Did not the will of God through this authoritarian Scripture fix on one point in history, namely, the death and resurrection of Jesus of Nazareth, as being all important for human life? How could there be any such identification of God's presence in history without his succumbing entirely to the irrationalism and indeterminism of history? Then—and this is again the important point—the Christians would appeal to analogies of such things as their opponents were required to believe on pure authority in the history of Greek philosophy or mythology. Was there not in Greek philosophy a place for a mediator, or at least for mediation?[7]

Here then we have these two facts, together constituting two aspects of one fact (a) the charge of rationalism and determinism lodged against the church Fathers was answered by means of the non-Christian idea of indeterminism, and (b) the charge of indeterminism lodged against them was answered by means of the non-Christian idea of determinism. They confused the Greek notion of determinism, or system, with the Christian idea of God's control of all things, which is the Christian system. Again they identified the non-Christian idea of indeterminism, namely, that of free will or human autonomy with the Christian

---

5. KSO: This is the case because the non-Christian idea of system wanted to "swallow up" all diversity into unity. This unity could not change or participate in any "becoming." Thus, human personality, with its freedom, and reason as individual, were all lost in a universal notion of the One.

6. KSO: Here Van Til uses the notion of "free will" as entailing human autonomy and thus as a pagan notion. There is a biblical, Reformed notion of "free will" as expressed, for example, in WCF 9.

7. KSO: For example, Plato and his followers posited a "Demiurge" (δημιουργός, craftsman) which was lower than god, but which created and controlled the universe.

idea of man's being a responsible creature of God. The reason for both these identifications lay in the fact that they did not observe that the Christian idea of God's control of all things—the Christian principle of continuity—requires a Christian principle of indeterminism. These two are correlative of one another, and the relationship between them cannot be penetrated by the mind of man. This relationship is not contradictory since in God there is full internal coherence. But for the human mind they must in the nature of the case have the appearance of being contradictory.[8] The idea of their unity must therefore be given on authority. Hence the need of supernatural revelation, and, after the fall, of the inscripturation of this supernatural revelation. The biblical idea of unity presupposes the self-identification of God and of his finished revelation to men in history. It involves the idea of God's giving in this self-identified revelation a system of truth, which is anthropomorphic in its expression and yet all-determinative in its content. These two ideas, that of self-identification and of an authoritative system, are involved in one another.

It was not till the contrast between the Christian principle, as involving its own continuity and discontinuity ideas, was seen to be the radical opposite in principle of the non-Christian principle with its own ideas of continuity and discontinuity that the idea of Scripture came to its own. Therefore it was not till the Augustinian and later the Reformed system of the content of Scripture was set forth that the Bible's idea of itself could have full justice done to it. But it must be added at once that this does not imply the idea that the substance of the matter was not present in the thinking of the church Fathers. It only means that there was no fully self-conscious biblical doctrine of Scripture till there was a fully self-conscious understanding of the content of Scripture.

C. THE APOSTOLIC FATHERS[9]

"The earliest Christian writings after the New Testament are customarily known under the title 'Apostolic Fathers.'"[10] We look at these very briefly.

---

8. KSO: As discussed in the foreword to this volume, Reformed Christianity holds that God ordains "whatsoever comes to pass," and it also maintains that human beings are always and everywhere responsible for their own choices. See, for example, Francis Turretin, *Institutes of Elenctic Theology*, ed. James T. Dennison Jr., trans. George Musgrave Giger, vol. 1 (Phillipsburg, NJ: P&R Publishing, 1992–1997), 607.

9. Cf. Chapter 11.

10. *Early Christian Fathers*, tr. and ed. by Cyril C. Richardson ("The Library of Christian Classics," Vol. I, gen. eds. J. Baillie, J. T. McNeill, H. P. Van Dusen; Philadelphia: The Westminster Press, 1953), p. 15.

A CHRISTIAN THEORY of KNOWLEDGE

1. Clement of Rome—Ethics[11]

There is no doubt of the fact that Clement was basically committed to the Christ of the Scriptures. But when he wants to present Christ and the resurrection to unbelievers he seeks to win them by showing that they need not accept a new principle of continuity at all when they come to Christ. Is not the resurrection of Christ easy to believe? Every spring all of us witness the resurrection of a new season. Is it not easy to believe in our own future resurrection! Surely, you have heard of that bird Phoenix. It rises repeatedly from the dead. Surely then when God "uses a mere bird to illustrate the greatness of his promise" we should live in holiness and unity, looking confidently to the future for our promised reward.[12]

Werner Jaeger says that Clement's concept of Christianity "is closer to Stoic moralism than to the spirit of St. Paul and his letter to the Romans."[13]

2. Ignatius—Heresy[14]

Ignatius is instructive because he deals with "heretics." To deal fairly and properly with "heretics" requires a clear insight into one's *criterion of judgment* between truth and falsity. But it is precisely on this point that Ignatius is weak.

He could not deal adequately with *Judaizers* because he himself had no adequate understanding of Paul's teaching on justification.[15]

He could not deal adequately with the Docetists[16] because he himself had no adequate understanding of the biblical teaching of the relation between the divine and the human in Jesus Christ as truly God and truly man.

---

11. KSO: Although Clement (died c. 100) "showed the influence of Stoic philosophy" in some of what he wrote, he "quoted extensively from the Old Testament as "Scripture" and from the words of Jesus, using sayings found in Matthew, Mark, and Luke. He also quoted Romans, 1 Corinthians, and Hebrews. Thus Clement provides important evidence that books which later became part of the New Testament canon were circulating among the churches by the end of the first century. Clement's letter also provides important evidence for the martyrdom of the apostles Peter and Paul, and for a mission of Paul to the "western boundary" (i.e., Spain)." J. Newton, "Clement of Rome," ed. J.D. Douglas and Philip W. Comfort, *Who's Who in Christian History* (Wheaton, IL: Tyndale House, 1992), 165.

12. Ibid., p. 56 (*Clement's First Letter*, 26:1).

13. Werner Jaeger, *Early Christianity and Greek Paideia* (Cambridge: Harvard University Press, 1961), p. 16.

14. KSO: Ignatius of Antioch (c. 35–107 A.D.). "The authentic epistles, and esp. that to the Romans, reveal a man passionately devoted to Christ. His consuming desire for martyrdom comes out esp. in the Ep. to the Romans. In the other epistles he warns the recipients against a Judaizing heresy with Docetic elements. He insists on the reality both of the Divinity and the Humanity of the Lord, whom he calls ὁ θεὸς ἡμῶν Ἰησοῦς Χριστός ('our God Jesus Christ'). His Birth, Passion, and Death were not appearances but realities." F. L. Cross and Elizabeth A. Livingstone, eds., *The Oxford Dictionary of the Christian Church* (Oxford; New York: Oxford University Press, 2005), 823.

15. *Early Christian Fathers*, pp. 78–79.

16. KSO: Docetism, in its various forms, held that the humanity of Christ only "seemed" (δοκέω, seem) to be real, but was in fact only apparent.

A true view of the relation between the divine and the human and a true view of justification go together. Having neither, Ignatius could not properly analyze either the heresy of the Judaizers or the heresy of docetism.

Not being able to analyze the heresies of the Judaizers and of the Docetists adequately, Ignatius was not able to analyze the heresy of the Gnostics[17] properly.[18]

Ignatius did not sense the fact that the Form-matter scheme of the Greeks which underlies all these heresies is diametrically opposed to the biblical scheme of creation, fall and redemption.

3. Polycarp—Authority[19]

Polycarp reasoned with men about the question of authority. Who is Christ? Does he claim to speak to man with the authority of God? If he does, are we expected to crucify our reason when we accept him as our Savior? Ignatius has no clear-cut view on the relation of authority to reason and does therefore not ask men to make their every thought obedient to the authority of Christ. From the 'Apostolic Fathers' we go on to:

D. THE APOLOGISTS[20]

1. Justin Martyr[21]

The most famous of the Apologists was Justin Martyr. Justin was a true believer in Christ. He gave his life for his faith. He was anxious to win men to Christ. It

---

17. KSO: "Gnosticism took many different forms, commonly associated with the names of particular teachers, e.g. Valentinus, Basilides, and Marcion. . . . A central importance was attached to 'gnosis', the supposedly revealed knowledge of God and of the origin and destiny of mankind, by means of which the spiritual element in man could receive redemption. The source of this special 'gnosis' was held to be either the Apostles, from whom it was derived by a secret tradition, or a direct revelation given to the founder of the sect." F. L. Cross and Elizabeth A. Livingstone, eds., *The Oxford Dictionary of the Christian Church*, (Oxford; New York: Oxford University Press, 2005), 687.

18. Ibid., p. 78.

19. KSO: "Born of a Christian family, Polycarp claimed to have been a disciple of John, presumably the apostle. Ignatius of Antioch, on his way to Roman martyrdom (c. 116), wrote letters both to Polycarp and to the church of Smyrna. The account of Polycarp's death (a letter from the church of Smyrna to the church of Philomelium) is the earliest extant Christian martyrology. The civil authorities importuned the bishop to apostatize because of his age, but he replied dramatically, 'I have served Christ eighty-six years and He has done me no wrong. How can I blaspheme my King? I am a Christian.'" A. Cabaniss, "Polycarp," ed. J.D. Douglas and Philip W. Comfort, *Who's Who in Christian History* (Wheaton, IL: Tyndale House, 1992), 573.

20. For a fuller development of the 'Apologists,' see the present writer's syllabus *Christianity in Conflict*, Vol. I/1 and 2 (Westminster Theological Seminary, 1962 and 1964).

21. KSO: "Of Greek parents, Justin (100–165) was born in Palestine near the modern city of Nablus in Samaria. He went to Ephesus and studied the philosophies of the time, especially

is Jesus Christ who has taught us the truth about the issues of life and death. It is Jesus Christ who is our final source of truth. Jesus was virgin-born. Jesus was crucified but rose again from the dead. He ascended to heaven. Do you find all this hard to believe? Yet in saying these things about Jesus "we introduce nothing new beyond (what you say of) those whom you call the sons of Zeus."[22]

Is it any wonder that the Greeks anticipated Christian teachings? Not at all. There are "seeds of truth in all men."[23] Christ is the "First-begotten of God" but he is, at the same time, "the Reason of which every race of man partakes."[24]

The basic reason why Justin is unable to set the Christ of Scripture clearly as a challenge over against Greek philosophy lies in the fact that he has, himself, no adequately biblical view of man. The Greeks assumed that man is free, i.e., autonomous. Justin should have challenged this idea in terms of the biblical teaching with respect to man's creation by God. But Justin is afraid to do this. The Greeks will then, he fears, charge him with holding to determinism or fate. So he virtually admits that he, as well as the Greeks, starts with the idea of man's freedom as the ability to act or not act, to act rightly or wrongly, without regard to the plan of God. Virtually committing himself to the same sort of freedom as that to which the Greeks are committed, he has thereby also committed himself to the principle of discontinuity as that to which the Greeks are committed, i.e., pure contingency.[25] Accordingly, Justin does not hesitate to follow Plato's example when he speaks of God as the nameless one. The god of the Greeks, being the god of all apostate thought, is utterly indeterminate. This god cannot name or identify himself because man has not identified him. Yet Justin identifies his own God with the God of the Greeks.

Justin should have set the self-naming Christ and God of Scripture as a challenge over against this anonymous god of the Greeks. But in his interest to win the Greeks to Christ, he compromised the Christ.

Platonism. Although deeply impressed by the death of Christian martyrs, he was actually converted (as he himself related) by a humble old Christian. For awhile he taught Christian philosophy at Ephesus, but left in 135 and went to Rome, where he taught and wrote until he was martyred under Marcus Aurelius. Only two or three of his treatises are still extant: his first *Apology* (the second may not be authentic) and his *Dialogue with Trypho.*" A. Cabaniss, "Justin Martyr," ed. J.D. Douglas and Philip W. Comfort, *Who's Who in Christian History* (Wheaton, IL: Tyndale House, 1992), 390.

22. *Early Christian Fathers*, p. 255 (First Apology of Justin, 21).
23. Ibid., p. 270 (44).
24. Ibid., p. 272 (46).
25. KSO: To be clear, Reformed theology has always affirmed contingency as itself established by God. By "pure contingency," Van Til means a notion of contingency that has presumed human autonomy as its foundation.

Holding to the idea of autonomy with the Greeks and holding to the same principle of discontinuity with the Greeks, Justin naturally also held to the same principle of continuity as the Greeks. As a Christian he believes his Christ is the Son of God, through whom the world is made, but as an anxious apologist his Christ is the principle of reason as found in all men.

Justin's failure to set his own Christian position clearly as a challenge over against the Greeks is matched by his failure to challenge Trypho the Jew to forsake his faith in work-righteousness and accept the grace of God in Christ.

Justin argues with Trypho as he argues with the Greeks. Justin seeks for an area of common interpretation with Trypho in order from that point to go on to the uniqueness of Christ. He grants the justice of Trypho's claim to being a true Jew. Justin should have shown Trypho that only he is a true Jew who believes in Christ as *the* seed of Abraham.

Undoubtedly Justin was concerned at heart to present to men the "Sacred Name" of his Savior. Yet, he confused this sacred name with the *Logos* idea of the Greeks.[26] Accordingly he speaks of Christ as the one who is "final law" to men. The Greeks had already, he argues, however obscurely, sensed the presence and coming of this law.

Instead of taking his views of God in his relation to man and his world exclusively from Scripture as the Word of the self-testifying Christ in order then with this "system" of truth taken from Scripture to challenge the wisdom of this world, Justin takes his view of God and his relation to man and his world partly from Scripture and partly from Greek philosophy.

The result is that he finds no unity of outlook in his own thinking. He remains a victim of the false problematics of apostate thought and, in spite of his best intentions, compromises his Christ.

In this basic respect Justin is the forerunner of Romanist and Arminian apologetics.[27] To this point we shall return.

---

26. KSO: The "*Logos* idea of the Greeks" is somewhat diverse. Generally speaking, the *Logos* was thought by the Greeks to be a kind of universal reason or truth with gave order and rationale to an ever-changing world. This idea was prominent during the time of the New Testament. The Lord inspired the apostle John to use the same word, but also to radically change its meaning and context. The *Logos* in Scripture is the second person of the Trinity. For more on the *Logos*, see Geehan, *Jerusalem and Athens*, 428–444.

27. KSO: One of the primary reasons that Van Til sees "Romanist and Arminian apologetics" as twins is that both compromise on key biblical doctrines, such as the self-attestation of Scripture, total depravity, and the absolute aseity and sovereignty of God.

2. Athenagoras[28]

Only a word need be said about Athenagoras. His general position is similar to that of Justin Martyr. Together they hold to the Logos theology. It is to be expected, therefore, that Athenagoras, like Justin, will think favorably of the efforts of Greek philosophy so far as it has spoken of God. Athenagoras thinks that Plato holds to one God and that Christians do not differ from Plato in this respect. Yet he also realizes that the philosophers have been unable to discover the truth that men need and the Christians therefore turn to "those guided by the Spirit of God."

In his brief treatise *On the Resurrection* Athenagoras argues that since God has created all things it should not be impossible for him to raise men from the dead. This is in itself true. But Athenagoras did not realize that, according to the views of Plato and others, God did not create all things. He apparently did not appreciate the fact that when he argued for the possibility of the resurrection in terms of the philosophy of his opponents he himself was no longer true to his own position. According to his own position the possibility of the resurrection is based on the God who has created the world.

Athenagoras also argues for the possibility of the resurrection by appealing to what his opponents should be willing to recognize on their own principles. He says that human life changes greatly from its inception till its end. The changes from the beginning of a human being till he reaches his end are so great and so much beyond our power of comprehension that those who see them ought to be willing to allow for the possibility of a resurrection of the dead.

But to argue thus for the possibility of resurrection is no longer to argue for its possibility on the grounds of the doctrine of creation. Athenagoras was not aware of the fact that in the two types of argument that he employed, the one based upon and the other not based upon the idea of creation, he was making use of two mutually exclusive notions of possibility. The Christian doctrine of resurrection fits in with and presupposes the Christian doctrine of creation and providence. The Christian doctrine of resurrection does not fit in with and would indeed not be "possible" without these doctrines as its presupposition. For on any other presupposition than that of creation and providence the idea of possibility

---

28. KSO: Athenagoras (2nd century) "is described in the earliest manuscript. of his works as 'the Christian Philosopher of Athens'. His 'Apology' or 'Supplication', addressed c. 177 to Marcus Aurelius and his son Commodus, sought to rebut current calumnies against the Christians: atheism (chs. 4–30), Thyestian banquets, and Oedipean incest. . . .As a writer Athenagoras was one of the ablest of the Apologists, lucid in style and forceful in argument. He was the first to elaborate a philosophical defence of the Christian doctrine of God as Three in One." F. L. Cross and Elizabeth A. Livingstone, eds., *The Oxford Dictionary of the Christian Church* (Oxford; New York: Oxford University Press, 2005), 122–123.

is that of Chance and the resurrection as a Chance fact is not the resurrection as spoken of in Scripture.

3. Irenaeus[29]

In the work of Irenaeus, *Against Heresies*, we have a comprehensive discussion of the gnostics. He attacks the idea of matter as eternal and as the source of evil. In particular he challenges the gnostic conception of salvation. He warns the gnostics that in using terms borrowed from the philosophers they are in danger of accepting their content too. He asks whether the men from whom they get their speculations, the philosophers, know or do not know the truth. If they know the truth then there was no need of the coming Savior at all and they might as well have spared themselves their elaborate discussion of intermediaries between God and man.

> Did all those who have been mentioned, with whom you have been proved to coincide in expression, know, or know not, the truth? If they knew it, then the descent of the Savior into this world was superfluous. For why (in that case) did he descend? Was it that he might bring that truth which was (already) known to the knowledge of those who knew it? If, on the other hand, these men did *not* know it, then how is it that, while you express yourselves in the same terms as do those who knew not the truth, ye boast that yourselves alone possess that knowledge which is above all things, although they who are ignorant of God (likewise) possess it?[30]

In contrast, Irenaeus asks,

> How much safer and more accurate a course is it, then, to confess at once that which is true: that this God, the Creator, who formed the world, is the only God, and that there is no other God besides him—he himself

---

29. KSO: "Irenaeus was likely born in Asia Minor ca. ad 140. Little is known about his personal life aside from what has been preserved in his own work and in Eusebius's *Ecclesiastical History*. Brief mentions of his boyhood around the time of Polycarp's martyrdom in the ad 160s would place his birth somewhere in the ad 140s. . . .Irenaeus' major contributions to the history of exegesis and doctrinal development are his two complete extant works, *Refutation and Overthrow of Knowledge Falsely So Called* (commonly called *Adversus Haereses*) and *Demonstration of the Apostolic Preaching*. Both were originally composed in Greek but now survive in the original language only through quotations." Charles Meeks, "Irenaeus," ed. John D. Barry et al., *The Lexham Bible Dictionary* (Bellingham, WA: Lexham Press, 2016).

30. *The Ante-Nicene Fathers*, ed. by A. Roberts and J. Donaldson, Vol. I (Grand Rapids: Wm. B. Eerdmans Pub. Co., n.d.), p. 378 (Irenaeus, *Against Heresies*, II:XIV.7).

receiving from himself the model and figure of those things which have been made—than that, after wearying ourselves with such an impious and circuitous description, we should be compelled, at some point or another, to fix the mind on some One, and to confess that from him proceeded the configuration of things created."[31]

The basic point of Irenaeus is that we must not seek the explanation of the course of the cosmos in that cosmos itself. That is what Valentinus and the gnostics have done. And that, he says, is characteristic of the heresies of "Marcion, and Simon, and Menander, or whatever others there may be who, like them, cut off that creation with which we are connected from the Father."[32]

In rejecting the doctrine of creation these heretics also take away the possibility of the performance of miracles which they themselves affect.[33]

In particular does Irenaeus attack the Platonic doctrine of reminiscence. He finds no difficulty in pointing out that if Plato himself was in the state of oblivion which came upon all men due to their having connection with the body, he cannot speak of a state of knowledge preceding that oblivion, "for if the cup of oblivion, after it has been drunk, can obliterate the memory of all the deeds that have been done, how, O Plato, dost thou obtain the knowledge of this fact (since thy soul is now in the body), that, before it entered into the body, it was made to drink by the demon a drug which causes oblivion?"[34] Irenaeus therefore contends that the souls of men had a beginning in creation.

In this it appears that Irenaeus is not afraid of seeking to meet the philosophers in philosophical debate; his position is that of the apologists in general. He too wants to show that the Christian faith is rational and he wants to show that it is more rational than opposing views. At the same time Irenaeus was apparently of the opinion that the Logos as the Christ was at work in essentially the same manner in the whole race of men from the beginning of their existence.

In rejecting the idea of the pleroma[35] he says:

"The disciple of the Lord, therefore desiring to put an end to all such doctrines, and to establish the rule of truth in the church, that there is one Almighty God, who made all things by his Word, both visible and

---

31. Ibid., p. 380 (II:XVI.3).
32. Ibid., p. 406 (II:XXXI.1).
33. Ibid., p. 407 (II:XXXI.2).
34. Ibid., p. 410 (II:XXXIII.2).
35. KSO: "Pleroma" is the Greek word for "fullness." In Gnosticism, for example, it indicated the fullness of the divine being, which could include the Unknown, Mind, Truth, and other such concepts.

invisible; showing at the same time, that by the Word, through whom God made the creation, he also bestowed salvation on the men included in the creation; thus commenced his teaching in the gospel: 'In the beginning was the Word, and the Word was with God, and the Word was God. The same was in the beginning with God. All things were made by him, and without him was nothing made. What was made was life in him, and the life was the light of men. And the light shineth in darkness, and the darkness comprehended it not.'[36]

It is in harmony with this universalism that he speaks of the conversion of Cornelius, to whom Peter the Apostle brought the message of the Son of God, in the following words: "He thus clearly indicates, that he whom Cornelius had previously feared as God, of whom he had heard through the law and the prophets, for whose sake also he used to give alms, is, in truth, God. The knowledge of the Son was, however, wanting to him."[37]

"The apostles, therefore, did preach the Son of God, of whom men were ignorant; and his advent, to those who had been already instructed as to God; but they did not bring in another god."[38] He also speaks of God as having "purified the Gentiles through the blood of His Son."[39]

In accordance with this, Irenaeus speaks of those among the heathen who were more moral than others as being acquainted with the governor of the world and therefore as speaking of him as the Maker of the Universe.

With genuine penetration he remarks in this connection that those who seek two ultimate principles back of the world, the one as the source of goodness, the other as the source of justice, lose both goodness and justice. But he thinks that Plato has not made the mistake of thus dividing God into two principles. "Plato is proved to be more religious than these men, for he allowed that the same God was both just and good. . ."[40]

In all this Irenaeus shows that though on the one hand he was committed to the Rule of Faith[41] and ready to maintain the truth against every form of heresy, he yet seemed to think of a general theism maintained by many men who are not Christians and of Christianity as something that is added to this general theism.

36. Ibid., p. 426 (III:XI.1).
37. Ibid., p. 432 (III:XII.7).
38. Ibid., pp. 432–433 (III:XII.7).
39. Ibid., p. 432 (III:XII.7).
40. Ibid., p. 459 (III:XXV.5; cf. all of XXV.5).
41. KSO: "*rule of faith*; in the early church, the credal expansion of the baptismal formula used to define the apostolic tradition of faith against the Gnostics. . ." Richard A. Muller, *Dictionary of Latin and Greek Theological Terms: Drawn Principally from Protestant Scholastic Theology* (Grand Rapids, Mich.: Baker Book House, 1985), 261.

Perhaps the most enlightening statement of the views of Irenaeus is found in the next to the last book where he sets forth the positive position of Christians as over against the gnostics. "There is therefore one God, who by the Word and Wisdom created and arranged all things."[42]

In this section the Logos theology of Irenaeus expresses itself. In it there is (a) the idea of God as unknown (b) the idea that this unknown God is made known through the Logos first in creation and then in the incarnation, through whom man, that is mankind, is brought back to God, that is, passes into the glory of God.

All in all, it may be said that Irenaeus was unable to work out a fully Christian doctrine (a) of the Trinity (b) of creation (c) of providence (d) of incarnation and (e) of redemption. He was too much under the influence of the philosophy of the Greeks to whom he sought to bring the gospel to really challenge them with the gospel.

4. Tertullian[43]

In dealing with Tertullian we deal with a most important figure for the history of theology and for the history of apologetics. He is called the founder of Latin Christianity. B. B. Warfield speaks of him as "the real father of the Christian doctrine of the Trinity."[44] If this estimate of Warfield's is at all correct, it will at once be apparent that Tertullian is of the utmost importance in the history of theology and apologetics. For it is the doctrine of the ontological Trinity that constitutes the very foundation of both sound theology and a sound apologetic. His treatise on the Trinity is found in *Against Praxeas*.

A second point on which Tertullian is found to make a striking contribution is connected with such phrases as *credo quia absurdum*.[45] It is the question of

---

42. Ibid., p. 488 (IV:XX.4).

43. KSO: Tertullian (c.196–c.212) "began writing in Carthage, North Africa, towards the end of the 2nd century, his undisputed works dating from *c.* ad 196 to *c.* ad 212. Some scholars claim to detect fresh doctrinal distinctives in his later work when he was sympathetic to Montanism. He has been characterized both as 'the last of the Greek apologists' and as 'the first of the Latin fathers'. Both descriptions are appropriate, since he preserves in his work a compendium of mainstream Christianity, while significantly foreshadowing the Latin Church's preoccupation with power and stressing such legal themes as confession, penance, renunciation and merit." Sinclair B. Ferguson and J.I. Packer, *New Dictionary of Theology* (Downers Grove, IL: InterVarsity Press, 2000), 675–676.

44. B. B. Warfield, "Tertullian and the Beginnings of the Doctrine of the Trinity," *The Princeton Theological Review* (Vol. IV, No. 2, April, 1906), p. 165; also, B. B. Warfield, *Studies in Tertullian and Augustine* (New York: Oxford University Press, 1930), p. 107. Future references will be to the volume of collected *Studies*.

45. KSO: That is, "I believe because it is absurd." Most agree that this statement is wrongly attributed to Tertullian. See, for example, Peter Harrison, "'I Believe Because it is Absurd': The Enlightenment Invention of Tertullian's Credo." *Church History*, (June 2017), 86(2), 339–364.

authority. Liberal theologians and their faithful followers tend to quote such a phrase as evidence of the fact that here was a man who was willing to believe anything however absurd or irrational it was, as long as the Bible asserted it to be true. And it is still customary to hail Tertullian in court as the representative of an unenlightened fundamentalism.

a. B. B. Warfield on Tertullian

But in looking into Tertullian's view of authority as he sets it forth in his work *The Prescription against Heretics* it is of importance at the same time to see what he says in his discussion of the soul (*A Treatise on the Soul*). In this treatise he makes his appeal to the soul of man in general for corroboration of the truth of God's Word in Scripture. This is a far different approach from that of a mere authoritarianism.

It is mainly with the three points mentioned, his doctrine of the Trinity, his doctrine of authority, and his doctrine of the soul, that we shall be concerned. In seeking light on these matters grateful use may be made of B. B. Warfield's article on Tertullian's doctrine of the Trinity, already referred to in the preceding footnote. Warfield's article, to be sure, limits itself to a discussion of the problem of the Trinity, but this discussion is so thorough and its outreach into the field of general apologetics is so great that it is highly valuable for our purpose.

To begin with it will help us if we listen to Warfield as he sets forth the general characteristics of Tertullian's theology. Warfield sums them up by saying that on the one hand Tertullian lived and moved and had his being under the spell of the Logos speculation, while on the other hand, "there was one thing . . . which was more fundamental to Tertullian's thinking than even the Logos Christology. That was the Rule of Faith—the immemorial belief of Christians, grounded in the teaching of the Word of God."[46] "This Rule of Faith had come down to him from 'the beginning of the Gospel,' as he phrased it; and he recognized it as his first duty to preserve it whole and entire."[47]

Let us assume for the moment the correctness of this analysis of Warfield's. And with this analysis let us imagine the struggle through which the fiery, penetrating, Christ-loving mind of Tertullian had to go in order to meet the theological needs of the hour. Here was the philosophical inheritance of his predecessors, the Apologists. Here was this Logos speculation on which he had been nurtured. "Its point of origin," says Warfield,

> lay in a conception of the transcendence of God which rendered it necessary to mediate his activity *ad extra* by the assumption of the interposition

---

46. Ibid., p. 26.
47. Ibid., p. 27.

of intermediary beings. In their highest form, the speculations indeed gave birth to the idea of the Logos. Under the influence of passages like the eighth chapter of Proverbs and the first chapter of John, the historical Jesus was identified with this Logos, and thus the Logos Christology was, in principle, completed. It will be observed that the Logos Christology was in its very essence cosmological in intention: its reason for existence was to render it possible to conceive the divine works of creation and government consistently with the divine transcendence: it was therefore bound up necessarily with the course of temporal development and involved a process in God. The Logos was in principle God conceived in relation to things of time and space: God, therefore, not as absolute, but as relative. In its very essence, therefore, the Logos conception likewise involved the strongest subordinationism. Its very reason for existence was to provide a divine being who does the will of God in the regions of time and space, into which it were inconceivable that the invisible God should be able to intrude in his own person. The Logos was therefore necessarily conceived as reduced divinity—divinity, so to speak, at the periphery rather than at the center of its conception. This means, further, that the Logos was inevitably conceived as a protrusion of God, or to speak more explicitly, under the category of emanation. The affinity of the Logos speculation with the emanation theories of the Gnostics is, therefore, close.[48]

It is readily seen that in the formulation of this Logos theology, the apologists were largely influenced by Greek modes of thought. The question for them was how they could protect the deposit of faith against those who were real heretics while they were themselves so largely controlled in their thinking by false modes of thought. Here were the gnostics; they thought of God as the featureless beyond. They brought this featureless beyond into contact with the world of space and time by means of a series of impersonal emanations. Now the acceptance of the Christian deposit of faith required of the apologists that they reject this doctrine of a featureless God. They did not really believe in such a God. They believed in the triune personal God of Scripture. Again the gnostics thought of the emanations of God into the world of space and time as necessarily involved in the nature of God's being. The apologists, on the other hand, according to the deposit of faith, thought of the creation or emanation of the Logos as a voluntary act on the part of God. But how would they be able to defend either their doctrine of God or their doctrine of the voluntary procession of the Logos from the personal God against the equivalent teachings of the gnostics so long

---

48. Ibid., pp. 19–20.

as they themselves admitted that God needed an intermediary to make contact with man? If they really held to the God of the Bible there was no room for such an intermediary and if they really held to the personality of God and to the exhaustively personal character of his work with respect either to himself or to the universe, then they would have to renounce their rationalistic efforts of explaining the relation of God to the movements of history. The God of the deposit of faith must be presupposed and the understanding of the relation of God to the world must be to the effect that unless one presupposes this God there is no possibility of reason understanding anything.

The problem of harmonizing the teaching of the Rule of Faith with the speculations of Greek philosophy would therefore, in the nature of the case, tend to become the problem of defending the deposit of faith against the encroachments of this speculation. This was especially true for Tertullian when he was confronted not only with the general gnostics' heresy but with that of the Monarchians.[49] The Monarchians, says Warfield, "did not come forward as innovators in doctrine, but as protestants in the interest of the fundamental Christian doctrines of the divine unity and of the Godhead of the Redeemer against destructive speculation which was endangering the purity of the Christian confession. They embodied the protest of the simple believer against philosophic evaporation of the faith. Above all they were giving at last, so they said, his just due to Christ."[50] Was not Christ fully God? If fully God then he was not identical with God. And there is only one God. Were not then the Monarchians more orthodox than the followers of the Logos theology? The answer is that they were not: The Monarchians were formally right in demanding that Christ must be all that God is. But while they demanded the equality of Christ with God they demanded the equality of the historical Christ in his human as well as in his divine nature, with God. In other words, they did not separate God, the triune God, from the cosmic process. They had no self-contained deity. For them the final subject of predication was reality; and the principle of unity found in this reality they called God. Their speculation was cosmological. If the Logos speculation tended to bring God down into the process of the temporal universe, the Monarchians tended to lift the process of time and history into deity.

So then when Tertullian was dealing with Praxeas, the Monarchian, he found himself confronted with a dilemma. He clearly saw that the Monarchian principle would destroy the Rule of Faith; if all the process of this universe is in God

---

49. KSO: Monarchianism was a term coined by Tertullian and was a Trinitarian heresy. It held that, because God is one, the manifestations of the three persons were only *modes* or *names*, rather than *persons*, of the one God.

50. Ibid., p. 23.

then there is nothing unique about the Christ and there is no need for his work of redemption. But how could the heretical Monarchians be met? Was not their basic fault their rationalistic effort to bring God and the universe into subjection to the one principle that is open to full inspection by man? What was required was the positing of the unity of God and of distinctness of personality within this unity in the Godhead as prior to any relationship to the course of history and as the one who is the creator and controller of history. But then what of the Logos speculation? If he was to answer the Monarchians effectively, Tertullian would first have to clean house with respect to his own Logos speculation. He would have to move on to ground higher than that on which he stood when speaking for, and seeking harmony between, the Christian and Greek views of life. From seeking harmony, he was driven first to notice the basic difference between the two positions and then to defense of the Christian position against the inevitable encroachment of the Greek spirit. And this necessity of defense led him to the necessity of an internal development of "the immanent movement of Christian thought," toward the development of an ontological trinity.

If he was to make an effective reply to Monarchianism he would have to cleanse his own thinking from the last remnants of Logos speculation. If he was to oppose the intermingling of the universe with God, he would have to remove from his own thinking the intermingling of God with the universe.

In some such way as this Warfield conceives of the struggle going on in Tertullian's mind when he is dealing with the trinity. We may use this approach of Warfield's as an heuristic principle by means of which to seek to understand the tenor of Tertullian's thought as a whole and in particular his view of the relation of the Rule of Faith to reason. Perhaps we shall be able to generalize the conclusion to which Warfield comes when he says that Tertullian, being basically true to the deposit of faith, made great progress toward the doctrine of a truly Christian doctrine of the trinity while yet he remained to some extent bound to the principle of Logos theology. Opposing the cosmological heresy of Monarchianism he cleared himself largely but not wholly of the cosmological speculation of the Logos theology.

b. "Apology"

In dealing with the main writings of Tertullian a beginning may appropriately be made with his *Apology*.

Like other apologies of early Christian theologians Tertullian first defends the rites and morals of the early Christians. Then he begins to set forth the Christian doctrine of God. "The object of our worship is the one God..."[51] This

---

51. *The Ante-Nicene Fathers*, Vol. III, p. 31 (Tertullian, Apology, XVII).

God, he says, is invisible and incomprehensible. Yet he is also revealed to us. He is presented to our minds in his transcendent greatness, as at once known and unknown. "And this is the crowning guilt of men, that they will not recognize One, of whom they cannot possibly be ignorant." Then Tertullian argues eloquently that round about and within men there is evidence of God's existence. He appeals here, as well as in his separate treatises on the soul, to the inherent nature of man's knowledge of God. To this natural revelation must be added the revelation through the prophets now given us in the Scriptures.[52] In particular this discussion pertains to the coming of Christ. And we must make a remark about his divinity. The Son of God is "made a second in manner of existence— in position, not in nature." "Even when the ray is shot from the sun, it is still part of the parent mass; the sun will still be in the ray, because it is a ray of the sun—there is no division of substance, but merely an extension. Thus Christ is Spirit of Spirit, and God of God, as light of light is kindled."[53]

In this connection Tertullian appeals to Zeno and to Cleanthes as also believing in the creation of the world by the Logos. He seems to assume that on this matter of the Logos there is therefore no basic difference between the views of the philosophers and the teaching of Scripture. Then as to why men should believe in this Christ as God, Tertullian says that even if Christ is a man and imposed a religion on his followers he did nothing that some of the heathen, such as Orpheus, and others have not done also. He adds: "Surely Christ, then, had a right to reveal Deity, which was in fact his own essential possession."[54] And if men find that belief in Christ changes them for their improvement they ought to believe in him.

In all this Tertullian is aware of the fact that there is a real difference between the religion of the heathen and his own. He employs great eloquence in exposing the folly of demon worship. Yet we find no very valuable argument for the basic doctrines of the Christian faith. The apologetic is largely practical; do not the Christians serve the emperor loyally; do they not pray for him as they should according to their books?

The nearest that Tertullian comes to a theoretical foundation for Christian ethics is when he says that Christians are "taught of God himself what goodness is" while the idea of goodness derived from the heathen poets and philosophers is based on human authority.[55] "Man's wisdom to point out what is good, is no greater than his authority to exact the keeping of it; the one is as easily deceived as the

---

52. Ibid., p. 32 (XVII; cf. XVIII, XIX).
53. Ibid., p. 34 (XXI).
54. Ibid., p. 36 (XXI).
55. Ibid., p. 50 (XLV).

other is despised." But here too he allows that even as the heathen had knowledge of God similar to that of Christians, they also had knowledge of the laws of ethics. Only the laws that the heathen possessed were derived "from the law of God as the ancient model."[56] "What poet or sophist has not drunk at the fountain of the prophets? Thence, accordingly, the philosophers watered their arid minds, so that it is the things they have from us which bring us into comparison with them."[57]

The basic difficulty with the apologetic of Tertullian at this point is that he does not realize that the "truths" recognized by the heathen are "truths" by which they seek to suppress the truth about themselves and the world. Tertullian seeks largely to connect Christian thought with heathen thought; there is, to him, a great difference between paganism and Christianity, but the difference remains one of gradation rather than of contrast.

c. "An Answer to the Jews"

A point of special interest in Tertullian is his discussion with the Jews. It is the question already discussed in the case of Justin Martyr. It is the question of how Tertullian seeks to prove to the Jews the identity of Jesus as the Messiah.

He argues, as did Justin with Trypho, that the Messiah is prophesied as having such traits as Jesus of Nazareth actually had. He also argues that the prophecy that all nations should believe in the Messiah has been fulfilled in Christ.[58] He goes on to show that the times and seasons as foretold by the prophets have been fulfilled in Christ. The destruction of the city of Jerusalem was foretold by the prophets. Thus he traces the "course of the ordained path of Christ, by which he is proved to be such as he used to be announced."[59]

In all this there appears to be a good answer to the Jew who really believes the Old Testament Scriptures. But a Jew who really believes the Old Testament does so because he believes in Christ. There is no attempt to settle the matter of identity as far as those who do not truly believe the Old Testament is concerned. There is no attempt made any more than there was in the case of Justin, to intimate that the real reason for the error of the Jews is their rationalistic unwillingness to accept their own Scripture as pointing toward Christ.

d. "The Soul's Testimony"

We come now to two exceedingly important writings of Tertullian. The first is *The Soul's Testimony*, and the second is *A Treatise on the Soul*. The question to be asked

---

56. Ibid.
57. Ibid., pp. 51–52 (XLVII).
58. Ibid., p. 157 (Tertullian, *An Answer to the Jews*, VII).
59. Ibid., p. 168 (XI).

is again whether Tertullian is here working largely under the influence of a sort of Logos speculation or whether he has outgrown such a speculation and has done justice to the deposit of faith as found in the oracles of the Christian religion.

To begin with, it is apparent that the approach in these treatises is not exclusively to the authority of Scripture but also to experience an ultimate. He wants in *The Soul's Testimony* to prove the existence of God from the testimony that any man's soul, whether Christian or not Christian, will give. "Thou art not, as I well know, Christian; for a man becomes a Christian, he is not born one. Yet Christians earnestly press thee for a testimony; they press thee, though an alien, to bear witness against thy friends, that they may be put to shame before thee, for hating and mocking us on account of things which convict thee as an accessory."[60]

The soul is asked to testify to the fact that there is one God, man's creator. Tertullian finds such testimony in the expressions of the people when they say instinctively "If God so will," "which may God grant," or when recovered from illness they give praise naturally to God. "In thine own forum thou appealest to a God who is elsewhere; thou permittest honor to be rendered in thy temples to a foreign god. Oh, striking testimony to truth, which in the very midst of demons obtains a witness for us Christians!"[61]

Secondly, the soul is asked to witness with respect to its own noble immortality. The Christian view of the soul, says Tertullian, is more noble than that of the Pythagoreans because it does not teach that man turns after this life into some beast. It is "more complete than the Platonic" view of the soul because it teaches the resurrection of the body as well as the survival of the soul. And it is more worthy of honor than the Epicurean view because it saves the soul from destruction.[62] "But we are not ashamed of ourselves if our presumption is found to have thy support."[63]

Tertullian does not seem to realize that the Christian idea of the soul and of man's position fits into the picture of Christian truth in general and cannot find and should not seek support from the testimony of the soul that seeks to interpret itself in terms of itself and of an immanentistic philosophy. How could the soul of Plato support the Christian doctrine of God and of its own immortality unless given primarily *in spite of* the system of Plato? If Tertullian had been fully aware of the difference between the general Christian and the general non-Christian view of things, he could hardly have said what he says in the following words at

---

60. Ibid., p. 176 (Tertullian, The Soul's Testimony, I).
61. Ibid., p. 176 (III).
62. Ibid., p. 177 (IV).
63. Ibid.

the conclusion of this treatise. "There is not a soul of man that does not, from the light that is in itself, proclaim the very things that we are not permitted to speak above our breath."[64] What he says is, of course, true in the sense in which Calvin later was to speak of the *sensus deitatis*. Every man knows that he is a creature of God. But the difference between Calvin and Tertullian is basic. They hold to the same doctrine of creation. But Calvin realizes that man seeks to suppress this truth and that therefore the soul's testimony for the truth must be wrung from him as from an unwilling witness. The sinner seeks as sinner to suppress and falsify the truth about himself as created. But Tertullian appeals to the system of the philosophers themselves. True, he does say that he appeals to the soul of the common man rather than to the soul of the sophisticated. He appeals to a *common consciousness*, so to speak. Nevertheless even this common consciousness to which he makes his appeal is still the consciousness of the unrepentant sinner who is supposed, in accordance with his own principles, to speak the truth about himself against the persecutors of the Christians. And this testimony is not forthcoming; in fact the reverse is true. The soul of the common man may speak of being created, but it does not take this as involving the necessity of repentance from sin any more than do the theories of the philosophers unless this soul of the common man is reborn by the Spirit of God. And it is not of this reborn soul that Tertullian speaks. In this treatise Tertullian does not ascribe any work to the Holy Spirit in the way of regenerating the soul before that soul will give forth the truth about itself; his appeal is to *experience as such*. And experience as such will not speak forth the truth about the origin or the nature of the soul; it will do the opposite since it is the experience of the sinner.

e. "A Treatise on the Soul"
In *A Treatise on the Soul*, Tertullian deals more fully with the philosophical theories about the soul. Again we are confronted with a measure of confusion in the midst of a brilliant and penetrating study. In *The Soul's Testimony* Tertullian seems to think that the experience of the non-sophisticated person directly corroborates the truth about the soul as taught in Scripture. He was appealing there to the common consciousness of man not in order to have it build up the whole doctrine of the soul, but in order to have it, at least in part, establish and corroborate the teaching of Scripture about the soul.

In similar fashion Tertullian argues in *A Treatise on the Soul* that the best of the philosophers have in their systems said that which, as far as it goes, is true about the origin and nature of the soul; they can therefore again serve, in part, for the establishment and corroboration of the Christian statement. He

64. Ibid., p. 179 (VI).

assumes that Christians must get their own full information about anything, and therefore about the soul, from the Scripture. His appeal is therefore not so largely to experience as it was in *The Soul's Testimony*. This point will be more fully discussed when we come to the consideration of his treatise *The Prescription against Heretics*. Our concern now is primarily to discern to what extent Tertullian has built up his doctrine of the soul from the Scripture and to what extent his desire for corroboration from the philosophers has forced him to defective notions of the soul.

There is no doubt that Tertullian's main desire is to be true to Scripture. Again, there is no doubt that he realizes that this often implies taking choice against the philosophers, even against Plato, whom he seems to think of as the best of them all. Let us first note some of the main points on which Tertullian sets off his doctrine from that of Greek philosophy and seeks to build it up on the foundation of Scripture.

1. Mention may be made first of the frequent appeal to Scripture as the Christian's final and sole source of information about basic truths.

Contrasting his own position with that of the philosophers, Tertullian says:

> To the Christian, however, but few words are necessary for the clear understanding of the whole subject. But in the few words there always arises certainty to him; nor is he permitted to give his inquiries wider range than is compatible with their solution; for 'endless questions' the apostle forbids. It must, however, be added, that no solution may be found by any man, but such as is learned from God; and that which is learned of God is the sum and substance of the whole thing.[65]

This basic assertion about the Scriptures ought to set the Christian's procedure off clearly from that of the philosophers, "those patriarchs of heretics, as they may be fairly called." And when we are forced "to try our strength in contests about the soul with philosophers" we should not allow the stage to be set and the problems to be stated by them in terms of their basic assumptions.[66] Tertullian is to a large extent aware of the necessity of setting the Christian position over against that of the philosophers.

As may be expected, the point about Scripture as the final authority of the Christian is strikingly brought out in his work *The Prescription against Heretics*. Says Tertullian: "Let our 'seeking,' therefore be in that which is our own, and from those who are our own, and concerning that which is our own—that, and

---

65. Ibid., p. 183 (Tertullian, *A Treatise on the Soul*, II).
66. Ibid., p. 183 (III).

only that, which can become an object of inquiry without impairing the rule of faith."[67]

2. It is therefore to be expected that the great and brilliant defender of the faith against various heresies, but in particular against the gnostic heresies, will single out the cosmological speculations of Plato as the source of them all. There, he says of Plato's views, is "the mystic original of the ideas of these heretics. For in this philosophy lie both their Aeons and their genealogies."[68]

3. More specifically, Tertullian sets off the Christian conception of the origin of the soul over against the Platonic theory. "For when we acknowledge that the soul originates in the breath of God, it follows that we attribute a beginning to it. This Plato, indeed, refuses to assign to it, for he will have the soul to be unborn and unmade." And again, in the same connection: "So far, therefore, as concerns our belief in the soul's being made or born, the opinion of the philosopher is overthrown by the authority of prophecy even."[69]

4. In addition to the fact of the creation of the soul Tertullian brings into consideration also the fact of its fall into sin. This is done over against Plato's idea that the irrational element of the soul is inherent in it and natural to it.

> That position of Plato's is also quite in keeping with the faith, in which he divides the soul into two parts—the rational and the irrational. To this definition we take no exception, except that we would not ascribe this twofold distinction to the nature (of the soul). It is the rational element which we must believe to be its natural condition, impressed upon it from its very first creation of its Author, who is himself essentially rational. For how should that be other than rational, which God produced on his own prompting: nay more, which he expressly sent forth by his own *afflatus* or breath?[70]

Moreover, Tertullian is perfectly aware of the implication of Plato's theory. "But, inasmuch as the same Plato speaks of the rational element only as existing in the soul of God himself, if we were to ascribe the irrational element likewise to the nature which our soul has received from God, then the irrational element will be equally derived from God, as being a natural production, because God is the author of nature."[71]

In this connection Tertullian appeals to the perfect man Jesus. The Platonic

---

67. Ibid., p. 249 (Tertullian, *The Prescription Against Heretics*, XII).
68. Ibid., p. 198 (*Treatise*, XVIII).
69. Ibid., p. 184 (IV).
70. Ibid., p. 194 (IV).
71. Ibid.

psychology, he argues, would not fit the case of our Lord. Plato divides the soul into three parts. There is the rational element which we have in common with God; then there is the irascible element (*thumikon*) which we have in common with the lions, and the concupiscible element (*epithumatikon*) which we have in common with the flies. But our Lord had all these three elements and none of the elements were in his case evidence of animality or imperfection.

> There was the *rational* element, by which he taught, by which he discoursed, by which he prepared the way of salvation; there was moreover *indignation* in him, by which he inveighed against the scribes and the Pharisees; and there was the principle of *desire*, by which he so earnestly desired to eat the passover with his disciples. In our own case, accordingly, the irascible and the concupiscible elements of our soul must not invariably be put to the account of the irrational (nature), since we are sure that in our Lord these elements operated in entire accordance with reason.[72]

5. The fact that Tertullian valiantly defends the validity of the knowledge obtained by sensation ought also to be mentioned. The validity of the senses, though impugned by Plato, is defended by Christ. "They are the faculties of seeing, and hearing, and smelling, and tasting, and touching. The fidelity of these senses is impugned with too much severity by the Platonists, and according to some by Heraclitus also, and Diocles, and Empedocles; at any rate, Plato, in the *Timaeus*, declares the operations of the senses to be irrational, and vitiated by our opinions or beliefs."[73]

To the argument that the senses deceive us, as when oars appear bent when immersed in water, or when we think a noise is in the sky and it is actually somewhere else, Tertullian answers in most penetrating fashion that "there cannot occur an illusion in our senses without an adequate cause."[74] And "whatever ought to occur in a certain manner is not a deception." It is no deception when oars appear bent when immersed in water because we can know that it is the nature of water to have such an influence on the oar. But most important of all is the fact that Tertullian signalizes the charge that the veracity and clarity of the revelation of God to man as it comes to him in things about him.

> Hence we are bound most certainly to claim for the senses truth, and fidelity, and integrity, seeing that they never render any other account

---

72. Ibid., p. 195 (XVI).
73. Ibid., p. 195 (XVII).
74. Ibid., p. 196 (XVII).

of their impressions than is enjoined on them by the specific causes or conditions which in all cases produce that discrepancy which appears between the report of the senses and the reality of the objects. What mean you, then, O most insolent Academy? You overthrow the entire condition of human life; you disturb the whole order of nature; you obscure the good providence of God himself: for the senses of man which God has appointed over all his works, that we might understand, inhabit, dispense, and enjoy them, (you reproach) as fallacious and treacherous tyrants![75]

6. Still further Tertullian points out that the Platonic theory of knowledge leads to the destruction of knowledge. He shows this by indicating that no theory of judgment can stand if it separates intellect and sense in the way that Plato did. "For is it not true, that to employ the senses is to use the intellect? And to employ the intellect amounts to a use of the senses? What indeed can sensation be but the understanding of that which is the object of sensation? And what can the intellect or understanding be, but the seeing of that which is the object understood?"[76]

He shows the same thing most basically by indicating that on Plato's theory the soul of man, when encased in the body, is out of touch with all principles of rationality and could attain to no knowledge at all.[77] In this connection Tertullian points out that Plato virtually identifies the soul with God, and that if the soul virtually has the character of divinity it is inexplicable why it should in any wise be without memory or knowledge in this world.

From the consideration of these several points one might conclude that Tertullian would surely set no value on the testimony of the soul to the existence of God and its own immortality if that testimony derives from a soul that is interpreted along the lines of Greek philosophy. We might be led to think that he would clearly discern that the testimony of the soul to its own creation by God is suppressed by the systems of the philosophers. But we find the contrary to be the case. He does not seem to sense that the systems of philosophy formed by non-Christian thinkers are the products of men who are sinners and who therefore, in their unregenerate hearts, do not love the truth about themselves. He seems rather to think of the mind of the sinner as though it were quite willing and able to see and speak forth the truth about itself and about the world. Right after asserting in the strongest terms that the Christian must get his information about God from God he says: "Of course we shall not deny that philosophers

---

75. Ibid., pp. 196–197 (XVII).
76. Ibid., p. 198 (XVIII).
77. Ibid., pp. 203–205 (XXIV).

have sometimes thought the same things as ourselves. The testimony of truth is the issue thereof. . ." Man may hit upon the truth accidentally. "In nature, however, most conclusions are suggested, as it were, by that common intelligence wherewith God has been pleased to endow the soul of man."[78] The philosophers have to an extent rafted to be true to nature. But the failure of philosophers in this respect is not connected by Tertullian with sin. It is simply something human. There is always an uncorrupted intelligence that can and does give forth the truth according to nature. Experience, as interpreted by non-Christian or Christian alike, is therefore for Tertullian one of the two sources of information about the soul.

Yet when thus interpreted, experience gives forth a testimony about the origin and nature of the soul totally different from the testimony of Scripture. But Tertullian is not aware of this discrepancy. He seeks, on the contrary, to force the two testimonies into harmony with one another. The result is that no coherent conception of the soul can be found in his writings, however penetrating and valuable they are with respect to many details. There is the truth of Scripture to which Tertullian wants to be true; according to it the soul is part of the man created by God and subject to the providence of God. But there is the rationalist-irrationalist theory of being that is characteristic of all forms of non-Christian thought. And it is as a matter of fact largely in accordance with such a non-Christian philosophy of being that Tertullian draws up his picture of the constitution of the human soul.

1. In the first place, though Tertullian holds that the origin of the soul is from the inbreathing of the breath of life by the Spirit of God, yet he also holds, and that first of all on purely philosophical grounds against the Platonists, that the soul is corporeal. He appeals to various philosophers and their arguments in support of his view. He turns to the great medical authority of Soranus who has proved, he thinks, that the soul "is nourished by corporeal ailments."[79] And then he also appeals to Scripture, and especially to the parable of the rich man and Lazarus as given by our Lord. The rich man, lifting up his eye in torment, seeks relief from thirst. This proves that he has a corporeal existence.

> But what is that which is removed to Hades after the separation of the body; which is there detained; which is reserved until the day of judgment; to which Christ also, on dying, descended? I imagine it is the souls of the patriarchs. But wherefore (all this), if the soul is nothing in its subterranean abode? For *nothing* it certainly is, if it is not a bodily substance.

---

78. Ibid., p. 182 (II).
79. Ibid., p. 186 (VI).

For whatever is incorporeal is incapable of being kept and guarded in any way; it is also exempt from either punishment or refreshment.[80]

2. On the question of the corporeality of the soul Tertullian holds with those who oppose Plato but on the question of simplicity he again agrees with Plato. He would speak of the soul as "an indivisible simple substance." More specifically it is identical with breath. Because it breathes, that is, because of its activity of breathing, the soul must be called spirit. "So that we are driven to describe, by (the term which indicates this respiration—that is to say) *spirit*—the soul which we hold to be, by the propriety of its action, breath."[81] As identical with breath, the soul may therefore be called spirit, "not because of its condition, but of its action; not in respect of its nature, but of its operation."[82]

There is here a very subtle distinction. Tertullian does not want to identify the soul with spirit as a substance for fear that this will place him in the camp of those who identify the spirit of man with the spirit of God. Hermogenes, he says, holds that man's soul came from matter, because if it were said to come from the Spirit of God, by the inbreathing of the Spirit of God, then the sin of this soul would virtually be the sin of the Spirit of God.[83]

The important point here is that in his reply to Hermogenes and other heretics Tertullian finds it necessary to insist that the soul is at the outset of its creation nothing but the breath of the living organism of the body. That is to say, he too, together with Hermogenes and the heretics, is afraid that if he says that the soul of man directly bears the imprint of the character of the spirit of God he cannot escape the charge of thinking of man as virtually identical with God. He therefore defines the soul as something that is as near as possible to non-being. It has as little of character as it can have consistent with any sort of self-conscious existence.

It is this point that is basic to the psychology of Tertullian. And this point that is basic to the psychology of Tertullian is of fundamental importance for his epistemology and therefore for his apologetic. We must look at it carefully. First let us quote Tertullian fully: He starts with a quotation of Isaiah 42:5: "He giveth breath unto the people that are on the earth, and Spirit to them that walk therein." In exegesis of this passage he then remarks as follows: "First of all there comes the (natural) soul, that is to say, the breath, to the people that are on the earth,—in other words, to those who act carnally in the flesh; then afterwards

---

80. Ibid., p. 187 (VII).
81. Ibid., p. 191 (XI).
82. Ibid., p. 190 (XI).
83. Ibid., pp. 190–191 (XI).

comes the Spirit to those who walk thereon,—that is, who subdue the works of the flesh; because the apostle also says, that 'that is not first which is spiritual, but that which is natural, (or in possession of the natural soul), and afterward that which is spiritual.'"[84] Adam first received the natural soul. Then when he "straightway predicted that 'great mystery of Christ and the church,' when he said, 'This now is bone of my bone and flesh of my flesh,' . . . he experienced the influence of the Spirit. For there fell upon him that ecstasy, which is the Holy Ghost's operative virtue of prophecy."[85]

In contrast to the Holy Spirit who may come upon a man after he exists as a soul in the natural sense, there is the evil spirit. Thus we have the picture of the natural soul of man, though brought into existence as the breath of life and as such, because of its action, called spirit. Yet this soul is placed before the choice of accepting either the Spirit of God or the spirit of evil as its dominating power. "Consequently, as the spirit neither of God nor of the devil is naturally planted with a man's soul at his birth, this soul must evidently exist apart and alone, previous to the accession to it of either spirit: if thus apart and alone, it must also be simple and uncompounded as regards its substance; and therefore it cannot respire from any other cause than from the actual condition of its own substance."[86]

In all this we have the assertion of the freedom of the will in the sense of autonomy over against the spirit of God and the spirit of evil. In other words Tertullian, though wishing to be faithful to Scripture in its teaching of man in the image of God, finds it still more necessary to be faithful to the supposed demands of "reason" according to which the idea of man as analogous of God would not be acceptable. Therefore he virtually substitutes for the biblical concept of freedom of the will of man as within the counsel of God and as in relationship to an environment constituted by the providence of God, the idea that man stands between God and the devil, both conceived as having some sort of ultimate power. That is to say, instead of thinking of man and Satan first of all as creatures of God and thus putting Satan and the power of temptation subject to the plan of God he puts Satan as a power next to God, and then he also puts man as still another power next to God.

3. It is to be expected that with such a view of the will of man there is a similar view of his rationality. Tertullian says that the *nous* of man is identical with the soul. It is therefore a function of this wholly autonomous man that he must, being ultimate, choose between ultimate good and ultimate evil.

---

84. Ibid., p. 191 (XI).
85. Ibid.
86. Ibid.

The burden of what Tertullian has to say about the origin and nature of the soul lies in his teaching of man's creation by God as a being endowed with free will and rational power. But there is great ambiguity in it all. As already noted he is afraid of ascribing any moral character to the soul as first created lest he be charged with attributing the origin of evil to God. Yet God who is rational and good must be said to be the origin of the soul.[87] But the basic concept remains that of the soul as so independent of God and so nearly without character at the outset of its career as is consistent with distinguishing it from non-being. "Now, if neither the spiritual element, nor what the heretics call the material elements, was properly inherent in him [Adam] (since, if he had been created out of matter, the germ of evil must have been an integral part of his constitution), it remains that the only original element of his nature was what is called the *animal* (the principle of vitality, the soul), which we maintain to be simple and uniform in its condition."[88]

In a section in which he recapitulates what has preceded he says: "The soul, then, we define to be sprung from the breath of God, immortal, possessing body, having form, simple in its substance, intelligent in its own nature, developing its powers in various ways, free in its determinations, subject to the changes of accident, in its faculties mutable, rational, supreme, endued with an instinct of presentiment, evolved out of one (archtypal soul)."[89]

4. There remains now, says Tertullian, the question how all the souls are derived from the one archtypal soul. Plato is certainly mistaken in deriving them from one the way he did. The loss and the origination of knowledge could not be explained on the Platonic basis of the idea that "learning is reminiscence."[90] After reviewing many philosophers he seeks the Christian answer on the derivation of all souls from Scripture: "Brother (in Christ), on your own foundation build up your faith."[91] His answer is given on the basis of such births as those of Esau and Jacob, of John the Baptist and others that "since God forms us in the womb, he also breathes upon us, as he also did at the first creation; when, 'the Lord God formed man, and breathed into him the breath of life.'"[92] The soul and body are "conceived, and formed, and perfectly simultaneously, as well as born together; and that not a moment's interval occurs in their conception, so that a prior place can be assigned to either."[93] Tracing this process back to Adam he says: "Accordingly from the one (primeval) man comes the entire outflow and

---

87. Ibid., p. 194–195 (XVI).
88. Ibid., pp. 201–202 (XXI).
89. Ibid., p. 202 (XXII).
90. Ibid., p. 203 (XXIII).
91. Ibid., p. 207 (XXVI).
92. Ibid.
93. Ibid., p. 207 (XXVII).

redundance of men's souls—nature proving herself true to the commandment of God, 'Be fruitful, and multiply.'"[94] We are not to conclude from this close interrelationship of the soul and body as to origin that they are identical and that the soul dies with the body. The body is as it were the house of the soul. The soul as well as the body does need food and drink, as we have seen before in the case of the rich man and Lazarus. But the soul needs nourishment because of "special necessity" while the "flesh" needs nourishment "from the nature of its properties." Accordingly the soul can depart safe and sound and "in possession, too, of its own supports, and the aliments which belong to its own proper condition, namely immortality, rationality, sensibility, intelligence, and freedom of the will."[95]

5. The derivation of individual souls from the one archtypal soul has a bearing upon the question of original sin. It is difficult to see how Tertullian with his view of the free will of man could hold to any such thing as original, or transmitted sin. It would seem that he could not hold to any form or representation of all men through Adam. But how could he even hold to any form of transmission at all? Should not on his view each soul be placed in the same position as was the soul of Adam? If later souls were in any way tainted with sin from the fact of their derivation from Adam, would not God, on Tertullian's logic with respect to Adam's free will, have to be charged with the origin of this sin?[96]

And indeed Tertullian seems to account for the universal presence of sin primarily on an empirical basis. "For to what individual of the human race will not the evil spirit cleave, ready to entrap their souls from the very portal of their birth, at which he is invited to be present in all those superstitious processes which accompany childbearing?"[97] Yet he also appeals to a common nature that all have in Adam as the reason for the need of regeneration. "Every soul, then, by reason of its birth, has its nature in Adam until it is born again in Christ; moreover, it is unclean all the while that it remains without this regeneration; and because unclean, it is actively sinful, and suffuses even the flesh (by reason of their conjunction) with its own shame."[98] Or again,

> There is, then, besides the evil which supervenes on the soul from the intervention of the evil spirit, an antecedent, and in a certain sense natural, evil which arises from its corrupt origin. For, as we have said before, the corruption of our nature is another nature having a god and father of

---

94. Ibid., p. 208 (XXVII).
95. Ibid., p. 219 (XXXVIII).
96. KSO: The point Van Til makes is that, once one affirms a notion of autonomous free will, *nothing* can influence that will, certainly not the sin of an ancestor.
97. Ibid., p. 219 (XXXVII).
98. Ibid., p. 220 (XL).

its own, namely the author of (that) corruption. Still there is a portion of good in the soul, of that original, divine, and genuine good, which is its proper nature. For that which is derived from God is rather obscured than extinguished. It can be obscured, indeed, because it is not God; extinguished, however, it cannot be, because it comes from God. . .Thus some men are very bad, and some very good; but yet the souls of all form but one genus: even in the worst there is something good, and in the best there is something bad. For God alone is without sin; and the only man without sin is Christ, since Christ is also God. Thus the divinity of the soul bursts forth in prophetic forecasts in consequence of its primeval good; and being conscious of its origin, it bears testimony to God (its author) in exclamations such as: *Good God! God knows!* and *Good bye!*[99]

• ⸻ •

The main elements of Tertullian's teaching with respect to the soul, its origin in paradise, its nature psychologically speaking, its ethical disposition at the first and after the fall, and its inheritance of evil and of good from the time of Adam to the present, are now before us.

In evaluating the matter as a whole the approach that Warfield has suggested is our guide. There is first the evident desire to be true to the Rule of Faith. Tertullian realizes that as a Christian his basic source of information about the soul is the Scripture. Yet there is also his allegiance to a sort of broad idealistic philosophy that is, in general, patterned after Plato. Even when he departs from Plato on important points he is yet of the opinion that there are basic points on which he can agree with the great master of Greek philosophy.

The result is that there is a basic confusion in all that is said about the soul. Some points are perfectly clear, to be sure. The soul is created; to hold with Plato that the soul is uncreated is to make it one with God. But at once the very Platonism just rejected, or at least some form of philosophy derived from the soul as interpreted without the doctrine of creation, tones down the far-reaching significance of the fact of creation. Appeal is virtually made to Being in general and to possibilities within this Being, rather than to God the Creator, in explanation of the nature of the soul. The soul's basic nature is interpreted in terms of the idea of slenderness of being, as existing near the abyss of non-being. The nature of man's freedom is sought in the fact that man is far removed from the fulness of the being of God.[100] Here also is the source of explanation of the possibility of

---

99. Ibid., pp. 220–221 (XLI).
100. KSO: That is, because man's will is autonomous, it is "far removed" from God, since God can have no control or authority over that will.

sin, even the likelihood of sin. Because of the slenderness of his being, man has very little power of resistance against the prince of evil. At the same time God is said not to be responsible for the entrance of sin because God made man free, which is to say that God himself is not at all, or is only remotely, present with man as he yields to temptation. Throughout all this, appeal is made to metaphysical discontinuity between God and man within a common unity of being.

It is this common unity of being that forms the basic presupposition of the discontinuity between God and man that is supposed to explain both the freedom of man and his fall into sin. Tertullian tries hard to defend the Christian doctrine of the soul against the charge of determinism. The heretics had argued that if God has made man perfect, and if therefore man's freedom lies within the plan of God, then evil too is traceable to God and God must be held responsible for its entrance into the world. Tertullian seeks to escape this charge by the notion of man's slenderness of being as already explained. Here he makes his basic mistake. *The idea of slenderness of being involves the idea of commonness of being between man and God.*[101] The non-Christian principle of discontinuity employed by Tertullian in order with it to defend the purity and holiness of God brings him into entanglement with the non-Christian principle of continuity which leads inevitably toward the identification of man with God.[102] The non-Christian principle of discontinuity can never be employed without also employing the non-Christian principle of continuity; the two are dialectically involved in each other. Irrationalism cannot find expression except in terms of rationalism, and indeterminism cannot find expression except in determinism; the result is that in all his efforts to absolve God from the responsibility for evil Tertullian succeeds only in immersing God with man in a common situation in which evil is as ultimate as the good.

The Creator-creature distinction is not made basic in Tertullian's thought and is not used in explanation of the freedom of man. It is in the notion of the commonness of being that there lies the rationalist and determinist tie-up of the human soul with God. Man has after all a bit of divinity in him. His being is itself divine. Thus Plato cannot have been so wholly wrong as he was said to be. Man gets his being from God and whatever he gets from God is and remains good. Therefore there always remains an element of good in all men. He cannot hold to total depravity. Reasoning along this line Tertullian would not be able

---

101. KSO: That is, God is the "fulness of being" and man, since he is less than God, is defined in terms of a "lack" or slenderness of being. God and man, therefore, occupy the same continuum of being and reality, but at different points on that same continuum. This is central to a "chain of being" as discussed in the foreword.

102. KSO: According to this scheme, there is, in other words, an identity *of being* between man and God (continuity), and the autonomy of man's will (discontinuity) within this identity.

to hold that Satan is wholly evil; has he not some measure of being and did he not get this being from God?

Then as to the matter of the inheritance of evil, here too the non-Christian principle of discontinuity comes into the picture. By the principle of discontinuity employed, Tertullian would be driven to the position that there is no such thing as inheritance at all.[103] For his principle of discontinuity was introduced by him in order to escape the charge of determinism. That is, if he would employ fully the Christian principle to which he stands committed he would be called a determinist by the heretics. So in order to escape this charge of determinism Tertullian again falls into the trap of using the non-Christian principle of indeterminism. But in using this he must at the same time use the non-Christian principle of determinism and rationalism. He therefore must hold that even that slender bit of being in man is really divine or participant in divinity. The doctrine of creation is virtually reduced to that of participation in divinity. At least it is the same being that is in God that is also in man, in however attenuated a form.

Moreover, it is this bit of being, participant in divinity, that is said to be in all men even after Adam has fallen into sin and even after individually men fall again into sin. Tertullian uses the notion of a common human nature. His principle of discontinuity would not entitle him to this. According to it, he should attribute to each man afresh a total independence of his fellows. But he must maintain some slender connection between all men. This slender connection by way of a common human nature presupposes back of it a common nature as between man and God. And it is this assumption of a common nature or being which, since it is participant in divinity, is said in some measure to be always good even in the midst of evil.[104]

The result of all this for Tertullian's view of the nature of sin is that its biblical character of ethical alienation from God is not fully appreciated. Tertullian's notion of sin is still largely controlled by the idea that sin is the metaphysical opposite of the good. It is, as it were, lower in the scale of being than is the good.[105] Sin is however inevitably, or almost inevitably, present in human nature on account of the slenderness of being that is man's character.

---

103. KSO: Said another way, there can be no inheritance of sin since man's will is thought by Tertullian to be independent from God. It is its own cause and nothing whatsoever can influence its choice.

104. KSO: That is, once it is thought that God's being and man's being are on the same continuum of being (in a "chain of being,"), every "being" will have some aspect of divinity given with its existence.

105. KSO: As I noted in the foreword, Van Til uses this notion of the "scale of being" in numerous places in his writings and in his teaching.

With this we must conclude our discussion of Tertullian's doctrine of the soul. In spite of his deep allegiance to a non-Christian philosophy, Tertullian, as noted, was able to render a great contribution not only to the doctrine of the trinity but also to the true doctrine of man. A consistently biblical doctrine of the trinity would have implied the complete rejection of all subordinationism. A completely biblical doctrine of man would have implied the complete rejection of all Platonism. In opposing heretics, while yet controlled to some extent by the same principles they used, he could not reach such heights as they who later made use of his constructions were able to reach. He was a true giant groping above himself for light, seeing it yet not seeing it.

f. Authority

Our discussion of Tertullian's doctrine of authority need not be long after what has already been said. It has already appeared that he means to hold to the authority of Scripture as the source of Christian doctrine. But it has been shown that he *also* appeals to experience as a final source from which both establishment and corroboration of doctrine may be derived. It is in *The Prescription against Heretics* that we have the most express statement with respect to the authority of Scripture. And it is to this treatise that appeal is frequently made by those who think that Tertullian stands for the idea of the acceptance of religious truth when wholly above and even contrary to truth discovered by reason.

As an illustration of such a view the words of Windelband[106] may be quoted. Windelband speaks of a growing "opposition between revelation and knowledge by reason" as developing during the early Christian era.[107]

> The more the Gnostics, in developing their theological metaphysics, separated themselves from the simple content of Christian faith, the more *Irenaeus* warned against the speculations of worldly wisdom, and the more violently *Tatian*, with oriental contempt of the Greeks, rejected every delusion of the Hellenic philosophy which was always at variance with itself, and of whose teachers each would exalt only his own opinions to the rank of law, while the Christians uniformly subjected themselves to the divine revelation.

---

106. KSO: "Wilhelm Windelband (1848–1915) was a German neo-Kantian philosopher. He is considered the founding father of the Baden (or Southwest) school of Neo-Kantianism. Windelband's main philosophical contribution consists in reformulating Kant's transcendental approach in terms of a "philosophy of values" that focuses philosophical analysis on questions of normativity." His most popular work was his *A History of Philosophy* (1873). https://plato.stanford.edu/entries/wilhelm-windelband/

107. W. Windelband, *A History of Philosophy* (London: The Macmillan Co., 1901), p. 224.

This opposition becomes still sharper with *Tertullian* and *Arnobius*. The former, as Tatian had already done in part, adopted the Stoic materialism in its metaphysical aspect, but drew from it only the logical consequence of a purely sensualistic theory of knowledge.[108]

This sensualistic theory of knowledge, says Windelband, allowed for no knowledge of the deity.

> Just for this reason it (he speaks of the soul) needs revelation, and finds its salvation only in faith in this. So *sensualism* here shows itself for the first time *as basis for orthodoxy*. The lower the natural faculty of man, and the more it is limited to the senses, the more necessary does revelation appear.
> Accordingly, with *Tertullian*, the content of revelation is not only *above reason*, but also in a certain sense *contrary to reason*, in so far as by reason man's natural knowing activity is to be understood. The gospel is not only incomprehensible, but is also in necessary contradiction with worldly discernment: *credible est quia ineptum est; certum est, quia impossibile est—credo quia absurdum*. Hence Christianity, according to this view, has nothing to do with philosophy, Jerusalem nothing to do with Athens. Philosophy as natural knowledge is unbelief; there is therefore no Christian philosophy.[109]

Only a passing remark need be made about the charge that Tertullian held to a narrow sensualistic theory of knowledge. This was not the case. As already noted, he defended the validity of knowledge derived from the senses, but he did this in the interest of showing that God's revelation, wherever given, is trustworthy. Moreover, he argued that sense knowledge and knowledge obtained through intellectual effort are directly involved in one another. Still further, Tertullian held that God could and did directly reveal himself to man by means of the prophets. Finally he even held that the soul was inherently in direct contact with God. All in all scepticism is about as far from his thought as anything could be.

But more basic is the charge that Tertullian believed what he believed because he thought it to be absurd and impossible. The quotation given from Tertullian's work *On the Flesh of Christ* does not bear this out. In the sections preceding the one from which the quotation is given he argues for the possibility

---

108. Ibid., pp. 224–225.
109. Ibid., p. 225.

of the incarnation. He argues for this against Marcion[110] and others who held to a docetic view of the human nature of Christ on the ground that a real incarnation was impossible. He puts the following words into the mouth of the heretic. "But, you say, I deny that God was truly changed to man in such wise as to be born and endued with a body of flesh, on this ground, that a being who is without end is also of necessity incapable of change. For being changed into something else puts an end to the former state. Change, therefore, is not possible to a Being who cannot come to an end."[111] To refute this argument against the possibility of the incarnation Tertullian argues that we must not apply our concepts of possibility to God since he is not subject to our conditions:

> But nothing is equal with God; his nature is different from the condition of all things. If, then, the things which differ from God, *and* from which God differs, lose what existence they had whilst they are undergoing change, wherein will consist the difference of the Divine Being from all other things except in his possessing the contrary faculty of theirs,—in other words, that God can be changed into all conditions, and yet continue just as he is? On any other supposition, he would be on the same level with those things which, when changed, lose the existence they had before; whose equal, of course, he is not in any other respect, as he certainly is not in the changeful issues *of their nature*.[112]

It is thus by an appeal to the fact that God is "wholly other" than man that Tertullian seeks to establish the possibility of his incarnation. To this he adds that all this will seem to be foolish and absurd to Marcion who does not realize that God hath chosen the foolish things of the world to confound the wise. God has

---

110. KSO: Marcion (died c. 160) "worked out his system and began to organize his followers as a separate community; and in 144 he was formally excommunicated. . . .from Rome as a centre, he devoted his gifts as an organizer to the propagation of his views and established compact communities over a large part of the Empire which admitted converts of every age, rank, and background. Marcion's central thesis was that the Christian Gospel was wholly a Gospel of Love to the absolute exclusion of Law. This doctrine, which he expounded esp. in his 'Antitheses', led him to reject the OT completely. The Creator God or Demiurge, revealed in the OT from Gen. I onwards as wholly a God of Law, had nothing in common with the God of Jesus Christ. Study of the OT indicated that this Jewish God constantly involved himself in contradictory courses of action, that he was fickle, capricious, ignorant, despotic, cruel. Utterly different was the Supreme God of Love whom Jesus came to reveal. It was His purpose to overthrow the Demiurge." F. L. Cross and Elizabeth A. Livingstone, eds., *The Oxford Dictionary of the Christian Church* (Oxford; New York: Oxford University Press, 2005), 1040.
111. *The Ante-Nicene Fathers*, Vol. III, p. 523 (Tertullian, *On The Flesh of Christ*, III).
112. Ibid.

chosen such things as are foolish in the eyes of those who measure God by their own conceptions. According to the world's wisdom, "it is more easy to believe that Jupiter became a bull or a swan, . . . than that Christ really became man."[113] If Marcion thinks it foolish to believe in the incarnation, why does he not also think it is foolish to believe in the death of Christ? But, then, "after all, you will not be 'wise' unless you become a 'fool' to the world, by believing 'the foolish things of God.'" So he cries out:

> O thou most infamous of men, who acquittest of all guilt the murderers of God! For nothing did Christ suffer from them, if he really suffered nothing at all. Spare the whole world's one and only hope, thou who art destroying the indispensable dishonor of our faith. Whatsoever is unworthy of God, is of gain to me. . . The Son of God was crucified; I am not ashamed because men must needs be ashamed *of it*. And the Son of God died; it is by all means to be believed, because it is absurd (*ineptum*). And he was buried, and rose again; the fact is certain, because it is impossible.[114]

Whatever may have been in Tertullian's mind when he wrote the last couple of sentences, the context shows that he certainly did not believe the death and resurrection of Christ because he himself thought these facts to be impossible or absurd. He argued for their possibility on the ground that God is not subject to the limitations of the creature. And he includes the birth and death of Christ among those things which appear foolish only to those who are so foolish as to measure the divine being with human concepts.

There remains, to be sure, something obscure in the manner of Tertullian's statement. He has often argued that the belief in the existence of God is very rational, even on the basis of the soul's testimony. And he appeals frequently for corroboration of his views to certain of the philosophical systems of unbelievers. On this ground he might well be charged with retaining elements of "rationalism" in his thought. And this would itself be evidence of how untrue to the evidence Windelband's statement about Tertullian holding to an irrational faith is. But then there is the other side of the story. He who retains elements of rationalism is bound also to retain elements of irrationalism. And this seems to find expression in the quotation given just before to the effect that God's nature is virtually wholly other than human nature. It would seem then that we

---

113. Ibid., p. 525 (IV).
114. Ibid., p. 525 (V).

may believe about God such things as are wholly contrary to what appears to be possible according to rational principles. In other words, Tertullian does not presuppose the ontological trinity at this point, and therefore does not think of human thought and experience as analogical of God's. Therefore he is unable to set off the Christian philosophy of life with any full consistency over against the non-Christian philosophy of life. When he seeks to defend the "rationality" of the Christian religion, he falls into a measure of univocism, or identity; he then argues that the God of the Christian and the God of the Stoic are virtually the same God. On the other hand when he must defend the transcendence of God above man against Marcion then he apparently falls into equivocism; he then argues that the God of the Christian is wholly other in nature than man. He has not clearly set the Christian principle of continuity and the Christian principle of discontinuity, together forming the Christian principle of analogy, over against the non-Christian principle of continuity and the non-Christian principle of discontinuity. So he is driven back and forth between two extremes. When he is attacked by a non-Christian principle of continuity he opposes to it what is, in part at least, a non-Christian principle of discontinuity. On the other hand when he is confronted by a heretic who stresses the non-Christian principle of discontinuity then Tertullian responds, in part at least, with setting over against it a non-Christian principle of continuity.

For all that Tertullian holds basically to the Christian principle of interpretation. And it is this fact that comes out magnificently in the expression frequently quoted from *The Prescription against Heretics*. In it he argues that as Christians we must live in our interpretations by the Scripture alone. That must be our final criterion of judgment. Our investigations must not allow for hypotheses that would undermine this criterion. And it is in this connection that he uses the famous words:

> What indeed has Athens to do with Jerusalem? What concord is there between the Academy and the Church? What between heretics and Christians? Our instruction comes from 'the porch of Solomon,' who had himself taught that 'the Lord should be sought in simplicity of heart.' Away with all attempts to produce a mottled Christianity of Stoic, Platonic, and dialectic composition! We want no curious disputation after possessing Christ Jesus, no inquisition after enjoying the gospel! With our faith, we desire no further belief. For this is our palmary faith, that there is nothing which we ought to believe besides.[115]

---

115. Ibid., p. 246 (*Prescription*, VII).

Is this vigorous attachment to Scripture as the only source and criterion of truth a mere irrational adherence to something about which nothing can be said in terms of rational propositions? What has been already adduced from Tertullian in the way of his refutation of the basic tenets of Platonism is in itself sufficient to prove the contrary. Tertullian knew and pointed out that if one assumes that man is not the creature of God, if man on the contrary assumes that he is of a piece with God, then there is no possibility of intelligent predication. He is therefore setting the Bible as the criterion for the believer, not as something irrational but as that which brings the God who, in the nature of the case, since he is man's creator, cannot speak otherwise than in terms of authority. Tertullian is simply asserting what all Christians should assert, namely, that in the Scripture they have the truth and that the truth has its own criterion of its truth within itself. It is the self-sufficiency of the truth of Christianity that Tertullian is bravely and more boldly than his predecessors asserting. Would that he had himself always been fully true to it! Then he would not have sought in the testimony of the "soul" as such for corroboration of the truth of Scripture statements about God or man. Then too, he would not have aligned himself in any way or to any extent with the "wholly other" god of the Greeks. Then he would not have been controlled by any irrationalist-rationalist principles in his many and brilliant discussions with the heretics. It is because he was not fully true to his own principles of Scripture that Tertullian did not offer a good defense of the truth of Christianity.

Summing up the matter discussed with respect to Tertullian we have the following: (1) In his doctrine of the soul he seeks to be faithful to Scripture but he is not fully so. (2) In his doctrine of Scripture as the supreme rule of faith and practice he again sets forth the Christian principle marvelously but again is in some measure unfaithful to his own principle. And so (3) with respect to the doctrine of the trinity he approaches the doctrine of the equality of their persons and their internal unity better than his predecessors but again he is not fully true to his own principles. Tertullian appears as a Samson doing mighty deeds of valor for the people of the Lord but then falling in love with the beauty that the Philistine offers.

5. *Alexandrianism (Clement and Origen)*[116]

From Tertullian we turn to a quite different sort of world, the world of Alexandria. Our concern will, of course, be primarily with Clement of Alexandria and with Origen.

In these two men, and especially in Origen, we meet with the first major

---

116. KSO: Clement of Alexandria (c. 150–c. 215). "Christian philosopher, probably born in Athens, who succeeded his teacher Pantaenus as head of a Christian (catechetical?) school in Alexandria some time after 180. He left Alexandria around 202. In many respects his thinking stands

attempt at a comprehensive statement of a world and life view in terms of principles that are true both to Greek thought and to Christian doctrine.

It is not our purpose to trace the thought of these two men as they historically developed it; nor do we intend to speak of the many subjects of which they spoke. Our intention rather is to confine ourselves to such matters as are of immediate and basic importance for Christian apologetics. In particular we limit ourselves to what they have to say on the question of authority.

We have seen that though the men discussed so far held to the absolute authority of Scripture, they themselves were not able to give a good account of their reasons for doing so. Their defense of Scripture was frequently in terms of "reason" or in terms of irrational faith, or in terms of a combination of these two. In practice, therefore, they were unable to escape a vacillating procedure; they sought to build up their epistemology, their metaphysic and their ethics both by an appeal to authority *and* by an appeal to reason.

The Alexandrians do not differ from these men on this point. The difference between them and such a man as Tertullian, for instance, lies not in that the latter appealed exclusively to authority while they appealed exclusively or primarily to reason. Both Clement and Origen appealed to the authority of Scripture. Origen did much work in determining the text of the Septuagint and spent a good part of his literary effort in exposition of the Scriptures. The difference would seem to lie rather in the greater degree with which the Alexandrians in practice allowed themselves to be controlled by principles of experience rather than by Scripture in working out their views. The Alexandrians, and particularly Origen, were far more speculative than was Tertullian. They were largely controlled by the idea of "thought in general," "being in general," and "good in general" that is, by the Greek approach to the problems of philosophy.[117] Accordingly they made

---

in the line of the Greek apologists, but he represents a contrast to contemporary (Western) writers in his positive evaluation of Gk. philosophy, his speculative bent and his deliberate lack of system. Alexandria having been the home of Philonic allegory (see Hermeneutics) and various brands of Gnosticism, it is necessary to note Clement's use of allegory (not yet systematized as it is by Origen) and his description of the perfect Christian as a 'true Gnostic'." Sinclair B. Ferguson and J.I. Packer, *New Dictionary of Theology* (Downers Grove, IL: InterVarsity Press, 2000), 148–149.

Origen (185–254) "was an early church Father and apologist for Christianity. He was heavily influenced by Platonic and Gnostic thought. As a consequence his defense of the faith tended to sacrifice important teachings. He denied the historicity of crucial sections of Scripture; he taught the preexistence of the soul and universalism (the belief that all will eventually be saved) and denied that Jesus was raised from the dead in a physical body. These positions were condemned as heretical by later church councils." Norman L. Geisler, "Origen," *Baker Encyclopedia of Christian Apologetics*, Baker Reference Library (Grand Rapids, MI: Baker Books, 1999), 565.

117. KSO: Any system of thought that studies such things as "being" and "thought" *in general* fails, at the outset, to begin with the distinction between God as the "I Am" and everything else as dependent on him.

extended use of the method of allegory in their interpretation of Scripture. By this method they were able, so they thought, to find harmony between teachings drawn from experience and teachings drawn from Scripture.

In practice, their recognition of Scriptural authority was therefore largely the same as the recognition given to the authority of an expert. And recognition of the authority of experts in religions was common in their day in Alexandria. Recognition of authority, says Windelband, was "the felt need of the time."[118] "For the farther the contrast between the systems [of philosophy] extended, the more it became evident how little able philosophy was to fulfill the task which it had set itself: namely, that of educating man by a sure insight to a state of virtue and happiness, to inner independence of the world."[119] It was "felt in every direction that man in his own strength can become neither knowing, nor virtuous and happy."[120] "Man's essential interest became thereby transferred for long centuries from the earthly to the heavenly sphere; he began to seek his salvation beyond the world of sense."[121] There was a readiness to accept "religions of authority" and this was geared to the solution of the problems of life and of thought alike. "The thought of antiquity described a peculiar curve, separating itself farther and farther from religion from which it proceeded, reaching its extreme separation in Epicureanism, and then again steadily drawing near to religion, to return at last entirely within it."[122] It was natural that under such circumstances it was Plato's system of thought, with its stress on the reality of the super-sensuous world, that should find much interest. "It was, therefore, this latter system which formed the controlling center for the religious closing development of ancient thought. A religious development of Platonism is the fundamental character of this period."[123]

> The philosophizing individual no longer had confidence that he could attain to right insight or to his soul's salvation by his own strength, and sought his help accordingly, partly amid the great monuments of the past, partly in a divine *revelation*. Both tendencies, however, are ultimately upon the same basis, for the confidence which was placed in the men and writings of a previous time rested only upon the fact that they were regarded as especially favored vessels of higher revelation. *Authority*, therefore, acquired its value as the mediate, historically accredited revelation, while the divine illumination of the individual as immediate revelation

---

118. Windelband, *op. cit.*, p. 210.
119. Ibid.
120. Ibid., p. 211.
121. Ibid.
122. Ibid., p. 212.
123. Ibid.

came to its assistance. Differently as the relation between these two forms was conceived of, it is yet the common mark of all Alexandrian philosophy that it regards *divine revelation as the highest source of knowledge*. Already in this innovation in the theory of knowledge, we find expressed the heightened value which this period put upon *personality*, and on personality as evincing itself in the feelings. The longing of this time desired that the truth might be found by experience, as an inner communication of man with the Supreme Being.[124]

What is to be particularly observed in this is that the view of "authority" as Windelband thus outlines it is a view which fully accords with the idea of human autonomy, and is wholly out of accord with the idea of absolute biblical authority. "The *appeal to authority* often makes its appearance in Greek and Hellenistic philosophy in the sense of a confirmation and strengthening of an author's own views, but not as a decisive and conclusive argument."[125]

It was the sort of authority that naturally developed out of the history of Greek speculation. It was when this speculation had become skeptical and irrationalist that it developed its idea of authority. The natural man, more than ever before, was impressed with his own failures to interpret reality exhaustively in terms of his immanentistic categories. It was as part of this general recognition of irrationalism that the Hellenistic idea of personality was developed. This idea was to the effect that man must be sufficient to himself in spite of what might happen in the universe. That is to say, it was assumed that the universe was not controlled by the providence of God as this providence is understood in the Christian sense of the term. Even the Stoic notion of providence was nothing but an intra-cosmic principle of supposed rationality, and this intra-cosmic principle found, as it were, over against itself an area of pure contingency. Therefore, man was still surrounded by forces over which there was no rational control and of which there was no rational knowledge. So man had to cultivate his own sufficiency within himself.

Thus there is a concomitant development of an irrationalist-rationalist notion of authority and of an irrationalist-rationalist notion of personality. In this development there may be said to be an intimation of the modern post-Kantian situation. In modern thought the autonomous man is quite willing to recognize authority. He has in modern times so clearly developed the idea of personality as autonomous and is so certain that there is no knowledge of God, in the historic Christian sense of the term, that he is perfectly safe in asking for authoritative information about that of which he himself virtually asserts that there cannot be any knowledge.

---

124. Ibid., p. 219.
125. Ibid.

Similarly at the time of the early church Hellenism had developed the idea of self-sufficient personality. It was based on two seemingly mutually exclusive reasons. The first is the idea that man knows that he is surrounded by an infinite ocean of possibility that may influence him for good or for evil and that he himself has no knowledge of this ocean. The second is that man "knows" that out of this ocean of possibility nothing can come in the way of a revelation from God in the Christian sense of the term. The first reason is irrationalist and the second is rationalist. And the two reasons are involved in one another.

The idea of personality and the concomitant appeal to authority, therefore, as these were developed in Hellenistic thought and as they operated in Alexandria, led directly to the mysticism of Plotinus. As such they were wholly exclusive of the Christian idea of personality as created in the image of God and of the Christian idea of authority. That is to say, the Hellenistic idea of personality and of appeal to authority implied the idea of pure mysticism and therefore the complete rejection of revelation in the orthodox sense of the term. According to Neo-Platonism man must seek absorption in deity. This is his practical, his ethical, not his theoretical idea. The idea of revelation that corresponds to this is the idea of immediate illumination of the individual by the deity. This illumination is not by way of information transmitted in thought communication but comes by way of ecstasy. "All thought, Plotinus teaches, is inferior to this state of ecstasy; for thought is motion,—a desire to know. Ecstasy, however, is certainty of God, blessed rest in him; man has share in the divine *theoria*, or contemplation (Aristotle) only when he has raised himself entirely to the deity."

"Ecstasy is then a state which transcends the self-consciousness of the individual, as its object transcends all particular determinateness. It is a sinking into a divine essence with an entire loss of self-consciousness: it is a possession of the deity, a unity of life with him, which mocks at all description, all perception, and all that abstract thought can frame."[126]

It is thus that the epistemology of Greek philosophy starts with the idea of the bold assertion of the autonomous man, that he can determine the nature of all possibility by means of his logical power, and ends by this self-same autonomous man cravenly seeking non-rational absorption into some impersonal non-determinate absolute.[127] Modern philosophy was to tell this identical story in aggravated form. The chief question is whether the Alexandrian theologians were able to distinguish between the true and false notion of personality and

---

126. Ibid., p. 228.
127. KSO: In other words, given the presumed autonomy of Greek philosophical thought, philosophy was bound to move to some kind of mysticism in order to "account" for that to which autonomous reason could not attain.

therefore also between the true and the false notion of authority. Or did they yield to the temptation to seek to combine the Christian and the pagan notion of personality and therefore the Christian and the pagan notion of authority? As is well-known, the latter was the case.

a. Clement on Authority

Both Clement and Origen appeal to the authority of Scripture. They even speak of this authority in very orthodox terms. But in the construction of their philosophical system they do not feel bound by this authority as basic to all else. The chief writings of Clement are his Exhortation to the Greeks, his Instructor, and his Stromata or Miscellanies. In all of them we find appeal to the authority of Scripture. So, for instance, in the Stromata we find the following words: "But we, who have heard by the Scriptures that self-determining choice and refusal have been given by the Lord to men, rest in the infallible criterion of faith, manifesting a willing spirit, since we have chosen life and believe God through his voice. And he who has believed the Word knows the matter to be true; for the Word is truth. But he who has disbelieved him that speaks, has disbelieved God."[128]

One might expect from the sound of these words that Clement would make faith in this Word as it speaks of the saving grace through Christ all-determinative in his thought. We soon discover, however, that Clement has interwoven the idea of faith in Scripture with the philosophical faith in first principles as the basis of the possibility of intellectual apprehension. "Well, Sensation is the ladder to Knowledge; while Faith, advancing over the pathway of the objects or sense, leaves Opinion behind, and speeds to things free of deception, and reposes in the truth."[129] Clement argues that faith is an ingredient in all Knowledge, especially of all knowledge with respect to ultimate things. "Should one say that Knowledge is founded on demonstration by a process of reasoning, let him hear that first principles are incapable of demonstration; for they are known neither by art nor sagacity."[130] Or again:

> For knowledge is a state of mind that results from demonstration; but faith is a grace which from what is indemonstrable conducts to what is universal and simple, what is neither with matter, nor matter, nor under matter. But those who believe not, as is to be expected, drag all down

---

128. *The Ante-Nicene Fathers*, Vol. II, pp. 349–350 (Clement of Alexandria, *The Stromata*, II:IV).
129. Ibid., p. 350 (*Stromata*, II:IV).
130. Ibid.

from heaven, and the region of the invisible, to earth, 'absolutely grasping with their hands rocks and oaks,' according to Plato. For, clinging to all such things, they asseverate that that alone exists which can be touched and handled, defining body and essence to be identical.[131]

"Now Aristotle says that the judgment which follows knowledge is in truth faith. Accordingly, faith is something superior to knowledge, and is its criterion."[132]

When therefore Clement speaks of the "infallible criterion of faith" this does not in his case imply the absolute authority of Scripture. He is speaking of a general faith which is required of man since, as the philosophers have shown, man cannot intellectually demonstrate first principles.[133]

In this, then, Clement's thinking is controlled largely by Greek thought rather than by Scripture. For him faith points to something supernatural. But he does not distinguish between faith and its place in a system of philosophy that deals with "thought in general" and "being in general," and faith as it fits into the Christian system. He does not distinguish between faith in the irrational and faith in the thought content communicated by Scripture. Standing at the fork in the road he is apparently trying to go in two directions, the one leading to the mysticism of Plotinus and the other to the gospel of Paul.

There is, therefore, a basic confusion running throughout the writings of Clement on the relation of the gospel to the wisdom of the world. The wisdom of the world as expressed in his day in Greek philosophy led straight to the irrational mysticism of Plotinus. Yet this wisdom of the world was for Clement a positive preparation for the coming of the Logos incarnate.[134] The prevailing view of Clement is that the Greeks knew the true God but knew him less perfectly than do Christians who have a fuller revelation than had the Greeks.

Much more might be said by way of indicating that for Clement faith in Scripture is the same faith that the best of the philosophers had and is faith in the same God that the philosophers owned, but is fuller faith in a fuller revelation of this same God through the Christ who is the Logos. Clement has failed to warn men to stay away from the road that leads to Plotinus. In particular he failed to

---

131. Ibid.
132. Ibid.
133. KSO: This is an important point that Van Til simply mentions here, but it is worthy of emphasis. At least since Aristotle, philosophy has recognized that not all principles are demonstrable. Specifically, those "first principles" or *principia* on which all others are based must be presupposed, since demonstrating them would require "first principles" behind "first principles" *ad infinitum*, which is absurd.
134. Ibid., pp. 515–518 (VI:XVII).

warn men clearly that only by grace can they be saved. He did not present the Son as saying: "No one cometh to the father but by me." Men already knew the Father; they had always known the Father; they had not offended the Father; they were not covenant breakers; they had no clear need of redemption. So even the work of the Son as the Savior could not be presented truly. His revelation among men when incarnate is taken to be nothing but the climactic expression of this self-same Christ, revelation found among all men, from the beginning. Clement virtually identifies the Christ incarnate with the general idea of the Logos. And since all men everywhere have been enlightened by the Logos it follows that all men everywhere, in some measure, have been enlightened by the Christ. Clement speaks of the Word as the "Song of salvation" but he assures the Greeks that this song is not new: it was from the beginning and even before the beginning.

> But we were before the foundation of the world, we who, because we were destined to be in him, were begotten beforehand by God. We are the rational images formed by God's Word, or Reason, and we date from the beginning on account of our connection with him, because 'the Word was in the beginning.' Well, because the Word was from the first, he was and is the divine beginning of all things; but because he lately took a name,—the name consecrated of old and worthy of power, the Christ,—I have called him a New Song.[135]

In all this the notion of "thought in general" and of "being in general" is more prominent than the notion of the gospel of Christ.

Basic to his inability to distinguish mysticism from the Christian doctrine of revelation was his conception of personality. On it, too, he was instructed by the Greeks rather than by Paul. Clement does not teach that Adam was in paradise in full possession of the knowledge of God by virtue of his creation by God and by virtue of his communication with God. Accordingly he has no concept of personality that would even allow for the possibility, let alone the actuality, of authoritative revelation on the part of God to man. His conception of personality is taken from the idea of being in general rather than from the Scripture. He assumes that Adam before the fall and his followers after the fall are in essentially the same sort of position with respect to their knowledge of God and with respect to virtue. Neither Adam, before the fall nor his posterity knew God by nature; they are made so that they can learn to know God. "Above all, this ought to be known, that by nature we are adapted for virtue; not so as

---

135. *Clement of Alexandria*, "The Exhortation to the Greeks," tr. G. W. Butterworth (New York: Putnam's Sons, 1919), p. 17.

to be possessed of it from our birth, but so as to be adapted for acquiring it."[136] Immediately following this general statement about man as a race he speaks the following words about Adam:

> By which consideration is solved the question propounded to us by the heretics, Whether Adam was created perfect or imperfect? Well, if imperfect, how could the work of a perfect God—above all, that work being man—be imperfect? And if perfect, how did he transgress the commandments? For they shall hear from us that he was not perfect in his creation, but adapted to the reception of virtue. For it is of great importance in regard to virtue to be made fit for its attainment. And it is intended that we should be saved by ourselves. This, then, is the nature of the soul, to move of itself. Then, as we are rational, and philosophy being rational, we have some affinity with it. Now an aptitude is a movement toward virtue, not virtue itself. All, then, as I said, are naturally constituted for the acquisition of virtue.[137]

It may be noted that the position of Clement is similar to that of Tertullian. Both seek to escape the charge of rationalism and determinism leveled against the Christian faith by the heretics. Both do this by using the idea that man was really not in possession of the true knowledge of God and of virtue at the beginning. Man began at the bottom of the scale of being. He therefore had free will. This notion of free will is the expression of an irrationalist philosophy of being. Or it is expressive of the non-Christian philosophy of being as far as such a philosophy is of necessity irrationalist. But to thus answer the charge of determinism and rationalism by means of irrationalism and indeterminism is but to prepare the way for a pendulum swing back to still greater rationalism. It is this rationalism that finds expression in Clement when he speaks of all men, whether Christians or not, as participating in the same knowledge of God through the Logos. In other words the correlative to his principle of indeterminism found in his teaching on the free will is found in the principle of continuity by which all men, whether they have knowledge of the historical Christ or not, are yet virtually said to be in him.

b. Origen on Epistemology
We need not now add much by way of discussion on Origen's conception of epistemology. It is generally speaking the same as that of Clement. He too asserts belief in Scriptural authority. This is the starting point of his famous work

---
136. *The Ante-Nicene Fathers*, II, p. 502.
137. Ibid., p. 502 (VI:XII).

on *First Principles*. Yet by his allegorical method he can make these Scriptures produce that which is largely in accord with the principle of Greek philosophy. When Scripture teaches plainly the idea of temporal creation out of nothing, Origen, controlled by the idea that the logic of man can determine what can be and what cannot be, says we cannot think of a moment when God was not creating. He must therefore have created all things from eternity. Thus he pays lip service to the Scriptures as the source of his information and quickly turns to Plato and asks him what can or cannot have been the case in all the ages past. It is the idea of thought in general that largely controls Origen in his speculation. Accordingly he does virtually the same things that Clement does when he wants to explain the nature and origin of evil in the world. He refers to the biblical idea of the fall of Satan and of man but he interprets this in terms of the idea of the chain of being. He interprets the Genesis narrative with respect to the fall figuratively, as intimating a pre-historic ultimate differentiation in reality. In this, too, he resembles Plato.

To escape the charge of determinism and therefore of making God the author of sin, Origen introduces the purely speculative notion of the souls of men as having sinned in a pre-existent state "for if it were not this way, and souls had no pre-existence, why do we find some new-born babes to be blind, when they have not committed sin, while others are born without any defect at all."[138]

This may suffice to indicate the nature of Origen's respect for Scripture. That Scripture is not really absolutely authoritative for him is clear from the fact that its whole message of grace is turned into the opposite so as to mean universal salvation. In other words, just as he seeks a non-Christian principle of discontinuity in order to explain the origin of evil, so he uses a non-Christian principle of continuity in order to have all men saved. The nature of being in general is such that all men will eventually participate in the being of God.

E. SAINT AUGUSTINE[139]

With a more biblical system of theology than that of any of his predecessors Augustine also had a more biblical idea of the Bible itself than they.[140] True, he only gradually realized the implications of his own basic principles. In fact he

---

138. *C. W. Butterworth, Origen on First Principles* (London: Society for Promoting Christian Knowledge, 1936), p. 67 (*De Principiis*, I:8–1, Greek text).

139. For a fuller discussion of Augustine, see the present writer's syllabus *Christianity in Conflict*, I/3 (Westminster Theological Seminary, 1962).

140. KSO: We should note here that this progression in the early church is to be expected. As the church grows in history, so her theology grows. Even with ebbs and flows, progress in doctrine is made as history moves forward.

was never able to reach full consistency in his teaching. But it is safe to say that his basic principles are derived from Scripture as the self-testifying word of God.

The opposite is maintained by such men as Harnack,[141] the historian of doctrine, and by Windelband, the historian of philosophy. For Windelband the essence of Augustine's system lies in the idea of self-sufficient internality. Augustine is thus taken to be the forerunner of Descartes and of modern philosophy, with its starting point in man as sufficient to himself. But B. B. Warfield has, we hold, shown that this interpretation of Augustine cannot be sustained by the chief body of his writings.[142]

Though in some measure subject to the principles of Platonism and particularly Neo-Platonism, Augustine yet produced from Scripture, more clearly than any one before him, such concepts as have enabled his followers to set off the Christian idea of Scripture and of its system of truth clearly against all kinds of non-Christian speculation.

1. Early Writings

In his early writings, Augustine was largely rationalistic in his defense of theism and largely irrationalistic in his defense of Christianity. In his early works he held to a rationalist principle of unity and to an irrationalist principle of diversity in his apologetic defense of Christianity. That is to say, he tended in this direction. Throughout his argument both for theism and for Christianity there appears a tendency to reason in a better way, a way that is more in accord with his own final theology. But then he had not yet worked out his final theology and it could hardly be expected that he should, therefore, at once be able to work out a true method of apologetics.

a. Augustine's Rationalism

In his *Confessions* he speaks of the time when he was converted to Christianity

---

141. KSO: Adolf Harnack (1851–1930) "was an immensely productive historian of the church of the first five centuries. He displayed his extensive research in over sixteen hundred publications. Significant among them were the History of Early Christian Literature to Eusebius (three volumes, 1893–1904), "a monument of exact learning and critical acumen," and The Mission and Expansion of Christianity in The First Three Centuries (1902; fourth edition, 1924), "the first detailed survey of the actual growth of Christian communities before the conversion of Constantine." His magnum opus was *Lehrbuch der Dogmengeschichte* (History of Dogma, 1886–1889), which traced the history of Christian doctrine down to the Reformation. He expounded there the thesis that as the original fervor of early Christians faded, Greek thought forms and institutions began to influence the church's development. Harnack was also a theologian of the school of Albrecht Ritschl (1822–1889). N.V. Hope, "Harnack, Adolf," ed. J.D. Douglas and Philip W. Comfort, *Who's Who in Christian History* (Wheaton, IL: Tyndale House, 1992), 303.

142. Cf. Warfield, *Studies in Tertullian and Augustine* (New York: Oxford, 1930).

and how he sought to relate his acceptance of Christ as his Savior to his philosophical speculations. He says that he found theism but not Christianity in the writings of the philosophers. In speaking of the books of the Platonists, he says,

> And therein I read, not indeed in the same words, but to the self-same effect, enforced by many and varied reasons, that, in the beginning was the Word, and the Word was with God and the Word was God. The same was in the beginning with God. All things were made by Him; and without Him was not anything made that was made. That which was made by Him is life; and the life was the light of men. And the light shineth in darkness; and the darkness comprehendeth it not. And that the soul of man, though it bears witness of the light, yet itself is not that light; but the Word of God, being God, is that true light that lighteth every man that cometh into the world. And that He was in the world, and the world was made by Him, and the world knew Him not. But that He came unto His own, and His own received Him not. But as many as received Him, to them gave He power to become the sons of God, even to them that believe on His name. This I did not read there.
>
> In like manner, I read there that God the Word was born not of flesh, nor of blood, nor of the will of man, nor of the will of the flesh, but of God. But that 'the Word was made flesh, and dwelt among us,' I read not there.[143]

Augustine continues to tell us what he found and what he did not find in the books of Platonists. The substance of his remarks is to the effect that he heard about God and about the Son and about men's participation in the Son, but not about the humiliation and exaltation of Jesus the Savior.

In other words, Augustine seems to think that a true theism is found among the Greeks and that therefore he can use the arguments given for the defense of theism as these have been worked out by the philosophers.

So when after his conversion he seeks to give himself an account of his faith he begins with defending theism. And he defends theism with a method that is essentially Platonic. At least he does not recognize the fact that there is a difference, and that a basic difference, between the Christian and non-Christian defense of the doctrine of God. Augustine does not realize that in defending a bare theism, a theism alike acceptable to Christians and to non-Christians, he is precluding the possibility of going on to a defense of Christianity. A bare theism

---

143. *The Nicene and Post-Nicene Fathers*, ed. by Philip Schaff, Vol. I (Buffalo: The Christian Literature Co., 1886), p. 108 (Augustine, *Confessions*, VII: Ch. 9 or Sec. 14).

is a theism which thinks it needs not Christianity; the God of a bare theism is such a God as does not need the work of Christ in order that men might be saved.[144]

In the *Soliloquies* Augustine personifies Reason and discourses with it. Reason asks Augustine what he would know. "A. God and the soul, that is what I desire to know. R. Nothing more? A. Nothing whatever."[145] A little later Reason asks whether then if Augustine cares to know nothing more than God and the soul he is not interested in learning truth. "R. What, do you not wish to comprehend Truth? A. As if I could know these things except through her. R. Therefore she first is to be known, through whom these things can be known."[146] But how shall we know the truth and how be sure that we know Truth? The answer given is essentially the Platonic one that Truth is the form in terms of which anything and in relation to which anything that is true must be called true. And the form cannot perish. Nothing that perishes must be said to be the truth. It must at most be said to participate in truth. Then "so also, if anything is true, it is assuredly from Truth that it is true."[147] And as nothing that perishes can be as such said to be true, so nothing that perishes can as such be said to be at all. Says Reason, "Nothing therefore is rightly said to be, except things immortal. Do you diligently consider this little argument lest there should be in it any point which you think impossible to concede. For if it is sound, we have almost accomplished our whole business, which in the other book will perchance appear more clearly."[148]

The second book then deals with the possibility of error. How is error to be distinguished from truth? This question must be answered if we are to know the truth. We must teach concerning falsity not falsely if we are to know the truth. The question of criterion is therefore all-important.

Well, we must hold that this criterion is in the mind because the mind is in the truth. Truth always abides in the subject and the subject always abides in the Truth. To be sure, when the matter is put this way the problem arises how an untrained mind, or the mind of an infant, may be said to contain or to be in the truth. "Or shall we rather inquire this, how a science can be in an untrained mind, which yet we cannot deny to be a mind."[149] But even this question will finally get its answer if only we think of Truth in sufficiently formal fashion. And here is the heart of the argument of Augustine. "R. From this truth, as I

---

144. KSO: The god of bare theism, in other words, is a false god, an idol. It cannot, by definition, be the true and Triune God.
145. Ibid., Vol. VII, p. 539 (Augustine, *Soliloquies*, I:7).
146. Ibid., p. 546 (I:27).
147. Ibid.
148. Ibid., p. 547 (I:29).
149. Ibid., p. 556 (II:27).

remember, that Truth cannot perish, we have concluded, that not only if the whole world should perish, but even if Truth itself should, it will still be true that both the world and Truth have perished. Now there is nothing true without truth: in no wise therefore does Truth perish, A. I acknowledge all this, and shall be greatly surprised if it turns out false."[150] Having thus established the idea of Truth as that which must always exist even when it itself perishes, it follows, argues Reason, that God and the soul exist and are known. The existence of God is immediately involved in the existence of Truth.[151] And as for the soul we need not worry, for it, too, exists and is immortal. Do you not at least know what a line is, asks Reason. And in answering that as you do, do you fear the Academicians? Not at all, is the answer.[152] For that much the wise men themselves grant as being independent of the reliability of the senses. "For whether the figures of Geometry are in the Truth, or the Truth is in them, that they are contained in our soul, that is, in our intelligence, no one calls in question, and through this fact Truth also is compelled to be in our mind. But if every science whatever is so in the mind, as in the subject inseparably, and if Truth is not able to perish; why, I ask, do we doubt concerning the perpetual life of the mind through I know not what familiarity with death?"[153]

In his book *On the Immortality of the Soul*, Augustine carries on the argument of the *Soliloquies*. To know the soul it must be, and to be it must be immortal. But to be immortal it must be within the Reason. "Reason is the aspect of the mind which perceives the true *per se* and not through the body. . . Nobody doubts that the first of these is in the mind."[154] But now comes the difficulty with respect to the "stupidity" which enters the mind. This difficulty is similar to the one mentioned above when the question was asked how a mind that is untrained can yet be said to be in possession of the truth. "But that very turning away from reason by which stupidity enters the mind cannot occur without a defect in the mind."[155] But how can there be a defect in the mind? How can that which is in the truth and in which the truth is, turn to stupidity? In other words, how can that, the very existence of which is truth and being, turn away to falsity and to non-being? The answer that Augustine gives is virtually to the effect that error and non-being are within truth and within being. And therefore the mind of man naturally, that is as the result of its inherent nature, turns to falsity and

---

150. Ibid., p. 556 (II:28).
151. Ibid., p. 558 (II:32).
152. Ibid., p. 540 (I:9).
153. Ibid., p. 558 (II:33).
154. *Basic Writings of Saint Augustine*, ed. by Whitney J. Oates, Vol. I (New York: Random House Pub., 1948), p. 306 (*On the Immortality of the Soul*, VI).
155. Ibid., p. 307 (VII).

to non-being. But for all that it must still be said to be within truth and within being. Irrationality and non-being must be dialectically related to truth and to being. And therefore in another way Truth and being must be both formal, that is they must be above all concrete differentiations.

> For if the mind has more being when turned towards reason and inhering in it, thus adhering to the unchangeable thing which is truth, both greatest and first; so when turned away from reason it has less being, which constitutes a defection. Moreover, every defect tends towards nothing [non-being], nor do we ever speak more properly of destruction than when that which was something becomes nothing. Therefore, to tend towards nothing [non-being] is to tend towards destruction. It is hard to say why this does not occur to the soul in which defect occurs.[156]

But can the process of stupidity or destruction go on so far as to have the soul perish altogether? The answer is again similar to the one given about the truth when it was said that even when truth perishes it is true that Truth perishes. In other words the mind can be deprived of "some of its form" but it cannot ever be wholly deprived of form. Even the body cannot be wholly deprived of that by which it is the body. Much less can the mind be wholly deprived of that by which it is mind. And so, if anything should be feared, it is that the mind may perish by defection, that is, may be deprived of the very form of its existence.

> Although I think enough has been said about this, and it has been shown by clear reasoning that this cannot be done, yet it should be also observed that there is no other reason for this fear except that we have admitted that the stupid mind exists defectively, while the wise mind exists in more certain and fuller essence. But if, as nobody doubts, the mind is most wise when it looks upon truth which is always in the same mode, and clings immovable to it, joined by divine love; and if all things which exist in any mode whatever exist by that essence which exists in the highest and greatest degree; then either the mind exists by virtue of that essence, inasmuch as it does exist, or it exists *per se*. But if it exists *per se*, since it is itself the cause of its existing and never deserts itself, it never perishes, as we also argued above. But if we exist from that essence there is need to inquire carefully what thing can be contrary to it, which may rob the mind of being the mind which the essence causes. So, then, what is it? Falsity, perhaps, because the essence is truth? But it is manifest and clearly

---

156. Ibid., pp. 307–308 (VII).

established to what extent falsity can harm the mind. For can it do more than deceive? And except he live is any deceived? Therefore, falsity cannot destroy the mind. But if what is contrary to truth cannot rob the mind of that being mind which truth gave it (for truth is thus unconquerable) what else may be found which may take from the mind that which is mind? Nothing, surely; for nothing is more able than a contrary to take away that which is made by its contrary.[157]

But suppose we seek the contrary of truth, not inasmuch as it is truth as the contrary of falsity, but inasmuch as it exists in the greatest and highest degree (although truth exists thus to the extent that it is truth, if we call that truth by which all things are true, in whatever degree they may exist, they exist inasmuch as they are true); yet by no means shall I seek to avoid that which this suggests to me so clearly. For if there is no contrary to that first essence inasmuch as it is essence, then much less is there a contrary to that first essence inasmuch as it is essence. Moreover, the antecedent is true. For no essence exists for any other reason than that it exists. Being, moreover, has no contrary except non-being: hence nothing is the contrary of essence. Therefore, in no way can anything exist as a contrary to that substance which exists first and in the highest degree. If the mind has its very essence from that essence (for since it does not have it from itself [*ex se*] it cannot have it otherwise than from that thing which is superior to the mind itself); then there is no thing by which it may lose its existence (being), because there is nothing contrary to that thing from which it has it. Hence the mind cannot cease to exist. But since the mind has wisdom because of turning to that by virtue of which it exists, so also when it turns away it can lose this wisdom. For turning away is the contrary of turning toward. But what it has from that to which there is no contrary is not a thing which it can lose. Therefore, it cannot perish."[158]

If truth perishes, it is still true that truth perishes and so truth still exists. If I am deceived, it is still I that am deceived and so I am immortal. It is thus that Augustine thinks he establishes the existence of God, of himself and of truth. Augustine is utterly unaware of the fact that by this mode of argument, if it were valid, the distinctions between God and man, truth and falsity, subject and object would be wiped out. For the validity of both sentences, the one about the perishing of truth and the one about the deceptions of man, depends upon the

---

157. Ibid., pp. 311–312 (XI).
158. Ibid., p. 312 (XII).

reduction of all concrete differences in existence to the formal identity of pure logic. A truth that is true even when it perishes is pure, formal truth. A mind that exists and lives as deceived but does not know that it is deceived, exists as a blank. A mind (or subject) that thus exists as a blank is in no wise different from the Truth (or object) which it knows as a blank. Moreover a mind that is a blank is in no way distinguishable from the truth that is a blank.

On the other hand, if anything of the distinctions mentioned is to be retained, if everything is not to be reduced to abstraction, this can only be done by a principle of irrationalism. In other words, concrete differences can be maintained only at the expense of the validity of the argument. The tendency toward non-being, or destruction, the stupidity of the mind, of which Augustine speaks, is assumed to be ultimate. Falsity, even as non-being or evil, as a defect of being, is assumed to be ultimate. It is *in spite of* this error, this evil, this defect of being as ultimate, that the argument is said to be valid. But then such validity as the argument may have depends precisely upon the ultimacy of all existential distinctions as being irrational. A formal theory of truth requires for its correlative the notion of brute fact. Modern philosophy since Kant has demonstrated this fact over and over. One can say that the *formality* of the theory of truth is the result of a desire to maintain the idea of truth in the face of an assumed brute factuality. Formal truth is therefore the result of a dialectical relationship between abstract universality and abstract particularity. The argument of Augustine depends for its validity upon its formality and its formality is the correlative of its irrationality. Thus truth is true as long as it has no content; as soon as it has any content it is no longer true.[159]

It follows that Augustine did not really have, as he thought he had, an adequate answer to the dualism of the Manichaeans or, for the matter of that, to the solipsism[160] of the Sceptics.

b. Augustine's Irrationalism

It has already been intimated that, if one employs an abstract non-Christian principle of unity, one is bound (if consistent) also to use an abstract principle of diversity. Accordingly we find that as Augustine uses a largely rationalistic principle by which to prove the rationality of belief in theism so he uses a largely irrationalist principle by which to prove the truth of Christianity. In fact he uses both a rationalist and an irrationalist principle in order to establish both theism

---

159. KSO: As long as truth remains "formal" without any "material" content, it can be affirmed. But such truth is merely abstract and thus, in the end, without meaning or significance.

160. KSO: Solipsism is the result of skepticism because all that can be affirmed, for a skeptic, is the self.

and Christianity. This could not well be otherwise. The one principle cannot be used at any point to the exclusion of the other. But in Augustine's case his rationalism is more prominent when he deals with theism and his irrationalism is more prominent when he deals with Christianity.

Let us, therefore, turn for evidence of irrationalism in Augustine to his discussion of *The Profit of Believing*. But before turning to his treatise on this subject a word must be said about another work, composed soon after his conversion, called *Concerning the Teacher*. In introducing this treatise, Whitney J. Oates says that it contains perhaps "the most concise statement of St. Augustine's theory of Divine Illumination."[161] Augustine's theory of divine illumination is, no doubt, as Warfield argues, theologically based upon the Christian doctrine of man's creation in the image of God. But in the earliest writings, its expression at least is largely controlled by neo-Platonic forms of thought. In other words Augustine was at this stage of his development unable to distinguish clearly between a Christian and a pagan form of the *a priori* element in human thought.[162] As already shown it is upon a neo-Platonic form of *a priori* knowledge that he is definitely dependent in his effort to defeat Manichaeanism.[163]

It is in the interest of showing his son Adeodatus that without *a priori* knowledge man could not know anything that he writes in this treatise. His argument is to the effect that there can be no intelligent communication between man and man if, generically speaking, man is not already in possession of the truth. He speaks of words and signs by which men seek to communicate with one another, and he asks what can be communicated by these means from one man to another. The answer is nothing less than startling. It is to the effect that nothing can be thus communicated. "For when a sign is given me, if it finds me not knowing of what thing it is a sign, it can teach me nothing, but if it finds me knowing the thing of which it is the sign, what do I learn from the sign?"[164] The use of words and signs is therefore to remind us of what is already known to us rather than to give us knowledge additional to what is already in our possession. "For it is the truest reasoning and most correctly said that when words are uttered

---

161. Ibid., p. 360.
162. KSO: "*A priori*" refers to aspects of human knowledge that are "prior to" experience. Rationalistic philosophies put emphasis on the *a priori*; empirical philosophies emphasize the *a posteriori* aspects of knowledge, which depend on experience.
163. KSO: "Manichæism is a religion founded by the Persian Mani in the latter half of the third century. It purported to be the true synthesis of all the religious systems then known, and actually consisted of Zoroastrian Dualism, Babylonian folklore, Buddhist ethics, and some small and superficial, additions of Christian elements. As the theory of two eternal principles, good and evil, is predominant in this fusion of ideas and gives color to the whole, Manichæism is classified as a form of religious Dualism." https://www.newadvent.org/cathen/09591a.htm
164. Ibid., p. 387 (*Concerning the Teacher*, X).

we either know already what they signify or we do not know; if we know, then we remember rather than learn, but if we do not know, then we do not even remember, though perhaps we are prompted to ask."[165] "To give them as much credit as possible, words possess only sufficient efficacy to remind us in order that we may seek things, but not to exhibit the things so that we may know them. He teaches me something, moreover, who presents to my eyes or to any other bodily sense or even to my mind itself those things which I wish to know."[166]

What this view does to history and the reporting of history may be gathered from Augustine's own treatment of the Scriptural story of the three young men who were thrown into the fiery furnace.

> But we do accept the story of the boys, that they triumphed over the king and over the fires by faith and religion, that they sang praises to God, and that they won honor even from their very enemies. Has this been transmitted to us otherwise than by means of words? I answer that everything signified by these words was already in our knowledge. For I already grasp what three boys are, what a furnace is, and fire, and a king, what unhurt by fire is, and everything else signified by those words. But Ananias and Azarias and Misael are as unknown to me as *saraballae*; these names do not help me at all to know these men, nor can they help me."[167]

There can, therefore, be no communication of truth about individual historical happenings. The whole point is startling expressed as follows: "Whenever we say anything, either the hearer does not know whether what is said is false or true, or he knows that it is false, or he knows that it is true. In the first mode he will either believe (or accept in good confidence), or he will form an opinion, or he will hesitate; in the second mode he will resist the statement and reject it; in the third he merely confirms. In none of these three cases does the hearer learn anything from what is heard."[168]

These passages have been quoted as evidence of irrationalism in Augustine. But it should be stressed that they might equally well be cited as evidence of rationalism in Augustine. For, as already observed, Augustine himself argues for the inability of signs and words to communicate truth in the interest of the idea that truth is within the mind itself. The negative argument against the possibility of truth communication by means of words and signs is meant to corroborate the *a priori*

---

165. Ibid., p. 389 (XI).
166. Ibid.
167. Ibid.
168. Ibid., p. 392 (XII).

argument employed to establish the abstract idea of truth as expressed in the idea that, if truth perishes, it is true that truth perishes and so Truth does not perish.

Augustine does not, in this connection, contend that knowledge obtained from the senses is of no value. He seems, on the contrary, to hold that knowledge obtained by pointing the finger at physical objects is true knowledge. Yet there is evidence enough to show that for him knowledge obtained from the senses is a lower type of knowledge than knowledge obtained from the mind itself. The logic of his position would lead him to hold to a distinction between a genuine knowledge of intellectual things by means of the intellect and a lower type of knowledge, hardly worthy of the name knowledge, obtained by means of the senses. For it is from Truth that anything is true. But sense objects cannot be shown to be "from truth." They are wholly individual. They do not participate in Truth. For Truth is defined as being Truth precisely because it is so abstract as to have no contact with concrete content of any sort. Or if it be said that Truth is true because the content which it contains is wholly flexible, then the content has at any rate no rational significance. The content must then be irrational in order to be content of purely formal Truth.

In his earliest writings Augustine is concerned to establish intellectual Truth as wholly or largely independent of the senses. "For even if you believe not your senses, and are capable of answering, that you are wholly ignorant whether it is a tree; yet this, I believe, you will not deny, that it is a true tree, if it is a tree: for this judgment is not of the senses, but of the intelligence."[169]

And it is this intellectualism, involved in a Platonic type of *a priori*, that requires for its correlative the idea of brute factuality. Of course Augustine's belief in the creation of the world by God did not allow for depreciation of sense knowledge. Nor did his Christian theology allow for either a non-Christian *a priori* or for a non-Christian type of *a posteriori* reasoning. Innate knowledge and acquired knowledge are involved in one another. They are interdependent. They are limiting concepts one of another. They are dialectically related to one another. But they must be placed upon the Christian presuppositions of the triune God as self-contained and the doctrines of creation and providence, and Augustine did so place them, especially in his later writings. But in his earliest writings, and especially when defending the Christian faith apologetically, he employed a non-Christian notion of abstract Truth and therefore also a non-Christian notion of brute fact.[170]

Accordingly, his concepts of reason and faith and their relations to one another

---

169. Ibid., p. 275 (*Soliloquies*, I:28).
170. KSO: In other words, once there is thought to be a separation between the *a priori* (abstract truth) and the *a posteriori* (experience), then experience cannot yield rational truth. The facts of experience, therefore, are uninterpreted and "brute facts."

are at this stage defined, the one in rationalist and the other in irrationalist terms. The notion of Aquinas that an object of knowledge cannot be at the same time an object of faith and that an object of faith cannot at the same time be an object of knowledge can find a good deal of support in Augustine's earliest writings.

If therefore we were to interpret the famous statement of Augustine to the effect that faith precedes knowledge (*credo ut intelligam*[171]) in accordance with the principles of his earliest writings, it would mean that faith is something practical by which we are brought into contact with objects which we already know from within. In other words the Platonic or neo-Platonic theory of truth requires a definition of knowledge which assumes that man inherently knows all things. Man is potentially omniscient. Does he not exist as participant in Truth? And truth is eternal. For the soul of man to exist it must exist as eternal and therefore as being virtually or potentially omniscient?

If man is virtually omniscient then all things of which he has omniscient or virtually omniscient knowledge must have existed from all eternity. To be at all is to be eternal. The soul is eternal. It has always been. Then the soul of Christ is also eternal and has always been. Everything that can be said to be soul in history has always been. In other words with the type of reasoning developed in Augustine's early writings we are back to a Platonic type of epistemology and ontology which would make historic Christianity wholly without meaning. Jesus of Nazareth would be reduced to the Word which is eternal. All men, all souls, would be eternal in him as God, and thus we would be back with all the heresies of Origen.

It goes without saying that these consequences were not drawn by Augustine and that he would have rejected them as utterly abhorrent to him. But that only shows how inconsistent with the principles of his theology his early apologetic method was.

On the other hand, if the objects of faith should be thought of as historical rather than as eternal then they would have to be thought of as wholly irrational. Or, we may turn this about and say that if the facts of the life and death of Jesus should be taken as individual historical facts rather than as mere illustrations of eternal principles of reason, then they would have to be taken as objects of an irrational faith. Of such objects nothing could then be known. That is to say, they would be objects of faith and therefore not objects of knowledge. The moment they would become objects of knowledge they would have to be eternally existent objects and therefore not temporal at all.[172]

---

171. KSO: "I believe in order to understand."
172. KSO: Van Til is pressing the consistency of Augustine's rationalism to its logical conclusion. Such rationalism cannot do justice to historical facts. Such facts, then, are thought to be separated from "truth" and can only be objects of a "faith" that is not directly connected to rational truth.

The whole method of apologetics followed in these first writings is therefore largely Platonic. The same dilemma that faces Platonic thought faces Augustine. When Plato took his line and divided it sharply between eternal being of which there was genuine or scientific knowledge, and non-being of which there was no knowledge at all, he was faced with the question of how learning by experience was possible. Either a man already knew all reality and he needed not to ask questions or he knew nothing and knew not how to ask questions.[173] Similarly with Augustine. For him Christianity is either true or it is not true. If it is true, it is known by man, by all men. But then if it is eternally existent and is not historical at all, it is no remedy for sin committed in history because the sin for which it would be taken as a remedy would itself not be an historical fact. On the other hand, Christianity may be taken as not true. Then it would be also non-existent, and the man for whom and in relationship with whom it would have come into existence would also be non-existent. Then all would be historical and therefore not eternal and therefore not existent and therefore unknown. In the first case, Christianity would be an object of knowledge but it would itself be an abstraction without content. In the second place, it would be an object of faith, but again an abstraction; it would have no intelligible content.

The only way that the dilemma was kept from plaguing Plato or Augustine too directly was through the fact that the rationalism which led to knowledge without content and the faith that led to an object without knowledge were kept in balance with one another. The abstract character of Truth involved in the idea that, if truth perishes, it is still true that truth perishes and therefore Truth does not perish, is hidden from view to some extent by the fact that there is a flavor of the concrete in it by means of the idea that truth *might perish*. An abstraction cannot perish. It has no content which can perish. On the other hand, if there were any content in truth and it really perished, how then could one know that it was truth that had perished? In other words, things perishable are without any intelligible content. For to have intelligible content a thing must exist and exist eternally. That is Augustine's definition of that which really exists and is really knowable. Therefore, if anything could perish, it could not exist and could not be known to perish, and therefore too, it could not be applied to truth. If the idea of perishing could in any wise be applied to truth it would not be truth to which it was applied, for truth is something that does not perish. But the abstract character of the perishable was kept from view by the fact that the perishable was said to be in contact with truth.

---

173. KSO: Van Til is referring here to Plato's doctrine of reminiscence (*anamnesis*). Plato taught that, given the immortality of the soul, anything we know in this world we know by "recollecting" what our soul already knew in eternity.

In other words, it was the measure of correlativism and dialecticism that was unavoidably involved in the very statement of an abstract theory of truth and an equally irrational and abstract theory of existence[174] that kept Augustine himself from observing how un-Christian and how utterly invalid his argument was.

But now we must still note in some detail the irrationalistic nature of Augustine's concept of faith in his earliest writings. Augustine's Platonic *a priori* theory of knowledge should have compelled him to say that there was no use at all in believing. How could one, first believing through means of the word spoken by other men, ever come to any knowledge of that which was spoken of? Even if we could ourselves go to see the things that were spoken of by words, we should then have only sense knowledge. And sense knowledge is not real or true knowledge at all. Even so, Augustine, in the very context in which he says that by means of words spoken by others we cannot learn anything, says that there is a certain utility in believing.

"From what has been said it follows, therefore, that in the case of those things which are grasped by the mind, anyone who is unable to grasp them hears to no purpose the words of him who does discern them; though we may make an exception in regard to the fact that where such things are unknown there is a certain utility in believing them until they are known."[175]

It is difficult to see the force of this contention. Suppose that we believe in the story of the historic Christ and his work. To be consistent, Augustine would have to treat that story the way he treated the story of the three "boys" in the fiery furnace. As shown above he argues that by our hearing that story we have learned nothing. On the other hand Augustine's theory of knowledge would require him to say that we do not need to be told the story for we know it already. "But, referring now to all things which we understand, we consult, not the speaker who utters words, but the guardian truth within the mind itself, because we have perhaps been reminded by words to do so. Moreover, he who is consulted teaches; for he who is said to reside in the interior man is Christ, that is, the unchangeable excellence of God and his everlasting wisdom, which every rational soul does indeed consult."[176]

Augustine's treatise, *The Profit of Believing*, was written with the Manichaeans in mind. As he has sought to meet the dualism of the Manichees (or their irrationalism) by means of a monism which itself destroyed the uniqueness of Christianity and even of theism, so now he seeks to meet the rationalism of the

---

174. KSO: By "existence" Van Til means *historical* or *concrete* existence, which is dialectically opposed to an abstraction.
175. Ibid., p. 392 (*Teacher*, XIII).
176. Ibid., p. 390 (XI).

Manichees by means of an irrationalism which destroys the possibility of putting intelligible content into the doctrines of Christianity.

The Manichaeans, he says, promise that "apart from all terror of authority" they would set men free from error's claims.[177] They made a "certain great presumption and promise of reasons." But they failed to give good reasons. Particularly they failed to show that man can do without authority in his handling of the problems of life. Is it so strange that we should have to receive information about many things from those who are experts in their fields? Are any of us omniscient? Surely if we err in seeking truth from such few as may have the truth we "err with the human race itself."[178] "I am not, am I, forcing you to believe rashly? I say that our soul entangled and sunk in error and folly seeks the way of truth, if there be any such. If this be not your case, pardon me, I pray, and share with me your wisdom; but if you recognize in yourself what I say, let us, I entreat, together seek the truth."[179] Here speaks the "humble inductivist" and not the "flaming rationalist." Are we not all human beings? Are we not all finite? Do we not all err? Is it then anything exceptional if we seek authority? Must not all men do the same?

Augustine now holds to something like a *tabula rasa*[180] theory of the human mind. He calls on his hearers to imagine a sort of Robinson Crusoe type of person, who has not heard of the truth.

> Suppose we have never heard any teacher of such a religion. We are undertaking an entirely new enterprise. We must first, I suppose, seek for men who profess to teach it. Suppose we have discovered that some hold one opinion, some another, and in the diversity of opinions all desire to attract inquirers, each to his own opinion. But suppose that among them there are some of notable celebrity, accepted by nearly all nations. Whether in fact they possess the truth remains a big question. But surely we must first find out about them, so that so long as we err, being human, we may seem to err with the human race itself.[181]

This approach is as irrationalist as the previous approach was rationalist! Certainly it is a flat denial of the Christian doctrine of man's creation in the image of God to think that any man can be without a teacher of any religion. All men have been from the beginning in Adam taught the true religion. All

---

177. Ibid., p. 399 (*On the Profit of Believing*, 2).
178. Ibid., p. 410 (15).
179. Ibid., pp. 409–410 (14).
180. KSO: "Blank slate."
181. *Library of Christian Classics*. Augustine, *Earlier Writings*, p. 303.

men are therefore in contact with the truth. To say this is not to fall back on the rationalism which we have so sharply criticized. It is rather to assert that there is such a thing as innate knowledge in every man by virtue of his creation by God. It is also to say that man's innate knowledge is correlative to his acquired knowledge, the knowledge that he obtains by a process of study of nature and self. Augustine, therefore, had to forsake his theology both when he first spoke as a rationalist and when he also spoke as an irrationalist.

To suppose such a Robinson Crusoe type of man as Augustine here supposes is, in effect, also to deny the fact of the fall of man as taking place by way of disobedience to the revealed will of God. If sin is disobedience to the revealed will of God, then there is such a thing as a revealed will of God. But instead of taking his notion of sin and error from Scripture Augustine at this point takes his conception of error from Plato. Error is for him here nothing more than the tendency toward non-being and therefore to metaphysical destruction of himself.[182]

We cannot discuss fully the question of the will of man as Augustine held to it in these first writings. In passing a word may be said about it. His doctrine of the will was at this time not clearly defined in Scriptural terms. It was rather defined in terms of the idea of the analogy of being. It was slenderness of being, so to speak, that accounted for man's free will. It is this will as consisting of slenderness of being that has in it a measure of stupidity. This stupidity is therefore inherent in the will because of the *slenderness* of the being that comes to expression in the will. It is thus by a measure of irrationalism that Augustine thinks he is answering the Manichaeans when they charge God with being the originator of sin. Augustine says it is rather the will of man that originates sin. But then since he must at the same time answer the dualism or irrationalism of these self-same Manichaeans and since this can be done only by a principle of monism, Augustine maintains this monism even while he maintains the autonomous will of man. Man is man and has real being because he participates in eternal or changeless being. He has being, and so he *is responsible*. He has only slender being and so he, not God, is responsible.[183] Thus he has, in effect, again forsaken Christianity and at the same time and for that very reason failed to answer the critics of Christianity.

How then can Augustine show there is any profit in believing? He tries to show that in the nature of the case all human beings, since they have but slender

---

182. KSO: That is, on a "scale of being" scenario, God, who is Truth, is the highest being. Anything opposing the highest being is tending toward non-being.

183. KSO: In other words, the monism of Augustine at this point is the monism of "Being" and both God and man are participants in it. God, as the highest being, and man as lower on the "scale." Thus, his "slenderness" of being.

being and are therefore full of stupidity, must of necessity believe at certain points. He places himself on neutral ground with his opponents. This implies taking for granted the truth of the epistemology and the metaphysics of these opponents, their virtual denial of the creation and of the fall of man. Augustine would now *seek* the true religion. Unbelievers and he together agree that they need the help of authority. Of course when he has virtually granted the truth of the unbeliever's epistemological and metaphysical assumptions about the nature of man and of sin the unbeliever can agree with him in his claim that man needs authority, for the authority that man then needs and all the authority that he can then claim man needs is that of experts in the field of religion. The place of experts is then the place of those who have had deep and long experience of sensing somehow what reality is like. It can then not be the authority of those who come with thought communication given to themselves by God. In other words when Augustine seeks on neutral ground with his opponents to establish a place for authority he has virtually chosen for the non-Christian rather than for the Christian notion of authority. But what then of the problem of criterion? How shall "we"—that is, all men together, unbelievers and believers alike—know where to find the right authority?

The answer is again nothing less than amazing. Augustine says: "The case standing thus, suppose, as I said, that we are now for the first time seeking unto what religion we shall deliver our souls, for it to cleanse and renew them; without doubt we must begin with the Catholic Church. For by this time there are more Christians, than if the Jews and idolaters be added together."[184]

But are we then to go by numbers only? That would be too absurd on the face of it. So to the idea of numbers is added that of the expert again. "But of these same Christians, whereas there are several heresies, and all wish to appear Catholics, and call all others besides themselves heretics, there is one Church, as all allow: if you consider the whole world, more fulfilled in number; but, as they who know affirm, more pure also in truth than all the rest."[185] Here it is "those who know" who must guide us, that is all men, in the choice of religion.

This tells the whole story. Augustine now tells how he himself, when he had been among the Manichees, had acted on these principles. "However, I continued to unsew myself more and more from those whom now I had proposed to leave." He then turns to his hearers to say: "If you see that you too have been long affected in this way, therefore, and with a like care for your soul, and if now you seem to yourself to have been tossed to and fro enough, and wish to put an end to labors of this kind, follow the pathway of Catholic teaching, which has

---

184. Ibid., p. 412 (19).
185. Ibid.

flowed down from Christ himself through the Apostles even unto us, and will hereafter flow down to posterity."[186]

It is to the Roman Catholic church indeed rather than toward a future Protestant church that the sort of Christ that would comport with such an approach would lead. It is the idea of expert authority on the part of the pope to which this reasoning leads. Involved in the argument for authority as thus constructed by Augustine is the assumption that there is no such authority as the Bible presents, for on the idea of biblical authority, which was part and parcel of Augustine's soul, the idea of analogy of being is to be rejected. Therefore his rationalism which led to virtual participation of man in the being of God would have to be rejected, and so also his irrationalism which presupposes that man is not in any wise connected with the truth of God and is therefore not responsible for any rejection of the truth is also to be rejected.[187]

While Augustine was thus untrue to his own theology when he reasoned by combining rationalism and irrationalism, he was at the same time also unable to answer the Manichaeans. It is one of the great blunders of Christian apologetics that it has sought to answer lower forms of non-Christian thought by higher forms of non-Christian thought. Particularly mistaken is the idea involved in the traditional method of apologetics such as is used by Bishop Butler[188] and his school, that non-Christian irrationalism can be cured by the application of non-Christian rationalism and that non-Christian rationalism can be cured by the application of non-Christian irrationalism, and that the truth of Christianity is therefore expressed in the nice combination of two, rather than in one, non-Christian principles. This is involved in the Romanist idea of the analogy of being which is still so largely used in the traditional form of apologetics used among Protestants. Of this we shall speak below.

But Augustine was the one who has more than all his predecessors worked out a theology which has put the church in possession of the means with which to meet the world of unbelievers. In working out the doctrine of the ontological trinity still more consistently than Tertullian had done, and in stressing the fact

---

186. Ibid., p. 413 (20).
187. KSO: That is, rationalism has to do with the "scale of being," such that man and God participate in it, and irrationalism has to do with experience, which can have no connection to abstract, *a priori*, truth.
188. KSO: Joseph Butler (1692–1753) "was an important eighteenth-century English apologist. . . .he is best known for *Analogy of Religion* (1736), in which he defends Christianity against Deism. . . .Butler was influenced by his older contemporary, Samuel Clarke, a disciple of Sir Isaac Newton and defender of the Christian Faith. Analogy of Religion was a defense of the plausibility of Christianity in terms of the analogy between revealed and natural religion." Norman L. Geisler, "Butler, Joseph," *Baker Encyclopedia of Christian Apologetics*, Baker Reference Library (Grand Rapids, MI: Baker Books, 1999), 108.

of the grace of God in Christ given by the sovereign disposition of God to his people, he has given us the foundation on which to build a principle of interpretation which shall be neither rationalistic nor irrationalistic nor a combination of these two, but which shall make sense of human experience. By presupposing the ontological trinity as taught by Christ in Scripture man is, to begin with, in contact with the truth. He does not know all the truth, but he does not need to know all the truth in order to know truth. Then error is explained not by slenderness of being but by willful transgression of the revealed will of God within and around man. Consequently there is the possibility of the communication of truth by God to man and through man to other men with absolute authority, and on the basis of absolute authority the reason of man may know and know truly.

2. *Later Writings*

As Augustine gradually began to fathom the depth of the grace of God in his heart he saw that his freedom did not consist in metaphysical slenderness of being but in ethical restoration to his Creator God through Jesus Christ his Redeemer God.

By the same token, Augustine learned that he must take his principle of continuity and his principle of discontinuity from Scripture rather than from Plato or Plotinus. The inwardness of the triune God of Scripture gradually wins out over the inwardness of Socrates and Plato. He learns to know himself not by some abstract interior principle but by the fact that he is known by God in Christ.

Knowing himself as known by Christ his Redeemer, Augustine is no longer plagued by the horrible uncertainty involved in being constantly tossed back and forth between an abstract principle of unity and an abstract principle of diversity. "It is not with a doubtful consciousness, but one fully certain that I love thee, O Lord. Thou hast smitten my heart with thy Word, and I have loved thee."[189] "What, then, am I, O my God? Of what nature am I?"[190]

Augustine now knows that he is not a compound between abstract impersonal being and equally abstract impersonal non-being. He is part of God's created world. He believes what Moses says about the creation of the world. Time is no longer a moving image of eternity. It is created by God. Time is no longer an aspect of pure, self-existent contingency. When he seeks to understand the nature of time he no longer tries to do so by a timeless principle of rationality. He merely seeks better to understand himself and his world in terms of God's

---

189. *Augustine: Confessions and Enchiridion*, tr. and ed. by Albert C. Outler (Vol. VII, "The Library of Christian Classics," gen. eds. J. Baillie, J. T. McNeill, H. P. Van Dusen; Philadelphia: The Westminster Press, 1955), p. 205 (Augustine, *Confessions*, X:VI).

190. Ibid., p. 217 (X:XVII).

revelation in Christ through Scripture. He has been rescued by Christ his Savior from the dizzy dialecticism between a timeless principle of logic which swallows up all temporal distinctions and therefore absorbs man himself and a featureless contingency which in turn swallows up every vestige of discernible identity.[191]

Augustine now realizes that in the triune God of Scripture he has found "the one and only and true God."[192] He knows that "in no other subject is error more dangerous, or inquiry more laborious, or the discovery of truth more profitable."[193] Augustine, still the searcher for truth, now finds the truth in Scripture because it alone speaks of the true, the triune God.

It is through an almost unbearable inward struggle that Augustine turns away from the wisdom of man to the wisdom of God, Augustine now seeks for a *Christian* view of himself and of history. He no longer looks for the consolation of philosophy but for the fulfillment of the promises of God. The "family of God" now has "a consolation of its own." When Christians are taunted for their faith they may in all humility but with all boldness say: "And that you are yet alive is due to God, who spares you that you may be admonished to repent and reform your lives."[194]

There are now clearly two distinct classes of people for Augustine, those who are redeemed by Christ and those who are not redeemed. The two kinds of people now have mutually exclusive principles for the interpretation of God's relation to man and his world. Believers in Christ must engage in an effort to win non-believers to an acceptance of Christ. The enemies of Christ must be called to repentance. "Let these and similar answers... be given to their enemies by the redeemed family of the Lord Christ, and by the pilgrim city of King Christ. But let this city bear in mind, that among her enemies lie hid those who are destined to be fellow-citizens, that she may not think it a fruitless labor to bear what they inflict as enemies until they become confessors of the faith."[195]

a. The Two Cities

So we are to read the narratives of Scripture not as though it were telling us "bare historical facts."[196] We are to read them as exhibiting to us the development of the struggle between two cities, the city of God and the city of the world. "Of things done, yet done prophetically; on the earth, yet celestially; by men, yet divinely!"[197]

---

191. Ibid., p. 257 (XI:XVII).
192. *Basic Writings of St. Augustine*, Vol. II, p. 669 (*On the Trinity*, I.II).
193. Ibid., p. 670 (I.III).
194. Ibid., p. 39 (*The City of God*, I.XXXIV).
195. Ibid., p. 39 (I.XXXV).
196. Ibid., p. 313 (V.XXVII).
197. Ibid., p. 358 (XVI.XXXVII).

The history of the patriarchs, the history of Israel, it all exhibits the conflict between the two cities.[198] "The enemies of the city of God, who prefer their gods to Christ its founder, and fiercely hate Christians with the most deadly malice,"[199] have been operative throughout the whole of the Old Testament period. It is in this way that Augustine interprets the Old Testament Christologically. All men are "bound together by a certain fellowship of our common nature."[200] But on the basis of this common human nature there is a hatred against Christians on the part of those who "live according to man." This hatred will find climactic expression in the last persecution of believers by the anti-Christ.

Only those who by grace have received true faith and therefore true virtue in their hearts will enter eternal blessedness. "But, on the other hand, they who do not belong to this city of God shall inherit eternal misery, which is also called the second death, because the soul shall then be separated from God its life, and therefore cannot be said to live, and the body shall be subjected to eternal pains."[201]

Here then is Augustine's total philosophy of history. By faith alone can we accept the existence of the triune God. By faith alone do we and can we accept the redemptive work of Christ and his Spirit in history. By faith alone can we accept the fact that we are creatures and sinners before God. By faith alone can we understand the progress of history to be that of the conflict of Christ against Satan. By faith alone can we accept the fact that the issue of each man's life and of history as a whole is that of eternal life and eternal woe with victory for Christ over his foes. But then "let those sceptics who refuse to credit the divine writings give me, if they can, a rational account of them."[202] That is, let sceptics give an account of the marvelous work of redemption of Christ in history. In the Bible alone do we read of the miracles of redemption. Accept then the Bible and with it the record of the redemption of God, or explain all things in terms of yourself as man.[203]

It is thus that the last of the great church Fathers becomes the means by which the stream of redemption, so nearly lost in the theology of the Alexandrians, is again brought to light. Having set forth this truly biblical philosophy of history and having challenged the sceptics to produce something intelligible in its place, he engages in "amicable controversy" with Origen and those who with him had no eye for the basic distinction between the city of God and the city of the world. He speaks of Origen who "believed that even the devil himself and his angels, after suffering those more severe and prolonged pains which their sins

---

198. Ibid., pp. 406–407 (XVIII).
199. Ibid., p. 406 (XVIII.I).
200. Ibid., p. 407 (XVIII.II).
201. Ibid., p. 506 (XIX.XXVIII).
202. Ibid., p. 569 (XXI.V).
203. Ibid., pp. 573–74 (XI.VII).

deserved, should be delivered from their torments, and associated with the holy angels."[204] "But the Church, not without reason, condemned him for this and other errors, especially for his theory of the ceaseless alternation of happiness and misery, and the interminable transitions from the one state to the other at fixed periods of ages; for in this theory he lost even the credit of being merciful, by allotting to the saints real miseries for the expiation of their sins, and false happiness, which brought them no true and secure joy, that is, no fearless assurance of eternal blessedness."[205] We must abide by the words of Christ, These shall go away into eternal punishment, but the righteous into life eternal.[206]

What, finally, can be said about the life of those who by grace have entered the city of God in this world and will, therefore, enjoy eternal life in heaven hereafter? Little enough indeed. But we do know that those "reasoners, whose thoughts the Lord knows that they are vain," who, with Plato, think such a life is impossible, need not detain us.[207] If for the sake of "ridiculing the resurrection" those who follow such men as Plato and Porphyry offer us the notion of everlasting alterations of happiness and misery or an immortality of the soul by "escaping from every kind of body," we pay no heed.[208] We abide by the promises of God in Christ. "True peace shall be there, where no one shall suffer opposition either from himself or any other. God himself, who is the Author of virtue, shall there be its reward; for, as there is nothing greater or better, he has promised himself. What else was meant by his word through the prophet, 'I will be your God, and ye shall be my people.'"[209]

It is thus that in his later writings Augustine attains to a vision of God, of himself and of his world that is, at bottom, the reverse of that which even the best of the philosophers, like Plato, had espoused. He has now found true inwardness for himself because he now sees that his inwardness rests upon the absolute Inwardness of the triune God of Scripture. He now sees that there are no abstract principles of truth, goodness and beauty above God but that God, as self-sufficient, and as revealed through Christ in Scripture, is for him the source and criterion of truth, goodness and beauty.

b. True Freedom
In his later days Augustine continued to engage in battle those who would lead the church back into the hopeless morass of non-biblical speculation. All his

---

204. Ibid., p. 587 (XXI.XVII).
205. Ibid.
206. Ibid., p. 553 (XXI.XXIII, quoting Matt: 25:46).
207. Ibid., p. 630 (XXII.XI).
208. Ibid., p. 634 (XXII.XII).
209. Ibid., p. 661 (XXII:XXX).

arguments against Pelagius and against the semi-Pelagians are carried on in the interest of preserving for sinful men the liberating insight into the fact that they have been saved from their involvement in the false speculations of sinful men by grace alone.

Pelagius was seeking to introduce the non-Christian view of human freedom, namely, autonomy, into the teaching of the church. If he had been successful, the whole structure of the Christian philosophy of history as Augustine had developed it on the basis of Scripture, would have crashed to the ground. The church might have continued to exist as a human uplift-society but no longer as the body of Christ. As a human uplift-society a church built upon the notion of human autonomy would no longer challenge the world to forsake its wisdom. The church would then have rejoined the men of the world in their hopeless effort at identifying themselves in terms of themselves and at finding meaning in their world.

The spiritual descendants of Pelagius in modern times are diligently seeking to do what he did in his time. They are doing this by "interpreting" Augustine's principle of "inwardness" as though it were an expression of the idea of human self-sufficiency.

It is thus that Wilhelm Windelband, the philosopher, interprets Augustine. He discounts the fact that in his maturest thought Augustine rejected the idea of human freedom as being identical with human autonomy altogether in favor of the idea that man's true freedom is ethical liberation from sin through the redemptive work of Christ in history.[210] Windelband contends that Augustine's idea of Inwardness leads right on to the modern philosophical idea of the self-sufficiency of man. All Augustine's teachings with respect to the doctrine of the sovereign grace of God are, from Windelband's point of view, nothing but indications of deflection from the main principle of his thought.[211] In teaching that man is chosen by God to true inwardness in Christ, says Windelband, Augustine forgot his own true principle of self-certainty altogether.

In similar fashion Adolf von Harnack, the church historian, asserts that the idea of predestinating grace leads to a *determinism* that conflicts with the gospel and imperils the vigor of our sense of freedom.[212]

It is thus that modern philosophers and modern theologians conspire to replace the doctrine of freedom in Christ with the doctrine of freedom without Christ.

---

210. Windelband, *op. cit*, p. 276.
211. Ibid., p. 284
212. Adolf von Harnach, *History of Dogma*, tr. by Neil Buchanan, Vol. V (Boston: Little, Brown, & Co., 1899), p. 217–221.

In our own day it is neo-orthodoxy that is seeking to do what Windelband and Harnack sought to do in their day.

Neo-orthodoxy tells us that we can now solve the problem of the relation of the true inwardness of man with the seemingly deterministic notion of the electing grace of God. The problem of the conflict between freedom and determinism is said to be a problem that pertains merely to the impersonal dimension of science. If only we have the vision of the personal dimension, the dimension of I-thou relation, then all contradiction ceases. Then we see that this I-thou dimension is paradoxically related to the I-it dimension. As God appears in history he is *wholly* revealed in it. This fact satisfies the autonomous man's legitimate demand for an all-penetrating unity of thought. At the same time, when God is wholly *revealed* in history he remains wholly *hidden* in it. This fact satisfies the autonomous man's legitimate demand for total independence.

It is thus that neo-orthodoxy seeks to reintroduce the apostate notion of human autonomy and with it (a) the notion of a principle of continuity that envelopes God the Creator as well as man the creature, and (b) the notion of a principle of discontinuity that also envelopes both God and man.

In his work on *Philosophie der Praktischen Vernunft*[213] (1927) Heinrich Barth asserts that it was not till Augustine set off his thought over against that of Pelagius that he employed the idea of paradox.[214] How marvelous, says Heinrich Barth, is the unity between freedom and grace in the final paradoxical expression given these concepts by Augustine.[215]

In this Heinrich Barth assumes, with Windelband, Harnack and others that Augustine's theology is a prefiguration of post-Kantian thought as this is based on the primacy of the practical reason.[216] Heinrich Barth thinks that Kant's view of the coincidence of freedom with determination by the moral law to be of permanent value.[217] Free will is a will placed under moral law.[218] Man is free as, moment by moment, of his own accord, he submits himself to the moral law.

In this analysis of Augustine's concept of freedom and grace we have an illustration of the modern practice of reinterpretation (*Umdeutung*).

Basic to an understanding of this practice as carried on in this instance is that Heinrich Barth assumes the Kantian distinction between the phenomenal and the noumenal world to be correct. In the phenomenal world there can be no

---

213. KSO: *Philosophy of the Practical Reason*.
214. Heinrich Barth, *Philosophie der Praktischen Vernunft* (Tubingen: Mohr Verlag, 1927), p. 128.
215. Ibid., p. 141.
216. Ibid., p. 185.
217. Ibid.
218. Ibid., p. 186.

free relations. When we think of freedom we must, therefore, forget our habit of thinking in terms of causal relations. All thinking about freedom in relation to grace must be done in terms of the noumenal realm. There we encounter no difficulty in combining freedom and grace. For there the God who gives grace is, in the first place, a projection of the man who receives it. Forthwith all is harmony.

On this basis we may accept the entire Augustinian theology of grace. We simply, à la Kant, reconstruct the ideas of creation, fall, incarnation and atonement by first refusing to identify them directly with anything that takes place in the phenomenal realm. Then positively we think of God, first projected by man, as revealing himself in grace to man as man and thereby enabling him to realize his true or free self.

This is what the modern principle of Inwardness does. Applied to Augustine it destroys his theology of grace. On the modern view of Inwardness there can be no direct revelation of God through Christ in history. There can be no transition from wrath to grace through the work that Christ did in the world of space and time. There can be no fall and there can be no redemption except metaphorically in the real, the historical world, the only world of which man knows anything.

Moreover, when Heinrich Barth, following many others, thinks that he finds unity between free will and grace by means of the modern nature-freedom scheme of Kant, he is mistaken.[219] Where is freedom on his view? He says it cannot be found anywhere in the world of causation. Freedom must be in the noumenal world where man stands in a purely negative relation to the world of causal determination. But no one has ever discovered this free man. Nor has anyone ever discovered the God this free man has projected for himself in the noumenal realm. Still less, if possible, can anyone see any effect of the work of grace on the part of this God toward the free man. The transaction between this God giving grace and this free man receiving grace must needs be mediated through the world of impersonal causation and in the process of mediation through the world of I-it relations the person-to-person relation is lost.

In contrast with this it was Augustine who attained to the notion of a wholly person-to-person relation between God and man. In his outlook there is no impersonal field which can act as a static between God and man. The whole world with all that is therein is created and sustained by God. The laws of this world are God's regular way of doing his work. The work of redemption is miraculous but the natural is built for the miraculous in advance in the one plan of God.

---

219. KSO: The "modern nature-freedom scheme" is a category utilized by Herman Dooyeweerd. Dooyeweerd rightly recognized "immanentistic" thought as inherently and foundationally dialectical. Modern thought presupposes a nature-freedom dialectic. Such a dialectic is irresolvable, and thus is a particular manifestation of what Van Til calls, more broadly, the rational-irrational dialectic of unbelieving thought.

The miraculous redeems and completes the natural. Christ lives and dies and rises again in the ordinary nature of man and takes our nature with him to heaven when, having finished his work, he returns to the Father.

Of course Augustine did not even in his latest writings attain to a fully self-conscious worked-out statement of his own basic position. But certainly his theology leads us forward to the truth because it works within the truth. Heinrich Barth does not lead us forward to the truth because he takes man out of the context in which truth alone is found. And this is typical of the modern theology that is based on the nature-freedom scheme of Kant. This nature-freedom scheme carries forth the slavery that was imposed upon man by the form-matter scheme of the Greeks. The Inwardness of the modern scheme was already latent in the form-matter scheme of the Greeks. The attitude of Socrates in the *Euthyphro*, where he wants to know what the holy is regardless of what gods or men say about it, points to and is the prefiguration of Kant's ethical dualism and ethical monism. The Inwardness of Socrates finds its modern expression in the Inwardness of Kant. It is upon the Inwardness principle of the Greek form-matter scheme supplemented by the Inwardness principle of the modern freedom-nature scheme that new Protestant theology and, in particular, the theology of Karl Barth and his disciples stands in order to challenge the theology of the Reformers.

V

FROM SOVEREIGN GRACE TO SYNERGISM

We have seen that with ever greater consistency Augustine gave forth the biblical doctrine of the sovereign grace of God. In his great work on *The City of God* he showed how those who live by grace have learned to see all the facts of life in a new light. They have a new philosophy of history. They have as, following Werner Jaeger, we may say, a new *paideia*.[1]

This *paideia* is Bible-centered, Christ-centered and therefore God-centered. As such it stands at every point opposed to apostate man's *paideia*, based on the idea of human autonomy.

The self-attesting Christ is moving on to victory over the hosts of darkness as history proceeds. Christ works through his church to the defeat of Satan and his hosts. The army of the living God had a great leader in Augustine. Christ became the victor over Augustine by way of a great internal struggle. Then Christ became the victor in the life of many believers through the teaching and the life of Augustine.

But did the church carry on the work of Augustine after his death? The answer is in the negative. There was a gradual decline from free or sovereign grace to synergism in the period from Augustine to Thomas Aquinas. We can do no more than indicate this fact by pointing to a few significant landmarks in this decline.

In the last of the great Greek philosophers the Greek *paideia* may be seen to be at every point hostile to the Christian *paideia*.

A. PLOTINUS[2]

In the philosophy of Plotinus all the major motifs of earlier Greek philosophy are molded into intricate interaction with one another. In Plotinus we have overt

---

1. KSO: Van Til is referring here to Werner Jaeger's three volume work on *paideia*. Jaeger sees the word *paideia* as difficult to define precisely. It includes, however, the shaping of a culture through a synthesis of civilization, culture, tradition, literature, and education. See, for example, Werner Jaeger, *Paideia: The Ideals of Greek Culture: Volume I. Archaic Greece: The Mind of Athens* Oxford University Press, 1986).

2. A fuller discussion of Plotinus will be found in the present writers' syllabus *Christianity in Conflict*, II/1 (Westminster Theological Seminary, 1964).

rationalism and overt irrationalism made correlative to one another. Plotinus wants to be true to the Parmenidean principle of pure logic as determinative of the nature of reality but he does not, in being true to this principle, want to deny the reality of the contingency of the world of sense.

"Intelligence," says Plotinus,

> is the first legislator, or rather, it is the very law of existence. Parmenides therefore was right in saying, 'Thought is identical with existence.' The knowledge of immaterial things is therefore identical with those things themselves. That is why I recognize myself as a being, and why I have reminiscences of intelligible entities. Indeed, none of those beings is outside of Intelligence, nor is contained in any location; all of them subsist in themselves as immutable and indestructible. That is why they really are beings.[3]

Over against this real world as identical with the intelligible world stands the world of pure, unrelated contingency.[4] There is an absolute dualism between these two words. Plotinus seeks to overcome this absolute dualism by means of the idea of participation. In this he follows Plato.

The facts of the world of sense, the world of contingency are unreal except so far as they participate in the world of timeless reality. Time is intelligible only if we think of it as timeless.

It is thus that in the philosophy of Plotinus the Greek *paideia* appears as utterly bankrupt. The principle of pure rationality and the principle of pure irrationality are made correlative to one another and thereby cancel out each other.

It is thus that the Socratic spirit of Inwardness, i.e., of the concentration of all interpretation upon man as the final point of reference stands over against the Christian spirit of Inwardness as expressed in Augustine's theology. In Plotinus and Augustine the Greek and the Christian *paideia* stand squarely over against one another, ready for the final duel.

It might seem that in the philosophy of Plotinus rationalism rather than irrationalism rules. Yet this is not the case. Even though thought and being must be said to be identical, Plotinus argues, no man can ever experience such an identification. The identification is always ideal. It is always above the discursive

---

3. *Plotinus Complete Works*, trans. by Kenneth S. Guthrie (London: George Bell and Sons, 2nd ed., 1918), p. 108 (V:9.5).

4. KSO: Knowledge, to be knowledge, must be "timeless" in that it cannot be knowledge at one moment and then no knowledge at another moment. Over against this is the contingency of the world, in which things that exist come and go with time. The two, in Greek thought, are seen to be in opposition with each other.

thought of any man. Discursive reason can only point to a unity that is higher than anything that man can say about it. If unity is to be objective then it must be above all the rational thought of man. Says Plotinus:

> (To attain Unity) we must therefore rise above science, and never withdraw from what is essentially One; we must therefore renounce science, the objects of science, and every other right (except that of the One); even to that of beauty; for beauty is posterior to unity, and is derived therefrom, as the day-light comes from the sun. That is why Plato says of (Unity) that it is unspeakable and undesirable. Nevertheless we speak of it, we write about it, but only to excite our souls by our discussions, and to direct them towards this divine spectacle, just as one might point out the road to somebody who desired to see some object.[5]

Again Plotinus says:

> There must indeed be some principle above Intelligence; for Intelligence does indeed aspire to be one, but it is not one, possessing only the form of unity... What is above Intelligence is Unity itself, an incomprehensible miracle, of which it cannot even be said that it is essence, lest we make of it the attribute of something else, and to whom no name is suitable. If however he must be named, we may indeed call him in general Unity, but only on the preliminary understanding that he was not at first something else, and then only later became unity. That is why the One is so difficult to understand in himself; he is rather known by his offspring; that is, by Being, because Intelligence leads up to Being.[6]

Plotinus gives us here the self-sufficient first principle of his philosophy. This first principle is altogether *beyond* the reach of reasoning. Yet reason says that the ultimate principle *must be* this super-rational sort of thing. Nothing can be said of the first principle. Yet it must be the source of all explanation of man and the cosmos.

Over against this comprehensive man-centered philosophy of Plotinus stands the comprehensive Christ-centered philosophy of Augustine. For all the many concessions Augustine makes, mostly in his earlier writings, to the man-centered principle of Plotinus it remains true that basically and, most consistently in his later writings, Augustine makes the triune God of the Scriptures

---

5. Ibid., p. 154 (VI:9.4).
6. Ibid., pp. 157–158 (VI:9.5).

the final reference point of his whole philosophy of history. The beginning, the development and the consummation of the *Civitas Dei* stands under the sign of the sovereign grace of God to man in Christ.

Consonant with the basic contrast on the matter of final reference point between Plotinus and Augustine is the difference between their views of logic.

Since the fall of Adam apostate mankind has assumed its own essential divinity. Man is assumed to be participant in deity. When he uses the laws of logic and in particular the law of contradiction, as he must, then he takes for granted this inherent divinity of man. He assumes that his logic is legislative for the nature of reality. Whatever exists, he assumes, must be exhaustively penetrable by the logical powers of man. As we have seen, Parmenides gave eloquent and terse expression to this assumption when he said that only that which I can think without contradiction, exists.[7] Plotinus carries this apostate view of logic through even when, in contrast to Parmenides, he seeks to ascribe some measure of reality to temporal things.

In complete contrast to this approach of Plotinus stands that of Augustine. To be sure, as noted, Augustine makes many a concession to the apostate point of view of logic. But at bottom his commitment is to the idea that man is the creature of God rather than participant in the being of God. In spite of his many concessions to the Greek *paideia* his main principle, as best expressed in his latest works, is that the sovereign God gives or withholds his grace to sinners according to his good pleasure. Therefore if those who operate from a Plotinian point of view charge him with determinism Augustine, following Paul, simply responds: "Who art thou O man that contendest with God." The judge of the whole earth will do right. Man, the creature, become the sinner, must admit mystery, but the mystery that he admits does not, as in the case of Plotinus, envelop God.

Still consonant with the basic contrast between Plotinus and Augustine on the question of the final point of reference and also consonant with the difference between them on the question of logic is their difference with respect to the philosophy of fact.

For Plotinus the world of space-time factuality exists by Chance. His principle of individuation is that of pure contingency and irrationality.[8] Over against

---

7. KSO: Parmenides, (c. 500 B.C.), was a Greek, Pre-Socratic philosopher, and is one of Van Til's favorite foils for monism and its consequent absurdities. Parmenides taught that only "being" *is* and everything else is "non-being," or non-existent. Thus, all presumed diversity is "absorbed" into the unity of being.

8. KSO: That is, because all things come to be by chance, and thus randomly, any particular "thing" (which is what is meant by "individuation") just "happens" to be (irrationality) and might not have been at all (pure contingency).

this purely contingent and purely irrational principle of individuality is the idea of Augustine that God, having created all things, having sent Christ to redeem the world, directs all things to the end appointed for them by himself. In spite of all the concessions that he makes to the Plotinian principle, especially in his earlier works, it is none the less true of Augustine that his basic commitment, best expressed in his later writings, is that the facts of reality are what they are, ultimately, by virtue of the all-encompassing plan of God.

It was not till Plotinus appeared upon the scene that the denial of God as creator and redeemer came to express itself fully in the idea of an abstract unity that is beyond all human predication. If Plato and Aristotle still kept up the pretense that it is by the laws of thought that men must come to the idea of a unity that is above the laws of thought, Plotinus maintained that "the principle of identity is derivative from the One and not applicable to it."[9] Says Richard Kroner, "Plotinus tried very hard to comprehend the Supreme Being logically and ontologically, but he knew very well that logic finally breaks down; only ecstasy can fill the gap that separates the human intellect from the mystery of the divine."[10]

B. THE AEREOPAGITE[11]

It is Pseudo-Dionysius[12] who brings this Plotinian motif into direct connection with the Christian principle. He does so by means of his idea of negative theology. If the Christian principle still keeps alive after its first encounter with the negative theology of Dionysius it does so with great distress. Says Sontag: "The Pseudo-Dionysius can be viewed within the Plotinian framework of perfection with little modification or distortion."[13] Of course as a Christian theologian Di-

---

9. Frederick Sontag, *Divine Perfection* (New York: Harper and Brothers Pub., 1962), p. 31.
10. Richard Kroner, *Speculation and Revelation in the Age of Christian Philosophy* (Philadelphia: Westminster Press, 1959), p. 89.
11. For a fuller discussion of Dionysius and Johannes Scotus Erigena along with the whole question of the pre-Kantian notion of a 'Scale of being' see the present writer's syllabus *Christianity in Conflict*, II/2 (Westminster Theological Seminary, 1964).
12. KSO: Pseudo-Dionysius, "(5th/6th centuries), the unknown author, probably a Syrian, of an extremely influential group of Greek theological works in the tradition of Christian Neoplatonism (see Platonism). . . The work of Pseudo-Dionysius is in fact a theology or a philosophy of theology (this is still much debated), which comprises three stages, the cataphatic, the symbolic and the mystical. These are respectively related to the three persons of the Trinity (theological dimension), to the soul's ascent to the Trinity (anthropological dimension) through purification, illumination and glorification (or deification or union with God), and also to the threefold structure of the cosmos." Sinclair B. Ferguson and J.I. Packer, *New Dictionary of Theology* (Downers Grove, IL: InterVarsity Press, 2000), 543.
13. Sontag, *op. cit.*, p. 33.

onysius speaks much of creation and redemption. And he says that as Christians we must not say anything about the Godhead "except those things that are revealed to us from the Holy Scriptures."[14] But the whole story of redemption from creation to the consummation of history is soon pressed into the framework of the scale of being. Above all other reality is the "Super-Essential Godhead" of which we must not dare "to speak, or even to form any conception."[15] Of course "not that the Good is wholly incommunicable to anything."[16] The principle of plenitude,[17] to which Dionysius is committed, takes care of both the idea of utter negation and, as correlative to it, of communication. For the super-essential Good "while dwelling alone by itself, and having there firmly fixed its super-essential Ray, it lovingly reveals itself by illuminations corresponding to each separate creature's powers, and thus draws upwards holy minds into such contemplation, participation and resemblance of itself as they can attain—even them that holily and duly strive thereafter."[18]

Through the beams that fall upon us in Scripture from the super-essential source of being we learn that it is the "Cause and Origin and Being and Life of all creation."[19] We even know that it is a "Power of Renewal and Reform."[20] As if to anticipate Paul Tillich's[21] idea of the *New Being*, the super-essential is said to be the "sacred grounding to them that feel the shock of unholy assault."[22]

As does Tillich, so Dionysius makes his theology Christocentric as well as biblical. But "even the plainest article of Divinity," says Dionysius, "namely the

---

14. *Dionysius the Areopagite on the Divine Names and the Mystical Theology*, trans. by C. E. Rolt (New York: The Macmillan Co., 1940), p. 51 (The Divine Names, I:1).
15. Ibid., p. 53 (*Names*, I:2).
16. Ibid.
17. KSO: For the relationship between the principle of plenitude and the scale of being, see the foreword. For more on this, see Lovejoy, *The Great Chain of Being; a Study of the History of an Idea*: esp. ch. 4.
18. Ibid., pp. 53–54 (*Names*, I:2).
19. Ibid., p. 55 (*Names*, I:3).
20. Ibid.
21. KSO: Paul Tillich (1886–1965). "Writing as a philosophical theologian, Tillich sought to mediate between Christian theology and secular thought. He viewed his task as one of apologetics, provided that we define apologetics in his own way, as an 'answering theology' which is offered on the basis of a shared area of common ground. He studied and subsequently taught in several German universities, and although he emigrated to the United States when Hitler came to power in 1933, his thought remains firmly rooted in German philosophical traditions. He is indebted to the Romantic movement (e.g. to Schleiermacher and to F. W. J. von Schelling, 1775–1854) but also to the phenomenology of Edmund Husserl (1859–1938) and Martin Heidegger (1889–1976). He also drew heavily on the psychology of Jung, especially in his work on symbols (cf. *Depth Psychology; Psychology of Religion*)." Sinclair B. Ferguson and J.I. Packer, *New Dictionary of Theology* (Downers Grove, IL: InterVarsity Press, 2000), 687.
22. Ibid.

Incarnation and Birth of Jesus in Human Form, cannot be expressed by any Language or known by any Mind—not even by the first of the most exalted angels."[23] If then there is any help in the person and work of Christ for the salvation of men, it is because of his identity with the super-essential. It is from this, the super-essential, that he emanates. It is not for anything that he has done for men by suffering for them on the cross and by rising for their justification from the dead but rather by virtue of his pointing them to the super-essential being that he saves them. It is this super-essential being that is a "Principle of Illumination to them that are being enlightened; a Principle of Perfection to them that are being perfected; a Principle of Deity to them that are being deified; and of Simplicity to them that are being brought unto simplicity; and of Unity to them that are being brought unto unity."[24]

It is thus that *negative* theology requires the idea of *symbolic* theology. Says Sontag: "Final statements are ruled out by the ultimate inappropriateness of a language that is necessarily based upon distinctions."[25] Even if one speaks of the super-essential being as perfect one has not done more than point to it. All human language is, in the nature of the case, symbolic, in the sense that it merely points to that of which it can say nothing in any conceptual form.

Modern philosophy and theology has tried to go beyond Dionysius in both his negative and in his symbolic approach to the idea of the wholly otherness of God. Following Kant, modern philosophers know with all possible certainty that God is unknowable. Even though they cannot show how man or the world can be known without God they are certain that man has knowledge and that he has this knowledge without God. Even though they admit that man is a product of chance and that the logical powers of his thought are products of chance yet they know that God cannot be man's creator or redeemer. On the other hand modern philosophers, and especially modern theologians, assert that man's constitution and the facts of the universe about him *somehow* point to God. They are sure that God is good and *somehow* the source of goodness in and to man. In other words the principle of plenitude controls modern philosophy and theology as it did St. Denis.[26] The only difference between the modern thinkers and St. Denis is that the moderns outdo him both in the irrationality of their affirmations and in the rationalism of their negations. But we need not pursue this point further here.

---

23. Ibid., pp. 75–76 (*Names*, II:9).
24. Ibid., pp. 55–56 (*Names*, I:3).
25. Sontag, *op. cit.*, p. 35.
26. KSO: "St. Denis" is another name for Dionysius.

C. JOHANNES SCOTUS ERIGENA[27]

We turn now briefly to Johannes Scotus Erigena. A few words about his justly famous work on the *Division of Nature* must suffice.

Erigena, as well as St. Denis, was a Christian theologian. When Erigena tells us about the divisions of those things that are and of those things that are not he is simply telling us, he says, what Scripture teaches. He is, says Gilson, simply seeking to give us a rational interpretation of the biblical text.[28] He is simply telling us about God and his creation.

And what does he tell us about God? Of course, says Erigena, we turn to the Bible to learn about God. There we learn about the triune God, about creation and about redemption. Says Henry Bett: "The system of Erigena is essentially Christo-centric, for the universe is conceived as created in Christ and restored in Christ."[29] But Bett adds at once that it is the "metaphysical Logos rather than the historic Jesus who is mostly in Erigena's thoughts."[30] Bett speaks of "an absence of all historic sense in Erigena's references to Christ."[31] What we learn by the affirmative theology of Scripture must be counterbalanced by the fact that God is infinitely above man. Every human thought involves limitation, and God is above all limitations. God is therefore more than Good and more than goodness. Every attempt that man makes to express the nature of God by means of superlatives is, in effect, to assert that God is wholly other than anything that man can assert about him. Says Bett in summarizing the view of Erigena: "God is indeed beyond all words, and all thought, for he surpasses all intellect, and is better known by not knowing, and is more truly denied in all things than affirmed."[32] All the distinctions that we make when we speak of God are not in God; they are only in our thought of God.[33] As if to anticipate Karl Barth, Erigena asserts over and over again that God is wholly beyond anything that man can say about him either by the way of negation or by the way of affirmation.

---

27. KSO: Erigena (or sometimes Eriugena), "John the Scot (c. 810–c. 877), philosopher. . . Erigena's philosophy, which was suspected of heterodoxy only at a much later date, is an attempted reconciliation of the Neoplatonist idea of emanation with the Christian idea of creation. . . Erigena was a deeply original thinker and a great scholar, with a knowledge of Greek which was quite exceptional for his time. He did an important work in translating the writings of Dionysius the Ps.-Areopagite into Latin and writing a commentary on his *Celestial Hierarchy*." F. L. Cross and Elizabeth A. Livingstone, eds., *The Oxford Dictionary of the Christian Church* (Oxford; New York: Oxford University Press, 2005), 561.
28. Etienne Gilson, *History of Christian Philosophy in the Middle Ages* (New York: Random House, 1955), p. 114.
29. Henry Bett, *Johannes Scotus Erigena* (London: Cambridge University Press, 1925), p. 106.
30. Ibid.
31. Ibid., p. 107.
32. Ibid., p. 24.
33. Ibid., p. 26.

When then Erigena speaks of the creation of the world by God this "creation" is in fact emanation. The super-essential good, which is above all our distinctions and sufficient to itself, turns out also to be the source of all that exists in the world. The principle of plenitude operates as much in Erigena as it did in St. Denis and in Plotinus. "The essence of all things is nothing but the knowledge of them in the mind of God. *Nihil enim est aliud omnium essentia, nisi omnium in divina sapientia cognitio.*"[34] The contention of Lovejoy that the rationalism of the principle of plenitude as used by such men as Plotinus and St. Denis is as determinist as is that of Spinoza is manifest with utmost clarity in the thought of Erigena.[35] The final significance of this fact is apparent when we see that according to Erigena the salvation of all men as accomplished by Christ and as shown in his resurrection, takes place in the strength of the power of nature, *naturali virtute.*[36] God realizes himself through the universe.[37]

D. NATURAL THEOLOGY

It has already become apparent from what has been said in the previous section that the ineffable God, who has no knowable character, somehow manifests himself in the world. It is an internal necessity for this God to reveal himself. Yet the world in which he manifests himself is not what it is exclusively by virtue of its coming from this god. There is a principle of non-being over against this God that contributes in an original manner to the nature of the world. To be sure, Erigena says that the world simply is what it is by virtue of the knowledge of God. And Erigena but expresses herewith the determinism that inheres in the principle of plenitude which controls his thinking. But in the time of Plotinus and his followers men were anxious to show the Christian world that it was they and not the Christians who really had an intelligible philosophy of history. Philosophy, they argued, does indeed point to the ideal world but it points to this ideal work as the principle of explanation of this world. Unfortunately Plotinus and his followers had to appeal to the idea of pure contingency for help in their explanation of the world of change. Without this principle of contingency the facts of space and time would, on their basis, be unreal. But with the principle of contingency as correlative to the principle of determinism this world was made utterly unintelligible.

---

34. Ibid., p. 51.
35. KSO: As noted in the foreword, the principle of plenitude is "determinist" because the principle maintains that it is necessary for the highest good to be good that it "create" or emanate more being. All possibles must become actual.
36. Ibid., p. 80.
37. Ibid., p. 94.

Early Christian theologians were not alert to this fact. They all too frequently did not realize that once they agreed that their notion of the incomprehensibility of God was the same, in effect, as the idea of the namelessness of God as held to by the Greeks, the gnostics and Plotinus, that then they could logically be compelled to deny the whole of the significance of the appearance of Christ in history. The God of Christianity is not nameless. He knows himself exhaustively. His creatures therefore also know him. They cannot help but know him. They do not, to be sure, know him exhaustively. God is not fully comprehensible to them. That is what is meant when in terms of the Christian principle God is said to be incomprehensible to man. This view of the incomprehensibility of God is the opposite of the notion of the incomprehensibility of God involved in the principle of plenitude. In the latter, God is wholly unknown and unknowable to himself. On this basis ultimate reality is utterly meaningless. If man says that the world has meaning for him in terms of such a god, he is merely deceiving himself. On this view no fact of history can be intelligently related to any other fact of history. Certainly the whole of the work of creation and redemption is then one colossal farce, a purely imaginary construction in the clouds on the part of man.

The natural theology that of necessity goes with this negative theology is well expressed by Plotinus and his followers when they all say that the facts of this world must somehow *participate* in the unity of the ideal world. If this natural theology is to have any rationality in it then it must be in terms of the Parmenidean aspect of the principle of plenitude. And the Parmenidean aspect of this principle leads to the idea of the absorption of the temporal into the eternal without residue. We shall discuss this point more fully when we deal with Thomas Aquinas. For the moment it is our purpose to stress the interdependence of the principles of negative and of natural theology. A wholly unknowable God lies back of the idea that the world has sprung by accident from this God and manifests this God only by contradicting him. If the God of the principle of plenitude really exists and rules the world then the world is, of necessity, that which this God of necessity must make it. This leads to pure determinism. The world therefore must be that in which, on the one hand, God is wholly revealed and, on the other hand, one in which God is wholly hidden.

It was not till Augustine saw clearly the fact that God is what the Scripture says he is, the light in whom is no darkness, when he saw clearly that the world is what the Bible says it is, the theatre of the creative and redemptive work of the Son of God and Son of man, that this combination of negative theology and natural theology was challenged to a duel. Of course, as has been repeatedly said, Augustine was himself often confused on the ultimate issue. But that he saw it, and in his later writings saw it clearly, cannot be doubted. Each in his own way, such men as Lovejoy, Gilson and Kroner do not have an eye for this fact. It is for this failure to see the basic contrast that they cannot describe the conflict of the Middle Ages for what it really was.

E. MYSTICAL THEOLOGY

Underneath the negative, the symbolical and the natural theology spoken of thus far lies that of mystical theology. As negative theology deals with the idea of the unknowable God and as natural theology deals with the unknowable world, so mystical theology deals with the unknowable man.

But this unknowable man thinks he knows himself very well indeed. In fact he starts from the idea that his knowledge of himself is so clear that he can easily take off from it into an intelligible search for the nature of God and the world. Of course it was not till modern times, beginning with Descartes,[38] that man frankly and openly asserted the claim that he knew himself whether or not God existed, and it has often been said that Augustine was really the forerunner of Descartes in stressing the principle of the self-sufficient inwardness of man. Nothing could be further from the truth. To be sure, Augustine did, especially in his earlier years, think in a Platonic-Plotinian manner. He tried to prove the existence of God by an appeal to an abstract principle of Truth. He talked as though the human mind or soul derives its illumination from the fact that it participates in this abstract principle of truth. But it is precisely from this Platonic and Plotinian approach that he was finally converted. He was converted to the idea that he was a sinner against the known will of God instead of being evil by accident, because participant in the principle of non-being. He was converted to the idea that God is the triune God as described in Scripture from the idea that God is some abstract principle above every form of diversity and differentiation that man makes in his speech about him. He was converted to the thinking of the Christ as the Son of God and Son of Mary, the mediator between God and man, dying under the wrath of God for sinful men. In short, Augustine learned the doctrines of salvation by grace. He therefore learned to worship the God of sovereign grace, and in terms of this God of sovereign grace he rejected the interpretation of God, of the world, and of himself in terms of the principle of plenitude.

Augustine learned, more particularly, to reject the mystical theory of salvation inherent in this principle of plenitude. This mystical principle implies

---

38. KSO: René Descartes (1596–1650) is considered to be the first prominent rationalist philosopher of the modern era, and the beginning of what came to be called "critical philosophy." In his philosophy, he sought for one clear and distinct indubitable truth that could ground all other knowledge. He concluded with his now famous, "*Cogito, ergo sum*," "I think, therefore I am." This principle, as Van Til notes, is meant to stand on its own, whether or not God exists. As such, Van Til calls it a "self-sufficient principle of inwardness."

that man has in himself the knowledge of the way of salvation and the power to walk in it.

This mystical principle was already expressed by Socrates in his principle of inwardness. To be sure, Socrates sought to answer the sceptics in his day by thinking of the individual soul as participant in an objective world of intelligence. But by the time of Plotinus this objective world of intelligence had shown itself to be something that was utterly beyond the reach of all human intelligence. If in Plato it is Diotema, the inspired, who must lift up the soul to the world of light, so it is by sheer concentration of its own powers that the soul of Plotinus takes its ecstatic flight into the world of light which is darkness now as well as light. In other words, it is the mysticism of Plotinus rather than the supposed inwardness of Augustine that is the steppingstone from the Socratic vision to that of the *Wesensschau* of Husserl and his existentialist followers.[39] Plotinus was not modern. He was still desirous of joining his soul with a somehow objectively existing principle of unity. The modern view thinks that this is to follow a mirage. Even so there is no essential difference between the ecstatic vision of Plotinus and of the idea of *Wesensschau* of most post-Kantian philosophy. Plotinus as well as those who follow Kant's primacy of the practical reason, want to transcend the realm of knowledge or of science by means of a grand *Entschluss*[40] of the will that is free because itself in principle lives in the world of the *noumenal*. Knowing that the *noumenal* realm is wholly unknowable and that man himself is therefore wholly unknowable to himself, modern theologians *postulate* the "existence" of a God of grace as also existing in that realm. Thus it is the primacy of the practical reason as over against the theoretical reason that leads to the postulation of the wholly unknown God and of his manifestation through Christ in the world. And this Christ is also both wholly known and wholly unknown. As such it is he that is supposed to help man who has in the first place constructed him.

If modern theology prides itself on having seen, with Kierkegaard[41], that truth is subjective and that man is existentially engaged when he finds this truth

---

39. KSO: Edmund Husserl (1859–1938) is the father of philosophical phenomenology, which informed existential philosophy, especially that of Jean Paul Sartre. Husserl's *Wesensschau* is often translated as "intuition."

40. KSO: "decision."

41. KSO: Søren A. Kierkegaard (1813–1855) "Kierkegaard's influence was not felt in America until the century after his death. Intellectually, Kierkegaard stood behind the development of existentialism which, through its many facets, emphasizes the priority of existence over essence. This philosophical movement has been one of the major currents of twentieth-century thought, particularly through the period 1920–1960. Christian existentialism is the appropriation of Kierkegaard's insights for Christian theology and ethics, stressing human experience, freedom and the commitment of faith." Daniel G. Reid et al., *Dictionary of Christianity in America* (Downers Grove, IL: InterVarsity Press, 1990).

in God as the Subject rather than as the object of thought, then the essentials of this thinking can be found in the *Enneads*.[42] Plotinus does not want the soul to be cold and detached when in itself, quite apart from any revelation through Christ in history it discovers "the intuition of the divine light." The soul must "feel a rapture such as that of a lover who sees the beloved object, and who rests within it, a rapture felt by him who has seen the true light, and whose soul has been overwhelmed with brilliance on approaching this light."[43] The modern theologian too has seen a vision. In the light of this vision he is certain that historic Christianity cannot be true. Historic Christianity, this modern theology asserts, has failed to see that truth is above the distinctions made by the human intellect. God as the subject or Person and man as subjects or finite persons must have a fellowship of love with one another in that realm which is wholly other than the realm of the phenomenal world. The principle of love that lives within all men by virtue of the fact that they are persons constructs the idea of Absolute all-inclusive love and personalizes as well as substantializes it. Having thus insisted that its ideal of universal love and universal forgiveness without the necessity or reality of an historical atonement is real, it builds the ecumenical church on this basis. All may enter into this church except those who believe historic Christianity to be true. Historic Christianity *cannot* be true. The modern theologian is willing to make this universal negative judgment about the nature of all reality in order to maintain his feeling that somehow all must turn out well with the world. What is God for except to make the world turn out well? What is God for except to obey man? What is God for except to reward all men because they are inherently good? What is God for except to forgive those who have somehow not followed the principle of goodness and being which was originally in them as fully as they might have done? All being is good and all who have any being therefore participate in ultimate being and good. Through history the good God in his goodness and generosity, withal needing the world in which to express himself, gives being and goodness to men and then takes these men, who are in the first place what they are because they emanate from him, further and further into communication of goodness and being with him.

It was this principle of inwardness or plenitude as represented so well by Plotinus that was brought into synthesis with the principle of Christianity by St. Denis and by Erigena. And surely it seemed as though the Plotinian myth was to swallow up the testimony of the Word of the self-attesting Christ. In neither St. Denis nor in Erigena does there seem to be much left of historic Christianity. To be sure, there is the verbal commitment to the self-attesting Christ. But then

---

42. KSO: The *Enneads* are six essays of Plotinus, put together by Porphyry, one of his students.
43. Plotinus, *op. cit.*, p. 155 (VI:9.4).

there follows immediately a reduction of his word and work in terms of the principle of plenitude.

We cannot now continue to trace the development of negative, of symbolic, of mystical and of natural theology further. Enough has been said to indicate the nature of the background of the Roman Catholic synthesis between Christianity and Greek thinking. It was the Roman Catholic *paideia* as a composite of the Greek and the Christian *paideia* that the Reformers rejected.

VI

AUTONOMY PLUS AUTHORITY: ROMAN CATHOLICISM[1]

We must now turn to the Roman Catholic doctrine of Scripture. The question to be asked is to what extent this doctrine is true to Scripture itself. As noted earlier a truly Scriptural doctrine of Scripture must ask Scripture to bear witness to itself. Moreover, a truly Scriptural doctrine of Scripture must think of Scripture as that light of God to sinful men to which all other lights are subject. For it is only by thinking of Scripture in this fashion, that the natural man is really challenged to forsake the autonomous principle by which he seeks to interpret all of life.

A. EARLIER OFFICIAL WRITINGS

We look first at the older official statements of the Roman Catholic church. These official documents do not say a great deal about Scripture. For further elucidation of them some of the discussions of certain Roman dogmaticians may be of help. In particular the general principles of epistemology as they appear in the works of St. Thomas Aquinas will shed light on the position found in the official confessions of the church.

1. Trent[2]

Of the various *Symbola Romana* the *Canons and Dogmatic Decrees of the Council of Trent* comes first. The Council of Trent met soon after the Reformation was

---

1. KSO: This is a centrally and foundationally crucial aspect of Reformed theology, and thus of Van Til's apologetic. Only in Reformed theology is the *principium cognoscendi* affirmed to be utterly self-attesting, and thus not dependent on anything for its authority except itself. Moreover, it seems the doctrine of Scripture, and what it teaches, has been the perennial target of detractors, both within and without Christianity.

2. KSO: "The Council of Trent was the definitive Catholic response to the Protestant Reformation. From 1545 to 1563, for a total of 25 sessions, the council of bishops deliberated. The council conceded that Protestantism resulted from the 'ambition, avarice, and cupidity' of Catholic bishops. It also ordered the systematic education and training of the clergy in established Catholic

in progress. Its deliverances are, accordingly, taken in relation to Reformation principles. This holds both for what it specifically says about Scripture and for the system of doctrine that it contains.

In the *Decree Concerning the Canonical Scriptures* it says that the truth and discipline of the gospel of God in Christ

> are contained in the written books, and the unwritten traditions (*sine scripto traditionibus*) which, received by the Apostles from the mouth of Christ himself, or from the Apostles themselves, the Holy Ghost dictating, have come down even unto us, transmitted as it were from hand to hand: [the Synod] following the example of the orthodox Fathers, receives and venerates with an equal affection of piety and reverence, all the books of the Old and of the New Testament—seeing that one God is author of both—as also the said traditions, as well those appertaining to faith as to morals, as having been dictated, either by Christ's own word of mouth, or by the Holy Ghost, and preserved in the Catholic church by continuous succession.[3]

Then follows a list of the sacred books to be thus venerated. This list includes the books of the Apocrypha as well as those of the Old and New Testaments. We are told that "if any one receive not [this list], . . . as they are contained in the old Latin vulgate edition; and knowingly and deliberately contemn the traditions aforesaid; let him be anathema."[4]

In addition it is asserted that in seeking to know what the sacred books teach in matters of faith and life men must not "presume to interpret the said sacred Scripture contrary to that sense which holy mother church,—whose it is to judge of the true sense and interpretation of the holy Scriptures,—hath held and doth hold; or even contrary to the unanimous consent of the Fathers; even though such interpretations were never [intended] to be at any time published."[5]

---

seminaries. In the seminaries, the church promoted the study of Thomas Aquinas, making him the dominant Catholic theologian. In a direct response to the Lutherans, the council likewise abolished indulgence sellers, listed and defined clergy obligations, regulated the use of relics, and ordered the restructuring of bishops within the church. The doctrinal work of Trent is summarized in the Tridentine Profession of Faith, which championed Roman Catholic dogma and provided the major theological response to the Protestants. Trent rejected justification by faith alone and promoted the necessity of meritorious works as necessary in the dynamic of salvation." James P. Eckman, *Exploring Church History* (Wheaton, IL: Crossway, 2002), 61.

3. Philip Schaff, *The Creeds of Christendom*, Vol. II (New York: Harper and Brothers, 1919), p. 80.
4. Ibid., p. 82.
5. Ibid., p. 83.

2. Vatican I

In the *Decrees of the First Vatican Council* (1870) Pope Pius IX begins with the idea that the church is the Spouse of Christ, and the teacher of truth and morals. The second chapter of the Decrees deals with Revelation. Some things may be known by reason; others must be made known by revelation. "The same holy mother church holds and teaches that God, the beginning and end of all things, may be certainly known by the natural light of reason, by means of created things; . . . but that it pleased his wisdom and bounty to reveal himself, and the eternal decrees of his will, to mankind by another and supernatural way: as the Apostle says, 'God, having spoken. . .'"[6]

It is to be ascribed to this divine revelation that such truths among things divine as of themselves are not beyond human reason can, even in the present condition of mankind, be known by every one with facility, with firm assurance, and with no admixture of error.

This, however, is not the reason why revelation is to be called absolutely necessary. Revelation is necessary because God in his infinite goodness has ordained man to a supernatural end, viz., to be a sharer of divine blessings which utterly exceed the intelligence of the human mind.[7] At this point appeal is made to what has been quoted above from the Council of Trent on the matter of the sacred books, the traditions, and the Vulgate edition. The sacred books and traditions, "having been written by the inspiration of the Holy Ghost, . . . have God for their author, and have been delivered as such to the church herself."[8] Appeal is also made to what was said by the Council of Trent on the fact that the church alone has the right to declare the sense and meaning of the sacred writings and traditions.

Chapter IV deals with Faith and Reason. It speaks of a "twofold order of knowledge distinct both in principle and also in object; in principle, because our knowledge in the one is by natural reason, and in the other by divine faith; there are proposed to our belief mysteries hidden in God, which, unless divinely revealed, cannot be known."[9]

The relation between faith and reason is further explained in the following words: "And not only can faith and reason never be opposed to one another, but they are of mutual aid one to the other; for right reason demonstrates the foundations of faith, and enlightened by its light cultivates the science of things divine; while faith frees and guards reason from errors, and furnishes it with manifold knowledge."[10]

6. Ibid., p. 240.
7. Ibid., pp. 240–241.
8. Ibid., p. 242.
9. Ibid., p. 247.
10. Ibid., p. 249–250.

Still further, stress is once more laid on the authority of the church as the final determiner of the meaning of sacred doctrine. "For the doctrine of faith which God hath revealed has not been proposed, like a philosophical invention, to be perfected by human ingenuity, but has been delivered as a divine deposit to the Spouse of Christ, to be faithfully kept and infallibly declared."[11] The infallible declaration of meaning by the church is never "to be departed from, under the pretense or pretext of a deeper comprehension of them."[12]

In order that the infallible declaration spoken of may be accomplished most effectively, the "Perpetuity of the Primacy of blessed Peter in the Roman Pontiffs" is then discussed (First Dogmatic Constitution on the Church of Christ, Ch. II). The end of this argument is that the Roman Pontiff is declared to be "the supreme judge of the faithful."[13] He has "supreme jurisdiction over the universal church."[14] He also has "the supreme power of teaching."[15] The supreme Pontiff is not to make known "new doctrine," but to teach conformably to the sacred Scriptures and the Apostolic traditions.[16] Speaking "*ex cathedra*, that is, when in discharge of the office of pastor and doctor of all Christians, by virtue of his supreme Apostolic authority" he gives such definitions of faith and morals as are "irreformable (*irreformabiles*) of themselves, and not from the consent of the church."[17]

In what has been quoted, two points may be distinguished. First there is that which deals directly with the sacred Scriptures. Second there is that which deals more broadly with the relation of faith and reason.

On the question of the place of Scripture the following elements stand out:

a. The place of the church is above the Scriptures instead of below it as in the case of Protestantism. Directly guided by the Holy Spirit the Church in turn guides, infallibly guides, the faithful.[18]

b. In performing the function of teaching the faithful the church uses the Bible as one of two main sources of revelation. The other source is that of Apostolic tradition. This tradition is supplementative to the sacred writings. It stands on a par with Scripture. Scripture is not the only source of revelation.

c. The church declares the sense or meaning both of Scripture and of the Apostolic traditions. Thus in practice it is the church with its infallible teaching authority that tells the faithful what "system of truth" they may find in Scripture.

---

11. Ibid., p. 250.
12. Ibid., p. 251.
13. Ibid., p. 265.
14. Ibid.
15. Ibid., p. 266.
16. Ibid., p. 269.
17. Ibid., pp. 270–271.
18. Cf. G. C. Berkouwer, *De Strijd om het Roomsch-Katholieke Dogma* (Kampen: J. H. Kok, n.d.).

AUTONOMY PLUS AUTHORITY: ROMAN CATHOLICISM

Professor G. C. Berkouwer in his *Conflict with Rome* points out that Romanist theology thinks of the church as "identical" with Christ. That is to say, the incarnation is a process. The incarnation is not a once-for-all and finished fact. He who speaks of the incarnation speaks therefore of a universal phenomenon. To be sure, Roman theology does distinguish between the historic Christ and the church. Its doctrine is not pure naturalism. Nor is it pure idealism. "But from the fact that Christ still is man and remains such eternally, it follows that the incarnation is as actual as it is historical."[19] Berkouwer quotes the Roman Catholic dogmatician, Brom, to the effect that the church is so filled with the idea of the actual living Christ that she may herself be called a continuous incarnation.[20]

This view of the church as in a sense a continued incarnation fits in with the notion of the analogy of being which so largely controls Romanist metaphysics. It is not the place here to discuss this doctrine. It is mentioned in passing only. This idea of the *analogy of being* compromises the biblical doctrine of creation. It tends to reduce the distinction of God as the Creator and man the creature to that of the Greek notion of man's participation in being as such. According to the Greek view of reality, especially as set forth in the philosophy of Aristotle, called "the philosopher" by Thomas Aquinas, all being is ultimately one. All individual beings are beings to the extent that they participate in this one ultimate being. According to Aristotle, God has the fulness of being. As such he is pure Act. At the lower end of being, not found in any actually existing thing that man can know, is pure potentiality of being. Man exists between pure actuality and pure potentiality of being. There is, therefore, a continuity of being between man and God. Man may increase in his participation of God as pure act. There is also discontinuity of being between man and God. Man is near the realm of pure non-being. He participates, as it were, in non-being as well as in being.

It is thus that for Aristotle the principle of potentiality and actuality control the relationship between God and man. This relationship is therefore one of process. It is activistic. It is the natural working out of the principles of continuity and of discontinuity of a general Being.

Only if the doctrine of the self-contained God and of creation is maintained as the presupposition of all that is said on any doctrine is it possible to maintain the full Christian position. Romanism is unwilling to make this doctrine of God basic to all its thinking. It seeks for a synthesis between the Aristotelian idea of analogy of being and the biblical idea of God as Creator and man as creature.

The reason for this lies in the Roman Catholic conception of the autonomy

---

19. G. C. Berkouwer, *Conflict met Rome* (Kampen: J. H. Kok, 1948), p. 273; cf., Eng. trans., *Conflict with Rome* (Philadelphia: Presbyterian and Reformed, 1958), p. 205.
20. Ibid.

of man. Man is said to be free. This does not merely mean that man is not ethically as corrupt as historic Protestant theology says that he is. It means this to be sure, but it also means that man is to some extent metaphysically ultimate. He partakes in ultimate being. His will is therefore of the same sort as the divine will. Man's will can initiate the wholly new. God does not control whatsoever comes to pass. Man determines in part what the ultimate issues of history will be like. God approaches man by way of the *infima species*, the lowest class. He never controls in the final sense the act of the individual man. For the individual as individual exists, in part at least, by virtue of his ultimate independence of his will.[21]

It was necessary to introduce this much of Thomist metaphysics in order to indicate the fact that its activistic conception of revelation is inherent in the basically activistic conception of the relation of God to man found in Roman Catholic thought. With God and man together, to some extent involved in a process of being, it is natural that the matter of knowledge should also be one of process.[22]

How then shall the matter of identification be settled? How could there be, on a Romanist basis, a finished revelation of God in history? There cannot be! There is not even a finished incarnation in history. Reality as a whole is a process. There is no once-for-all act of justification of the sinner by God in history; justification too is a process, a process of participation of the sinner in the supernatural righteousness of God in Christ.

On the other hand, the matter of identification must be settled. So it is settled arbitrarily. According to its theory of reality Romanism cannot even attribute infallible knowledge to God. For God cannot know what will come to pass. He is dependent upon millions of human wills, each in some measure able to initiate that which is wholly new.[23] God can send his son into the world. He may intend to save all men. But men can resist this grace; they have autonomy; who can decide their ultimate fate but they themselves? So there can be no infallible Bible in the Protestant sense of the term as there can be no finished acts of redemption

---

21. KSO: Van Til is referring here to libertarian free will, according to which no one other than the individual ultimately ensures what he would choose in various circumstances. Molinism is a popular Roman Catholic belief that incorporates this view of human freedom. According to one Romanist encyclopedia, "Molinism combats the heresy of the Reformers, according to which both sinners and just have lost freedom of will. It maintains and strenuously defends the Tridentine dogma that teaches that freedom of will has not been destroyed by original sin, and that this freedom remains unimpaired under the influence of Divine grace." https://www.newadvent.org/cathen/10437a.htm. Arminianism also depends on aspects of Molinism.

22. KSO: In other words, since Romanism affirms the autonomy of the will, the "actualization" of given events in the world depends *both* on God and man equally. Things in the world "come to be" by virtue of this mutually cooperative effort, which is initiated by man's autonomous choices.

23. KSO: In Molinism, God has "middle knowledge." This knowledge is "pre-volitional" for God, and thus *dependent on* what possible human creatures would do in all possible situations. For God to "know" these possibilities, humans must be able freely and autonomously to choose. Thus, God only knows by virtue of what humans would freely choose.

in history in the Protestant sense of the term. What is to be done about it?

An idea of finality that is correlative to the idea of process must be discovered. A principle of identification that shall furnish continuity as well as discontinuity must be found. It is this combination of continuity and discontinuity that finds expression in the idea of the church as, on the one hand, continuing the incarnation and, on the other, as possessing irreformable truth and as infallibly teaching this irreformable truth by means of the supreme Pontiff as the supreme teacher of the faithful.

Thus Romanism seeks to serve both God as supreme in his field and the autonomous man as supreme in his field.

The result is that man is, in practice, made more ultimate than God. There is no place for sovereign grace.

B. THE ATTRIBUTES OF SCRIPTURE

It will not be difficult now to see why the Protestant Reformation developed its so-called attributes of Scripture in opposition to the Romanist position. With a different system of theology went a different view of Scripture. In Protestantism it is by one act of faith that the believer embraces the Christ and the Scriptures which tell of the Christ.[24] It is a matter of interdependence. The believer comes to Christ through the Bible and with it to the divinity of Christ.

The Christ of God came once for all to finish his work of redemption for his church. He finished his work. Through his apostles and prophets he gave a finished interpretation of this, his work. All the elements of that work are finished in Christ. The faithful are justified; justification is an act of the judgment of God. Men are certainly saved, and on the basis of the promises of God may know that they are certainly saved. They will certainly be glorified. God's program for history will be accomplished; he controls whatsoever comes to pass.

The church therefore stands *under* the Scripture. It first recognizes the Scriptures by way of identification. It determines the canon simply because it sees what books carry the message of God. No supplementative tradition can stand next to the self-attesting word of God. The Holy Spirit does not directly and independently guide the church; he guides the church in understanding the Scriptures as the self-attesting word of Christ. Nothing but the autographa[25] can be said to be infallibly inspired. The Scripture must be interpreted by Scripture. The church must subject itself in its explanation of the system of truth of Scripture as well as in its identification of Scripture to the self-attested Word as found in Scripture.

---

24. Bavinck, *op. cit.* Vol. I, p. 610.
25. KSO: That is, the original manuscripts of the books of Scripture.

No interpretation as such may be said to be infallible. There is an ever deeper insight into the truth of Scripture promised to the church if it submits its efforts at interpretation to the Scripture itself.

In presenting the Scripture as self-attesting and as interpreting the finished work of redemption through Jesus Christ the motives of credibility must themselves be interpreted in terms of the self-attesting Word of God. Only that is credible which is in accord with the system of truth set forth in this Bible. The more clearly this system of truth be set forth in its contrast with the systems of men, based as they are on a theory of being and of knowledge that involves both God and man in a common process or that places man with God into a common changeless substance, the more clearly will the natural man be driven to turn away from himself to the living God. It is only if the Holy Spirit gives him repentance that he will submit his every thought captive to the obedience of Christ.

1. Necessity

The Protestants therefore argued for the necessity of Scripture because man, the creature, has sinned against God. He has broken the covenant. Salvation is an ethical matter. Man was created perfect. He needed no grace as a creature. To be sure, he needed and received God's favor. Sometimes Reformed theologians have called this grace. But then the word is used in a broader sense. So Bavinck speaks of it.[26] Then too, man as a creature, though perfect, needed supernatural revelation. God's revelation to him in nature was supplemented by God with his supernatural word communication. This was to tell man of his destiny and to make him self-conscious as a covenant being. But all this betokens no defect in the creature as such. The ideas of creation and covenant are supplemental one to another.

Over against this, the Romanist conception of the need of supernatural revelation is quite different. According to Romanism, grace is necessary for man before he has sinned. This is because man, as finite, is inherently defective to some degree. Therefore supernatural revelation is, for Romanist theology, a matter of grace from the beginning.

> According to Rome grace is thus a *donum supernaturale per se* and not *per accidens*, not only because of sin. Sin has not changed the nature of grace. Perhaps it has increased because of sin. But both before and after the fall it was the same, namely, an *elevatio supra naturam*. That is its character

---

26. KSO: For example, "True religion, accordingly, cannot be anything other than a covenant: it has its origin in the condescending goodness and grace of God. *It has that character before as well as after the fall.* For religion, like the moral law and the destiny of man, is one." (my emphasis) Herman Bavinck, John Bolt, and John Vriend, *Reformed Dogmatics: God and Creation*, vol. 2 (Grand Rapids, MI: Baker Academic, 2004), 570.

and essence; Christianity may then also be an *Erlösungsreligion*; it is not in the first place *reparatio*, but *elevatio naturae*, it serves the purpose of lifting nature above itself, to make man divine. It was that purpose that was served in Adam's case by the *gratia gratum faciens*; it is that purpose that is now served by Christianity. Grace was then and now the same; i.e., the real, the essential thing in Christianity has not been made necessary through sin; it was necessary before the fall."[27] [28]

The incarnation was necessary for man as finite, not for man as a sinner. In order that man should become like God, God had to become like man. "This law held as well before as after the fall. . . Now (after the fall) the incarnation brings redemption to man as something subordinate. The emphasis for Rome lies not in reconciliation and forgiveness of sins, but in God becoming man and in man becoming divine."[29]

It was against this view of Christianity that the Reformation set itself. It opposed in particular the proposition that *supernaturale amissa, naturalia adhuc esse integra*.[30] For corresponding to the idea that man is by virtue of finitude inherently defective is the idea that even so he is normal. To reach his supernatural goal he needs, even apart from sin, supernatural grace. But even without supernatural grace he is normal. In Roman thinking man can exist without *justitia supernaturalis*[31] and yet be a good, true, completely sinless man, having a *justitia naturalis*,[32] which in its kind is without fault.[33] [34] At most it can be said that without supernatural grace man is wounded. But to be wounded is mainly

---

27. KSO: Translated in the English edition of Bavinck as "Hence, according to Rome, grace is a supernatural gift as such and not incidentally (*per accidens*), not only because of sin. Sin has not in any way changed the nature of grace. Perhaps grace has been increased by sin; but both before and after the fall it was identically the same, namely, an *elevation* [of man] *above nature*. That is its character and essence. Christianity, accordingly, may also still be a religion of redemption; but preeminently it is not a *reparation* but an *elevation* of nature; it serves to elevate nature above itself, that is, to divinize humanity. In the case of Adam the *gratia gratum faciens* [sanctifying grace] served that goal; now Christianity serves that goal. Hence, then and now his grace is the same; that is, the essential element in Christianity was not necessitated by the fall; it was already necessary before the fall." Herman Bavinck, John Bolt, and John Vriend, *Reformed Dogmatics: God and Creation*, vol. 2 (Grand Rapids, MI: Baker Academic, 2004), 547.
28. Ibid., p. 587.
29. Ibid.
30. KSO: "when the supernatural is lost, the natural is still intact."
31. KSO: "supernatural righteousness."
32. KSO: "natural righteousness."
33. KSO: The reference to Bavinck says this, "In Rome's view a human being can lose the '"supernatural righteousness"' and still be a good, true, complete, sinless human, with a natural justice that in its kind is without any defect." Herman Bavinck, John Bolt, and John Vriend, *Reformed Dogmatics: God and Creation*, vol. 2 (Grand Rapids, MI: Baker Academic, 2004), 551.
34. Ibid., p. 591.

to be incomplete, that is, incomplete as far as man's ultimate end is concerned. Supernatural grace is therefore basically a matter of supplementation.

Bavinck lays great stress on the ethical character of Reformation theology. The work of Christ, his incarnation, his death and his resurrection, together with the infallible setting forth of the meaning of this work in Scripture and the testimony of the Holy Spirit by which the Scripture and the Christ are accepted—is all because of sin.

It is readily understood that there is therefore in Roman theology no place for Scripture in the true sense of the term. There is no strict need for redemption from sin. Since men are not as sinners hostile to God they would not, if left to themselves, hate God and their neighbor. They would not oppose the coming of supernatural revelation. They would not seek to suppress it. Scripture would not need to be once-for-all inscripturated against the ravages of sinful men.

2. Authority

With the Romanist doctrine of the church as standing above Scripture, there is no *necessity* for Scripture in the Protestant sense of the term. Similarly for Romanism there is no place for the authority of Scripture. To be sure, Rome does not deny the authority of Scripture in so many words. On the contrary, she affirms it along with its inspiration. But in practice the Scriptures are made to be dependent upon the church.

"The authenticity, the integrity, the inspiration and authority of Scripture is determined by the church."[35] [36] *Quoad se*[37] the Scripture is said to be independent, but *Quoad nos*[38] it is dependent upon the church. The church does not claim to have inspired the Scriptures, to have made it canonical, etc. But she alone can recognize these characteristics of Scripture infallibly.[39]

The ideal of papal inability is but the logical climax of the Roman concept of the church and of Christianity in general. If Christianity is primarily

---

35. KSO: "The authenticity, integrity, inspiration, canonicity, and authority of Scripture are all established as certain by the church."" Herman Bavinck, John Bolt, and John Vriend, *Reformed Dogmatics: Prolegomena*, vol. 1 (Grand Rapids, MI: Baker Academic, 2003), 455.
36. Ibid., p. 481.
37. KSO: "With respect to itself."
38. KSO: "With respect to us."
39. KSO: "And Roman Catholic theologians distinguish between the authority of Scripture with respect to itself (*quoad se*) and with respect to us (*quoad nos*). But this distinction cannot be applied here. For if the church is the final and most basic reason why I believe Scripture, then the church, and not Scripture, is trustworthy in and of itself (αὐτόπιστος). We have to make a choice: either Scripture contains a witness, a teaching about itself, its inspiration and authority, and in that case the church simply accepts and confirms this witness; or Scripture itself does not teach such an inspiration and authority, and in that case the church's dogma about Scripture stands condemned for a Protestant." Herman Bavinck, John Bolt, and John Vriend, *Reformed Dogmatics: Prolegomena*, vol. 1 (Grand Rapids, MI: Baker Academic, 2003), 457–458.

supplemental to nature, then the idea of the absolute authority of God over man is out of place. The idea of expert authority is then appropriate.

This idea of expert authority is perfectly in "accord with reason." The autonomous man can very well admit that he needs information supplemental to that which he can obtain by reason. The ideal of Christianity as possibly leading him to a super-human destiny is not out of accord with his basic desires. He may even admit that through sin, his reason is *wounded*, that is, even more than otherwise in need of supplemental information and help.

But how can we harmonize this view of Romanism with the following words? "Man being wholly dependent upon God, as upon his Creator and Lord, and created reason being absolutely subject to uncreated truth, we are bound to yield to God, by faith in his revelation, the full obedience of our intelligence and will."[40] The answer lies in the fact that this is to be taken as correlative to what follows: "Nevertheless, in order that the obedience of our faith might be in harmony with reason, God willed that to the interior help of the Holy Spirit there should be joined exterior proofs of his revelation. . ."[41] Thus, on the one hand, men must be "wholly dependent upon God," live by supernatural grace, and receive the interior light of the Holy Spirit, and, on the other hand, man can yield "voluntary obedience to God himself, by assenting to and with his grace, which he is able to resist."[42] Thus the authority of God as it comes to man is never absolute. It is correlative to the idea of human autonomy.

As noted earlier the idea of papal authority is therefore purely arbitrary. The promises of God in Christ as given in Scripture for man's salvation may not be believed as certainly true. That such is the case is asserted on the basis of the infallible authority of the supreme teacher of the church.

3. Perspicuity

From the official documents of the Roman Catholic church we learn not only that there are apostolic traditions supplementing the sacred writings as the church's source of revelation, we learn also that the church alone authoritatively and irreformably interprets both of these sources. Without this infallible interpretation on the part of the church the faithful would be sure to misunderstand its meaning. For the Scriptures are not inherently clear in their presentation of the Christ and his work of redemption. How could there be in the phenomenal world any fully clear interpretation of the course of history? Is not Reality in part controlled by millions of men whose wills are not ultimately under the control of God?

---

40. Schaff, *op. cit.*, Vol. II, pp. 242–243.
41. Ibid., p. 243.
42. Ibid., p. 244.

But this is not the reason given by the church for the necessity of its exclusive explanatory and declarative function. If it gave this reason it would, to be consistent, have to maintain that there can be no full clarity of interpretation anywhere. For on the assumption of the philosophy involved in the idea of human autonomy, as noted before, clarity would have to be by complete or exhaustive logical description. Only if the relations of everything to everything are exhaustively set forth can there then be full clarity. But when the relations of anything would be thus exhaustively set forth, the individuality of the thing would have disappeared. There would then be no change, no history, nothing new, no increment of being. Accordingly, to provide for individuality, for change and for history, there is need of another idea, the idea of pure contingency or chance. This idea must be made correlative to the idea of exhaustive rationality.

The result is that there can be no actually ascertainably clear revelation of God to man in history. And, of course, there can then be no Scripture that is clear in the presentation of its system of truth. For the idea of the system of truth as found in Scripture presupposes the notion of the self-contained God. This God is, naturally, "incomprehensible." That is, he is not fully comprehensible to man, made in the image of God. The idea of the perspicuity of Scripture, therefore, does not mean that its system of truth is logically penetrable to man. On the contrary, as noted above, its system presupposes mystery between God and man. But the mystery between God and man itself presupposes the internal perspicuity of God to himself and therefore a true apprehension of the meaning of the revelation of God by creatures made in his image.

Accordingly man must make every thought captive to the obedience of Christ. Obedience is the mark of true covenant submission. Scripture must be the *supremus judex controversarium*.[43]

The Reformation therefore rejected the idea of the correlativity between reason subjecting itself wholly to revelation and revelation being *quite* in accord with reason. For the false ideal of a rationalistic system made correlative to the false ideal of independent, irrational individuality, it substituted the biblical notion of God attesting himself clearly to men who are as creatures analogous to him in thought and being and who, as sinners, need to be unmistakably challenged by a revelation that cannot be confused with the speculations of the autonomous man. The declarative function of the church must therefore be *ministerialis* rather than *magisterialis*.[44]

---

43. KSO: "supreme judge of controversies." The Roman church declared the pope to be the *supremus judex controversarium*; Van Til's point, along with Protestantism, is that only the Scripture can fulfill this role.

44. KSO: "ministerial rather than magisterial."

AUTONOMY PLUS AUTHORITY: ROMAN CATHOLICISM

4. Sufficiency

Coming now to the question of the sufficiency of Scripture we are again confronted with the idea of tradition; this time with the idea of declarative as added to constitutive tradition. Supernatural revelation comes to the church, says Rome, both through the sacred oracles and through tradition (*in libris scriptis et sine scripto traditionibus, quae ipsius Christi ore ab Apostolis acceptae, aut ab ipsis Apostolis Spiritu Sancto dictante quasi per manus traditae, ad nos usque pervenerunt*).[45][46] The Scriptures without this apostolic tradition are therefore, on this view, not a complete or finished revelation of God. And the Holy Spirit does not testify to the Old and New Testament Scriptures as being alone the Word of God.

So far we have constitutive tradition. Tradition, together with Scripture, constitutes the source of the doctrine of grace. But who is to interpret, i.e., declare, the meaning of the truth as found in Scripture and tradition? Tradition is said to be infallible, but what is contained in this tradition is ultimately determined by the church. Since the Pope, with consent of the church, has declared the infallibility of the supreme teacher of the universal church, it is this teacher who practically determines the content of the traditions.

> When the Pope pronounces a dogma it *ipso facto* becomes apostolic tradition. The criterion of tradition has been successively found in apostolicity, in episcopal succession and in papal declaration. Therewith the end has been reached. The infallible Pope is the *principium formale* of Romanism. *Roma locuta, res finita*. Pope and church, Pope and Christianity are one; *Ubi Papa, ibi ecclesia, ibi religio Christiana, ibi Spiritus*. From the Pope there is no appeal not even to God. Through the Pope God himself speaks to humanity.[47][48]

---

45. KSO: ". . . in the written books, and the unwritten traditions which, received by the Apostles from the mouth of Christ himself, or from the Apostles themselves, the Holy Ghost dictating, have come down even unto us, transmitted as it were from hand to hand:. . ." Philip Schaff, *The Creeds of Christendom, with a History and Critical Notes: The Greek and Latin Creeds, with Translations*, vol. 2 (New York: Harper & Brothers, 1890), 80.

46. Ibid., p. 241.

47. KSO: "For Rome, when the pope proclaims a dogma, it is by that very fact apostolic tradition. The criterion of tradition has therefore been successively found in apostolicity, in episcopal succession, and in papal decision. With that the process has reached its conclusion. The infallible pope is the formal principle of Romanism. When Rome has spoken, the matter is settled (*Roma locuta, res finita*). Where the pope is, there the church is, there the Christian religion is, there the Spirit is (*Ubi Papa, ibi ecclesia, ibi religio Christiana, ibi Spiritus*). One cannot appeal from the pope to a higher authority, not even to God. Through the pope God himself speaks to humanity." Herman Bavinck, John Bolt, and John Vriend, *Reformed Dogmatics: Prolegomena*, vol. 1 (Grand Rapids, MI: Baker Academic, 2003), 485.

48. Bavinck, *op. cit.*, Vol. I, p. 516.

It is thus that with the rejection of the necessity, the perspicuity and the authority of Scripture goes the rejection of its sufficiency. And the rejection of the Scriptures in each instance is due to the desire to make Christianity acceptable to the autonomous man. The idea of the autonomous man is that gods and men are alike expressive of and subject to the conditions of one universe. Accordingly, when man seeks a system of truth this system must be identical with the divine system. The human system cannot be an analogical reproduction of the system revealed by God. The two systems must be one system. There must be identity.

But this identity cannot be attained. This is admitted. Even God has no absolute system. There is no such system. Reality is open. Time is ultimate. Change is one of the ingredients of ultimate reality. The universe or Reality is *open* as well as closed. So God is wholly hidden as well as wholly revealed.

It is because of this correlativity between reality as wholly hidden and wholly revealed that non-Christian thought speaks of the analogy of being and the analogy of thought. The idea of God is then projected as the ideal of complete comprehension of reality. Accordingly, the god of the autonomous man is frequently spoken of as if he had attributes similar to those of the God of Christianity. But the attributes of the god of the autonomous man are projections of his own ideals. He speaks *as if* such a god exists. He speaks *as if* such a god were revealing himself and giving commandments to man. In reality no such god exists.

Since Romanism seeks, on the one hand, to be true to historic Christianity and, on the other hand, to please the autonomous man its "system" is a combination of two mutually opposed systems and even of two mutually opposed ideas of system. When the Roman Catholic speaks of his idea of analogy it is this confusion of two mutually exclusive ideas of system that he is really presenting. On the contrary, the Protestant idea of analogy does not seek to please the autonomous man. It would call the natural man to repentance. It would have him accept the Christian instead of the non-Christian idea of system; the Christian instead of the non-Christian idea of being and knowledge. It would have him submit himself and his thoughts to the obedience of God in Christ.

With a "system" that is itself a confusion of two ideas of system it is quite impossible for Romanism to present the challenge of the gospel to the natural man effectively. Granted that Romanism has in it a large element of true Christianity, this element is counterbalanced and modified by so much that is taken from non-Christian philosophy that it is impossible for the light of the gospel to shine through with clarity and challenge to the man who thinks of himself as properly the final point in predication.

C. THE THOMISTIC PAIDEIA

A few words must now be added concerning the theology of Thomas Aquinas as far as it involves the relation of supernatural revelation to natural theology. This will help to understand the official position of the Roman Catholic church as intimated in the quotations given from its confessions.

In the encyclical letter of Pope Leo XIII the study of St. Thomas is recommended to the teachers of the church in the interest of the spreading of the faith in the following words: "We, therefore, while we declare that everything wisely said should be received with willing and glad mind, as well as everything profitably discovered or thought out, exhort all of you, Venerable Brothers, with the greatest earnestness to restore the golden wisdom of St. Thomas, and to spread it as far as you can, for the safety and the glory of the Catholic Faith, for the good of society, and for the increase of all the sciences."[49][50]

The first thing to note about the approach of Thomas is that he begins his identification of God, in both the *Summa Contra Gentiles* and in the *Summa Theologica*, by means of the natural reason. In other words, at the outset of his theology and controlling everything that he says, he not only assumes but assures us that reason can prove the existence of God. He argues that it cannot say much about the nature of God but he insists that it can prove the existence of God. At first he seems, in the *Contra Gentiles*, to assert that reason can only know of the fact *that* God exists, but cannot know anything about what God is. "Now, in considering the divine substance, we should especially make use of the method of remotion. For, by its immensity, the divine substance surpasses every form that our intellect reaches. Thus we are unable to apprehend it by knowing what it is."[51]

But this very way of remotion, he adds, tells us *something* at least of what God is by telling us what he is not.[52] We shall approach all the nearer to a knowledge of the nature of God even by the way of remotion

> as through our intellect we are able to remove more and more things from Him. For we know each thing more perfectly the more fully we see

---

49. KSO: The full title of this encyclical is *Encyclical Letter of Our Holy Father by Divine Providence, Pope Leo XIII on the Restoration of Christian Philosophy, According to the Mind of St. Thomas Aquinas, the Angelic Doctor.*

50. *The 'Summa Theologica' of St. Thomas Aquinas*, tr. by The Fathers of the English Dominican Province, Vol. I (London: Burns Oates and Washbourne, 1920), p. 31.

51. Thomas Aquinas, *On the Truth of the Catholic Faith* (*Summa Contra Gentiles*) tr. by Anton C. Pegis, Vol. I (Garden City: Hanover House, 1955), p. 96 (I:14.2).

52. KSO: The "way of remotion" is also called the *via negativa*, or way of negation, wherein God is described according to what he *is not*. For example, to say God is infinite is to say he is *not* finite.

its differences from other things; for each thing has within itself its own being, distinct from all other things. So, too, in the case of the things whose definitions we know. We locate them in a genus, through which we know in a general way what they are. Then we add differences to each thing, by which it may be distinguished from other things. In this way, a complete knowledge of a substance is built up.[53]

It is in this way that Thomas combines one principle which, if carried through, would lead to the idea that man can know nothing of God and another principle which, if carried through, would lead to the idea that man can know everything of God. On a Protestant basis the way of remotion or negation cannot be applied at all unless there be first a positive identification of God by himself. Since men are sinners this positive way of identification must be by the way of the self-attesting Christ speaking in the Scriptures. To apply the way of remotion in the manner of Thomas is evidence that one has accepted a way of affirmation that is not based on the Creator-creature distinction, but on the assumption of a unity that is above this distinction. In other words, the irrationalism that is involved in Thomas' way of remotion presupposes and is correlative to the rationalism involved in the idea that man can directly participate in a process of definition by which all reality can be exhaustively known.[54]

It is thus that Thomas seeks to reach the natural man with the teachings of Christianity. He would show to those who do not stand with him on the position of authority that many truths about Christianity are attainable by reason, and that those which are not attainable by reason are at least not contrary to reason. "Some truths about God exceed all the ability of the human reason. Such is the truth that God is triune. But there are some truths which the natural reason also is able to reach. Such are that God exists, that he is one, and the like. In fact, such truths about God have been proved demonstratively by the philosophers, guided by the light of the natural reason."[55]

Thus the natural reason, as employed by the philosophers, can attain to the knowledge of the existence of God and of the nature of God to the extent at least that it knows of his unity. This must be done primarily by the way of remotion. Thomas analyzes this method further when he speaks of univocism,

---

53. Ibid., p. 97 (I:14.2).

54. KSO: Van Til's point is that, because Thomas fails to begin his inquiry into God's existence and character from Scripture, such an inquiry will vacillate between a foundation of "natural reason," or rationalism, on the one hand, and "remotion," or irrationalism, on the other. Both reason and remotion must be grounded in Scripture in order to be properly applied, and to provide "concrete" rather than abstract content.

55. Ibid., p. 63 (I:3.2).

equivocism, and analogy. He says that nothing is predicated univocally of God and of other things.[56] On the other hand, not all names applied to God and creatures are purely equivocal.[57] We must therefore say that terms applied to God and creatures are employed analogically.[58]

He gives several reasons for saying that we cannot predicate univocally of God and creatures. But all the reasons given rest upon the idea that pure univocism implies virtual identity. Parmenides argued that only that can exist which is fully subject to the laws of human logic. In other words Parmenides assumes that the reach of human logic is the limit of possible existence. This involves the ideal identification of the human with the divine mind. There is no divine mind that stands above the human mind at all. In other words this position is purely rationalistic and deterministic. If it were held, the whole of Christianity would at once disappear. This same rationalistic and deterministic motif controls Plato in much of his thinking. His ideal is, as it were, to have men disappear into God. Man's separate self-existence is evil. To the extent that man is individual he has no true being. To be sure, even Plato did not carry this rationalistic motif through completely. Particularly in his later dialogues he saw that such an ideal is destructive of human experience. So he thought to "save appearance" by making concessions.

But Aristotle from the start of his major work contends that rationalism and determinism must not be taken as the only and all-controlling principle. We must not be definition-mongers. We must not hold that even our first principles of thought are demonstrable; they must rather be taken as intuitive lest we go about in circles. Thus what seemed to be a defect to Plato, namely, that the idea of substance is not wholly reducible by definition, is from the point of view of Aristotle a great virtue.

Thomas follows Aristotle rather than Plato in this idea of primary substance as being individual as well as specific. It is this point that he begins from in both of his *Summae*. When arguing for the existence of God, we must not, he says, hold that this existence is self-evident. To be sure, the existence of God is self-evident in itself. But it is not self-evident to us. The reason for this is that we do not know the essence of God. "But, because what it is to be God is not evident to us, the proposition is not self-evident to us, and needs to be made evident. This is done by means of things which, though less evident in themselves, are nevertheless more evident to us by means, namely, of God's effects."[59] Accord-

56. Ibid., p. 143 (I:32).
57. Ibid., p. 145 (I:33).
58. Ibid., p. 147 (I:34).
59. *St. Thomas Aquinas Summa Theologiae*, gen. ed. Thomas Gilby, O. P., Vol. II (New York: McGraw-Hill, 1964), p. 7 (1a.2).

ingly, Thomas also contends constantly that all human knowledge begins from sensation. Our knowledge must to this extent be empirical.[60]

With this rejection of Parmenidean rationalism in its various forms considered in itself we can have no quarrel. But what is the foundation that underlies the notion of equivocism in the name of which Platonic univocism is rejected? Is it the positive idea of God's creation of the world? Is it the idea that in each fact of the universe surrounding man he is confronted with the plan of God, and therefore with an element of mystery? Certainly this is not the case with Aristotle. His principle of individuation is wholly irrational. So when he argues for the existence of God he argues by way of remotion till he reaches the idea of deity as a specific or generic unity as an ideal rather than that of numerical individual existence.

As for Thomas, he does defend the idea of creation. One would therefore expect that he would set his principle of individuation clearly over against that of Aristotle. One would think that he would say that we must start from the senses because in the world about us we are surrounded with the created reality of God. But Thomas does not do this. To be sure he does say that "Now, the knowledge of the principles that are known to us naturally has been planted in us by God; for God is the Author of our nature. These principles, therefore, are also contained by the divine Wisdom."[61] He constantly falls back on the idea of creation of man by God. Yet, so far as he does this, he has already taken the Christian point of view for granted, and it is his purpose to prove the truth of the Christian position to "reason." He assumes that even those who do not think of man as created by God have used their reason correctly in essentials.

So when he constantly refers to the fact that human knowledge is derived from the senses he must, to be true to his method, assume with Aristotle and others, that there is a non-rational, wholly contingent, principle of individuation.[62] The only principle of equivocism that those who hold to a non-Christian principle of univocism can understand and accept is an irrationalist one. And this is the kind of principle of equivocism that Aquinas constantly employs. For him the fact that our knowledge as human beings is derived from the senses is evidence of its lack of universality and therefore of its uncertainty. Accordingly, knowledge is defective to the extent that the senses are involved. But such a view is not consistent with the idea of creation and providence. If God has made all things and if he controls

---

60. KSO: For further discussion of Thomas's metaphysical and epistemological problems, including his view of self-evidence, see K. Scott Oliphint, *Thomas Aquinas (Great Thinkers)* (Phillipsburg, NJ: Presbyterian and Reformed Publishing Company, 2017): esp. chapter 2.

61. Thomas Aquinas, *On the Truth of the Catholic Faith*, Vol. I, p. 74 (I:7.1).

62. KSO: That is, the principle of individuation is "non-rational" because it is necessarily empirical (thus, based on the senses, not on the rational) and is "wholly contingent" because any individual thing that exists does not exist *necessarily*; it might not have existed.

all things by his plan, then knowledge from sensation is no less certain and true than is knowledge obtained more directly by intellection proper.

One further point must be mentioned in connection with Thomas' idea of analogy. It indirectly establishes the point made just now about the non-Christian character of his principle of individuation. The point is that just as Thomas supplements the non-Christian idea of univocism by means of a non-Christian idea of equivocism so in turn he supplements the non-Christian idea of equivocism by a non-Christian idea of univocism. In other words what Thomas does is to seek to avoid the extremes of univocism and equivocism by keeping the two in balance with one another.

Using the idea of equivocism without first placing it upon the Christian doctrine of creation leads him to complete skepticism. He could not then rightfully claim that we can argue from effect to cause. There is no justification for thinking that the cause and effect relation obtains between the things with which human knowledge deals unless it be based upon the presupposition of the doctrine of the comprehensive plan of God.

But the whole approach of Thomas is to the effect that man does know the relations and even the essences of created things without at all referring them to their Creator and controller. It is quite in accord with his basic principle of theology as well as in accord with his basic principle of apologetics that he should assume this. If one holds to the idea of human autonomy in theology to such an extent that he thinks man can resist the plan of God, he has therewith set aside the all-comprehensiveness of that plan; he has to some extent introduced the non-Christian notion of individuality as being what it is by chance.[63] He has also introduced the non-Christian notion of universality as being above God and man. So then Thomas thinks he has the right to argue from effect to cause without first inquiring into the differences in meaning between the idea of cause when used by Christians and the idea of cause when used by those who do not take the Christian position.

And it is this uncritical assumption that vitiates the entire argument for the existence of God that he offers, and in fact vitiates his approach to every other problem in philosophy and in theology. For Aristotle the idea of cause is not that of production. It is rather that of a principle of explanation. Particularly when he speaks of God as the first cause or the prime Mover, this does not mean for him that God has created the world. For him God does not even exist as a numerical being. God does not know himself. He is not self-conscious. He is an "it." This sort of god is the logical outcome of Aristotle's method. With his assumption of

---

63. KSO: "By chance," because man's autonomous choices are outside God's control, thus, in that sense, arbitrary.

human ultimacy and therefore with his further assumption of the idea of rationality as inherent in a reality that envelops gods as well as men, and still further with his assumption that Chance is ultimately the source of individuality, there was no other god that Aristotle could logically find. His god is the logical result of following the way of remotion in the way that Thomas too employs it.

Thomas argues that God is his own essence. In God essence and existence are the same. But on his principle of knowledge Thomas cannot relate the existence and the essence of God at all. One cannot relate these two except by presupposing their mutual implication and then starting from this God as the presupposition of all predication. The way of remotion can tell us nothing of the nature of God unless we have first determined the significance of the way of remotion itself by the way of positive creation and revelation.[64] We could know nothing about a thing by knowing how that thing differs from other things unless we presuppose that all things that we know have intelligible relations to one another by virtue of God's providence. This is the critical point. Thomas assumes the non-Christian principle of abstract Parmenidean rationalism even while he rejects it. How could man know what God is by knowing what he is not, unless we have first enveloped God with ourselves in a common universe of abstract rationality? It is only if first with the early Greeks we assume that all reality has one character, that we can also with Anaximander assert that God is indeterminate. So also the method of Thomas should lead him to say that God is both wholly determinable and wholly indeterminable by man. But as a Christian theologian he does not believe this. The result is that he confuses that which he believes as a Christian and that which his method requires him to hold as a would-be neutral reasoner.[65]

It remains now to indicate the significance of what has been said about the general principles of Thomas' theory of knowledge for the idea of scriptural revelation.

The idea of Scripture as the word of the self-contained God of Christianity cannot be accepted if Thomas' principles are true. If these principles are true, there is no necessity for Scripture in the Protestant sense of the term. For man is then not a sinner in the sense that he is spiritually blind to the truth. The principles of the natural man, even when they are inherently destructive of the Christian position are, nonetheless, assumed to be such that man can by means of them know the truth about reality.

Man can by means of them know much about the nature of God. There are

---

64. KSO: Van Til is emphasizing the point that "brute facts" cannot lead to a first cause, or to anything else, since their interpretation is entirely dependent on the interpreter. To understand facts properly, and thus apply a proper "way of remotion," one needs to see them as created by God and as revealing him.

65. KSO: This sentence is a helpful summary of the problems in Thomas.

many things about God, the fact that he is eternal, that he knows all things, that he knows singulars, etc., which Thomas *proves* about God. But the god about which all this is proved is at most a god who is correlative to the universe. So the god thus proved as existing does not stand above man. He cannot give a finished revelation of his will to man. He cannot even clearly speak to man. He is not a person; he is an "it."

All this is not to say that as a Christian theologian Thomas does not hold in some sense to Christian teaching. It is to say that the natural theology as worked out by him fits in with the natural theology of the official documents of the Roman Catholic church and is, therefore, inherently inimical to the Protestant idea of Scripture.[66]

The conclusion of the matter is that the Roman Catholic view of Scripture cannot be understood for what it is unless it is seen as the climactic expression of the Roman Catholic synthesis of the Greek and the Christian *paideia*. This synthesis consists of negative theology, of mystical theology, of symbolic theology and of natural theology. It is a synthesis of Aristotle plus Christ.[67]

D. VATICAN II[68]

We ask now whether the situation has changed because of the decisions of Vatican II.[69] Through the official decisions of Vatican II, Mother church is again calling

---

66. KSO: Note: *"natural theology of the regenerate*; in the context of the universal Protestant assumption that fallen natural reason and/or pagan philosophy could produce no saving knowledge of God, the connection between natural and revealed theology was necessarily severed, raising the question of the possibility of finding truths about God in the created order. Beza is usually credited with the formal statement of a natural theology of the regenerate, a sense of the divine work in creation, useful to Christian theology, but possible only in the context of a prior saving knowledge of God." Richard A. Muller, *Dictionary of Latin and Greek Theological Terms: Drawn Principally from Protestant Scholastic Theology* (Grand Rapids, Mich.: Baker Book House, 1985), 302–303.

67. KSO: It is crucial to recognize the inextricable link between Aquinas and the Roman Catholic Church. There may be bits and pieces that can be extracted from Thomas's writings and incorporated into a Reformed systematic theology, but, to the extent that Thomas was consistent, his system holds together only in a Roman Catholic context. To see one example of the end result of Protestants embracing Thomas, see Douglas Beaumont, *Evangelical Exodus*, (Ignatius Press, 2016) and K. Scott Oliphint, "Review of Evangelical Exodus: Evangelical Seminarians and Their Paths to Rome," *Themelios* 41, no. 2 (2016).

68. More detailed discussions of recent movements within Roman Catholicism will be found in the present writer's "Hans urs Von Balthasar" and "Hans Küng" in *Christianity and Barthianism* (Presbyterian and Reformed. 1962), pp. 319–386. For a study of modern work among Roman Catholic philosophers, see the writer's "Pierre Teilhard de Chardin—Evolution and Christ" (*Westminster Theological Journal*, Vol. XVIII, No. 2; May, 1966; available in reprint from Presbyterian and Reformed Pub. Co.).

69. KSO: "Vatican II, also termed the Twenty-first Ecumenical Church Council, was convened by Pope John XXIII in October 1962, and reconvened for several separate sessions by Pope Paul VI

the present writer, together with all Protestants, back to its bosom.[70] The council of Trent and Vatican I also called this writer back to the fold. But at that time her voice was stern. He was said to be a "heretic." All his labors for the kingdom of Christ would be lost and he himself stood in jeopardy of losing his part in Christ as his Savior, unless he returned to Mother Church. Through Vatican II Mother church speaks with a soft and pleading voice. The present writer is now one of the "departed brethren." He has really all the while been in the "soul" of the church. How wonderful it would be if he could now at last, after all his wandering, join its body too.

At this point then the writer will give his reasons why, even now, he cannot return to Mother church. He appreciates greatly the difference in the tone of voice used in Vatican II as over against that used at Trent. He would emulate the fine courtesy with which representatives of Mother church now seek him out for dialogue. Even so, the writer believes the theology of the Mother church as expressed in Vatican II is not significantly different from the theology of Trent. The theology of Trent was basically unacceptable to the Reformers. The theology of Vatican II is basically unacceptable today to the sons of the Reformers.

1. Herman Bavinck on Trent[71]

We have already set forth some of the main teachings of the Council of Trent and of Vatican I as these are found in the official documents of the church. At this point we add a summary of what Herman Bavinck says about the historical influence of the teachings of Trent.[72]

Speaking of the doctrines formulated at Trent with respect to the concepts of tradition, sin, free will and justification, Bavinck says that in them the true nature of Roman Catholic thought, as opposed to Protestantism, has come to light.[73] Says Bavinck: "Pelagianism and Curialism have developed themselves further after Trent and attained to a complete victory."[74]

This development appears in the fact that the order of Jesuits became

---

from September 1963 until its conclusion in 1965." Paul P. Enns, *The Moody Handbook of Theology* (Chicago, IL: Moody Press, 1989), 603.

70. KSO: "No longer calling for a return to the Roman Catholic church as the true church, Vatican II recognized non-Catholics as legitimate Christian communities. Non-Catholic Christians were now referred to as "separated brethren," and Vatican II allowed for Catholics to engage in public worship together with Protestants." Ibid., 604.

71. KSO: See Herman Bavinck, John Bolt, and John Vriend, *Reformed Dogmatics: Prolegomena* (Grand Rapids, MI: Baker Academic, 2003), 143–144.

72. Bavinck, *op. cit.*, Vol. I.

73. Ibid., p. 143.

74. Ibid., p. 145.

prominent after Trent. In general the Jesuits followed the theology of Thomas Aquinas but departed from him in their Pelagian view of sin, of free will and of grace.[75]

At the beginning of the eighteenth century the influence of the rationalistic spirit of Descartes and other modern philosophers influenced Roman Catholic as well as Protestant theologians.[76] As a consequence "confessional differences were forgotten. . . An attack on freethinkers replaced that of polemics against Protestantism."[77]

Even in the beginning of the nineteenth century many Roman theologians ascribed to reason the right to determine what is revelation.[78]

After the period of rationalistic influence the church experienced a renewal of its spirit.[79] The general movement of romanticism proved advantageous to the church.[80] Friedrich Schleiermacher's views on Scripture, regeneration, justification and the church had their appeal.[81] But this new theology à la Schleiermacher was too concessive to Protestantism.[82] Another neo-scholasticism appeared. The Jesuit movement waxed stronger and stronger again. And in 1870 Vatican I declared the infallibility of the Pope.[83] In 1879 Pope Leo XIII commended the study of St. Thomas in his encyclical *Aeterni Patris*.[84]

Again a new theology appeared in the form of Americanism or Reform-Catholicism. This new theology saw much that was good in modern culture and strove to have the church make concessions with respect to it.[85] But positive Protestantism would be unwise, says Bavinck, to expect anything favorable from such a new theology. This new theology has no intelligible principle by which properly to determine the nature of the gospel.[86]

In 1899 the Pope condemned this Americanism in a letter to Cardinal Gibbons. But even this condemnation could not arrest the development of the modern spirit in the church of Rome.

Then, concluding his survey of the Roman Catholic development of dogma, Bavinck draws an all-important conclusion. The serious significance of every

---

75. Ibid., p. 147.
76. Ibid., p. 148.
77. Ibid., p. 149.
78. Ibid.
79. Ibid., p. 150.
80. Ibid.
81. Ibid., p. 151.
82. Ibid.
83. Ibid.
84. Ibid.
85. Ibid., p. 152.
86. Ibid., p. 153.

tendency within the Church of Rome since the time of Trent does not lie in the fact that she may lose a few or more of its members to *positive* or *negative* Protestantism. The whole significance of all the internal dissensions within the Roman church lies in the question as to how far these dissensions reveal a deep, inner conflict between the old faith and the modern consciousness in the church itself.[87]

2. G. C. Berkouwer on Vatican II

Today Dr. G. C. Berkouwer speaks of a "new climate of life and thought in the Catholic church."[88]

Through the influence of such men as Yves Congar[89] and others there has come about, says Berkouwer, "a more open-mindedness toward the Reformation which in turn has created a far better possibility for dialogue than has been known since the sixteenth century."[90] "Roman Catholics are putting increasing emphasis on the new possibility of an existential encounter between Rome and the Reformation."[91] "Van de Pol,[92] for example, . . . rejects the traditional black-white picture and speaks of the *providential* task that the Reformation shall one day fulfill."[93] There is, says Berkouwer, in the church "a more inclusive vision of the truth" than was formerly present there. He adds that "obviously, to speak of a simple 'return' to the Mother church does not fit well with this. Rather, we hear of a 'growing together toward the fulness of Christ.'"[94] "Catholic theologians are insisting urgently that Catholic theology refuses to sacrifice *sola fide-sola gratia* to the Reformation, that Catholicism too seeks to preserve the truth of the complete gratuity of grace."[95] Was not this the "deepest intent of Trent?" they say.[96] The

---

87. Ibid.
88. G. C. Berkouwer, *The Second Vatican Council and the New Catholicism*, tr. by L. B. Sinedes (Grand Rapids: Wm. B. Eerdmans, 1965), p. 34.
89. KSO: Georges-Yves Congar (1904–95). "After publishing a controversial article in which he ascribed the alienation of French culture from the Church to the latter's 'disfigured visage', in 1936 he announced a series of ecclesiological studies under the title '*Unam Sanctam*'. The first of these was his own *Chrétiens désunis* (1937; Eng. tr., Divided Christendom, 1939), in which he sought to work out 'principles for Catholic ecumenism' in the light of the different conceptions of unity, and so of ecumenism, among liberal Protestants, Anglicans, and the Orthodox." F. L. Cross, ed., *The Oxford Dictionary of the Christian Church*, third edition, (Oxford University Press, 2005), 401.
90. Ibid., p. 39.
91. Ibid., p. 40.
92. KSO: Willem Hendrik van de Pol (1897–1988) was a Dutch theologian. Originally in the Dutch Reformed Church, he wrote his dissertation on the life and thought of John Henry Newman. Like Newman, he converted to Roman Catholicism and was ordained a priest in 1944.
93. Ibid.
94. Ibid.
95. Ibid., p. 41.
96. Ibid., p. 43.

new theologians, says Berkouwer, are bringing into the arena of discussion new insights into the Catholic doctrines of justification, Scripture and tradition, the infallibility of the church and so forth. We contend that we are observing a new interpretative phase of Roman Catholicism.[97] A basic question facing Protestants is, whether the new theology aims merely at "new forms of expression" of the old faith or at radical revision of the Confession of the Church.[98]

In our estimation of the nature of the tensions within the Mother church the question of Scripture is, says Berkouwer, all important. The new theologians argue that Trent "leaves Catholics free to identify themselves with the notion that tradition is not a source of revelation on the same level with Scripture, but is only an *interpretative* source. Trent, it is argued, leaves Catholics free to identify themselves with the very ancient tradition of the church according to which *all the truth of salvation is contained in Scripture.*"[99]

Berkouwer speaks of "the new accent on Scripture" found in the "new theology" of recent Roman Catholic writers. The exponents of the "new theology" object to understanding Trent as though it spoke of tradition as a source of revelation on a par with Scripture. Can we then now speak of "a Roman Catholic version of *sola Scriptura*? Rahner[100] considers it *absurd* to suppose that God's revelation 'in broad outline' is contained in the Scriptures while there are other elements of revelation so different from the content of Scripture that they are derived from *another* source."[101]

"All kinds of questions rise out of the new situation" says Berkouwer, "foremost of which in our minds is whether a new outlook is now possible in regard to the Reformation doctrine of *sola Scriptura* which, until now, has been considered, along with *sola fide*, *sola gratia* and *solo Christo*, an exclusive Reformation credo."[102]

"If the disagreement no longer can be centered on the question of a single or a plural source of revelation, where does the disagreement lie?" Geiselmann[103]

---

97. Ibid., p. 53.
98. Ibid., p. 54.
99. Ibid., p. 97.
100. KSO: Karl Rahner (1904–1984). "Rahner was the author of a very large number of books and articles. The ultimate source of his thought is to be found in Joseph Maréchal's vast work *Le Point de départ de la métaphysique* (1923–49), which attempted to construct a revised system of Thomist metaphysics which would take account of and be immune to the criticism of I. Kant." F. L. Cross, ed., *The Oxford Dictionary of the Christian Church*, third edition, (Oxford University Press, 2005), 1371.
101. Ibid., p. 98.
102. Ibid., p. 97.
103. KSO: J. R. Geiselmann (1890–1970) was for years the authority of the Tübingen school for the Roman Catholic church. One of his most influential works was *Scripture and Tradition (Die Heilige Schrift und die Tradition)* (1962).

speaks of a "'rehabilitation' of tradition among Reformed writers."[104] Must we join Geiselmann when he says that: "the turning of Catholic theology to Scripture and the return of evangelical theology to tradition offers us the hope for a fruitful dialogue on Scripture and tradition."[105] If we do we shall find encouragement in Oscar Cullmann[106] who says that the Roman Catholic and the Protestant viewpoints on Scripture and tradition "have drawn astonishingly close together."[107] Says Berkouwer: "Cullmann calls for a discussion 'without polemical motives,' and his plea is even more relevant in the light of recent events."[108]

·———·

Berkouwer should have added two additional points, which Cullmann makes, in this connection. The first is to the effect that Cullmann calls for discussion between Roman Catholics and Protestants not only "without polemical motives" but "with complete openness." But what does Cullmann mean by this "new openness?" Cullmann wants, to be sure, to "start from a New Testament foundation." He does not want faith in Christ to be endangered.[109] Both Catholics and Protestants want to be faithful to Christ.[110] What "prevents the Protestants from returning to Rome is primarily the concept of the church, of infallibility, of unity just as our concept of the church and her unity must prevent the Catholic church from recognizing the Protestant churches as legitimate churches."[111]

Yet "it cannot be the will of God that several churches exist which exclude one *another*... Thus unity is the most important characteristic of the church." And "this unity is basically connected with the fact that it is the *Holy Spirit* which constitutes the church... It is the Spirit's nature to bring men together after having touched them."[112]

---

104. Ibid., p. 98.
105. Ibid.
106. KSO: Oscar Cullmann (1902–99). "NT scholar and theologian. Born at Strasbourg, he studied at the universities of Strasbourg and Paris, and in 1930 he became professor in the former. In 1938 he became professor at Basle and from 1948 to 1972 he was simultaneously also professor in the Protestant faculty of the University of Paris. Cullmann's work lay in the area of Biblical Theology, and he was specially concerned in developing a theory of Heilsgeschichte. This was expounded in *Christus und die Zeit* (1946; Eng. tr., *Christ and Time*, 1951)." F. L. Cross, ed., *The Oxford Dictionary of the Christian Church*, third edition, (Oxford University Press, 2005), 442.
107. Ibid., p. 99.
108. Ibid.
109. Oscar Cullmann, *A Message to Catholics and Protestants* (Grand Rapids: Eerdmans, 1959), p. 27.
110. Ibid., p. 21.
111. Ibid., p. 22.
112. Ibid., p. 12.

We "must consider one another as brothers in Christ."[113] When we consider one another as brothers, we can appreciate one another's publications in the field of dogmatics. Says Cullmann:

> As an example I point to the works of my colleague, Karl Barth: certainly no one can say that he has Catholic tendencies. Various Catholic books have appeared recently, stamped with the Imprimatur. They draw attention to basic differences; but, on the other hand, they discover a profound agreement on essential questions of faith. We might mention the book by Hans Urs von Balthasar,[114] which was published several years ago, the three volumes by Pere Bouillard, a Jesuit in Paris, and even a dissertation on justification in the theology of Karl Barth, which Hans Küng,[115] a young priest in Lucerne, now professor in Münster, defended at the Catholic faculty a short time ago. Karl Barth agreed to write a foreword to this book, in which he declared that, if what Küng represents as the Roman doctrine of justification actually is their doctrine, then he would have to recognize that his doctrine agrees with theirs.[116]

Now "this change in relations among the theologians should become visible to the layman. . ." We "should not continue a cold war when among the theologians peace was declared long ago."[117]

If now the "solidarity which has existed for a period of years among theologians" is to appear more publicly what can we do? In the first place we must pray, since "prayer always unites."[118] But when we pray for unity we must not, while praying

---

113. Ibid., p. 27.
114. KSO: Hans Urs von Balthasar (1905–1988). "From 1940 to 1948 he was university chaplain at Basle. Here he met K. Barth, on whom he published an important study in 1951. . . His greatest achievement, however, lay in his theological trilogy: *Herrlichkeit: Eine theologische Ästhetik* (3 vols. in 7, 1961–9 [incomplete]; Eng. tr., *The Glory of the Lord*, 7 vols., 1982–91), to which *Glaubhaft ist nur Liebe* (1963; Eng. tr., *Love Alone*, 1968) was an introduction; *Theodramatik* (4 vols. in 5, 1973–83; Eng. tr. 5 vols., 1988–98), and *Theologik* (1985)." F. L. Cross, ed., *The Oxford Dictionary of the Christian Church*, third edition, (Oxford University Press, 2005), 149.
115. KSO: Hans Küng, (1928–2021). "A Swiss Roman Catholic theologian, who has taught at Tübingen since 1960. Küng's theological work has been dominated by three main concerns: apologetics, ecumenism, and reform in the Roman Catholic Church. He sees his most important task as a theologian to be that of using all the resources of modern theology to present the Christian gospel as a credible and relevant message for the modern world." Sinclair B. Ferguson and J.I. Packer, *New Dictionary of Theology* (Downers Grove, IL: InterVarsity Press, 2000), 373.
116. Ibid., p. 28–29.
117. Ibid., p. 30.
118. Ibid., p. 31.

think about the *manner and means* of realizing the unity of the church.... When the Catholics pray as believing Catholics for the unity of the church, they must be exclusive, they must pray for our subjection to Rome. We conceive of unity in an entirely different manner, and when we pray for unity, we must pray that the Catholics stop being Catholics, i.e., change their concept of the church. To be sure, our prayers meet in heaven, and God knows which is the true unity. But we must recognize, although it may be painful, that we remain separated even when we pray for unity if we think at all about the manner and means of achieving unity. When prayer for unity is not offered in an ecumenical spirit, then it may even deepen the chasm between us. I have heard of cases in which the week of prayer became a time of hunting for 'heretics.' The danger always exists that prayer for unity will become the prayer of two opponents, each praying for the defeat of the other. I do not wish to assert that it necessarily comes to this, but the danger exists. Everything depends on the spirit in which unity is prayed for. It can deepen the separation between brothers instead of strengthening their brotherhood. And yet, although the danger cannot be avoided as soon as we think of how to achieve unity, we must continue the practice of praying for unity; God will hear and purify our prayers."[119]

In addition to thus praying for unity without thinking about differences pertaining to the concept of the church we must practice charity toward one another as "brother *in* Christ—in the same Christ, our mutual Lord. An offering for one another should be a symbol of an actual fact, not of the unity of the church, but of the solidarity of all who are baptized into Christ and invoke his name."[120] It is thus that we might give "an ecumenical demonstration"[121] of "the brotherhood which exists in a divided Christianity."[122]

It is clear that if Protestants were to act on Cullman's proposal they would thereby indicate that the historic Protestant view of Scriptural teaching as normative for the idea of the church is no longer of significance to them. And further, in spite of Cullmann's contention the Christian solidarity that he proposes to establish is nothing more than humanitarianism decked with a "Christian symbol." On Cullmann's proposal the Bible, as it was held by Luther and Calvin, disappears altogether. Mother church might seem to gain by this but she too would eventually lose all that is left of historic Christian teaching in her faith

---

119. Ibid., p. 32.
120. Ibid., p. 36–37.
121. Ibid., p. 38.
122. Ibid., p. 39.

and practice. The "complete openness" with which Cullmann wants Protestants to reconsider their doctrine of Scripture is, in effect, already a complete denial of the historic Protestant view of Scripture. It shows itself to be this in Cullmann's proposal of union between Protestants and Catholics.

The second point that Berkouwer should have considered flows from the first. It is to the effect that Cullmann refers to Karl Barth as a representative of the Protestant position. He says that such Catholic writers as Hans Urs von Balthasar, Henri Bouillard and Hans Küng find basic similarities between Roman Catholic theology and the theology of Barth. This is obviously true. But it corroborates the contention made just before that it is the "new" Protestantism rather than historic Protestantism that Catholics think of when they think of a possible agreement with respect to the relation of Scripture to tradition. Cullmann says that no one suspects Karl Barth of having Catholic tendencies. This is true enough. It is equally true, and of far deeper significance, that no one should suspect Barth of having any orthodox Protestant tendencies. However much he may be concerned to stress his contention that the Bible *is* the Word of God he is, if possible, more deeply concerned to point out that this word *is* must not be taken in the historic orthodox sense of direct revelation. If it were to be so taken we should fall back, Barth argues, into the position of the blessed possessors (*beati possidentes*). Revelation must, to be sure, be historical, but history must never be taken as directly revelational.

Is it any wonder that Catholic theologians are more than happy to see a great Protestant theologian cast away the historic Protestant doctrine of Scripture? Why worry any longer about the question whether tradition should be set next to Scripture as a second source of revelation?

Has Trent, has the first, has the second Vatican council, has any Catholic theologian, past or present, ever gone further than has Barth in virtually denying the *sola scriptura* principle of Luther and of Calvin? They have not. They could not.[123]

Moreover, what is true with respect to the doctrine of Scripture is true with respect to the content of Scripture teaching. The content of Scripture centers in Christ. And who is Christ? The historic Christian church has answered this question in the Chalcedon creed. But lest the words of Chalcedon be taken to be what the *beati possidentes* want them to be, namely, directly revelational of God Barth has, he says, actualized the incarnation.

Again, Catholic theologians have more than they could have wished for from any Protestant in Barth's theology. If, on their view, the church is the

---

123. Cf. the writer's *The New Modernism* (Presbyterian and Reformed, 1947) and his "Has Karl Barth Become Orthodox" (*Westminster Theological Journal*, Vol. XVI, No. 2; May, 1954).

continuation of the incarnation, for Barth God is wholly identical with his revelation in Christ. Moreover as God *is* his revelation in Christ so he *is* his work of salvation of all men.[124] Has Trent, has the first, has the second Vatican council ever gone further than this in virtually denying the *solo Christo* principle of Luther and of Calvin? They have not. They could not.

What such recent Catholic theologians as Balthasar now visualize as their goal is to catch up with such Protestants as Barth in presenting a philosophy of history in which Christ is the "integrating principle" alike of man and of nature.[125] Barth unites all things in heaven and on earth by means of his "Christ-Event." Balthasar follows the same path.[126] Balthasar realizes that Barth has out-distanced all previous Catholic theology by means of his modern existentialist categories of thought. Lest Roman Catholic theology should fall behind Protestantism in striving for the ideal of uniting all things, natural and supernatural, in the Christ-Event Balthasar proposes that modern existential categories of thought be added to the essentialist categories of Aristotle in the construction of the church's philosophy of history.[127]

We must now be true to Trent while going beyond it. We must now be true to Thomas Aquinas while going beyond him. Speaking of Thomas Aquinas, Balthasar says: "He does indeed do justice to the intimately Christological form of grace, and it is not difficult to go on from there to deduce its ecclesiological form and scope. But high scholasticism was too essentialist in its thinking to bring into prominence the personal power of Christian grace as creative of situations."[128]

As Christian believers we must see that Christ "assumed our history and tradition into himself."[129] "All existences, both before him and after him, receive their meaning from Christ's existence."[130] In "recapitulating history" Christ "becomes its norm."[131]

In taking an essentialist-existentialist approach to theology we do better

---

124. Cf. the writer's "Karl Barth on Chalcedon" (*Westminster Theological Journal*, Vol. XXII, No. 2; May, 1960). See also his *Barth's Christology* (1962) and *Karl Barth and Evangelicalism* (1964). Both by Presbyterian and Reformed Pub. Co.

125. Hans Urs Von Balthasar, *A Theological Anthropology* (New York: Sheed and Ward, 1967), p. 86.

126. Ibid., p. 79.

127. KSO: By "existential categories of thought" Van Til means, roughly, that history must be defined, not simply by virtue of what it is *essentially*, but also by its *becoming*. In that way, Barth's "actualizing" of the incarnation fits perfectly, in that it focuses on an "*Event*" rather than on the doctrines taught in Scripture.

128. Hans Urs Von Balthasar, *A Theology of History* (New York: Sheed and Ward, 1963), p. 69.

129. Ibid., p. 70.

130. Ibid., p. 71.

131. Ibid., p. 79.

justice both to the uniqueness and to the universal significance of the Christ-Event than historic scholasticism was able to do. There is no longer any danger that the contingency aspect of God's revelation through Christ in history be prematurely eternalized by the overbearing claims of eternal universals. "There is no moment at which he is *universale ante rem*, [i.e., universal prior to the thing] an essence *preceding* existence, in so far as the *res* [i.e., thing] is his own historical existence."[132] On the other hand, there is no longer any danger that the universal aspect of God's revelation through Christ in history will be lost in pure contingency. "He is the *universale in re*, [i.e., universal in the thing] the supra-temporal *in* time, the universally valid *in* the here-and-now, necessary being *in* concrete fact; in the thirty-three years of his life the accent is on the *res*, and during the forty days on the *universale*."[133]

From this point, argues Balthasar, we can go on to the second level of universalization, the sacramental level.[134] Christ's existence, "and hence his mode of duration" is the same in the sacraments as it was in the forty days.[135] Accordingly "by becoming contemporaneous with the believer in the sacrament, the Lord bestows upon him the possibility, given him in faith, of becoming like him who became man."[136] Balthasar continues: "In this communion between the Lord and his church there comes into existence a kind of time which is sacramental, and most especially eucharistic. Its peculiar character is that the eternal Lord is constantly coming afresh into contemporaneity with his Bride, but without becoming subject to or measurable by passing time."[137]

We must go one step further with Balthasar. "The third level," he says, "perfects the work of the forty days and the sacraments by placing the church and the individual spiritually under the abiding norm of the life of the Lord."[138]

On this third level of universalization it is the Spirit "who comes to the fore. . . in the fulness of his personal sovereignty."[139] The Spirit "allows the individual his own will, his choice, his freedom. He does not impose himself from without, but works in the inner source of the created spirit, not as 'another' but as exalted

---

132. KSO: The point Van Til is highlighting here, both from von Balthasar and from Barth, is that the historical has become all-encompassing; there is nothing "before" the historical that can give history its meaning. Since "existential categories of thought" are now predominant, it is the *process*, the *Event*, that has significance.
133. Ibid., p. 89.
134. Ibid., pp. 90–91.
135. Ibid., p. 91.
136. Ibid., p. 93.
137. Ibid., p. 95.
138. Ibid., p. 97.
139. Ibid., p. 98.

above all otherness (*de non aliud*: Nicholas of Cusa), so immanent that he is often indistinguishable from the natural spirit."[140]

As the divine norm working within man the Spirit works as the "Spirit of Christ, of the Logos." This excludes every form of arbitrariness. In his interpretations the Spirit "is not only subjective and personal, but objective, absolute Spirit, containing in himself a whole cosmos of super-personal truth." The Spirit "forms and gives life to the church founded by Christ, which proceeds from his humanity sacrificed on the cross." Thus "the whole structure of the church's being is formed of his inmost spirit. She embodies the meaning of his coming, of the fact that he is, of the way that he is."[141]

And so completely is the faith of the individual believer taken up into the church, that the church may be called "the collective consciousness of all believers. . . . There is a point in each individual consciousness when thinking with the church (*sentire cum ecclesia*) becomes *sentire ecclesiae*, the thinking of the church, which is not ultimately separable from thinking of the Holy Spirit, *sentire Spiritus Sancti*."[142]

It is in this framework of thought that Balthasar sets his view of Scripture and tradition. They are organs which play their part in the normative function of the church:

> Scripture is the Logos objectified and made the norm for all ages by the Holy Spirit in the context of the Incarnation. According to Origen it is the body of the divine Son *in so far as* he is the Logos, the truth-word. It is a 'body' formed by the Holy Spirit, the first 'hearer' of the Word. As the Spirit 'receives' the Word, so, and not otherwise, in just that form, with that shape, with that emphasis, he causes it to be written for the Church. And since that which he has heard in truth is infinitely richer and deeper than what can be comprised in a body made of letters, he has also undertaken, as the Spirit, to explain to the Church that which he has heard, in the Church's *tradition*. Because letter cannot of its very nature be the same thing as spirit, and because what is written is necessarily fragmentary (Jn 20:30; 21:25), the Church is the interpreter of what has already been uttered in revelation, but is continually being illuminated in new ways as the meditation of the Church, guided by the Holy Spirit, presents it to the light of conscious faith. Ultimately, the continuity of this interpretation does not reside in the human consciousness of believers

---

140. Ibid., p. 99.
141. Ibid.
142. Ibid., p. 100.

or of the Church, but in the Holy Spirit. And what is continuity for him is apt, often enough, to look incomprehensibly disjointed to men. It is not only that the Spirit is not limited to any one stage or interpretation of truth that has already been attained; it is not only that the outpouring of his sovereign power can seem at first sight like a sweeping away of all the dykes and containing banks, and is only recognizable by hindsight as having been in fact under the control of a different and much deeper continuity. It is also that, in a sort of *generatio aequivoca*, he can bring up what seem to be new mysteries out of the depths of the revelation accomplished in Christ; mysteries which were indeed present in it, but hitherto not noticed or suspected or regarded as possible by anyone at all. When he does this, he never fails, indeed, to show the point at which the 'new' things are linked on to the old, the crater out of which they erupt, the 'letter' which they interpret.[143]

It is in this way that the "mysteries concerning the Mother of God" become intelligible to the believer.[144] It is obvious that "the quality of marvelousness belongs here to the innermost constitution of truth; it is the very opposite of anything obvious, anything inoffensively self-evident. Mariology is surely the supreme example of how the Holy Spirit interprets the Lord's life: the necessary unfolding by the Third Person of a part of divine revelation that had necessarily been left in semi-obscurity by the Second Person."[145]

We observe now that, if we are to take Balthasar's view of Scripture and tradition as representative of what the Catholic church believes with respect to them, then all neo-orthodox Protestants may rejoice and all orthodox believers must weep. The main point of the two books discussed above, as well as the main point of his earlier book dealing with Karl Barth,[146] is to the effect that neo-orthodox Protestantism and Roman Catholicism are basically at one in holding that the Christ-Event is the supreme integrating principle of life.

Orthodox Protestantism has, we are told, no such integrating principle. It has no eye for the freedom of God and for the freedom of man as participant in the freedom of God in the Christ-Event. In consequence orthodox Protestantism has no eye, on the one hand, for the uniqueness of the incarnation and, on the other hand, for its universal saving significance. Orthodoxy has no eye for the fact that Christ is the electing God and the elected man. Orthodoxy speaks of a

---

143. Ibid., pp. 100–102.
144. Ibid., p. 104.
145. Ibid.
146. Hans Urs Von Balthasar, *Karl Barth—Darstellung und Deutung Seiner Theologie* (Köln: Verlag Jakob Hegner, 1951).

God in himself and a man in himself, not realizing that God is what he is in his saving acts toward man in Christ and that man is what he is in his being saved by and in participation with the saving activity of God in Christ.[147]

From the orthodox point of view this indicates anew the fact that the forces of neo-orthodox Protestantism and the forces of Roman Catholicism have united in a common attack on the self-attesting Christ of the Scriptures. The Christ as speaking in the Scriptures and the Scriptures as the Word spoken by Christ are alike rejected in the name of what is, basically, a speculative concept, namely, the Christ-Event. The former Aristotle-Christ synthesis and the former Kant-Christ synthesis[148] have joined hands to form the Aristotle-Kant-Christ synthesis. The absolute authority of the Creator-Redeemer God speaking directly to man through the words of Scripture has virtually been replaced by the self-sufficient, autonomous man putting his own ideal self on a pedestal and bowing down before it.

It is in this manner that Roman Catholicism and neo-orthodox Protestantism, reaching out hands toward each other and already regarding each other as brothers in the Christ-Event, bring the "message of salvation" to all men. But this message means nothing more than that all men are already elect in Christ, and that they would do well by themselves to become more deeply imbued with this fact.

3. The Documents of Vatican II

But we must now look into *The Documents of Vatican II* in order to see whether we can possibly find something better than this in them. Is the new interest in Scripture perhaps indicative of a new desire to listen directly to the voice of Christ speaking in Scripture?

In his opening address to the Council, Pope John says that its meetings will be held "under the auspices of the virgin Mother of God." Then he adds: "In calling this vast assembly of bishops, the latest and humble successor to the Prince of the Apostles who is addressing you intended to assert once again the *magisterium* (teaching authority), which is unfailing and perdures until the end of time, in order that this magisterium, taking into account the errors, the requirements, and the opportunities of our time, might be presented in exceptional form to all men throughout the world."[149]

"The greatest concern of the Ecumenical Council is this: that the sacred

---

147. Cf. the writer's *Christianity and Barthianism*, pp. 67–113.
148. KSO: Van Til sees the "Aristotle-Christ synthesis" as Roman Catholic, following Thomas Aquinas, and the "Kant-Christ synthesis" as neo-orthodox, following Karl Barth.
149. *The Documents of Vatican II*, gen. ed. Walter M. Abbott, S. J.; trans. ed. Very Rev. Msgr. Joseph Gallagher (New York: Guild Press, 1966), p. 710.

deposit of Christian doctrine should be guarded and taught more efficaciously. That doctrine embraces the whole of man, composed as he is of body and soul. And, since he is a pilgrim on this earth, it commands him to tend always toward heaven."[150]

The "sacred patrimony of truth received from the Fathers" must be preserved.[151] We must build upon the teachings of the church "as it still shines forth in the Acts of the Council of Trent and First Vatican Council. . ."[152] "The substance of the ancient doctrine of the deposit of faith is one thing, and the way in which it is presented is another. And it is the latter that must be taken into great consideration with patience if necessary, everything being measured in the forms and proportions of a magisterium which is predominantly pastoral in character."[153] "Nowadays, . . . the Spouse of Christ prefers to make use of the medicine of mercy rather than that of severity."

The Catholic church "desires to show herself to be the loving mother of all, benign, patient, full of mercy and goodness toward the brethren that are separated from her." To mankind in general, the church "distributes. . . the goods of divine grace which, raising men to the dignity of the sons of God, are the most efficacious safeguards and aids toward a more human life."[154]

God wills all men to be saved. "All men who are born were redeemed by the blood of Christ. . ." But "the greater part of the human race. . . does not yet participate in those sources of divine grace which exist in the Catholic Church." Hence the church "whose light illumines all, whose strength of supernatural unity redounds to the advantage of all humanity" seeks to envelop all within its bosom.[155] The church "prepares, as it were, and consolidates the path toward that unity of mankind which is required as a necessary foundation, in order that the earthly city may be brought to the resemblance of that heavenly city where truth reigns, charity is the law, and whose extent is eternity."[156]

"O Mary, Help of Christians, Help of Bishops, of whose love we have recently had particular proof in thy temple of Loreto, where we venerated the mystery of the Incarnation, dispose all things for a happy and propitious outcome and, with thy spouse, St. Joseph, the holy Apostles Peter and Paul, St. John the Baptist and St. John the Evangelist, intercede for us to God."[157]

150. Ibid., pp. 713–714.
151. Ibid., p. 714.
152. Ibid., p. 715.
153. Ibid.
154. Ibid., p. 716.
155. Ibid., p. 717.
156. Ibid., p. 718.
157. Ibid., p. 719.

Listening, as it were, to this opening address we are not very hopeful that the Council will reveal any open-mindedness toward the principles of the Reformation. The teaching magisterium is, at the outset, said to be absolutely authoritative. And this—it is unnecessary to indicate in detail—is taught throughout the documents.

In the light of the absolute character of the teaching magisterium of the church the question whether Scripture and tradition are two coordinate sources of revelation becomes virtually academic. Two young boys may argue as to which is to be "the boss" but they always know that "mother" is "the boss" of both. And herewith the Reformation principle is, in effect, as clearly rejected by Vatican II as it was by Vatican I and by Trent.

Of still greater importance, if possible, is the fact that the content of what Mother church teaches in the documents of Vatican II is as definitely anti-Reformational as is the content which she taught in the documents of Vatican I and of Trent.

Vatican II does not discuss some of the teachings of Trent and of Vatican I, but it does assume their truth. Everything that was said in the earlier documents about "the natural light of reason" and about the "freedom" of man Vatican II presupposes as true. What Vatican II does say is unintelligible unless we realize that she builds upon the work of her predecessors.

It is impossible to establish the truth of this contention by a detailed comparison of the documents of Vatican II with those of its predecessors. We must restrict ourselves to a comparison between the general teleology of history that faces us in Vatican II and the teleology of history that faces us in Trent and Vatican I.

The teleology of history that faces us in the documents of Trent and in the documents of Vatican I is a composite. The documents of Trent and of Vatican I give ecclesiastical expression and authority to a synthesis of Aristotle's philosophy and Christian theology. The "natural light of reason" spoken of in these documents refers to the idea that the methodology of Aristotle[158] is a proper method for the interpretation of "nature" and for the proof of the existence of God. The Christian believer need only to *add* Christian teaching about the realm of the supernatural in order to have a rounded, comprehensive teleology of history.

In the synthetic teleology of history that is found in the documents of Trent and of Vatican II the relation of God to man is largely expressed by an intermingling of the Parmenidean notion of pure static being and of the Heraclitean

---

158. KSO: The "methodology of Aristotle" was brought into the Catholic Church through Aquinas.

AUTONOMY PLUS AUTHORITY: ROMAN CATHOLICISM

notion of being as pure flux.[159] In this notion of the analogy of being pure determinism and pure indeterminism, pure rationalism and pure irrationalism seemed to be given equally ultimate standing. Yet Aristotle assumes that somehow the rational will prevail over the irrational.

The philosophers and the theologians of the church combined this product of "the natural light of reason" with the "truths of faith." From the Scriptures they took the notion of God's overruling providence and of the kingdom of Christ as victorious over evil. They fused this teleology of history as presented by Christ in Scripture with the teleology of Aristotle.

It was in terms of this Aristotle-Christ teleology that Trent rejected the teachings of the Reformers as heretical. The Reformers spoke of a God whose decree settles the ultimate destiny of man *ad bonam partem* or *ad malum partem*.[160] Surely such determinism must not be tolerated. We must defend the genuine significance of *natural* or else what meaning has the *supernatural*?

We must defend the genuine significance of the "natural reason" and of the "free will" of man, or else what meaning has human responsibility in relation to the gospel call? We must defend the living dynamic character of God's revelation to man and in man, or else how can that revelation really touch man at all?

We must therefore maintain that the living voice of Christ is, through his Spirit, here and now, speaking in the church, and, more specifically, in the teaching magisterium of the church. As he continues his incarnation in the church and therefore continues his speaking in the church, "the faithful" can be at ease. Here and now, through every priest in every parish, the faithful may partake of Christ. Here and now Mother church will instruct the faithful on every question in every aspect of life. The scientist and the philosopher may search for truth with complete openness of mind. If they have difficulty in finding truth, Mother church, through her teaching magisterium will enable them to see that all things find their ultimate significance through Christ as incarnate in his church. God meant mankind to participate in the nature of Christ and God. The church helps mankind onward toward its supernatural destiny of participation in God.

If now there is any difference between the teleology of history of Vatican II as over against the teleology of history of Trent and of Vatican I, this difference is obviously not to be found in a new openness toward Reformation principles. The difference is rather to be found in a new openness toward modern existentialism.

---

159. KSO: The problem, in unbelieving thought, lies in its attempt to deal with unity and diversity. The unbeliever cannot show how facts might be related, thus he is unable to justify categorization as such. Neither can he apply the laws of logic without absorbing the individual into a unified whole. Van Til characterizes this in terms of two influential pre-Socratic philosophers—Heraclitus, who argued that all was flux, and Parmenides, who argued, against Heraclitus, that all was, at bottom, one.

160. KSO: That is, roughly, with respect to blessing and cursing.

There is somewhat more of Heraclitus and somewhat less of Parmenides in Vatican II as over against its predecessors.

How can church dogma be said to be in some sense changeable without contradicting the unchangeable, the irreformable teachings of the Councils of the past? The new theologians of Vatican II have found how this may be done. If Newman[161] sought to show how this may be done by the idea that universal truth pronounced by earlier councils has certain *implications* that were not seen by them but may be drawn out by later councils, this is now too logicistic. Existential thinking has, in modern times, opened our eyes to the complete openness of reality. This new insight enables the church to discover new teachings, in no wise logically deducible from earlier teachings and in no wise directly deducible from any Scriptural or traditional teaching. How much more generous the church can now be toward all men. "Since God the Father is the origin and purpose of all men, we are all called to be brothers." All men "have been summoned to the same destiny, which is both human and divine. . ."[162] The "Church has been sent to unbelievers to be the 'sacrament of unity of the whole human race.'"[163]

This "Second Vatican Council, having probed more profoundly into the mystery of the church, now addresses itself without hesitation, not only to the sons of the church and to all who invoke the name of Christ, but to the whole of humanity."[164] The whole world is emancipated by Christ. The human person, "deserves to be preserved; human society deserves to be renewed. . . Therefore, this sacred Synod proclaims the highest destiny of man and champions the godlike seed which has been sown in him.[165]

The church may therefore say, "*Nihil humani mihi alienum est.*"[166] "What does the church think of man?"[167] The answer given in terms of the new and

---

161. KSO: John Henry Newman (1801–1890). "Although Newman was made a cardinal in 1879 and officially cleared of modernism in 1908, his theology was generally neglected or misunderstood until Vatican Council II (1962–65) focused the whole Roman Catholic Church's attention on many parallel issues. It then became clear that Newman had touched on many questions of enduring importance, even if his own answers had proved to be fragmentary, illustrative rather than explanatory, inspirational rather than definitive. Newman's relevance to recent theology can be seen in two of his works in particular: the *Essay on the Development of Christian Doctrine* (London, 1845, 1891) and *An Essay in Aid of a Grammar of Assent* (London, 1870)." Sinclair B. Ferguson and J.I. Packer, *New Dictionary of Theology* (Downers Grove, IL: InterVarsity Press, 2000), 466.
162. Ibid., p. 307.
163. Ibid., p. 580.
164. Ibid., p. 200.
165. Ibid., p. 201.
166. KSO: That is, "nothing of humanity is alien to me."
167. Ibid., p. 209.

more interior insight that the church has discovered is that man was created "to the image of God." Sacred Scripture teaches this.[168]

Then, further, there is the question of sin. "Although he was made by God in a state of holiness, from the very dawn of history man abused his liberty, at the urging of personified Evil. Man set himself against God and sought to find fulfillment apart from God. Although he knew God, he did not glorify Him as God, but his senseless mind was darkened and he served the creature rather than the Creator."[169]

Every human being "feels as though he is bound by chains. But the Lord Himself came to free and strengthen man, renewing him inwardly and casting out that prince of this world (cf. Jn 12:31) who held him in the bondage of sin. For sin has diminished man, blocking his path to fulfillment."[170]

The fulfillment of man cannot be stopped by evil. Man "outstrips the whole sum of mere things. He finds reinforcement in this profound insight whenever he enters into his own heart. God, who probes the heart, awaits him there. There he discerns his proper destiny beneath the eyes of God. Thus, when man recognizes in himself a spiritual and immortal soul, he is not being mocked by a deceptive fantasy springing from mere physical or social influences. On the contrary he is getting to the depths of the very truth of the matter."[171]

"Steeped in wisdom, man passes through visible realities to those which are unseen. It is, finally, through the gift of the Holy Spirit that man comes by faith to the contemplation and appreciation of the divine plan."[172] "In fidelity to conscience, Christians are joined with the rest of men in the search for truth, and for the genuine solution to the numerous problems which arise in the life of individuals and from social relationships."[173]

"Our contemporaries make much of this freedom and pursue it eagerly; and rightly so, to be sure."[174] God wants men to serve him spontaneously. When man thus spontaneously seeks God he need fear nothing. In particular he need not fear death. By his death Christ "freed man from death. Hence to every thoughtful man a solidly established faith provides the answer to his anxiety about what the future holds for him. At the same time faith gives him the power to be united in

---

168. Ibid., p. 210.
169. Ibid., p. 211.
170. Ibid.
171. Ibid., p. 212.
172. Ibid., p. 213.
173. Ibid., p. 214.
174. Ibid.

Christ with his loved ones who have already been snatched away by death. Faith arouses the hope that they have found true life with God."[175] Thus it is

> only in the mystery of the incarnate Word that the mystery of man takes on light.
>
> All this holds true not only for Christians, but for all men of good will in whose hearts grace works in an unseen way. For, since Christ died for all men, and since the ultimate vocation of man is in fact one, and divine, we ought to believe that the Holy Spirit in a manner known only to God offers to every man the possibility of being associated with this paschal mystery.
>
> Such is the mystery of man, and it is a great one, as seen by believers in the light of Christian revelation. Through Christ and in Christ, the riddles of sorrow and death grow meaningful. Apart from His gospel, they overwhelm us. Christ has risen, destroying death by His death. He has lavished life upon us so that, as sons in the Son, we can cry out in the Spirit: Abba, Father![176]

It is of importance to note that with the help of the new theology found in its midst Mother church has "solved" the problem of the relation of God's decree to human responsibility. She can now say to modern man that his concept of freedom is quite proper. God wants spontaneous service. At the same time she can assure all men that it is God's "plan to dignify men with a participation in His own life."[177] Can God's plan be frustrated by men endowed with free will? "All men are called to salvation by the grace of God."[178] But could all men too resist this call and defeat the plan of God? No, indeed, for "the promised restoration which we are awaiting has already begun in Christ," and "is carried forward in the mission of the Holy Spirit, and through Him continues in the church."[179] Then too there is the never to be forgotten help of "the Blessed Virgin who was eternally predestined, in conjunction with the incarnation of the divine Word, to be the Mother of God."[180] "In an utterly singular way she cooperated by her obedience, faith, and hope, and burning charity in the Savior's work of restoring supernatural life to souls. For this reason she is a mother to us in the order of

---

175. Ibid., p. 215.
176. Ibid., pp. 221–222.
177. Ibid., p. 15.
178. Ibid., p. 32.
179. Ibid., p. 79.
180. Ibid., p. 91.

grace... This maternity will last without interruption until the eternal fulfillment of all the elect."[181]

All men may rejoice in the fact that Mother church dwells in her midst for she is "the universal sacrament of salvation." In her presence Christ is present. And in the presence of Christ we know that "the renovation of the world has been irrevocably decreed and in this age is already anticipated in some real way."[182] In and through the church men may hear the voice of Jesus Christ, telling them the innermost realities about God.[183] How richly blessed are all men because of the fact that the church, through the Roman Pontiff or the body of bishops together can and do infallibly define these ultimate mysteries of God "in accord with revelation itself."[184]

We observe now that the "innermost realities of God" as infallibly revealed by the church very largely resemble current existentialist patterns of thought. Vatican II has, it appears, added the categories of the freedom-nature scheme of Kant to the categories of the form-matter scheme of Aristotle.[185]

The church is now able to add the teleology of Kant to the teleology of Aristotle and use the new synthetic theology thus constructed in order by means of it to proclaim the teleology of the church. The church has rediscovered and renewed herself. She once proclaimed her anathema upon those who sought salvation through Christ alone by means of its Aristotle-Christ synthesis. By means of this Aristotle-Christ synthesis the Church then knew infallibly what the innermost nature of God was like. She knew that it was not what the Reformers said it was. She knew that "the faithful" must be warned against the pollution of the teachings of Luther and Calvin.

Today the church no longer anathematizes heretics. She now accomplishes the same end by enveloping departed brethren. The church has enlarged the vision of herself and of her mission by means of adding the Kant-Christ synthesis with which neo-orthodox Protestantism operates to its own Aristotle-Christ synthesis.

Karl Barth has, apparently, been the envy of many Roman Catholic theologians. By putting new presuppositions underneath the doctrine of election, Barth says that he has "solved" all formerly insoluble problems with respect to divine

---

181. Ibid.
182. Ibid., p. 79.
183. Ibid., p. 113.
184. Ibid., p. 49.

185. KSO: As noted earlier, the "freedom-nature" and "form-matter" schemes are categories of "dialectical ground motives" that were developed by Herman Dooyeweerd, and which he argues to be inherent in various historical manifestations of unbelieving thought. According to Dooyeweerd, "form-matter" is the dialectic of medieval philosophy, "freedom-nature" is the dialectic of post-Kantian thought.

sovereignty and human responsibility. To be sure, says Barth, men are under the wrath of God. They are reprobate. But this reprobation (a) does not refer to persons, and (b) is never the last word with respect to any man. All men are therefore elect. All men are elect because man cannot be man unless he is elect in Christ.

It is thus that both the absolute freedom of man and the absolute comprehensive election of all men are seen to be harmonized with one another.

This sort of theology might well be the envy of Roman Catholic theologians. They were not slow to invite Barth to give up his opposition to the *analogia entis*[186] idea and to join with them in their opposition to the idea of the *Alleinwirksamkeit Gottes*[187] of the Reformers.

Vatican II has now pronounced as the Word of Christ a type of teleological interpretation of history that is virtually identical with a synthesis of medieval essentialism and modern existentialism.

Thus authority and autonomy have been "harmonized" once more. The church now sends out its theologians to have dialogue with departed brethren. Her emissaries now anesthetize the departed brethren. Did not she, long before Luther and Calvin, preach the primacy of sovereign grace? Did not she, long before Luther and Calvin, preach Christ as the Savior of the world?

Come join us then as together we preach this Christ to all men. Outside of Christ there is no salvation for man and no man can be truly man outside Christ.

Neo-orthodox Protestant theologians are now urging union with neo-orthodox Roman Catholicism. Believers in the Christ of the Scriptures will not allow themselves to be put to sleep by the siren voice of a new theology of self-righteousness plus grace any more than the Reformers in their day allowed themselves to be frightened by the anathemas of the theology of self-righteousness plus grace.

---

186. KSO: That is, the "analogy of being" as set forth by Aquinas.
187. KSO: That is, Luther's emphasis on salvation as the "alone work of God."

VII

EVANGELICALISM AND SCRIPTURE

In the preceding chapter, frequent mention was made of the Protestant as over against the Roman Catholic view of Scripture. In conjunction with that, frequent mention has been made of the Protestant as over against the Romanist system of truth that goes with and is involved in the Protestant view of Scripture. But Protestants are not fully agreed among themselves about the system of doctrine contained in Scripture. The difference between them on the system of doctrine contained in Scripture can largely be traced to the difference in their estimate of the autonomy of man. At any rate it is from this point of view that we shall look at it in this chapter. It is not the whole Protestant doctrine of Scripture that we wish to discuss. It is only the apologetical significance of this doctrine that comes before us. For that purpose the all-important question is, What estimate is put upon the natural man and his ability to accept the gospel when it is presented to him? Does his decision with respect to the gospel ultimately rest with himself or with God? Is his decision autonomous or is it analogical? Is it possible to say in answer to these questions that the decision is partly with God, even largely with God but that it is also partly, even if in a very small degree, with man?

On these questions there are two answers given among Protestants. The first answer is that of evangelicalism. By this term we would indicate those who hold to either the Lutheran or the Arminian view of the human will. The evangelical view of the human will is that it does have some measure of ultimate power of its own over against the overtures of the gospel as presented in Scripture. There may be, especially as over against Romanism, a very great stress on the sovereignty of the grace of God. Yet there is, in the last analysis *also* a power of ultimate resistance against God.

The Reformed view of the human will is, on the contrary, that man has no ultimate power either to accept or to resist the overtures of the gospel. It is, to be sure, man who accepts, and it is man who rejects the gospel, and this acceptance or rejection of the gospel on the part of man is of the highest importance. But if it is not to be action in the void it must take place in relation to and in dependence upon the all-embracing counsel of God.[1]

It is this difference between the evangelical and the Reformed view of man which, in practice at least, involves at the same time a somewhat different view of Scripture. At least it involves a different attitude toward Scripture. Each party will, of course, charge the other with not being true or at least with not being fully true to Scripture. But the difference goes beyond that. Each will charge the other with not having an adequately Protestant view of Scripture. That is, each will charge the other with imposing upon Scripture a system of interpretation derived from human experience as such instead of from Scripture.

The nature of these charges may at once be indicated. The evangelical will charge the Reformed person with being both irrationalist and rationalist with respect to Scripture. The Reformed position is said to be *irrationalist* in that it presents the Bible as the word of a wholly arbitrary God, and as therefore teaching things contrary to reason, which itself is given by God to man. The Reformed position is said to be *rationalist* in that it presents the Bible as teaching one major doctrine, the sovereignty of God, with all other doctrines as logically deducible from it.

On the other hand the Reformed person will charge evangelicalism with both irrationalism and rationalism. There would be no issue from these charges and countercharges except for the fact that the charges in each case spring from a clearly distinguishable source. This difference in source, as already intimated, springs from the difference with respect to the idea of human autonomy. The evangelical holds to some measure of human autonomy. It is this that colors the nature of the charges of irrationalism and rationalism that he brings against the Calvinist. The Calvinist, on the other hand, does not hold to any human autonomy. It is this that colors his charges of irrationalism and rationalism that he brings against the evangelical.

It is to be expected that this difference between the evangelical and the Reformed view of human autonomy has a direct bearing upon the attitude toward Romanism manifested in each of the two cases. This is often only a practical difference. Both parties avow their utter loyalty to the Scriptures as the infallible word of God. Both parties are equally set against papal authority. But, as noted in the previous chapter, it is a compromising view with respect to human autonomy that lies back of the idea of papal authority. It is because Romanism seeks to interpret human life in terms of a method derived from Aristotle in order then to supplement it with supernatural revelation, that it really has no truly Christian concept of Scripture at all. Similarly evangelicalism, still retaining some

---

1. KSO: See WCF 3.1., and also 9.3.

measure of the idea of human autonomy, is unable to do full justice to the idea of Scripture. Thus it is unable at the same time to set off the Protestant position with full consistency over against Romanism.

It follows then that not being able to distinguish clearly in practice between a Romanist and a truly Protestant notion of authority in relation to human autonomy evangelicalism is weak in its presentation of the gospel to the natural man. It does not clearly distinguish the position of Christianity based as it is upon the idea of the internal self-contained character of God from the position in which man is his own ultimate interpreter.

With B. B. Warfield, we may say then that the Romanist position can be called Christian, but with a large admixture of naturalism.[2] Evangelicalism is Protestant but with some, though a much smaller, admixture of naturalism.[3] It is only in the Reformed system that the idea of the Bible and the system of truth contained in it comes to its own.[4] This is not to contend that every one professing the Reformed faith therefore has a more truly biblical attitude toward Scripture than any one professing some form of evangelicalism. The question is only what the system of doctrine calls for. Those holding the best of systems often live at a far distance from their own confessions.

With these introductory remarks as background we turn to a discussion of the evangelical position on Scripture.

In the Confessions of the evangelical churches the Romanist conception of the church and of traditions is vigorously rejected. So for instance in the Formula of Concord (1576) the following words appear: "We believe, confess, and teach that the only rule and norm, according to which all dogmas and all doctors ought to be esteemed and judged, is no other whatever than the prophetic and apostolic

---

2. KSO: "Evangelicalism does not cease to be fundamentally antinaturalistic, however, in becoming antisacerdotal: its primary protest continues to be against naturalism, and in opposing sacerdotalism also it only is the more consistently supernaturalistic, refusing to admit any intermediaries between the soul and God, as the sole source of salvation." Benjamin B. Warfield, *The Plan of Salvation: Five Lectures* (Philadelphia: Presbyterian Board of Publication, 1915), 20.

3. KSO: "There are other evangelicals whose conceptions are similarly colored by an underlying naturalism, out of which they have formed their better confession by a like process of modification and correction. . . . The other party is represented by the evangelical Arminian, whose evangelicalism is a correction in the interest of evangelical feeling of the underlying semi-pelagianism of the Dutch Remonstrants." Benjamin B. Warfield, *The Plan of Salvation: Five Lectures* (Philadelphia: Presbyterian Board of Publication, 1915), 21.

4. KSO: Speaking of the Calvinist, Warfield says, "Thus, and thus only, he contends, can either the supernaturalism of salvation which is the mark of Christianity at large and which ascribes all salvation to God, or the immediacy of the operations of saving grace which is the mark of evangelicalism and which ascribes salvation to the direct working of God upon the soul, *come to its rights* and have justice accorded it." Benjamin B. Warfield, *The Plan of Salvation: Five Lectures* (Philadelphia: Presbyterian Board of Publication, 1915), 111, my emphasis.

writings both of the Old and of the New Testament, as it is written (Ps 119:105): 'Thy word is a lamp unto my feet, and a light unto my path.' And St. Paul saith (Gal 1:8): 'Though an angel from heaven preach any other gospel unto you, let him be accursed.'"[5]

The Five Remonstrant Articles (1610) contain no separate statement on Scripture; these articles were written by those who were officially committed to belief in the Belgic Confession (1561). And this Belgic Confession was the confession of the Reformed Churches of the Netherlands.[6]

The difference then between the evangelical and the Reformed view of Scripture must be garnered from the way in which those adhering to these positions have dealt with Scripture. Do they really make it the Word of God attesting to itself? Do they really interpret all things in terms of its principles? In particular do they, like Romanism, allow that the natural man can, in terms of his adopted principles, truly identify and order large areas of life? That is to say, what is their attitude toward the Romanist conception of natural theology as related to revealed theology? No attempt will be made to give anything like a comprehensive survey of the history of evangelical thought dealing with the doctrine of Scripture in relation to natural theology. What will be said will be by way of giving illustration of the main point, namely, that evangelicalism cannot, because of its system of doctrine, provide for a fully self-attesting Scripture. On this point we shall deal first with Lutheranism and then with Arminianism.

A. LUTHERANISM

1. Francis Pieper

For an excellent work on evangelical Lutheranism, for one dealing directly with the question at hand, we can do no better than take the *Christian Dogmatics* of Francis Pieper.[7] Dr. Pieper was, according to John Theodore Mueller, "for over half a century the outstanding teacher of dogmatics at Concordia Seminary" in St. Louis, Missouri. The work has been translated from the German. More recent teachers of Lutheran theology, like Engelder and Mueller himself, make grateful acknowledgment of indebtedness to Pieper.

Pieper makes a searching analysis of the "theology of self-consciousness," that is, the modern theology of Schleiermacher and his followers. "Invented for

---

5. Philip Schaff, *op. cit.*, Vol. III, pp. 93–94.
6. It was revised by the National Synod of Dordt in 1619. It is this form which is now generally accepted in the Reformed Churches of the Netherlands.
7. KSO: Francis Pieper (1832–1941). Pieper was the fourth president of the Missouri Synod, Lutheran Church from 1899–1911. He authored the three volume *Christian Dogmatics*.

the purpose of insuring the scientific character of theology, this theology makes its advocates play the role of the man who, in order to brace his toppling Ego, takes a tight hold on his Ego. Furthermore, the Ego theology is a form, the worst form, of idolatry—self-deification."[8]

But what of Reformed theology? Does Pieper share the frequently stated position that all orthodox Protestants have essentially the same view of Scripture? Does he think that all "fundamentalists" should unite in common opposition to all "modernists," calling them back from their confidence in "experience" to belief in the Word of God? Far from it! Pieper is convinced that orthodox Reformed theology is deeply tinged with the principles of "ego-theology." Says Pieper: "The desire to go beyond Word and faith and to walk by sight already in this life has given rise to Calvinism, to synergism, and lies at the bottom of the entire modern 'construction theology' (*Konstruktions-theologie*)."[9]

The main objection raised against Calvinism is that of rationalism as based upon and proceeding from an ego-theology. "What we object to in the Reformed theology is this, that in all doctrines in which it differs from the Lutheran Church and on which it has constituted itself as the Reformed Church alongside the Lutheran Church, it denies the Scriptural principle and lets rationalistic axioms rule."[10]

As for Calvin himself, says Pieper, he virtually forsook the revealed will of God. "The depths of the Godhead are not hidden to Calvin; they are so clear to him that by them he cancels the revelation in the Word (the *gratia universalis*)."[11]

Calvin's "particularism" is said to have its roots in his rationalistic appeal to the hidden will of God. "Luther lets the Word of God, Scripture itself, tell him what the gracious will of God is, how far it extends, and what it effects. Calvin lets the result (*effectus*) of the historical experience (*experientia*) determine what God's gracious will is."[12] "True, also Calvin says that we should not seek to explore the hidden will of God, but rely on Christ and the Gospel. But how can Calvin direct men to rely on Christ and the Gospel since he teaches that only some of the hearers of the Word have a claim on Christ? As a matter of fact, he does not direct men to Christ and the Gospel, but to their inward renewal and sanctification, or to the *gratia infusa*."[13] "Calvin's theology, therefore, is not basically biblical, but rationalistically motivated."[14]

---

8. Francis Pieper, *Christian Dogmatics*, Vol. I (Saint Louis: Concordia Pub. Co., 1950), p. 127.
9. Ibid., Vol. II, p. 389.
10. Ibid., Vol. I, p. 186.
11. Ibid., Vol. II, p. 47.
12. Ibid., p. 48.
13. Ibid., p. 46.
14. Ibid., p. 276.

In following Calvin, Reformed theology "through the use of rationalistic axioms, fixes an unbridgeable gulf between itself and genuine Christian theology."[15] So, for instance, we are told, Calvinism holds to the purely speculative maxim that the finite cannot contain the infinite (*finitus non est capax infiniti*). In virtue of this "rationalistic axiom" Calvinism virtually denies the incarnation. "In so far as Reformed theology, in its effort to disprove Lutheran Christology, applies the principle that the finite is not capable of grasping of the infinite, it inevitably denies the incarnation of the Son of God, and Christ's vicarious atonement, and so destroys the foundation of the Christian faith."[16] In this way, Reformed men commit "theological suicide."[17] Again Calvinism is said to deny the "Scripture doctrine of *gratia universalis*" because of another "philosophical axiom," namely, "whatever God earnestly purposes must in every case actually occur; and since not all men are actually saved, we must conclude that the Father never did love the world, that Christ never did reconcile the world, and that the Holy Ghost never does purpose to create faith in all hearers of the Word. This is the chief argument of Calvin in the four chapters of his *Institutes* (III, 21–24) on Predestination. He disposes of the Scripture declarations which attest universal grace with the statement, repeated again and again, that the result must determine the extent of the divine will of grace."[18]

John Theodore Mueller, professor of systematic theology, takes essentially the same position as that of Pieper. Speaking of the confessional Lutheran church, he says, "Its theology is that of the Holy Bible, and of the Bible alone; its doctrine is the divine truth of God's Word. *The Lutheran Church is therefore the orthodox visible Church of Christ on earth.*"[19]

Pieper's charge is not merely that individual Reformed theologians have been rationalistic in their approach to Scripture. His charge is that it is of the genius of Reformed theology as such to be rationalistic. The system of Reformed theology, he argues in effect, is rationalistically constructed. This we deny.

Pieper has not sought to refute the painstaking exegesis of Calvin and his followers as they deal with the doctrines of predestination, the two natures of Christ, and particularism. If Calvin and his followers had been moved by rationalistic considerations in the formulation of these and other doctrines they would have tried to show how such doctrines are "in accord with reason," in accord with "the experience of freedom." On the contrary, Calvin and his followers

---

15. Ibid., p. 271.
16. Ibid.
17. Ibid., p. 167.
18. Ibid., p. 26.
19. John Theodore Mueller, *Christian Dogmatics* (St. Louis: Concordia Pub. House, 1934), p. 24.

have interpreted "the laws of reason" and "the experience of freedom" in terms of Scripture as the only final authority for man. At the very beginning of Calvin's *Institutes* we are told that man does not see himself for what he really is except he recognize himself as a creature of God. And to recognize himself as a creature of God he must own himself to be a sinner before God. Moreover, Calvin argues further on, that to recognize one's sinfulness, he must have learned to know himself in the light of Scripture, of Scripture as understood by the regenerating and illuminating operation of the Holy Spirit.[20]

According to Calvin, man as the interpreter of Scripture must first be interpreted by Scripture, and Scripture is the Word of God. The idea of Scripture as the Word of God and the idea of God as speaking through Scripture are involved in one another. Scripture tells us that God is infinite, eternal and unchangeable in his being, wisdom, power, holiness, justice, goodness and truth. Scripture tells us that this God cannot deny himself. It is this self-contained, wholly self-dependent God who speaks in Scripture. It is not rationalism to assert that Scripture *cannot* also reveal a God who does deny himself, a god who creates man with powers equal to himself. For Scripture speaking is God speaking. Is God indeterminate? Has he no character?

At this point, Calvinism and Lutheranism, as set forth in Pieper's work, part company. With unquestioned desire to follow Scripture wherever it may lead him, Pieper virtually holds that it may lead anywhere. It may teach "that God intends what is never accomplished." God "intends to save the world through Christ." Nevertheless "God's purpose is not accomplished in a part of mankind."[21]

This approach is irrationalist in character. If God's will of decree can be resisted, he is, as Luther would say, "a ridiculous God."[22] The nature of his power would be indistinguishable from the nature of man's power. The distinction between God as original or ultimate and man as derivative and dependent would be done away. Then Luther's words are applicable:

> For if I am ignorant of the nature, extent and limits of what I can and must do with reference to God, I shall be equally ignorant and uncertain of the nature, extent and limits of what God can and will do in me—though God, in fact, works all in all (1 Cor 12:6). Now, if I am ignorant of God's works and power, I am ignorant of God himself; and if I do not know God, I cannot worship, praise, give thanks or serve him, for I do

---

20. Calvin: *Institutes of the Christian Religion*, I:1–9.
21. Pieper, *op. cit.*, Vol. II, p. 27.
22. KSO: This statement can be found in Martin Luther, tr. J. I. Packer, and O. R. Johnston, *Martin Luther on the Bondage of the Will: a New Translation of De Servo Arbitrio (1525) Martin Luther's Reply to Erasmus of Rotterdam* (London: J. Clarke, 1957): 182.

not know how much I should attribute to myself and how much to him. We need, therefore, to have in mind a clear-cut distinction between God's power and ours, and God's work and ours, if we would live a godly life.[23]

Moreover, the irrationalist doctrine of the human will leads away from the Protestant doctrine of Scripture. Romanism required men to have implicit faith in the church. From this slavery of men to other men Luther appealed to Scripture. "What do you mean, Erasmus? Is it not enough to have submitted your judgment to Scripture? Do you submit it to the Church as well?—why, what can the Church settle that Scripture did not settle first? And what room do you leave for that liberty and authority to judge the framers of these decisions of which Paul speaks in 1 Cor 14, when he says: 'let the others judge'? (v. 29)"[24] The very idea of the Bible as a final standard of judgment becomes meaningless on the assumption that there is no God who controls whatsoever comes to pass. Faith would be blind trust in the guesses of men themselves surrounded by Chance.

We must now inquire about the nature of Lutheran apologetics as Pieper and others think of it. Do we not expect him to call upon men simply to believe in the Scriptures as the Word of God? If his doctrine of Scripture is irrationalistic in nature, how then can he appeal to reason at all? Yet, to "reason" he does appeal. "When we compare the Holy Scriptures according to content and style with other 'Bibles' in the world, e.g., with the Koran, . . . then a reasonable reason cannot do otherwise than conclude that the Scriptures must be divine and confess that it is more reasonable to grant the divinity of Scripture than to deny it. This is the domain of apologetics."[25] Again, "Christ is appealing not only to the Scriptures, but also to something which is known even to natural reason—to the omnipotence of God."[26]

This conception of apologetics as held by Pieper and other Lutherans is essentially the same as that of other "evangelicals" or "conservatives." Together with other "conservatives" Pieper appeals to the "natural man" as having within him a standard by which he can judge the truth or falsity of the Scriptural claim to its own authority.

The final question now presses itself upon those who hold to the Reformed Faith. The Calvinist certainly believes in the Scriptures as self-authenticating. For believing this, he is virtually labeled as *irrationalist*. Again, the Calvinist certainly believes that it is God, the self-contained and self-determinate God, who speaks

---

23. Martin Luther, *The Bondage of the Will*, tr. by J. I. Packer and O. R. Johnson (Westwood: Fleming H. Revell Co., 1957), p. 78.
24. Ibid., p. 69.
25. Pieper, *op. cit.*, Vol. I, p. 310.
26. Ibid., p. 311, fn.

in Scripture. For believing this he is called a rationalist by the "conservatives" as represented by Pieper.

From Pieper's argument it appears that he is willing to take his view of being from the Bible as the word of the self-attesting God without qualification. To say that God testifies to himself in his Word is to say that he makes himself unmistakably known in the facts of the phenomenal world. In particular it means that he makes himself unmistakably known in the work of redemption as this is accomplished in the phenomenal world. But according to Pieper the Bible might teach *anything* about God. It might say such things as can in no wise be identified by man. In other words, God's revelation may be of a God whose character is indeterminate and whose actions in the world in consequence cannot be identified. Thus Pieper is not willing to maintain that the idea of possibility is wholly subject to the self-contained God of Scripture. He constructs his system, in part at least, upon the idea that possibility is above God. It is this that makes identification in history impossible.

It is not that we first wish to claim for man the right and ability of identification in history, in order that then he may identify Scripture as the Word of God. On the contrary, it is because we would maintain that identification of any fact or truth in the phenomenal realm is possible to man in history only because all things in history are controlled by God back of history that we object to Pieper's position. Identification of fact or truth in history by human reason must be frankly based upon identification by God. Only if the authority of God's self-identification and of his self-authenticated revelation to man in history is assumed can there be any intelligible predication by man. But such self-identification of God cannot be obtained if it be allowed that God may reveal anything at all. God can reveal only that which is consistent with his nature as a self-identified being. The law of identity in human logic must be seen to be resting upon the character of God and therefore upon the authoritative revelation of God. But to say that God is both omnipotent and not omnipotent, because conditioned by the ultimate determinations of his creatures, is to remove the very foundation of the law of identity.[27] This is irrationalism. It allows the legitimacy of the non-Christian principle of individuation, namely chance. It is quite impossible, once this is allowed, to challenge the non-Christian position effectively.

Corresponding to this concession to the non-Christian principle of individuation is a concession to the non-Christian principle of unification. Pieper holds that Scripture cannot teach that the ultimate differences between men come from

---

27. KSO: Said another way, once it is granted that man can thwart what God wills, then possibility is outside of God's power, and thus "controls" all facts. What is possible and impossible, therefore, is a matter of chance, not of God's power and sovereign control.

the plan of God. He argues that God's overtures to men are ultimately in terms of classes. The individual finally decides to which class, the elect or the non-elect, he will belong. Man can finally resist the grace of God.

This position involves an appeal to a principle that is higher than the counsel of God. It is in effect an appeal to a unity in which God orders only the relations of parts. It is to reduce the Christian conception of causation as actual determination to the non-Christian procedure. For the essence of non-Christian methodology is to appeal to rationality that is above God and man as well as to possibility that surrounds them both.

2. *Karl Francke*[28]

Lutheranism thinks that its doctrine of Scripture is taken from Scripture itself. Its doctrine of the freedom of the will is supposed to come from Scripture by exegesis. In a book dealing specifically with this problem Karl Francke gives a detailed exegesis of Scripture in defense of the Lutheran position. His book gives a thorough analysis of the noetic effects of sin as set forth in Scripture. The title is *Metanoetik*. He calls it "the science of thought that has been redeemed." It is impossible to do more than intimate something of the nature of the argument as a whole, and to point out the notion of the human will that results from it.

Francke's starting point is 2 Corinthians 5:17, "Therefore if any man be in Christ Jesus, he is a new creature, old things are passed away; behold all things are become new." He speaks accordingly of regenerated thought as thought that is radically changed. This change is designated in the New Testament with the term *metanoein*.

Francke's interest is not in seeking to determine the ethical consequences of regeneration as much as it is in seeking to determine the nature of the "purely noetical" consequences of regeneration.

The three main divisions of the book deal with the necessity, the possibility, and the actuality of regenerated thought.

In the first section, the author collects the biblical material that has bearing on the blinding effects of sin. The author brings out very well the fact that non-regenerated thought seeks at one time to know all reality and at another time maintains that nothing can be known. "*Einerseits soll es Wahrheit überhaupt nicht erkenner, anderseits umspannen, was höher als der Himmel, tiefer als die Unterwelt*[29]

---

28. KSO: Karl Francke is a rather obscure German Lutheran theologian and author. Apparently, Van Til worked on Francke's book, *Metanoetik*, during his Th.M. studies at Princeton. Francke's book was published in 1913.

29. KSO: That is, roughly, "On the one hand, it should not recognize truth at all, on the other hand, it should include what is higher than the heavens, lower than the underworld."

(Job 11:7ff.)."³⁰ This is the point to which we have called attention by saying that anti-theistic thought wants to use language univocally or give up the possibility of knowledge altogether. Anti-theistic thought will not be receptive. "*Es will sich nicht mehr passiv und rezeptiv verhalten.*"³¹ ³² Accordingly it loses itself in the artificial fabrication of insoluble antinomies. It refuses any help. It will accept nothing but what has come out of the depth of its own wisdom.

The stages throughout which this process of sinful thought comes to its completion are three. The first stage is that of deceit, *apaty*.³³ This deceitfulness of sin may be subdivided into the deceitfulness of philosophy (Col 2:8), the deceitfulness of riches (Mt 13:22), and the deceitfulness of false morality (2 Thes 2:10). It is this first stage that places the seeds of separation from God in the heart of man. The second stage is that of *erring* in thought, *plany*.³⁴ Psalm 95:10 speaks of a people that do always err in their hearts. The same thought is expressed by Isaiah when he says, "All we like sheep have gone astray." It was this "spirit of error" (1 Jn 4:6) that moved the false prophets of old to oppose the realization of the kingdom of God. Error gives a more external expression to that which lives in the heart through deceit. The third stage is that of stupor, *katanuxis*.³⁵ This marks the climax of the process of anti-theistic thought. To it the wisdom of God is foolishness. It hardens the heart (Rom 11:25). Truth is obnoxious to the victim of the spirit of stupor. It closes the ears to the witnesses of the Truth (Is 9:10). This third stage is often given to men as a punishment for falling into the earlier stages Rom 1:26–27. In this third stage the first and second stages reach their natural climax. It may therefore be said that the first stage is the determining point. It is not only when matters have come to such a pass as is portrayed in the first chapter of Romans that God is displeased. Since the third stage is often the result of a punishment of the first and second stages it follows that in the eyes of the Lord it is the first stage that is already decisive. At first this natural thought *will* not see and hear, and at last it can not see and hear.³⁶

The picture of the noetic effect of sin as painted by Francke is black enough. Yet the Lutheran conception of man's independence underlies the whole discussion. Man, as it were, starts this whole course of error without any relation to God's plan. Francke will, of course, grant the doctrine of creation, but he fails

---

30. Karl Francke, *Metanoetik* (Leipzig: A. Deichertsche Verlagsbuchhandlung, 1913), pp. 14–15.
31. KSO: "It no longer wants to behave passively and receptively."
32. Ibid., p. 13.
33. KSO: The Greek word would be transliterated *apatē*.
34. KSO: The Greek word would be transliterated *planē*.
35. KSO: The Greek word would be transliterated *katanyxus*.
36. Ibid., p. 44.

to see the full significance of it. He says that God had to respect the freedom he himself had given to his creatures. "*Er muss die ihm schöpfungsmassig garantierte Freiheit respektieren.*"[37] [38] And this freedom is interpreted as meaning that man can do some things without any reference to God. The whole process of deflection is pictured as beyond God's operation till he sees fit to intervene when things have gone too far.

This independence of man is still more apparent in the second section of the book which deals with the possibility of regenerated thought. After the dark picture given of the position of sinful man, it would certainly seem that only God could take the initiative in the process of restoration. The "natural man" would seem to be so dead that it would require the Holy Spirit to blow into his nostrils the breath of life. We thought we saw the natural man as dead in trespasses and sins, i.e., as a corpse. But we were mistaken. The "corpse" is not a corpse. It breathes and moves. Not only did God have to respect the freedom given it at creation, but even the sinner is given strength to search for and desire the truth, apart from the operation of the Holy Spirit. Of his own accord he "comes to himself" and reflects upon his lost condition without any help from the Holy Spirit. Not as though the natural man could get out of his predicament without the help of the Spirit. "*Die dämonischen Geister des Irrsals können nur durch Mittel und Kräfte eines uber dämonischen d.i. göttlichen Geistes verbannt werden.*"[39] [40] But the sinner seeing his predicament can at least cry for help. There is a longing to get out of the misery and into the truth. Francke is here unbiblical and pelagianising in his thought.

Francke establishes his point, he thinks, by referring to Christ's promise to the apostles that he would give them the spirit of truth. He also pictures Paul's crying for release from his awful conflict with sin as an instance of the natural man seeking light. But these examples only prove the poverty of an argument of this sort. The apostles, with the exception of Judas, were true disciples of Christ, according to his own word. We would naturally expect that they would ask for the Spirit of Truth. Paul tells us in the immediate context of Romans 7:24, that the new life within him is seeking to throw off the bondage to the remnants of the old man that he finds within himself against his will. Thus Paul thought of himself very definitely as a regenerated man when he uttered that famous cry for relief. So then, the very examples adduced in proof are the best of testimony that the position of Francke is unbiblical. Moreover, if man is really unable to seek

---

37. KSO: "He must respect the freedom guaranteed by creation."
38. Ibid., p. 48.
39. KSO: "The demonic spirits of error can only be banished by means and powers of one over the demonic, that is, by the divine spirit."
40. Ibid., p. 51.

God by nature, as Francke himself says that he is not, where does this new ability to seek God suddenly come from? Either we must accept the exegesis of Francke in his first section in which he portrays the result of sin seriously, and reject his second section as in opposition to it, or we must maintain his second section and hold that in his first section he was all the while clinging to a false independence idea. It would seem fair to choose the second alternative since Francke is most anxious to reserve for man a freedom as a creature by which he is able to do all manner of things that seem to be beyond God's control.

Francke's argument might be called the very opposite of that of Luther in *The Bondage of the Will*. Luther proves in great detail that man is by nature unable to do any good, and we have seen that in many ways the argument of Francke in the first section of his book resembles that argument of Luther. But the swerving from the first to the second position on the part of Francke resembles that which happened when the semi-mechanism of Luther turned into the synergism of Melanchthon. In both cases it was really a development rather than a reversal. And it could not be a development if there were not already some germ of the second position found in the first position.

We may say, then, that in the second section of his book Francke is unfaithful to the redemptive principle as a whole. If one maintains a soteriological theory in which the "natural man" is conceived of as able of his own accord to seek the truth because he has a true insight into his own sorrowful condition, one cannot but become anti-biblical epistemologically in the sense that he must then think of certain facts as existing in such a way that man can have knowledge of them without having knowledge of the true God.[41] If no one can come to the Father but by Christ and no one can say Christ is Lord except through the Spirit, it is equally possible or equally impossible for man to come into contact with the Father or the Son or the Spirit. If one maintains that he can approach Christ of his own accord even though he is a sinner, he may as well say that he can approach the Father too. If one can say that he knows what the fact of sin means without the enlightenment of the Holy Spirit, he may as well say that he can know any and every fact without reference to God. If one fact can be known without reference to God, there is good reason to hold that all facts can be known without reference to God.

Francke is unable to do justice to the identification of Scripture as a unit. He identifies the desire for the Spirit of truth as he thinks it exists in the "natural man" with the desire on the part of Old Testament saints for the fulness of

---

41. KSO: When Van Til says here, ". . . without having knowledge of the true God." he means *saving* knowledge of the true God, since all people have, through general revelation, true knowledge of the true God.

the promise of the Shiloh, as given in Genesis 49:10. But such an identification presupposes that these Old Testament saints were unbelievers while actually we are told that Abraham is the father of the faithful. Hence, Franke's appeal to the Old Testament saints weakens rather than strengthens his position. His further argument that as this longing for the Shiloh on the part of Old Testament saints became ever stronger and stronger in the course of the history of the Old Testament, so the longing for the truth on the part of the "natural man" may become ever stronger, also falls to the ground. "The natural man can learn to wait for the Spirit of Truth." "*Da natürliche Denken kann die Kunst lernen, auf den Geist der Wahrheit zu warten. Und wo dieses Warren brünstig aufrichtig und zielbewusst geübt wird, gestaltet es sich unwillkürlich zum Bitten um denselben.*"[42] [43] This picture of the natural man as conscious of the end he has in view, that is, of seeking the truth and then praying for it, is about as far removed from the picture Scripture gives of the "natural man" as it could be. Once one starts on the decline toward the idea of autonomy there is no stopping.

That Francke has no very deep conception of sin is further evidenced by the fact that he minimizes original sin. To him the conception of inherited sin is a logical contradiction.[44] This is an important point. Why should original sin be considered a logical contradiction? It can be so considered only if it is taken for granted that personal covenantal representation is an impossible conception. We are not now concerned to prove that the principle of personal representation is biblical. That cannot easily be denied by any one who reads Romans 5:12, "Therefore as through one man sin entered into the world, and death through sin; and so death passed unto all men, *for that all have sinned.*" But, for the moment, we are only concerned to know that this representational principle can be denied only on the supposition that a personal act must necessarily be a *uni*personal act. In other words, on this basis an act can be truly personal only if the surroundings of the person be impersonal. To be truly personal on this view, there really should be no more than one person. If there were more than one person, the surroundings would not be entirely impersonal, and to that extent the act would not be fully personal. This reduces the position to an absurdity, because if there were only one person there could be no personal relationship at all. It were quite legitimate and true to say that the foundation of all personal activity among men must be based upon the personality of one ultimate person; namely, the person of God, if only it be understood that this ultimate personality of God is a triune personality. Within

---

42. KSO: "The natural man can learn to wait for the spirit of truth. And where this is practiced fervently, sincerely and purposefully, it automatically becomes a plea for it."
43. Ibid., p. 56.
44. Ibid., p. 73.

the Trinity there is completely personal relationship without residue. For that reason it may be said that man's actions are all personal too. Man's surroundings are shot through with personality because all things are related to the infinitely personal God. But when we have said that the surroundings of man are really completely personalized, we have also established the representational principle. We have not only established the *possibility* of the representational principle, but its *necessity* and *actuality* as well. All of man's acts must be representational of the acts of God. Even the persons of the Trinity are mutually representational of one another. They are *exhaustively* representational of one another. Because man is a creature he must in his thinking, his feeling and his willing be analogically representative of God. There is no other way open for him. He could, in the nature of the case, think nothing at all unless he thought God's thoughts after him, and this is analogical, representational thinking. Thus man's thought is representative of God's thought, but not exhaustively reproductive.

The biblical doctrine of original sin is based upon this purely biblical and therefore purely theistic concept of representation. Since the whole being of God, if we may in all reverence say so, is built upon the representational plan, it was impossible for God to create except upon the representational plan. This pertains first to every individual human being, but it pertains just as well with respect to the race as a whole. If there was to be a personal relationship between finite persons—and none other is conceivable—there would have to be representational relationship. Every act of every finite person affects every act of every other finite person that comes after him by virtue of the one general plan of God with respect to the whole of creation. Hence, it could not be otherwise than that the acts of Adam *should affect, representationally, every* human being that should come after him.[45]

---

45. KSO: Van Til's use of the "representational principle" is fairly sparse in his writings, and for good reason. The word "representational" remains too ambiguous to provide clear and substantive theological direction. As he is sometimes wont to do, Van Til takes a prominent notion of philosophical idealism and gives it Christian-theistic content. To put the matter simply, and less in terms of idealism, Van Til is saying that all that we know and do and think as human beings presupposes the triune God, who exhaustively knows himself in his triunity. So, when he says that the being of God is "built on" the representational principle, he only means that the persons of the Trinity exhaustively know, love, will, etc. each other in and through the one God. This exhaustive knowledge "filters down," as it were, in creation such that we know, think, act, etc. only because we are creatures of the self-sufficient triune God. Also, Adam, as the first man, is representational because, as image of God, he will reflect the representational principle as it is originally in God. That "reflection" means, in part, that he is the first representational man, and thus is our representative, even in his original sin. This is all to say that Van Til's use of the representational principle is not a clear way to explain Reformed theology. I am convinced that he was influenced by Bavinck here. See Herman Bavinck, *The Philosophy of Revelation: The Stone Lectures for 1908–1909*, Princeton Theological Seminary (New York: Longmans, Green, and Co., 1909), 53–82.

To reject the doctrine of original sin may therefore be characterized as a concession to the anti-biblical idea that the acts of human personalities are surrounded by a universe over which God has no complete control, i.e., an impersonal universe. Thus it comes to pass that the rejection of the doctrine of original sin on the part of Francke is merely another indication and proof that our interpretation of his idea of the "natural man" is correct. If there is an element of anti-biblical thinking at one point, it is sure to reappear elsewhere. A suit of clothes usually shows signs of wear at several places simultaneously.

Summing up the whole teaching of Francke on the question of the possibility of renewed thought, we may say that according to him, the possibility of renewal does not lie so much in the fact that the Holy Spirit is all-powerful—though this is a *sine qua non*—as in the fact that the "natural man" is after all quite powerful for good because he always remains a rational creature, and no rational creature is ever quite helpless. Thus Francke has given to man a vicious independence to begin with.

Summing up the whole of modern Lutheran epistemology as far as we have discussed it, our conclusion can be none other than that Lutheran epistemology has not lived up to its early promise. There is in Lutheranism a great advance upon the scholastic position, which is found in every direction.[46] Yet that advance might have been much greater if Lutheranism had had the courage to carry the Reformation a little farther than it did. Lutheranism is too largely anthropological instead of theological. Its theology at some stages of the process speaks as though there were matters that pertain to the welfare of man without affecting the position of God. Lutheranism has not been quite biblical enough in the sense of making God the completely original and exclusively original personality which serves as the foundation for the meaning of all human predication.

B. ARMINIANISM

Turning now to the general Arminian conception of Scripture, it is well to look briefly at the works of Arminius himself. It is his theology that underlies, in large measure, the five articles of the Remonstrants against which the Reformed Synod of Dort set forth the Reformed view in five counter articles.[47] We are not

---

46. KSO: Almost every time Van Til mentions the "scholastic position," he is referring to medieval scholasticism and its "form-matter" dialectic. For a helpful analysis of this scholasticism from a historic, Reformed perspective, see William Cunningham, "Scholastic Theology," in *Historical Theology: A Review of the Principal Doctrinal Discussions in the Christian Church since the Apostolic Age* (Edinburgh: T&T Clark, 1863), 413–425

47. KSO: "The Synod of Dort was an assembly of divines from the Reformed tradition that met

now concerned with the Arminian system as a whole except in so far as it has a bearing on its view of Scripture.[48]

"Let Scripture itself come forward, and perform the chief part in asserting its own Divinity. Let us inspect its substance and its matter." It is thus that Arminius begins his discussion of the divinity of Scripture.[49] Corresponding to this assertion of the objective divinity of Scripture is his position with respect to the necessity of the internal testimony of the Holy Spirit in witnessing to the Scriptures as the Word of God. He says that the "Holy Spirit is the author of that light by the aid of which we obtain a perception and an understanding of the divine meanings of the word, and is the Effector of the certainty by which we believe those meanings to be truly divine; and that he is *the necessary author, the all-sufficient Effector.*"[50] In stating his position on Scripture he opposes the Roman view of tradition and papal authority.

But it soon appears that Arminius holds to a view of human autonomy that is out of accord with the idea of Scripture as self-attesting. This fact appears again and again in his several disquisitions on predestination. Predestination is not, for Arminius, a part of the actual control of whatsoever comes to pass. "I could wish also that the word 'ordaining' were used in its proper sense, from which they seem to me to depart, who interpret it—to decree that something shall be done. For its true meaning is to establish the order of things done, not to appoint things to be done that they may be done; though it is used sometimes by the fathers in the latter sense."[51] That man has autonomy is involved in this notion of ordering rather than controlling. God cannot determine in advance what man will do. He can order reality in accordance with what he foresees man will do. Thus election is not an actual determination on the part of God with respect to man. It is rather a determination to order the relations of the events in history in

---

in the city of Dordrecht, Holland, from the fall of 1618 to the spring of 1619. The chief purpose of the synod was to respond to the theology of the followers of Jacob Arminius (1560–1609). Arminius had taught a subtle doctrine of predestination wherein God chose some to salvation and others to damnation, but God based his decision on his foreknowledge of how an individual would respond to the free offer of his grace. Arminius's followers expanded on his teachings, claiming that Christ's death was fully atoning for the entire human race (though only those who believed in Christ derived benefit from it), that all humans had the power to assent to or resist grace, and that true believers could fall away so far as to lose justifying faith. The Synod of Dort rejected these positions." David M. Whitford, ed., *T&T Clark Companion to Reformation Theology*, T&T Clark Companion (London; New York: T&T Clark, 2012), 399.

48. *The Works of James Arminius*, tr. by James Nichols and W. R. Bagnall, Vol. I (Buffalo: Derby, Miller and Orton, 1853), esp. pp. 113–145.
49. Ibid., p. 123.
50. Ibid., p. 140.
51. Ibid., Vol. III, p. 284.

such a way that those whom God foresees will believe shall then be saved. Again and again Arminius makes the point that God's foresight of their faith precedes God's election of men. "This decree has its foundation in the foreknowledge of God, by which he knew from all eternity those individuals who *would*, through his preventing grace,[52] *believe*, and, through his subsequent grace *would persevere*, according to the before described administration of those means which are suitable and proper for conversion and faith; and, by which foreknowledge, he likewise knew those who *would not believe and persevere*."[53]

It is in this manner that Arminius repeatedly tones down the doctrine of election, from that of ultimate control to that of ordering aspects of reality that exist in part at least beyond the control of God. Since the doctrine of election is based upon the doctrine of providence, Arminius quite consistently also tones down this doctrine till it resembles the idea of an abstract formal unity more than that of the control of God. To be sure, Arminius speaks of providence as preserving, regulating, governing and directing all things. In addition to asserting this he says: "Besides this, I place in subjection to Divine Providence both *the free-will and even the actions of a rational creature*, so that nothing can be done without the will of God, not even any of those things which are done in opposition to it; only we must observe a distinction between good actions and evil ones, by saying, that 'God both *wills* and *performs* good acts,' but that 'he only *freely permits* those which are evil."[54] Of the natural man Arminius says: ". . . it is necessary for him to be regenerated and renewed in his intellect, affections or will, and in all his powers, by God in Christ through the Holy Spirit, that he may be qualified rightly to understand, esteem, consider, will, and perform whatever is truly good."[55] So the only question remaining between him and his opponents, says Arminius, is whether the influence of God is irresistible. "That is, the controversy does not relate to those actions or operations which may be ascribed to grace, (for I acknowledge and inculcate as many of these actions or operations as any man ever did), but it relates solely to the mode of operation, *whether it be irresistible or not*. With respect to which, I believe, according to the scriptures, that many persons resist the Holy Spirit and reject the grace that is offered."[56]

Arminius' doctrine of the relationship between the idea of necessity and contingency are in accord with this formal notion of God's providence. "My opinion

---

52. KSO: "Preventing grace" is better and more often termed "prevenient grace." It means the grace that comes before one exercises faith.
53. Ibid., Vol. I, p. 248.
54. Ibid., p. 251.
55. Ibid., p. 252.
56. Ibid., pp. 253–254.

concerning Necessity and Contingency is 'that they can never be applicable at once to one and the same event.'"[57] Again,

> For every being is either necessary or contingent. But those things which divide the whole of being, cannot coincide or meet together in any single being. Otherwise they would not divide the whole range of being. What is contingent, and what is necessary, likewise, differs in their entire essences and in the whole of their definition. For that is *necessary* which *cannot* possibly not be or not be done. And that is *contingent* which *is possible* not to be or not to be done. Thus contradictorily are they opposed to each other; and this opposition is infinite, and, therefore, always dividing truth from falsehood: as, 'this thing is either *a man* or it is *not a man*'; it is not possible for anything to be both of these at once that is, it is impossible for any thing *of one essence*.[58]

On the basis of this fundamental difference between necessity and contingency Arminius says it is impossible that an event would be 'necessary' with regard to the first cause, which is God,—and *contingent* with respect to second causes. "It is not only a rash saying, but a false and ignorant one, 'that a thing which, in regard to second causes, is done *contingently* is said to be done *necessarily* in regard to the divine decree.'"[59] The relation between the will of God and the will of man is to be resolved rather by saying that God's power is adjusted "to the mode of a thing." In the case of the events accomplished through the will of man, God's power is persuasive only. Thus the event that occurs will be said to be done contingently.[60] Its eventuation will be "certainly foreknown by God, according to the infinity of his understanding."[61]

This mode of reasoning, it will be noted, is in terms of ideas of necessity and contingency borrowed from non-Christian philosophy. It is basically subversive of the idea that human thought and human action are analogical to divine

---

57. Ibid., p. 289.
58. Ibid., p. 290.
59. Ibid., pp. 290, 291.
60. KSO: The Reformed worked hard to set forth a proper, biblical notion of necessity and contingency, especially as those modes relate to God's and man's choices. Thus, they incorporated a distinction, broached in the foreword, between the necessity of the consequence and the necessity of the consequent. In the former, God's decree (which itself was possible not to be until and unless God freely determined it would be) will eventuate. In the latter, there is real contingency with respect to our choices. See the discussion, for example, of the Reformed in Willem J. van Asselt, J. M. Bac, and R. T. te Velde, eds., *Reformed Thought on Freedom: The Concept of Free Choice in the History of Early-Modern Reformed Theology* (Grand Rapids, MI: Baker Academic, 2010).
61. Ibid., p. 291.

thought and divine action. It assumes, as was the case with Pieper and Francke above, that all human thought and action must, at some-point, be autonomous. Human thought and action, it is argued on the basis of abstract possibility and abstract logic, cannot be derivative and receptively reconstructive; it must, at least in some measure, be ultimate. Human thought and human action must be unipersonal.

With a system of thought thus taken in part from non-Christian principles of interpretation Arminius cannot consistently allow that Scripture is self-attesting. For he has found that man can identify facts and laws in nature and history, in reality as man sees it, without reference to the self-attesting deed of God in his revelation. The thinking of Arminius is carried on in part in terms of a system of reality apart from God, and in part in terms of Scripture. The result is that though his position is far better than that of Romanism, it is nonetheless infected with something of the same naturalism that marked the latter view.

1. Richard Watson[62]

The tendency to think in principles other than those derived from Scripture is more prominent in later Arminian theologians than it is in Arminius himself. We shall look at some of them.

Richard Watson's *Theological Institutes* begins by asking why it is that revelation is necessary for man. His reply is that the nations had confused ideas about God and morality previous to the coming of revelation; he does not make a clear distinction between general and special revelation. But it soon appears that he thinks of man as originally having some defect because of his finitude. "No creature can be absolutely perfect because it is finite; and it would appear, from the example of our first parents, that an innocent, and, in its *kind*, a perfect rational being, is kept from falling only by 'taking hold' on God; and as this is an act, there must be a determination of the will to it, and so when the least carelessness, the least tampering with the desire of forbidden gratification is induced, there is always an enemy at hand to make use of the opportunity to darken the judgment and to accelerate the progress of evil."[63]

This view of the nature of man as first created is frequently found in Arminian theologians. It naturally goes with the idea of autonomy. For this idea involves the notion that man must ultimately accomplish his own character. He was not created perfect; he could not be created perfect. Creation is finite and

---

62. KSO: Richard Watson (1781–1833) was a British Methodist who was the first to systematize John Wesley's theological position.

63. Richard Watson, *Theological Institutes*, 13th ed., Vol. II (New York: Phillips and Hunt, n.d.), p. 33.

therefore itself imperfect. It needs from the outset some sort of supernatural gift in order to attain its end.

This position is very similar to the idea of the *donum superadditum* of Roman Catholic theology.⁶⁴ In both cases grace is something supplementative to nature that would be defective without it. Like Thomas Aquinas, Arminius uses the idea of man as a creature tending toward non-being from which he was taken at the first. Having so little of being in it this creature easily sways back and forth between the forces of evil and good. He has to make a habit of choosing for the good. Then his character will gradually be formed. At last he will be inclined toward the good all the time.

But this view of man is out of accord with the narrative of Scripture. Man was created perfect.⁶⁵ His character or nature was given him by God. To be sure man was subjected to a test. And this test would elicit from man greater self-conscious reaction to the gifts of God. But the idea of this test does not imply that man was not perfect at the outset of his existence. As Jesus was perfect and yet was subjected to the test of obedience so original man was also perfect. Original man could fall while Jesus could not fall. But in both cases the test came to a perfect man.

From Watson's views of the will of man as the ultimate source of man's character it follows that the necessity of Scripture and its redemptive revelation is not exclusively due to sin. If evil and finitude are involved in one another, it is no longer possible to distinguish clearly between an argument for special or redemptive revelation and an argument for natural revelation. For in that case redemption is necessary just because man is finite. The incarnation would have been necessary even apart from sin. Man was subject to forces not under God's control. The facts about him did not speak to man exclusively of God but also of other, equally ultimate forces. Man's own consciousness was then not inherently revelational. Man's actions had to be unipersonal to be personal at all.⁶⁶ At

---

64. KSO: The *donum superadditum* is a "superadded gift; specifically, the gift of grace superadded to human nature after creation but before the fall, a concept debated in the medieval theory of grace and merit and rejected by the Protestant orthodox. The concept arises out of the problem of explaining the hypothetical ability of Adam and Eve to have retained their original righteousness.... Aquinas maintained that the *donum superadditum* was part of the original constitution of man and that its loss was the loss of the original capacity for righteousness. Since the superadded grace was not merited in the beginning, it cannot be regained by merit after the fall." Richard A. Muller, *Dictionary of Latin and Greek Theological Terms: Drawn Principally from Protestant Scholastic Theology* (Grand Rapids, Mich.: Baker Book House, 1985), 96.

65. KSO: By "perfect" here Van Til means "without sin."

66. KSO: By "unipersonal" Van Til means that, for Watson and Arminians generally, man's action has to be *only* his and cannot in any way be in conjunction with God's ordination, concurrence, or providence.

the outset man found himself in a sea of abstract possibility. Reality would be basically of one sort; God and man would be together in a universe surrounding both. Watson does not hesitate to subject God to the same condition of temporality as man. "Duration, then, as applied to God, is no more than an extension of the idea as applied to ourselves; and to exhort us to conceive of it as something essentially different, is to require us to conceive what is inconceivable."[67] What man can conceive is the limit of possibility, and since man cannot conceive eternity as other than an extension of time, therefore it must be an extension of time.

This line of reasoning is quite out of accord with Watson's generally orthodox position. He seeks to satisfy the demand for univocism or continuity as the autonomous man thinks of it. To satisfy the autonomous man's demands he is willing to subject his God to the conditions of finitude. For it is only thus that, according to the autonomous man, God can have any definite characteristics. On the other hand, he seeks to satisfy the autonomous man's demands for equivocism or discontinuity. So he says that man, according to Scripture, has not been given a character by God; he must accomplish his own character by actions that are exclusively his own.

Watson's soteriology agrees with his views about original man. The natural man has, according to Watson, the power to resist the overtures of the gospel. Salvation is merely made *possible* for him by God. God approaches him only as a member of a class. The individual man must make the ultimate decision; Christ's active obedience is not attributed to his people; Christ has done no more than remove the obstacles in the way of man's salvation. The work of the Holy Spirit, too, is limited to a removal of obstacles. By regeneration the power of sin over man is broken so that with free choice man can serve God.

Of peculiar interest is the fact that Watson not only claims to hold to the biblical doctrine of total depravity but claims to be able to do so more consistently than the Reformed Faith can. For on the Arminian position he says the good deeds done by the natural man are seen to be the effect of an influence on them by the Holy Spirit, while in the Reformed Faith these good deeds must be explained by the artificial doctrine of common grace.[68] This mode of reasoning resembles that of Schleiermacher when he argues that it takes full independence in man for him to feel "absolute dependence." For without such full independence man cannot with full self-consciousness submit himself to God. On any basis but that of full independence the relation between God and man would not be exclusively personal. However, as noted above, the exact reverse is the case. There can be only one final reference point in predication. If man is taken

---

67. Ibid., Vol. I, p. 357.
68. Ibid., Vol. II, p. 48.

to be this final reference point, his environment becomes dependent upon him, and any other personality that may exist is not more ultimate than he. Therefore there is no God on whom he can feel himself dependent. He is his own god.

It is of interest to note that though Watson claims to do full justice to the biblical teaching on total depravity, in reality his conception of grace, like that of Rome, reduces the differences between the virtues of the believer and those of the unbeliever to a matter of gradation. Grace supplements and perfects nature. For Watson this means that nature is inherently in need of such supplementation. It is thus the gradation motif inherent in the idea of reality as a chain of being is given a determining influence in Christian theology.[69]

Watson does not take the Scriptures as the exclusive source of ultimate identification. Watson's basic principles are taken in part from Scripture and in part from the autonomous man.

2. Joseph Butler[70]

Similar to the position of Watson is that of Bishop Butler. His work, *The Analogy of Religion Natural and Revealed to the Constitution and Course of Nature*, is a classic on the method of apologetics current in evangelical circles.

According to Butler the course and constitution of nature is perfectly intelligible to man in terms of principles not taken from the Christian religion. Christianity is said to be in analogy with what man has already found in the course of his own independent investigations of nature and history. Christianity is therefore first a republication of natural religion adapted to the present circumstances of mankind. Secondly Christianity tells of a dispensation not discoverable by reason. "And in consequence of this revelation" several distinct precepts are enjoined us. "By reason is revealed the relation, which God the Father stands in to us. Hence arises the obligation of duty which we are under to him. In Scripture are revealed

---

69. KSO: That is, as noted in the foreword, nature, as limited, is lower on the "scale of being" than nature supplemented by grace. But everything is on the same scale. Without grace, one tends toward non-being. Grace moves one up on the scale, further from non-being.

70. KSO: Bishop Joseph Butler (1692–1752) was the most influential Protestant apologist of the 18th century. The book to which Van Til refers—*The Analogy of Religion Natural and Revealed to the Constitution and Course of Nature* (1736)—was a defense of Christianity against the prevalent deism of the day. Butler uses a double negative argument to attempt to argue from the natural religion of the deists to the probability of revealed religion as well (given 'x' in natural religion, it is not so irrational to believe 'y' in revealed religion). The basic thrust of Butler's argument is this: this (observed) life and the (unobserved) afterlife, taken together, exhibit features which resemble known features of this life taken alone. For example, we can infer that this life is a training-ground for the next life from the way in which the early years of this life are a training-ground for the later ones. Parenthetically, the reader should note that the term "analogy" is not used in the same way by Butler, Aquinas, or Van Til, which is one reason why confusion remains with respect to the term itself in apologetics.

the relations, which the Son and the Holy Spirit stand in to us. Hence arise the obligations of duty, which we are under to them."[71]

It is apparent that the idea of gradation and supplementation largely controls Butler's thinking. It is not the fact that man has sinned against the triune God which accounts for his need of redemption and therefore for his need of an infallible interpretation of the work of redemption. It is merely that by reason man has met only the Father. It would enrich him if he also met the Son and the Holy Spirit. For this purpose Christianity is given.

As with Romanism, so with Butler, original man hovered near the realm of non-being. As such man was naturally inclined to "external objects." He had to exercise his will and thus establish a habit in order to overcome his natural propensity to those external objects. Not that this propensity in itself was an evil. But if not resisted it would keep him from turning to higher things. "*Thus the principle of virtue, improved into a habit, of which improvement we are thus capable, will plainly be, in proportion to the strength of it, a security against the danger which finite creatures are in, from the very nature of propension, or particular affections.*"[72]

When original man did yield to his natural propensities for external objects and thus failed by discipline of will to establish habits of virtue, then God through the Son and the Spirit came to his assistance. Not that the Father's laws were too rigid. Even in nature, where the will of the Father is revealed, we find not only severity but also indulgence.[73] Even so the Son and the Spirit in a special sense reveal the mercy of God. "Revelation teaches us, that the unknown laws of God's more general government, no less than the particular laws by which we experience he governs us at present, are compassionate, as well as good in the more general notion of goodness: and that he hath mercifully provided, that there should be an interposition to prevent the destruction of human kind; whatever that destruction unprevented would have been."[74] God "gave his Son in the same way of goodness to the world, as he affords particular persons the friendly assistance of their fellow-creatures; when, without it, their temporal ruin would be the certain consequence of their follies: in the same way of goodness, I say; though in a transcendent and infinitely higher degree."[75]

On such a theology as this, it is evident the Protestant doctrine of Scripture cannot well be maintained. There is no longer any strict necessity for Scripture on account of the sin of man. This sin is, in part, due to man's finitude. So man is scarcely, at least not exclusively, responsible for his sin, and his sin is not

---

71. Butler, *op. cit.*, Vol. I, p. 197.
72. Ibid., p. 122 (italics are Butler's).
73. Ibid., p. 256.
74. Ibid., p. 261.
75. Ibid., p. 262.

self-conscious disobedience against the known will of God. Man was not at the first clearly surrounded by the will of God. God's revelation was not clear because it was not all-inclusive. So redemptive revelation cannot be clear. It too comes in a universe that contains forces over which God has no control. The authority ascribed to such a revelation can be no higher than that of expert advice to the largely autonomous man. The relation between God and man is not that of the covenant as pictured in Scripture, but is a matter of claims and counter-claims of one person who is greater than the other to whom he gives good advice about the arrangements of the universe. There could be no finality to the revelation or advice given by this greater, more experienced person to this lesser, less experienced person. For the greater person would find himself in a process of development too.

Of course this view of Christianity and of its function in the world is not typical of the average Arminian Christian. The average Arminian evangelical has a much more Scriptural view of Christianity. Even Butler had a better view of Christianity than is expressed in his mode of reasoning for its defense. But the point of importance to note is that when the idea of autonomy in man is accepted in any measure the Protestant view of Scripture is to that degree compromised. We are then back with the chain of being idea, the gradation motif of Romanism.[76] Christian men have undertaken to satisfy the supposed needs of the natural man as this natural man himself defines those needs. Christian theologians undertake to prove the truth of Christianity by reducing it to such an extent that it is scarcely distinguishable from the higher types of non-Christian thought. Scripture is then no longer what it intends to be, the self-testifying Word of God, basic and controlling in the principles of those who give their thoughts over to the subjection and obedience of Christ Jesus.

3. John Miley[77]

The theology of John Miley is also Arminian. Miley also interprets Scripture in terms of a philosophy in which the idea of the autonomous man plays a prominent part. According to Miley, Adam lived in a sort of pre-moral state. Adam's nature, he argues, "certainly could possess no proper ethical element, such as can arise only from free personal action."[78] Adam had a non-ethical and therefore

---

76. KSO: Meaning that even at creation and before the fall, we needed something else in order to move us further away from non-being. The "scale of being" applies to our finitude, even before the fall.

77. KSO: John Miley (1813–1895) was a Methodist theologian who taught systematic theology at Drew University in Madison, NJ. He authored a two-volume systematic theology that showed his adherence to Wesleyan/Arminian theology.

78. John Miley, *Systematic Theology*, Vol. I ("Library of Biblical and Theological Literature," ed. by G. R. Crooks and J. F. Hurst, Vols. IV, V, New York: Eaton and Mains, 1892), p. 409.

non-meritorious holiness. Human action to be moral action, according to Miley, must not be done in relation to the all-encompassing plan of God; it must rather be done in a vacuum. Only a series of acts resulting exclusively from the determination of man himself could result in a good character. The idea of created ethical character is rejected by Miley and by Arminian theologians in general.[79]

It is clear that by this insistence on human autonomy Arminianism has involved itself in the hopeless problematics of non-Christian thought. How could moral action originate from a moral amoeba? How could it operate in a vacuum, granted it could originate? How could a moral action be distinguished from a non-moral or an immoral action? In other words, how could the *ought* ever be set off over against the *is*? How, that is, could there then be any authoritative revelation of God over man?

The fact that Miley cannot consistently carry through the idea of an absolute beginning of moral action through man in a moral vacuum appears from the fact that he finds it necessary to insert some distinction between good and evil actions in man from the beginning.

"While Adam and Eve were constituted holy in their moral nature, the spontaneous tendencies of which were toward the good, yet in their complete constitution there were susceptibilities to temptation which might be followed into sinful action."[80] But there is no justification for instituting any difference between good and evil unless it be upon the presupposition of God who identifies himself as good, who makes man good and unavoidably aware of the good. It is this identification of good by God himself and by God to man in his nature and in the direct commandment given him that is presented in Scripture. For that reason Scripture is self-authenticating. In being self-authenticating it authenticates clearly and unmistakably in man and to man the distinction between good and evil.

It follows from this view of Scripture as self-authenticating and as indicating to man what is true and false, what is good and evil, that man lives by the absolute authority of God. All identification in history is therefore ultimately by way of God's authoritative statement. Therefore man cannot expect to understand exhaustively the reason for any particular commandment of God. The commandment as given to man in paradise with respect to the forbidden fruit was not based upon some easily discernible difference between the fruit of that tree and the fruit of other trees. It was, as far as man could discern, a matter of

---

79. KSO: Elsewhere, Miley says, "A mere initial tendency to the good in Adam could have no ethical character. It could not become an active disposition until duty in some form was presented. Simply as spontaneously active it could constitute only a motive, not an ethical action." John Miley, *Systematic Theology*, Volume 1 (New York: Hunt & Eaton, 1892), 411.

80. Ibid., p. 434.

indifference. But God's setting aside the tree as forbidden indicated to man that the good for him is that which God says is good and because God says it. To be sure, God would say only what is in accord with his holy nature. But there is for man no direct knowledge of this nature of God except through the expressed will of God. The will of God as expressed supernaturally in conjunction with the revelation of God already manifest in created reality is the source of man's knowledge.

It is this idea of Scripture as thus making God known to sinners through his will, requiring obedience to that will, which the autonomous man will not allow. He insists that he has the right of self-determination, the right of distinguishing for himself the true from the false and the right from the wrong, and it is this claim that Miley and other Arminians are owning as fit and proper for the sinner to make. They hold it to be right and proper for the sinner because they, in the first place, have reduced the idea of man's creation in the image of God into something resembling the non-Christian notion of man as participating in the being of God.

That the Arminian conception of man leads readily to the modern position in which man is frankly made the standard of right and wrong can readily be seen from O. A. Curtis'[81] book, *The Christian Faith*. In his case Arminianism has practically lost its Scriptural moorings and placed itself upon a non-Christian philosophy of experience. Curtis acknowledges the influence of the personalist philosophy of experience of Bordon P. Bowne[82] upon him. This personalist philosophy is based upon the assumption of Immanuel Kant that man is his own interpreter. Albert C. Knudson,[83] also a personalist philosopher, claims that Methodist theology was peculiarly fortunate in adapting itself to modern thinking inasmuch as it is empirical in its method from the beginning.[84]

He interprets the emphasis of early Methodism upon the "primacy of

---

81. KSO: Olin Alford Curtis (1850–1918) taught systematic theology at Drew University from 1896–1914.

82. KSO: Bordon P. Bowne (1847–1910) was one of the leading Boston Personalists. He taught philosophy at Boston University. Van Til discusses Boston Personalism in his *The Case for Calvinism*.

83. KSO: Albert C. Knudson (1873–1953) spent the majority of his teaching career at Boston University as an Old Testament professor, then as a professor of systematic theology. "Deeply influenced by Boston University's Borden P. Bowne, Knudson emphasized the personalist themes of the immanence of God, an understanding of God in terms of personal categories, and religious knowledge as a fundamental and valid aspect of human experience. His systematic and speculative thought was published in *The Philosophy of Personalism* (1927); *The Doctrine of God* (1930); *The Doctrine of Redemption* (1933); and *The Validity of Religious Experience* (1937)." Daniel G. Reid et al., *Dictionary of Christianity in America* (Downers Grove, IL: InterVarsity Press, 1990, n.p.).

84. Albert C. Knudson, "Emphases in Methodist Theology," *The Christian Advocate* (Vol. 106, No. 10 and 11; March 5 and 12, 1931), pp. 291–292, 325.

religious experience" as something that was bound to eventuate in a change of attitude toward the traditional objective view of Scripture, and Christian doctrine in general. Then he goes on to say, "The important thing here, however, is to note that the primacy of religious experience, which may be said to be the basic principle of our church, makes theological finality impossible, and that, if we are to be true to this principle, our theology must continually adapt itself to the changing thought of the world—must, in a word, be progressive."[85]

Whatever our reaction may be to this claim of Knudson's, it remains true that the Arminian point of view makes compromise with the natural man. In this it resembles the position of Rome and cannot be said to represent Protestantism at its best. Arminianism therefore cannot place the Christian system of truth squarely over against the non-Christian system. It has granted that non-Christian thought, which is based upon the idea of the autonomy of man, upon the idea of a principle of continuity that stands above both God and man, and upon a principle of discontinuity that surrounds both God and man with chance, can, for all that, make intelligible distinctions between right and wrong, between one fact and another fact, and between truth and falsehood. To make such an admission involves a failure to present Christianity as expressed in the self-authenticating Scriptures of the Old and New Testaments as requiring man to turn away from his sin to the living God through the Christ whom he has sent to be the Savior of men.

---

85. Ibid., p. 292.

VIII

NATURAL THEOLOGY AND SCRIPTURE[1]

We have now reached the point in our discussion where we may ask how Christians who believe the Bible for what it is, the self-attesting word of Christ as God, should present this Bible to those who live by the principle of the autonomy of man. From time to time that question has already been answered, at least by implication. In general the answer implied or suggested is that the Bible must be presented to men as the principle in terms of which the whole of human life is to be explained. It cannot come to men other than as the Word of God. It must come in terms of authority. It must therefore require the obedience of men. It comes to men as the rightful sovereign comes to rebels who have usurped authority in his realm. It must come the way King Shaddai and Prince Immanuel did to the diabolonians in Bunyan's *Holy War*. At the same time it must come the way Jesus himself the Son of God came to Jerusalem weeping over its children, softly and tenderly offering them rest from the toil and burden of sin. God seeks spontaneous and loving acceptance of his Word. As he wanted this in paradise, so he wants it now. Christians must be, like the Apostle Paul, all things to all men in order to save some. Firm and insistent in their ultimate objective, they must approach their goal *suaviter in modo*.[2]

It is to be expected that Roman Catholics will not wish to present Scripture as authoritative in the sense described. They do not believe in the absolute authority of Scripture in any practical way. Theirs is a formal adherence to Scripture. Their philosophy of reality allows for the notion of expert authority but not for that of absolute authority. According to Romanism God does not control all things and therefore he is not in a position to give an authoritative interpretation of all things nor really, of any one thing.[3]

---

1. The material in this chapter presupposes the argumentation found in the present writer's "Nature and Scripture" in *The Infallible Word*.
2. KSO: "mild in manner."
3. KSO: "God does not control all things" because Romanism holds that man's choices must be free in a libertarian sense and therefore completely free of God's control.

Evangelicals too, though of course they actually do constantly speak of the authority of Scripture, have a philosophy of being that cannot do justice to this idea. So they too, though to a much smaller extent than the Romanists, make compromise with the idea of human autonomy.

The way this compromise appears in connection with the presentation of Scripture is a matter of great interest for us. How do sincere Christians who truly want to accept the Scriptures as the self-attesting Word of God but who also want, in some measure, to own the claims of human autonomy, present the Scriptures to men?

The answer is that they seek to do this in piecemeal fashion. They would interpret Paul's words to the effect that they must be all things to all men in order to win some in such fashion as to present the natural man with what are to him the least objectionable features of Christianity first. Surely, they say, we must not antagonize men from the outset. We must not tell them at once that as ambassadors of the King of kings we demand unconditional surrender and will be satisfied with nothing less. We must rather begin from what, as Christians, we have in common with men. Perhaps men have not stopped to think that even in their own view of the world there is room for the idea of the *Beyond*. It is no disgrace surely for anyone to admit that one is not omniscient. Do not all things end in mystery? In particular do not modern scientists, such as James Jeans and Arthur Eddington and others, stand reverently at the borders of the universe bowing before a god that is wholly beyond anything that man has discovered? Do not the best of philosophers interpret the lower things of the universe in terms of that which is higher, the material in terms of the spiritual? So why should not men accept the idea of the supernatural? It is but an extension of the principle of discontinuity which they themselves, in terms of their own philosophy, admit. The *possibility* of the existence of God, of his revelation to men, of his miraculous work in history, ought to be granted by all but extreme determinists and rationalists.

From this point on, the evangelical will say to his non-Christian friend: We can look together at the facts of nature and history in neutral fashion to see *whether* there is evidence there of God's presence and of Christ's redeeming work of mercy. Does it not look as though *in all probability* the facts can be *better* explained in terms of the Christian *hypothesis* than in terms of any other? Let reason by all means be adhered to; you are yourself the final judge, but will you not be compelled to admit that there is at least a *probability*, even a *high* probability that theism and Christianity are true? Should not probability be our guide in life? Does not one act upon it when, in the nature of the case, no demonstrative certainty can be obtained? In the case of ultimate things we should not expect demonstrative but only moral certainty. About the question of existence, that is all that can be expected. So then it is wholly reasonable that you should submit yourself to the authority of the Christ of the Scriptures. We are not asking you forthwith to accept the Scriptures as the infallible Word of God. We are asking you first to regard them merely as trustworthy *historical* documents. As such they speak of Jesus of Nazareth. They portray him to us and let him speak for himself. If you look at that portrait, you will see that it has all the signs of verisimilitude upon it. You be the judge. Is he not divine? If you cannot trust him and his words, what else is there that you can trust? Then human nature in its deepest needs and in its highest aspirations cannot be satisfied.

It is in some such fashion that the evangelicals argue for the idea of the Scriptures as the Word of God. They seek to show that it is quite in accord with "reason" to believe in the Bible as the Word of God. It is in accord with reason because reason itself points beyond itself, and what is presented in Scripture is not so far beyond anything that reason teaches but that it can be shown to be in accord with it. The principles of discontinuity and of continuity, of equivocism and of univocism as these are involved in the notion of human autonomy, are not challenged by this method of the evangelical.

Historically, it is in Bishop Butler's famous *Analogy* that this method of argument has been first worked out fully. Butler argues that both he and his opponents agree on a known area of interpretation, the course and constitution of nature. From that known area he seeks to have his opponents go with him by the principle of analogy onto an acceptance of Christianity. Butler's principle of analogy is to all intents and purposes the same principle as was employed by Aquinas.[4] We have already shown how this principle is inherently destructive of the Protestant idea of Scripture. Butler's concept of analogy starts with the idea of man as ultimate. How then is it possible to reach the idea of man as derivative from the idea that man is ultimate? It is a foregone conclusion that on the principle employed by Aquinas and Butler the god that is discovered is not the absolute God of Scripture. He will be an abstract universal obtained by the way of negation based on the idea of autonomy or he will have only metaphorical characteristics when obtained by way of eminence from the same idea of autonomy. The authority of the Scriptures that is involved in this method is therefore nothing higher than that of the expert.

---

4. KSO: There are significant differences between Aquinas and Butler in the way that they employ the notion of analogy. The reason Van Til says that their principles of analogy are "to all intents and purposes the same principle" is, as he goes on to say, they both begin with a notion of man as autonomous and of reason as neutral. Their differences, therefore, are not *foundational* differences in that sense.

In practice, of course, the position of the evangelical is far, very far, better than this. But it is his adherence to the idea of autonomy, in some measure at least, that keeps him from doing justice to that which lives in his heart.

·———·

It might be expected then that Reformed theology would have nothing to do with such an essentially Roman Catholic method of presenting the doctrine of Scripture. Its basic philosophy of reality, itself taken from Scripture, is that God controls whatsoever comes to pass. This is true because God is what he is, the necessary self-existent One. God cannot possibly not exist. *This fact too is taken from Scripture.* On a non-Christian basis it must be maintained on the one hand, that existence and being are coterminous and, on the other hand, that they have no necessary connection at all. Those who work on the idea of human autonomy have to be both utter rationalists and utter irrationalists. They have to hold that God knows all things even as man also knows all things and that God does not know anything even as man does not know anything. There is on this basis one law of rationality and one law of being to which God and man are alike subject. By its principle of continuity a god is obtained who is wholly rational and quite necessary for man as man is wholly rational and quite necessary for this god. By its principle of discontinuity a god is obtained who is wholly other than man, or rather, who is wholly unknown to man.

Over against this sort of god who springs from the principle of the autonomous man is the God of Scripture. He presents himself in Scripture as the One in terms of whom man himself is to forsake his autonomy and permit himself to be interpreted by God. In other words the Scripture presents God as ultimate. Accordingly Scripture presents itself as the final principle by which all things must be measured. The gods produced by the thinking of man apart from Scripture are idols. To hold to any such god is to break the first commandment of the God of the Scriptures.

Involved in this doctrine of the God who controls whatsoever comes to pass is the notion that all things in the world are revelational and that man as created by God knows himself in relation to this revelation of God. He knows himself to be analogical to God in his being, his thought and his action. Even the sinner after the fall knows that his idea of autonomy is a false idea. He "knows" that he is a creature of God; yet his idea of autonomy would make him think as though he were not. Thus sin is always sin against better knowledge. But the sinner's depravity is such that he cannot but sin against this better knowledge. His evil nature has become second nature to him. He is controlled in his thinking by the idea of his own ultimacy. That is his *adopted* principle. It is that principle with which he confronts the challenge that comes to him in the idea of the Bible as the Word of God.

Not as though he is in every sense self-conscious of his own adopted principle. In practice the natural man is much better than his principle. He does not fully live up to his principle. He is not a finished product. He is restrained by the non-saving grace of God from "being as bad as he can be," and as bad as he will be when his principle has full control of him.[5]

In practice, therefore, the man of the street is a complex individual. He is first the creature made in the image of God. He was represented in Adam at the beginning of history. In Adam he broke the covenant of God. He is now in principle opposed to God. He is dead in trespasses and sins. He is wholly polluted in all the aspects of his being. So far as he lives from this principle he will not because he cannot, and he cannot because he will not, accept the overtures of the grace of God unless by the regenerating power of the Holy Spirit he is made alive from the dead. But he does not live fully from his principle. Therefore he does not react in the exclusively negative way that we would expect him to, if we look at the principle that ultimately controls him. Like the prodigal of the scriptural parable he cannot forget the father's voice and the father's house. He knows that the father has been good and is good in urging him to return. Yet his principle drives him on to the swine trough. On the one hand he will do the good, in the sense of that which externally at least is in accord with the will of God. He will live a "good" moral life. He will be anxious to promote the welfare of his fellow men. In all this he is not a hypocrite. He is not sufficiently self-conscious to be a hypocrite.

It is therefore of the utmost importance to distinguish between what the natural man is by virtue of his adopted principle and what he still is because of the knowledge of God as his creator that he has within him and because of the non-saving grace by which he is kept from working out his principle to the full and by which he is therefore also able to do the "morally good."

When presenting the Scriptures as the Word of God to men it is necessary to do so with due consideration of all of these facts. Men have the knowledge of God within them. At bottom they know that not to glorify God is to be disobedient to God, is to break the covenant of God. When challenged with the idea of the Bible as the Word of God this challenge finds an immediate and unavoidable response in the deepest of men's beings. Men know at once that they ought to accept this challenge; they know that they are rebels and ought to

---

5. KSO: For a discussion of this "non-saving grace of God," see Van Til, *Common Grace and the Gospel*.

resubmit themselves to their rightful sovereign. It is as "knowing God" Paul says, that men rebel against God (Rom 1:32).

It is therefore a fatal mistake on the part of Christians not to demand absolute surrender of the natural man. He can understand the language of absolute surrender; he can understand no other language. This is not to say that he will forthwith surrender when the challenge is made. He will not surrender till the Spirit of God, who himself inspired the Bible as the Word of God, will give him life from the dead. But the challenge will be intelligible to him. It requires him to accept his original sovereign, from whom he has turned in a false effort at autonomy, as his rightful Lord. He understands that in the nature of the case his Lord cannot accept a compromise peace. The diabolonians of Bunyan's parable sought such a peace; they were not offered anything but the promise of life on the basis of surrender, and death on the basis of anything less.

Does this idea of challenging the natural man with the demand for absolute surrender violate the principle of human personality? It would do so only if it were first granted that human personality should be thought of as inherently autonomous. But if human personality is inherently analogous of God's personality, then it is natural and proper and good for this personality to own its Lord. Then too its rightful claims will be met. In paradise God did not force his requirements upon Adam. He presented him with a choice. He asked him to do that which is right from a deep desire to love and serve his Maker. It is that which must again be done when the sinner is confronted with the gospel as presented in Scripture. But the idea of choice, such choice as is incumbent upon and proper for human personality, cannot be of any significance if it is to take place in a void. Only upon the presupposition that is in relation to the commandment of God does human choice not take place in a void.

What needs to be done then in presenting the Scriptures to the natural man is to appeal to his "sense of deity," to the fact that in the very *penetralia* of his consciousness he does always confront the same God who now asks him to yield obedience to him. The gospel of God's grace to sinners comes to creatures who know God but who have rebelled against God and therefore do not know God lovingly. It comes to those who now have needs such as they at the first did not have. They are now subject to the wrath of God due to their disobedience. If they are to be reinstated to favor with God, there must be atonement made for them. The Son of God has made that atonement for men. He now everywhere calls men to accept this atonement. Whosoever believes will be saved. That is, whosoever turns from his evil ways of unbelief, whosoever now accepts the finished work of Christ in his death and resurrection as paying in his stead for the penalty that was due to him for his sin, the penalty of eternal death, will be saved. He can learn about this salvation from no other source than from the Bible.

Nor can he learn of this salvation from the Bible as being merely an historical record. The idea of the Scriptures as telling about the work of the Christ merely as historical records is inherently unintelligible. The idea is that these documents are supposed to be historically trustworthy even though they are not to be taken as the Word of God. That is to say the idea why Christian apologists approach the unbeliever with this idea of the essential trustworthiness of the gospels as historical documents rather than as the infallible word of God is to make the acceptance of what they teach easier for the natural man. But how could the natural man consistently allow that what the Scriptures say about the idea of human autonomy with its principle of continuity and of discontinuity, and what is said about Christ and his work is even possible? From the point of view of his principle of continuity, the autonomous man must deny the uniqueness of Christ and his work, and from the point of view of his principle of discontinuity this same autonomous man must hold that Christianity as a fact is unique as everything else is unique.[6]

Put in other words, on the principle of autonomy there is no intelligible principle of identification of anything in history. In the words of Goethe it may be said, on this basis, that, "if the individual speaks, it is no longer the individual that speaks." If a fact is identifiable in history, it is identifiable only in terms of a rationalist system that at the same time sublates its identity into relations.

The implication of what has been said is this: If Christians ask non-Christians merely to accept the gospels or some other part of Scripture as historically trustworthy documents, they are allowing the legitimacy and efficacy of the principle of autonomy. They are allowing that it is possible intelligently to identify and set in order the elements of human experience in history by means of the principle of autonomy. But if this were true, if by the principle of autonomy such identification and ordering could take place, there is no need for the idea of God speaking to men. It is just because man *cannot* speak intelligently to himself without God and because the sinner has sent God out of his life that God in condescending grace comes back to him. But he asks men to accept him at his word for what he is, the indispensable presupposition of all intelligent human predication.

It is in consonance with this approach that the Reformed Confessions assert that our final acceptance of the Scriptures as the Word of God rests upon the internal testimony of the Holy Spirit. All the indications of the divinity of Scripture

---

6. KSO: See the foreword for an elaboration of this idea. The non-Christian principle of continuity is a rationalistic, "law-like" principle that cannot abide any irregularities of nature; thus, no Incarnation, miracles, etc. The non-Christian principle of discontinuity is a principle of random chance, so that anything can happen.

would lose their effectiveness and would indeed accomplish the very opposite of what they are meant to accomplish if they were taken out of their relation of dependence upon the testimony of the Holy Spirit. These indications do, of course, objectively show the Scriptures to be the Word of God. The whole Bible in all respects shows itself objectively to be the Word of God. The majesty of its style, the harmony of its parts and other such things, all indicate the Scriptures to be the Word of God.[7] Prophecies fulfilled and miracles performed, the works as well as the words of Christ, all that Scripture contains, shows its divinity. The record of these works and words of the Christ is *ipso facto* as a record identified by God as the Word of God. But the acceptance of both the Christ and his word, both the personal word and the spoken word, comes by virtue of one and the same act of submission and surrender. And this act of surrender and faith comes in consequence of the testimony of the Holy Spirit.

This testimony of the Holy Spirit is therefore not a new revelation of God that would in turn need a new testimony for its corroboration. Nor does it work apart from the objective evidence of the divinity of Scripture. It appeals to man as made in the image of God with full ability to see and understand the significance of his deeds.[8] It speaks to this same man as the sinner with utter inability to understand spiritually and to respond obediently to the demands of the gospel. It speaks to him through the content of the Bible and only through the content of the Bible. It actually convinces the sinner and practically convicts him of sin and of judgment. It compels him to believe that which he knows he ought to believe but which because of the perverseness of his will and the darkness of his mind he otherwise cannot believe, namely, that the Bible is the Word of God and what it contains is the system of truth as given to man by God.

What has been said so far in this chapter has not been universally agreed upon by Reformed theologians. There are among them at least two generally distinct points of view with respect to the matter discussed. It is well that these two distinct points of view be considered.

The difference between these two points of view hinges largely on the question of the method of apologetics to be followed in presenting the Christian faith to men. This general difference of method of apologetics involves and is centered in a difference of evaluation of the place and value of natural theology in relation to Scripture. At least in connection with our general purpose of dealing with Christian epistemology it is this question that interests us.

---

7. KSO: See WCF 1.5.
8. KSO: Note Van Til's affirmation that total depravity does not preclude a certain kind of understanding of the "natural man."

NATURAL THEOLOGY AND SCRIPTURE

[A.] KUYPER AND WARFIELD ON APOLOGETICS

It will not be possible to do more than deal with some of the outstanding representatives of each of the two points of view. In fact it is around two names in particular that we wish to center the discussion of this subject. There is first the name of Dr. Abraham Kuyper, Sr., founder of the Free University of Amsterdam. Then there is the name of Benjamin Breckinridge Warfield, outstanding theologian of Princeton Theological Seminary. Frequently the difference between the two points of view on apologetics is spoken of as the difference between the Princeton and the Amsterdam point of view. (It should be noted that since the reorganization of Princeton Seminary in 1929, neither the theology nor the view of Scripture entertained by Warfield are now taught at that institution. The representatives of the new Princeton should be classified with the modern rather than with the orthodox theologians. This fact has become particularly clear now that in his book *The Westminster Confession for Today* Dr. George Hendry[9] has completely rejected the theology of Dr. Warfield and the other earlier Princeton theologians.)

In looking into the differences between the Amsterdam and the Princeton schools of apologetics it should be noted first that there is little difference between them on the theology of Scripture. Barring relatively minor matters, the school of Princeton as represented by Warfield and that of Amsterdam as represented by Kuyper are remarkably similar in the presentation of what Scripture teaches. More than that, there is as equally close a similarity between the views of Scripture as there is between the views of the content of Scripture. Both hold to the idea of God as controlling whatsoever comes to pass. Both hold with Calvin to man's having a sense of deity that is ineradicable because he is made to be in the image of God. Both are therefore equally opposed to the "evangelical" view of man, to the extent that it attributes autonomy to him in relation to God. Both hold with Calvin to the idea of the necessity of the testimony of the Holy Spirit if the natural man is to accept the Bible as the Word of God.

It is because of this large measure of agreement on the doctrine of Scripture as well as of the content of Scripture that the difference between them on the matter of natural theology is so remarkable.

---

9. KSO: George Hendry was the Charles Hodge Professor of Systematic Theology at Princeton Theological Seminary from 1949–1973. Van Til notes that Hendry is "the greatest expositor of Karl Barth on this continent, as he tells us that the static God of the Westminster Confession must be replaced by the living god of the Confession of 1967." Cornelius Van Til and Eric H. Sigward, *The Sermons and Addresses of Cornelius Van Til*, Electronic ed. (Labels Army Company: New York, 1997).

Generally speaking, Warfield's method of apologetics implies a much higher view of natural theology than does that of Kuyper. But in saying this a word of explanation is in order as to what each of these two men mean by natural theology. Kuyper frequently uses it as synonymous with the idea of general, non-soteriological revelation. Again he speaks of it as being that natural knowledge which man has by virtue of the fact that he is made in the image of God and has within him the sense of deity. So when he deals with the Belgic Confession and particularly with its statement to the effect that there are two ways of knowing God, one through nature and one through Scripture, he says that this must not be taken to mean what rationalists have made of it but must be taken to mean simply that "without the substratum of natural theology there would be no redemptive theology."[10] [11] It is not therefore the idea of the autonomous man that Kuyper thinks of when he speaks of natural theology. When he discusses the sinner and the fact that this sinner has usurped the authority of judging the work of redemption that God has wrought for man, he speaks of the natural principle, *principium naturale*.[12] He then contrasts with it the special principle, the principle by which God has in Christ and through the Spirit come to save sinners. These two principles, he argues, stand utterly opposed to one another. "Since the *revelatio specialis* presupposes the fact that the operation of the natural principle has been disturbed in its healthful function through sin, it follows as a matter of course that this natural principle has lost the power of judgment. Whoever attributes this power of judgment to it recognizes it *eo ipso* as sound, and has therewith done away with the *ratio sufficiens* of special revelation."[13] [14]

Warfield also uses the idea of natural theology sometimes as referring to natural revelation within and about man. Usually, however, he refers to the conclusions which men in general, whether Christian or not, have drawn from natural revelation. And the issue with respect to natural theology is with respect to this latter matter. It does not refer to natural revelation, either round about or within men. It does not refer to what men ought to infer from this natural revelation whether external or internal. Nor does it refer to what those who have been redeemed have learned to infer from natural revelation inasmuch as they regard it in the light of Scripture. The question is, What evaluation is to be placed upon the interpretation of natural revelation, internal and external,

---

10. Abraham Kuyper, *Encyclopaedie der Heilige Godgeleerdheid*, Vol. II (Kampen: J. H. Kok, 1909), p. 328.
11. KSO: See Kuyper, Abraham, *Encyclopedia of Sacred Theology; Its Principles* (New York. C. Scribner's Sons, 1898), 374.
12. Ibid., p. 355.
13. Ibid.
14. KSO: Ibid., 381.

that the natural man, who operates with the principle of autonomy, has given of it? Can the difference between the principle of autonomy and that of Christian theism be ignored so that men can together seek to interpret natural revelation in terms of one procedure?

It is on this point that Kuyper and Warfield differ materially. At first sight at least it seems as though the difference between them is irreconcilable. It is this apparently irreconcilable difference that must first be delineated.

Kuyper's position has already been indicated in the telling sentence quoted. The idea of two ultimate principles is, he insists, a contradiction in terms. Either allow that the natural principle has within itself the legitimate powers of self-interpretation and then expect the special principle to be destroyed by it, or else maintain that the natural principle is in any case finite and more particularly sinful and then present the special principle to it with the demand of submission. Of course Kuyper chooses the second of these alternatives. Of course, says Kuyper, the natural man has power to observe the facts of the physical universe, to weigh them and arrange them. He can reason logically; sin has not made man insane. But the direction of the human person has changed. The power of thought may be compared to a sharp blade. If this blade is put into a mower but it is put too high so that it cannot reach the grass, there is no good result.[15][16] The result is, says Kuyper, even worse than this illustration would indicate. For the action of sinful human thought is not merely fruitless; it is destructive of the truth. Sinful man is out to destroy the special principle when it comes to him with its challenge. The natural principle takes an antithetical position over against the special principle and seeks to destroy it by means of logical manipulation.[17][18] The natural principle lives from *apistia*; its faith is fixed upon the creature instead of upon the Creator.[19][20] It will therefore use its principles of discontinuity and of continuity in order by means of them to destroy the witness of Scripture to itself. The natural man is perfectly consistent with himself and intellectually honest in doing so. He is simply true to his principle in doing so. A principle, a first premise, cannot be proved. It is the basis of proof. If proof were given of a principle, it would cease to be a principle.[21][22] The Christian realizes that the non-Christian does not know the truth about himself and of his

---

15. Ibid., p. 241.
16. KSO: Ibid., 288.
17. Ibid., p. 242.
18. KSO: Ibid., 290.
19. Ibid., p. 254.
20. KSO: Ibid., 280–81.
21. Ibid., p. 338.
22. KSO: Ibid., 384.

power of reason. He should therefore expect that the non-Christian will, from his natural principle, seek to destroy the special principle. He will do so by saying that the "irrational" element, that is the supernatural, is like the irrational element found everywhere. He will by means of his principle of continuity absorb all the claims of Scripture into a system of logical gradation. "*Zelf toch erkent ge van uw eigen standpunt, dat wie buiten* phōtismos *staat het werkelijk bestand van zijn eigen wezen, en dus ook van zijn rede, niet inziet en niet inzien kan.*"[23] [24] When you as a Christian present the unbeliever with the fact of miracles performed, this has no power of compulsion for him who, because on his principle, cannot even allow for the possibility of miracles.[25] [26]

Kuyper makes a special point of the necessity of holding that Scripture is not merely a *record of* but is itself revelation. One cannot separate cool atmosphere from the ice through which it comes. Without the Scripture as revelation there is no revelation. If one does not take the Scripture itself as revelation, then one ends by way of Origen in the philosophy of Plato or of Aristotle.[27] [28]

Similarly the idea of the testimony of the Spirit, too, is part of the special principle the whole of which one makes the foundation of his thought or the whole of which one rejects in the name of the natural principle.[29] [30] With the light of Scripture it is possible for man to read nature aright. Without that light we cannot, even on the Areopagus, reach further than the unknown God.[31] [32]

It is thus that the enlightened consciousness of the people of God stands over against the natural consciousness of the world. For the believers, Scripture is the principle of theology. As such it cannot be the conclusion of other premises, but it is *the* premise from which all other conclusions are drawn.[33] [34]

From what has been said it is not to be concluded that Kuyper had no great appreciation of the knowledge of God that may be obtained from nature. The contrary is true. He lays the greatest possible stress upon the idea that the Bible is not a book that has fallen from heaven. There is a natural foundation

---

23. Ibid., p. 339.
24. KSO: "From your own point of view you acknowledge that he who stands outside of spiritual illumination does not perceive, and cannot perceive, the real condition of his own being, nor of his reason," Ibid., 384–85.
25. Ibid., p. 341.
26. KSO: Ibid., 387.
27. Ibid., p. 316.
28. KSO: Ibid., 362.
29. Ibid., p. 320.
30. KSO: Ibid., 357.
31. Ibid., p. 332.
32. KSO: Ibid., 378.
33. Ibid., p. 517.
34. KSO: Ibid., 562.

for it. This natural foundation is found in the fact that "nature" is itself the creation of the same God who, in the special principle, comes to man for his redemption. In form at least Kuyper would therefore agree with Aquinas when he says that the supernatural or spiritual does not destroy but perfects nature. But Kuyper's ideas of the natural and the supernatural are quite different from those of Aquinas. For Aquinas the natural is inherently defective; it partakes of the nature of non-being. Hence sin is partly at least to be ascribed to finitude. For Kuyper the natural as it came from the hand of God was perfect. To be sure, there was to be development. Historically, this development has come by way of grace. But for all that, grace is an "accident," something that is incidental to the fulfillment of the natural. Christ came into the world to save, and in saving it developed to its full fruition the powers of the natural. Thus grace is not reduced to something that is to be naturally expected as a development of the natural. The gradation motif of Aquinas is replaced by the idea of grace as "accidental," as the means by which sin, which is wholly unnatural or contrary to the natural, and destructive of the natural, is removed, in order that the truly natural may thus come to expression.

The natural man, working on his principle, working from the principle of his second nature, must not be given the opportunity of destroying the "accidental" character of redemption. He would be given this opportunity if his principle of autonomy were not challenged. Working on his principle he would destroy the "accidental" character of grace altogether. He would do what Romanism has so largely done. He would seek to show that the redemptive is to be expected by man. He would show, on the other hand, that the redemptive is something without determinate character in history so that every man may regard it as he pleases.

It will now be seen that what has been advocated in this work has in large measure been suggested by Kuyper's thinking. The interdependence of the various aspects of what Kuyper so effectively speaks of as the special principle is something that would seem to be of the essence of a sound doctrine of Scripture. It is difficult to see how else the Scriptures can be presented as self-attesting. As soon as the elements of the special principle, such as the indications of divinity, the testimony of the Spirit, or the words of Christ are set next to one another, as largely independent of one another, the natural man is given an opportunity to do his destructive work. He is then allowed to judge at least with respect to one or more of these elements apart from the whole. If he is allowed to judge of the legitimacy or meaning of any one of them, he may as well be given the right to judge of all of them. If the natural man is allowed the right to take the documents of the gospels as merely historically trustworthy witnesses to the Christ and his work, he will claim and can consistently claim also to be the judge of the Christ himself. For it is only if the Christ be taken as the Son of God that he can be said legitimately to identify himself. If he is not presupposed as such, his words have no power. Then they too are absorbed in what is a hopeless relativity of history.

Kuyper then has done great service to Christian apologetics by thus stressing the interdependence of the various elements of the special principle, and by stressing also its "incidental" or "accidental" nature. It is thus alone that the idea of Scripture as self-attesting, and as at the same time based upon the natural as it came from the hand of God, is really maintained.

There is one main conclusion that Kuyper has drawn from this his general position, and that is that because of it there is virtually no use in Christian apologetics. Not that Kuyper has himself always been true to his virtual rejection of apologetics. But he frequently argues that since the natural man is not to be regarded as the proper judge of the special principle and since this is true because his understanding is darkened, there is no use and no justification for reasoning with the natural man at all. The question is whether this conclusion can be harmonized with the fact that Christianity is the true religion and has the criterion of truth within itself. In his *Institutes* Calvin greatly stresses that men *ought* to see God's presence as Creator, Provider, Benefactor, and Judge in nature and in history because this presence is clearly there. Men have not done justice by the facts, by the evidence of God's presence before their eyes, unless they burst out into praise of him who has made all things. Christ himself says that men should believe him as being in and with the Father because of his words, but if not for his words then for his works' sake. Does not this imply that there is a clearly distinguishable presence of God in history? Does not the doctrine of Scripture itself maintain that this book has in it the marks of divinity so that it is clearly distinguishable from all other books as being the very Word of God? And does not the Holy Spirit testify to the Word with definite content as being the Word of God?

Shall we then simply say that since the natural man is blind there is no purpose in displaying before him the rich color scheme of the revelation of God's grace? Shall we say that we must witness to men only and not reason with them at all? How would witnessing to them be of any more use to them than would reasoning? If men cannot in the least understand what he who witnesses is speaking of, will the witnessing be any challenge to him at all?

To find an answer to such questions as these it is well that we turn to the objection that Warfield raised against the position of Kuyper. In the 'Introductory Note' to the work on *Apologetics* written by Francis R. Beattie, Warfield expresses vigorous dissent from Kuyper's view of Christian apologetics. He speaks of the "widespread misprision of apologetics" that has come about because of rationalism and because of Mysticism. For rationalism religion is expressed only in value judgments; hence it is impossible to know anything of God. Then, Warfield adds: "In a somewhat odd parallelism to this (though, perhaps, it is not so odd, after all) the mystical tendency is showing itself in our day most markedly in a widespread inclination to decline apologetics in favor of the so-called *testimonium Spiritus Sancti*. The convictions of the Christian man, we are told, are not the product of reasons addressed to his intellect, but are the immediate creation of the Holy Spirit in his heart. Therefore, it is intimated, we cannot only do very well without these reasons, but it is something very like sacrilege to attend to them."[35]

Warfield recognizes that this mysticism is often the expression of modern irrationalism. As such, he says, it is to be expected. But he adds that

> the case is very different, however, when we encounter very much the same forms of speech on the lips of heroes of the faith, who depreciate apologetics because they feel no need of 'reasons' to ground a faith which they are sure they have received immediately from God. Apologetics, they say, will never make a Christian. Christians are made by the creative Spirit alone. And when God almighty has implanted faith in the heart, we shall not require to seek for 'reasons' to ground our conviction of the truth of the Christian religion. We have tasted and seen, and we know of ourselves that it is from God. Thus, the sturdiest belief joins hands with unbelief to disparage the defenses of the Christian religion.[36]

Then he speaks of the work of Kuyper as follows:

> He has written an *Encyclopedia of Sacred Theology*, and in it he gives a place to apologetics among the other disciplines. But how subordinate a place! And in what a curtailed form! Hidden away as a subdivision of a subdivision of what Dr. Kuyper calls the 'Dogmatological Group' of disciplines... one has to search for it before he finds it, and when he finds it, he discovers that its function is confined closely, we might almost say jealously, to the narrow task of defending developed Christianity against philosophy, falsely so-called.[37]

Apologetics comes for Kuyper at the end of the process whereby Christianity has been set forth thetically. "Meanwhile, as for Christianity itself, it has remained up to this point—let us say frankly—the great Assumption. The work

---

35. B. B. Warfield, "Introductory Note," in Francis R. Beattie's *Apologetics*, Vol. I (Richmond: The Presbyterian Committee of Publication, 1903), p. 20.
36. Ibid., p. 21.
37. Ibid.

of the exegete, the historian, the systematist, has all hung, so to speak, in the air; not until all their labor is accomplished do they pause to wipe their streaming brows and ask whether they have been dealing with realities, or perchance with fancies only."[38]

Has not Kuyper himself engaged in apologetics of a much more basic sort than he speaks of when he calls it a defense against false philosophy? Has he not defended the idea of the sense of deity independently of Scripture?

> We must, it seems, vindicate the existence of a *sensus divinitatis* in man capable of producing a natural theology independently of special revelation; and then the reality of special revelation in deed and word; and as well, the reality of a supernatural preparation of the heart of man to receive it; before we can proceed to the study of theology at all, as Dr. Kuyper has outlined it. With these things at least we must, then, confessedly, reckon at the outset; and to reckon with these things is to enter deeply into apologetics.[39]

Then after noting this "inconsistency" in Kuyper he offers his basic criticism. Kuyper shows how the various disciplines of theology are to be organized, ending with practical theology. Its system of truth may be drawn from Scripture. "But certainly," says Warfield,

> before we draw it from the Scriptures, we must assure ourselves that there is a knowledge of God in the Scriptures. And, before we do that, we must assure ourselves that there is a knowledge of God in the world. . . . Thus, we inevitably work back to first principles. And, in working back to first principles, we exhibit the indispensability of an 'apologetical theology,' which of necessity holds the place of the first among the five theological disciplines.
>
> It is easy, of course, to say that a Christian man must take his standpoint not *above* the Scriptures, but *in* the Scriptures. He very certainly must. But surely he must first *have* Scriptures, authenticated to him as such, before he can take his standpoint in them. It is equally easy to say that Christianity is attained, not by demonstrations, but by a new birth. Nothing could be more true. But neither could anything be more unjustified than the inferences that are drawn from this truth for the discrediting of apologetics. It certainly is not in the power of all the demonstrations

---

38. Ibid., p. 22.
39. Ibid., p. 23.

in the world to make a Christian. Paul may plant and Apollos water; it is God alone who gives the increase. But it does not seem to follow that Paul would as well, therefore, not plant, and Apollos as well not water. Faith is the gift of God; but it does not in the least follow that the faith that God gives is an irrational faith, that is, a faith without grounds in right reason. It is beyond all question only the prepared heart that can fitly respond to the 'reasons'; but how can even a prepared heart respond, when there are no 'reasons' to draw out its action? One might as well say that photography is independent of light, because no light can make an impression unless the plate is prepared to receive it. The Holy Spirit does not work a blind, an ungrounded faith in the heart. What is supplied by his creative energy in working faith is not a ready-made faith, rooted in nothing, and clinging without reason to its object; nor yet new grounds of belief in the object presented; but just a new ability of the heart to respond to the grounds of faith, sufficient in themselves, already present to the understanding. We believe in Christ because it is rational to believe in him, not though it be irrational. Accordingly, our Reformed fathers always posited in the production of faith the presence of the '*argumentum propter quod credo*,'[40] as well as the '*principium seu causa efficiens a quo ad credendum adducor.*'[41] That is to say, for the birth of faith in the soul, it is just as essential that grounds of faith should be present to the mind as that the Giver of faith should act creatively upon the heart.

We are not absurdly arguing that apologetics has in itself the power to make a man a Christian or to conquer the world to Christ. Only the Spirit of Life can communicate life to a dead soul, or can convict the world in respect of sin, and of righteousness, and of judgment. But we are arguing that faith is, in all its exercises alike, a form of conviction, and is, therefore, necessarily grounded in evidence. And we are arguing that evidence accordingly has its part to play in the conversion of the soul; and that the systematically organized evidence which we call apologetics similarly has its part to play in the Christianizing of the world. And we are arguing that this part is not a small part; nor is it a merely subsidiary part; nor yet a merely defensive part—as if the one end of apologetics were to protect an isolated body of Christians from annoyance from the surrounding world, or to aid the distracted Christian to bring his head into harmony with his heart. The part that apologetics has to play in the Christianizing of the world is rather a primary part, and it is a conquering

---

40. KSO: That is, "the grounds on account of which I believe."
41. KSO: "the principle or efficient cause from which I am led to believe."

part. It is the distinction of Christianity that it has come into the world clothed with the mission to *reason* its way to its dominion. Other religions may appeal to the sword, or seek some other way to propagate themselves. Christianity makes its appeal to right reason, and stands out among all religions, therefore, as distinctively 'the apologetic religion.' It is solely by reasoning that it has come thus far on its way to its kingship. And it is solely by reasoning that it will put all its enemies under its feet. Face to face with the tremendous energy of thought and the incredible fertility in assault which characterizes the world in its anti-Christian manifestation, Christianity finds its task in thinking itself thoroughly through, and in organizing, not its defense only, but also its attack. It stands calmly over against the world with its credentials in its hands, and fears no contention of men.[42]

The idea that faith comes ultimately by virtue of the testimony of the Holy Spirit upon the minds of men does not exclude apologetics, argues Warfield. He cannot understand why Kuyper should minimize the significance of apologetics because he makes much of sin.

Perhaps the explanation is to be found in a tendency to make too absolute the contrast between the 'two kinds of science'—that which is the product of the thought of sinful man in his state of nature, and that which is the product of man under the influence of the regenerating grace of God. There certainly do exist these 'two kinds of men' in the world—men under the unbroken sway of sin, and men who have been brought under the power of the palingenesis. And the product of the intellection of these 'two kinds of men' will certainly give us 'two kinds of science.' But the difference between the two is, after all, not accurately described as a difference in kind—*gradus non mutant speciem*.[43] Sin has not destroyed or altered in its essential nature any one of man's faculties, although— since it corrupts *homo totus*—it has affected the operation of them all. The depraved man neither thinks, nor feels, nor wills as he ought; and the products of his action as a scientific thinker cannot possibly escape the influence of this everywhere operative destructive power; although, as Dr. Kuyper lucidly points out, they are affected in different degrees in the several 'sciences,' in accordance with the nature of their objects and the rank of the human faculties engaged in their structure. Nevertheless,

---

42. Ibid., pp. 24–26.
43. KSO: That is, degrees of change do not change the species.

there is question here of perfection of performance, rather than of kind. It is 'science' that is produced by the subject held under sin, even though imperfect science—falling away from the ideal here, there and elsewhere, on account of all sorts of deflecting influences entering in at all points of the process. The science of sinful man is thus a substantive part of the abstract science produced by the ideal subject, the general human consciousness, though a less valuable part than it would be without sin.[44]

In this passage Warfield rejects the idea of a twofold science so fully developed in Kuyper's work. We cannot here enter upon a discussion of Kuyper's conception of a twofold science, the one based upon the idea of autonomy and the other based upon the idea of regeneration. His main point is that those who have not experienced the working of the special principle regard all that they see as normal. On the other hand he who has experienced the special principle realizes that due to sin the mind of man has been darkened, and a great disturbance has taken place in nature by which the transparency or clarity of God's revelation has been obscured.[45] Warfield argues that the difference between the scientific effort of the regenerated and the non-regenerated consciousness is, though a great difference, yet after all no more than a gradational difference. Otherwise "there would be no 'science' attainable at all." The regenerated man himself is not perfect in degree. He remains a sinner. Says Warfield:

> Only after his sanctification has become complete can the contrast between him and the unregenerate sinner become absolute; not until then, in any case, could there be thought to exist an absolute contrast between his intellection and that of the sinner. In the meantime, the regenerated man remains a sinner; no new faculties have been inserted into him by regeneration, and the old faculties, common to man in all his states, have been only in some measure restored to their proper functioning. He is in no condition, therefore, to produce a 'science' differing in *kind* from that produced by sinful man; the science of palingenesis is only a part of the science of sinful humanity, though no doubt its best part; and only along with it can it enter as a constituent part into that ideal science which the composite human subject is producing in its endless effort to embrace in mental grasp the ideal object, that is to say, all that is. Even if the palingenesis had completed its work, indeed, and those under its sway had become 'perfect,' it may be doubted whether the contrast between the

---

44. Ibid., pp. 26–27.
45. Kuyper, *op. cit.*, Vol. II, p. 171.

science produced by the two classes of men could be treated as absolute. Sinful and sinless men are, after all, both men; and being both men, are fundamentally alike and know fundamentally alike. Ideally there is but one 'science,' the subject of which is the human spirit, and the object all that is. Meanwhile, as things are, the human spirit attains to this science only in part and by slow accretions, won through many partial and erroneous constructions. Men of all sorts and of all grades work side by side at the common task, and the common edifice grows under their hands into ever fuller and truer outlines. As Dr. Kuyper finely says of himself, in the conflict of perceptions and opinions, those of the strongest energy and clearest thought finally prevail. Why is not the palingenesis to be conceived simply as preparing the stronger and clearer spirits whose thought always finally prevails? It is not a different kind of science that they are producing. It is not even the same kind of science, but as part of a different edifice of truth. Through them merely the better scientific outlook, and the better scientific product, are striving in conflict with the outlook and product of fellow-workers, to get built into the one great edifice of truth ascertained, which is rising slowly because of sin, but surely because of palingenesis.[46]

From this quotation it seems as though Warfield is altogether ignoring the fact that there is a difference of principle between those who work from the basis of regeneration and those who do not. He seems to regard the fact that there cannot in history be any actually complete manifestation of the victory of one principle over the other as sufficient warrant for ignoring Kuyper's contention that the two types of people spoken of see themselves and all things else differently from one another. Yet Warfield realizes full well that there is a conflict of principle going on in the world. What he is deeply concerned to avoid is the separation of the Christian from the non-Christian in the field of knowledge, for then the conflict of principles would be stifled. We quote again:

And no mistake could be greater than to lead them to decline to bring their principles into conflict with those of the unregenerate in the prosecution of the common task of man. It is the better science that ever in the end wins the victory; and palingenetic science is the better science, and to it belongs the victory. How shall it win its victory, however, if it declines the conflict? In the ordinance of God, it is only in and through this conflict that the edifice of truth is to rise steadily onwards to its perfecting.

In the fact thus brought out, the ultimate vindication of the supreme

---

46. Warfield, *op. cit.*, pp. 27–29.

importance of apologetics lies, and as well the vindication of its supreme utility. In the prosecution of the tasks of apologetics, we see the palingenesis at work on the science of man at its highest point. And here, too, the 'man of stronger and purer thought'—even though that he has it is of God alone—'will prevail in the end.' The task of the Christian is surely to urge 'his stronger and purer thought' continuously, and in all its details, upon the attention of men. It is not true that he cannot soundly prove his position. It is not true that the Christian view of the world is subjective merely, and is incapable of validation in the forum of pure reason. It is not true that the arguments adduced for the support of the foundations of the Christian religion lack objective validity. It is not even true that the minds of sinful men are inaccessible to the 'evidences,' though, in the sense of the proverb, 'convinced against their will,' they may 'remain of the same opinion still.' All minds are of the same essential structure; and the less illuminated will not be able permanently to resist or gainsay the determinations of the more illuminated. The Christian, by virtue of the palingenesis working in him, stands undoubtedly on an indefinitely higher plane of thought than that occupied by sinful man as such. And he must not decline, but use and press the advantage which God has thus given him. He must insist, and insist again, that his determinations, and not those of the unilluminated, must be built into the slowly rising fabric of human science. Thus will he serve, if not obviously his own generation, yet truly all the generations of men.[47]

It is well that at this point the criticism made by Warfield of the position of Kuyper be supplemented with a brief statement of what he has elsewhere said on the nature of apologetics. We turn first to his article *Apologetics*, first printed in the *New Schaff-Herzog Encyclopedia of Religious Knowledge*, and reprinted in his collected works, *Studies in Theology*.

Apologetics, says Warfield, has its basic justification not in any accident, "not even in that most pervasive and most portentous of all these accidents, the accident of sin; but in the fundamental needs of the human spirit."[48] If the Christian is to give an orderly account to himself and to all men of his faith he may conveniently divide his work into five parts:

(1) The first, which may perhaps be called philosophical apologetics, undertakes the establishment of the being of God, as a personal spirit, the Creator, preserver, and governor of all things. To it belongs the great

---

47. Ibid., pp. 29–30.
48. B. B. Warfield, *Studies in Theology* (New York: Oxford University Press, 1932), p. 4.

problem of theism, with the involved discussion of the antitheistic theories. (2) The second, which may perhaps be called psychological apologetics, undertakes the establishment of the religious nature of man and the validity of his religious sense. It involves the discussion alike of the psychology, the philosophy, and the phenomenology of religion, and therefore includes what is loosely called 'comparative religion' or the 'history of religions.' (3) To the third falls the establishment of the reality of the supernatural factor in history, with the involved determination of the actual relations in which God stands to his world, and the method of his government of his rational creatures, and especially his mode of making himself known to them. It issues in the establishment of the fact of revelation as the condition of all knowledge of God, who as a personal Spirit can be known only so far as he expresses himself; so that theology differs from all other sciences in that in it the object is not at the disposal of the subject, but vice versa. (4) The fourth, which may be called historical apologetics, undertakes to establish the divine origin of Christianity as the religion of revelation in the special sense of that word. It discusses all the topics which naturally fall under the popular caption of the 'evidences of Christianity.' (5) The fifth, which may be called bibliological apologetics, undertakes to establish the trustworthiness of the Christian Scriptures as the documentation of the revelation of God for the redemption of sinners. It is engaged especially with such topics as the divine origin of the Scriptures; the methods of the divine operation in their origination; their place in the series of redemptive acts of God, and in the process of revelation; the nature, mode, and effect of inspiration; and the like.[49]

Apologetics therefore has great value.

Though faith is the gift of God, it does not in the least follow that the faith which God gives is an irrational faith, that is, a faith without recognizable ground in right reason. We believe in Christ because it is rational to believe in him, not even though it be irrational. Of course mere reasoning cannot make a Christian; but that is not because faith is not the result of evidence, but because a dead soul cannot respond to evidence. The action of the Holy Spirit in giving faith is not apart from evidence, but along with evidence; and in the first instance consists in preparing the soul for the reception of evidence.[50]

49. Ibid., pp. 13–14.
50. Ibid., p. 15.

NATURAL THEOLOGY AND SCRIPTURE

From what has been quoted of Warfield's position the following points of importance emerge:

(1) Warfield agrees with Kuyper that the natural man is dead in trespasses and sins. It is not because of any lower view of sin that Warfield defends against Kuyper the right and value of apologetics.

(2) Warfield stresses the objective rationality of the Christian religion. This is not to suggest that Kuyper does not also believe in such an objective rationality. But by pointing out again and again that the Christian faith is belief on evidence not blind belief, Warfield makes plain that Christianity is "rationally defensible." This has direct significance for apologetics. Kuyper seems sometimes to argue from the fact that the natural man is blind to the truth, to the uselessness of apologetics. But Warfield points out that this does not follow. On this point he closely follows Calvin. Men ought to conclude that God is their Creator, their Benefactor and their Judge. They ought to see these things because the revelation of God to them is always clear. The fact that men do not see this and cannot see this is due to the fact that their minds are darkened and their wills are perverted through sin. Such is the argument of Calvin. And Warfield's insistence that we believe Christianity because it is "rational," not in spite of the fact that it is irrational, is fully in accord with it. To the extent that Warfield differs on this point with Kuyper and has called us back to Calvin, he has done great service for Christian apologetics.

That such is the case may be observed from the fact that Romanist apologetics lowers the objective clarity of God's revelation. Romanist apologetics argues that men have done justice by the evidence for God's existence and government of the world if they conclude that God *probably* exists. But it is of the essence of the Reformed doctrine of God and his revelation to men that his existence is objectively clear to men. Men cannot look at any fact whether within or about them but they must see in it the presence of God. Even when men have fallen into sin they cannot eradicate their sense of the presence of God. Sin is what it is precisely because it is a *negative ethical reaction to God's inescapable presence*. Sin is not due to some slenderness of being, to some nearness to non-being, to some lack of supernatural grace; it is direct rejection of the known will of God. The sinner is a sinner by virtue of the suppression of the revelation of God within him. Only thus can the Protestant doctrine of sin as ethical alienation from his Creator rather than physical defect be maintained. Only thus can the fact that Christianity is ethical in character, rather than a means by which men are lifted up to a higher place in the scale of being, be maintained.

It is therefore of the utmost importance to stress what Warfield stressed, when he said that we believe Christianity because it is "rational." When the Scriptures are presented to the natural man and with it the system of truth that it contains, he knows at once that he ought to accept it. He knows that if he rejects it he does so in spite of the fact that he knows its claim is true and just. Scripture speaks in the name of God to the sinner asking that he repent from his sin. The natural man, having usurped authority to himself is asked to recognize his legitimate sovereign. A son that has gone away from home and has been away for a long time might suddenly be put face to face with his father. Would it be possible for him not to own and recognize his father for what he actually is? So impossible is it for the sinner to deny that Christianity is true. The sense of deity within him constantly gives the lie to all his theories short of the recognition of God as Creator and Judge. So also when confronted with Scripture as the Word of God the natural men can apply his reductionistic theories only at the cost of an evil conscience. He may be intellectually honest in his research. But at bottom he maintains his theories against better knowledge.

(3) Having stressed the objective rationality of Christianity, Warfield does not adequately stress the difference between the principle of the natural man and the principles of the Christian.

(a) This appears primarily in the fact that he attributes to "right reason" the ability to interpret natural revelation with essential correctness. It is not easy to discover just what Warfield means by "right reason." But clearly it is not the regenerated reason. It is not the reason that has already accepted Christianity. It is the reason that is confronted with Christianity and has some criterion apart from Christianity with which to judge the truth of Christianity. Sometimes it appears that in Warfield this "right reason" springs from or is identical with the sense of deity that men have within them. In fact there is little doubt but that this is what Warfield has in mind. He speaks as though man by virtue of his natural endowments is able to interpret natural revelation correctly. Even though he speaks of the struggle that must go on between the Christian and the non-Christian view of things this struggle must not be regarded as destroying the approach to a unified result between them. Since Christians as Christians have received no new natural endowments, they cannot be said, according to Warfield, to have some interpretation of natural revelation that cannot be made by all men.[51]

In spite of the fact that Warfield, as much as Kuyper, believes in the ethical alienation of the natural man from God he does not give this fact its rightful significance in Christian apologetics. He criticizes Kuyper for concluding to the uselessness of apologetics from the fact of the depravity of men. We hold this criticism to be essentially just. An Arminian would argue to the uselessness of preaching if one holds that the sinner to whom this preaching comes is dead in

---

51. KSO: This notion of "right reason" is due, in part, to the influence of common sense realism on Old Princeton. For more on this, see my foreword in Van Til, *Christian-Theistic Evidences*.

trespasses and sins. The Reformed Christian replies that though he is dead in sins, this deadness of the natural man is an *ethical* deadness, not a metaphysical escape from God. As the image of God and therefore endowed with the sense of deity, man can very well understand intellectually what is meant when the preacher tells him that he is a sinner and that he ought to repent. He *knows* God as Paul says so specifically in his letter to the Romans (*gnontes ton theon*[52]). Yet ethically he does not know God. His mind is darkened and his will perverted, as Paul says with equal clarity. So then in his preaching the Reformed theologian is anxious to do justice to both aspects of biblical truth on this matter. He should stress on the one hand, the objective clarity of God's revelation to man. He should stress that this revelation is unavoidably present to the natural man since it always enters into the *penetralia* of his consciousness. On the other hand he should stress the ethical darkness of the mind of man. As a consequence of this darkness of mind, this spiritual blindness, the natural man does not know truly that which, in the sense above defined, he knows and cannot help but know. Warfield has greatly stressed the point that God's revelation is present to every man and sometimes draws from it the illegitimate conclusion that therefore the natural man, disregarding his ethical alienation from God, can give an essentially correct interpretation at least of natural revelation. Kuyper has stressed the natural man's ethical alienation from God and sometimes draws from it the illegitimate conclusion that the natural man is unable to understand the intellectual argument for Christianity in any sense.

(b) The fact that Warfield has not sufficiently stressed the difference between the principles of the natural man and those of the regenerate man appears also from the fact that he attributes to "right reason" the ability to judge of the credibility of redemptive revelation in terms of principles not taken from this redemptive revelation. "Right reason" must "establish the reality of the supernatural factor in history" by a method identification that does not itself come from this supernatural reality.

This second point follows naturally from the first. If "right reason," or a man "in the natural use of reason" can discover that God, that is the true God, exists, he has therewith already found the possibility of supernatural revelation. Having established the possibility of supernatural revelation he needs only to engage in actual historical research in order to look for the reality of such a revelation. In doing so he will then be asked first to look at the New Testament as a human document written by trustworthy men. He must not be asked directly to regard these documents as being the Word of God. The Christian knows that they are such. He is anxious to have the non-Christian also believe that they are such. But

---

52. KSO: That is, "knowing God..." Rom. 1:21.

for the sake of letting "right reason" judge for itself *whether* they are such, these records must first be presented as being ordinary historical records. As historical records written by the apostles they tell us about the life and labors, the death and resurrection of Jesus Christ. The picture given in these records leaves the impression of verisimilitude. Jesus of Nazareth appears from them as being the very son of God. He promised to his disciples the Spirit of truth so that they would be inspired to write the New Testament as the Word of God. It is thus that we get to the idea of infallible inspiration by way of a process of reasoning that involves several steps. The doctrine of inspiration is the end result of this process of reasoning. We must not, argues Warfield, begin with it as immediately and directly a part of the Bible that as Christians we present unto men.

In some such way the general argument of Warfield may be summarized. We proceed to show from his writings what he says on the subject.

In an article "The Real Problem of Inspiration," Warfield seeks to show that the rejection of the doctrine of the plenary inspiration of Scripture leads ultimately to the confusion of those who reject it.

> Now if this doctrine is to be assailed on critical grounds, it is very clear that, first of all, criticism must be required to proceed against the evidence on which it is based. This evidence, it is obvious, is twofold. First, there is the exegetical evidence that the doctrine held and taught by the Church is the doctrine held and taught by the biblical writers themselves. And secondly, there is the whole mass of evidence—internal and external, objective and subjective, historical and philosophical, human and divine—which goes to show that the biblical writers are trustworthy as doctrinal guides. If they are trustworthy teachers of doctrine and if they held and taught this doctrine, then this doctrine is true, and is to be accepted and acted upon as true by us all. In that case, any objections brought against the doctrine from other spheres of inquiry are inoperative; it being a settled logical principle that so long as the proper evidence by which a proposition is established remains unrefuted, all so-called objections brought against it pass out of the category of objections to its truth into the category of difficulties to be adjusted to it.[53]

Again and again Warfield falls back on this point that the last basis to which appeal must be made when men are doubtful about the doctrine of inspiration is

---

53. B. B. Warfield, "The Real Problem of Inspiration," *Revelation and Inspiration* (New York: Oxford University Press, 1927), p. 174. This essay originally appeared in *The Presbyterian and Reformed Review* (Vol. IV, No. 14; April, 1893), pp. 177–221.

NATURAL THEOLOGY AND SCRIPTURE

that they are forced also to reject the apostles as trustworthy guides of doctrine. "Are the New Testament writers trustworthy guides in doctrine? Or are we at liberty to reject their authority, and frame contrary doctrines for ourselves?"[54] Again: "First, we emphasize the fact that, this being the real state of the case, we cannot modify the doctrine of plenary inspiration in any of its essential elements without undermining our confidence in the authority of the apostles as teachers of doctrine."[55] Or again, "It follows on the one hand that it [the doctrine of inspiration] cannot rationally be rejected save on the ground of evidence which will outweigh the whole body of evidence which goes to authenticate the biblical writers as trustworthy witnesses to and teachers of doctrine."[56]

It is by the appeal to the apostles as trustworthy teachers of doctrine that Warfield would avoid the charge of making all teaching of Scripture to depend upon the doctrine of inspiration.

> Let it not be said that thus we found the whole Christian system upon the doctrine of plenary inspiration. We found the whole Christian system on the doctrine of plenary inspiration as little as we found it upon the doctrine of angelic existences. Were there no such thing as inspiration, Christianity would be true, and all its essential doctrines would be credibly witnessed to us in the generally trustworthy reports of the teaching of our Lord and of his authoritative agents in founding the Church, preserved in the writings of the apostles and their first followers, and in the historical witness of the living Church. Inspiration is not the most fundamental of Christian doctrines, nor even the first thing we prove about the Scriptures. It is the last and crowning fact as to the Scriptures. These we first prove authentic, historically credible, generally trustworthy, before we prove them inspired. And the proof of their authenticity, credibility, general trustworthiness would give us a firm basis for Christianity prior to any knowledge on our part of their inspiration, and apart indeed from the existence of inspiration. The present writer, in order to prevent all misunderstanding desires to repeat here what he has said on every proper occasion—that he is far from contending that without inspiration there could be no Christianity. 'Without any inspiration,' he added, when making this affirmation on his induction into the work of teaching the Bible—'without any inspiration we could have had Christianity; yea, and men could still have heard the truth and through it been awakened,

54. Ibid., p. 180.
55. Ibid., p. 181.
56. Ibid., p. 209.

and justified, and sanctified, and glorified. The verities of our faith would remain historically proven to us—so bountiful has God been in his fostering care—even had we no Bible; and through those verities, salvation.' We are in entire harmony in this matter with what we conceive to be the very true statement recently made by Dr. George P. Fisher, that 'if the authors of the Bible were credible reporters of revelations of God, whether in the form of historical transactions of which they were witnesses, or of divine mysteries that were unveiled to their minds, their testimony would be entitled to belief, even if they were shut up to their unaided faculties in communicating what they had thus received.' [57]

A little later Warfield adds:

We must indeed prove the authenticity, credibility and general trustworthiness of the New Testament writings before we prove their inspiration; and even were they not inspired this proof would remain valid and we should give them accordant trust. But just because this proof is valid, we must trust these writings in their witness to their inspiration, if they give such witness; and if we refuse to trust them here, we have in principle refused them trust everywhere. In such circumstances their inspiration is bound up inseparably with their trustworthiness, and therefore with all else that we receive on trust from them.[58]

A point of particular interest is the relation between the written and the incarnate word. As stated above, Warfield would accept what the Apostles say about Jesus Christ on the ground that they are trustworthy teachers of doctrine. For if we trust them at all we will trust them in the account that they give of the person and in the report they give of the teaching of Christ; whereupon, as they report him as teaching the same doctrine of Scripture that they teach, we are brought face to face with divine testimony to this doctrine of inspiration. "The argument, then, takes the form given it by Bishop Wordsworth: 'The New Testament canonizes the Old, the INCARNATE WORD puts his seal on the WRITTEN WORD. The Incarnate Word is God; therefore the inspiration of the Old Testament is authenticated by God Himself.'"[59]

Once more, and finally, Warfield would base the work of the Holy Spirit in relation to Scripture also upon the apostles as trustworthy teachers of doctrine.

---

57. Ibid., pp. 209–211.
58. Ibid., p. 212.
59. Ibid.

"And, again, the general trustworthiness of the writers of the New Testament gives us the right and imposes on us the duty of accepting their witness to the relation the Holy Ghost bears to their teaching . . ."[60] In summing up this approach Warfield says:

> It is not on some shadowy and doubtful evidence that the doctrine is based—not on an *a priori* conception of what inspiration ought to be, not on a 'tradition' of doctrine in the Church, though all the *a priori* considerations and the whole tradition of doctrine in the Church are also thrown in the scale for and not in that against this doctrine; but first on the confidence which we have in the writers of the New Testament as doctrinal guides, and ultimately on whatever evidence of whatever kind and force exists to justify that confidence. In this sense, we repeat, the cause of distinctive Christianity is bound up with the cause of the biblical doctrine of inspiration.[61]

Warfield realizes that his method of establishing the doctrine of Scripture as inspired of God can produce no more than probable truthfulness. "Of course, this evidence is not in the strict logical sense 'demonstrative'; it is 'probable' evidence. It therefore leaves open the metaphysical possibility of its being mistaken."[62] This probable evidence is, to be sure, so great as to amount in practice to demonstration itself. Even so it must be stressed that the force of the argument is no more than probable. How else could we with open minds consider the phenomena of Scripture that are sometimes alleged as militating against its divinity? "Their study is not to be neglected; we have not attained through 'probable' evidence apodeictic certainty of the Bible's infallibility."[63] It is not, of course, that Warfield himself entertains any doubts about the plenary inspiration and therefore the divinity of Scripture. On the contrary he was one of its greatest advocates. Nor can we disagree with him when he says that the Christian faith is not a blind faith but is faith based on evidence. At every turn where Warfield militates against mysticism of every sort he has made all believers his debtor. At the end of the article from which the last quotations have been taken he exclaims: "If then we ask what we are to do with the numerous phenomena of Scripture inconsistent with verbal inspiration, which, so it is alleged, 'criticism' has brought to light, we must reply: Challenge them in the name of the New Testament

---

60. Ibid., pp. 212–213.
61. Ibid., pp. 213–214.
62. Ibid., p. 218.
63. Ibid.

doctrine, and ask for their credentials. They have no credentials that can stand before that challenge. No single error has yet been demonstrated to occur in the Scriptures as given by God to his Church."[64]

But if we are to follow Warfield in making this bold challenge we shall have to follow him when elsewhere he asserts his convictions with respect to the system of truth that the Scriptures teach, and the doctrine of Scripture that is involved in that system. That system is the system of the Reformed faith. It is based upon the idea that God is the necessary self-existent Being, the ontological trinity, the God who controls whatsoever comes to pass. All the works proceeding from this one God, whether directly and immediately from the Father, the Son or the Holy Spirit, are yet the works of this one God. All the facts of creation, and all the facts of redemption, objectively through what Christ did in history once and for all, and subjectively through what the Holy Spirit has since done in his work of applying the redemption wrought by Christ to men, is self-attesting. All testimony for the truth of the Word and work of this God is through human agency. Even the writings of Scriptures are given through human agency. But this makes them no less the self-attesting Word of God. The identification of Scripture as the Word of God is, of necessity, also the work of the self-attesting God, in this case effected through the testimony of the Holy Spirit. The identity of Scripture as the Word of God can, therefore, be effected no other way than by way of the self-testimony of Scripture. And it can be accepted, in the last analysis, in no other way than through the testimony of the Holy Spirit to the Scripture as self-attesting.

It follows that, if we accept this view of theology and of the doctrine of Scripture as Warfield has himself often enough set it forth, it is impossible to follow him in his method of apologetics as outlined above. This method would lead to the very mysticism or rationalism which it is his great desire to oppose. For mysticism is involved in the principle of equivocism and rationalism is involved in the principle of univocism, and they are both based upon the idea of human autonomy.

This idea of human autonomy lies back of the idea of abstract possibility as a substitute for the idea, as defended by Warfield in his theology that God himself is the source of possibility. Unfortunately Warfield recognizes the legitimacy of the idea of abstract possibility in his apologetic methodology. His whole procedure as outlined above is based upon the idea that in studying the facts, either of natural or of special revelation, men have every right to start from the idea that God can possibly not exist and that the Bible at least can possibly be the word of men rather than the word of God. He insists that men have a right and a duty to

---

64. Ibid., p. 225.

be open-minded with respect to the claims of God for himself, and the Christian must not claim more than probable certainty for his position.

In thus allowing for the idea of abstract possibility Warfield cannot do justice to the claims of God's revelation either in nature or in history or in Scripture. He cannot do justice to the fact that the God of his own theology is the source of necessity and "possibility" and therefore of necessity self-attesting. He cannot do justice to the evidence of God's existence in nature and history. He cannot say with Calvin that men ought to see God, the true God, in nature and history since this true God and he alone is clearly revealed there. No other God could possibly be revealed there. A theism that is merely said to be more probably true than its rivals is not the theism of the Bible. It is the God who cannot but exist that is the one who is clearly and unavoidably present to every man created by this God. Man's sense of deity speaks of this God, not of *a* god who *probably* exists and probably does not exist.

Again, in allowing for the idea of abstract possibility, Warfield cannot do justice to his own principle of the trustworthy character of the apostolic witnesses to Christ and his work. It is utterly impossible that there should be trustworthy witnesses to the incarnate Word unless these trustworthy witnesses are trustworthy because they are the servants of the self-attesting God, speaking through the Son of God. This is only to say that any identification of any fact can take place in terms of the truth of the Christian religion alone. It is but to say that Christianity *alone* is rational. It is but to say that if one leaves the foundation of the presupposition of the truth of the Christian religion one falls into the quagmire of the utterly irrational. No intelligent predication is possible except on the basis of the truth, that is the *absolute* truth of Christianity.

How otherwise would supposedly trustworthy witnesses after observing the person and the work of Jesus proceed to make a report of it? They would have to do so in terms of their independent and ultimate principles of knowledge and being. But these principles make it impossible that there should be any such thing as the incarnate Word of the Bible. These principles would require that this supposed Son of God be explained in terms of general laws of which he would be an instance, leaving what uniqueness might remain to spring from the realm of the non-rational. In other words these principles would require such men as used them to think of the incarnate Word as they do of all other phenomenal appearances. These phenomenal appearances are said to be the result of some dialectical relationship between abstract logic and pure brute factuality. The incarnate Word would not be allowed to have either the internal and eternal rationality that he is said to have with God the Father, or the identifiable and knowable human nature that he is also said to have in the gospels.

Going on from here it follows that by Warfield's method there would be no divine witness given by the incarnate Word to the written Word. Since the incarnate Word could not be identified by those who were merely trustworthy witnesses rather than divinely inspired interpreters, the witness of Jesus would in turn be no more than that of a trustworthy man as unable to identify himself or the Word of God.

How could this incarnate Word, not knowable as such either by himself or by others, promise the Spirit of truth to his apostles? Or how could the apostles tell us about "the relation the Holy Ghost bears to their teaching" when any witness that would come to them from that Holy Ghost could not be identified by them?

Finally, how could those who are asked to study the evidence for the divinity of Scripture for themselves, with a method that is not itself clearly based upon the presupposition of this divinity itself, be given an opportunity to identify the Scriptures for what they are at all? The only way by which the Scriptures can be placed before men so that they can even intellectually recognize it as being the Word of God is by placing the sharpest possible contrast before men between the principles involved in the idea of divine ultimacy and human ultimacy. The natural man must be shown that, on his principle, no intelligible identification of any fact in human history is possible. He must not be encouraged to think that he can make such an identification in terms of his principle. If it be allowed that he can make any such identification, he is, by implication, also given the right to identify both the incarnate and the written Word. The result will be that in identifying them he will destroy them by his principles of univocism and equivocism. He will reduce the Word as found in Scripture to that which is as penetrable to man as is anything else in principle and to something that is as meaningless as in anything else in history.

It has not been possible to avoid a discussion of the difference between these two great modern Reformed theologians Kuyper and Warfield. The difference between Kuyper and Warfield on the matter of apologetics is there and it is important. It is impossible to ignore it and to speak as though there were only minor differences of emphasis between them. It is impossible to follow both Kuyper and Warfield, however much lovers of the Reformed Faith may revere them both. On the other hand the difference between them should not be overstressed. It was only an inconsistency on Warfield's part to advocate a method of apologetics that is out of accord with the foundation concepts of his own Reformed theology. Kuyper too was inconsistent when, after rejecting such a method of apologetics, he yet sometimes employed it. There is no need here, nor space, to give the evidence for this contention. Both men have also been most fortunately inconsistent in another direction. Warfield again and again in his writings shows how the principles of those who work with the idea of autonomy lead to the destruction of human experience. When he does this he does basically what Kuyper does, i.e., appeals to the sense of deity in men, rather than to the principles that follow from the idea of autonomy. In other words Warfield then rejects the idea of autonomy. He seems to hold that because of the sense of deity within men they really in practice do not proceed from the idea of autonomy, and that they are therefore in a position to be to some extent ready to recognize the special principle for what it is. And it is this that is also true of Kuyper. He does set forth the idea of autonomy and of its opposition to any manifestation of the truth of God. But he too stresses again and again the fact that no man is a finished product. Man has the sense of deity within him, and in particular he is the recipient of the common grace of God. In practice he is therefore more ready to give consideration to the presentation of the special principle than one would expect him to be.

With grateful acknowledgment of indebtedness to both Kuyper and Warfield, to Herman Bavinck and other associates and followers of Kuyper, to the various associates and followers of Warfield, to J. Gresham Machen in particular, we would take their common basic contribution to the idea of the full Christian faith and the self-attesting Scripture and build as best as we can upon it. The great contribution of Kuyper discussed in this chapter is that of his analysis of the idea of autonomy. Never again can we forget that the natural man, working from his adopted principle, will seek to weave the special principle into the natural principle, and that he will seek to do this in philosophy and science no less than in theology. The great contribution of Warfield discussed in this chapter is his insistence that Christian theism is the only internally intelligible system of truth.

Combining these two great principles, held by both men, but not equally emphasized by both, we shall claim that the Christian system is undoubtedly true, that it is distinguishable intellectually by men because it has been distinguished for them by God through his Word, and that unless one therefore presupposes its truth there is no theology, no philosophy, and no science that can find intelligible meaning in human experience.[65]

---

65. KSO: As noted above, Van Til's studies in apologetics at Princeton Seminary included a basic commitment to common sense realism by his professor, which appears to be, in part, what Warfield advocates above as well. Van Til does not mention common sense realism as a culprit here, but it seems clear that it is.

IX

HAMILTON'S *BASIS OF CHRISTIAN FAITH*

We have to this point been attempting by way of historical study to indicate a truly biblical epistemology. In the following four chapters we shall deal with modern approaches to the question concerning the possibility of knowledge and experience. In the first two of these chapters we shall look in detail at two modern exponents of the Warfield type of epistemology-apologetic, Floyd Hamilton and James Oliver Buswell, Jr. They are interested in *defending* the Reformed faith. In the last two chapters we shall look at many 'post-Barthian' philosophers and theologians who, in terms of their epistemology attempt to both make sense of the world and science and destroy the Reformed faith. We shall indicate in those chapters what we believe to be the dilemma of all western thought. We hope to show that both the friends and the enemies of the Reformation fail in their efforts because they refuse to put the self-attesting Christ at the center of their system. In failing to do this, even the friends of the Reformation become its enemies.

We turn now to a discussion of the Reverend Floyd E. Hamilton's recent work on apologetics. Hamilton was a student at Princeton Seminary in the days of Warfield and has been, except for an intermission, an advocate of the probability method of Bishop Butler as taught at Princeton.[1]

In the fourth revised edition of his work on *The Basis of Christian Faith*,[2] Floyd E. Hamilton once again turns to what he calls "the old Princeton method

---

1. KSO: As argued in the foreword of *Christian-Theistic Evidences:* xi–xxxii., esp. xi–xvii, William Brenton Greene, Jr., Van Til's apologetics professor at Princeton, was committed to common sense realism in his apologetic. Hamilton was also a student of Greene's. The way in which Greene's common sense approach filtered down can be seen in Floyd Hamilton. After Princeton, Hamilton wrote a book entitled, *The Basis of the Christian Faith* (1927). In the preface to that book Hamilton says: "Special thanks are due to Dr. William Brenton Greene, Jr., former professor of Apologetics in Princeton Theological Seminary, for his assistance in revising and criticizing the whole book." See Cornelius Van Til, *Defense of the Faith* ed. K. Scott Oliphint, (Phillipsburg, N.J.: Presbyterian and Reformed Publishing Company, 2008), 361.
2. Floyd E. Hamilton, *The Basis of Christian Faith*, 4th rev. ed. (New York: Harper, 1964). We have discussed Hamilton's earlier position in *Defense of the Faith* (1955).

of apologetics."³ Says Hamilton: "During the past thirty-five years the method has been attacked by the 'presuppositionalists,' led by Dr. Cornelius Van Til, of Westminster Theological Seminary. They have held that it is impossible to prove the existence of God to an unbeliever; that one must *assume* his existence as a basis for argument with an unbeliever, because the unbeliever and the believer have no common ground on which they can meet in argument."

> The presuppositionalists are so persuasive in their reasoning that I have been much influenced by their arguments. Before this revision could be undertaken, therefore, I had to come to some definite conclusion regarding the method to be used in the book. It was the fact that the old Princeton method has been blessed by the Lord so greatly in the salvation of souls that led me to conclude that it was the truest and best method. Unbelievers, as a matter of history, *have* been met on so-called 'neutral' ground of facts and argument and *have* been brought to the belief in God and the Bible as the Word of God, and the Holy Spirit has used these methods to prepare them for his regenerating act. I have in my files many letters from those who have been brought to the Lord through reading *The Basis of Christian Faith*. As a matter of fact this old method really *works* in reaching unbelievers with the gospel.⁴

As we read this new work of Hamilton's it is not necessary to repeat our criticism of the old Princeton method in detail. A few remarks must suffice.

Hamilton says that the old Princeton method "really *works* in reaching unbelievers with the gospel." In this fact we rejoice. We also rejoice when Arminians "reach unbelievers with the gospel." It is God who reaches unbelievers through Arminian preachers *in spite of* their Arminianism. In its preaching Arminianism ascribes a measure of autonomy to the natural man. It is not *because of* but *in spite of* this fact that the Holy Spirit regenerates unbelievers through Arminian preaching.

The old Princeton method also ascribes autonomy to the natural man. With this ascription of autonomy to the natural man goes the approval of the use of a principle of continuity that wipes out the distinction between God the Creator and man his creature, as well as a principle of discontinuity in which pure contingency or chance is made the ultimate source of differentiation in the world.

So far then as the old Princeton method "has been blessed by the Lord," it is, we believe, in spite of these fatal flaws. Would that Hamilton, now that he

---

3. Ibid., p. xiv.
4. Ibid., pp. xiv–xv.

has returned to this method, had dealt with this basic criticism of it. He has not done so. He has merely repeated and enlarged what he said in the first edition of his work.

There is nothing more that really needs to be said. It is only by way of courtesy that we fallow Hamilton's later argument to see if he has in it offered anything that may possibly escape the criticism we made of his first edition. His argument is similar to that of his first work.

Hamilton requests unbelievers not to reject Christianity out of mere prejudice. Will they not inquire *what* Christian belief is?[5]

Take, to begin with, the question of the nature of man. Christians believe

> the Bible teaching that, after being created, man disobeyed God and brought sin upon the whole human race. Since then, all men are naturally rebels against God, seek to ignore him and try to interpret the universe with God left out. Unless God changes their minds, men are either indifferent to him or at enmity with him. They will not believe that God is the creator, preserver, and controller of the universe.
>
> The Bible teaches that the mind of man is sinful and corrupt. The seriousness of this corruption cannot be overemphasized. Apart from the grace of God, man wants his own way in everything. No matter how he may try to be unprejudiced, his assumption that there is no God enters all his reasoning processes.[6]

Accordingly, says Hamilton,

> we cannot expect him to *believe* the arguments in this book, even when he understands them.
>
> If that is so, it may be asked, 'What is the use of arguing about such matters?' Well, in so far as our facts and arguments are true, they may be used by the Holy Spirit of God in applying the truth to the hearts of such people and, by changing their hearts, enabling them to believe and accept as well as understand the truth about God, man, and the Bible.[7]

The reader will be puzzled at this point. As a Reformed theologian Hamilton analyzes man in terms of the biblical concepts of creation and fall with its consequent total depravity of man. In consonance with this analysis Hamilton

---

5. Ibid., p. 1.
6. Ibid., pp. 1–2.
7. Ibid., p. 2.

asserts that when the natural man is confronted with the truth about himself and his world he will not accept this truth unless the Holy Spirit enlightens his mind.

The "presuppositionalist" agrees with this. He does not hold that it is useless to present the truth of God as revealed in Scripture to the natural man. The believer *must* preach to the natural man even while he knows that this natural man is dead in trespasses and sins and is spiritually blind. Christ spoke to Lazarus who was in the tomb. He made his word to Lazarus effective toward life anew. So those who bring the Word of Christ to men that are spiritually dead may expect that Christ will, in his sovereign grace, cause the deaf to hear and the blind to see.

But the whole point of the old Princeton method, based as it largely is on Butler's *Analogy*, is to the effect that sinners are *not* spiritually dead and that, therefore, it does *not* take the regenerating act of the Holy Spirit for them to see and accept the truth.

The point that Hamilton makes with respect to the need of "common ground" between believer and unbeliever corroborates this point. The "presuppositionalist" does not, as Hamilton thinks he does, deny that there is common ground between the believer and the unbeliever. Neither party denies the fact of the existence of common ground. The question pertains to the *nature* of the common ground. The present writer has repeatedly asserted that metaphysically believers and unbelievers have *all reality in common*. The unbeliever and the believer are, alike, image-bearers of God. Together they operate in the God-created and Christ-redeemed world. Paul says of all men that, "knowing God," they have not kept him in remembrance.

It is, therefore, because all men are image-bearers of God and because the "facts" and "laws" of the world are what they are, as revelatory of God's acts of revelation in and through them, that the natural man remains accessible to God. No man can escape the call of God which confronts him in his own constitution as well as in every fact of the world that surrounds him.[8]

On the other hand, the unbeliever does *not* believe that he is a creature of God and that he is spiritually blind because of his fall in and with Adam. The unbeliever *assumes* his non-createdness, his autonomy. He *assumes* the non-createdness, the just-thereness, of the facts of the universe. He *assumes* the existence

---

8. KSO: It should be noted here that Van Til sees the *sensus divinitatis*, that is, the sense of deity in all people, as *including* some kind of knowledge of reality. Since reality is revelatory, and since all people know God through reality as created by God, there is a knowledge of reality as well. This knowledge of reality, however, is *in spite of*, not because of, the unbeliever's basic principles and commitments. That knowledge, too, is, in various ways, suppressed and distorted in order to avoid the God revealed in it.

of the laws of "causality" and of "logic" as having no reference to the Creator-redeemer God of Scripture.

Such being the case, the "presuppositionalist" refuses to speak of a common ground between believers and unbelievers, in which this all-determinative difference between them is ignored. When the believer *interprets* the world he interprets it in terms of the biblical teaching with respect to God and his relation to man and his world, and therefore every word he speaks when ultimately considered is colored by this fact. When the unbeliever *interprets* the world, he interprets it in terms of his assumption of human autonomy, and with it a non-created or purely contingent factual space-time cosmos and of a non-created, timeless, abstract principle of logic. In consequence every word he utters, when it is completely 'talked out,' is seen to receive its definition from this underlying structure.

The unbeliever is the man with yellow glasses on his face. He sees himself and his world through these glasses. He cannot remove them. His *interpretation* of himself and of every fact in the universe relating to himself is, unavoidably, a *false* interpretation. The conclusion that he, quite logically, draws from his assumption of his own autonomy is that the Christian position with respect to the creation, fall and redemption of man is the projection of a man who has illusions. There simply *cannot* be any such thing as creation. There *can* be no judgment after death. There *can* be no eternal punishment for sinners. There are no sinners.

It is therefore the idea of a common ground of *interpretation* that the "presuppositionalist" rejects.[9] Such a common ground would be a meaningless monstrosity. Can any one intelligently assume that he is both a creature and not a creature, a sinner and not a sinner? Can any one intelligibly assume, with Hamilton, the Reformed theologian, that God is the source of possibility and with Hamilton, the apologist, that possibility is the source of God.

We turn now to a consideration of the arguments as used by Hamilton the apologist. Doing so will give evidence of the fact that the antithesis posited just now is not too strong.

A. THE EXISTENCE OF THE SOUL

Hamilton starts out to prove the "existence of the soul." "The only possible conclusion," that follows from empirical observation of man says Hamilton, "is that

---

[9]. KSO: This is a significant, and often overlooked, point of Van Til's Christian epistemology. To the extent that what the unbeliever *knows* he knows by way of his own *interpretation*, he cannot know truly. His knowledge of reality, which comes by way of his sense of deity, therefore, as affirmed above, can be seen as "pre-interpretive" knowledge, in that it comes to all people *immediately*, that is, without inference.

there is an active *ego* or *soul* behind the activities of the brain."[10] "Here we have *reality*. We are not mere chemical or physical machines. We are living souls."[11]

Here then is to be our starting point. It is our *ultimate* starting point. Man can say that here he has "reality." The unbeliever will agree. He does not need the Holy Spirit to convince him about the correctness of taking man, just man, not as a creature of God and a sinner against God, as our starting point. But the Holy Spirit will not convince men of the truth that here is reality. The Holy Spirit may convict a man, who thus takes himself to be the self-intelligent subject of predication, of sin, of righteousness and of judgment. If he does, then this supposedly self-sufficient "living soul" will repent and say with Calvin that he is utterly unintelligent to himself unless he, from the start, takes his own self-consciousness as having its meaning in terms of his simultaneous God-consciousness.[12]

But Hamilton may object that he is going to lead us on toward the idea of man's being a creature and a sinner in need of redemption through Christ. We reply that he cannot do so if he intends to reason consistently with the starting point that he has taken. If he comes to the conclusion that man is what the Bible says he is, then this will be by means of a logical jump. Then, if he looks back upon the process of reasoning he has followed, he will realize that his starting point would lead him logically to a philosophy of factual time-space existence as not-created, as self-existent and to a philosophy of logic that is also self-existent.

In other words, if Hamilton's unbeliever is only alert, he will gladly agree on Hamilton's starting point. Granting this starting point, Hamilton's unbeliever need only to reason consistently on the basis of it and he can compel Hamilton to forsake the whole of his biblical teaching with respect to God and man. Hamilton the theologian will then, no doubt, still hold to his Christian convictions but he will have to do so *in spite of* the method that he has as an apologist employed.

B. THE NATURE OF THE REASONING PROCESS

"We are now ready," says Hamilton, "to examine the reasoning process going on in our minds."[13] The soul "is the *subject* of all our experiences, sensations, and thoughts."[14] The "soul" has "*sensations*."[15] "My eye sees a red object and the

10. Ibid., p. 5.
11. Ibid.
12. KSO: The argument for the existence of the soul overlaps with current arguments for the existence of consciousness. For a helpful apologetic argument for consciousness, see Nathaniel Gray Sutanto, "Covenantal Apologetics and Common-Sense Realism: Recalibrating the Argument From Consciousness as a Test Case," *Journal of the Evangelical Theological Society* 57/4, (2014).
13. Ibid.
14. Ibid., pp. 5–6.
15. Ibid., p. 6.

retina and optic nerve report the red color to the brain."[16] "But the mind or soul is not like a white paper on which sensations are registered, as if by a pen."[17] The ideas of space and time are innate. "The mind claps these space and time forms on every sensation as it is received and cannot think without thinking in space and time forms."[18] There are other innate ideas. Two of them are *being* and *cause*.

Thus there are "three factors in the thinking process: the thinking soul, the sensations or memories used as material by the soul in constructing thought, and the innate ideas which are the tools used by the soul in the construction of thoughts. The simplest kind of thought is a *judgment*. A judgment is the action of the soul in *interpreting* sensations or mental states, and the result of that action."[19]

With this analysis of the soul and its equipment Hamilton has, as he thinks, all that he needs, as a believer, for a point of contact with the unbeliever. He now knows that

> the content of the knowledge of man, either unregenerate or regenerate, coincides with the content of God's knowledge of the same facts in so far as what is known by man is the truth which God knows. This means that there is definitely a point of contact between the regenerate man and the unregenerate man, and also that total depravity does not make it impossible for the unregenerate man to know truly, though partially, the truth of God in revelation and in the natural creation. It is this fact that rescues us from skepticism and makes it possible to present an objective argument for the existence of God, with the hope that the unregenerate man will understand and be convinced that God exists, even *before* he is regenerated. In fact it is often such argument that is used by the Holy Spirit to condition the individual for the sovereign act of the Spirit in regeneration.[20]

Hamilton refers in this connection to Stuart C. Hackett's[21] work on *The Resurrection of Theism* which, he says, gives a "devastating rebuttal of the idea that we cannot prove the existence of God apart from the Bible."[22] Hackett is

---

16. Ibid.
17. Ibid.
18. Ibid., p. 7.
19. Ibid., p. 9.
20. Ibid., p. 34.
21. KSO: Stuart Hackett (1925–2012), taught at Western Conservative Baptist Seminary in Portland, OR, Denver Conservative Baptist Seminary in Denver, CO, Louisiana College in Pineville, LA, Wheaton College in Wheaton, IL, and finally at Trinity Evangelical Divinity School in Deerfield, IL.
22. Ibid.

of the opinion that "the presuppositionalist approach lands one ultimately in an extreme Calvinistic atmosphere."[23] As an Arminian, Hackett argues that on the view of presuppositionalism, man is not, properly speaking, given a free choice between metaphysical systems.[24] Calvinism reduces rational men to puppets. "But if it seems to be the case that man is under *obligation* to believe the Gospel and that he must accept Christ as Savior *before* the Spirit of God regenerates the heart . . . then let the presuppositionalist framework be consigned to the irrationalism that is written so plainly through its structure."[25]

In contrast to Hackett, Hamilton is a Calvinist. He believes that God controls whatsoever comes to pass. He cannot agree with Hackett "that man must accept Christ as Savior *before* the Spirit of God regenerates the heart." Even so, Hamilton thinks that Hackett's refutation of presuppositionalism "is convincing and thorough."[26] As a Calvinist, Hamilton disagrees with Hackett when he says that the natural man can accept Christ *before* the Spirit regenerates the heart. As a Calvinist, Hamilton can say that the natural man "will view every argument from his anti-God point of view, and until God's power changes his heart he will disbelieve every argument proving God's existence and sovereignty."[27] Yet as a follower of the old Princeton method Hamilton maintains that the natural man can "understand and be convinced that God exists, even *before* he is regenerated."[28] How will Hamilton make his total view intelligible?[29]

C. THE INSUPERABLE PROBLEM

Hamilton himself speaks of an "insuperable problem" confronting him at this point.

> As Christians and believers in the God of the Bible, we know that the Christian God is Triune: God the Father, God the Son, and God the Holy Spirit. We know that the Bible tells us that this Triune God created and controls the universe. We know that the Bible teaches us that this God is infinite, eternal and unchangeable, in his being, wisdom, power, holiness,

---

23. Stuart Hackett, *The Resurrection of Theism* (Chicago: Moody Press, 1956), p. 174.
24. KSO: This common misconception of Calvinism displays a basic ignorance of the Reformed view of human free choice. See WCF 9; see also van Asselt, *Reformed Thought on Freedom: The Concept of Free Choice in the History of Early-Modern Reformed Theology*.
25. Ibid.
26. Hamilton, *op. cit.*, p. 34.
27. Ibid., p. 2.
28. Ibid., p. 34.
29. KSO: This problem, we should note, is intrinsic to any Reformed theologian who chooses to adopt an Arminian, or "classical" apologetic; the two cannot be made consistent.

justice, goodness, and truth. We know that God the Son came, was born of the Virgin, lived sinlessly on earth, was crucified, died and was buried, rose from the dead on the third day, and ascended into heaven.

As Christians we know all this about God from the Bible record, but we also know that most of these things depend upon the Bible record itself for their proof, and that we cannot prove them apart from the Bible record. The unbeliever to whom we are trying to prove the existence of God, however, will not accept the Bible as true. Can we show him that the Christian God exists? Unless he is first shown that the Bible is true, he will not accept what the Bible says about God. But the Bible, from the beginning to end, teaches the Christian God, so we are faced with the problem of trying to prove the existence of the God in whom the unbeliever has no faith, from a Book which he will not accept![30]

The task that Hamilton now sets for himself is much more difficult than the task that Hackett sets for himself. Hackett simply resurrects his "theism" in the way that Thomas Aquinas and others first built it, namely on the idea of human autonomy. The God of Hackett's theism is not the triune God of Scripture. Of course, even Hackett, as an evangelical, builds Christianity as a second story upon his theism as a first story. Like Thomas, he then *believes* that there is some sort of coherence between his theism and his Christianity.

But this way is not open to Hamilton. He believes that it is the triune God of Scripture who "created and controls the universe." Every fact confronting any man, therefore, brings him face to face with the revelation of this triune God of Scripture. Every fact of the space-time world is what it is, in the last analysis, because of its relation to the activity of the triune God of Scripture. Man himself, as the subject who knows, knows himself and his universe for what they are only if he sees himself and his universe in their relation to the triune God of Scripture.

When fallen man therefore says or presupposes that he is intelligible in and of himself apart from his relation to the triune God of Scripture, then he does not know himself for what he is. When such a man asks *whether* he is created in the image of God, his question is, in one sense, meaningless. Yet, in the last analysis, it is worse than meaningless. It is an insult to God. A child who asks *whether* his parents, with whom he has lived from birth, are his parents is not neutral in relation to his parents. He insults them. It is only as a covenant-breaker that man asks *whether* the triune God of Scripture exists.

If then, this covenant-breaking man also asks *whether* the space-time facts are what they are, ultimately, because of the activity of the triune God of Scripture,

---

30. Ibid., p. 35.

Creator and Controller of them, he again insults God. The presupposition of asking such a question is that Chaos and Old Night are back of God. To ask *whether* the triune God of Scripture exists and *whether* the space-time world is what it is because of this God, is to presuppose that abstract possibility is back of God. A God of whom it is possible to ask intelligently *whether* he exists is not the God of Scripture. The God of Scripture is back of all possible eventuation in the space-time world. It is an insult to this God to argue for his *possible* existence. An argument for his possible existence *presupposes* the idea that he may possibly not exist. But *the God of Scripture tells us that he cannot possibly not exist. He presents himself as the self-referential source of all that exists in the universe.*

Finally, when this covenant-breaking man asks *whether* the triune God of Scripture is the Creator of the laws of the mind of man and the laws of the universe surrounding man he is, again, insulting this God.

How then will Hamilton solve his "insuperable" problem? He wants to bring the unbeliever to an acceptance of the triune God of the Bible and the Bible as the authoritative word of this triune God.

Hamilton's unbeliever "is sinful and corrupt. . . . Apart from the grace of God, man wants his way in everything. No matter how he may try to be unprejudiced, his assumption that there is no God enters all his reasoning process. . . . He will view every argument from his anti-God point of view. . ."[31] Through the fall "he became spiritually dead."[32] His soul "became evil, and this total depravity affected his thinking processes as well as his whole personality."[33] When the unbeliever begins to reason in the field of philosophy or theology, the very nature of the subject matter, dealing as it does with the ultimate muses of the universe, makes it impossible for him to reason correctly.[34]

Because of sin and the fall of man into sin, man's soul, before regeneration, is spiritually dead and morally corrupt. It is this fact that warps man's intellectual processes, so that he continually ignores or rejects the spiritual implications of the evidence for the existence of God that is all around him in the created universe.[35]

Yet as believers we must seek to bring the unbeliever to an acceptance of the fact that the triune God of Scripture exists. We must seek to make him realize that if man is to know this triune God, it is God who must take the initiative in revealing himself. Moreover we must seek to make the unbeliever see that

---

31. Ibid., p. 2.
32. Ibid., p. 10.
33. Ibid.
34. Ibid., p. 14.
35. Ibid.

as a sinner, Christ and the Holy Spirit must take the initiative in saving him from his sin.

At times Hamilton seems to undertake the solving of his insuperable problem in the way the presuppositionalist undertakes to solve it; i.e., by saying that man and his world are what the triune God of Scripture says they are and that, unless man believes this to be true and makes it the basis of his predication, all is chaos. Says Hamilton: "While the unbeliever does not acknowledge God's creation and control of the facts, they are still the same facts for him and for the Christian."[36]

But the point is that Hamilton *rejects* the position of the presuppositionalist in the main argument of his book. The presuppositionalist has always maintained that the revelation of God to man is alike present to all men. He has stressed the fact that man as, knowing God (*gnontes ton theon*),[37] represses this knowledge. He does so by means of his basic assumption of human autonomy, of the contingency of the space-time facts of the world and the self-existence of its laws.

In returning to the old Princeton method Hamilton undertakes to show that the unbeliever need not be challenged on these his basic assumptions. The believer need not, from the outset, challenge the unbeliever when he simply speaks about "the soul," about "innate ideas" like that of "being" and "cause." Hamilton undertakes to show against the presuppositionalist not merely that the unbeliever can formally understand the position of the believer. Hamilton undertakes to show that "the content of the knowledge of man, either unregenerate or regenerate, coincides with the content of God's knowledge of the same facts in so far as what is known by man is the truth which God knows."[38]

There is a constantly recurring confusion in Hamilton's book. Against the presuppositionalist he quotes from Scripture to the effect that the heavens declare the glory of God. "In other words the fact of creation by God can be shown through the study of 'nature.' The Bible also declares that we can know God's power and deity from the created universe and can recognize that we should worship him."[39]

But this is not what the presuppositionalist denies. On the contrary he affirms it in the strongest possible fashion. It is the final basis for his idea of the point of contact with the unbeliever. The unbeliever cannot escape God. An Oriental cannot even make himself believe that he is not an Oriental. The

---

36. Ibid., p. 17
37. KSO: That is, "knowing God. . ." Rom. 1:21.
38. Ibid., p. 34.
39. Ibid., p. 39.

knowledge of God as his Creator is indelibly fixed in the constitution of every man. Calvin says it is "infixed in his bowels."[40]

But the perversion of sin in the natural man is such that he constructs a view of himself and his world by which he seeks to suppress what, deep down in his being, he knows to be true about himself. Surrounded by the light of God's revelation the natural man, in his spiritual blindness perverts it and makes himself believe that it is a revelation of himself.

Hamilton simply assumes from the fact of the presence of God's revelation to man that the natural man *interprets* it correctly. He confuses the *revelation* of God to man with sinful man's false *interpretation* of this revelation.

It is in consonance with this confusion that Hamilton undertakes to *prove* the existence of God to the unbeliever. Here is "the soul." Here are "sensations" of "the soul" and its innate ideas of being and of cause. "Our starting point is in our own souls. We *know* that *we* exist. This knowledge is immediate and cannot be doubted. Now in making such a statement we are not assuming that we are uncreated. *We* know that God created us because the Bible so tells us, so *that* knowledge is back of our whole argument."[41]

We, i.e., as *believers*, know that we are created. But the unbeliever does *not* believe this. It is true as Hamilton says, that the unbeliever cannot doubt his existence. But it is equally true that the unbeliever assumes his non-createdness.

Hamilton now sits down with this unbeliever so as to discuss their common problems. He says to Mr. Jones, the unbeliever: "We know that we did not produce our own souls and bodies. We must have been caused by someone with power sufficient to produce our souls and bodies. We must have been caused by either a Person or an impersonal force. Here we appeal to the axiom that the cause must be adequate to produce the effect. How could an impersonal force produce a personal being? How could that which neither thinks nor wills produce that which thinks and wills?"[42] "Only a powerful being could produce a thinking, willing person."[43]

Now we "look about us." We see other persons. "The similarity of their

---

40. KSO: Van Til may be referring to this from Calvin: "Men of sound judgment will always be sure that a sense of divinity which can never be effaced is engraved upon men's minds. Indeed, the perversity of the impious, who though they struggle furiously are unable to extricate themselves from the fear of God, is abundant testimony that this conviction, namely, that there is some God, is naturally inborn in all, and is *fixed deep within, as it were in the very marrow.*" John Calvin, Institutes of the Christian Religion, ed. John T. McNeill, trans. Ford Lewis Battles, vol. 1 of *The Library of Christian Classics* (Louisville, KY: Westminster John Knox Press, 2011), 45–46, my emphasis.

41. Ibid., p. 40.
42. Ibid.
43. Ibid., p. 41.

natures to ours suggests a common cause. They too must have been caused by a powerful Person."[44]

We again look about us. "What is life? Is life intelligent? Does life itself think or will? Are these vital forces a manifestation of a Power back of them, not human, that thinks or wills?"

"All this evidence points to a *personal* cause, with power adequate to produce the world of thinking, willing human beings. The God of the Bible is an obvious answer."[45] "A Person must be in control."[46]

We look about us more widely. In nature, as well as in other persons, we find evidence of plan and purpose. "The fact that cells in plants and animals divide according to a plan points to a rational Cause. All these items and a million others point to a Designer and Planner who has prepared this earth for our occupancy."[47]

Look at that beautiful rose, Mr. Jones. "The blossom is about six inches in diameter." And listen to that beautiful music. You must agree that "only a planning Person could produce all these things."[48]

But, to change the subject, Mr. Jones, did your conscience ever trouble you? You agree, of course, that man is a creature not only of appetites, but "of standards of right and wrong." Surely then "it seems probable that the Cause which produced him is likewise moral in nature."[49] "A moral man must have a moral God as his Maker."[50] "The only true standard is the Word of God."[51]

Here we have several arguments for the existence of God. "Each adds proof to the others, and their force is felt only when they are taken together." They are "cumulative."[52]

When Hamilton told us about his "insuperable problem" he added: "unwillingly we are forced to admit that we cannot offer mathematical proof of the existence of God."[53] At the conclusion of his arguments he repeats this point and adds: "The kind of proof we are discussing is *inferential proof*, the culmination of innumerable lines of evidence all pointing to what seems an *inescapable conclusion*."[54] Of course, because of sin men will seek to escape the proper conclusion

---

44. Ibid.
45. Ibid.
46. Ibid., p. 42.
47. Ibid., p. 43.
48. Ibid.
49. Ibid., p. 45.
50. Ibid., p. 48.
51. Ibid., p. 47.
52. Ibid., p. 48.
53. Ibid., pp. 35–36.
54. Ibid., p. 48.

of the arguments. "The evidence for God is there, but only the Holy Spirit can make men accept it."[55]

Hamilton now goes on to consider the world today and its origin. There is nothing added in this chapter to the argument already given. We already have "what seems an inescapable conclusion" that there is a Cause back of the universe and that "it seems probable" that this cause is moral in nature. Surely then "if there is a rational God at all, he could make the world of life at one stroke as easily as through a long process."[56] "But if the evolutionary theory be rejected, however much special creation may be disliked, it is the only alternative."[57]

Going on from this point Hamilton establishes "the reasonableness of supernaturalism."

Says Hamilton: "If the arguments advanced in the preceding chapters are sound, we have shown that a power which we call 'God' exists, and that his nature is such that he has both the power and the knowledge to intervene in the universe."[58] Alternative positions have been shown to be "logically impossible." The evolutionary hypothesis has been shown to be "improbable."

"The only conclusion possible, then, is to say that there is such a God, having power, intelligence, personality, and will, capable of producing the world of today, with its manifold forms of life culminating in man. Certainly if such a God exists, and reason compels us to believe that he does, no rational man would deny the possibility of his intervening in the universe which he has made."[59] It is "absurd" if any one denies the possibility of supernatural revelation.

But is it probable that God should intervene in the universe? Of course it is: "God would not logically create man and leave him alone."[60] "A person with free will might possibly do things contrary to the will of God, so it would be natural for God to warn him and help to guard him against such disobedience."[61] And wouldn't God tell man what he is here for and what is his ultimate destiny? "If it is true that there is a heaven and a hell, to one of which places every soul will go, God would hardly leave man in ignorance of this momentous fact."[62] "Most of all, after the fall of man, if God intended to redeem man's life from destruction in a definite way, and intended, as the Bible teaches, to have this redemption applied to a man's life through faith in a risen Lord, he would most certainly

---

55. Ibid.
56. Ibid., p. 91.
57. Ibid.
58. Ibid., p. 94.
59. Ibid.
60. Ibid., p. 99.
61. Ibid., p. 100.
62. Ibid.

tell men about this fact in some way or other. We thus see that there is a very great probability, if the God represented in the Bible exists, that he would reveal certain vital facts to man."[63]

But we have so far dealt only with the possibility and the probability of supernatural revelation. There remains the question: Has there actually been such a revelation? This question is "one purely of fact."[64] It is a question of evidence. "What are the laws of evidence?"[65] They are three: Is the witness competent? Is he reliable? Was he "in a position to know the facts."[66]

Apply these tests to the question of the resurrection of Christ from the dead. Looking at "all possibilities" we find "that the only conclusion possible is that Christ actually rose from the dead."[67] The "resurrection establishes beyond a doubt the truth of Christianity. But not only does it prove that Christianity is the one true religion. It also proves that all that Christ said and did was true, and this in turn proves that the Bible is the Word of God written."[68]

It is in this manner that Hamilton seeks to solve his "insuperable problem." His aim is to bring the unbeliever to a belief in the triune God of the Bible and in the Bible as the authoritative Word of God.

Yet, at no point in his argument does Hamilton as much as present the triune God of Scripture for what he is to the unbeliever. As a Reformed theologian Hamilton knows that the "Christian God" has created man in his image, and that every sinner is aware of this. *Knowing God*, says Paul, and knowing therefore that as creatures they *ought* to obey God, men seek to repress this knowledge. In every moment of self-awareness every man experiences God's call to the recognition of himself as man's Creator.

Secondly, as a Reformed theologian Hamilton knows that every sensation that any man experiences is of God-controlled and God-directed facts. God controls "whatsoever comes to pass."

It is "the Soul" which, by its innate ideas of being and cause orders its experience. As a believer Hamilton knows that "the soul" is what the Bible says it is. But as an apologist he merely asks the unbeliever to admit that he has "a soul." Hamilton will lead him on from this point toward belief in the Bible with all that it teaches in the name of the triune God. The process goes step by step. The argument is cumulative. The result is that God *probably* exists.

It appears then that Hamilton's great problem remains unsolved. His method

---

63. Ibid.
64. Ibid., p. 105.
65. Ibid.
66. Ibid., pp. 105–106.
67. Ibid., p. 304.
68. Ibid.

of apologetics is based upon the assumption that the unbeliever is right in thinking that he can properly start with himself as "free" in order then to accept or to reject the Christian position as an hypothesis about the nature of reality. Instead of showing his unbeliever that on his assumption he cannot identify himself and cannot, therefore, even begin a process of rational inquiry, Hamilton establishes him in his folly. How could "the soul" say *I*, and ask questions about himself and his world if the God of the Bible had not first said *I am* and then told man who he is? All that "the soul" of Hamilton's unbeliever "knows" is *that* he exists. He does not know *what* he is. But then unless he knows *what* he is, he cannot really know *that* he is. Hamilton, the apologist, agrees with his unbeliever, when this unbeliever in effect claims to be able to do what according to Hamilton, the theologian, only the triune God can do, namely, identify himself in terms of himself.

By definition Hamilton's unbeliever does not wish to be thought of as deriving himself, his free personality, from the creative activity of God. He refuses to operate responsibly within the plan of God. He operates, therefore in the Void. His "sensations" spring from the Void. If he is "free" they cannot, he thinks, have their source in the all-controlling power of God.

If then, for the moment, we grant that his "soul" can say *I*, he will never be able to distinguish one sensation from another. It is too much even to say of his sensations that they will always be the same. He has no standard by which to distinguish what is different and what is the same.

Yet it is this "open universe" that Hamilton's unbeliever insists he needs lest his freedom of inquiry be strangled. From his point of view as an apologist the position of Hamilton the theologian is that of pure determinism. A properly scientific procedure, "the soul" insists, requires that at the outset of any empirical investigation every hypothesis is as legitimate as every other hypothesis. Pure contingency, as the source of his every sensation, is the presupposition of Hamilton's unbeliever. The "soul" of Hamilton's unbeliever cannot distinguish himself from other selves and cannot distinguish one sensation from any other sensation. The unbeliever is free from the God of Christianity, by being free in Chaos.

But let us, for the sake of the argument, grant that the soul has sufficient coherence within itself to identify itself and distinguish one sensation from another. Let us watch the soul as it then leads us on to the idea of the existence of God. Hamilton tells Mr. Jones, the unbeliever: "We must have been caused by someone with power sufficient to produce our souls and bodies. We must have been caused by either a Person or an impersonal force. Here we appeal to the axiom that the cause must be adequate to produce the effect."[69]

Here then causation is a general axiom. It is also an innate idea "formed by

---

69. Ibid., p. 40.

the mind when sensations are received."[70] Hamilton speaks of "the bridge of cause which we have erected."[71]

As a *theologian* Hamilton believes that "the 'self,' the idea of 'cause,' and the external universe are created 'facts.'"[72] But his unbeliever does not interpret them so. Says Hamilton: "But when the non-Christian scientist or philosopher begins to reason in the field of philosophy or theology, the very nature of the subject matter, dealing as it does with the ultimate causes of the universe, makes it impossible for him to reason correctly. The distortion brought about by the fall of man into sin completely blocks the intellectual channels of such a non-Christian thinker and prevents him from reasoning correctly."[73]

Of course the unbeliever as well as the believer "is still a creature made in the image of God (even if he will not acknowledge that fact) and may therefore reason correctly as far as the form of his reasoning steps and his conclusions are concerned. When we substitute Christian assumptions for his non-Christian premises, the steps of his reasoning process may be correct."[74] Hamilton agrees with the presuppositionalist that the truth about man and his world is what Scripture says it is. He says: "The judgments 'Every effect has an adequate cause' and 'My experience is taking place' are self-evidently true because God has ordained them to be true as the primary thoughts of a rational creature made in the image of God. . . Yet when an unbeliever makes them, his underlying assumption that God cannot be the cause of any experience makes even these primary judgments only partially and formally true for him."[75]

But now look again at Hamilton the *apologist*. He knows that the unbeliever *assumes* his autonomy. He knows that the unbeliever *assumes* the self-existence of the space-time facts. And he knows that the unbeliever assumes that God cannot be the cause of any experience.

Knowing all this Hamilton none the less reasons with Mr. Jones, his unbeliever, as though he need not reject these assumptions. On the contrary he talks to Mr. Jones as though, if only he thinks orderly he will come to the proper conclusions about God and his world.

Start from your own idea of the soul, and from your own idea of your sensations, Mr. Jones. Then apply your own idea of causation to the self and its sensations and you will arrive at the conclusion: "A Person must be in control."[76]

---

70. Ibid., p. 7.
71. Ibid., p. 16.
72. Ibid.
73. Ibid., p. 14.
74. Ibid., p. 12.
75. Ibid., p. 11.
76. Ibid., p. 42.

If you have not felt the force of the argument from cause by itself then add the arguments from design, from beauty and from morality. Each of these arguments "adds proof to the others, and their force is felt only when they are taken together."[77]

Now if one thing is obvious it is that the God that is constructed by this approach *is not* the God of the Bible. The God that is thus constructed in this fashion is a *god* who confronts an ultimately autonomous human self and a purely contingent universe. The God to whom Hamilton leads his unbeliever has not created the world and does not control both it and man. The idea of cause as employed by Hamilton's unbeliever cannot be shown to be "innate" in the soul. The soul is at best, an island of foam floating on an ocean of Chance. This island cannot support the human end of the "bridge of cause." Neither can this bridge of cause be shown to be supported on the other end by God. The God who is to support the further end of the bridge of cause must first be constructed by materials taken out of the world of contingency by the soul that has first taken itself out of the world of contingency. Of course the bridge itself must also be built of the timbers of foam taken out of the bottomless ocean of contingency.

Hamilton says that as a sinner the unbeliever will not believe his argument for the existence of God, for the possibility, the probability and the actuality of the revelation of God unless the Holy Spirit open his eyes to see that the argument is sound.

But surely the unbeliever will gladly accept Hamilton's argument. Indeed some unbelievers may prefer a materialistic and mechanistic interpretation of the universe to Hamilton's teleological one. Yet many others may gladly accept Hamilton's theism. It will give them the comfortable feeling of the Pharisees that they are not like other men, like materialists and mechanists or even like this God-is-dead theologian, Altizer.[78]

Surely, too, the Holy Spirit will not exert himself in order to change men from atheists to theists that are not Christian theists. The Holy Spirit operates in the world to convict men of sin, of righteousness and of judgment. He testifies to the fact that such arguments as Hamilton presents are used by sinners in order to make themselves believe that they have done justice by the evidence if they conclude that some sort of God may possibly or even probably exist and that Christ is his Son.

We may continue to expect Roman Catholics and Arminians to construct

---

77. Ibid., p. 48.
78. KSO: Van Til is referring to Thomas J. J. Altizer (1927–2018). Shortly before the publication of this book, in 1965 and 1966, *Time* magazine featured Altizer and the "God is dead" movement.

arguments of this sort despite their personal belief in the "Christian God." We *should* expect that Reformed thinkers would come to unbelievers with the full gospel of the self-identifying Christ of the Scripture, as *the* way, *the* truth and *the* life. Unless man presupposes the God and the Christ of the Scriptures, he cannot identify himself, nor any fact of his world, or even relate any fact to any other fact.

Predication is meaningless except upon the presupposition of the truth of Christianity. The unbeliever can intellectually understand this. It is the task of the Christian apologist to present the absolute contrast between predication carried forth upon Christian premises and predication carried forth on the premise of human autonomy. Roman Catholicism and Arminianism fail to present men with the full significance of the gospel because they do not challenge the starting point and the methodology of the unbeliever. Those who hold the Reformed Faith in theology can be of inestimable blessing to the unbeliever if, instead of following the Romanist and the Arminian, they apply the principles of their theology to the method of their apologetics.[79]

---

79. KSO: This is an important point. We should not expect anyone holding to an Arminian theology to adopt an apologetic that relies on Reformed theology, especially its view of the self-attestation of Scripture as described, for example, in *Westminster Confession of Faith*, 1.4. On the other hand, we should expect anyone holding to Reformed theology to apply that theology, in all of its fullness, to the apologetic enterprise.

X.

BUSWELL'S *SYSTEMATIC THEOLOGY*

A position similar to that of Floyd E. Hamilton is set forth by Dr. J. Oliver Buswell, Jr.[1] In distinction from Hamilton, Buswell has, from his earlier to his later writings, been true to the "inductive methodology" of Bishop Butler.

We shall deal with Buswell's recent work on systematic theology[2] and in passing, touch on his recent work on philosophy, *A Christian View of Being and Knowing*.[3] We shall, for the sake of clarity, first look at this work on philosophy.

Buswell says he is setting forth "a Christian view of philosophy."[4] He is setting forth a Christian metaphysics and a Christian epistemology in detail and offers a "summary statement" of a Christian ethics.[5]

"In *metaphysics* we believe that God is the supreme personal Intelligence, Creator of the finite universe." The doctrine of temporal creation "is entirely consistent with God's eternal triune existence."[6] In the created universe we

---

1. KSO: Dr. J. Oliver Buswell, Jr. (1895–1977), after serving in pastoral ministry, was called to be the third president of Wheaton College in 1926, where he remained until 1940. After a short stint at Faith Seminary, he became president of National Bible Institute of New York City in 1941. In 1956, he became Dean of Covenant Seminary, where he remained until his retirement in 1970. Buswell was involved, with J. Gresham Machen and others, in opposing the Presbyterian Church U.S.A. He helped found the Orthodox Presbyterian Church in 1936, was a leader in forming the Bible Presbyterian Church in 1937, out of which he along with a large group began the Evangelical Presbyterian Church. This church united in 1965 with the Reformed Presbyterian Church in North America to become the Reformed Presbyterian Church, Evangelical Synod. Buswell was the first one to coin the term 'presuppositionalism' in print after it was suggested to him by Allan A. MacRae; see J. Oliver Buswell, "Presuppositionalism – A Book Review," *The Bible Today* 41, no. 8 (May 1948): 235. For an extended discussion of Buswell and his interactions with Van Til, see David O. Filson, *A Fountainhead of Misunderstanding: J. Oliver Buswell, Cornelius Van Til, and the Context and Contours of an Apologetic Debate*, Ph.D. dissertation, (Westminster Theological Seminary, 2018).
2. James O. Buswell, Jr., *A Systematic Theology of The Christian Religion* (Grand Rapids: Zondervan, 2 vols., 1962, 1963).
3. James O. Buswell, *A Christian View of Being and Knowing* (Grand Rapids: Zondervan, 1960).
4. Ibid., p. 8.
5. Ibid., pp. 8–9.
6. Ibid., p. 8.

find "an important difference between beings which think, and beings which are spatially extended, or spiritual beings and material beings. This is Descartes' distinction between *res cogitans* and *res extensa*."[7] [8]

"In *epistemology*, we believe that God, the supreme personal Intelligence, has created us to be in some measure capable of intelligent apprehension of truth. We regard the basic laws of logic as derived from the character of God's intelligence."[9] "We believe and accept the Bible as the infallible Word of God, and we are prepared to submit reasonable evidence, open to public investigation, in support of the system of doctrine set forth therein."

"Most important are our presuppositions in the field of ethics. We find a calamitous situation existing. We call it the problem of moral evil. There is a basic disharmony in man's spiritual world."[10] Moral evil is obviously universal. We conclude that: "(1) There must be some primitive cause of moral evil at the historical source of the race, and (2) a wrong relationship with the Creator of the race must have come about in connection with this primitive cause."[11]

When we consider how I was representatively present at the signing of the declaration of independence then we see how reasonable it is to believe what Genesis 3 and Romans 5 tells us about "a primitive representative, or federal head, of the race." How reasonable to believe that the whole race of man was involved in "some primitive human act in violation of the moral character of God." What these passages of God's infallible revelation teach us is so reasonable that if they had not been given us "we should be compelled to postulate the substance of what they say. Universal moral evil can reasonably be interpreted as resulting from an original sin against the character of God."[12]

Still further, it is the cross of Christ "which constitutes the distinctive feature of Christian ethics." Still further, our Christian philosophy has an answer for the removal as well as for the entrance of moral evil. "The Christian ethic centers in the good news that the Son of God voluntarily bore human sin, and offers both pardon and cleansing to all who will accept him."[13] "We take the act of the crucifying of Jesus as a world representative event, on the analogy of original sin. It was a deed committed by the representatives of the entire human race, typifying and comprehending all our moral corruption."[14] "In Christian ethics, the

---

7. Ibid.
8. KSO: Descartes's distinction is, very generally, between consciousness (*res cogitans*—thinking thing) and matter (*res extensa*—extended thing).
9. Ibid., pp. 8–9.
10. Ibid., p. 9.
11. Ibid.
12. Ibid., p. 10.
13. Ibid.
14. Ibid.

individual acknowledges his implication in the original sin of the race. . . but. . . repudiates the primitive federal head and his act of original sin, and experiences a change of orientation. He specifically accepts the One who bore his sin on the cross as his federal head and representative."[15] "Christian ethics recognizes that not all humanity will repudiate moral evil and accept the cross. . ."[16] How then are those who do accept the cross, who are members of "the redeemed humanity" to present their Christian philosophy to those who do not accept the cross?

Buswell answers as follows: "We who accept this system of philosophy accept these presuppositions [basic concepts of the Judeo-Christian tradition] in a manner similar to that in which the geophysicists accepted the maps and charts scientifically prepared prior to the elaborate studies of the International Geophysical Year which began in July 1957. The scientists were quite conscious that there were discrepancies in their findings. They were prepared to re-examine anything and everything for greater accuracy."[17] But though ready to re-examine everything, they did not begin in ignorance. "They would not have been in any position to advance the cause of science if they had not had reasonably reliable presuppositions to begin with."

"Similarly we believe that our attitude toward philosophy, as we state our presuppositions, is the truly scientific one—the attitude most likely to lead to a clearer understanding."[18]

More particularly, our method of presenting our Judeo-Christian view of reality is that of induction. In this we must follow the example of our Lord and of biblical writers in general.

> One epistemological trait is characteristic of the biblical writers throughout, that is the appeal to empirical evidence in verification of the divine authority of their message. In the tenth chapter of the Gospel according to John it is recorded that Jesus was accused of blasphemy because he said, 'I am the Son of God,' thus, in the Jewish way of thinking, 'making himself equal with God.' His reply is in two steps. (1) Man is created in the image of God. There is a God-related element, even in fallen man (Ps 82:6–7). Therefore Jesus' claim to be God in the flesh *might* be true. It is *not necessarily* blasphemy. (2) Jesus next appealed to the empirical evidence 'If I do not the works of my Father, believe me not. But if I do, though ye believe not me, believe the works: that ye may come to know, and continue to know, that the Father is in me, and I in him.' (vss. 37, 38)

---

15. Ibid., p. 11.
16. Ibid.
17. Ibid., pp. 11–12.
18. Ibid., p. 12.

Compare the empirical evidence for the resurrection of Christ cited in the fifteenth chapter of 1 Corinthians, and the reference to 'many infallible proofs' in Acts 1:3.[19]

If we follow the example of our Lord and of Paul then we are also in line with "common Christian practice." "The common Christian practice in regard to theistic evidences is analogous to the ordinary practice with reference to the existence of the sun, the existence of the material world, or any other matter of commonly accepted fact."[20]

"There are devout Christian scholars of the present generation who hold to an inflexible deductive rationalism."[21] Buswell here refers to "Professor Hackett's new book, *The Resurrection of Theism*."[22] There are other "influential Christian scholars" who hold

> that since man exists in a fallen condition, and since his mind is distorted by sin, there is no common ground, in reason or in evidences, between the Christian and his message, on the one hand, and the unbeliever on the other. This view has been called 'presuppositionalism,' not because those who oppose it do not frankly state their presuppositions, but because, according to this particular *a priori* view, there is no intellectual common ground *unless* one adopts distinctly Christian presuppositions.[23]

As a result of this unbiblical method of teaching "many young men have been impressed with the idea that it is improper to present evidences and reasons to the unsaved man."

"This position is taken to such extremes that the historical inductive arguments for the existence of God are said to be not only false but harmful. As one of the presuppositionalists puts it, 'Whereas Professor Hepp [of Amsterdam] says that the cosmological and teleological arguments cry out day and night to the glory of God, as a matter of fact the cosmological and teleological arguments cry out day and night 'there is no God.'"[24] The quotation given is from the present writer's little book *Common Grace*.[25]

Buswell informs us that he has called this position "presuppositionalism"

---

19. Ibid., pp. 169–170.
20. Ibid., pp. 171–172.
21. Ibid., p. 173.
22. Ibid., p. 174.
23. Ibid., p. 175.
24. Ibid., p. 176.
25. The writer's *Common Grace*, Philadelphia, 1964, p. 61.

and that, contrary to its claims, it is out of accord with Calvin's approach. "Calvin's constant assumption, like the assumption of the writers of the Scriptures, is that fallen man may hear and understand something of the Word of God and may, by the convicting power of the Holy Spirit, be convinced and believe."[26] Having said this Buswell concludes, "I would urge the use of the inductive processes of presenting evidence, not as the only method, but as a method of pointing to the truth useful and profitable in many situations."[27] Those who, like Hackett, advocate "the rationalistic *a priori* method" need not fear that if they should follow the inductive procedure, logic would not receive its due. "I believe that all that is contained in the Christian revelation is reasonable. Nothing violates the principles of logic. We do not believe contradictory propositions. But factual existences never can be deduced from mere abstract logical principles. God has spoken!"[28]

A. NATURAL THEOLOGY

We now turn to Buswell's *Systematic Theology*, Part I, the section dealing with theism. It is marked, among other points, by an "emphasis upon the value of inductive evidence."[29]

Of course "our one complex primary presupposition" of the Christian religion is "*Jesus Christ as the Second Person of the sovereign triune Godhead, as presented in the Bible, his infallible Word.*"[30]

Buswell finds it necessary at this point to explain in what sense "we students of theology presuppose our basic presuppositions."[31] The answer is that "we take our supposition as a conclusion arrived at on the basis of what we consider good and sufficient reasons. We are at all times ready to re-examine our basic presupposition and state our reasons for holding it (1) for the purpose of clarifying and confirming our position and (2) for the purpose of convincing those who have not yet arrived at our presupposition and not yet taken it as their own conclusion."[32]

If some one who "is not familiar with inductive processes of reasonings" thinks that such a position is "obviously absurd," we reply that "this objection

---

26. *Christian View*, p. 177.
27. Ibid.
28. Ibid., pp. 174–175.
29. *Sys. Theol.*, I p. 5.
30. Ibid., p. 15.
31. Ibid.
32. Ibid.

confuses the chronological beginning, which may be anywhere, with the pedagogical beginning, which is selected for the purposes of exposition."[33]

Of course it would be quite wrong for a Christian to doubt the foundations of his own position but this is not the case when he deals "with one who does not yet believe in God."[34]

Let us then proceed to the proof for the existence of God. "We shall argue that God is known by his effects, that is by revelation, in Christ, in Scripture, and in his creation, when we present the theistic proofs. Inductive reasoning in theology carries us as far, and is as reliable, as inductive reasoning is, or claims to be, in any sphere."[35]

If some one still suggests that our procedure is not really inductive because we speak of Christ as we do, then let him rest assured that

> in interpreting the Bible we do not ask any favors which we do not believe are proper rules for the reading of any serious literature. When we presuppose, as we have clearly indicated, that the Bible is the infallible, inerrant, Word of God, all we ask unbelievers to accept is merely the rules for dealing seriously with important writings. Give a fair hearing to any one of the several authors or books of the Bible; allow due proportionate weight to such interpretation of what is said as would reasonably be coherent and non-contradictory. Then apply the same rule to the Bible as a whole. Give a fair chance for the Bible to speak consistently. Assume a reasonable presumption in favor of consistency and non-contradiction, at least to the extent that such presumptions would be allowed in any great and influential writings.[36]

B. WHAT IS GOD?

But is there any point seeking to prove *that* God exists unless we know *what* God is? Well let the Bible tell us *what* God is. We may sum up what the Bible teaches in the words of the *Westminster Shorter Catechism*: "God is a Spirit, infinite, eternal and unchangeable in his being, wisdom, power, holiness, justice, goodness and truth."[37] If we should meet Professor Edgar Sheffield Brightman[38]

---

33. Ibid.
34. Ibid., p. 16.
35. Ibid., p. 23.
36. Ibid., pp. 24–25.
37. Ibid., p. 30.
38. KSO: Edgar Sheffield Brightman (1884–1953) was, with Bowne and Knudson, a Boston personalist.

and he should seek to convert us to his idea of a finite God we shall tell him, "I am a Calvinist."[39] A Roman Catholic would likely object to this procedure. He might quote from Thomas to the effect "that nothing is predicated *univocally* of God and of other things."[40]

To this sort of objection we should say: "I reject the Thomistic doctrine of analogy."[41] Analogical statements are true only in a figurative sense of the word. What we need are *univocal* statements about God. They are "literal."[42] There are, to be sure, analogical statements about God in the Bible. But "there are also literal statements about God and his attributes, which are comprehensible even to our finite minds."[43] A summary of such statements is found in the answer to question four of the Westminster Shorter Catechism just given.[44]

We are now ready to proceed. "If we accept the Bible, we accept it as true. If we accept it as true, in that very act we regard whatever contradicts it as false. Whatever propositions are taught in the Bible are to be believed and their contradictories are to be rejected."[45]

If the followers of Thomas object that we have taken our "primary presupposition" from revelation and that we are therefore, when we use it, no longer standing on common ground with those who do not believe in revelation, this does not stop our effort. We are frankly out to establish the truth of *Christian* theism, not theism in general. We are Protestants. We accept "the laws of logic not as superior to our basic presupposition but as implied in them and derived from them."[46] We therefore "hold Thomas' denial of the possibility of univocal statements about God to be wholly arbitrary and contrary to fact."[47]

Moreover, we do stand on common ground with those who do not believe in Christian theism. We believe "that all that is contained in the Christian revelation is reasonable. Nothing violates the principles of logic."[48] But though we insist that the laws of logic are *implied* in our basic presupposition we would urge Christian scholars to use the inductive procedure in their presentation of the good news of the gospel.

In inductive reasoning

---

39. Ibid., p. 63.
40. Ibid., p. 29.
41. Ibid., p. 29 fn.
42. Ibid., p. 29.
43. Ibid., p. 30.
44. Ibid.
45. Ibid., p. 20.
46. Ibid.
47. Ibid., p. 30.
48. *Christian View*, p. 176.

facts are observed and implications of facts are inferred, leading to more or less probability in conclusions, with more or less cogency. There is no argument known to us which, as an argument, leads to more than a probable (highly probable) conclusion. For example, most of us believe that the sun will rise tomorrow morning, but if we were to analyze the evidences, the arguments which lead to such a conclusion, we should be forced to admit that the arguments, good as they are, are characterized by probability. The theistic arguments are no exception to the rule that *all* inductive arguments about what exists are probability arguments. This is as far as the arguments, *qua* arguments, claim to go.[49]

1. The Cosmological Argument

Buswell now proceeds to suggest how we may properly use the cosmological argument for the existence of God. He would use such words as these: "'If anything does now exist, then either something must be eternal, or something not eternal must have come from nothing.' The argument then proceeds to show that it is more reasonable to believe that something is eternal; and that among the many hypotheses of eternal existence, the God of the Bible is the most reasonable, the most probable eternal Being."[50]

Buswell wants to distinguish his method of argument from that of Thomas Aquinas. We can give only a sample of Buswell's criticism of the arguments set forth by the great Roman Catholic apologist.

Thomas' first argument is, says Buswell, basic for his position. He holds that we must think of an unmoved mover back of all cosmic motion because an eternal series of motions is inconceivable. But "there is no logical reason why one motion after another could not have been continued from eternity past." Buswell would therefore re-express the argument from motion in the following words: If motion does now exist, then either motion must have been eternally actual or potential, or on the other hand, motion must have arisen from nothing. Among the various hypotheses it is most probable that the God of the Bible existed eternally as the potential Originator of motion.[51]

Similarly, Thomas' argument from cause should say: "If there now does exist a chain of causality, then either it is itself eternal as a chain, or it originated in an eternal potential Cause, or it originated from nothing." The God of the Bible is then shown to be the most probable eternal potential cause.

"We must reject the notion that an infinite regress of causes is impossible to

---

49. *Sys. Theol.*, I p. 72.
50. Ibid., p. 79.
51. Ibid.

conceive. Rather, it is the case that it is difficult to conceive of the opposite. To argue that since every event has a cause, therefore there must be some event at the beginning which has no cause, is clearly a fallacy."[52]

Again Thomas' argument from contingency must be restated. "There is no ground for saying that an infinite chain of contingent beings could not have existed. I suggest that here, as above, emergentism be shown to be improbable, and the eternal existence of the God of the Bible be shown to be most probable."

"That the conditional demands that which is absolute and unconditional is but another form of the same fallacy which we find in the two preceding arguments. There is no logical reason why the entire universe might not be made up of inter-dependent contingencies."[53]

Once more, Thomas is quite wrong in saying that "the imperfect implies the perfect." There is, therefore, no validity in Thomas' argument from degrees. "It suggests, however, an induction from the fact of valuation to a perfect standard of value, similar to my inductive statement of 'the moral argument' in *What Is God*. How did the idea of value, or the fact of valuation, come to be, if there is no true norm? Each historical view of the norm is self-contradictory without Theism, but each of the norms set forth in great historical systems of ethical philosophy proves to be a true subordinate norm, if 'the kingdom of God and his righteousness is taken as the supreme norm.'"[54]

Finally Thomas' argument from teleology is, says Buswell, "essentially sound but extremely meager. I should criticize it for not including an outline of the biblical answer to the problem of evil."[55]

Buswell justifies what he calls his long discussion on the Thomistic proofs as follows: (1) some unbelieving philosophers think that Thomas "exhausted the possibility of theistic evidences and failed; and therefore all time spent on theistic evidences is wasted"; (2) there are those who favor *a priorism*; (3) some Christians feel that in Thomas "they have their chief defense against atheism." It must therefore be shown that the inductive arguments for the existence of God, when properly restated, are sound.[56]

Take then, again, the cosmological argument. We start from the fact that "at least something, the cosmos, now exists, and since it is highly improbable that something comes from nothing, something must be eternal. Further, it is highly improbable that the material universe is eternal."[57]

52. Ibid.
53. Ibid., pp. 75–80.
54. Ibid., p. 80.
55. Ibid.
56. Ibid., p. 81.
57. Ibid., p. 84.

We ask in the second place, whether this something that is eternal can be identified with "unconscious intelligence." This nothing "seems contradictory."[58] "It is," therefore, "simple and reasonable to believe that eternal personal Intelligence is the explanation of the universe. It is unreasonable to believe in any other theory."[59]

"In conclusion," says Buswell, "let me emphasize again that belief in an eternal Being of some End is necessary for all hypotheses except the absurdity of uncaused emergence from nothing. The atheistic materialist must believe that the cosmic process is eternal. The non-theistic idealist must believe that some kind of mind or spirit or will is eternal. In postulating faith in the eternal God as the explanation of the cosmos, we are advancing the most simple and reasonable hypothesis of all."[60]

2. The Teleological Argument

As for the teleological argument, it "is used in the Scripture. 'He that planted the ear shall he not hear?' (Ps 94:9). The implicit argument is quite transparent. Can we believe that the purposiveness of our sensory organs can be explained without an intelligent Purposer?"[61] Think also of Psalm 19. Think especially of Romans 1:18–22. Paul does not formulate his thought technically. "But the cosmological and teleological arguments are imbedded in these Scriptural words in such a sense that if these arguments are unsound, then these words of Scripture are false. If these arguments are sound then the created universe is sufficient evidence, and unbelievers who possess the evidence are inexcusable."[62]

If "young men" only read this plain statement of Paul they will no longer be led astray into thinking "that it is improper to present evidences and reasons to the unsaved man."[63]

It should be noted too, says Buswell, that "the theistic argument from teleology is not in the slightest degree inconsistent with recognition of what we call mathematical, or mechanical chance."[64] "The teleological argument simply recognizes that there are many things in the universe which our minds cannot ascribe to chance. As Eddington says, a monkey playing with a typewriter might accidentally type a word or two, but who can believe that such a process has produced an intelligible book?"[65]

---

58. Ibid., p. 85.
59. Ibid.
60. Ibid.
61. Ibid., p. 86.
62. Ibid.
63. *Christian View*, p. 176.
64. *Sys. Theol.*, I p. 88.
65. Ibid., p. 89.

"It must be remembered that mathematical or mechanical chance is an entirely different concept from theological or cosmic chance."[66]

Finally if the fact of evil is brought forward as evidence against teleology we reply, "moral, spiritual, ethical values are immeasurably deepened by the fact that God has permitted sinners to sin and has allowed the abstract possibility of evil to become an actuality. So we find that what we call 'natural evil' in the universe is morally good for the discipline of our souls."[67]

We may say as Christian believers that our claims do not outreach the evidence. All we claim is that: "*It is possible to believe rationally in cosmic teleology.*" Finally: "Even though it were equally possible (which it is not) to interpret all the data of human experiences in terms of chaotic irrationalism, would it not be preferable to adopt the hypothesis of theism?"[68]

However, we need not stop with this minimal claim with respect to cosmic teleology, for "there is one factual pattern in cosmic data which throws the balance of probability entirely on the side of theism. This is the pattern of data centering in the Jesus of history. . . In *Behold Him* I approached the entire field of biblical doctrine from the point of view of the historical Jesus. Who and what was he? I sought to show that the indisputable facts relating to him can be explained in no other category than biblical theism."[69] From a proper philosophical point of view "Christ and the Bible are just as much in the data as any other facts open to public investigation."[70] The Bible speaks of "the Supernatural." Believing in the "supernaturalistic view" of the cosmos means for us "that God is a Person and that he is just as capable of acting in and upon and through his creation as a human person is capable of acting in his own proper sphere."[71] If you ask how we can identify the presence of the supernatural among other cosmic data, we reply that "we should not be able to distinguish a supernatural event if it could not be placed in comparison with the usual course of nature."[72]

3. The Anthropological Argument

We pass on now to the anthropological argument. Buswell relates this argument to the cosmological and the teleological arguments by saying: "As indicated above I conceive the theistic arguments as a series of concentric circles; first, the

---

66. Ibid., p. 88, fn.
67. Ibid., p. 89.
68. Ibid.
69. Ibid., p. 90.
70. Ibid., p. 90, fn.
71. J. O. Buswell, *Behold Him!* (Grand Rapids: Zondervan, 1937), p. 24.
72. Ibid.

cosmos as a whole, second, purposiveness within the cosmos. The third circle is the nature of man within the area of purposiveness. What is the explanation of man?"[73] Basing the anthropological argument on the former two we may well say: "'Shall he who created purpose and will and thought and all that is included in character and personality, shall he be regarded as impersonal and devoid of conscious intelligence?'"[74]

4. The Moral Argument

Under this heading Buswell refers to his earlier book with the title *What is God?* "In *What is God?* I developed the moral argument at some length, showing that in the great historical systems of ethical philosophy, where the God of the Bible is left out, the criteria assumed lead to contradiction. But where God is accepted as the ultimate criterion, the criteria in the various theories contain important subordinate truths."[75]

5. The Ontological Argument

When Buswell finally comes to the ontological argument he rejects it, as might be expected, when it is expressed in "the deductive *a priori* form."[76] But the argument can also be stated in "the inductive *a posteriori* form." "The latter, the inductive form, is, I think, acceptable if properly stated."[77] Descartes suggests the inductive form of the argument rather obscurely. And even Anselm, "Platonist that he was, felt the need of inductive reasoning *a posteriori* from effect to cause, in defending his theism."[78] Leibniz too, "like Anselm and Descartes before him, also had room for inductive arguments *a posteriori*."[79]

Stating the ontological argument in its proper inductive form Buswell says: "The idea of the God of the Bible, 'He who is,' is a *datum*. The inductive ontological argument simply says, What is the explanation of this *datum*?"[80]

"The point is that the idea of God as set forth in the Bible is not explicable from any non-theistic data. The God of the Bible is a Spirit without corporeal existence. He is omnipresent. He is omniscient, not through quickness of

---

73. *Sys. Theol.*, II, p. 90.
74. Ibid., p. 91.
75. Ibid.
76. KSO: The ontological argument, set forth by Anselm and others, is an *a priori* argument; it does not require empirical evidence in order to be stated. Thus, Buswell, the inductivist, would reject it as originally formulated.
77. Ibid., p. 93.
78. Ibid., p. 94.
79. Ibid., p. 95.
80. Ibid., p. 98.

intellectual discursive processes like Thor or Hercules. He is powerful, not by relative measure of strength, but by the total control of all the power that is or could be. The idea of such a God with such attributes is not conceivable as a composite of non-theistic human experiences."[81] Stated in words such as these the ontological argument "has considerable weight. As Descartes says, this idea must have God as its cause."[82]

Summing up the whole matter Buswell says:

> Concluding then the inductive arguments for the existence of God, we hold that these arguments do establish a presumption in favor of faith in the God of the Bible. It should never be held that these arguments have the demonstrative quality of mathematical processes. It ought to be recognized, on the contrary, that, as we have indicated above, all existential propositions are logically qualified by a greater or lesser degree of probability.
>
> As Bishop Joseph Butler said in his *Analogy*, the evidence for the God of the Bible is sufficiently cogent to place upon us a moral responsibility. We must choose for or against God. Dr. Machen used to say it is as though we were on an island which is certain to sink. We are in an earthly life which is certain to come to an end. We may not have intellectually one hundred per cent demonstrative arguments, but we are bound, being on such an island, to take the best passage available to the most probable place of safety. We are in a world where sin and misery abound. The Christian Gospel *might* be true. The evidence is strong enough so that we are morally culpable if we fail to give heed. Indeed the evidence, compared with evidence in other matters, is overwhelming, so that Paul is justified in saying that those who have the evidence and who do not accept of the grace of God are 'without excuse.'
>
> The unbeliever may well be convinced, and the Christian is greatly helped by the arguments. But we have far more. We have the convicting and regenerating work of the Holy Spirit, energizing faith in our hearts (Eph 2:8–10; Phil 2:13). We are not groping uncertainly, not merely 'following a gleam,' not taking 'a leap in the dark'; we are 'walking in the light.' (1 Jn 1:7).[83]

---

81. Ibid., p. 99.
82. Ibid., p. 100.
83. Ibid., pp. 100–101.

C. EVALUATION

1. Buswell Modifies Thomas

In the first place Buswell modifies Thomism. Buswell agrees with Thomas in rejecting Anselm's form of the ontological argument for the existence of God.[84] "A Platonic idealist could accept it, but a realistic dualist scarcely could."[85] Fortunately Anselm, "Platonist that he was, felt the need of inductive reasoning *a posteriori* from effect to Cause, in defending his theism" against Gaunilon.[86]

The case of Descartes is similar to that of Anselm. He "presented the argument of Anselm chiefly in a deductive, *a priori* manner," but he also "states the ontological argument" inductively.[87]

In general, however, in spite of his modifications, Buswell's *approach* to the theistic proofs is similar to that of Thomas. Thomas does not use his five arguments as "demonstrations." On the contrary he uses them as "inductive probability reasonings."[88] The clear evidence of this fact, Buswell argues, is found in the fact that Thomas "concludes his presentation of each with a reasonable induction to a conclusion far short of deity, such as 'first mover,' 'original cause,' 'necessary being,' etc. Then, without the slightest pretense of complete 'demonstration' in the deductive sense, Thomas concludes, 'and this everyone understands to be God . . . to which everyone gives the name God, this all men speak of as God,' etc."[89]

Buswell has no objection of any sort to all this. On the contrary he approves it. Buswell's criticism of Thomas is restricted to the idea that he is *not inductive enough*. Thomas has some leftovers of deductivism in his thought. These must be removed. "There is no logical reason why one motion after another could not have continued from eternity past. The question whether this is the case is merely a question of fact. . ."[90] Similarly "we must reject the notion that an infinite regress of causes is impossible to conceive. Rather, it is the case that it is difficult to conceive of the opposite."[91] We must, therefore, not make such universal negative assertions about the realm of possibility as Thomas does. We must be more consistently inductive than Thomas.

Then, when we are more consistently inductive we can at the same time prove much more than Thomas did. Our argument then runs as follows: "If there now does exist a chain of causality, then either it is itself eternal as a chain, or it

---

84. Ibid., p. 93.
85. Ibid.
86. Ibid., p. 94.
87. Ibid., pp. 96–97.
88. Ibid., p. 75.
89. Ibid., p. 76.
90. Ibid., p. 79.
91. Ibid.

originated in an eternal potential Cause, or it originated from nothing." To this he adds: "The God of the Bible is then shown to be the most probable eternal potential cause."[92] [93]

Herewith Buswell has reached "common ground" with modern science, modern philosophy and modern theology as they make pure contingency their basic principle of individuation. "There is," says Buswell, "no ground for saying that an infinite chain of contingent beings could not have existed."[94] Buswell agrees with Kant and his followers that *nothing* can be said in advance of any empirical investigation as to what can or cannot exist. "There is no logical reason why the entire universe might not be made up of inter-dependent contingencies."[95] Nobody knows in advance of any empirical investigation what may prove to be the fact of the matter. For this reason the Christian must not expect a "privileged position" for the Bible as an authoritative interpretation of the facts of which it speaks. The "system of truth" which the Bible presents must be offered as an hypothesis which may or may not be proved true by the facts that are to be investigated. "The idea of the God of the Bible, 'He who is,' is a *datum*. The inductive ontological argument simply says, What is the explanation of this *datum*?"[96] Let us together find the explanation of this "*datum*." Jesus shows us how to proceed. He tells the Jews that he is the Son of God. The Pharisees reply to that by saying that he blasphemes. Jesus points out that, because man is created in the image of God, "there is a God-related element, even in fallen man (Ps 82:6–7)." On this basis he argues that for him to claim to be the Son of God in the flesh *might* be true. "It is *not necessarily* blasphemy." It is thus that Jesus does not ask that his words be accepted on authority. Whether his words are true the Pharisees themselves may judge by looking at his works. It is only after having cleared the ground of all rationalistic *a priori* assertions about what is possible and impossible in the existential realm that Jesus appeals to empirical evidence when he says, "If I do not the works of my Father believe me not."[97]

It is in this way that we must understand what Buswell means when he speaks of Christian presuppositions. "The primary presupposition of the Christian religion is, of course," says Buswell, "Jesus Christ."[98] Moreover the laws of

---

92. Ibid.
93. KSO: It should be noted that there is equivocation in the notion of "eternal" employed here. Even if a series of causes *were* eternal, that eternity would have no direct or coincident relation to God's eternity. God's eternity is not a series of anything; it is an infinite and immutable eternity. A series of causes, by definition, could not be such.
94. Ibid.
95. Ibid., p. 80.
96. Ibid., p. 98.
97. *Christian View*, p. 170.
98. *Sys. Theol.*, I, p. 15.

logic are implied in the Christian's basic presuppositions. According to Buswell the Christian should say: "We take our presupposition as a conclusion arrived at on the basis of what we consider good and sufficient reasons."[99] These good and sufficient reasons were obtained by a purely inductive procedure. This inductive procedure involves the idea of pure contingency.[100]

For Buswell presuppositions are not the conditions which make experience intelligible. As a *Christian*, Buswell *believes* that when Jesus said he was the Son of God he spoke the simple truth. As a *Christian* Buswell *believes* the Bible and what it says about God and man, about sin and redemption on its say so as the absolutely authoritative word of God.

However, as an *apologist* Buswell presents the Bible and "the system of truth" it contains as an hypothesis which may or may not be proved true by an empirical investigation carried on in terms of principles which are not openly Christian but which are distinctively *pre*-Christian which means, of necessity, from a biblical point of view, *non*-Christian.

Believers and unbelievers stand on absolutely common ground with respect to the investigation to be undertaken. The one as well as the other must agree to exclude *any* and every *a priori* prejudice in favor or against Jesus' claim to be the Son of God. The Christian merely offers the claim of Jesus as the hypothesis which is more probably true than its opposite. But we must ask what are Buswell's and what are the non-Christian's ontological foundations which allow them to make such probability statements intelligible. If the non-Christian is able, apart from Christianity, to make his notion of probability intelligible then for what purpose does he need Christianity? He is thoroughly able to make himself and his world intelligible to himself in terms of himself without God and his revelation.

2. Buswell Rejects Presuppositionalism

Buswell's real opponent on the question of apologetic methodology is the "presuppositionalist." And what is wrong with the presuppositionalist is that he advances a "negative thesis, denying that there is a common ground of reasoning between those who accept Christian presuppositions and engage in the spread of the Gospel, and those who do not accept Christian presuppositions and reject the Gospel." How obviously wrong this is! If the believer and the unbeliever in "the God of the Bible" did not have "some element of common meaning in the

---

99. Ibid.
100. KSO: It should be highlighted here that Van Til's notion of presupposition is contrary to Buswell's. By definition, a presupposition, for Van Til, is *before* (pre-) any inference or conclusion. For Buswell, presuppositions come at the end of inference. Buswell's use of the term is wholly unique.

terms employed" between them how could the "conception of 'unbelief'" have any meaning at all?[101]

The "presuppositionalist" whom Buswell opposes is his fellow Calvinist. But he is an *extreme* Calvinist, and it is the extreme character of his Calvinism that leads the presuppositionalist to the assertion that there is no common knowledge at all between the believer and the unbeliever. The extreme Calvinist does not leave adequate room for human freedom. He does not realize that God has given man "absolute freedom" in certain areas of life so that the outcome of certain of his actions may be spoken of as "indeterminate." Moreover, as he does injustice to the idea of human freedom so the extreme Calvinist also does injustice to man's power of logical penetration. Seeing an apparent contradiction between the all-controlling providence of God and human responsibility the extreme Calvinist seeks to escape his dilemma by appealing to Paul's "merely arbitrary answer" given in Romans 9:20, 21[102] instead of going on to the more profound and more ultimate answer given in verse 22.[103]

The "fountainhead of presuppositionalism" Buswell referred to in his article of 1948 is the present writer. In 1960 Buswell was, if possible, more deeply convinced than he was in 1948 of the evil effects of teachings of this presuppositionalist. Even though "this type of presuppositionalism is never consistently carried out. . . the teaching goes on, and many young men have been impressed with the idea that it is improper to present evidences and reasons to the unsaved man." Just think of telling young men that "the cosmological and teleological arguments cry out day and night 'there is no God.'"[104] Is it not obvious that the cosmological and teleological arguments are "embedded in" such passages of Scripture as Romans 1?[105] As the presuppositionalist flies in the face of Scripture so also he flies in the face of Calvin. "Calvin's constant assumption, like the assumption of the writers of the Scripture, is that fallen man may hear and understand something of the Word of God and may, by the convicting power of the Holy Spirit, be convinced and believe." We must therefore reject presuppositionalism in its "negative attitude toward such broken fragments of the truth as may be found in the minds of ignorant and wayward men."[106] "We know that a great

---

101. J. O. Buswell, Jr., "The Fountainhead of Presuppositionalism," *The Bible Today* (Nov., 1948), p. 41.

102. KSO: "But who are you, O man, to answer back to God? Will what is molded say to its molder, '"Why have you made me like this?"' Has the potter no right over the clay, to make out of the same lump one vessel for honorable use and another for dishonorable use?" (Rom. 9:20–21).

103. KSO: "What if God, desiring to show his wrath and to make known his power, has endured with much patience vessels of wrath prepared for destruction. . ." (Rom. 9:22).

104. *Christian View*, p. 176.

105. *Sys. Theol.*, I, p. 86.

106. *Christian View*, p. 177.

multitude of humanity are not committed to a denial of the existence of God, and are ready to believe that he exists, if his character and his plan of redemption are made plain and simple."[107]

To be true to Scripture and to Calvin who taught us how to obey Scripture we must reject presuppositionalism and make use "of the inductive processes of presenting evidence, not as the only method, but as a method of pointing to the truth useful and profitable in many situations."[108]

[a.] A Basic Misunderstanding

When in 1948 Buswell charged that I did not believe in the idea of common ground, I replied in *The Defense of the Faith* (pp. 253–267).[109] Since this reply does not appear in the revised edition (1967) of this book it is included here, with but slight technical alteration.

Coming now to a brief statement of the method of defense that I use for the propagation of what I believe and how it differs from the traditional method I may note first that Buswell has not, for all the length of his article, anywhere given a connected picture of my argument. He at once characterizes it in contrast with his own as being "negative and universal." Without the least bit of qualification I am said to deny "that there is common ground of reasoning between those who accept Christian presuppositions and engage in the spread of the gospel, and those who do not accept Christian presuppositions and reject the gospel."[110] The facts are far otherwise.

I am, to be sure, opposed to the traditional method of apologetics as this has found its most fundamental expression in the *Summae* of Thomas Aquinas the Roman Catholic and in Bishop Butler the Arminian. I seek to oppose Roman Catholicism and Arminianism in Apologetics as I seek to oppose it in theology. Does that make my main thesis universally negative? I think there is a better and more truly biblical way of reasoning with and winning unbelievers than the Romanist-Arminian method permits.

To begin with then I take what the Bible says about God and his relation to the universe as unquestionably true on its own authority. The Bible requires men to believe that he exists apart from and above the world and that he by his plan controls whatever takes place in the world. Everything in the created universe displays the fact that it is controlled by God, that it is what it is by

---

107. Ibid., p. 172.
108. Ibid., p. 177.
109. KSO: See Van Til, *The Defense of the Faith*, 240–267.
110. J. Oliver Buswell, Jr., "The Fountainhead of Presuppositionalism," *The Bible Today*, (Nov. 1948) p. 41.

virtue of the place that it occupies in the plan of God. The objective evidence for the existence of God and of the comprehensive governance of the world by God is therefore so plain that he who runs may read. Men cannot get away from this evidence. They see it round about them. They see it within them. Their own constitution so clearly evinces the facts of God's creation of them and control over them that there is no man who can possibly escape observing it. If he is self-conscious at all, he is also God-conscious. No matter how men may try they cannot hide from themselves the fact of their own createdness. Whether men engage in inductive study with respect to the facts of nature about them or engage in analysis of their own self-consciousness they are always face to face with God their maker. Calvin stresses these matters greatly on the basis of Paul's teachings in Romans.

In maintaining the essential clarity of all of the created universe as revelational of God's existence and his plan Calvin is not daunted even by the fact of sin and its consequences. If there has been any "obscuration" in the revelation situation on account of sin this sin is in any case the fault of man. If in Adam, the first man, who acted for me representatively, I have scratched the mirror of God's general revelation round about and within me, I know in my heart that it is I who have scratched it. Men ought therefore, says Calvin, to conclude that when some individual sin is not punished immediately it will be punished later. Their consciences operate on this basis.

One thing should be particularly stressed in this connection. It is the fact that man today is sinful because of what happened at the beginning of history.

> We are told that man could never have had any fruition of God through the revelation that came to him through nature as operating by itself. There was super-added to God's revelation in nature another revelation, a supernaturally communicated positive revelation. Natural revelation, we are virtually told, was from the outset incorporated into the idea of a covenant relationship of God with man. Thus every dimension of created existence, even the lowest, was enveloped in a form of exhaustively personal relationship between God and man. The 'ateleological' not less than the 'teleological,' the 'mechanical' no less than the 'spiritual,' was covenantal in character.[111]

Even in paradise, therefore, supernatural revelation was immediately conjoined with natural revelation. Revelation in and about man was therefore never

---

111. The writer, "Nature and Scripture," *The Infallible Word*, p. 259.

meant to function by itself. "It was from the beginning insufficient without its supernatural concomitant. It was inherently a limiting notion."[112] [113]

Having taken these two, revelation in the created universe, both within and about man, and revelation by way of supernatural positive communication as aspects of revelation as originally given to man, we can see that natural revelation is even after the fall perspicuous in character. "The perspicuity of God's revelation in nature depends for its very meaning upon the fact that it is an aspect of the total and totally voluntary revelation of a God who is self-contained."[114] God has an all comprehensive plan for the universe. "He has planned all the relationships between all the aspects of created being. He has planned the end from the beginning. All created reality therefore actually displays this plan. It is, in consequence, inherently rational."[115]

At this point we may add the fact of Scriptural revelation. God has condescended to reveal himself and his plan in it to sinners. It is the same God who speaks in Scripture and in nature. But in Scripture he speaks of his grace to such as have broken his covenant, to such as have set aside his original revelation to them. And as the original revelation of God to man was clear so is the revelation of grace in Scripture. "The Scriptures as the finished product of God's supernatural and saving revelation to man have their own evidence in themselves."[116]

In all of this there is one thing that stands out. It is that man has no excuse whatsoever for not accepting the revelation of God whether in nature, including man and his surroundings, or in Scripture. God's revelation is always clear.

The first and most basic point on which my approach differs from the traditional one is therefore that: (a) I start more frankly from the Bible as the source from which as an absolutely authoritative revelation I take my whole interpretation of life. Roman Catholicism also appeals to Scripture but in practice makes its authority void. Its final appeal is to the church and that is, in effect, to human experience. Even Arminianism rejects certain Scripture doctrines (e.g., election) because it cannot logically harmonize them with the general offer of salvation. (b) I stress the *objective clarity* of God's revelation of himself wherever it appears. Both Thomas Aquinas and Butler contend that men have done justice by the evidence if they conclude that God *probably* exists. (I have discussed the views of

---

112. Ibid., p. 267.
113. KSO: For Van Til, a limiting notion is a biblical-theological notion entailed by, and defined by, another notion in order properly to be understood. Natural revelation and special revelation are, in that sense, limiting notions. They are always meant to go together and each is properly understood in light of the other.
114. Ibid., p. 269.
115. Ibid.
116. Ibid., p. 271.

Aquinas in *The Infallible Word* and those of Butler in the syllabus on *Evidences*.)[117] I consider this a compromise of simple and fundamental Biblical truth. It is an insult to the living God to say that his revelation of himself so lacks in clarity that man, himself through and through revelational of God, does justice by it when he says that God *probably* exists.

> "The argument for the existence of God and for the truth of Christianity is objectively valid. We should not tone down the validity of this argument to the probability level. The argument may be poorly stated, and may never be adequately stated. But in itself the argument is absolutely sound. Christianity is the only reasonable position to hold. It is not merely as reasonable as other positions, or a bit more reasonable than other positions; it alone is the natural and reasonable position for man to take. By stating the argument as clearly as we can, we may be the agents of the Holy Spirit in pressing the claims of God upon men. If we drop to the level of the merely probable truthfulness of Christian theism, we, to that extent, lower the claims of God upon men."[118]

Accordingly I do not reject 'the theistic proofs' but merely insist on formulating them in such a way as not to compromise the doctrines of Scripture.[119] "That is to say, if the theistic proof is constructed as it ought to be constructed, it is objectively valid, whatever the attitude of those to whom it comes may be."[120] (c) With Calvin I find the point of contact for the presentation of the gospel to non-Christians in the fact that they are made in the image of God and as such have the ineradicable sense of deity within them. Their own consciousness is inherently and exclusively revelation of God to themselves. No man can help knowing God for in knowing himself he knows God. His self-consciousness is totally devoid of content unless, as Calvin puts it at the beginning of his Institutes, man knows himself as a creature of God. There are "no atheistic men because no man can deny the revelational activity of the true God within him."[121] "Man's own interpretative activity, whether of the more or less extended type, whether in ratiocination or intuition, is no doubt the most penetrating means by which

---

117. KSO: Thomas was clear that the existence of God was *not* self-evident to us. This was due, in part, to his misreading of Romans 1, and also to his abstract view of essence. See Oliphint, *Thomas Aquinas (Great Thinkers)*, esp. 33ff.
118. The writer, *Common Grace*, Phila., 1964, p. 62.
119. KSO: For an attempt to formulate a cosmological argument that does not compromise the Reformed doctrine of Scripture, see K. Scott Oliphint, *Covenantal Apologetics: Principles and Practice in Defense of Our Faith* (Wheaton, IL: Crossway Books, 2013), 110–122.
120. Ibid., p. 49.
121. Ibid., p. 55.

the Holy Spirit presses the claims of God upon man."[122] Even man's negative ethical reaction to God's revelation within his own psychological constitution is revelational of God. His conscience troubles him when he disobeys; he knows deep down in his heart that he is disobeying his creator. There is no escape from God for any human being. Every human being is by virtue of his being made in the image of God accessible to God. And as such he is accessible to one who without compromise presses upon him the claims of God. Every man has capacity to reason logically. He can intellectually understand what the Christian position claims to be. Conjoined with this is the moral sense that he knows he is doing wrong when he interprets human experience without reference to his Creator. I am therefore in the fullest agreement with Professor Murray when, in the quotation given of him, he speaks of the natural man as having an "*apprehension of the truth of the gospel* that is *prior* to faith and repentance."[123] But I could not thus speak with assurance that the natural man could have any such apprehension of the truth of the gospel if I held with the traditional view of Apologetics that man's self-consciousness is something that is intelligible without reference to God-consciousness. If man's self-consciousness did not actually depend upon his God-consciousness there would be no meaning to Romans 1:20. Each man would live in a world by himself. No man could even have that intellectual cognition of the gospel which is the prerequisite of saving faith. In short if the universe were not what the Calvinist, following Paul, says it is, it would not be a *universe*. There would be no system of truth. And if the mind of man were not what Calvin, following Paul, says it is, it could not even intellectually follow an argument for the idea that the universe is a *universe*. All arguments for such a universe would come to him as outside that universe.

Yet it is the very essence of the positions of Aquinas and Butler that human self-consciousness is intelligible without God-consciousness. Both make it their point of departure in reasoning with the non-believers that we must, at least in the area of things natural, stand on the ground of neutrality with them. And it is of the essence of all non-believing philosophy that self-consciousness is taken as intelligible by itself without reference to God. Moreover the very theology of both Romanism and Arminianism, as already noted, requires a measure of subtraction of the self-consciousness of men from its creaturely place. (d) Implied in the previous points is the fact that I do not artificially separate induction from deduction, or reasoning about the facts of nature from reasoning in *a priori* analytical fashion about the nature of human-consciousness. I do not artificially abstract or separate them from one another. On the contrary I see induction and

---

122. Ibid., p. 62.
123. J. Murray, "Common Grace," *Westminster Theological Journal* (Vol. V, No. 1, Nov. 1942).

analytical reasoning as part of one process of interpretation. I would therefore engage in historical apologetics. (I do not personally do a great deal of this because my colleagues in the other departments of the Seminary in which I teach are doing it better than I could do it.) Every bit of historical investigation, whether it be in the directly biblical field, archaeology, or in general history, is bound to confirm the truth of the claims of the Christian position. But I would not talk endlessly about facts and more facts without ever challenging the non-believer's philosophy of fact. A really fruitful historical apologetic argues that every fact *is* and *must be* such as proves the truth of the Christian theistic position.

A fair presentation of my method of approach should certainly have included these basic elements that underlie everything else.

It is only in the light of this positive approach that my statements to the effect that epistemologically believers and non-believers have nothing in common can be seen for what it is. Even in *Common Grace* it is evident that by the sinner's epistemological reaction I mean his reaction as an ethically responsible creature of God. Does the sinner react properly to the revelation of God that surrounds him, that is within him and that comes to him from Scripture? As I have followed Calvin closely in stressing the fact that men *ought* to believe in God inasmuch as the evidence for his existence is abundantly plain, so I have also closely followed Calvin in saying that no sinner reacts properly to God's revelation.[124] Is this too sweeping a statement? It is simply the doctrine of total depravity. All sinners are covenant breakers. They have an axe to grind. They do not want to keep God in remembrance. They keep under the knowledge of God which is within them. That is they try as best they can to keep under this knowledge for fear they should look into the face of their judge. And since God's face appears in every fact of the universe they oppose God's revelation everywhere. They do not want to see the facts of nature for what they are; they do not want to see themselves for what they are. Therefore they assume the non-createdness of themselves and of the facts and the laws of nature round about them. Even though they make great protestations of serving God they yet serve and worship the creature more than the Creator. They try to make themselves believe that God and man are aspects of one universe. They interpret all things immanentistically. Shall we in the interest of a point of contact admit that man can interpret anything correctly if he virtually leaves God out of the picture? Shall we who wish to prove that nothing can be explained without God, first admit that some things at least can be explained

---

124. KSO: When Van Til says "no sinner reacts properly to God's revelation," he includes, especially, God's revelation in and through all of creation. That means that no sinner acts properly to anything in the world. And, as he reiterates, he's thinking of sinners and their "ethical reaction" against God, in *everything*. So, his much-maligned notion that those outside of Christ can't properly know anything must always be seen within this context.

without him? On the contrary we shall show that all explanations without God are futile. Only when we do this do we appeal to that knowledge of God within men which they seek to suppress. This is what I mean by presupposing God for the possibility of intelligent predication.[125]

It is asked what person is consistent with his own principles. Well I have consistently argued that no one is and that least of all the non-Christian is. I have even argued in the very booklet reviewed that if men were consistent they would be end products and that then there would be no more reasoning with them. However since sinners are not consistent, and have what is from their point of view an old man within them they can engage in science and in the general interpretation of the created universe and bring to light much truth.[126] It is because the prodigal is not yet at the swine trough and therefore still has of the substance of the Father in his pockets that he can do that and discover that, which for the matter of it, is true and usable for the Christian. In a booklet largely written in the defense of the idea of 'commonness' as between believers and unbelievers against those who deny it Buswell finds nothing but the opposite. If his contention is that I have said precisely the opposite of what I wanted to say he should in fairness at least have discussed the points just now discussed.

What then more particularly do I mean by saying that epistemologically the believer and the non-believer have nothing in common? I mean that every sinner looks through colored glasses. And these colored glasses are cemented to his face. He assumes that self-consciousness is intelligible without God-consciousness. He assumes that consciousness of facts is intelligible without consciousness of God. He assumes that consciousness of laws is intelligible without God. And he interprets all the facts and all the laws that are presented to him in terms of these assumptions.[127] This is not to forget that he also, according to the old man within him, knows that God exists. But as a covenant breaker he seeks to suppress this. And I am now speaking of him as the covenant breaker. Neither do I forget that

---

125. KSO: Hendrik Stoker gave a helpful summary, from a Calvinistic philosopher's perspective, of what Van Til is saying here. See Stoker, "Reconnoitering the Theory of Knowledge of Professor Dr. Cornelius Van Til," esp. 44–62.

126. KSO: By "an old man within them," Van Til is referring to man's original creation in God's image, and the remnants of that image in all of us, including the true knowledge of the true God.

127. KSO: This illustration is particularly apt to help explain the totalizing effects of sin. It is not as though the sinner has no eyes at all. Instead, he *can* see, but everything he sees is "colored" by his sin. So, for example, an unbeliever and a believer say together, "There is a tree." But the same tree is "colored" by the unbeliever so that it is not an aspect of God's creation, but is, in some sense, "just there." It is not something God has providentially made and controls. It is not something given to man as a gift to be nurtured to God's glory. It is thought to have no context or use beyond the sinner's own. For that reason, even as the unbeliever says, "There is a tree," he makes a statement for which he will be judged. He "knows," in his suppression of the truth, that it could not in any way be "God's tree."

no man is actually fully consistent in working according to these assumptions. The non-believer does not fully live up to the new man within him which in his case is the man who worships the creature above all else, any more than does the Christian fully live up to the new man within him, which in his case is the man who worships the Creator above all else. But as it is my duty as a Christian to ask my fellow Christians as well as myself to suppress the old man within us, so it is my duty to ask non-believer to suppose not the old man but the new man within them.

The necessity for this can be observed every time there is some popular article on religion in one of the magazines. There was a questionnaire sent out recently by one of them asking a certain number of people whether they believed in God. By far the greater number of them said that they did. But from further questions asked it appeared that only a very small number believed in the God of the Bible, the Creator and Judge of men. Yet they said that they believed in God. From such an article it is apparent that every sinner has the sense of deity and therefore knows God as his Creator and Judge. But from such an article it is also apparent that *every* sinner seeks in one way or another to deny this. They are therefore without God in the world. They must, as Charles Hodge so well points out, be renewed *unto* knowledge (Col 3:10) as well as unto righteousness and holiness (Eph 4:24).[128]

Now neither Aquinas nor Butler makes any such distinctions as I have made. And in that they are but consistent. They do not make the Creator-creature distinction absolutely fundamental in their own thinking. How then could they consistently ask others to do so? It is of the essence of their theology to maintain that God has made man so that he has such freedom as to be able to initiate something that is beyond the counsel of God. For them the human self therefore is supposed to be able to think of itself as intelligible and of the facts and laws of the world as manipulable and therefore intelligible apart from their relationship to God. I have already pointed out that for this reason the traditional view of apologetics has no universe and has no real point of contact in the unbeliever. If either Romanism or Arminianism were right in their view of the self-consciousness of man there could be no apologetics for Christianity at all. There would be no all-comprehensive plan of God. This much being clear it can be seen that the Romanist and the Arminian will, in consistence with their own theology, not be able to challenge the natural man's false assumptions. The traditional apologist must somehow seek for a point of contact within the thinking of the natural man as this thinking has been carried on upon false assumptions. He cannot seek

---

128. KSO: See Charles Hodge, *Systematic Theology* (Oak Harbor, WA: Logos Research Systems, Inc., 1997), 2: 99–102.

to stir up the old man in opposition against the new man in the non-Christian. He makes no use of such a distinction. He will allow for gradational differences within the natural man. He will even make a great deal of these. To him therefore the passages of Paul to the effect that every man knows God and that man is made in the image of God are interpreted so as to do injustice to other equally important teaching of Scripture to the effect that the natural man knoweth not God. All this is compromising theology. It is no wonder that the Romanist and the Arminian will also follow a compromising apologetics.[129]

The basic falseness of this apologetics appears in the virtual if not actual denial of the fact that the natural man makes false assumptions. Aquinas and Butler hold that the natural man, whom the Calvinist knows to be a covenant breaker and as such one who interprets God himself in terms of the universe, has some correct notions about God.[130] I mean correct notions as to content, not merely as to form. Anyone who says "I believe in God," is formally correct in his statement, but the question is what does he mean by the word *God*? The traditional view assumes that the natural man has a certain measure of correct thought content when he uses the word God. In reality the natural man's 'God' is always a finite God. It is his most effective tool for suppressing the sense of the true God that he cannot fully efface from the fibers of his heart.

The natural man's god is *always* enveloped within a Reality that is greater than his god and himself. He always makes Reality, inclusive of all that exists, the *All* the final subject of which he speaks. With Thales[131] he will say *All* is water, with Anaximenes[132] *All* is air. With others he may be a dualist or a pluralist or an atomist, a realist or a pragmatist. From the Christian point of view he still has a monistic assumption in that he makes Reality to be inclusive of God and himself.[133] And there is not much that the traditional apologist can do about this.

---

129. KSO: Note that this is the case because both Romanism and Arminianism have (1) a weak view of sin, such that its effects are less than total, especially with respect to knowledge, and (2) a strong view of man's freedom such that, for man to be responsible, God can have no control over his decisions.

130. KSO: So, for example, the "Catechism of the Catholic Church," paragraph #841 states, "The plan of salvation also includes those who acknowledge the Creator, in the first place amongst whom are the Muslims; these profess to hold the faith of Abraham, *and together with us they adore the one, merciful God,* mankind's judge on the last day." See http://www.scborromeo.org/ccc/ccc_toc.htm, my emphasis.

131. KSO: Thales (c. 624–c. 548 B.C.) of Miletus was a pre-Socratic philosopher, regarded by Aristotle as the first philosopher of the Greeks.

132. KSO: Anaximenes (c. 586–c. 526 B.C.) of Miletus was, like Thales, a pre-Socratic philosopher.

133. KSO: In other words, no matter to what philosophical "-ism" one is committed, such "parts" of one's philosophy are always subsumed under the notion of "*Reality*." This is what Van Til means by a "monistic assumption." There is, and can be, no proper Creator/creature distinction if "*Reality*" is a unity which includes everything.

He has bound himself to confusion in apologetics as he has bound himself to error in theology. He must tie on to some small area of thought content that the believer and the unbeliever have in common without qualification when both are self-conscious with respect to their principle. This is tantamount to saying that those who interpret a fact as dependent upon God and those who interpret that same fact as not dependent upon God have yet said something identical about that fact.

All this is bound to lead to self-frustration on the part of the traditional apologist. Let us watch him for a moment. Think of him first as an inductivist. As such he will engage in 'historical apologetics' and in the study of archaeology. In general he will deal with the 'facts' of the universe in order to prove the existence of God. He cannot on his position challenge the assumption of the man he is trying to win. That man is ready for him. Think of the traditional apologist as throwing facts to his non-Christian friend as he might throw a ball. His friend receives each fact as he might a ball and throws it behind him in a bottomless pit. The apologist is exceedingly industrious. He shows the unbelieving friend all the evidence for theism. He shows all the evidence for Christianity, for instance, for the virgin birth and the resurrection of Christ. Let us think of his friend as absolutely tireless and increasingly polite. He will then receive all these facts and toss them behind him to the bottomless pit of pure possibility. "Is it not wonderful," he will say, "to see what strange things do happen in Reality. You seem to be a collector of oddities. As for myself I am more interested in the things that happen regularly. But I shall certainly try hard to explain the facts you mention in accord with the laws that I have found working so far. Perhaps we should say that laws are merely statistical averages and that nothing can therefore be said about any particular event ahead of its appearance. Perhaps there are very unusual things in reality. But what does this prove for the truth of your view?"[134]

You see that the unbeliever who does not work on the presupposition of creation and providence is perfectly consistent with himself when he sees nothing to challenge his unbelief even in the fact of the resurrection of Christ. He may be surprised for a moment as a child that grows up is surprised at the strange things of life but then when he has grown up he realizes that 'such is life.' Sad to say the traditional Christian apologist has not even asked his unbelieving friend to see the facts for what they really are. He has not presented the facts at all. That is he has not presented the facts as they are according to the Christian way of looking at them. Every fact in the universe is what it is by virtue of the place

---

134. KSO: In other words, as the Queen said to Alice, "Why, sometimes I've believed as many as six impossible things before breakfast." See Lewis Carroll, *Through the Looking Glass* (Courier Dover Publications, 2017), ch. 5.

that it has in the plan of God. Man cannot comprehensively know that plan. He must therefore present the facts of theism and of Christianity, of Christian theism, as proving Christian theism because they are intelligible as facts in terms of it and in terms of it alone.

But this is also in effect to say that the Christian apologist should never seek to be an inductivist only. He should present his philosophy of fact with his facts. He does not need to handle less facts in doing so. He will handle the same facts but he will handle them as they ought to be handled.

Now look at the traditional apologist when he is not an inductivist but an *a priori* reasoner.[135] He will first show his fellow worker, the inductivist, that he defeats his own purposes. He will show that he who does not challenge the assumptions of his non-Christian friends has placed himself on a decline which inevitably leads down from Locke through Berkeley to Hume, the skeptic. Then for his own foundation he will appeal to some internal ineffable principles, to some *a priori* like that of Plato or of Descartes. He will appeal to the law of contradiction either positively or negatively and boldly challenge the facts to meet the requirements of logic. Then he will add that the facts of Christianity pass his examination *summa cum laude*. Well, they do. And in passing the examination they invariably pass out of existence too. He can only prove the immortality of the soul if with Plato he is willing to prove also that man is divine. He can only prove the universe to have order if with the Stoics he is also willing to say that God is merely its principle of order. With the Hegelian idealists such as Bradley and Bosanquet or Royce[136] he will prove all the facts of the Bible to be true by weaving them into aspects of a Universe that allows for them as well as for their opposites.

But usually the traditional apologist is neither a pure inductivist nor a pure *a priorist*. Of necessity he has to be both. When engaged in inductive argument about facts he will therefore talk about these facts as proving the existence of God. If anything exists at all, he will say, something absolute *must* exist. But when he thus talks about what must exist and when he refuses even to admit that non-believers have false assumptions about their 'musts,' let alone being willing to challenge them on the subject, he has in reality granted that the non-believer's conception about the relation of human logic to facts is correct.

---

135. KSO: "The inductivist" follows the empirical evidence; the "*a priori* reasoner" follows the laws of thought.

136. KSO: This is a reference to two British idealists, Bernard Bosanquet (1848–1923) and F. H. Bradley (1846–1924), with whom Van Til interacts in many of his writings. The absolute idealists were opposed to logical methods such as linear inference, insisting that all inference must necessarily presuppose some universal system, and to Josiah Royce (1855–1916). Royce was the leading American proponent of Absolute Idealism.

It does not occur to him that on any but the Christian theistic basis there is no possible connection of logic with facts at all. When the non-Christian, not working on the foundation of creation and providence, talks about 'musts' in relation to 'facts' he is beating the air. His logic is merely the exercise of a revolving door in a void, moving nothing from nowhere into the void.[137] But instead of pointing out this fact to the unbeliever the traditional apologist appeals to this non-believer as though by his immanentistic method he could very well interpret many things correctly.

That this traditionalist type of apologetics is particularly impotent in our day I have shown in my review of Dr. Richardson's and Dr. Carnell's books on Apologetics. Dr. Richardson is a modernist. But he says he holds to the uniqueness of the facts of Christianity. At the same time he believes that this holding to the uniqueness of Christianity and its facts is not inconsistent with holding to a form of coherence that is placed upon human experience as its foundation. Dr. Carnell is an orthodox believer. To an extent he has even tried to escape from the weaknesses of the traditional method of apologetic argument. But he merely rejects its inductivist form. By and large he falls back into traditional methodology. And just to that extent he has no valid argument against Richardson. To the extent that he admits the type of coherence which Richardson holds to be valid he has to give up the uniqueness of the events of Christianity as he himself holds them. On the other hand, to the extent that he holds to the uniqueness of events the way Richardson holds to them, to that extent he has to give up the coherence to which he himself as an orthodox Christian should hold. (See *The Westminster Theological Journal*, November, 1948.)[138]

Buswell's handling of the question of the immutability of God exhibits exactly the same difficulty. He speaks of the dynamical self-consistency of God as a concept that will make it quite easy to see how God's immutability can be consistent with the genuine significance of facts in the course of history. But to the extent that he explains how the immutability of God can be consistent with the actuality of historical change he explains it away. He goes so far as to define that very immutability in terms of God's constancy of relationship to the created temporal universe. "God's immutability consists in his perfectly unified plan in dealing with the world, which he created, God's absoluteness is in his perfectly

---

137. KSO: Generally speaking, the challenge for laws of thought, such as logic, is to apply such "unchanging" laws to the changing world. "A is not non-A" is true, but if applied, say, to something in the world that is physical and is always changing, its truth can quickly become ambiguous and vague.

138. KSO: Review of *Christian Apologetics*, by Alan Richardson, *Westminster Theological Journal* 11/1 (Nov 1948): 45–53; Review of *An Introduction to Christian Apologetics*, by Edward J. Carnell, Ibid., 45–53.

consistent relatedness."[139] Now if God's immutability is not first to be spoken of as an attribute that pertains to the character of God as he is in himself apart from his relation to the universe, then there is no problem any more because in that case one of the factors of the problem has been denied. To the extent that he has explained he has also destroyed the fact to be explained. To speak of self-consistency after first reducing the self to a relationship is meaningless. On the other hand he does not really hold to the identity of the being of God in himself with his relationship to the world. That is also plain from his general discussion of God. But then if you are to speak to an unbeliever with respect to the God who is really self-contained and ask him to think of this God along the lines of his own procedure, without challenging the assumptions that underlie his procedure, then he will simply say that such a God is so wholly beyond his experience that he can make nothing of him and that such a God is therefore meaningless to him. To this he can on his method offer him no answer.[140]

The general conclusion then is that on the traditional method it is impossible to set one position clearly over against the other so that the two may be compared for what they are. Certainly there can be no confrontation of two opposing positions if it cannot be pointed out on what they oppose each other. On the traditional basis of reasoning the unbeliever is not so much as given an opportunity of seeing with any adequacy how the position he is asked to accept differs from his own.

All this comes from following the Roman Catholic, Thomas Aquinas, or the Arminian, Butler. If one follows Calvin there are no such troubles. Then one begins with the fact that the world is what the Bible says it is. One then makes the claims of God upon men without apologies though always *suaviter in modo*. One knows that there is hidden underneath the surface display of every man a sense of deity. One therefore gives that sense of deity an opportunity to rise in rebellion against the oppression under which it suffers by the new man of the covenant breaker. One makes no deal with this new man. One shows that on his assumptions all things are meaningless. Science would be impossible; knowledge of anything in any field would be impossible. No fact could be distinguished

---

139. J. Oliver Buswell, Jr., *What Is God?*, p. 32.

140. KSO: As noted in the foreword, Van Til was particularly aware of this problem of God's relatedness, given his own studies of Idealism at Princeton University. In his dissertation, he shows how the affirmation of some "Absolute" in Idealism is really no absolute at all since it requires, for its definition, that which is relative. This is his concern with Butler here. Orthodox theology maintains, for example, that God's immutability is what it is *even if* there is nothing else existing. It is not, in the first place, an immutability of relationship. So also with God's absoluteness. It could not be "absoluteness in relationship" unless such a relationship is intrinsic to, and required by, God's absolute character. Orthodox theology affirms God as most absolute, even if/when he relates himself to what he has made.

from any other fact. No law could be said to be law with respect to facts. The whole manipulation of factual experience would be like the idling of a motor that is not in gear. Thus every fact—not *some* facts—every fact *clearly* and not probably proves the truth of Christian theism. If Christian theism is not true then nothing is true.[141] Is the God of the Bible satisfied if his servants say anything less?

And have I, following such a method, departed radically from the tradition of Kuyper and Bavinck? On the contrary I have learned all this primarily from them. It is Kuyper's *Encyclopedie* that has, more than any other work in modern times, brought out the fact of the difference between the approach of the believer and of the unbeliever. It is Bavinck's monumental work which set a "natural theology" frankly oriented to Scripture squarely over against that of Romanism which is based on neutral reason. It is Bavinck who taught me that the proofs for God as usually formulated on the traditional method prove a finite god. I have indeed had the temerity to maintain that these great Reformed theologians have in some points not been quite true to their own principles. But when I have done so I have tried to point out that when they did so they had departed from Calvin.[142]

It is obvious from this reply to Buswell made in 1955 that I have *never* denied that there is a common ground of *knowledge* between the believer and the unbeliever. I have *always* affirmed the kind of common ground that is spoken of in Scripture, notably in Romans 1 and 2, and in Calvin's *Institutes*.[143] As creatures made in God's image man cannot help but know God. It is of this revelation *to* man through "nature" and through his own constitution that Paul speaks of in Romans.

But as I have always *affirmed* the fact that all men, even the most wicked of men, have this *knowledge* so I have always *denied* that fallen man's *interpretation of this revelation* of God to him is *identical* with the revelation itself. *Natural revelation must not be identified with natural theology.*[144] Paul does not identify these. He says that the natural man has given a false *interpretation* of the revelation within

---

141. KSO: This statement is a nice summary of what Van Til means by a "transcendental" approach to apologetics. It includes the impossibility of the contrary—"If Christianity is not true, then nothing is true."

142. Cf. the writer's *Common Grace*.

143. Cf. the writer's syllabus—Introduction to Systematic Theology.

144. KSO: The point Van Til is making here is that which the apostle Paul makes in Romans 1:18–20. In that passage, Paul affirms that all people know God. That knowledge cannot be due to fallen man's own rational inferences. We know because God *reveals* himself. Once we *take* that true knowledge of God as a datum of our cognitive faculties, we inevitably suppress and distort it. The knowledge of God is due to *natural revelation*. Our (sinful) cognitive response to that true knowledge is *natural theology*. In other words, *revelation* is what God does; *theology* is what we do.

him and about him. He "holds back" the truth (Rom 1:18).[145] We can understand why Thomas, the Roman Catholic, and Butler, the Arminian, should identify natural revelation and natural theology but we cannot understand why Buswell, the Calvinist, should do so.

The natural theology of Thomas as expressed, particularly, in his "proofs" are constructed by means of the methodology of Aristotle's philosophy. Aristotle's methodology assumes that man is *not* created in the image of God, that the *facts* of the universe which man interprets are *not* created and that the laws of logic are *not* imprinted on man's mind by his Creator. When this methodology is consistently applied it does indeed "prove" God's existence. That is, it proves the existence of Aristotle's god, *a god who did not create the world,* who does not know the world, who does not know "himself" because "he" is no self. "He" is an "it," an abstract principle of all-absorbing rationality. *Thomas himself admits this!*[146]

It is the god who is *not* man's Creator, the god against whom man has *not* sinned, the god who, as an abstract principle cannot think or will and who as an abstract principle can have no Son, it is this "it" who yet *sends his son* into the world to save men from their sin! This son, as exemplifying pure comprehensive rationality, saves all men even though as participant in his ultimate rational being, they need not be saved. If men refuse to be saved it is because they already participate in rationality and are already compassed about by pure contingency.

Bishop Butler, the Arminian, follows Thomas, the Roman Catholic, in offering this synthesis of paganism and Christianity to the natural man for his salvation. Now Buswell, the Calvinist, follows both.

Of course as a "simple believer" Buswell disagrees with the theology of Romanism and of Arminianism. He believes the "system of doctrine" taught in the Westminster Confession. But this makes the synthesis between the "truth" that he establishes by reason and the truth that he accepts by faith all the more monstrous, even more so than the admitted synthesis of Thomas. One can, in a measure, understand how Thomas and Butler can build their theology on their philosophy. The philosophy of both of these men is built upon the idea of man as autonomous, upon a non-rational or purely contingent principle of factual individuation and upon a purely formal, impersonal, all-absorbing principle of unification. The theology of these men is, in large measure, adjusted to this kind of philosophy. In the theology of both of these thinkers man is, to some extent free, i.e., ontologically independent of God; the facts of man's world are to some

---

145. Cf. John Murray, *Commentary on Romans,* loc. cit.
146. *Summa Contra Gentiles,* I:13:29, 30.

extent contingent; they are not clearly revelatory of their Creator, and with his own laws and thought man determines whether or not God can or cannot exist.

However, when Buswell as a Calvinist builds his Calvinist theology upon his natural theology and this in turn upon a philosophy of being and knowing built upon his "inductive" method, then the monstrous nature of his synthesis becomes glaringly apparent, indeed almost inconceivable!

If Buswell wanted men to become Roman Catholics or Arminians, then he might well use the method he uses. But Buswell wants men to become Calvinists, albeit not "extreme" Calvinists. All Calvinists will say that the atonement of Christ is particular. They will join with Dr. J. Gresham Machen: "When Christ sets out to save a people, he saves them." But, unless they are extreme Calvinists, they will also say that the atonement is universal. Is not the atonement sufficient for all and applicable to all? Is it not offered to all: "On these three points of the universality of the atonement, there is no essential difference between the evangelical Arminian and the true Calvinist."[147]

When extreme Calvinists speak of immutability as an attribute that characterizes God as he is in his relation to this world and then have difficulty in relating such an immutable God to the changing scene of the space-time universe, Buswell solves the problem with his view of the "dynamic nature of God's immutability."[148] "God's immutability consists in his perfectly unified plan in dealing with the world, which he created."

"God's absoluteness is in his perfectly consistent relatedness."[149] It is by means of his idea of the "dynamic nature of God's immutability" and his idea that there is "absolute freedom within certain areas of human life,"[150] that Buswell finds it possible, in opposition to the extreme Calvinist, i.e., the presuppositionalist, to discover "some elements of common meaning" in the terms employed between those who believe and those who do not believe in the God of the Bible.[151]

Having found these "elements of common meaning" between the believer and the unbeliever concerning the God of the Bible, Buswell is again able to join with the Arminian and the Roman Catholic in identifying God's revelation *to* man in the created world with sinful man's *response* to that revelation. In other words, it is his 'moderate' as over against 'extreme' Calvinism that enables him to identify natural *revelation* with natural *theology*. It is, therefore, only the extreme

---

147. *Sys. Theol.*, II, p. 142.
148. Ibid., I, p. 5.
149. James Oliver Buswell, Jr., *What is God?* (Grand Rapids: Zondervan, 1937), p. 32.
150. James Oliver Buswell, Jr., *Sin and Atonement* (Grand Rapids: Zondervan, 1937), p. 49.
151. "Fountainhead," *loc. cit.*

Calvinist who cannot join the traditional Thomistic type of reasoning for the existence of God and the Butler type of reasoning for the truth of Christianity.[152]

As a moderate Calvinist Buswell says: "I believe that God will somehow get the Gospel to every soul who is willing to believe."[153] And as the work of Christ's atonement is universal so also is the work of the Holy Spirit. "By its universality I mean that, although I cannot cogently prove it from the Scripture, I postulate that the convicting work of the Holy Spirit is absolutely universal to the entire human race in all ages and in all areas."[154]

We must, of course, "not say that men are saved without the Gospel" but we must say "that Christ, the Second Person of the Trinity, and the Holy Spirit, the Third Person of the Trinity, in addition to the light of nature (Rom 1:20) do communicate with lost souls in ways which human intelligence cannot directly connect with the main stream of revelation in the Judeo-Christian tradition."[155]

Finally, we note more particularly what Buswell, as a "moderate" Calvinist, says about the relation of men to God as Creator and providential controller of the universe. As over against the 'extreme' Calvinist who virtually holds a determinist view of God's relation to man, Buswell again finds it possible to join with the Arminian and the Roman Catholic in saying that "God has constituted man in such a way that man himself is the originating cause of his own responses."[156] Man's "realm of freedom may be a very small fraction of the totality of human behavior, nevertheless it is the determining factor in responsibility."[157]

With his view of human freedom as "the determining factor" one is, argues Buswell, protected from any tendency toward determinism. Since 1930, Buswell says, he has observed the tendency toward determinism in the "fountainhead of presuppositionalism."[158] In unpublished syllabi Van Til "has made many statements which imply that the actual temporal processes of sequence in the historical world cannot be real in the ontological experiences of God in his eternal state of being." One can scarcely distinguish Van Til's doctrine on the relation of time

---

152. KSO: Van Til's point about Buswell's view of God's immutability and absoluteness, is that each of those attributes are themselves dependent on man's freedom in order to be what they are. Thus, immutability is "*dynamic*" because man's autonomous choices impinge on how and if God will act. Absoluteness is "related" because its definition must include man's "sovereign" choices, which themselves move God in particular ways. Once the notion of the absolute freedom of man is established, all Christian doctrines must be adjusted to it, and thus, Reformed theology cannot be maintained.
153. *Sys. Theol.*, II, p. 161.
154. Ibid., p. 160.
155. Ibid., I, pp. 353–354.
156. *Sin and Atonement*, p. 48.
157. Ibid.
158. "Fountainhead," *loc. cit.*

to eternity from that of Spinoza.[159] When, as moderate Calvinists, we hold to the "dynamic self-consistency of the God of the Bible," we escape all appearance of determinism and, at the same time every appearance of contradiction.

Still further, with our dynamic view of God, Buswell argues, we can also see that the relation between hereditary sin and individual freedom is easily solved. We now see that "In Adam all die." This is determinism so far as the individual is concerned. The extreme Calvinist maintains that men are bound over to eternal death because of the fact that God regards them as sinners in Adam. The moderate Calvinist knows that "the guilt of hereditary sin is removed by the blood of Christ. Complete pardon has been purchased and is freely offered to 'whosoever will receive it.'"[160]

In a conversation with a young man who sought to blame heredity and therefore God for his own ill behavior, Dr. Buswell tells us, "I sought to show this young man that his responsibility was not so much in the nature of responsibility for his sinfulness as responsibility for his attitude toward the remedy."[161] "Man is himself responsible for accepting or rejecting the grace which is freely bestowed upon him in the gospel."[162] "Jew and Gentile together, the whole race of humanity participated in the murder of God's Son." It would have been perfectly right if the curse of the sixty-ninth Psalm had then "broken over the heads of humanity." "Instead of the curse, however, Christ died in our place as our substitute. He forgave the lowest sin, the all-comprehensive sin of humanity."[163] "The entire incident is the act of the triune God in forgiving sin."[164]

With this insight into Buswell's espousal of a moderate rather than an extreme Calvinism we can, to some extent, understand why Buswell can join with the Catholic and the Arminian in their method of presenting theism and then Christianity to men.

When Thomas presents his theistic philosophy, he makes a point of telling us that he does so on the basis of reason alone. He stands, he says, on the same ground with all men. To be sure, Thomas argues, his philosophy is a theistic philosophy and only a theistic philosophy can furnish a sound basis for a Christian theology. Even so his philosophy has not been formed in any sense under revelational duress.

In similar fashion Buswell works out his philosophy which he calls "dualistic realism" or "integrated dualism" or "dualistic integrationism" without benefit of

---

159. Ibid., p. 47.
160. *Sin and Atonement*, p. 41.
161. Ibid., p. 44.
162. Ibid., p. 46.
163. Ibid., p. 82.
164. Ibid., p. 83.

revelation.[165] We are all together in the same situation, he says to his unbelieving friends. Let us then together study the general nature of being.[166] Let us also together study the principles of knowledge and of morals. If you should meet a "presuppositionalist" please ignore him. His extreme Calvinism requires him to hold that he has no "intellectual common ground" with you. In this he goes contrary to Scripture. He simply asks you to submit to the Bible and its teaching with respect to the nature of being, of knowing and of morals. He thinks that because of your fall in and with the first man, Adam, you are unwilling and spiritually unable to accept the truth about yourself, about the world and about God unless you are one of the group for whom Christ died to save you from the wrath to come and unless the Holy Spirit regenerates you and gives you the ability to see the facts for what they are.

In all this the presuppositionalist goes contrary to the very Scripture to which he appeals. And, above all, the presuppositionalist goes contrary to the example of him who died for us all.

"The point is that, apart from empirical evidence, we have no such thing as revelation, no such thing as the Bible."[167] Our method, says Buswell, as well as yours is, therefore purely empirical. We expect no such general opposition to our position of "Christian theism" on your part as the presuppositionalist does, for the Holy Spirit works in the hearts of all men so that they are not necessarily adversely disposed to the Christian message. To be sure, "there are many who have been instructed in the idea that God is an impersonal principle, or a pantheistic influence." To them we "outline our reasons" for believing in "the existence of God as the Bible proclaims Him."[168] We show them that "all that is contained in the Christian revelation is reasonable. Nothing violates the principles of logic. We do not believe contradictory propositions. But factual existences never can be deduced from mere abstract logical principles. God has spoken."[169]

3. Buswell's Natural Theology

Buswell's natural theology is, as noted, based upon his philosophy of being, of knowing and of morality. He thinks he has shown that the biblical position is quite possible because it is not against logic and explains the "phenomena of the human mind,"[170] better than Materialism can. It is also better than Idealism.

Believers in the God of the Bible should present their God as a *datum* to

---

165. *Christian View*, p. 19.
166. Ibid., p. 15.
167. Ibid., p. 170.
168. Ibid., p. 172.
169. Ibid., pp. 174–175.
170. Ibid., p. 96.

be interpreted by the ordinary canons of inductive procedure.[171] When we as believers, says Buswell, present the Bible as being "the infallible, inerrant, Word of God," then all we ask unbelievers to do is to consider the Bible in the way that they do other serious writings. If they do this, they can admit that our claim with respect to the Bible is true.[172]

4. The Unbeliever Replies to Buswell
We have, by this time, a pretty full view of Buswell's notion of the Christian believer's standing on common ground with the unbeliever in order to persuade him to accept the truth of the Christian religion. Buswell offers the body of teachings of the Bible as an hypothesis by which men, if they accept it, may be able to interpret experience *better* than they otherwise could.

To do this is, in effect, to admit that the natural man is actually what he thinks he is, namely, the proper judge of truth and morality. To do this, is secondly, to admit that the world is actually what the unbeliever thinks it is, namely, an infinite bottomless ocean of chance. To do this is, thirdly, to admit that all that man can do in this world is to swing the logician's postulate and assert that no such thing as absolute truth *can* exist.

To obtain his "common ground" with the unbeliever Buswell is, in effect, willing to grant that man, though not thinking of himself as a creature of the God of the Bible and as a sinner against this God, and as not needing the salvation wrought by Christ or the regeneration of the Holy Spirit, *yet knows* correctly who and what he is.

To obtain his "common ground" with the unbeliever, Buswell is, in effect, willing to grant that when this man, though not thinking of the world of space-time facts as belonging to God its Creator-controller-redeemer but thinking of it as so many items in a grab-bag, yet handles these facts properly.

Finally, to obtain his "common ground" with the unbeliever, Buswell is willing, in effect, to grant that when this man, though not thinking of the laws of logical thought as implanted in his mind by his Creator, but using them as a means by which to "prove" to himself that the God of Scripture *cannot* possibly exist, yet handles these laws properly.

In reality when the unbeliever says "*nobody knows*," Buswell, in effect, agrees with him. When Christ disputed with the Pharisees and claimed to be the Son of God, he spoke as one having authority. He *knew* who he was. He alone of all the sons of earth could identify himself. He could not, without denying himself, speak otherwise than with authority. He told the Pharisees that in not taking

---

171. *Sys. Theol.*, I, p. 88.
172. Ibid., p. 25.

him at his word they showed that they misinterpreted every fact of which the Old Testament spoke. Moses and the Prophets spoke of him because through them he was speaking of himself. The Apostles spoke on his authority as they set forth the significance of his claim. Through him all things are made. By him all things consist. All history has its significance and comes to its proper climax because of what he was and did.

They who are scientists and love him as they work, will gather together all the facts they can in terms of the master-plan that is given them through Christ in Scripture. No induction is possible outside this plan, *for if the God of Christianity did not exist there could be no inductive process!*[173]

They who are philosophers and love him in their work seek for ever more comprehensive coherence in human experience by combining the facts and the principles of human thought in terms of the self-identifying Christ. No basic coherence is found anywhere except in terms of the self-identifying Christ, for without him who holds all things together by the word of his power there could be no coherence.

For all this Buswell, the philosopher, in effect, assumes that the unbeliever's view of (a) man, (b) of the facts surrounding man in the world and (c) of the laws of human thought as legislative for all possible reality, are right. Buswell is willing to make these fatal admissions in the interest of having common ground with the unbeliever. But the common ground that he thus obtains is *common quicksand*.[174] It is the "common ground" of those who are in the ocean drowning even as the Queen Elizabeth passes by.

One wonders why as a Calvinist, Buswell did not seek for a common ground where Calvin, following Paul, found it. Calvin found common ground in the fact that however sinful men may be, they recognize deep down in their being that they are creatures made by God. It is as "knowing God" (*gnontes ton Theon*)[175] that they rebel against God. Unbelief and rebellion can have meaning only because of this ineradicable knowledge of God that every man has within himself. Then, too, every fact of man's environment speaks clearly of its divine origin.

How then can Buswell seek for common ground with the unbeliever in this unbeliever's false interpretation of the clearest possible revelation of God within

---

173. KSO: This is one of Van Til's key points, and it is one of the ways he is "transcendental" in his approach. Every Christian should be able to agree with this statement: it is, in fact, absolutely true, that "if the God of Christianity did not exist there could be no inductive process." Since that statement is true, it should be a substantial aspect of our defense of Christianity. That is, its truth must have practical and applicable apologetic implications.

174. KSO: See Oliphint, *Covenantal Apologetics: Principles and Practice in Defense of Our Faith*, 76–85.

175. KSO: Rom. 1:21.

and about him? By seeking common ground in this way Buswell does not properly present men with the Christ through whom alone men can be saved from their frustration and rebellion.

The modern scientist or philosopher who does not work on the presupposition of the absolute truth of what Scripture says about God in Christ as the Creator-Redeemer of the world centers all his interpretative efforts about himself as the central point of reference but has no coherence within himself at all. This is the first and most basic fact that he should learn. Only a Christian believer can tell him this.

The Christian has been saved by grace from the futile and sinful effort of knowing himself without knowing himself in terms of the self-identifying Christ. He alone can properly diagnose the disease of man. He says there is only one disease. It is sin. And the wages of sin is death. All men are under the wrath of God by virtue of their sin in Adam. All men daily add to their burden of sin. All scientists and philosophers who daily engage in gathering and arranging the facts of their own constitution and of the world about them without owning Christ as their King and the King of the universe add still further to the load of their sin.

Why does Buswell the philosopher not tell them this? As a theologian, he knows all this to be true.

Again the modern scientist and philosopher who do not work on the basis of the absolute truth of what God through Christ tells men about the world, reduce this world to pure contingency. If the world were what they assume it is, it would, as it were, consist of an infinite number of beads no two of which can be strung because they have no holes in them.[176]

Instead of warning men of this, Buswell urges his fellow Christians who may be scientists or philosophers to join their unbelieving co-workers in the hopeless task of accumulating facts no one of which can even be distinguished from another.[177] Yet Buswell, the theologian, knows full well that all the individual facts of the world are what they are because of the place that they occupy in the plan of God for the world as a whole.

Finally the modern non-Christian scientist assumes that he can *somehow*

---

176. KSO: In other words, a world of pure contingency is a world of disparate and unrelated, even unrelat*able*, facts. There is nothing, no "string" to bring one fact into relation with another, and there are no "holes" in the facts through which they could be unified. If all is contingent, then all is nothing but random and meaningless.

177. KSO: Van Til recognizes that facts *can* be distinguished one from another, even by unbelievers. His point here is that a non-Christian philosophy or science has no *system* available to him by which the facts can be distinguished. He is pressing Buswell on his view of man's autonomy, and thus of man's ultimate contingency, such that God cannot bring together, by way of his all-comprehensive plan, the facts of creation. If man is indeed autonomous, then God can have no all-comprehensive plan at all. It is "up to" man to contribute to what God can plan on his own.

say something about what is possible or impossible in a world of pure chance. Buswell the philosopher does not point this out to them. Rather, his "dynamic" view of the immutability of God is calculated to appease those who determine what can or cannot exist in the realm of being by this standard: what man can or cannot say is in accord with their logical comprehension and inductive procedure.

XI

THE DILEMMA OF WESTERN THOUGHT

We turn now to a consideration of the dilemma of western thought. It has become plain to us that the traditional Butler-type of apologetics does not present Christianity as a challenge to modern relativist thought. Modern man must be challenged to forsake his sinful and therefore futile effort to find meaning in life in terms of himself as a law unto himself.

The believer in Christ must therefore place himself upon the position of the unbeliever for the sake of argument. The believer can then show the unbeliever that he cannot as much as find a place on which to stand in order to oppose the Christian position. The unbeliever must presuppose the truth of the Christian position in order to deny it. Unless the unbeliever repents and in humble faith accepts the authority of the self-attesting Christ as he speaks in Scripture, he can say nothing about himself as the interpreter of the world or about the world as interpreted by himself. So far as modern thought is not based upon the presupposition of the truth of Christianity it is lost in utter darkness. Christianity is the only alternative to chaos. The traditional method of apologetics fails to bring out this fact. It is the business of a Reformed and therefore truly biblical apologetics to do what Romanist-Arminian apologetics has not done and cannot do.

In the present chapter we, therefore, deal with the dilemma of western thought in general and in the final chapter with the dilemma of recent theological thought in particular.

For the sake of convenience we may divide western thought into theology, philosophy and science. When we speak of the dilemma that faces western thought today, we refer to the fact that theology, philosophy and science are and have been both purely rationalist and purely irrationalist.

On the one hand, Reality can only be what the intellect of man, using the law of contradiction, says that it must be. On the other hand, Reality can only be that about which the intellect of man, again using the law of contradiction, can say nothing at all.

That is, man says in one breath that the nature of Reality and therefore all events (facts) within that Reality cannot be other than the law of contradiction will allow. He thereby tells us what Reality is. Yet man, in the next breath, tells us that we have no absolutely certain knowledge about the nature of Reality at all, for Kant has shown us that the law of contradiction as posited by *man* is not applicable to Reality. Reality, the Real, transcends logic. He thereby tells us that he cannot utter one word about what Reality is.[1]

The theologian today vies with the philosopher and the scientist in seeking to assure us that when he speaks to us of God and of Christ, he is not saying anything that is against reason. The scientist vies with the philosopher and the theologian in seeking to assure us that he would not start with any absolute *a priori* principles which would preclude the appearance of facts that are *wholly* new.

It may be objected here that theology, philosophy and science no longer speak of the universe as a whole. Immanuel Kant has taught the theologian as well as the philosopher and the scientist to give up the old metaphysic which applied logic to Reality. One cannot speak conceptually about a God who is eternal and unchangeable in all his attributes. All that man can speak of conceptually is that which he himself has, by the forming process of his mind, molded into such categories as space and time, substance and cause: categories which exist in the mind but which may, or may not, apply to Reality.[2]

Man may indeed continue to speak about God as 'transcendent' but then he must realize that he is not speaking conceptually, but only symbolically; he is using words about that of which he *knows* nothing.

So then modern theology, modern philosophy and modern science alike assert that *nothing* can be said conceptually about a God who is above what Kant calls the *world of phenomena*, the world of experience. But even when men thus claim not to be able to say anything about God, they are, by implication, saying *everything* about God. They are, in effect, making universal negative propositions about God.[3]

---

1. KSO: This is Van Til's summary of Kant's phenomenal/noumenal distinction. Though the noumenal consisted of the "things-in-themselves," according to Kant, they could not themselves be known. They simply supplied the transcendental ground for whatever understanding we might glean from our experiences of the phenomena. Thus, we "know" the phenomena, and we can't *really* know them.

2. KSO: This, again, is a summation of Kant's view. All knowledge begins with experience, but all knowledge does not arise from experience. Our experiences are "synthesized" with the categories of understanding so that we might make proper judgments about those experiences.

3. KSO: That is, for Kant to insist that God must be *noumenal*, and thus cannot be experienced, is to preclude any notion of a God who creates and reveals himself in and through his world and his Word.

A. DEMYTHOLOGIZATION[4]

What needs to be done, we are told, is to 'demythologize' the history of theology, the history of philosophy and the history of science. The theologians hasten to demythologize first the confessions of the church and then the Bible on which these confessions are based. Man views himself

> as a unified being and attributes his experience, thought and volition to his own agency, not to divine or demonic causes. If, as a naturalist, he acknowledges himself in the highest degree dependent, he still does not look upon this dependence as a subjection to higher powers distinguishable from the orderly processes of nature. On the other hand, if he understands himself as 'spirit,' he is aware of his own freedom and responsibility, and even though he recognizes his conditioning by natural forces, he distinguishes his true being from them.[5]

Similarly, when philosophy speaks it no longer speaks with Plato of eternal ideas of goodness, truth and reality or of man as essentially participating in such eternal entities. Man has learned to look within for an understanding of himself. Carrying through the principle of true inwardness as once suggested by Socrates, man sees himself as intelligible to himself in terms of himself and without any reference to any transcendent being.

Finally, science, following or preceding philosophy, has learned to think of *time* and *change* as *ultimate*. Scientists today no longer search for changeless eternal substances. For them nature is explained in terms of functions and correlations.

B. EXISTENTIAL INTERPRETATION

It might seem that the phenomenal world is now enough for man. Whether as a theologian, as a philosopher or as a scientist, modern man needs only to show

---

4. KSO: "Rudolf Bultmann (1884–1976) . . . claimed that much of what the Bible sets forth as historical fact is myth. To him, myth in Scripture was anything which could not be accepted by modern scientific man—*That is*, the entire supernatural element of Scripture had to be dismissed as myth. Thus, according to Bultmann, there was no evidence in the Gospels of the historical Jesus. He set out to *demythologize* the Bible, and by removing those elements which modern man found unacceptable, to render the *Kerygma*, or essence of the gospel, credible to him." Alan Cairns, *Dictionary of Theological Terms* (Belfast; Greenville, SC: Ambassador Emerald International, 2002), 294.

5. Schubert M. Ogden, *Christ Without Myth* (New York: Harper & Brothers, 1961), pp. 35–36.

the utter intellectual untenability of traditional theology, traditional philosophy and traditional science.

However, it has become obvious to modern man that, in order to understand nature, and himself in relation to nature, he still needs some sort of transcendence. Nature deals not only with what is fixed and changeless; nature deals with novelty as well. To be sure, when the modern scientist is engaged in demythologizing, he operates with the principle that nature is wholly perspicuous to man's intellect, because wholly changeless. How else can he exclude what to him are archaic ideas of a transcendent changeless God remaining changeless while, and after, creating a changing world? Nature simply *must* be such that this "logical contradiction" cannot be. The scientist *must* therefore make a universal negative statement about all that surrounds nature in order to preclude the possibility of any of God's interferences with the laws of nature. In short, the process of demythologizing in which the modern scientist engages requires him to be a pure rationalist and therefore a pure determinist.[6]

But then the modern scientist is not and cannot be a pure rationalist and a pure determinist without at the same time being a pure irrationalist and a pure indeterminist. The modern scientist cannot merely negate the 'irrational,' the 'supernatural,' the 'miraculous,' in short the 'mythology' of the past. He must offer his own substitute for these. He must have his own mythology. With Kant he therefore holds that *time is ultimate*. Its products are those of pure contingency, of pure indeterminism.[7] Thus, the universe of science must be at the same time absolutely closed and absolutely open.

It appears then that even when science seeks to limit itself to the so-called phenomenal realm it is both determinist and indeterminist.

As for philosophy, it too, and more obviously so, cannot stop with the purely negative attitude toward 'metaphysics.' Kant says that as *free*, man is *above* the laws of nature because he is the *source* of them. This concept of the freedom of man as the virtual source of order in the world of phenomena presupposes the demythologizing of the idea of God as the Creator either of man or of nature.

On Kant's view (so largely adopted by subsequent philosophers, be it with modifications) man is utterly free as a citizen of the noumenal realm, the Real world, the world prior to the categorizing process of the mind of man, and utterly

---

6. KSO: Here Van Til uses the notion of "demythologization" as equivalent to any notion of a transcendent God. Science "demythologizes" nature by assuming it is simply and only governed by laws, i.e. there can be nothing from "outside nature" that might interfere with nature's regularity.

7. KSO: In other words, if time itself is "ultimate," in that it governs all that exists, then everything is contingent. All that is comes into, and goes out of, existence. So, in a dialectical fashion, there is both determinism and indeterminism.

determined as a citizen of the phenomenal realm.⁸ As a citizen of the noumenal realm he cannot know himself or his fellow man. As soon as he tries to explain himself as free he has to do so by means of the categories of the phenomenal realm. He must explain himself causally and when he explains himself causally then he has explained his freedom out of existence. To be sure, there is the contingency idea which, as already noted, is one constituent element of the world of phenomena. But then when man appeals to this pure contingency in nature for an explanation of his moral freedom, he reduces his freedom to the freedom of pure chance. Thus man seeks to explain himself in terms of nature but this nature is itself explained in terms of a combination of pure fate and pure chance. The result is the purely meaningless and therefore chaos.⁹

But then modern theology comes to help the modern scientist and the modern philosopher. Of course, the theologian would not intrude upon either the domain of science or of philosophy. Not at all! The modern theologian makes plain first that he is not falling back into mythology or metaphysics. What he says about God or about Christ will be in accord with modern science and modern philosophy. The theologian is thoroughly sensitive to the fact that man's understanding of himself in terms of himself as autonomous, i.e., self-sufficient and self-defining, is basic to everything that he may say about God or about Christ. "The picture of the world formed by modern science and man's understanding of himself as a closed inner unity" are basically determinative as to what the theologian will want to say either about God or about Christ.¹⁰ Does this attempt on the part of the theologian to make his assertions about God and about Christ then mean that the theologian has nothing to say that the scientist and the philosopher cannot of themselves discover? Does it mean also that all the theology of the past and indeed the "gospel" of the New Testament must simply be ignored?

Not at all, says Rudolf Bultmann, the great exponent of the demythologization of the New Testament. To be sure, argues Bultmann, when the New Testament speaks of God in the mythological categories of Gnosticism, this is "not only rationally unimaginable" by man today but also "says absolutely nothing to him. For he cannot understand that his salvation, . . . his authentic existence, should consist in such a condition."¹¹

---

8. KSO: For Kant, the "noumenal" realm, which must both be what it is and be unknowable, consisted of God, things in themselves, and the "self," the latter of which Kant called the "transcendental unity of apperception."
9. KSO: This paragraph is Van Til's summation of the dialectical thought of Kant and his followers, which relates the noumenal (freedom) to the phenomenal (determined).
10. Ibid., p. 37.
11. Ibid. Ogden quotes from Bultmann's *Kerygma und Mythus*, I, p. 21.

Says Schubert Ogden:[12] "For man to 'exist,' in the technical sense that Bultmann presupposes, means he is a being who must continually face and answer the question of what it is to be a man. It means, in a word, that he is *a moral or religious being*, one who always has to deal with the problem of what he *ought* to be. What he is to be is never already determined, but, rather, is something he himself is required to decide freely and responsibly by his *existentiell* understanding of himself in his world."[13]

But, if all this might seem to us to indicate that Bultmann's theology seeks to be nothing more than what an existential philosopher such as Martin Heidegger already tells us about the possibilities of man's authentic existence in terms of his own freedom, then we are, says Ogden, quite mistaken. Bultmann insists that faith in Christ is all important. Expounding Bultmann's view Ogden says: "Faith is not simply one among several possible self-understandings that can arise spontaneously out of human existence itself. Rather, it is a self-understanding that is realized only in response to the word of God encountered in the proclamation of Jesus Christ."[14] "In this sense, theology is indeed *ministerium verbi divini*,[15] for its sole norm is the revealed word of God that has its origin and legitimation in Holy Scripture; and the purpose of every genuine theological statement is to explicate the self-understanding, or, in different words, the *existentiell* understanding of God, the world, and man, that is the real content of the New Testament itself."[16]

Of course, by thus referring us to "the revealed word of God" Bultmann is not reverting to type. He is not making any 'objective' statements about a reality that is not an 'object.' Together with the "entire neo-Kantian tradition, including contemporary existentialism, that provides the philosophical background of his thought," Bultmann lifts everything that the New Testament says out of the phenomenal into the noumenal realm.[17] When the New Testament "presupposes the Old Testament Jewish Mythology of creation and speaks in

---

12. KSO: Schubert Ogden (1928–) "American theologian associated with process theology—the application of the philosophy of Charles Hartshorne and Alfred North Whitehead to theological projects. Ogden was also influenced by the theologian Rudolf Bultmann. For Ogden, Christian theology includes the task of philosophy. Philosophical theology has two criteria which it must meet. First, it must be appropriate to the religious commitments from which it arises. Second, it must be credible within the context of contemporary understanding (i.e., not merely among those who share a religious commitment). Ogden's application of process thought seeks to find an alternative to both liberal theology and neo-orthodoxy." *A Dictionary of Philosophy of Religion*, Charles Taliaferro and Elsa J. Marty, eds. (New York: Bloomsbury Academic, 2018), 202.
13. Ibid., p. 48.
14. Ibid., p. 23.
15. KSO: "servant of the word of God."
16. Ibid., pp. 23–24.
17. Ibid., p. 25.

reportorial fashion of the woes of the last days, the resurrection of the dead, and the final judgment," then Bultmann knows there is a twofold or double history.[18] If the New Testament message is to be made relevant to the present and intelligible to modern man, faith in Christ and the New Testament requires that we look for noumenal history, or *Geschichte*, within and behind phenomenal history, or *Historie*.[19]

The important point is that *"demythologization is a demand of faith itself."*[20] If the Christ or the word of Christ were to be directly identified with any fact of ordinary history, it would fall *ipso facto* within the realm of science, the realm of universal law, and as such it could never serve as that which is above and beyond man's self-understanding.

It is in this manner that Bultmann combines "the Christian understanding of existence" with a philosophy such as that of Heidegger "in which the phenomena of human existence may be appropriately described in a nonmythological way."[21]

It is thus by his demythologization and by his existential interpretation of the New Testament that Bultmann sees its message as freed from every traditional encumbrance and its benediction poured upon all men.[22] Those who accept the gospel of the New Testament now enjoy freedom from the past and openness for the future. They now enjoy "eschatological existence."[23] The "decisive eschatological occurrence" is, for them, no longer some "imminent cosmic catastrophe, but the fact that God is now judging the world in Jesus Christ and thereby calling men to decide for life or death (cf. John 3:19; 9:39)."[24]

What then does theology have to offer the scientifically minded philosopher? Bultmann not only admits but insists that "the Christian understanding of existence... can be known apart from Christ."[25] While philosophy asserts that man can live the authentic life through powers of his own, the New Testament says man must be freed by an act of God. Therefore, the Christian understanding

---

18. Ibid., p. 28.
19. KSO: In modernist and neo-orthodox theological thinking, Van Til rightly sees influence from the Kantian structure of the "phenomenal/noumenal." There are multiple aspects to this structure, but, generally speaking, the phenomenal is the historical dimension in which are found the data of history. The reason for a "noumenal" realm is so that the data of history can, somehow, be understood in a meaningful way. Apart from the noumenal, history is nothing more than the ever-flowing stream of brute factuality. Here, *Geschichte* is the "noumenal" aspect and *Historie* is the mere historical.
20. Ibid., p. 43.
21. Ibid., p. 56.
22. Ibid., p. 60.
23. Ibid., p. 62.
24. Ibid.
25. Ibid., p. 72.

of existence may be *known* but not *realized* apart from Bultmann's Christ. The New Testament speaks of a "salvation-occurrence that has taken place in Christ." Says Ogden: "In other words, the New Testament asserts that without the saving act of God, the human situation is one of utter despair. For philosophy, on the other hand, man's situation neither is, nor can be, as desperate as theology is wont to portray it."[26] Philosophy says: "You can because you ought!" "In the New Testament's judgment, however, man has lost his factual possibility and, indeed, even his knowledge of his authenticity is falsified by being bound up with the assumption that he has power over it."[27]

Two points are here to be noted. First the Christ-occurrence is said not to be mythical in the Gnostic meaning of the term. This is the case because "its central elements are the person and destiny of the actual historical figure Jesus of Nazareth."[28] Secondly, the Christ-occurrence is not mythical because the "'true intention' of the Christological myths cannot be discerned in the meaning of their objective contents, but must be uncovered through critical interpretation."[29] All the New Testament's Christological statements are therefore to be "interpreted not in terms of their objective contents, but as statements of existential significance. . ."[30]

"Thus the New Testament speaks of the cross as 'the eschatological event,' which never becomes an event of the past, but rather is constantly present both in preaching and sacraments. . ."[31]

It is thus that for Bultmann the traditional view of Christ and his work are spoken of as being mythological, and his own view of the Christ-Event as taking place within the present as genuinely historical.

It is clear that Bultmann's interpretation of the New Testament is accomplished in terms of a modified form of Kantian noumenal-phenomenal philosophy. This means that his theology, together with modern philosophy, is faced with the dilemma of being purely rationalist and purely irrationalist at the same time. All three of them support each other in asserting that nothing *can* be said about ultimate reality. How could anything be said about ultimate reality if man and nature alike are the products of pure chance? How can there be any intelligent speech about what can or cannot be according to logic if logic itself is the product of pure contingency? If man is himself but a white-cap of an ocean wave and if

26. Ibid.
27. Ibid., p. 73.
28. Ibid., p. 77.
29. Ibid.
30. Ibid., p. 78.
31. Ibid., pp. 79, 80.

the ocean has neither bottom nor shore, how can he make any universal statements at all?[32] Yet the post-Kantian man, either as theologian, as philosopher or as scientist, implies universal statements about ultimate reality in every utterance that he makes. He does so both negatively and positively.

He does so negatively in his program of demythologizing. When he says what ultimate reality 'cannot' be he is not coming back from a trip into space to tell us he has not seen God there. He is doing something much more ambitious than that. He is saying, in effect, that by logic he has penetrated all reality and has cleared every square inch of territory in it and is sure that God is not now, never has been and never will be there!

But then there is the positive as well as the negative side. Post-Kantian man assumes as self-evident that he is himself the ultimate source of all predication, all definition and interpretation. What he speaks of as his freedom implies a definite view of all reality. His freedom involves for him a definite view of his total environment. His view of freedom requires that the environment be of such a nature as will never interfere with his plans for the future. Modern man assumes as self-evident a philosophy of reality, a philosophy of history, in which he is himself the center. Modern man assumes that he and he alone can make good any claim of "ownership" in the universe.

In being utterly anti-metaphysical, the modern theologian is, if possible, more metaphysical than his forbears.[33] Ancient and medieval man tended to lay out their claim in the realm of being. The realm of non-being or contingency was, largely, a matter of indifference. Who cares if wild beasts live in the heart of Africa? Who cares what happens in "outer space?" What can one even mean by "outer" space?

But now the last of earth's wildernesses are opened up and Russia and the United States are equally mindful of the fact that the one may destroy the other by using outer space. Similarly modern man realizes that he must pre-empt non-being and pure contingency as well as being and pure determinism in order to maintain his autonomy, his independence, as over against the Creator-God. He does so by means of the method of dialecticism. By means of dialecticism, modern man proves to himself that no one can say anything about being except as correlative to non-being.

---

32. KSO: That is, if *everything* is contingent, there can be no absolute, thus, no possibility of a "universal" statement. Whatever statement is made would itself be contingent and therefore subject to change.

33. KSO: One of the implications of Kant's *Critique of Pure Reason* is that the "noumenal" was argued to be necessary but unknowable. Given its unknowability, it rendered metaphysics utterly irrelevant and thus, for many, unnecessary.

With a sense of great exhilaration modern man now realizes that all the future is his, not God's. God never did exist except in the imagination of man. God is dead. Christ, as Chalcedon pictured him, with two distinct natures, one divine and one human, is dead. We can now have a *Christ Without Myth*. We have no *Angst* with respect to the idea of eternal punishment. There is no hell but only victory over hell.

In early Greek philosophy Parmenides and Heraclitus seemed to be utterly opposed to one another. Parmenides said that all reality was static while Heraclitus said that all reality was flux. One had to choose between these antagonists. But now Parmenides and Heraclitus have become friends. Modern man holds that both were wrong and both were right. One cannot say that all reality is what logic says it must be; Heraclitus has his rights. One cannot say that all reality must be identical with ultimate Chance; Parmenides has his rights. All reality is both changeless and changing. Pure rationalism and pure irrationalism have embraced each other. Dialecticism has come; paradox has been discovered. We are free in every sense at last!

For all this, modern man finds himself, now that he has found his new freedom, in great distress! He is beginning to see, ever increasingly, that he is playing a game with himself. It is obvious, and it is becoming more obvious to him, that, if he uses the law of contradiction on the assumption of his own freedom or ultimacy, then his logic must be legislative for all reality. Whatever creator-gods there be, they can create nothing that is not in accord with man's understanding of what is logically possible. This being the case, Parmenides was right; there simply *cannot* be anything that has not from all eternity existed.[34] In fact there can be no God, that is, no divine mind which is, in any basic sense, higher than the human mind.

So far so good. Following Parmenides, the philosophy of logical analysis proves to itself beyond peradventure of doubt that it is meaningless to speak one word about God. Following Parmenides, Bultmann demythologizes the New Testament. Following Parmenides, Paul van Buren[35] has done away, once for all, with everything that savors of transcendence above human experience.

Thomas J. J. Altizer, following Nietzsche, whom he considers "the greatest

---

34. KSO: This is the case because if logic legislates what is logically possible, it must have existed from all eternity or it would be contingent. If contingent, it would be able to be or not to be.

35. KSO: Van Buren, Altizer and others were instrumental in the "death of God" movement, which was, "A theological movement popularized by Protestant theologians Thomas J. J. Altizer, William Hamilton and Paul van Buren in the 1960s, which declared that the traditional concept of God had ceased to play any significant role in the life of modern people. The movement was highly publicized by popular media but had a relatively short lifespan." Stanley Grenz, David Guretzki, and Cherith Fee Nordling, *Pocket Dictionary of Theological Terms* (Downers Grove, IL: InterVarsity Press, 1999), 35.

modern master of understanding man,"[36] calls upon modern man to accept the "gospel of Christian atheism" instead of the gospel of the New Testament, and Harvey Cox invites him to buy a building site in his "secular city" because then the future is his, but the modern man discovers that the future has already moved through a corridor into the dead past. Just as modern man is about to engage in a transaction which will insure him a future over which no one has any control but himself, he discovers that to be intelligibly real this transaction has to be thought of as having taken place in eternity. Worse than that, just as the free modern man takes a good look at himself as free, he discovers that, knowing himself to be free, he knows himself as having been determined from all eternity. When he sputters against this his own conclusion, he discovers that he has nothing that he can call his own for the horrifying reason that he is what he is because he is nothing in himself but is identical with God. Finally, this free man now discovers that he has been wholly absorbed into the "wholly other" God of whom he had just persuaded himself so joyfully that he could say nothing at all.[37]

Just then Heraclitus appears upon the scene and offers to return his hard-won freedom to him. "'*Statt der lebendigen Natur,*' we say, '*da Gott die Menschen schuf hinein,*'[38]—that nebulous concoction, that wooden, that straight-laced thing, that crabbed artificiality, that musty schoolroom product, that sick man's dream! Away with it. Away with all of them! Impossible! Impossible."[39] Why bother about logic? Opposites do flow into one another. This is true for the whole of reality.

This gospel of Heraclitus has been brought to us in recent decades through Henri Bergson's *L'Evolution Creatrice*,[40] through Samuel Alexander's *Space-Time and Deity*,[41] through James' *Pragmatism*,[42] through John Dewey's *The Quest for Certainty*, through Martin Heidegger's *Sein und Zeit*,[43] and through many others. As true followers of Kant, they have, one and all, seen the vision of time and pure contingency as ultimate.

---

36. Thomas J. J. Altizer, *The Gospel of Christian Atheism* (Philadelphia: Westminster Press, 1966), p. 139.
37. KSO: This is Van Til's summary of the "rational/irrational" dialectic of modern theology. Man is absorbed into the wholly other God (rational) of whom he could say nothing at all (irrational).
38. KSO: This is a quote from Goethe's *Faust* and expresses human despair, "Instead of living nature, in which God created man. . ." the quote continues, "you are surrounded with smoke and decay, the skeleton of animals. . ."
39. William James, "The Nature and Value of Philosophy" in *An Anthology of Recent Philosophy* compiled by Daniel Sommer Robinson (New York: Thomas Y. Crowell Co., 1929), p. 9.
40. KSO: Henri Bergson (1859–1941), French philosopher, *Creative Evolution*.
41. KSO: Samuel Alexander (1859–1938), British philosopher.
42. KSO: William James (1842–1910), American pragmatist philosopher.
43. KSO: Martin Heidegger (1889–1976), German existentialist philosopher, who wrote *Being and Time*.

So modern man makes his escape from the abstract realm of the true, the good and the beautiful and follows Heraclitus down into the freedom of pure non-being. Down and down he goes, down through the realm of the phenomenal, till he reaches, or rather is lost in, the bottomless ocean of pure contingency. Down he goes, did I say? No, in pure contingency there is neither down nor up.

Having lost his identity in the realm of non-being he calls to Parmenides for help. No, not to Parmenides but to the god of Parmenides. But this God, too, has lost himself. The god of Parmenides now appears to the modern man to be no more than an abstract principle of rationality which has relation to the pure flux of temporal reality only by being correlative to it.

But the half has not been told. Modern man must maintain his identity and therewith his freedom by riding off in opposite directions simultaneously. Hence his *Urangst*.[44] In order to escape being absorbed into the blank identity of an eternal timeless principle he must flee toward the utter flux and to escape being swallowed up by the Chaos and Old Night of pure contingency he must, at the same time, flee toward the god of utter staticism.

Thus the freedom or identity of modern man consists of two mutual negations which keep canceling out each other.

This problem of the relation of the "free self" to its environment is found alike in science, in philosophy and in theology. In all three of these fields of endeavor man seeks to show that his assertions are both according to logic and according to fact. But when he thinks that his assertions are fully in accord with the law of contradiction and therefore fully clear, they are purely tautological. In that case science has no contingency, philosophy no synthesis, theology no revelation. His logic hovers above the field of fact, like a turnpike in the sky[45] with no approaches to it. He can go as fast as he wills on this turnpike in either direction; it makes no difference in which direction he goes for going is the same as standing still.

Then when his assertions start from facts and purport at all costs to be about facts, he can say nothing about these facts. He has no principle by which to distinguish one fact from another; in Chaos and Old Night all cows are black and all cats are grey. How do you even distinguish cows from cats if time and chance as such are the ultimate principles of individuation? With time as the ultimate principle of individuation one cannot account for counting. In seeking for facts you are then in the swamp that has no bottom, and from which there is

---

44. KSO: "primal fear."
45. KSO: Van Til was asked why he referred to logic as a turnpike in the sky. See Cornelius Van Til, "At the Beginning, God: An Interview With Cornelius Van Til Christianity Today," XXII, (1977).

no approach to the turnpike of logic. Science has no system, philosophy has no coherence and revelation has no intellectual content.[46]

How then, to ask Kant's question, are synthetic *a priori* judgments possible?[47] How can there be systematic knowledge that develops as man engages in research? How can one explain the fact of human knowledge? It cannot be explained by science, it cannot be explained by philosophy and it cannot be explained by theology.

C. DIMENSIONALISM IS NO HELP

It follows, too, that the idea of dimensionalism[48] so frequently employed by some scientists, philosophers and theologians against the naturalism of their brethren is of no validity. There are naturalists in science, there are naturalists in philosophy and there are naturalists in theology.

Over against them stand the spiritualists in science, in philosophy and in theology. The argument of the naturalists is, in each case, to the effect that there is no meaning in things in themselves, in Absolutes or in a transcendent God. How can anything intelligible be said about that which is, by definition, wholly above and beyond human experience? The answer of the spiritualist to the naturalist is, in each case, to the effect that there is no meaning to experience unless there be a principle of permanence, a systematic whole, a God that is thought of as above and beyond anything that science by itself presents. And is not the spiritual built into human experience itself? Is not our sense of 'Oughtness' the best evidence of the actual existence of a freedom that is above the laws of science? Naturalism is bound to deny this fact of freedom. A broader and deeper interpretation of the universe is needed. We must not only recognize the fact of human freedom, but we must also postulate it as being higher than the necessities of nature. We must even say that it is the free man who, by his logical thought, deals with the impersonal facts of nature as if they were amenable to the purpose of man.

Then the theologian comes in order to build upon the spiritual interpretation

---

46. KSO: The point of this paragraph is that those who embrace philosophy, science, or theology, to the extent that it begins with and is consistent with its own autonomous principle, have no way to distinguish fact from fact, or to apply logic to facts. By virtue of God's common grace, such people cannot be consistent with their own rebellious principles. But that is no testimony to the principles themselves. Based on those principles, people who can count, are not able to account for counting.

47. KSO: This was the question, owing to Humean skepticism, that Kant set out to ask and answer in his *Critique of Pure Reason*.

48. KSO: For Van Til, dimensionalism is any philosophy, science, or theology that posits two "dimensions" as necessary for meaning and an understanding of "reality." Plato's "Real and Ideal" and Kant's "phenomenal and noumenal" are two examples of dimensionalism.

of the world, already given by spiritually minded scientists and philosophers, the house of a spiritualist theology. A transcendent free self points to a still more transcendent self which we may properly call God.

It is thus that modern dimensionalist theology builds upon what it considers the solid foundation of modern dimensionalist philosophy and science.

Two points must be made with respect to this dimensionalist theology.

In the first place such a theology can say nothing about its transcendent God or about its Christ that the philosopher and the scientist cannot know of himself. The God and the Christ of modern theology are projections and, in fact so far as intelligible content is concerned, the same projections that modern spiritualist philosophy and science make.[49] When with Karl Barth modern theology speaks of God as the wholly other, it says but the same thing that Sir Arthur Eddington says when he speaks of the mysterious universe. The god of modern theology is but the god of pure negation. In modern philosophy and science this idea is expressed by the insistence that no interpretation of life so far given by any so-called system of truth can be final.

Supported by spiritualist science and philosophy, modern theology carries out its negative program of demythologization with relentless courage. In the name of this wholly other god Bultmann exorcises the Calvinist and Lutheran ideas of creation and redemption in and through the course of history. Modern theologians criticize one another for not having sterilized the house of their theology thoroughly enough from the last vestiges of a supposedly direct identification of any event or word in *Historie* with that which, they argue, can only take place in *Geschichte*. The original sin of historical theology, particularly of orthodox Protestantism, is that, together with the naturalists, it reduces the spiritual relations between men and their God to the level of the phenomenal world.[50] Orthodox theology, we are told, simply has no eye for the higher, the spiritual, dimension of life. With all his talk about a transcendent and sovereign God, Calvin, in particular, had no eye for the wholly otherness, and therefore for the true sovereignty and freedom of God.

Let us, then, as modern Christians, follow the modern theologians, supported by modern philosophers and modern scientists, as they join the naturalists in their program of excluding every last vestige of a transcendent God who is at all conceptually knowable and historically identifiable by man.

But, having brought home to ourselves and to our children the fact that all

---

49. KSO: By "projections" Van Til means that these ideas and concepts are products (projections) of human consciousness, rather than revealed by God.

50. KSO: That is, for dimensionalists, the "higher" order must *not* be historical. For orthodox theology, the resurrection of Christ, for example, is a *fact* of history. For a dimensional theology, the meaning of the resurrection *must* be "above" the historical dimension.

the gods of orthodox historical theology are idols and that we must bow to the god of pure negation alone, we must think of this god of pure negation as being also the god of pure or absolute affirmation.

It is here that theology must take the lead. Once the slate is cleared of the last remnant of any directly knowable revelation of God in history, the theologian takes the initiative in saying that God, while wholly unknowable, is wholly known. Having made clear that no one knows *that* God exists, the theologian proceeds to tell us *what* God is and *what* he is saying.

But, while theologians may lead the philosophers and the scientists in telling us all about God, they do not say anything beyond what has always been said by philosophy and science.

When Paul Tillich says that philosophy can ask the proper human questions but that only theology can give the answers or when Bultmann says that philosophy knows the needs of man but only theology can bring the message of redemption for the fulfilment of those needs, we are bound to take issue with them. Tillich and Bultmann tell us that theology must give the answer and offer the power that it hears about from the revelation of God through Christ. But the God of their theology is the same unknowable wholly other of which philosophy already speaks. The Christ of modern theology is as unknowable as is the god of modern theology. If theology differs at all from philosophy or from science, it is only in that it pretends to have a bigger flashlight and can therefore have a little deeper glance (*Blik*) into the infinite impenetrable mists that surround fallen man. When modern theology speaks of man's sin and of the saving grace of God in Christ, it merely uses religious language for ideas that philosophy has all the while expressed in concepts of its own.

In the second place, if what has been said so far is true, a basic consequence follows for the Christian thinker. The Christian thinker must beware of misunderstanding the issue of modern thought. A common misunderstanding is to the effect that the great debate that rages is one between secular and religious thought.

There is, says Karl Heim,[51] first the "mature secularist." This "mature secularist"

---

51. KSO: Karl Heim (1874–1958), "Lutheran theologian. A native of Frauenzimmern in Württemberg, he studied at Tübingen and was for some years a pastor and schoolmaster. In 1907 he became a Privatdozent at Halle, in 1914 Professor of Theology at Münster i.W., and in 1920 at Tübingen. For several years he was one of the leading opponents of the (pagan) German Faith Movement. His theology, which developed out of a Pietistic background, stressed the Ritschlian contrast of faith and reason and, while fully accepting the achievements of modern secular culture and science, emphasized the transcendence of faith. He was esp. concerned to analyse the conditions governing the valid apprehension of supernatural truth. In his personalism (the 'I–Thou' relationship; cf. M. Buber) and his doctrine of 'perspectives', his teaching had affinities with certain existentialist doctrines." F. L. Cross, ed., *The Oxford Dictionary of the Christian Church* (Oxford: Oxford University Press, 2005), 751. As we will see below, Heim's dimensionalism, dependent on Kant, is the "polar and suprapolar."

lives in the conviction that he alone has returned to the solid ground of reality and that the rest of us are still pursuing chimeras which have long since lost their significance. For this "serene secularism" the "landscape is suddenly filled with light and the outlines become clear and distinct. There comes into being a new, self-contained, comprehensive conception of reality." He perceives "the cosmic stream of events, however extravagant the multiplicity of forms it comprises and however astonishing the wealth of varying shapes which it produces, is still ultimately subject to a single universal fundamental law."[52]

"That is," says Heim, "the clear, perspicuous, overall picture of reality on the basis of which the genuine secularist conducts his life and thinking."[53]

Throughout the book from which we have quoted, and in many other works, Heim seeks to show that

> there is something which lies from the outset outside the whole scope of natural science, some position which is entirely beyond the range of the scientific method, a firm point which cannot be subjected to the spatial and temporal measurements with which natural science works, and which lies even beyond the incalculable dimensions of the cosmos in comparison with which Man sinks into nothingness. We need a position which does not have to be defended against scientific objections, a position from which, if the necessity should arise, we could go over from the defensive to the attack in our relations with natural science.[54]

Heim then proceeds to show that the "serene" secularist is not entitled to serenity. He may boast of basing his "comprehensive view" of reality upon the clearly perceived facts and laws of science. Actually he is already shown to be mistaken in the fact that "the world of nature, which is experienced, measured and computed" is not the first but "always only the second *datum*" with which even the scientist deals. For each of us, it is his own ego which is the "first *datum*." Fichte[55] had this first *datum* in mind when he said, "Look at yourself. Turn your

---

52. Karl Heim, *Christian Faith and Natural Science* (London: S. C. M. Press, 1953), p. 21.
53. Ibid., p. 22.
54. Ibid., p. 32.
55. KSO: Johann Gotlieb Fichte (1762–1814). "Fichte claimed that his philosophical doctrines were implicit in those of I. Kant, which he sought to develop on the lines of 'spontaneity' and 'autonomy'. Acc. to him the objects of our knowledge are the products of the consciousness of the ego as regards both their matter and their form. This ego, however, is not the individual 'I', but the Absolute Ego, which can be known only by philosophical intuition. It develops in three phases. In the first it posits itself, in the second it posits a non-ego against itself, and in the last it posits itself as limited by the non-ego. Acc. to Fichte God is the Absolute Ego, 'the living operative moral order'; but He is not to be conceived as personal. True religion consists in 'joyously doing right'. When

gaze away from all that surrounds you and towards your own inner self. This is the first demand which philosophy makes of its pupil. Nothing outside you matters here, but only you yourself."[56]

It is thus, at one stroke, says Heim, that the whole naturalist position is seen to be untenable. "The great discoverer in the West of the ego and of its separateness from the whole objective world was Plato." For him the "soul" is "the Archimedean eternal fulcrum, the one invisible reality."[57] We have now gone beyond Plato but have never renounced his basic insight. We no longer speak of the soul as an "indestructible being." We follow Kant as he excludes from Plato's soul "all the metaphysical consequences which the Greeks had drawn from it."[58] Then we go beyond Kant with the help of existential philosophy as we went beyond Plato with the help of Kant's critical philosophy. The ego of Kant's "transcendental apperception can be present only in the singular."[59] For Kant it is in "'consciousness in general' that we as individual persons participate when we think and when by means of the categories of understanding we penetrate into the world of experience."[60] And this point is, as such, "unassailable." Fichte even strengthened this position of Kant's ego by insisting that man's "relative ego" is in its deepest essence one with the "absolute ego." And Fichte was altogether justified when in a triumphant spirit he challenged every form that naturalism, materialism, mechanism or solipsism might take. "'When the newest-born of the millions of suns which shine above my head has long since poured out its last spark of light,' says Fichte, 'I shall still be, unscathed and untransformed, the same person that I am today.'"[61] It is in terms of this "epistemological subject," as Rickert called it, that we are unafraid of nature. We are not subject to nature; nature is subject to us.

But with the help of existential philosophy we are able to go far beyond the idealism of Fichte. A "radical change in the whole conception of reality" has come about through such men as Kierkegaard and Jaspers[62].[63] We now realize that the "epistemological subject" need not, as Kant thought, exist only in the singular. It is true that logically Kant was right. Kant's inference, that because the ego is

---

society will have reached a condition in which morality is the norm, the existence of the Church will be unnecessary." F. L. Cross, ed., *The Oxford Dictionary of the Christian Church* (Oxford: Oxford University Press, 2005), 611.

56. Ibid., pp. 35–36, quoting Fichte's introduction to his *Theory of Science*.
57. Ibid., p. 49.
58. Ibid.
59. Ibid.
60. Ibid.
61. Ibid., p. 51.
62. KSO: Karl Jaspers (1883–1969), German existentialist philosopher and psychiatrist.
63. Ibid.

not objective it can exist only in the singular, is logically absolutely cogent and evident. But it is precisely at this point, says Heim, "that logic is incomprehensibly refuted by the reality of our existence."[64] Existential philosophy has brought home to us that self-existence is, at the same time, "coexistence" or "as Jaspers says, 'I exist only in communication with another.'"[65]

"Isolation," Heim tells us by quoting Heidegger, "is a deficient mode of coexistence. The possibility of isolation is the proof of coexistence."[66]

In saying this, we have not abandoned the Kantian and idealist principle of the "transcendental ego" as existing "only in the singular."

As Moses saw the promised land "from the summit of Mount Nebo," so Kant pointed to the promised land in which we now live. "Together with Fichte he had recognized that on this side of the whole observable space there lies a region which is not observable; and he had seen that between this observable world and that non-observable region in which I stand as the cognitive ego there is a great gulf fixed."[67] He saw, too, that these two worlds, for all that great gulf that separates them,

> belong together so intimately that they cannot be separated by any 'concrete detachment' but can only be distinguished from one another by means of an abstraction. Only one step now remains to be taken in order to reach the final recognition which brings to an end the whole process which began with primitive thought. The reason must still be made clear why only an abstract distinction between the two worlds is possible. It is because the opposition here is not between two *worlds* but between two *spaces*, the relation between which can therefore not be compared with any intra-spatial relation.[68]

But now that the "new mathematics and the new physics have begun to reckon with a multiplicity of spaces" and existential philosophers have, at the same time, "begun to devote attention to the thou," we are in a position to have a rounded out dimensional outlook on life. We have now left behind every form of primitive thought. That is Heim's equivalent for "demythologization." We do justice to science, to philosophy and to religion alike. Secularists are now seen to be like "Flatlanders. . . who can see reality only in two dimensions."[69] They live

64. Ibid., p. 52.
65. Ibid.
66. Ibid.
67. Ibid., p. 114.
68. Ibid.
69. Ibid., p. 231.

in "polar space." They cannot conceive of any such thing as suprapolar space.⁷⁰ For us, however, who now live in suprapolar space, the question is: "Is there a key which I need only to put into the keyhole and turn, in order to open, for people from whom the suprapolar space is still hidden, the door which leads into this space?"⁷¹ Can we infer the existence of "the omnipotent God" from what we see in nature? The answer is *no*. There is always an "infinite qualitative difference"⁷² between "the eternal God, who alone is absolute, unconditioned and omnipotent" and the greatest cause of that any Flatlander can conceive. No "*causal inference* leads us out beyond the frontiers of the polar space. . ."⁷³

Can there then be "*empirical proof* whereby forces from the world beyond make themselves so clearly perceptible that it is no longer at all possible to deny the existence of a suprapolar space?"⁷⁴ The answer must again be in the negative. Such a thing would be possible only if in science we had a 'closed system'

> comprising an ascertainable energy quantum with a constant energy content. Only on this condition could it be shown that some particular occurrence, say the resuscitation of a dead man, cannot be explained by reference to the forces of this world and must arise from some supramundane source of energy. But in fact the totality of the polar cosmic space in which the secularist lives is not a closed system. Consequently, even the most incomprehensible occurrence, which looks like a violation of all the causal relations, can always be attributed to some intramundane force, which had hitherto remained unknown but which is easily able to counteract the effects of other forces.⁷⁵

Still further, what holds true for such possibly physical occurrences as the resurrection of a human body from the dead, holds equally for such experiences as a sense of guilt, or the pangs of conscience. The believer attributes these to an

---

70. KSO: This notion of "suprapolar" space was conceived by Heim in order to transcend the phenomena of this world. For Heim, suprapolar space was not beyond this world, but was another dimension of existence. According to Heim, "what we have here is two spaces, each of which embraces the whole universe but each in quite a different aspect . . ." So, "while we are encompassed on all sides by the temporal world, we stand at the same time even now in the midst of eternity and are enclosed within the archetypal space (*Urraum*) of God,"(*Christian Faith and Natural Science*, 169, 171). As Van Til is articulating Heim's view, he wants us to recognize that it is nothing but an application of Kant's phenomenal/noumenal distinction to Christianity. What is lost in this application is orthodox Christianity *in toto*.
71. Ibid., p. 232.
72. Ibid., p. 234.
73. Ibid., p. 235.
74. Ibid.
75. Ibid., pp. 235–236.

action that originates in a "higher dimension." But the secularist can always try to "analyze them by the techniques of parapsychology or depth psychology. . ."[76]

Theologians should, says Heim, be warned against "drawing theological inferences, particularly from the non-causal character of certain processes within the atom."[77] Even if scientists should speak of a "meaningfulness" and of a "conformity to plan which are apparent in the laws of nature as a whole" and should then think of this as an "imposing revelation of God in nature"[78] the theologian should not fall into the trap that is therewith set for him. The theologian must make it quite clear to himself and to others that when he speaks of the "space of eternity" he does so "quite independently of the impression which the meaningfulness and the planned regularity of the laws of nature make upon himself or even upon the critical scientist."[79]

Finally we ask whether perhaps we can help the Flatlander to work his way up into suprapolar space by means of what Kant and others call a postulate of the practical reason. We sense in ourselves as free men, says Kant, the absolute claims of the moral law. And this, he argues, should lead to the belief "that there stands behind the moral law an omnipotent Will which guarantees its realization."[80] We might even extend Kant's idea of the moral postulate to the idea of truth. We would then hold that to "achieve complete clarity" science as a whole needs the notion of a "mind which is immanent in the entire cosmos, a mind in which the mind of every single individual is rooted."[81]

But this last way, too, is not open to us for:

> If we acknowledge in our conscience a moral law which is unconditionally valid, then we have already passed beyond the frontiers of the polar space, in which there are always only relative values and validities. In other words, when we speak of the moral law, we already find ourselves within the ambit of the eternal archetypal space, in the center of which stands the personal God. It is the same thing if we believe in a truth which is unconditionally valid for all mankind. . . Any postulate from which we may set out is already a bridgehead which we have won in the suprapolar space. A postulate consists in our advancing from one point which we have already secured within the eternal space of God and taking

76. Ibid., p. 236.
77. Ibid.
78. Ibid.
79. Ibid., p. 237.
80. Ibid.
81. Ibid.

possession of everything else which this space comprises. But all that we have done thereby is to render ourselves clearly conscious of that which was vouchsafed to us from the beginning by virtue of the disclosure of this space.

From this it follows that we have no means at our disposal of breaking open the endless prison of the polar space and gaining entrance to the suprapolar space.[82]

"For anyone who has access only to the polar space" any such thing as a knowledge of suprapolar space "appears totally inconceivable. For him it is quite incomprehensible that such a thing should even be possible."[83]

Yet it is "this knowledge, the very possibility of which stands or falls with the existence of a suprapolar space without which it is unthinkable" that we need in order to understand what the Bible means by faith.[84]

Faith in God is to live in the realm of eternal space. From the vantage point of this eternal space the believer has a new "overall view of the world."[85] This new overall view of the world is radically different from that of the secularist. There is even a conflict between the two: "The conflict between these two conceptions, from which there always also result two contrary views of nature, is the deepest root of all the tensions in which we live, including all the ideological struggles which affect even political and economic life. . . This conflict is the underlying feature of the world-form in which we are now living."[86]

We have now found, argues Heim, the true insight into the "riddle of life."[87] As free men we live in suprapolar space. And in suprapolar space "God is present for us." This supra-space is, to be sure, "not the reality of God itself."

> This ultimate reality remains that which is 'wholly other,' totally incomprehensible and entirely inaccessible to our thought and observation. It confronts us neither as an object, in the way in which solid objects are disclosed to us, nor as a Thou, in the sense in which the I and the Thou confront one another in polar space. When we speak of the suprapolar space, we cannot be referring to the eternal reality of God itself, but only

---

82. Ibid., pp. 238, 239.
83. Ibid., p. 239.
84. Ibid.
85. Ibid., p. 247.
86. Ibid.
87. Karl Heim, *The Transformation of the Scientific World View* (London: S. C. M. Press, 1953), p. 200–258.

to one aspect, a side which is turned toward us, the only side from which God can be accessible to us, to you and me, if He is willing to disclose himself to us at all.[88]

It is only by thinking of God as "totally incomprehensible and entirely unaccessible to our thought and observation" that we can, according to Heim, escape the "peril with which our religious life is threatened" in the idea of the *analogia entis*.[89] The *analogia entis* idea is, as is well known, an expression used to indicate the Roman Catholic idea of natural theology. Natural theology starts *von unten*,[90] and seeks by logical implication from the world, space and time, to prove the necessary existence of God. But, together with other modern Protestant theologians, Heim argues that any God obtained by such reasoning is finally no more absolute than they who manufacture him.[91]

To reach God at all we must first realize we can never reach him if we merely reach out toward him from where we are without him. If we merely reach out for him by means of logic, we must, with Kant, say that God is one, but one as an abstract logical principle which swallows up our individual existence. But we have already discovered in the awareness of ourselves as individuals that "logic is incomprehensibly refuted by the reality of our existence."[92] "The word 'ego' can only be used in the singular; for otherwise it loses its non-objective character and becomes an object possessing number like other objects. And yet we are forced to use the word 'ego' in the plural! We are so accustomed to this paradoxical situation that in every day life we are already scarcely aware of the contradiction which it involves. We notice it all the more clearly in all the crises of human intercourse."[93]

D. DEMYTHOLOGIZATION AGAIN

We see then that Heim obtains to a position "'on this side of' the whole range of scientific research" by the following steps:

---

88. Karl Heim, *Christian Faith and Natural Science*, pp. 163–164.
89. Ibid., p. 163.
90. KSO: "from below." The natural theology of Romanism moves from the empirical to a god who is posited as the first cause.
91. KSO: The *analogia entis* is a teaching of Thomism. It presupposes the "scale of being" to which Van Til has already referred. Heim's critique that such a god "from below" and according to the *analogia entis* is not absolute is correct. He is the "highest" on the scale of being, but is, nevertheless, an aspect of that scale.
92. Ibid., p. 52.
93. Ibid., p. 53.

1. There is first our direct experience of the non-objectivisable ego. In this ego we have "'a point outside,'. . . which is placed from the outset beyond the range of scientific explanation because it precedes it. . ." With the experience of this non-objectivisable ego we, at the same time, experience an absolute victory over naturalism and secularism. For it is at once obvious, it is self-evident, that it is because of the fact that we experience ourselves as "outside" of the correlativities of nature that the idea of nature has meaning for us. Without the pre-supposition of the non-objectivisable ego science would be chaos. Now "I can face 'the measureless cosmos at the very thought of which my sense-bound soul trembles' and cry: 'It is you who change, not I; all your metamorphoses are no more than a stageplay; I shall forever soar unscathed above the wreckage of your puppets.'"[94]

But have we perhaps proved too much? We rejoiced in the discovery of the non-objectivisable ego because now we no longer needed to fear the loss of our identity in the relativities of the world of "objects." Are we now to lose our identity by being swallowed up into the Absolute? Does not the very claim I make for escape from the morass of relativism depend upon my being essentially identical with the "absolute ego" of idealist philosophy?[95]

2. The solution lies, for Heim, in going on beyond Idealism to the recognition of the fact now observed by existentialism that "'Existence (*Dasein*) is also essentially coexistence (*Mittsein*)' or, as Jaspers says, 'I exist only in communication with another.'"[96] Thus "the basis upon which we can take our stand has become firmer."[97] For on the idealist position "encounters between persons belonged to the world of objects and so to the field of scientific investigation. . ." Idealism "had not yet remarked the paradoxical state of affairs which confronts us on every encounter with the Thou."[98] We now see that our person-to-person confrontation takes place in the realm of the non-objectivisable.[99]

3. One final step remains for Heim. A new fear for the loss of our identity arises. When with the existentialism of such men as Heidegger and Jaspers we insist that I as a non-objectivisable ego exist only in communication with other non-objectivisable egos, I can make no sense of this communication at all. For each of us, as non-objectivisable egos, is bound to his own body. And "by being bound, once and for all, to this one body, I am irrevocably shut out from all

---

94. Ibid., p. 50.
95. Ibid.
96. Ibid., p. 52.
97. Ibid., p. 54.
98. Ibid.
99. Ibid., p. 56.

others. The interior of these others remains hidden from me. I am like a prisoner sentenced for life to solitary confinement in a single cell within a vast prison of cells."[100] What is the answer? The answer lies, says Heim, in returning to or retaining the idealist argument to the effect that the "transcendental ego. . . exists only in the singular, since it is agreed that only objects have number."[101]

If then we are really to escape the secularist claim "that grass will grow over us all" at last we need the "hypothesis" that "there is an omnipresent 'Thou'. . . before whose eyes all the hidden background of existence stands exposed. All the cards we are playing are on the table before him. All that goes on within us is open before him like a book. He alone has no need to deduce from outward appearances, as we must, what moves us from within. This and this alone can mean the end of my solitude. For only in this case is there one to whose sight the prison walls which divide us are transparent. He looks down from above into every cell simultaneously."[102] And herewith the hopeless struggle between individual egos, each, of necessity, seeking the center of the stage in all cosmic happening, is overcome. In God "we are all understood."

We now have personal encounter with God. With Fichte we see that concentrating "solely on ourselves" is, at the same time, to concentrate on God.[103] "I can base my whole life on faith in the one who has put me here."[104] Secondly, we now have personal encounter with one another. As all of us are understood by God, we all understand each other in him. Thirdly, we can now even have at least potential personal encounter with the secularist. I can show him that all modern scientific investigation points toward the idea of an "entelechy" that is back of all temporal and spatial succession. The whole of scientific development points beyond the absoluteness of the object, the absoluteness of objective time and space and the absoluteness of causal relations to a vision of the fact that "the process of nature in its deepest essence is not a dead mechanism whose course is laid down in fixed terms, but that it is something which in some sense is alive; something which man may influence by the interposition of the will in the same way in which he can affect a human opponent."[105]

Thus we find that "we are inexorably driven by the principle of continuity,"[106] to the idea of "a non-objective reference point for self-defense and self-regulation

---

100. Karl Heim, *The Transformation of the Scientific World View*, p. 247.
101. Karl Heim, *Christian Faith and Natural Science*, p. 52.
102. Karl Heim, *The Transformation of the Scientific World View*, p. 248.
103. Ibid., p. 247.
104. Ibid.
105. Ibid., p. 174.
106. Ibid., p. 240.

which we observe in wholeness, though in a different form from anything which is available in human experience."[107]

With the help of this notion of a God who is wholly other than anything discovered by human experience and is, at the same time, the everywhere present principle of continuity within all finite reality, animate and inanimate, those who are religious can speak to those who are secularists without seeming to be fantastic in what they say. "A concept has been found which bridges the gulf that gapes between the polar and the suprapolar zones. This is the concept of space, which is here applied to the suprapolar realm but is at the same time one of the fundamental concepts with which modern physics works."[108]

Heim's conception of God as wholly other than nature and at the same time omnipresent in nature aims to harmonize the biblical point of view with that of the latest scientist. Now that we think of the processes of nature as not absolutely determined but as having "a structure which is reminiscent of vital processes,"[109] we can accept the biblical account of the miraculous. We can now understand how Jesus could drive out demons. We may start from the lowest rung of the ladder of existence and climb up to the highest and always we shall meet the whole mysterious.[110] *Omnia abeunt in mysterium*. Miracle confronts us everywhere. The "inner structure of every act of will" is miraculous.[111] Realizing this everywhere present character of the utterly mysterious, we sense the fact that the causal relations of which science speaks and the scriptural stories of miracles do not exclude but rather support one another.[112]

Basic to all, however, we can with our concept of the mysterious universe show men that it is reasonable to call Jesus 'Lord.'[113] We accept the authority of Christ on his own word. We do not need to prove that Christ possesses authority.

---

107. Ibid., p. 241.
108. Karl Heim, *Christian Faith and Natural Science*, p. 162.
109. Karl Heim, *The Transformation of the Scientific World View*, p. 173.
110. Ibid., p. 175.
111. Ibid., p. 177.
112. KSO: Van Til has been attempting to show the "dimensionalism" present in Heim's thought as Heim tries to relate Christianity to science. The relationship, whether focused on the "nonobjectivisable" ego, or in the "suprapolar," is akin to Kant's phenomenal/noumenal relationship. The domain of science is knowledge; the domain of religion is faith. As long as each stay in their proper place they can "support" one another.
113. KSO: Heim's Kantian dimensionalism is explicit just after this quote from Van Til on Christ's Lordship, "From the standpoint of the polar space this experience is totally incomprehensible. For it is the reverse of the convulsive effort by which positivism is constrained to posit its supreme value and to hold fast to it. It is comprehensible only if there is a suprapolar space within which reality as a whole, which in the polar space resolves itself into a number of interminable series, is viewed synoptically in a higher order as a unity." Karl Heim, *Christian Faith and Natural Science*, p. 192.

A CHRISTIAN THEORY *of* KNOWLEDGE

To prove the authority of Christ would be to appeal to a criterion beyond himself. "But if any such criterion were found, then Christ would no longer be the *Kyrios*, the supreme authority."[114]

・――・

Looking back we see that in Heim's position we have a very carefully articulated view of reality as a whole. Heim's position interrelates with utmost care the basic principles of recent science, of existentialist philosophy and of dialectical theology. What interests us now is that the dilemma between an abstract rationalism and an equally abstract irrationalism spoken of earlier appears in striking fashion in the synthesis of thought offered us by Heim.

This dilemma appears in what Heim affirms with respect to the non-objectifiable ego. The plurality of the world of nature, Heim's world of the *I-It dimension*, depends for its unification upon this non-objectifiable ego. But to serve as the principle of unification of the I-It dimension this non-objectifiable ego must as Fichte, following Kant, made abundantly clear, be *one*. As *one* this non-objectifiable ego answers perfectly to the eternal changeless principle of Parmenides. That is to say, the assumption of Parmenides is that the presupposition of all logical analysis is the free or autonomous human self. On this assumption logic must devour its master. If the existence of the individual self is to be logically related to reality as a whole, then this reality reveals itself as being an abstract unity that allows for no plurality at all.

The 'God' of Heim thus makes a plurality of non-objectifiable egos impossible. But with the disappearance of the *individual* non-objectifiable ego and existence of the *plurality* of such egos, goes the disappearance of the plurality and temporality of the I-It dimension. The I-It dimension depends upon the I-Thou dimension and the I-Thou dimension depends upon 'God' as an abstract unitary principle.

Thus we see that Heim's "principle of continuity" leads to the destruction of the significance of all history. According to this principle, history is conceived of in purely determinist lines.[115]

But Heim supplements his "principle of continuity" with his principle of discontinuity. His principle of discontinuity is that of pure contingency or pure irrationalism. This, too, appears in what he says about the non-objectifiable ego. He says that it is absolutely against the demands of logic that this ego exists in

---

114. Karl Heim, *Christian Faith and Natural Science*, p. 191.
115. KSO: "Determinist lines," because the principle of continuity, as a rationalist principle, is the law-like principle of the natural. No freedom can be admitted into the "course of nature" because such freedom would introduce discontinuity. For more on this, see the foreword.

plural form. The individual non-objectifiable ego cannot say anything about itself except it do so in terms of pure relativity and solipsism. Each individual non-objectifiable ego is bound to an individual body in the world of the I-It dimension. This casts them into pure contingency. It is impossible for two such non-objectifiable egos to converse with one another. Neither of them can know himself, for he must be both on the way upward to absorption into abstract unity and on the way downward into abstract diversity. How then can they converse with one another? They live at the same time in the world of utter diversity and in the world of blank identity.

Finally, when Heim says that these non-objectifiable egos, living in utter isolation from one another are understood by God, this is assumed to be true because in God the principle of pure identity and of pure differentiation is the same as that of the I-It and the I-Thou dimension. On the one hand, the God of Heim is wholly other than the I-It and the I-Thou dimension while on the other hand this God is wholly identical with both. God is, in short, wholly what man's abstract logic demands and at the same time the wholly opposite of what this logic demands. God is the inward principle of identity and diversity of which the world is the outward expression.

We turn now, at the conclusion of this chapter, to the question of the duty of evangelical Christians with respect to this situation. By evangelical Christians we refer to such Christians as believe that in the Christ of the Old and New Testaments the answer to the modern dilemma is found. This Christ is the Christ of the creeds of the early and of the Reformation church.

If the evangelical Christian is to seize his opportunity and do his duty with respect to the dilemma of modern thought, he must, by all means, understand its implications for the historic Christian Faith. He must realize that the modern theologian, the modern philosopher and the modern scientist are agreed on the necessity of demythologization. Every major teaching of the evangelical faith is openly or covertly, expressly or by implication, demythologized. Then, secondly, the existential or dialectical interpretation of man and his environment may or may not use biblical terminology but in either case it is hostile to the historic Christian Faith. Then, thirdly, having noted the destructive character of modern thought, the evangelical Christian must plead with men to forsake it, and to return to the faith of Augustine, of Luther and of Calvin lest they be crushed between the upper and nether millstones of abstract rationalism and abstract irrationalism. A word must now be said about each of these three points.

The evangelical Christian should note that the faith he has accepted on the assumption that God has clearly revealed himself in nature and in Scripture is, in effect, if not openly, said to align him with the Flatlanders who wander about in the mazes of polar space. In spite of the light of supra-polar space, and therewith of the I-Thou dimension, evangelical Christians still reduce the revelation of God to something that is directly ascertainable in the I-It dimension of life. Evangelical Christianity or fundamentalism, as it is usually called, has no eye for the 'mysterious' nature of the universe. It has no eye for the fact that as God is the wholly other of whom nothing can be said by way of analogy, so man in his freedom is also the wholly other in relation to nature, and so nature itself is also wholly mysterious. In short, fundamentalism has no proper principle of discontinuity. This explains what might otherwise appear to be strange, namely, that the fundamentalist is found to be in alliance with rationalism in theology, determinism in philosophy and naturalism in science. If we are to have a purified Christianity, we must, argues the modern Christian, seek to persuade the fundamentalist to see the suprapolar dimension. Of course, we know that the vision of the suprapolar dimension has fallen as a gift into our laps.

We know that we ourselves did not see the true nature of the sovereignty of God's grace in Christ toward us until it had already enveloped us. But now that we have seen the light, we see, too, that we have in reality always been surrounded by it. We realize, when we saw ourselves as non-objectifiable with the help of the existentialist philosopher and the modern physicist, that even the men of the New Testament and, in particular, Jesus, already had this point of view. In fact we realize that the whole ladder of animate existence, from the molecule to the angel can, in no sense, be seen for what it is except we presuppose that which is wholly beyond understanding, namely, that there is vitality or soul behind and in it all. This gives us courage to hope that although analogically we can say *nothing* for the idea of the pure contingency in science, the idea of the non-objectifiable self in philosophy and the idea of the wholly unknowable God in theology, yet the Flatlander fundamentalist or naturalist may yet see what we now see. After all, if only we, like Socrates of old, bring out into the open what is within man but still hidden to him then all will be well. Has not Karl Barth, for all his stress on the wholly other God, also emphasized that to be man at all, man must be man in Christ?

If we thus press upon our fundamentalist and naturalist friends the utter necessity of adopting (a) our conception of the non-objectifiable self, (b) our principle of discontinuity and (c) our principle of continuity, then they may yet see the spiritual dimension of reality.

E. PEACE ON EARTH

When then the fundamentalist and the naturalist are lifted with us into the suprapolar dimension, they will, without further consideration, give up all their past quarrels, whether in science, in philosophy or in theology. All these quarrels were carried forth on the assumption that absolute truth or falsehood could be established in the I-It dimension. In particular, the fundamentalist thought that men who did not hold the same views that he held about certain supposed "facts" in the I-It dimension must be excluded from fellowship with Christ. The benighted bigotry by which men were divided into two classes, the elect and the reprobate, the saved and the lost, was carried on by well-meaning but self-deceived men in terms of a God and a Christ who was thought to be known directly in the I-It dimension. Even the creeds of Protestantism, and in particular the Westminster Confession of Faith, centered all their teachings in a Christ who is to be directly identified with the man Jesus of Nazareth.

Imagine the joy when the fundamentalists and the naturalists in philosophy, as well as the "positivists," find that the true Christ is the Christ of the suprapolar dimension, and that communion in and with him between all men takes place in the Eternal Now in which all men live. Then will the fundamentalists weep for all the exclusiveness with which they have treated their brethren in Christ. But their weeping will soon be turned to joy when they fully realize that they, and all men with them, are one in Christ. When they have received the "new birth" and true faith, the fundamentalists will, with us and with all men of every nation and kindred and tribe, sit at the marriage supper of the Lamb who was slain before the foundation of the world.

Meanwhile, the evangelical Christian will, if he has been truly critical, see that the Christ of modern non-objectifiable man is a snare and a delusion. He who seeks to interpret himself and his environment in terms of this Christ has no intelligible view either of man or of his environment. The man who has constructed this Christ and has reconstructed himself and his world by the help of this Christ, has therewith destroyed the intelligibility of science, of philosophy and of theology. In seeking in the non-objectifiable self the presupposition on the basis of which human experience is to be made intelligible, modern man condemns himself to absolute and perpetual meaninglessness. He cannot, while yet he must, find himself in relation to the relativities of his I-It dimension. When, recognizing this, he projects his God and his Christ into the realm of the wholly unknown so that this Christ may help him, he soon discovers that this Christ, too, must be wholly relative in order to be wholly absolute. Thus whatever non-objectifiable man may do it is always like a running off into opposite directions simultaneously. He can prove nothing to be either wrong or right. In his discussions with the fundamentalist, he may first insist that nobody knows or can know a Christ who can be identified with any human being found in the I-It dimension. Having stated this he cannot with meaning say: "But you are wrong and I am right." When the modern man says: "Science has proved," or "We now know," the evangelical Christian knows that such statements are made on the assumption that man, and especially modern man, understands himself. Yet modern man cannot offer an intelligible interpretation of himself. He may seek to demythologize the historic Christian faith but he has to attempt doing this by means of the myth of the non-objectifiable self.

F. TRADITIONAL APOLOGETICS

The real struggle for the soul of man and with it for the intelligibility of science, philosophy and theology can be seen for what it is only if the two totality views of man and his environment, the one represented by historic Protestant thinking and the other by modern dimensionalism are set squarely over against one another. There can be nothing but a head-on collision between these two totality views. If men are to be won to Christ, they must learn to see that in him alone is there significance in life at any point. They must therefore, at the same time, see that the Christ-construct of modern man is the product of man who has, in and since Adam, declared himself independent of God and has actually demonstrated to the world the fatal folly of his choice against God and his Christ.

The Reformers and, especially Calvin, following the Apostle Paul, based their interpretation of life in its totality on the teaching of the Christ of the gospels, who said that he was the Son of the Living God. Heim is formally quite right when he says that he who appeals to a criterion beyond the Christ in order to establish the truth or falsity of the claims of Christ to the effect that he spoke with absolute authority, has already denied the Christ. But Heim, and the average modern theologian with him, has done just that which he says we must never do. In the name of the non-objectifiable man, supposedly already living in the Eternal Now, Heim has excluded the possibility of ever knowing Christ or of ever having any help from anything that he did on the cross or through his resurrection for sinful men.

By way of complete contrast to this position of Heim we consider that of Calvin. The whole of Calvin's theology is based on the scriptural teaching to the effect that man can never know himself or his world unless he, from the outset, sees himself and his world created by God and redeemed by Christ.

Christ identifies himself as the one through whom all things of the I-It dimension are created and by whom they consist and are brought to their consummation.[116] Christ identifies himself as the one who, though he knew no sin, became sin for men that they might have everlasting life and not remain under

---

116. KSO: This is an example of Van Til using modern theology's language (the "I-it dimension") to persuade modern theologians of the truth of orthodox Christianity. Van Til does not mean, by using this language, that there is legitimacy to modern theology's use of such dimensionalism.

the wrath of God. They who through the regenerating power of the Holy Spirit have confessed their sin have received life from the dead. They have therewith been given that unity between their scientific, their philosophic and their theological enterprise without which human experience has no coherence at all.

In particular the critical evangelical has denounced for himself the futile and fatal autonomy involved in the ideal of the non-objectifiable man. In doing this he has at the same time denounced for himself the futile and fatal principle of discontinuity by which man and his world are from the beginning cut off from the unity that can alone be found in the creating-redeeming Christ of the Scriptures. Finally in doing this he has, at the same time, also denounced for himself the futile and fatal principle of continuity by which man, as soon as he speaks of himself, is lost in the abstract principle of rationality in terms of which he tries to speak.

The recent developments in theology, philosophy and science, such as dialectical theology, existential philosophy and logical analysis have shown the evangelical believer more clearly than ever before that the battle is between *two mutually exclusive totality views of life*. In the past evangelical apologists may not have seen this fact, but now there is little excuse for them not seeing it. It is clear now that if, in the interest of a point of contact with the non-believer, Christian apologists start with the "soul" in order then "by the bridge of cause" to prove the existence of God and after that the possibility, the probability and factuality of the revelation of God as found in the Christ of the Scriptures, then they are defeating themselves. He who begins his argument for the truth of Christianity from the "reality" of the "soul's" existence after the fashion of Descartes will immediately be told that this is the position of the "old metaphysic" and that no one can believe any such thing any more. "What do you mean" by the "soul" anyway? To say *that* the soul exists is meaningless unless you tell us *what* you mean by the soul. When you undertake to tell us *what* you mean by the soul you, of necessity, employ concepts that are valid only within the I-It dimension. We appreciate, of course, the fact that you too want to defend the suprapolar dimension. But, if you really want to defend the existence of the "soul" over against materialism and naturalism, you will have to follow with us in the train of the great Kant and his modern followers and speak of the non-objectifiable ego. If this is what you mean when you speak of "an active *ego* or *soul* behind the activities of the brain,"[117] then you mean essentially the same thing that Karl Heim and many other recent thinkers also believe. Then you will stand with us in the vanguard of the defenders of dimension of spiritual values.

---

117. Floyd E. Hamilton, *The Basis of Christian Faith*, Fourth Edition (New York: Harper & Row, 1964), p. 5.

Further, when you say that the soul is "an active agent, not a passive substance" and that "here we have *reality*,"[118] so we again agree. Here, in fact, we have our ultimate staring point. Again Kant has shown us that unless we presuppose the free creative self as that without which space-time experience is unintelligible all science and philosophy and theology is meaningless.

Still further, if starting from the "soul" you give "reasons why we must believe in God,"[119] we again agree. Have we not just heard from Heim that Kant is logically quite right in saying that the possibility of any intelligible interpretation of the I-It dimension presupposes that there is *One* non-objectifiable ego?

Finally, we are sure that you will want to go further with us as, following the existentialists, we assert that there are many souls or egos. Even if logically there *must* be one ego, our experience of reality teaches us that there are many and that there may be an infinite number of egos.

It is thus that the unwary evangelical, yielding the claim to the validity of the principles of continuity and discontinuity of the would-be independent or autonomous man is led ever more deeply into a position that is utterly destructive of the position that he is so earnestly trying to defend.[120]

We have quoted from the Reverend Floyd E. Hamilton's book on *The Basis of Christian Faith*. Himself a Calvinist, he wants his readers to adopt with him the view of Christianity set forth in the historic Reformed Confessions. Yet, by starting with the fact of the soul's existence without, after the example of Calvin, and by saying that man is what he is in the configuration of the creation, the fall and the redemption of the world through the self-identifying Christ of the Scripture, Hamilton gives himself over to the tender mercies of those who hold that man is not a creature made in the image of God, is not a sinner who has broken the law of God and cannot be redeemed by anything that happens in the "objective," the I-It, dimension.

Hamilton appeals for support of his position to a work on *The Resurrection of Theism*, written by Stuart Cornelius Hackett.[121] [122] But Hackett adopts the starting

---

118. Ibid.
119. Ibid., pp. 35 ff.
120. KSO: These previous paragraphs illustrate the evangelical apologist agreeing with the dimensionalist in order, eventually, to introduce the truth of theism. Van Til is arguing that such initial agreement concedes the Christian point at the outset.
121. S. C. Hackett, *The Resurrection of Theism* (Chicago: Moody Press, 1957).
122. KSO: Stuart C. Hackett (1925–2012) "taught philosophy of religion at Western Conservative Baptist Seminary in Portland, OR, then Denver Conservative Baptist Seminary in Denver, CO, then Louisiana College in Pineville, LA, then Wheaton College, Wheaton, IL and finally Trinity International University in Deerfield, IL. He authored several books on philosophy," http://a2z.my.wheaton.edu/faculty/stuart-hackett. Dr. Hackett was an Arminian theologian who was critical of Van Til's view because it required Reformed theology. *The Resurrection of Theism* was published

point of human autonomy because as an Arminian he is strongly opposed to the "determinism" that he finds in the Calvinistic view of life.[123] Hackett argues for the "free" self in precisely the same way that the modern non-evangelical thinker today argues for the free self. Hackett assumes that if man were thought of from the outset as operating within the configuration of biblical truth, then the "philosopher's ass" must first have eaten one of the two bales of hay before him, unless he had already eaten it. Hackett does not see that his "ass" would be blind, and both bales of hay beyond his reach.[124] The only alternative to the biblical idea of human freedom as operating within the concrete situation of the creative-redemptive work of Christ is the idea of man as free in a vacuum. It is no wonder that in adopting modern man's view of the human self as the non-objectifiable ego, Hackett, with it, also adopts the modern view of an abstract principle of rationality as a criterion of meaning for man,[125] and the modern view of an abstract principle of discontinuity. Hackett has no argument against the position of modern thinking as this displays itself in perpetual motion between absorption of man by absolute determinism and absolute indeterminism alike.

But unavoidable as such an approach as that of Hackett may be for him as an Arminian, it is a matter of regret for one who loves the gospel of the sovereign grace of God in Christ, as does Hamilton, to fall back on Hackett for help thereby cutting himself loose from all intelligible speech about himself in the interest of a point of contact with the unbeliever.

It would have been better if he, together with other Reformed thinkers such as Herman Dooyeweerd, had demonstrated that the human self, logic and fact can never be brought into intelligible relation with one another unless they are, from the outset, taken as standing in that relation with one another as is portrayed in Scripture. To do this is to do what the Apostle Paul did when he said: "Where is the wise? where is the scribe? where is the disputer of this world? hath not God made foolish the wisdom of this world? For after that in the wisdom of God the world by wisdom knew not God, it pleased God by the foolishness of preaching to save them that believe" 1 Cor 1:20, 21).

---

in 1957, then republished, with a foreword by Vernon Grounds, in 2003. For an informative review of Hackett's book, see Review: Stuart Cornelius Hackett: *The Resurrection of Theism*. Chicago: Moody Press, 1957. *Westminster Theological Journal*, XXII (November, 1959), 49–52. It should be noted that any and all Arminian approaches will, by definition, object to a Reformed approach to apologetics.

123. Ibid., p. 174.

124. KSO: Van Til is referring here to John Buridan (1300–1358) and his tale of the donkey. The donkey is between two bales of hay. Since, according to some notions of free will, the donkey lacks any cause whatsoever to choose, he starves to death. This is a critique of a "causeless" notion of free will.

125. Ibid., pp. 59 ff.

XII

THE DILEMMA OF MODERN THEOLOGY[1]

We turn now to a more specific discussion of the dilemma that is found in recent theology. In doing so we shall deal with theologians that come after such men as Bultmann, Barth and Tillich.

A. A NEW QUEST OF THE HISTORICAL JESUS

It is natural that we should, in this connection, first take up the question as to what current theology does with Jesus. Jesus stands at the heart of the gospel which any Christian theology claims to bring to men for their help. It is through their faith in Jesus that theologians would go beyond philosophy. We have seen that Bultmann thinks of existential philosophy as not able to give man the answer that he needs to his deepest question. After all, it is only through revelation that men are given light from above, and this light from above shines among men in Jesus of Nazareth.

But what can be known of Jesus of Nazareth? Surely so far as any one ever saw or heard anything of him this took place in the I-It dimension. But we cannot directly meet any man there. We must therefore meet Jesus in the I-Thou dimension. But if he is living in the I-Thou dimension, Jesus lives in the prison cell of his own isolation. How then could he possibly give us any help? As one non-objectifiable self among millions of others, he could not know himself unless he, with all other men, were taken into and lost in an abstract principle of unity made after the pattern offered by Parmenides. In other words, the relation of Jesus to other men must, for existential theology, be explained by means of the

---

1. KSO: In this chapter, Van Til attempts to summarize the influence of philosophy on modern theology, including Bultmann and others. His assessment of modern theology will conclude that, whether in Bultmann, Barth, Ogden, or Ott, the "dilemma" will be a dialectical affirmation of an "abstract, changeless unity" and "abstract change." Put simply, Van Til's argument will show that when theology abandons orthodoxy, with its fundamental premise of the ontological Trinity, it will never be able to identify who we are as human beings, and what the world is as God's creation. Through all of the twists and turns in this chapter, that point should be kept in the forefront.

principle of continuity and discontinuity that at once explains and explains away the difference between him and other men.

How then shall we discover Jesus Christ as the Savior of men? If the older liberal theology was not able to discover him and if Bultmann and his generation were not really able to discover him, how shall we, of the younger generation, proceed to look for him? We shall ask for information on this point from James M. Robinson.[2] Robinson has published a very enlightening book dealing with the post-Bultmann period in theology. The title of his book is *A New Quest of the Historical Jesus*.[3]

In renewing our quest for the historical Jesus, argues Robinson, it would be nothing short of Quixotic to return to the historic orthodox method of approach. Orthodoxy cannot even be improved. On the other hand there is today no need to worry about such efforts as were made in the past by men like Arthur Drews or P. L. Couchod.[4] No one cares today to deny the actual historic existence of Jesus.[5] We must therefore continue to walk in the way that the liberal theology of the previous century opened for us.

The liberal theologians sought to be genuinely anti-metaphysical. They would have nothing to do with the doctrines of orthodoxy that were based upon the old metaphysic. Even so the quest for the historical Jesus, as it was carried on in the previous century, failed to see that in all historical research the human self is involved. At least they failed to see this fact in its full significance. They were looking for "Jesus of Nazareth as he actually was." But for them this Jesus as he actually was tended to coincide with "the reconstruction of his biography by means of the objective historical method" of their day.[6]

But now in the twentieth century "we have come to recognize that the objective factual level upon which the nineteenth century operated is only one dimension of history, and that a whole new dimension in the facts, a deeper and more central plane of meaning, had been largely by-passed. . . The dimension

---

2. KSO: James M. Robinson (1924–2016) was a New Testament scholar. "It fell to. . .James M. Robinson to coin the slogan 'A New Quest of the Historical Jesus' and thereby to create something of a myth (in the popular sense of the term). Robinson argued that there could be no going back on the conclusions of Bultmann, and that no methods to rescue something from the wreck could work. Nevertheless, he saw the possibility of progress in a new kind of historical approach which would interrogate the gospels to find out something about the 'selfhood' of Jesus through determining his understanding of his existence." Sinclair B. Ferguson and J.I. Packer, *New Dictionary of Theology* (Downers Grove, IL: InterVarsity Press, 2000), 305.

3. J. M. Robinson, *A New Quest for the Historical Jesus* (London: S. C. M. Press, 1959).

4. KSO: C. H. Arthur Drews (1865–1935) was a German philosopher who opposed the historicity of Jesus. Paul-Louis Couchoud (1879–1959) was a French philosopher who wrote various books and articles on the historicity of Jesus.

5. Ibid., p. 88.

6. Ibid., p. 28.

in which man actually exists, his 'world,' the stance or outlook from which he acts, his understanding of his existence behind what he does, the way he meets his basic problems and the answer his life implies to the human dilemma, the significance he had as the environment of those who knew him, the continuing history his life produces, the possibility of existence which his life presents to me as an alternative—such matters as these have become central in an attempt to understand history. It is this deeper level of the reality of 'Jesus of Nazareth as he actually was' which was not reached by the reconstruction of his biography by means of objective historical method.'"[7]

There is therefore no escape from the verdict that the twentieth century theology must make about the first quest for the historical Jesus. That quest "ended in failure."[8] "'Historicism' is gone as the idealogical core of historiography, and with it is gone the centrality of the chronicle. 'Psychologism' is gone as the idealogical core of biography, and with it is gone the centrality of the *curriculum vitae*. Consequently the kind of history and biography attempted unsuccessfully for Jesus by the nineteenth century is now seen to be based upon a false understanding of the nature of history and the self. As a result it has become a *completely open question*, as to whether a kind of history or biography of Jesus, consistent with the contemporary view of history and human existence, is possible."[9]

Such men as Heidegger and R. G. Collingwood have, says Robinson, given us an "interpretation of history in terms of the historicity of the self."[10]

"History is," Robinson tells us, "the act of intention, the commitment, the meaning for the participants, behind the external occurrence."[11] "The first effect of the modern view of history and human existence upon New Testament study was . . . to focus attention upon the *kerygma* as the New Testament statement of Jesus' history and self-hood."[12] In the *kerygma* "God calls upon me to accept his judgment upon me in Jesus' death, and to live from his grace in Jesus' resurrection."[13] As such it is an "eschatological event," and therefore does not impose upon me the patterns with which it originally operated.[14]

Herewith we have in principle gone beyond every positivist view of history[15]

---

7. Ibid., pp. 28, 29.
8. Ibid., p. 66.
9. Ibid., pp. 66, 67.
10. Ibid., p. 71.
11. Ibid., p. 67.
12. Ibid., p. 69.
13. Ibid., p. 48.
14. Ibid., p. 49.
15. KSO: A "positivist" view of history is committed to historical *fact* as autonomously interpretable.

and beyond the temptation of identifying Jesus of Nazareth with some historically identifiable personality. We can, in short, get to an appreciation of the absolute uniqueness of Jesus in a way that was not open to the liberal theologian. We now see that the humiliation of Jesus does not for us need to be legitimized by any particular historical acts or sayings of Jesus.[16]

We no longer separate the steps in the humiliation of Jesus from those of his exaltation. These are always present together. Therein lies the paradoxical nature of the *kerygma*. The *kerygma* contains the whole story of Jesus beginning with his pre-existence and ending with his glorification. The whole of this story shines forth for us in history. Herewith the possibility of a new quest for the historical Jesus is opened to us. In seeking for the historical Jesus we no longer look for a reproducible *curriculum vitae*.[17] We look for history as "occurrence and event."[18] "Of such history the Gospels provide information which is more than abundant."[19] The sources that we have in the gospels "*do* make possible a new kind of quest working in terms of the modern view of history and the self."[20] The new quest for the historical Jesus fits in with modern "man's quest for meaningful existence."[21]

Using the philosophical analysis of the meaning of human life of such men as Heidegger, the New Quest carries the work of demythologizing further than has ever been done before. Bultmann and his followers have helped us to see that "in the process of demythologizing, the objectified language of the *kerygma* loses its own concreteness, and becomes, so to speak, transparent, so that its existential meaning may be grasped."[22] The all-important question then is: what is it which becomes apparent to us when we have demythologized the objective language of the gospel? "Does one encounter in the *kerygma* a symbolized principle, or interpreted history?"[23] In the first case we should fall back into an objective view of the *kerygma*. Or, with Fritz Buff, we should lose the *kerygma* altogether. Demythologizing would then force us into *dekerygmatizing*.

But surely the *kerygma* does not merely offer to us that which even philosophical analysis finds to be the possibility of authentic human existence. We must at all costs avoid the idea that the *kerygma* is identical with mysticism. We must therefore maintain that "what is encountered when the objectified language

---

16. Ibid., p. 51.
17. KSO: That is, a historical "life story."
18. Ibid., p. 71.
19. Ibid.
20. Ibid.
21. Ibid., p. 75.
22. Ibid., p. 80.
23. Ibid., p. 81.

of the *kerygma* becomes transparent is Jesus of Nazareth, as the act of God in which transcendence is made a possibility for human existence. The *kerygma* is not the objectification of a new, 'Christian' religious principle, but rather the objectification of a historical encounter with God."[24]

Herewith we have come to a full appreciation of the paradoxical nature of the *kerygma*. We no longer identify the *kerygma* with Jesus according to the flesh. Nor do we seek the *kerygma* by wiping out Jesus according to the flesh. We now see that no matter how mythological the *kerygma* presents itself in the New Testament it does not proclaim mythological ideas. What it does proclaim is the "existential meaningfulness of a historical person."[25] The "emphasis in the *kerygma* upon the historicity of Jesus is existentially indispensable, precisely because the *kerygma*, while freeing us from a life 'according to the flesh,' proclaims the meaningfulness of life 'in the flesh.'"[26] It is this "concern of the *kerygma* for the historicity of Jesus which necessitates a new quest."[27] Thus though the *kerygma* does not lie on "the level of objectively verifiable fact," it is "interested in historiography of the twentieth century kind, for the *kerygma* consists in the meaning of a certain historical event, and thus coincides with the goal of modern historiography."[28]

In what then does the new quest differ from the existential interpretation given by Bultmann? The answer that Robinson gives is, in effect, that we must go beyond Bultmann as Bultmann went beyond Heidegger.

The distinctiveness of the new quest lies precisely in the fact that it seeks to go more deeply even than did Bultmann both into the uniqueness and into the universality of Jesus as the Christ. "Contemporary methodology consists precisely in the combination and interaction of objective analysis and existential openness, i.e., it seeks historical understanding precisely in the simultaneous interaction of phenomenological objectivity and existential 'objectivity.'"[29]

We have, argues Robinson, in our new quest, applied fully the insight that has been afforded us by the distinctions made between the I-It and the I-Thou dimensions in human experience. It is only in the I-Thou dimension that I encounter Jesus. If one should say that then our encounter with Jesus is, in its nature, the same as our encounter with any other human being, then we answer, according to Robinson, that this is not the case because I "disengage the kerygmatic fragments from the New Testament before I can encounter them

---

24. Ibid., p. 84.
25. Ibid., p. 87.
26. Ibid., p. 88.
27. Ibid.
28. Ibid., p. 90.
29. Ibid., p. 96.

existentially."³⁰ Thus we are led into a "further dimension, in which historical encounter becomes revelation."³¹

It is thus that the new quest for the historical Jesus, on the one hand finds the *kerygma* in every historical detail of the life of Jesus and on the other hand does not directly identify the *kerygma* with any of those historical details. When the historiographical method requires us to put in suspension even the historicity of the claims of Jesus to the effect that he himself is the Son of Man then this does not trouble us in the least.³² "The material whose historicity *has* been established is sufficient in quality and quantity to make a historical encounter with Jesus possible. His action, the intention latent in it, the understanding of existence it implies, and thus his selfhood, can be encountered historically. And this can in turn be compared with the *kerygma*, once the meaning the *kerygma* conveys has begun to shine through the language in which it is communicated."³³

This must suffice to give some indication of the new quest of the historical Jesus in which theologians are today engaged. It appears that the new quest is an attempt to carry through more consistently than ever the modern distinction between the I-It and the I-Thou dimension of human experience. There is therefore nothing basically new about the new quest. So far as the new quest may be said to be new it is new in the sense that it seeks to apply the idea of the non-objectifiable ego even more consistently than such men as Bultmann did. Applying the idea of the non-objectifiable ego more consistently than it has been done by Bultmann and his generation implies that both the principle of discontinuity and the principle of continuity implied in that idea are applied more consistently than they were before. This means that the demythologizing process must be more relentlessly carried through than it was by even Bultmann. It means that the process of existential interpretation of the gospel must be effected more consistently than by such men as Bultmann.

Accordingly we find that the new quest, as Robinson outlines its effort, seeks in the first place to get absolute freedom with respect to the *ipsissima verba*³⁴ of the New Testament. There is absolutely nothing in what the New Testament records with respect to the life and work of Jesus that needs to be taken at face value. What needs to be done is to look for the inner meaning behind what the New Testament says. When Jesus says he is the Son of Man and the Son of God then we are not to take this as an authoritative statement by himself about himself. We are rather to take this as so much historical evidence, which we as

---

30. Ibid., p. 98.
31. Ibid.
32. Ibid., p. 99.
33. Ibid., p. 105.
34. KSO: The precise language of the New Testament.

THE DILEMMA OF MODERN THEOLOGY

historians, seeing all history in relation to our internally self-sufficient selves, may use. It is the historian himself who decides what is and what is not existentially significant. It is the historian himself who independently of the "objectivity" of the gospel narrative decides on the nature of the *kerygma*.

But to give this measure of independence to the historian in relation to the New Testament documents is (no matter how much Robinson rebels against the idea) to lead directly into pure mysticism. It is, in effect, to take away all distinction between Jesus and other men. Beyond that it is to take away the significance of all uniqueness in history. But this is where the principle of continuity that has been adopted by the non-objectifiable ego takes one. It is the same principle that Parmenides accepted in his day. It is the principle of pure rationalism and pure determinism.

But then just as we hear Robinson take away from Jesus all right to say anything about himself, we find that he nonetheless wants to retain contact with something that is historical in the ordinary sense of the term. Robinson divides the material found in the gospels into the *kerygmatic* and *non-kerygmatic*. We are no longer to make our appeal to the fact that Jesus himself proclaimed the *kerygma*.[35] We are rather to look into the "non-kerygmatical material." For the very objectivity of the method of our study now shows us that it is these materials which enable us to have an "historical encounter with Jesus."[36]

It is in this manner that Robinson would save us from mysticism, the pure mysticism toward which he has been leading us. But it is obvious that, if he is to succeed, he cannot, according to his own principle, escape going back of this history, too, in order to find the uniqueness of Jesus. So far as ordinary history is concerned Jesus is like every other man, a non-objectifiable ego bound by the fact of his bodily existence to a fate that all men have in common. Jesus as well as all other men is, because really human, *wholly* human, and if possible more deeply and *really* human than are other men. This means, on Robinson's principle of discontinuity, that Jesus is as deeply, and if possible, more deeply, hidden in the realm of non-being than are other men.

Here then the dilemma of modern theology appears in the clearest possible fashion. It is the same dilemma that we have spoken of in the preceding chapter. It is the dilemma which modern man faces when he starts his interpretation of himself and his work from himself as ultimate. He must, of necessity, simultaneously go off into the two opposite directions, the one of total absorption into featureless being, the other of absorption into featureless non-being. On this basis it is utterly impossible to find in Jesus anything that makes him different from

---

35. Ibid., p. 100.
36. Ibid., p. 105.

other men. All that Robinson actually says is that Jesus lives from transcendence. Well, so do all other men, of necessity, live from transcendence. They would not be non-objectifiable egos if they did not live in self-sufficient transcendence above the I-It dimension.[37]

The new quest for the historical Jesus has, therefore, if Robinson's picture of it is accurate, once more and more clearly than ever, shown that the wisdom of man has been made foolishness with God.

Moreover the new quest has shown more clearly than ever that the traditional method of apologetics is inadequate. If anything has come out of the new quest, it is the fact that the struggle between evangelical and non-evangelical or modern theologians is not a matter of this or that point. It is a matter of interpreting *every* fact from the outset either in terms of the self-attesting Christ or in terms of the self-attesting man. As noted earlier, it is meaningless or worse to start with the fact that the "soul" exists in order then by "the bridge of cause" to prove that *a* God exists. The question is as to *what* man is and *what* God is. Every man in effect gives his answer to this question in the first sentence he utters about himself. Simply to say *that* the "soul" exists is, in effect, already to say, that its nature, its *what*, is not what Scripture says it is but is, in effect, identical with the non-objectifiable ego of modern philosophy and theology. Only God in Christ can tell us what God is. Only God in Christ can tell us what man is. To look at man and his work without doing so in the light of the revelation that God through Christ gives in the Bible is to turn off the light of the sun and to ask *whether* a sun exists and to look for it with a flashlight whose light is a derivative from the sun. What the evangelical Christian must do is to show that he who does not look for the meaning of man in the light of the revelation that comes from Christ directly revealed in Scripture is like one who shakes off all the apples of the apple tree, grubs out the tree, and *then* asks *whether* there must not have been some sort of something that is higher than the apples in order to account for them. This "some sort of something" or at most some sort of tree may, possibly or probably, tell us that it is an apple tree.

B. CHRIST WITHOUT MYTH

The fact that current theologians who go beyond Bultmann cling to their hopeless dilemma as Linus does to his blanket is even more clearly evident in the

---

37. KSO: In other words, once the dimensionalism of Kant is adapted to theology, the "non-objectifiable ego," which is to say, the ego that transcends the historical dimension, becomes the proposed starting point for all theology. This will inevitably produce the dialectic of continuity, with its proposed unity of "featureless being," and discontinuity, which results in "featureless non-being."

work of Schubert Ogden than in that of Robinson. Ogden deals with essentially the same question: whether any unique significance can and must be attributed to Jesus by modern man who, by virtue of his manhood, already lives from transcendence.

Here is an existentialist philosophy such as we have in Heidegger's *Sein und Zeit*. It pretends to give us an all-comprehensive interpretation of human life. It is built on the idea of the free self. It shows man what he ought to do. Man ought, according to Heidegger, to live an authentic human existence, and man has, according to Heidegger, the resources for leading an authentic existence within himself. Says Ogden: "The rule here, of course, is the one stated by Kant: *Du kannst, denn du sollst. . .*"[38] [39]

Then comes Bultmann. He is a Christian theologian. He seeks to make the significance of the cross and resurrection of Jesus intelligibly significant to modern man. And modern man understands himself best in terms of an existential philosophy. If Bultmann is to bring the cross of Christ to men, he must make this cross intelligible to men in terms of their existential interpretation of themselves. Why should men feel the need of the cross of Christ? They have all they need without it. If Bultmann wants modern man to accept the cross and resurrection of Christ, he must assuredly *not* identify this cross and this resurrection with anything that took place in the past in Palestine. Absolutely nothing that has taken place in the objective, or the I-It dimension, can as such be taken as revelatory of a transcendence other than the transcendence that is of necessity involved in the idea of the non-objectifiable ego. The transcendence of the non-objectifiable ego *must* be taken as the source of the intelligibility of what can take place in the I-It dimension and for that very reason the transcendence of God must be excluded as making itself in any wise apparent in this I-It dimension. Bultmann knows that in presenting the cross and resurrection of Christ to men today he is bound to meet not only the objection of modern science, but, back of that, of "*modern man's understanding of himself.*"[40] "Modern man is confronted by a curious dilemma. He may regard himself as pure nature, or as pure spirit. In the latter case he distinguishes the essential part of his being from nature. In either case, however, *man is essentially a unity.* He bears the sole responsibility for his own feeling, thinking and willing. He is not, as the New Testament regards

---

38. Ibid., p. 118. See Schubert M. Ogden, *Christ Without Myth* (New York: Harper & Row, 1961).

39. KSO: "You can, because you should. . ." This refers to Kant's "categorical imperative" in ethics which he thought was an objective moral standard that we are obligated to follow, despite any contrary desires.

40. R. Bultmann, "New Testament and Mythology," *Kerygma and Myth—A Theological Debate*, Vol. I (London: S.P.C.K., 1957), p. 6.

him, the victim of a strange dichotomy which exposes him to the interference of powers outside himself. If his exterior behavior and his interior condition are in perfect harmony, it is something he has achieved himself, and if other people think their interior unity is torn asunder by demonic or divine interference, he calls it schizophrenia."[41] In short, modern man thinks of "human nature as a self-subsistent unity immune from the interference of supernatural powers."[42] Man is, in short, a non-objectifiable ego.

But there are a practically infinite number of finite non-objectifiable egos. And, as Heim has indicated, each one of these numberless egos must logically seek to posit itself as the source of all intelligence and action in the whole world. In other words, each finite self must, on the modern view of man, claim to do what, in the historic Christian creeds, God is said to do. If each self makes this claim and then speaks of this his claim to other selves who make the same claim for themselves, then there is Chaos and Old Night. Only if by some happy accident these numberless would-be omnipotent and omniscient selves meet in conclave and appoint a ruler over themselves does this warfare of every one against every one else have any hope of solution. But the king they then appoint will be a tyrant. He will offer to rule over them only if they first agree to have their eyes taken out and their hands cut off. If there is to be real unity, "he," or rather "it," says that there must be no others beside himself who have any knowledge or power that is not identifiable with his own. But finally, so long as this elected ruler *speaks*, "it" is still *merely one objectifiable ego, among at least other possible egos*, that speaks. Why then not an *infinite number of other egos*? If therefore the conclave of finite non-objectifiable egos really wants to pay the price for unity in the interest of communication, they might better follow the example of Socrates who demanded to see the nature of the holy regardless of what men or gods say about it. Only when they have done that do the isolated egos really have One who is wholly other and wholly above them. This God or this One is then up so high that he can look down into the individual prison cells of each of the finite non-objectifiable egos, except for the fact that he has then no thought of them nor any power to act with respect to them. He cannot as much as think of himself, since he is no self. Thus it appears that without this all-absorbing Moloch the infinite number of human selves live in utter isolation from each other. If they seek to communicate with one another, they must do so via the I-It dimension. They must build a "bridge of cause" in the I-It dimension across which they can walk in order to meet one another. But this bridge must first be built by these utterly isolated selves and each self must build his own bridge. There is no bridge

41. Ibid.
42. Ibid., p. 7.

already existing before they walk on it. To say that there is such a bridge before they walk on it would be sheer mythology. For who could then build such a bridge except a God whose existence the selves would first have to prove by way of this bridge which, without his existence, does not exist?

Now the younger theologians such as we are discussing know that in the theology of such men as Bultmann no answer has been found as to how Jesus can have any significance if, in order to bring him to modern man, this modern man has already interpreted him. So Ogden himself speaks of a consensus among recent theologians that Bultmann's proposal is intrinsically problematic. He even says that there is a consensus of opinion to the effect that "Bultmann's solution is inherently inadequate"[43] and "structurally inconsistent."[44]

As for Ogden himself he sums up Bultmann's internal inconsistency by saying: "Bultmann's theology in its present form is characterized by the *Problematik* that its ostensibly unlimited demand for demythologization and existential interpretation, which, as it rightly sees, is unavoidable, is in fact limited by its appeal to an event that is mythological and inexpressible in existential terms."[45]

What then is to be done? Are we as modern theologians to admit failure? Are we to look back and take into our theology the idea of the transcendent God as everywhere clearly revealed in the I-It dimension? Are we to think of man as the image of God? Are we to say that man has fallen into sin and that the effects of this fall are everywhere clearly apparent in the I-It dimension? Are we then to think that Jesus Christ the Son of God died for us in the I-It dimension and that by his Spirit we must be born again in the I-It dimension if we are to believe in him and come into his presence at the end of the history of the I-It dimension? Never! That is sheer mythology! No modern man who prizes his self-sufficient freedom will take back anything of this orthodox mythology!

When Ogden near the end of his book sets forth his constructive position he makes it as clear as mountain air that, whatever the structural weakness of Bultmann's theology, Bultmann was not mistaken when he made all his theology rest upon the non-objectifiable ego. Says Ogden: "*Christian faith is to be interpreted exhaustively and without remainder as man's original possibility of authentic existence as this is clarified and conceptualized by an appropriate philosophical analysis.*"

"This first thesis, which summarizes the essential *method* of our position, records once again our complete acceptance of Bultmann's demand for demythologization and existential interpretation."[46]

---

43. Ogden, *cit.*, p. 96.
44. Ibid., p. 99.
45. Ibid., p. 110.
46. Ibid., p. 146.

This is the first thesis of Ogden's proposed post liberal theology. The second, like it, follows in these words: "*Christian faith is always a 'possibility in fact' because of the unconditioned gift and demand of God's love, which is the ever-present ground and end of all created things; the decisive manifestation of this divine love, however, is the event Jesus of Nazareth, which fulfills and corrects all other manifestations and is the originative event of the church and its distinctive word and sacraments.*"[47]

Combining these two theses, Ogden argues, we are both building upon and going beyond Bultmann.[48] We must demythologize the New Testament even more thoroughly than Bultmann did. However man thinks of himself he cannot think of himself as "'open' to the seizure of alien and supernatural powers. He views himself, rather, as a unified being and attributes his experience, thought and volition to his own agency, not to divine or demonic causes. If, as a naturalist, he acknowledges himself in the highest degree dependent, he still does not look upon this dependence as a subjection to strange powers distinguishable from the orderly processes of nature. On the other hand, if he understands himself as 'spirit,' he is aware of his own freedom and responsibility, and even though he recognizes his conditioning by natural forces, he distinguishes his true being from them."[49]

With Bultmann, Ogden would, accordingly, look for the "true intention" of the New Testament, back of its mythological form. This is especially true of the Christ-occurrence. However mythologically this Christ-occurrence is presented in the New Testament, we understand that it is not really a "mythical event" at all.

The real purpose of the New Testament is "not simply to express the existential 'significance' (*Bedeutsamkeit*) of the historical figure of Jesus as the salvation-occurrence. This clearly seems to be so of the statements concerning pre-existence and virgin birth; for what they evidently intend to say when they present Jesus as having come from heaven or as having had a non-natural origin is that his 'significance' for faith is not exhausted by ordinary historical observation."[50]

Bultmann does not always have the courage of his convictions. He sometimes speaks as though the object of the Christian faith needs something in the I-It dimension as an objective foundation. But, if it did, how then could the gospel message be seen to be inherently for all men everywhere? It is therefore all-important, argues Ogden, that true objectivism be sought, not at any point in the I-It dimension, but totally beyond it.

The new and true objectivism which Ogden offers us is seen to correspond

---

47. Ibid., p. 153.
48. Ibid.
49. Ibid., pp. 35–36.
50. Ibid., p. 77.

perfectly with modern man's conception of human nature as a closed unity. The Christ of this new objectivism is not the dead Christ of a dead past. He is rather a power of transcendence that reaches out higher than the transcendence inherent in man's non-objectifiable existence.

"To be sure," says Ogden,

> the decisive manifestation of this divine word is none other than the *human word* of Jesus of Nazareth and thence of its own authentic proclamation. But the point of this claim is not that the Christ is manifest only in Jesus and nowhere else, but that the word *addressed to men everywhere*, in *all the events of their lives, is none other* than the word spoken in Jesus and in the preaching and sacraments of the church.
>
> One of the most pressing tasks of a post liberal theology is so to formulate the doctrine of revelation that *this* point is made its *controlling center*.[51]

Again: "Faith has nothing to gain and much to lose if it is not made unmistakably clear that no other word is spoken in Jesus than is everywhere spoken in the actual events of nature and history and specifically witnessed to with more or less adequacy by 'the law and the prophets.'"[52] It is this "'objective' reality of the revelatory event Jesus the Christ" that Bultmann fails to express adequately.[53]

It is thus by this new objectivism that special grace and common grace, special revelation and general revelation are harmonized. It is thus that the whole question of modern man's self-understanding through philosophy is not altered but deepened by theology.

Bultmann claims that *philosophy* can only speak of the *possibility of man's authentic existence* while *theology* may speak of its *actuality in the Christ-occurrence*. But now the Christ-occurrence is seen to include even the search of the philosopher. The possibility of authentic human existence presupposes its actuality, in principle, in all men everywhere. What is true of philosophy is also true of science. It, too, is seen finally to rest upon the Christ-occurrence.

Ogden is certain that his new "objectivism" carries forth the Reformation principle of *sola scriptura—sola gratia*.[54] Those who hold to the new objectivism freely choose Scripture to be their norm. For them salvation is the free gift of God: God is free to give it and man is free to receive it. The whole transaction between God and man, the whole Christ-occurrence, is no longer lettered to the

---

51. Ibid., p. 156 (Italic added).
52. Ibid.
53. Ibid., p. 158.
54. Ibid., p. 55.

mechanical and relativist relations of the I-It dimension. Bultmann speaks of the historic "doctrine of atonement" as "primitive mythology." Well, if Bultmann did not altogether succeed in setting us free from the old *Heilsgeschichte*, the new objectivism has fully finished the work he so nobly began.

Modern man, as Bultmann said earlier, "*is essentially a unity.*" As such "he bears the sole responsibility for his own feeling, thinking and willing. He is not, as the New Testament regards him, the victim of a strange dichotomy which exposes him to the interference of powers outside himself."[55] The new objectivism has brought full harmony between the "real intention" of the New Testament and the principle of inwardness of the modern man. *The New Testament's real intention was to give expression to the principle of inwardness which modern man, especially since the days of Kant, has seen to be the truth, the way and the life.* All that we need to do is to peel off its disfiguring detritus of mythology and the men of the New Testament appear before us as those who were groping for the light which only later ages, when man should come of age, could express.

C. PRIMAL THINKING

If then the Christian minister is to speak truly of the saving acts of God for man and in man, he must do so in terms of this new objectivism. The Christian minister must reinterpret the New Testament. There is, says Bultmann,

> a curious contradiction which runs right through the New Testament. Sometimes we are told that human life is determined by cosmic forces, at others we are challenged to a decision. Side by side with the Pauline indicative stands the Pauline imperative. In short, man is sometimes regarded as a cosmic being, sometimes as an independent 'I' for whom decision is a matter of life or death. Incidentally, this explains why so many sayings in the New Testament speak directly to modern man's condition while others remain enigmatic and obscure.[56]

The new objectivism enables us to see that what the New Testament really intended to say is that God is wholly free to turn into the opposite of himself and man is wholly free, on God's return journey, to be taken up into the free being of God.

The reader may know that this gospel of the freedom of God has been, for these many years proclaimed by Karl Barth and his followers. Barth, too, has

---

55. Bultmann, *New Testament and Mythology*, p. 6.
56. Ibid., p. 12.

demythologized the New Testament in the interest of the sovereign and universal grace of God. Barth's argument, like that of Bultmann, is that, if we are really to preach the grace of God, we must never directly identify the Christ-occurrence with anything that has happened in the past., i.e., in the I-It dimension. The resurrection of Christ, Barth like Bultmann argues, must be related to what happened on certain calendar days in the land of Palestine, but it must never be directly identified with any calendar event. The objectivity of the Christian faith, argues Barth, must rest on a *Real Event*. Our faith must not rest in itself. The objectivity of the gospel of sovereign universal grace rests on a real confrontation of the disciples with their risen Lord.

But *for this very reason* the resurrection must not be identified with a fact of *Historie*, a fact of the I-It dimension. Real objectivity lies primarily in the I-Thou dimension, the real world, the dimension of *Geschichte*.

It thus appears that though Barth does not, after the fashion of Bultmann, speak of demythologizing the New Testament, and that though Barth is critical of Bultmann for having no objective foundation for the gospel, he himself finds such objectivity by thinking of God and man as living together in one supra-temporal presence.[57]

In this supra-temporal presence there is no past and no future in the calendar sense of the term. The resurrection does not follow upon the crucifixion. Together they are *one Event*. The resurrection of believers does not follow upon that of their Savior in Palestine; the Christ and his church are *one Event*. The redemption of man, whether through what Christ did for or what the Holy Spirit does within man, does not follow man's creation. Creation is the external ground of redemption as redemption is the internal ground of creation. Both together form the *one Christ-Event*.

Thus the whole of what takes place in the I-It dimension is subject to the I-Thou dimension. When all things of the I-It dimension have thus been made subject to the I-Thou dimension, then the God whom no one knows and yet whom everyone knows absolutely becomes all in all. That is what Paul meant in 1 Corinthians 15:28. This is the new objectivism which Ogden, following the lead of Barth and others, offers to ministers.

D. PREACHING THE NEW OBJECTIVISM

But how do I as a minister preach this new objective, this universal sovereign grace of God?

Suppose that I am a young minister entering with enthusiasm upon my

---

57. KSO: The "supra-temporal presence" is what Van Til means by *Geschichte*.

work. Suppose I have been trained in the Presbyterian tradition. While a student I was troubled with the "contradictions" in the Reformed Confessions. Imagine being required to believe in a God who controls whatsoever comes to pass and at the same time to believe that man is responsible for his deeds. I must tell men that as the heirs of the first man, Adam, they are, in him, under the wrath of God and I must also tell men that, if they finally open their eyes in torment, they have no one to blame but themselves.

I have heard the Arminian, the Lutheran and the Roman Catholic compromises on these points and I have rejected them as mere reshufflings of the dilemma of the Calvinists. And now I have suddenly been set free from this dilemma. I no longer worry about the contradictions in the creeds. I no longer bother even to employ the artificial exegesis of Arminians. With their Kantian helicopters such men as Bultmann and Barth have suddenly lifted me out of the I-It dimension.

But all this, the evangelical Christian sees, is purely negative. And this purely negative attitude toward the dilemma of the Calvinist presupposes that its pilot finds himself already in the I-Thou dimension. Bultmann in demythologizing presupposes modern man's existential self-understanding. In other words, the young preacher, seeking to be a sky-pilot to his people, must already be up in the air before he can look down with pitying eye on his obscurant fellow ministers who still do their preaching in terms of the I-It dimension. In other words, the whole presupposition of the process of demythologizing presupposes the internal intelligibility of the non-objectifiable ego.

But alas when this non-objectifiable ego speaks, it is no longer the non-objectifiable ego that speaks. The non-objectifiable ego finds that he is still bound to the I-It dimension. He must speak to himself about himself as free from the I-It dimension in terms of concepts which glue him back into that dimension. The helicopter pilot cannot explain to himself how he ever became liberated from the I-It dimension and he also finds that he must fall back into it in order to take off from it again.

In other words, the would-be-free modern man finds that he cannot reject the "contradictions" of the New Testament except in terms of God who is, utterly unlike himself, *wholly* free from all contact with the I-It dimension. Only in terms of a wholly other God can man himself be free. And then, in particular, the free self must think of himself as wholly absorbed into this wholly free God. How else is he really free? A God who is wholly free from all contact with the world of space and time (and a man who is wholly free because he is wholly absorbed into this wholly free God)—it is only such a God, the God of sovereign grace, that I as a young Presbyterian preacher may now preach. I may now rejoice in the fact that the leaders of American Presbyterianism have, in their *Confession of*

1967, enabled me to be a true follower of the New Testament, a true follower of Calvin, because I am a truly modern man.

But now I discover to my dismay that as soon as I begin preaching to men about this universal sovereign grace or rather as soon as I start thinking about myself and of my person-to-person confrontation with other men in terms of this wholly other God, I can preach only if I keep absolute silence and stop thinking, even about myself.

But this I cannot do. I must therefore repudiate the idea of my absorption unto God. I must reaffirm the imperviousness of my individual temporal ego. But then I can assert this imperviousness of my own ego only if, at the same time, I assert the imperviousness of an infinite number of actual or possible finite egos together with mine. And then, when I do this, I-find myself slipping into utter separation both from my fellow egos and from the I-It dimension of reality.

I have thus freed myself from enmeshment in the contradictions of the New Testament, not because I can now say something without contradicting myself, but because I am now an imaginary point of intersection between a logical urge that leads me upward toward extinction in the static universe of Parmenides and an illogical urge downward toward extinction in the eternal flux of Heraclitus.

With Bultmann I have bravely rejected everything of the New Testament that does not speak to me as a modern man, as a man free from all divine and demonic intrusions. But now I discover that I am twice over a child of the "hell of the irrevocable." I now have no freedom at all. I am an amalgam of pure fate and pure chance. I know enough to be sure that the historic Christian faith, with its foundation in the "contradictions" of the New Testament, *cannot* be true and yet I know nothing at all. Dissatisfied with knowledge that is short of omniscience I end up with not knowing anything. Insisting that all reality must be what I, by logical manipulation, must say that it must be, I find that, on my new view, logic has no application to reality at all.

In conclusion, we listen briefly to what Heinrich Ott,[58] the successor to Karl Barth, in Basel, tells his students about preaching. Ott seeks to combine the theology of Bultmann and of Barth. Ott, too, as well as Ogden, sets forth a new objectivism. This new objectivism is primarily that of Barth. Barth has, more consistently than has Bultmann, says Ott, outreached the restrictions of the philosophy of Heidegger as this was set forth in his early work on *Sein und Zeit*. Ott argues that only in Barth's notion of *Geschichte* does the Christ-Event of which the New Testament really wants to speak, come to its own. Barth insists that man must not first seek to understand himself in terms of an existential

---

58. KSO: Heinrich Ott (1929–2013) was a Swiss Protestant theologian who taught theology in Basel from the 1960s through the 1990s.

philosophy like that of Heidegger and after that accept the gospel as agreeing with this self-understanding. Rather all of man's interpretation, including that of himself, must come from above, in terms of the revelation of God in Christ. Man may use any philosophy he pleases if only he makes every thought, even of his philosophy, subject to God speaking to us in the Christ-Event.

But now an extremely interesting thing has happened. Heidegger himself now sees that, if man is to be intelligible to himself, he must be so in view of a being that transcends him and from its transcendence manifests itself in man. Heidegger is now as anxious to reach out beyond science and beyond metaphysics as any theologian ever was.

The great help that we may derive from the "later Heidegger" comes from the fact that he has taught us, to our amazement, that true thinking is not conceptual thinking at all. At "a meeting of old Marburgers" Heidegger spoke on the subject *Christian Faith and Thinking*. On that occasion he made the amazing statement: "Science does not think."

What can I as a young minister do with that? I have just been told by Bultmann, basing himself upon Heidegger's philosophy, that it is because of the *thinking* of modern science that I must no longer believe in the three-decker universe of orthodox theology. What then can Heidegger now mean when he says that science does not think?

Well relief comes at once, it would seem, when we realize that Heidegger makes this seemingly negative statement about the thinking of science, in the light of a higher kind of thinking, a thinking in terms of faith. So we listen with great yearning as we hear Heidegger speak of "the nature and the specific movement of the thinking in which faith thinks."[59]

And then we hear Heidegger tell the story of his conversion. He speaks of the vision of a new concept of reality and a new concept of understanding.[60] Acceptance of this new concept of reality and of understanding leads us beyond existentialism. We now have a transcendence that is, at one and the same time truly prior to immanence and yet is the structural principle of immanence. We are now lifted up much higher into space than the Kantian helicopters were able to lift us while at the same time we are down to earth in the realm of the I-It dimension.

We were not wrong then in demythologizing the New Testament. Seeing

---

59. Heinrich Ott, "What is Systematic Theology," *The Later Heidegger and Theology* ("New Frontiers in Theology," Vol. I, New York: Harper and Row, 1963), p. 78.

60. See the present writer's *The Later Heidegger and Theology* (Phila.: Presbyterian and Reformed Press, 1964), for fuller discussion and references of these points on Heidegger.

ourselves now in the light of a wholly transcendent being we are above all dualisms and contradictions.

Ott goes with Heidegger into 'his space ship, saying all the while that "a theology of saving facts is empty-headed thoughtlessness." We may now combine Barth's theology of the Christ-Event speaking to us from above with Heidegger's philosophy of Being as "clearing-being," *Lichtunggeschichte*.[61] The philosophy of the "later Heidegger" at least opens up to us the possibility of the existence of a God such as Barth preaches. Therewith our preaching has become in principle the preaching of the unobjectionable man of modern philosophy.

We conclude then that modern theology exhibits, if possible, with more consistency than is true of either modern philosophy or modern science, that once man forsakes the obedience to the self-identifying Christ of Scripture he loses himself because he is at the same time identical with abstract changeless being and with abstract change. Modern man is, as we earlier saw from Karl Heim's analysis of him, one of an infinite number of selves, each in his own prison, unable to communicate with other selves except in terms of the light, the life and the Word of a self who is wholly other than and, therefore, wholly above all these finite selves. But this wholly other self turns out himself not to be a self who can communicate except he be taken up into an impersonal principle of unity above himself and all finite selves. In short, if this wholly other self finds that he is really a self, he finds that he is a finite self together with an infinity of finite selves, and then, in that case he, together with this infinite array of actual or possible finite selves, must look for ability to speak to these others selves for their enlightenment of themselves by means of the light of a *Being* that is above all selves.

It appears then that Ott's, as well as Ogden's new objectivism, for all its bold demythologizing of the old "objectivism" of such men as Luther, of Calvin and of the Apostle Paul, disappears into the mist of the unknown and the unknowable. Enthusiastically rejecting the "dilemma" of the historic Christian faith, the new objectivism of the modern theologian, philosophically and scientifically orientated, with its notion of the non-objectifiable ego, is lifted by its own petard.

---

61. Ibid., p. 13.

INDEX OF SUBJECTS AND NAMES

A
Activism 61, 66, 159, 160
Adam 10, 19, 20, 34, 38, 39, 40, 46, 62, 61n64, 95–8, 100, 113, 114, 129, 144, 163, 211, 217, 221, 222, 229, 230, 262, 297, 313, 314, 317, 348, 368
Alexander, Samuel 329
Alexandrianism 106, 107, 109–11, 135
Altizer, Thomas J. J. 59n52, 276, 328, 329n36
Americanism (Reform–Catholicism) 177
Amsterdam, Free University of 12, 42, 233, 282
Analogia entis (see Analogy of Being)
Analogical thought 7, 8, 29, 39, 62, 105, 168, 171, 197, 211, 215, 228, 285, 346
Analogy of being 132, 139, 159, 168, 190, 196n186, 340n91
Analogy of Religion Natural and Revealed to the Constitution and Course of Nature by Joseph Butler 11, 132n188, 219, 227, 262, 291,
Anaximander 174
Anglican Communion 53
Anselm of Canterbury 290, 292
Apologetics by Warfield 12n20
Apologetics xi, xxix, xxxv, 11–14, 34, 37, 38n5, 80, 81, 107, 232, 277, 319
    of Augustine 116, 126, 132,
    Arminian 75, 296, 319
    evangelical 219
    of Hamilton 274
    of Kuyper and Warfield 233–4, 238–42, 245–8, 254, 256–60

    Lutheran 204
    of Paul Tillich 146n21
    Reformed xxxv, 9, 11
    Roman Catholic 75, 296, 319
    of Thomas Aquinas 173
    traditional view of 296, 299, 300, 301, 303–5, 307, 348, 360
    of Van Til 309
Aquinas, Thomas 9n14, 67, 126, 141, 150, 155, 156n2, 159, 169, 170–5, 177, 184, 188n148, 190n158, 196n186, 217, 219n70, 227, 237, 267, 285–7, 292, 296, 298–300, 303, 304, 308, 310, 313
Aristotle 33n2, 35, 67, 110, 112, 143, 159, 171, 172, 173, 174, 175, 184, 188, 190, 191, 195, 198, 236, 304n131, 310
Arminianism xiv, xixn16, xxn17, xxiii, xxvi, 4, 49, 75, 160, 197, 199n3, 200, 212, 213, 216, 217n66, 218, 221, 222–4, 248, 260, 266, 276, 277, 296, 298, 300, 303, 304, 308, 310–3, 319, 350, 351, 368
Arminius, Jacobus 212–7
Arnobius 102
Athenagoras 76–7
Augustine 71, 80, 115–45, 151, 152, 345
Authority xii, xxi, 8n13, 33, 40, 41, 49, 54, 69, 71, 81, 85, 90, 93, 109, 110, 129, 131, 133, 170, 179n103, 190, 196, 199, 204, 248, 316, 348
    of the church 158, 251
    of experience 53,
    of the expert 51, 52, 55, 64
    of God 5, 7, 73, 98n100, 106, 188, 205, 227, 315, 343–4, 358
    of revelation 2, 20, 23, 29, 113, 211, 222, 234, 298,

of Scripture xx, xxxiii, 17n1, 18–9, 21–2, 26–7, 29, 31, 44, 48, 50, 53, 55–7, 62, 67, 68, 70, 87, 89, 101, 107, 108, 111, 112, 114, 115, 132, 155, 164, 168, 203, 225–7, 268, 273, 281, 293, 294, 296, 319
    of the Roman Catholic Church 188, 198, 213, 298
Autonomy viii, xi, xii, xviii, xxv, 2n1, 4, 5, 8–9, 13, 49, 52, 66, 70, 74n25, 75, 95, 99n102, 109, 110n127, 137–8, 141, 155, 159–60, 165, 166, 173, 196, 197–9, 210, 213, 216, 221, 222, 224, 225–8, 230–1, 233, 235, 237, 243, 254, 256–7, 260, 262–3, 267, 269, 275, 277, 317n177, 327, 334n55, 349, 351

B

Balthasar, Hans Urs von 175, 181, 183–7
Barth, Heinrich 138–40
Barth, Karl 54–5, 56n42, 58–61, 62–6, 148, 181, 183–4, 185n132, 187, 188n148, 195–6, 233n9, 332, 346, 353, 366–7, 368–9, 371
Basis of Christian Faith, The, by Hamilton
Bavinck, Herman ix, xx, xxv, xxvii, xxxv, 7n11, 12, 15, 17, 18, 25n13–14, 27, 29, 161n24, 162–4, 167n47–48, 176–7, 211n45, 257, 309
Beattie, Francis R. 238, 239n35
Behold Him, by Buswell 289
Belgic Confession 200, 234
Bergson, Henri 329
Berkeley, George 306
Berkouwer, G. C. ix, 44n17, 63–5n64, 158n18, 159, 178–80, 183
Bett, Henry 148
Bondage of the Will, by Luther 203n22, 204n23, 209

Bosanquet, Bernard 306
Bouillard, Henri 183
Bradley, F. H. 306
Brightman, Edgar Sheffield 284
Bowne, Bordon P. 223
Brunner, Emil 54, 56n42, 66
Bultmann, Rudolph 321n4, 323–6, 328, 332–3, 353–4, 356–8, 360–1, 363–6, 367, 368–70
Bunyan, John 225, 230
Buff, Fritz 356
Buswell, James Oliver, Jr. ix, xxxiii, 259, 279, 281–3, 286–7, 288, 289, 290–1, 292–4, 295, 296, 302, 307, 308n139, 309–14, 315–8
Butler, Joseph ix, 11, 14, 132, 219–21, 227, 259, 262, 279, 291, 296, 298–300, 303–4, 308, 310, 312, 319

C

Chalcedon, Creed of 183, 184n124, 328
Calvin, John xxix, xxxiii, xxxv, 13, 18n3, 23–4, 64n64, 88, 182–4, 195–6, 198, 199n4, 201–3, 233, 238, 247, 255, 264, 270, 283, 295–6, 297, 299–301, 308–9, 316, 332, 345, 348, 350, 369, 371
Calvinism xxxv, 201–2, 223n82, 266, 311, 313–4,
Carnell, E. J. 307
Chance xviii, 2–3, 7, 40, 46, 48, 49n24, 58n44, 64n64, 77, 144, 147, 166, 173–4, 204–5, 224, 231n6, 260, 276, 284, 288–9, 315, 318, 323, 326, 328, 330, 369
Christ
    and the church
    incarnation of xxvii, 18, 53n31, n33, 55, 60, 63, 80, 103–4, 139, 147, 159–61, 163–4, 183–4, 186, 187, 189, 191, 194, 202, 217, 231n6
    historicity of 354n4, 357–8

INDEX OF SUBJECTS AND NAMES

Christ and the Jews, by Van Til 67n1
Christ Event 184–5, 187–8, 326, 367, 369–71
Christian Dogmatics, by Francis Pieper 200, 201n8, 202n19
Christian Faith, The, by O. A. Curtis 223,
Christian Faith and Thinking, by Heidegger 370
Christian View of Being and Knowledge, A, by Buswell 279
Christliche Dogmatik (Eng.: *Church Dogmatics*), by Karl Barth 54, 58, 59n49, n52, 61n57
Church, Roman Catholic 2n1, 132, 155, 165, 169, 175, 176n70, 179n103, 181n115, 192n161,
City of God, The, by Augustine 134–6, 141
Clement of Rome vii, 72
Collingwood, R. G. 355
Common Grace, by Van Til xxvi, xxix, xxxi, xxxiii, 229n5, 282, 299n118, 309n142
Common grace 13–4, 35–6, 38, 218, 257, 331n46, 365
Concerning the Teacher, by Augustine 123
Concord, Formula of 199
Confession of 1967 233n9
Conflict with Rome, by Berkouwer 159
Couchod, P. L. 354
Covenant of Grace 22
Cox, Harvey 329
Creation xiv, xvi, xix, xxii, xxiii, xxviii, xxxvin2, 2n3, 5n7, 6n10, 10n15, 33n1, 37, 39n7, 42, 43n15, 55, 65n64, 68, 73, 74, 76, 78–80, 82, 85, 80, 90, 92, 94, 96, 98, 100, 113–4, 115, 123, 125, 129–31, 133, 139, 146, 148–9, 150, 159, 162, 172–4, 175n66, 207–8, 211, 216, 217n64, 221n76, 223, 237, 239, 254, 261, 263, 265, 269, 272, 279, 284, 289, 297, 301n124, 302n126, n127, 305, 307, 309n144, 317n177, 324, 332, 350, 353n1, 367
Cullmann, Oscar 180–3
Curtis, O. A. 223

D

Defense of the Faith, by Van Til xxvi, xxix, xxxi, xxxiii, 52n28, 54n38, 259n1, 296
Descartes, René 116, 151, 177, 280, 290–1, 292, 306, 349
Dialecticism 54n38, 66, 128, 134, 327–8
Dialectical theology vii, xv, xvii, xxviii, 54, 55n41, 58, 62, 66, 99, 120, 122, 125, 128n174, 139n219, 195n185, 255, 322n7, 323n9, 344, 345, 349, 353n1
Diocles 91
Dionysius the Aereopagite (Pseudo-Dionysius, or St. Denis) 145–7, 148–9, 153
Dimensionalism x, 43, 331, 333n51, 343n112, n113, 348, 360n37
Division of Nature, by Scotus Erigena 148
Dooyeweerd, Herman xxxvi, 42, 49, 139n219, 195n185, 351
Dort, Synod of 212, 213n47
Drews, Arthur 354

E

Ecumenism 178n89, 181n115
Eddington, Arthur 226, 288, 332
Encounter 54n38, 59n52, 139, 145, 178, 239, 341–2, 356–9
Encyclopedia of Sacred Theology, by Kuyper 234n11, 239
Engelder, Theodore 200
Erasmus 203n22

Erigena, Johannes Scotus viii, 145n11, 148–9, 153
Ethics 39, 85–6, 107, 123n163, 152n41, 279–81, 361n39
Evangelical xxxv, 4, 8–9, 11, 14, 17, 59n52, 180, 197ff, 267, 311, 345–7, 350–1, 360, 368,
Event xxiv, xxv, 55, 59–60, 63, 215, 287, 289, 334, 356–7, 363–5, 367,
   eschatological 326, 355
Evidence of God 12, 24, 50, 56, 85, 91, 226, 232, 238, 241, 245ff, 268, 271–3, 276, 280–3, 286ff, 301, 305,
Evil xiii, xxiv, 35–6, 39–40, 45–7, 50, 57, 68, 77, 95, 97, 100, 115, 151, 171, 193, 214, 216, 217, 220, 222, 228, 230, 268, 280–1,
   as privation 122
   Christ's triumph over 191
   knowledge of 40, 110, 248
   origin of 77, 96, 98, 99,
   problem of 57, 287
Existentialism 15, 152n41, 191, 196, 324, 341, 370

F

Fact xx–xxvi, 2ff, 26ff, 63n64, 69ff, 78, 126ff, 134, 141, 142, 145, 147, 150, 172, 185, 205, 216, 224, 226, 235, 238, 254–6, 260, 261, 262–3, 265, 267, 273, 275, 277, 283, 289, 292–3, 297, 300–10, 314, 315–16, 320, 325, 330, 347, 349, 351, 354, 360,
   brute 122, 125, 174n64, 255, 325n19
   philosophy of 144, 191n159, 209, 255, 264, 269, 273, 286, 314, 316–17, 334, 355n15, 371
Ferrier, J. F. 53
Ferré, Nels F. 55,
Feuerbach, Ludwig 54

Fichte, Johann Gottlieb 334–6, 342, 344
Fisher, George P. 252
Francke, Karl ix, 206–10, 212, 216
Freedom xxviii, 49, 50, 66, 74, 99, 133, 136ff, 185, 187, 190, 193, 194–5, 206, 208–9, 303, 346, 351, 364, 366, 369
   as autonomy xii, 49n24, 70, 95, 196, 311–13, 321ff, 331–2, 358, 363
   and Calvinism 295
   according to Molinism xxn17, 160n21
   as nonbeing 330
   of will xxiii, 95, 97–8, 129
Freud, Sigmund 46
Fundamentalism 81, 201, 346, 347

G

Geiselmann, J. R. 179–80
Gilson, Etienne 148, 150
Goethe 231, 329n38
Geschichte 60, 64n64, 325, 332, 367, 369,
Grace 10, 14–15, 30, 35, 37, 45–7, 63, 111, 113, 115, 133, 135, 136–9, 141, 143–4, 262, 268, 291, 298, 313, 317, 333, 346, 351, 355, 365, 367, 368–9
   Arminian view of 213n47, 214, 217
   common (see common grace)
   Protestant view of 162–7, 199n4, 229–31, 237–8,
   Roman Catholic view of 160–1, 175, 178, 184, 189, 194–7, 202, 206, 217, 219
   triumph of 65n

H

Hackett, Stuart 265–7, 282–3, 350–51

Hamilton, Floyd E. xxxiii, 259ff, 349n117, 350, 351,
Hamilton, William 328n35
Harnack, Adolf von 116, 137–8
Heidelberg Catechism 46
Heidegger, Martin 46, 146n21, 325, 329, 336, 341, 355, 356, 357, 361, 369–71
Heim, Karl 333–45, 348–50, 362, 371
Hendry, George 233
Hepp, Valentine 14, 15, 282
Heilsgeschichte 180n106, 366
Heraclitus 91, 191n159, 192, 328–30, 369
Hermogenes 94
History xii, xxi, 2, 3, 7, 18–22, 26, 28, 38, 39, 40, 45, 50, 53, 57, 58, 60, 63n64, 68–71, 83, 84, 124, 126, 127, 134, 135, 137–9, 141, 144, 146, 149, 150, 153, 160–1, 165–6, 183–5, 190–1, 193, 196, 205, 210, 213, 216, 219, 222, 226, 229, 231, 237, 238, 244, 246, 249, 254, 255, 256, 260, 289, 297, 301, 307, 316, 325, 327, 332, 333, 344, 354, 355, 356, 359, 363, 365
    of the church xxii, xxix, 115n140,
    of thought (various) xix, 41, 43, 80, 109, 116n141, 200, 321
Hodge, Charles xxxv, 12, 233n9, 303
Holy Spirit xi, 10, 11n16, 12–13, 23–5, 44, 46–8, 88, 95, 158, 161–3, 164–7, 180, 186–7, 193–4, 208–9, 212, 213–14, 218, 220, 229, 231–2, 233, 238–9, 241–2, 246, 252, 254, 260–2, 264–6, 269, 272, 276, 283, 291, 295, 299–300, 312, 314, 315, 349, 367
Homrighausen, Elmer George 55
Hume, David 306, 331n47
Husserl, Edmund 40n10, 146n21, 152

I

Ignatius 72–3
Inductive Apologetics 279, 282–7, 290–4, 296–7, 306, 311, 315–16, 318 (see also 40)
Infallible Word, The, by faculty of Westminster Seminary 24, 225, 297, 299
Inspiration xx, 23–4, 27, 61, 155n1, 157, 161, 164, 230, 246, 250–3
Institutes of the Christian Religion, The, by Calvin 18, 23–4, 202, 203, 238, 270n40, 299, 309
Intellect 10, 31, 37–8, 43, 68, 92, 125, 145, 146, 153, 169, 173, 214, 239, 319,
Intellection 173, 242, 243, 291
Intelligence 41, 93, 97, 119, 125, 157, 165, 272, 312, 362
    Buswell's view of 279–80, 288
    Plontius' view of 142, 143, 152
Inwardness Principle 140
Irrationalism 6, 15, 39, 40, 48–50, 58, 70, 99, 104, 109, 114, 122, 128, 132, 142, 170, 191, 198, 239, 289, 328, 344–5
Irenaeus 77ff, 101

J

Jaeger, Warner 72,141
Jaspers, Karl 335, 336, 341
Jeans, James 226
Jesuits 176–7, 181
Justification (epistemic) 31, 238
Justification (salvific) 72–3, 147, 156n2, 160, 161, 176, 177, 179, 181, 252
Justin Martyr 73–6, 86
Jesus of Nazareth 18, 31, 51, 72, 82, 86, 90, 117, 126, 147, 148, 217, 227, 250, 289, 326, 347, 353ff, 364–5
    resurrection of 70, 74,

K

Kant, Immanuel xxxiii, 7, 8n12, 43n15, 46, 49–50, 52, 66, 139, 140, 147, 152, 188, 195, 223, 329, 322–7, 329, 331, 335–8, 340, 343n112, 349, 350, 360n37
Kerygma 355–9
Kierkegaard, Søren 54n38, 152, 335
Knudsen, Albert C. 223n84
Kroner, Richard 145, 150
Küng, Hans 175n68, 181, 183
Kuyper, Abraham xxxiii, 12, 15, 233ff, 256–7, 309

L

Law of God 34, 42, 43, 86, 350
Leibniz, Gottfried Wilhelm 290
Leo XIII 169, 177
L'evolution Creatrice, by Bergson 329
Lichtunggeschichte 371
Locke, John 306
Logic xxvii, 9, 26, 28, 122, 134, 142, 216, 255, 283, 314, 320, 326–31, 336, 344–5, 351, 369
    human capacity for 62, 115, 144, 171, 306–7, 340,
    laws of 3, 33, 191n159, 205, 263, 280, 285, 293–4, 306–7, 310,
    philosophy of 264
Lovejoy, Arthur xiii–xvii, 146n17, 149–50
Lutheran Theology 200ff, 368
    on autonomy 4, 207
Luther, Martin 203–4, 209

M

Machen, J. Gresham 257, 279n1, 291, 311
Mackay, John A. 55
Manichaeans 122, 123, 128, 128–30, 132
Marcian 73n17, 78, 103–5

Mary 18, 151, 189
Masselink, William 13, 14
Melanchthon, Philip 209
Metaphysics of Apologetics, by Van Til 44n17
Methodist theology 216, 221, 223
Miley, John 221–3
Mueller, John Theodor 200, 202
Murray, John 24n10, 26, 300, 310n145
Mythical Theology 326, 364

N

Natural Theology 149ff, 200, 340
    of Bavinck 309–11
    of Buswell 283, 311, 314
    of Kuyper 240
    and Scripture 225ff
    of Thomas Aquinas 169, 175, 310
    of Warfield 234
Negative Theology 145, 147, 150–51, 175
Neo–Orthodoxy 138, 324
New Quest for the Historical Jesus, A, by Robinson 354–60
New Schaff–Herzog, Encyclopedia of Religious knowledge, Article by B. B. Warfield in 12n20, 245
Nicolas of Cusa 185–6, 288
Niebuhr, Reinhold 55
Niebuhr, Richard 55
Nietzsche, Friedrich 328
Noumenal 43n15, 55n41, 138–9, 152, 320, 322–7, 331n48, 337n70, 343n113

O

Oats, Witney J. 119, 123
Ogden, Schubert 321n5, 323n11, 324, 326, 361, 363–5, 367, 369, 371
On the Flesh of Christ, by Tertullian 102, 103

INDEX OF SUBJECTS AND NAMES

On the Immortality of the Soul, by Augustine 119
Origen 106–7, 111, 126, 135, 236
    epistemology of 114–5
    cited by Balthasar 186
Ott, Heinrich 353n1, 369–71

P

Paideia 141–2, 144, 154,
    in Thomas 169, 175
Parmenides xvi–xvii, 142, 144, 171, 191–2, 328–30, 344, 353, 359, 369
Pelagianism 176
Pelagius 137
Personality 49–52, 66, 68, 70, 83–4, 109–111, 113, 210–12, 219, 230, 268, 272, 274, 290, 356
Phenomenal 39n7, 43n15, 57, 64n64, 138–9, 153, 165, 205, 255, 320n1, 321–6, 331–2, 337n70, 343n112
Philo Judaeus 67–9
Philosophie der Praktischen Vernunft, by Heinrich Barth 138
Philosophy xxxvi, 26, 39, 41, 43, 87, 102, 112, 114, 141, 152, 159, 166, 173, 190, 221, 226, 275, 319–23, 325, 330–3, 346–7, 348, 350
    ancient 42, 50, 142–5, 236
    of Aristotle 159, 310
    of Augustine 134–5, 137
    of Buswell 279–81, 311, 314
    per Bultmann 365, 369
    Christian xiii–xv, xix, 41, 105
    of Erigena 149
    existentialist 45, 336, 344, 349, 353, 361, 370–1
    Greek 68, 70, 74–6, 80, 83, 89–90, 92–3, 98, 107–10, 115, 328
    of history 20, 135, 137, 141, 144, 149, 184, 327
    idealist 98, 341
    of Kant 49, 335,
    Kuyper's view of 239–40,
    modern 52–5, 66, 116, 122, 145, 293, 327, 360
    non–Christian 41, 101, 168, 207, 215, 223, 300
    of reality 225, 228, 327
    Reformed 20
    Roman Catholic xxxiii, 225
    of Thomas Aquinas 313
Pieper, Francis 200ff, 216
Pius IX 157
Plato xiv, xvi, 51, 74, 76, 78–9, 89, 91, 92, 93–4, 96, 98–9, 108, 112, 143, 171
    Platonism 74n21, 98, 101, 106, 108, 110, 116, 145n12
Plotinus viii, 110, 112, 133, 141–5, 149–53
Pol, Van de 178
Polycarp vii, 73, 77n29
Pragmatism, by William James 329
Predestination 137, 194, 202, 213
Predication 2–4, 6, 8–9, 20, 27, 33–4, 106, 145, 174, 212, 255, 269, 277, 302
    final reference point of 39, 57, 65, 67, 83, 168, 218, 231, 327
Prescription Against Heretics, The, by Tertullian 81, 89, 90n67, 101, 105
Presupposition xviii, 6, 9, 10, 12, 76, 125, 159, 173, 174, 222, 230–1, 255–6, 281
    presuppositionalist 260, 262–3, 266, 269, 275, 277, 294, 295, 311, 314
Princeton Theological Seminary xxiiin24, 11–2, 14, 80n44, 206n28, 211n45, 233, 248n51, 257n65, 259–60, 262, 266, 269, 308n140
Principles of Sacred Theology, by Abraham Kuyper 12

Probability 226, 273, 276, 286, 289, 291, 294, 299, 349 (see also Chance)
Proofs of God (see Evidence of God) 190, 235, 271, 276, 282, 284, 287, 292, 299, 309–10, 337
Providence of God xix, xxi, xxii, xxiii, xxiv, xxv, xxix, 1, 20, 46–7, 58n44, 76, 80, 92–3, 95, 109, 125, 172, 174, 191, 214, 217n66, 295, 305, 307

Q

Quest for Certainty, The by Dewey 329

R

Rationalism viii, 48–50, 58, 62, 70, 99–100, 104, 114, 116, 123–4, 126n172, 127–32, 142, 147, 149, 170–2, 174, 191, 198, 201, 203, 238, 254, 282, 328, 344–6, 359
Rawlinson, Alfred E. J. 53
Reason 5n8, 8n13, 9–13, 50, 52–6, 67, 70, 73, 75, 83–4, 91, 95, 97, 101–2, 107, 113, 116, 118–21, 125–6, 129, 133, 138, 143, 152, 157–9, 165, 166, 169–72, 175n66, 177, 190–1, 198, 202–5, 219–20, 226–7, 235–42, 245–50, 260, 264, 268, 272, 275, 282, 288, 293, 295, 300, 309–10, 313, 320, 333n51, 338
    human faculty 4n6, 5, 9n14, 55, 67, 157, 170, 205,
    autonomous 54, 110n127
Reality xiii, xviii, xxiv, xxv, xxvi, 2n3, 6–8, 19, 39–43, 45–9, 51–4, 62, 63n64, 69, 72n14, 83, 92, 99n101, 108, 109, 115, 127, 131, 142, 144, 145, 146, 153, 159, 160, 165, 168, 170, 172, 174, 192, 206, 213, 214, 216, 218, 219, 223, 225, 228, 240, 246, 249, 262, 263n9, 264, 274, 281, 298, 304–6, 315, 316, 319–21, 324, 326–30, 331n48, 334–6, 339, 340, 343, 344, 346, 349, 350, 355, 365, 369, 370
Real Problem of Inspiration, The, by Warfield 250
Reform–Catholicism 177
Reformed Theology xi, xii, xix, xx, xxi, xxix, xxxv 5, 11, 17n1, 30n22, 74n25, 201, 202, 211n45, 228, 256, 277n79, 312n152, 350n122
Remonstrant Articles 200, 212
Resurrection of Theism, by Hackett 265, 266n23, 282, 350, 351n122
Revelation xxi, xxvi, xxix, 2, 5, 7, 8, 10, 12, 13, 19–23, 25, 29–31, 33, 34, 37–9, 42n13, 44n18, 45, 46, 48, 52–5, 57–61, 63–5, 69, 71, 73n17, 85, 91, 101, 102, 108–10, 112–3, 134, 139, 145n10, 153, 157, 158, 160, 162, 164–7, 169, 174–5, 177, 179, 183–7, 190–1, 194, 195, 198, 201, 205, 209n41, 216, 217, 219–23, 226, 228, 232, 234–6, 238, 240, 243, 246–9, 252, 254, 255, 262, 265, 267, 269, 270, 272, 273, 276, 280, 283–5, 294, 297–301, 309–14, 316, 330, 331, 333, 338, 349, 353, 358, 360, 365, 370
Richardson, Alan 307
Rickert 325
Ritschl, Albrecht 52, 58, 66, 333n51
Robinson, James M. 354–61
Roman Catholic Theology xiv, xx, 8, 17, 183, 184, 217
Royce 306

S

Satan 39–40, 95, 100, 115, 135, 141
Science xii, xx, xxi, 13, 14, 26, 27, 28, 43, 49, 66, 118, 119, 138, 143, 152, 157, 169, 206, 242–6, 248, 257, 259, 281, 293, 302, 308, 317,

319–23, 325, 330–50, 361, 365, 369–71
Schleiermacher, Friedrich vii, 52, 54, 58, 66, 146n21, 177, 200, 218
Scripture
    allegorical intrepretation of 68, 115
    authority of xx, 18, 31, 48, 53, 57, 68, 87, 101, 107, 111–2, 164, 168, 225–6
    modern view of 25
    necessity of vii, 21, 44, 48, 50, 56, 162, 217
    perspicuity of vii, viii, 44, 61–2, 165–6, 168, 298
    phenomena of vii, 26–7, 253
    Protestant doctrines of 17, 183, 197, 204, 220
    Reformed doctrine of xx, 18, 299n119
    Roman Catholic doctrine of 155
    sufficiency of vii, 18, 57–8, 62, 167
Sein und Zeit, by Martin Heidegger 329, 361, 369
Sensualism 102
Septuagint 107
Simon 78
Sin xxiii, xxvi, 4n6, 10, 13, 18–22, 25, 34–8, 44–8, 50–1, 54n38, 56, 62, 65n64, 67, 88, 90, 93, 94, 97–100, 115, 127, 130–1, 135–7, 162–4, 165, 176–7, 193, 206–12, 217–8, 220, 224–5, 228–30, 232, 234–5, 237, 241–9, 261–2, 264, 268–71, 275–6, 280–2, 289, 291, 294, 297, 302n127, 304n129, 310, 313, 317, 332–3, 348–9, 363
Socrates 133, 140, 152, 321, 346, 362
Soliloquies, by Augustine 118–9, 125n169
Sontag, Frederick 145, 147
Soranus 93

Soul 31, 68, 78, 81, 85–108, 114–20, 126–32, 135–6, 145n12, 151–3, 189, 193–4, 241, 263–5, 268–76, 306, 335, 346, 349–50, 360
Soul's Testimony, by Tertullian 86–9
Sovereignty of God 11, 14, 64, 75n27, 198, 346
Space-Time, and Deity, by Alexander 329
Spinoza, Baruch 149, 313
Stromata, by Clement 111
Studies in Theology, by B. B. Warfield 245
Summa Contra Gentiles, by Thomas Aquinas 169, 310
Summa Theologica, by Thomas Aquinas 169
Survey of Systematic Theology, A, by Van Til 44n17
Symbolic Theology 147, 175

T
Tatian 101–2
Taylor, A. E. 52–3
Temple, Archbishop William 53–4
Tertullian 81ff, 114, 132
Theological Institutes, by Watson 216
Tillich, Paul 146, 333, 353
Timaeus, by Plato xvi, 91
Treatise on the Soul, by Tertullian 81, 86, 88, 89
Trent, Council and Canons of 155–7, 176
    Bavinck on 176–8

U
Universalization 185

V
Valentinus 78
Vollenhoven, D. H. Th. xxxvi, 42, 49
Van Til, Cornelius 260, 312
Vatican I 157, 176, 177, 190, 191

Vatican II 175–6, 190, 191–2, 195–6
   Berkouwer on 178
   Documents of 188
Vos, Geerhardus 12

W

Warfield, Benjamin Breckenridge xxxv, 12, 80–4, 98, 116, 123, 199, 233, 233–5, 238–40, 242–5, 247–9

Watson, Richard 216–19
Wesensschau 40, 152
Westminster Confession of Faith
   xxi–xxiii, 30, 310, 347
Westminster Shorter Catechism 284–5
Westminster Theological Seminary 260
What Is God, by Buswell 284f, 287, 290, 308, 311
Wordsworth, Bishop 252

INDEX OF SCRIPTURE REFERENCES

Genesis
1   103n
3   280
49:10   210

Job
11:7ff   207

Psalms
19   288
19:1-2   6
82:6-7   281, 293
94:9   288
119:105   200

Proverbs
8   82

Isaiah
1:18   56
9:10   207
42:5   94
53:6   207
55:9   45

Matthew
13:22   207
25:46   136

John
1:7   291
3:19   325
4:6   207
9:39   325
10:37-38   281
12:31   193
20:30   186
21:25   186

Acts
1:3   282
17:25   3
17:29   xxix
17:30   31

Romans
1   34, 207, 295, 299, 309
1:18   11, 13, 19, 310
1:18-22   288
1:18-32   46
1:19-20   13, 37
1:20   300, 213
1:21   34, 249, 269, 316
1:25   34
1:26-27   207
1:32   230
2   309
2:14   13
5   280
5:12   10, 34
7:24   208
8:6   34
8:6-8   10
9:20-1   295
9:22   295
11:25   207

1 Corinthians
1:20-1   15, 351
10:5   xxviii
12:6   203
14   204
15   282
15:28   367

2 Corinthians
5:17   206
10:1-5   3

Galatians
1:8   200

Ephesians
1:11   xxii
2:1   10, 34
2:2   34
2:3   34
2:8-10   291
4:18   34
4:24   303

Colossians
2:8   207
3:10   303

1 Thessalonians
4:5   37

2 Thessalonians
1:8   37
2:10   207

Philemon
2:13   xxv, 291

1 John
1:7   291
4:6   207

Westminster Seminary Press (WSP) was founded in 2011 by Westminster Theological Seminary in Philadelphia, Pennsylvania. WSP is a uniquely Reformed academic publisher dedicated to enriching the church, the academy, and the Christian through the printed word. WSP collaborates widely—including with faculty, staff, and students at Westminster—to publish new and classic books that foster faith in and obedience to Jesus Christ from an orthodox, Reformed perspective. For more information, visit www.westminsterseminarypress.com, email wsp@wts.edu, or write to us at 2960 Church Road, Glenside, Pennsylvania 19038.